Harold F. Hartman

FOREIGN
GOVERNMENTS

The Dynamics of Politics Abroad

Edited by Fritz Morstein Marx

FOREIGN
GOVERNMENTS

The Dynamics of Politics Abroad

ANDREW GYORGY   PAUL M. A. LINEBARGER
JOHN N. HAZARD   JOHN BROWN MASON
HENRY P. JORDAN   FRITZ MORSTEIN MARX
EDWARD G. LEWIS   W. HARDY WICKWAR

Second Edition

New York   PRENTICE-HALL, INC.   1952

L.C. Cat. Card No.: 52-8606

To
That Influential Figure in World Affairs—
The Man
Who neither Knows nor Cares

PREFACE TO THE SECOND EDITION

A book like this cannot shut itself off from the march of events. That is true even when the daily headline is intentionally subordinated to longer-range political influences. Periodically an analysis and interpretation of foreign governments must be tested against subsequent occurrences. Moreover, the reader is entitled to find yesterday's news laced into the treatment of an evolution that has no end.

The revision proved the general plan of the book in no need of change, beyond allowing recognition of recent developments. On the other hand, all chapters have benefited from the revision, especially by consideration of the suggestions of thoughtful critics, who deserve much of the credit for such improvements as the users of the book will discover. Certain sections required more work than others because of the increasing momentum of previously noted tendencies, particularly the sections dealing with the Soviet Union, China, Japan, and Germany.

In order to satisfy the wish expressed by many colleagues for a separate presentation of France and Italy, this part has been completely rewritten. Unfortunately, Mario Einaudi, whose chapters on the two European neighbor-republics will be remembered as an outstanding contribution to the first edition, found himself unavailable for this new task at the time it had to be done. Fortunately, when he generously gave the team a free hand to search for a replacement, we were able to win a scholar as able as Edward G. Lewis to fill the breach.

Washington, D. C.   *Fritz Morstein Marx*

PREFACE TO THE FIRST EDITION

Like other great wars, World War II has wrought political changes of revolutionary character. It has played havoc not only with the designs of the vanquished but also with the hopes of the victors. It has laid the foundations for an international structure of power that renders peace highly insecure. And it has deeply affected the course of developments in many countries. The postwar world in which the United States is called upon to exert enlightened leadership is a much changed world.

To measure and appraise these changes is therefore a timely task. It is also one beset with obvious difficulties. Tendencies that seem to be of world-wide scope often take on a different appearance in different countries. Close familiarity with many parts of the globe is required to paint the whole canvas with sufficient accuracy. Firsthand knowledge adequate to this assignment is not given any single mind. That is the reason why a fresh investigation of political life abroad turned necessarily into a group venture.

The men who banded together in this combined operation have been for many years students of the particular areas for which they assumed responsibility. Each knows his area not only from primary sources but also from field observations. Each for his area has acquired a feeling for the pulse of politics as it beats today. It is no less important that each member of this team has been drawn by his wider professional interests beyond a narrow expertship. Such breadth of perspective enabled the team to achieve agreement on the project in all of its aspects and to carry it out jointly as one enterprise.

But agreement on the project was not intended to produce a Procrustean uniformity of treatment. Each country has an individuality of its own, born of its own culture. Each also has its own troubles. There is no standard test by which the vitality of different political systems may be gauged with assurance. Guidance in determining what is relevant has come from deliberate emphasis on the living reality of government. This emphasis has invited attention to factors of enduring significance rather than photographic precision in recording the ephemeral.

None of the members of the team has been willing to claim for his findings and conjectures anything like authoritative finality. Indeed, the very traditions of free inquiry tend to deny all such claims. This book is written as an expression of the faith of its authors in the reader's capacity for employing information to bolster rather than weaken the independence of his judgment. As a result, while each team member because of his training accepts the discipline of objectivity, none has felt it desirable to conceal either his personal point of view or his general bias in favor of the democratic way as we know it.

As a very small matter, a word should perhaps be said about the charts and tables in the book. They appeared justified to elaborate particular points of interest where the burden of detail would have made lengthy reading. Several of these charts and tables are published here for the first time. Another matter, though much more important to the team, is the tribute due many good friends—too many to name—who have helped to make this book what it has come to be. It is a pleasant obligation to acknowledge a large debt of gratitude to these silent partners.

Washington, D. C.   *Fritz Morstein Marx*

INTRODUCING THE TEAM

Professor *Andrew Gyorgy* is a research associate in Foreign Area Studies at Yale University, where he was formerly on the faculty of the Department of Political Science. A research fellow of the Rockefeller Foundation in 1938, he has taught also at the University of California, the University of New Hampshire, Johns Hopkins University, and Louisiana State University, specializing in comparative government and international relations, with particular emphasis on Eastern Europe. He is the author of *Geopolitics: The New German Science* (1944), *Governments of Danubian Europe* (1949), and of contributions to various periodicals. During World War II he served as instructor in area training courses administered under auspices of the War Department, especially at the Infantry School, where he was stationed. He has traveled widely in eastern Europe. In 1949 he served as faculty leader of Yale's Mediterranean Study Tour.

John N. Hazard, a fellow of the Institute of Current World Affairs at the Moscow Juridical Institute from 1935 to 1937, is professor of public law and a member of the staff of the Russian Institute at Columbia University, where he gives particular attention to Soviet political and administrative institutions. He has formerly been on the faculties of the University of Chicago and of the School of Advanced International Studies. In addition to *Soviet Housing Law* (1939), his numerous writings have been published in such works as *A Foreign Policy for the United States* (ed. Quincy Wright, 1947) and professional journals like *Columbia Law Review, Annals of the American Academy of Political and Social Science*, and *International Journal* (Canada). He is the editor of *Soviet Legal Philosophy* (1951). In World War II he served as Deputy Director, USSR Branch, Office of Lend Lease Administration and successor agencies, and later as adviser on state trading to the Department of State. He revisited the Soviet Union toward the end of the war.

Professor *Henry P. Jordan*, until recently a member of the Department of Government of New York University, has been lecturing in Germany since 1950, partly under auspices of the High Commissioner's Office, including service as a visiting professor at the University of Marburg. He has also been associated with Carleton College, the University of Colorado, Queens College, the University of Puerto Rico, and Rutgers University. His main fields of teaching are comparative government and political philosophy; Latin American affairs and international relations have claimed much of his professional interest. He is the editor of *Problems of Postwar Reconstruction* (1942), to which he contributed the chapter on hemisphere policy as implemented by economics. His section on international law and relations has been a recurrent feature in the *Annual Survey of American Law* (1945 and later). Special aspects of Latin American

xii INTRODUCING THE TEAM

developments have been analyzed by him in such periodicals as *International Postwar Problems* and *Current History* and in works like *The Evolution of Latin American Government* (ed. Asher Christensen, 1951). Besides several visits to Latin America, he was officially concerned with the area while serving with the Pan-American Branch of the Foreign Economic Administration during World War II.

Professor *Edward G. Lewis,* who is teaching comparative government in the Department of Political Science at the University of Illinois, has also taught at the University of California and at the University of Texas. He has held a scholarship to the Peace Academy in The Hague and a fellowship at the Faculty of Law of the University of Paris, and has also studied at the London School of Economics. His travels in Europe have brought him to other countries as well. He is the author of *British By-Elections as a Reflection of Public Opinion* (1943) and joint editor of *Outside Readings in American Government* (rev. ed., 1952). Other writings of his have appeared in the *American Political Science Review* and similar professional journals. In World War II he served with the Navy, and was a military government officer on the island of Guam.

Paul M. A. Linebarger, professor of Asiatic politics at the School of Advanced International Studies, was reared in China. Before assuming his present post, he taught at the University of Chicago, Harvard University, Duke University, and the University of Michigan. His books include *The Political Doctrines of Sun Yat-sen* (1937), *Government in Republican China* (1938), *The China of Chiang Kai-shek* (rev. ed., 1943), and *Psychological Warfare* (1948). He has also written for popular and learned journals, like *Yale Review* and *Journal of Politics.* During World War II he was on military duty with the Intelligence Section of the United States Army Headquarters in China under General Stilwell and General Wedemeyer. At war's end he was chief of the Far Eastern Section, Propaganda Branch, G-2, General Staff, United States Army. Since then he has repeatedly revisited the Far East, including Korea, in both official and private capacities.

John Brown Mason has been serving recently as chief of the Civic Activities Division in the Office of Political Affairs of the High Commissioner's Office in Germany. He has taught at the University of Wisconsin and after World War II at Oberlin College. His special fields are comparative government and international relations. His writings include *Hitler's First Foes: A Study in Religion and Politics* (1936), *The Danzig Dilemma: A Study in Peacemaking by Compromise* (1946), and contributions that have appeared in such periodicals as *American Political Science Review* and *American Journal of International Law,* and in other works, like *New Constitutions and Constitutional Developments* (ed. Arnold Zurcher, 1951). During World War II he organized and directed at Stanford University the European area section of the Civil Affairs Training School for prospective military government officers. Later, as chief of the Training Division of the Foreign Economic Administration, he was in charge of civilian training for overseas duty. As a member of the historical mission of the Secretary of

War, he interrogated such Nazi leaders as Göring, Rosenberg, and von Ribbentrop on the inner working of the Nazi party and state. In 1946 he took part in the Hoover Food Mission to Europe.

Fritz Morstein Marx, a research fellow of the Rockefeller Foundation in 1930-31, is an adjunct professor of political science at American University. He has been a faculty member at several other institutions of higher learning, including Princeton, Harvard, and Yale. He was the first chairman of the Special Committee on Comparative Administration, sponsored by the Committee on Public Administration of the Social Science Research Council. Much of his writing has been devoted to comparative government and politics. Prior to his enlistment as a private in World War II, he served as a staff aide on the Combined (American-British) Production and Resources Board.

W. Hardy Wickwar, until recently professor of social science and head of the Department of Political Science at Hamilton College, is now Social Affairs Officer in the United Nations Secretariat. A research fellow of the Rockefeller Foundation in 1927-31, he has been associated with various academic institutions, including the London School of Economics. Comparative government and political theory are two of his fields of specialization. His publications include *The Struggle for the Freedom of the Press* (1928), *Baron d'Holbach* (1935), *The Social Services* (rev. ed., 1949), and articles for such periodicals as *Social Service Review* and *American Political Science Review.* During World War II he was on duty as a specialist in comparative welfare administration with the United Nations Relief and Rehabilitation Administration. His postwar travels have led him repeatedly to England as well as to other parts of Europe.

CONTENTS

PART I. IDEAS AND IDEALS

CHAPTER 1. MAN AND THE STATE, *Fritz Morstein Marx*

CHAPTER 2. ALTERNATIVES OF IDEOLOGY, *Fritz Morstein Marx*

xv

CHAPTER 4. GOVERNMENT BY CONSENT AND DISCUSSION,
W. Hardy Wickwar

CHAPTER 5. THE STRUCTURE OF PUBLIC ADMINISTRATION,
W. Hardy Wickwar

CONTENTS xix

2. NATIONALIZATION 132

Monopoly and Public Control, 132; National versus Local Control, 133; Nationalization Procedure, 133; Management of Nationalized Undertakings, 135.

3. SOCIAL SERVICES 135

The Economic Floor, 135; Income Security, 136; Welfare Services, 137; National Education, 137; Special Problems of Education, 138; Socialized Medicine, 139; Neighborhood and Community Planning, 140; A Nonequalitarian Society, 141.

4. DEFENSE SERVICES 141

Sea Power and Air Power, 141; Role of the Army, 142; Defense of the Empire, 142.

5. FOREIGN AFFAIRS 143

Britain's Regional Interests, 143; Participation in Regional Bodies, 144; Participation in International Bodies, 145.

CHAPTER 8. FROM EMPIRE TO COMMONWEALTH,
W. Hardy Wickwar

1. COLONIAL STATUS 146

Powers of the Mother Country, 146; Privileges of the Colonial Territory, 146; Relations between Colony and Mother Country, 147.

2. DOMINION STATUS 148

Cabinet Responsibility, 148; Continental Union, 148; Foreign Policy, 149; Claims of Independence, 149.

3. THE STATUTE OF WESTMINSTER 150

Equality of Status, 150; Powers of the Imperial Parliament, 151; Bill of Rights for the Dominions, 152.

4. COMMONWEALTH UNITY 152

Common Citizenship, 152; Reciprocal Aid, 153; Commercial Regulation, 154; New Regulatory Means, 155; Nature of Relationship, 155; Parallel Partnership, 156; Political Significance of the Commonwealth, 156.

5. THE DEPENDENT EMPIRE 157

Diversity in the Tropics, 157; International Position of Dependencies, 158; Economic Progress, 158; Governmental Advance, 159; Responsibility of the Colonies, 159; The Colonial Governor, 160; Unsolved Problems of Government, 161.

6. SELF-GOVERNMENT IN THE DEPENDENCIES 161

Uncertainties of Approach, 161; Practical Examples, 162; Malayan Federation, 163; Indirect Rule in Africa, 163; Other Areas, 164; International Implications, 165.

PART V. FEDERAL GOVERNMENT: THE CENTRAL EUROPEAN RECORD

CHAPTER 16. THE GERMAN EMPIRE AND THE WEIMAR REPUBLIC, *John Brown Mason*

CHAPTER 17. THE HITLER NIGHTMARE AND POSTWAR RECONSTRUCTION, *John Brown Mason*

PART VI.   THE SOCIALIST STATE: THE SOVIET UNION AND ITS ORBIT

CHAPTER 20.   RUSSIA AND MARXISM, *John N. Hazard*

CHAPTER 21. THE ONE-PARTY SYSTEM, *John N. Hazard*

CHAPTER 22. GOVERNMENTAL STRUCTURE AND POLITICAL CONTROL, *John N. Hazard*

CHAPTER 23. SOCIALIST ADMINISTRATION AND THE PUBLIC INTEREST, *John N. Hazard*

CHAPTER 24. INDIVIDUAL INTERESTS AND COLLECTIVE NEEDS, *John N. Hazard*

PART VII. RECONSTRUCTION GOVERNMENT: CHINA AND JAPAN

CHAPTER 27. IDEOLOGICAL DYNAMICS OF THE POSTWAR FAR EAST, *Paul M. A. Linebarger*

CHAPTER 28. SOURCES OF POWER IN THE POSTWAR FAR EAST, *Paul M. A. Linebarger*

PART VIII. LATIN AMERICA: MEXICO AND BRAZIL

CHAPTER 31. MEXICO: FROM REVOLUTION TOWARD
CONSTITUTIONALISM, *Henry P. Jordan*

TABLES AND CHARTS

PART I

IDEAS AND IDEALS

CHAPTER 1

MAN AND THE STATE

1. The Nature of Political Man

Human Need and Human Knowledge. All government has its ultimate foundation in the needs of man. Foremost among these, from the standpoint of political organization, are those needs arising from man's existence as a social being. Living as he does in association with his kind, he has a fundamental interest in the establishment of authority to help him both in reaping the benefits and meeting the dangers of such association. If we would understand the problem of government, we shall do well to keep in mind the social nature of man. A purely architectural appreciation of political institutions, or of alternatives of constitutional design, is indicative of little insight into the problem. The primary fact is that government everywhere is government by men and for men, with the number of direct participants and beneficiaries ranging from the few at the one end of the scale to the many at the other.

In focusing their attention on the social nature of man, students of politics spare themselves some of the embarrassment of groping their way in the darker regions of the abstract. But they do not escape the enigmatic aspects of human behavior. Man, individually, is concrete enough. Moreover, he has generally thought it easy to understand his own nature, to know what was good for himself, to recognize what he wanted; consequently, his needs, too, have a seductive appearance of being at once obvious and concrete. But if politics could really be reduced to equations about people who know their own minds and can judge their own needs, it would be child's play, not the art and science it is. As poets like Aeschylus, Shakespeare, and Goethe knew intuitively, long before psychiatric verification was possible, man has little basis for claiming that he understands his own personality and his own good. Too often he cannot explain his actions. Too often he is his own worst enemy.

Comprehension and Emotion. Man's capacity for becoming his own worst enemy stems in part from limitations upon his intellectual perception. His place in the social order has given rise, through all the ages of recorded history, to questions that his intellect lacked the power to answer with finality. Of late, moreover, the questions have tended to get tougher. Modern industrial civilization, supported by the twin pillars of science and technology, is certainly not the simplest structure to comprehend. Because scientific and technical knowledge has pushed ahead at so many points and in so many different directions, no human mind can hope to see the total development except in broadest outline; few minds are good enough even to trace all the outline with some assurance. The great body of humanity is guided by crudely simplified versions of what the best minds say they see. It is thus only too easy for man to become sorely confused over ends and means.

Moreover, man hears different voices within himself. The rational ego lives in constant battle with the irrational ego; nor are the two neatly separated. On the contrary, mental processes are tightly intertwined with emotional processes. As everyone knows, when people are swayed by emotions, their ability to think and act rationally is sharply curtailed if not completely suspended. The extreme testimony to this fact is mob action, which can turn mature and ordinarily restrained individuals into hysterical killers. Emotional urges defying self-control have their origin in a great variety of personal factors, especially in those that cause oppressive feelings of insecurity or inadequacy. The triumph of emotion over reason may also result from an equally burdensome awareness of the growing insignificance of the individual in a society of increasingly large-scale organization. Broadly speaking, when conscious achievement of purpose is smothered by obstacles, smoldering frustration often sets off an explosion.

Political Man's Complexity. Although the only truly concrete element in the structure of government, man therefore is not a standard unit in the calculus of politics. Whether one likes it or not, it is undoubtedly true that no unduly simplified concept of man can long survive in political science. The greatest errors of political theory have had as cause the oversimplification of human nature. Some thinkers have built the entire edifice of their theory of government on the contention that man is essentially evil. Others have reversed this position, insisting that man is essentially good. Whatever the criteria of good or evil, today the psychologist is rare who would tie himself to either alternative.

Discomforting though it may be, the sounder view is at the same time less categorical. Man is both good and bad, both wise and foolish, both courageous and timid, both strong and weak; and, as the primary factor in politics, he transmits to the latter his own problematic nature by showing in his individual conduct all these characteristics in varying degrees. Complicated rather than simple, he is not seldom baffled by his inability to predict his own behavior. It is therefore obvious that the generalizations of political science must be framed in recognition of the quicksand nature of human motivation.[1]

Political man has done and will continue to do many strange things. To

---

[1] Two extraordinarily illuminating documents are *The Diaries of Franz Kafka, 1910-1913,* ed. Max Brod (New York, 1948), and *The Journals of André Gide, 1914-1927,* II, trans. Justin O'Brien (New York, 1948). These books are an eloquent record of man's struggle with himself. A classic is Graham Wallas, *Human Nature in Politics* (4th ed., New York, 1950).

mention but a few within the range of our immediate experience: He has persistently voiced a preference for as little government as possible, yet has not found it incongruous to exert steady pressure for an expansion of governmental protection and assistance. He has come to admit the appalling risk of an uncontrolled business cycle, yet has been very slow to dismiss his strong mental reservations toward governmental planning to avert this risk. In hours of exaltation, he has seen the glory of popular rule and acknowledged it as a grand venture in cooperation, yet more often he has cursed government as a scheming agent of interference. He has not remained ignorant of the uncounted ways in which the modern service state sustains the national economy, yet his most familiar nightmare has been the vision of a despotic bureaucracy feasting on the fruits of the people's toil like a swarm of locusts. The fact that there is no familiar cartoon figure portraying government as a source of benefits or services further illuminates this complicated rather than simple nature of political man.[2]

Abstract Man's Trickery. A heroic interpretation of history would find most of its raw material in particular personalities. Political science, on the other hand, deals in the main with the behavior of large numbers of people and so must necessarily place great emphasis upon man in general. Man in particular is concrete, but man in general is always abstract. In fact, so much of an abstraction is abstract man that he has never been met, engaged in conversation, or interviewed. He was not born, nor does he die; he lives as an immortal figment of statistics. In him we have a convenient symbol that is supposed to furnish some idea of what most of us are thinking and doing or are likely to think and do next.

In examining abstract man, we are confronting the conformities of social life, which have a tendency to mask individual characteristics and so inevitably fail in many ways to indicate accurately what particular men are actually thinking and doing or are likely to think and do next. Abstract man, therefore, may claim for himself more consideration than he is justly entitled to receive: there is always the question of for precisely how many of us he has a right to speak. Unless we are careful, he may trick us by his quantitative pretenses. We must correct his exaggerations. We must watch him closely. We must doubt him often.

2. The Value of Comparison

Use of Comparative Study. In such corrective effort, the primary step is to accept nothing at face value. We should be on guard against giving too much weight to the conformities of social life and the political institutions they support. Change is constant as well as vital; and every set rule has its exceptions to challenge it. It is therefore highly advisable to scrutinize the terrain of politics from as many different vantage points as are accessible.

---

[2] To borrow a point from H. D. Lasswell, *Politics: Who Gets What, When, How* (New York, 1936), p. 37.

One of the best vantage points is that gained in comparative study. The comparison of types of behavior, for instance, is an illuminating approach in the identification of the bounds within which man in the abstract is a helpful concept. Comparative study is still more revealing when we place side by side different systems of government or, as integral parts of such systems, different institutions that serve the same political purpose. This book, by supplying the reader with a foundation for comparative analysis, attempts to make possible the extension and rounding out of his knowledge of politics.

Comparative study of government is nothing new. It had its first boom many centuries ago. Aristotle, considered by many the father of political science, gave the comparative approach a central place in his methodology. Dissatisfied with Plato's freely roaming speculative reasoning, he instructed the students gathered about him in the Lyceum in the discipline of empirical research. This discipline brought forth a substantial collection of case studies dealing with the political organization of individual Greek city-states, exemplified by the surviving *Constitution of Athens.*

Such investigation of comparable institutions and dispassionate comparison of findings widened the field of intellectual vision, made established facts more meaningful, encouraged a systematic grouping of all that was known, and so made possible a theory of government subject to the test of observation. Since Aristotle's day these advantages have been sufficiently obvious to commend the comparative method to students of government, not excepting those who were unable or were disinclined to equal Aristotle's scientific zeal. In his *Prince,* Machiavelli bolstered shrewd advice to Italy's statesmen with telling references to the wisdom and folly of rulers in other times and places. Harrington reinforced the tenor of his *Oceana* with evidence drawn from the political practices of various nations, ancient and contemporary. Montesquieu derived some of the most influential ideas in his *Spirit of the Laws,* especially that of the separation of powers, from the comparison of different political systems. Rarely affected by the feuds between different schools of thought, comparative study of government has outlived passing methodological fashions.

Extension of Comparability. When most of the world moves in the same general direction, especially in economic development, comparative study of politics extends its area. An isolated social system may present particular lessons—for example, the tribal way of life of the Hopi Indian could teach metropolitan man much about the avoidance of conflict. But Hopi governance offers few significant parallels to the manner in which the political institutions of a progressively urbanized society function. This society is primarily industrial. The industrial revolution has been a great equalizer of continents and regions; together with the drive for foreign markets, the sweeping advances of a scientific and technological character made during the nineteenth and twentieth centuries have fostered the establishment of a world-wide minimum standard of existence. This standard is acknowledged in every part of the globe, if only for the purpose of measuring relative local inadequacies.

Notwithstanding differences in national economic levels, large masses of people in many different countries live in about the same way, share about the same material values, and enjoy about the same basic amenities of life; were it not for the destructions of World War II, these masses would be even larger than they are. Productive resources in most of the world are harnessed in approximately the same technical manner and under similar legal forms. Where the economy has remained predominantly agrarian, pressure for native industries has been rising: the equalizer continues to be active. In the twentieth century, more human beings go through their day in roughly the same way than at any time since man left the cave.

These uniformities in the general mode of living have been multiplied by wider contact, which, in turn, is the result of the rapid shrinkage of distance. In 1790 it took six wearying days to travel, by stagecoach, from Boston to New York. In less time, the modern traveler, whether or not he gains anything by the rush, can comfortably circle the globe by plane; and we are far from having reached the practical limits of speed in ordinary air transport. When Karl Marx wrote his *Capital,* the prognostications he made had immediate meaning only for a few industrial countries. One century later, the problems of industrial society are written all over the political structure and processes of the modern nation-state.

Common Features of Government. The common impact of these problems becomes evident as soon as one considers some of the most characteristic features of contemporary government. In little more than two generations, all the highly developed countries have witnessed an extraordinary growth in government functions, especially in such critical fields as those of economic regulation, employer-employee relations, and public welfare or social insurance. Progressive extension of governmental responsibility has carried with it a corresponding expansion and increase in the number of administrative agencies. Because governmental machinery for the handling of administrative business has become so much larger, proportionately greater political importance has accrued to the executive branch. The increasing importance of the latter derives essentially from its power of control over administrative operations coupled with its competence for policy coordination: thus can be met the problem of incorporating far-flung regulatory and service operations into coherent programs related to the needs of the economy. To attend to these needs is not usurpation; hence, the recent spread in the relative ascendancy of the executive branch has not ushered in any general decline of legislative control. Rather, legislative determination has been raised to a higher and more consequential plane. Yet it is clear that a common feature of government today is the administrative nature of the quantitative bulk of government.

In the economic sphere, the sensitivity of industrial production to fluc-

tuations in markets and purchasing power has made unemployment a ter-
rifying prospect to large portions of mankind. They therefore yearn for
"full employment." This widespread yearning has drawn forth equally
widespread governmental commitments to counter depressions through appropriate action based on constant and continuing economic diagnosis.

Still larger portions of mankind have faced, more than once during their
lives, the horror of war. Their anxious quest for security against aggression
has translated itself not only into heavy defense budgets but also into public
obligations of military training and service, as well as into a noteworthy range
of governmental restraints upon private action for security reasons.

Finally, government everywhere has come to take a much greater interest
in both the formation and the expression of public opinion, a development
that has led to differing degrees of governmental influence in the operation of
various means of communication, such as broadcasting. It has also led to
technical arrangements by which chief executives and other political leaders
are enabled to reach national audiences of record size. Another result has
been a proliferation of informational services rendered by government departments. Within proper restraining limits, government comes closer to the
people by playing an active rather than a passive part in the crystallization of
public opinion. In its extreme form, such activity has encompassed an integrated system of propaganda directed by political officers.

Comparison and Imitation. Perhaps it should be emphasized that comparative study of politics has only one legitimate goal—to advance knowledge. Its ability to attain this goal is due to the fact that what is treated as
commonplace or is habitually confined to a particular meaning in the governmental experience of one country usually has a deeper significance when
looked at afresh against the background of political institutions in other countries. Such fresh examination in a wider frame of reference is always a broadening influence. It guards against the errors of nearsightedness. It extends
the range of observation by adding another dimension, as it were.[3]

Comparative analysis, on the other hand, does not have as its guiding
principle the assumption that there is one best way of government, which,
when discovered, is to be adopted everywhere. Advocates of wholesale imitation would find little comfort in comparative study, for one point it makes
plain is the limited practicability of transferring the fruits of political ingenuity from one country to another. But one country's example of success
or failure may provide others with welcome experience or specific pointers to
be applied discriminatingly to their own affairs. These are the very grounds
on which Mr. Justice Brandeis rested his praise of the experimental potentialities of federalism.

Current Benefits of Comparative Analysis. Moreover, in an era in
which the decisive influence of the United States in world affairs has become

---

[3] This point is well illustrated by such a broadly conceived comparative treatise as that of
C. J. Friedrich, *Constitutional Government and Democracy* (rev. ed., Boston, 1950).

a momentous fact, it should be easy for Americans to see the larger practical value of comparative politics. It is now a matter of grave importance that we raise our eyes from the domestic scene long enough to learn as much as we can about the political characteristics and tendencies of other countries. Only such knowledge can bring into being the kind of informed public opinion that is needed to make possible and to maintain a wisely conceived American foreign policy.

Most of the factors that exert a controlling influence on international affairs are factors arising from national need or national self-interest, real or imagined. The individual's response to either is affected by the political ways and governmental traditions of his nation. In turn, however, the individual affects these national ways and traditions. Here, once more, we come face to face with vast throngs of human beings—contented, miserable, boastful, desperate, callous, frenzied. They crowd the stage of politics, milling about legislatures, executive offices, and courts of law. The more prominence comparative study succeeds in giving to the human element, the less danger there is that it will end up in a meaningless comparison of empty form and ossified ritual. Like all social sciences, political science can be truly scientific only to the degree in which it contributes to the creation of a science of man.[4]

3. Political Man as Organized Man

Man under Government. We have seen, then, that to live as a social being is an expression of the nature of man. At bottom, all society is both part and product of man's social nature. In the social organization and in the processes of social life around him, he always meets in some measure his own social self, or, more specifically, he meets the institutional embodiment of the social nature and needs of his kind.

Because man is a social being, he is also a political being, for in seeking a mode of life satisfying to his social nature, he is forced to create a system of authority that will provide him with at least the rudimentary elements of law and order. In doing so, however, he also creates a dilemma, and one that he has never been able to solve. It exists in the possibility that any system of authority he sets up may evade his control—that is, the control exerted in common by the great body of men. When that happens, and to the extent to which it happens, political power usually becomes an instrument of exploitation used in the interest of the few to the disadvantage of the many. Social man needs government sorely; but in equal measure he needs to exert enough control over it to keep it in his service and to prevent it from being turned against him. These needs make social man political man.

It is thus evident that political man cannot be thought of as belonging to a

---

[4] An indication of the extent to which this point of view is becoming common may be found in some of the more recent general treatments of political science, especially C. E. Merriam, *Systematic Politics* (Chicago, 1945).

functional or occupational category—as does the policeman, the meteorologist, or the businessman. In particular, political man is not one whose paid job it is to handle political affairs. There have always been governmental functionaries—lawmakers, diplomats, soldiers, administrative officials, judges —but these political man likes to denounce as politicians, or bureaucrats, or brass hats. Typically, he suspects the motives of any expert in politics and takes pride in his low opinion of the breed. Political man is political not by occupation, but because he lives under government.

Foundations of Political Organization. Society is formed and constantly reinforced by the social behavior of its members. In the same way, government, as the basic structure of authority within the social order, draws its vitality from the political initiative and response of the great mass of men. Consequently, since government is capable of touching him at any time and in a number of ways, each individual is a political being, at least in a passive sense. In order to be consciously effective as a political being, however, he must accept his part in the political process. As political man, he is called upon to assume the burdens of politically organized man.

In one sense, political man is organized man independent of personal civic effort on his part, by virtue of his status as a compulsory member of any particular nation-state. For the consequences of this status, it does not matter whether he happens to exercise the privileges of a free citizen or whether he trudges along under the heavy load of duties assigned to a mere subject without effective rights. But in either case his national status is that of organized man, since for all practical purposes he is unable to strip it off.

Compulsion of National Status. Under the auspices of the modern state, the organizational implications of government for the life of everyone have steadily unfolded. At the same time, the condition of the intentionally or unintentionally stateless individual has been made ever more precarious. To a striking degree the state today has become what a philosopher of individualism once decried it as being, "an imposed fate." It is a fate that has engaged millions of common folk, eager to live in peace, in the cataclysmic wars of the twentieth century.

To most of us, the compulsory nature of the organization that goes with nationality is so obvious as to appear completely normal. It is true that if one starts with the premise of personal freedom, the exact opposite—mobility at pleasure—might more appropriately be considered normal. But how is any individual to engineer his escape from the state? Even though he were suited for a solitary existence, he still has only a small chance of remaining undisturbed in whatever backwoods he may retire to. However well-hidden his lair, he is likely to be tracked down by such agents of government as the tax collector, the sanitation officer, the draft board, the census taker, the security investigator, and the fire guard. This annoyance is yet little compared with the virtual impossibility of slipping out from under one sovereignty and quietly assuming allegiance to another. Passports and visas may be withheld in the exercise of discretionary power. Emigration and immigration proceed through barely opened doors and require elaborate certificates and permits, issued or refused by administrative agencies in the light of circumstances.

Conscious Self-Organization. If, on the other hand, the individual sees no reason to shun his community or to flee his government; if he is ready to meet at least his basic civic obligations; if he is even eager for an active part in political life—under these conditions, his first task is one of reflection. He must himself clearly recognize the full significance of his status as politically organized man. This he will be able to do only by seeking an understanding of the essence of citizenship. Next he must adjust his political behavior to the rules of conduct emanating from such an understanding.[5] In no other way can he organize himself for his role as political man. If he does not attain this understanding, if he does not undertake this self-organization, he cannot hope to make himself felt politically. On the contrary, he is likely to dissipate his civic efforts, to despair of his contribution as a member of the community, and to take eventual refuge in the wholly negative attitudes of the uncooperative grumbler.

But although political man is organized in either a passive or an active sense, even his most active political self-expression does not claim him fully. As a rule, he is organized politically only in part, and to varying degrees. Of course, as long as he fails to understand his civic role, he is always only partly organized; on each occasion on which the necessity arises, he has to be talked into filling his place in the ranks or into taking on particular chores.

Interfering Factors. But political man appears only partly organized for still other reasons. Even when he consciously accepts his role in the community, he repeatedly breaks with his organized self—in most instances when irresistibly driven by the irrational forces within himself. Prejudice, fear, hatred, or mere inertia sometimes overwhelm his reason; his emotional response sweeps him along, away from such standards of judgment as he would ordinarily respect in appraising political issues. To this extent, and for so long as such conditions exist, he may be said to disorganize himself as political man. Needless to say, the limits on his insight and his knowledge are bound to have the same effect.

No less important an interfering factor is the circumstance that political man is organized in more than one manner. The primary organization— that from which his status as a national is derived—competes with other organizations for his attention and cooperation. The latter organizations are nearly all inferior in power and size to the basic type provided by the nation-state, but they may have a primary appeal to the minds of their members. Political man thus finds himself torn between the conflicting claims of many organizations devoted to special causes and interests. His

---

[5] For an outstanding exposition of this need, see John Dewey, *The Public and Its Problems* (New York, 1927; reissued Chicago, 1946).

involvement in these is largely voluntary. He may choose to be a member of a labor union or of an employer association; he may belong to an organized farm group or be tied in with such other special interests as mining, shipping, or food distribution. He may think of himself primarily as a consumer and in consequence give most of his free time to a consumer organization. He may be principally active as a member of a church, a professional organization, or an association for the advancement or care of particular groups of the population.

Such activities may deepen political man's civic sense. All too often, however, they restrict his perspective and weaken his concern with the general interest.[6]

Effect of Personal Interests. Finally, man is a politically organized being in part only precisely because citizenship is not a gainful occupation. He must earn his living elsewhere. His full-time job is in the factory, on the farm, in the office, in the store. As a consequence, his activity as a citizen can be at best only a part-time business.

In addition, there is the matter of personal preference. In some ways, social man likes to be entirely nonpolitical; in some ways, entirely private. He has a family, friends, neighbors, and wider social circles devoted to fun and play or even to enlightenment. There are times when he doesn't care at all for public affairs; when his personal worries have a monopoly on his mind; or when his private affairs run along so splendidly that he is reluctant to do anything but enjoy himself. At such times, his part-time concern as a citizen may reach a completely inactive state.

Variables of Political Behavior. All these variables of motivation, interest, ability, and circumstance give man's political conduct characteristics of great diversity. For the political scientist, therefore, the propriety of generalization comes to depend upon imaginative and sophisticated analysis made simultaneously at many different points, inasmuch as individual governmental institutions as well as the entire political process are subject to many subtle changes that fail to strike the eye at first glance.

For example, although the constitutional allocation of power and the structure of government remain exactly the same, shifts in civic morale may produce a vastly different degree of political unity and public spirit. When large masses of people succumb to apathy or hopelessness, a corresponding change is felt in the pulse of politics. Conversely, when crisis shakes up a nation, the spreading awareness of peril and simultaneous evidence of leadership may combine to arouse political man to vigorous civic action. He may wholeheartedly subordinate his private interests to public needs. He may be eager

---

[6] For a general introduction to the pattern of multiple allegiances arising from the structure of associations within contemporary society, see C. E. Merriam, *The Making of Citizens* (Chicago, 1931). This book provides a broad summary of findings arrived at in a series of studies dealing with training for citizenship in various countries.

to contribute his leisure hours to community service. He may even clamor for a chance to offer tangible sacrifices for the common good.[7]

Impact on Political Life. These variables of behavior—especially the fluctuations in the extent to which man makes himself felt as a politically organized being—introduce a considerable element of change into public life, national or local. Not surprisingly, the spirit of civic participation and the operative rhythm of government in the United States, for example, have been quite different at different times. They were of one kind in the gloom of economic disintegration in 1932; of quite another in the early glow of the New Deal in 1933. Again, they were of one kind at the height of the war effort in 1944, but of another in the postwar uncertainties of 1946. Or, to take an example in the municipal sphere: The temper of a local community may be one thing in the stagnant condition of boss rule, but quite another after a successful campaign for the council-manager plan has been undertaken.

On the same grounds, one can establish distinctions in the inner strength of any other country at different points in its history. Such a line of inquiry would go far to explain why France collapsed under Hitler's assault, while England stood up under an equally severe test. The historic fact that England did meet this test, however, says little about her capacity for living through a comparable ordeal some other day. No people is consistent with itself all the time. Each shows measurable variations in its vital processes. Political man functions in constantly changing degrees of intensity or indifference.

Self-Organization and Political Theory. In the first and most necessary instance, political man organizes himself by gaining an understanding of his own role in the community. There are of course more formal methods of self-organization. For instance, the citizen registers for voting purposes; works as member of a political party getting out the vote on election day; enrolls in a nonpartisan campaign to build support for a civic program. But none of these specific activities can mean much unless political man first succeeds in defining in his own mind what government is entitled to demand of him and what he may demand of government.

This matter is one of ideas, not of membership cards. In order to provide a framework within which man can find place both for the structure of authority and himself, such ideas must be capable of linking up with one another to form a working theory of government. Purely as an intellectual edifice, a theory of government has little general appeal. Typically, its architect is a political philosopher, whose blueprints are seldom widely read. But popular versions of his thought may gain sufficient circulation to be acted upon at a strategic moment. All government rests on theories. Even in

---

[7] Except in the *Iliad*, the interplay of motives under conditions of common strain has been depicted nowhere more memorably than in Leo Tolstoy's *War and Peace.*

its most erratic manifestations, political practice bears some relation to precepts of theory. Moreover, most men of practical affairs, though they sometimes like to affirm the opposite view, make a success of what they are doing only because they have a definite mental orientation toward their work—that is, are guided by a theory.

In the market place of public affairs, political ideas have currency mainly in the form of a crude type of shorthand; they are handed about as images, symbols, or slogans. However inadequate intellectually as a substitute for full-bodied ideas, the political images men carry in their heads, the symbols and slogans to which they respond, do exert a controlling influence over their actions. Political conduct is, therefore, in large part a reflection of political ideas. The latter aid man in visualizing the political structure and the political process; in determining his own share in affecting both; and in working out for himself a point of view and a practical approach toward citizenship. In all these respects, he acts upon ideas about government, fragmentary or comprehensive, simple or elaborate. In organizing himself as a citizen, he relies heavily on those ideas he has learned to accept as basic in any explanation of what the relationship between man and authority ought to be.

4. Ideas, Institutions, and Realities

Ideas as Institutional Supports. Ideas do not live in a vacuum. They express themselves through institutions. Ideas endow institutions with a purpose; generate an institutional will, as it were; and, by the directive force of this institutional will, govern the general operation of the institution. Ideas equip institutions with defensive armor, keeping intact the institutional rationale; or, conversely, they spearhead the attack of change on institutional purpose. But in all the instances in which they play an active role in relation to the institutional structure, social, economic, or political, ideas have to contend with what man accepts as the given realities of his condition.

Thus, a selective process is at work whose outcome determines the survival of particular ideas. Some ideas may soar to lofty heights but never find a place in man's mind because they fail to tally with the fundamental facts of his experience. Although experience is not stationary, it refers our sense of reality to the familiar and rejects the unfamiliar. It follows that ideas in harmony with a *status quo* usually have wider appeal than ideas running counter to it—unless the *status quo* is disintegrating. For example, a property system based on individual gain will keep itself surrounded by a cluster of ideas arguing the benefits of the system, but will at the same time supply an inhospitable soil for the growth of ideas stressing the collective use of property. Conversely, ideas about personal liberty, even when officially promoted, may never take hold if the government at the same time contradicts its words about individual freedom by its practice.

In brief, a close relationship exists between ideas, institutions, and realities.

The relationship is so intimate that it seems foolish to raise the question once asked of the late philosopher Alfred North Whitehead, "What is more important, ideas or things?" His answer was very much to the point—"Why, I should imagine ideas *about* things." Perhaps one might amplify the answer by giving first place to ideas about things that relate to man's experience.

Ideas as Unified Frame of Reference. It is significant that the most enduring ideas about the place of man under government have been those of comprehensive sweep, of bold vision, of inner coherence. Political ideas likely to impress themselves upon man's mind are ideas integrated in a system, ideas that make sense in relation to one another. The need for system in political theory can probably be best appreciated when one considers the all-pervasive effects of the structure of political authority. Living under this structure is man, who is at once parent, worker, neighbor, and citizen, all in the same frame of ideas. This frame of ideas must show a high degree of unity if it is to serve him adequately.

Political theory may confine itself to an explanation of the organization and uses of power in a particular setting. Or it may set out on the more ambitious undertaking of demonstrating generally the essential features of the best kind of government as the ideal type. In either case, an integrated body of ideas is alone adequate for the purpose. The point of departure, of course, is man—man wanting to be himself individually as well as socially. In order to be himself, he needs safeguards against intrusions on his peace, freedom for his self-development, and justice to prevent abuse. Government, which extends these guaranties to him, is therefore a principal factor in his scheme of values, and consequently becomes part of the ordered universe in which man seeks his own purpose. His concern with a purposeful universe, as it is carried over into politics, leads him to look for a broadly inclusive system of political values.

Ideas as Moral Law. Concern with values is the core of all political theory. The logic of human action centers upon this core. Because man, as a political being, sooner or later learns that he gets nowhere by aimlessly pushing or being pushed about, he seeks a working formula of politics by which to go. Because such a working formula is apt to let him down if it is just a jumbled assortment of unrelated particulars, he gropes for some systematic theory of government. But in formulating such a theory, he needs a guide, not only to what is, but also to what ought to be.

Merely to know politics in an empirical way is not sufficient. Any definition of citizenship, for example, implies that there is in general reasonable certainty about what a good citizen should and should not do. In other words, the question of the moral law in politics is broached. In order to answer it, political theory must commit itself on its order of values, on things good and things evil.

In formulating its system of values, political theory is bound to encounter other systems. To begin with the most obvious, there is the system of values put forth by religious faith, usually the most highly developed. But primitive superstition, too, boasts some system of values; and any body of personal ethics autonomously conceived, even that of the agnostic or the atheist, represents a value system. This coexistence of different systems of values raises important questions of interrelation.

Interrelations of Value Systems. Acknowledgment of God's order as the order of the universe reduces any system of political values to a subordinate place. No system of political values, on this basis, could be thought of as departing from the harmony inherent in God's order. On the contrary, political values could be only an elaboration of religious values. Of course, on the premise of compatibility, religion may take a relatively neutral attitude toward the value system of politics; this situation is particularly likely to occur when religion is no longer a strongly effective force in society. But even under such conditions, the air of neutrality could not be maintained if the value order of politics appeared to challenge the religious system of values in any significant respect.

If fundamental breaks occur between the religious and the political system of values, continuous conflict is inevitable. Such conflict would tear into the very heart of man's basic allegiance.[8] If he follows the voice of religion, he must sharply reject the irreconcilable counterclaims of politics. If he takes the opposite side, he will come to turn away either from religion or from those who speak for it. The attitude of the Holy See toward Marxist communism is a clear illustration of the fundamental conflict that may arise between a religious and a political value system.

The same alternative is offered when the place of the value system of religion is taken by one of personal ethics independent of religious faith. But a greater risk is faced by the rebel who, for reasons springing from his personal ethics, defies the prevailing system of political values. He usually must meet the consequences of such defiance without the comfort of institutional support.

Another condition results from the revolutionary or evolutionary ascendancy of systems of political values in periods of declining religious vigor or progressive moral confusion. Such tendencies have long been in evidence. As man's moral vision of a divine order has grown dim, the waning strength of religion has left him either to flounder unsupported or to put his faith in various secular prescriptions. One such prescription is a naïve pseudo-religion of science claiming cultish deference for every scientific finding, a position that is anathema to true science, as leaders of science have pointed out frequently. At another extreme, unchallenged primacy has been claimed for a system of political values consolidated into an all-embracing ideology.

---

[8] The position of a leader of Protestant theology is set forth with great distinction in Reinhold Niebuhr, *Nature and Destiny of Man* (New York, 1941); that of an equally outstanding Catholic philosopher in Jacques Maritain, *Scholasticism and Politics,* ed. Mortimer Adler (New York, 1940) and *Christianity and Democracy,* trans. D. C. Anson (New York, 1944).

In this last case, political theory in actual fact transforms itself into a secular religion. It will insist upon settling all issues of right or wrong on its own terms. It will present itself as the sole foundation of all morality, arguing that all morality at its source is identical with political morality. Indeed, on this premise, a political ideology may be able to ally itself with a dependent religion, as the relationship between the Kremlin and the Russian Orthodox church indicates. It is evident that the rank claimed for political theory among the systems of values that influence man's choice is a fundamental factor in distinguishing among different systems of government.

Harmony of Political Values. A political system, then, though presenting itself in a set of institutions, is at bottom an enactment of values and ideas. It is truly a political system in exact proportion to the support it commands from a systematic body of ideas grounded in an order of values. This does not mean that either the body of ideas or the underlying value system must be original or pure, underived or unmixed. It does mean that both the ideas, however extensively blended, and the values, however heterogeneous by pedigree, must be integrated. They must form, or be susceptible of being considered to form, a harmonious whole.

For example: The value of individual liberty cannot be reconciled with the diametrically opposite value of unconditional obedience demanded in the interest of maximum political strength. Personal freedom can be reconciled, however, with the different value of the general welfare. The value of liberty, in turn, correlates with maxims of political theory. One such maxim is that authority must always be held in check. This maxim cannot, of course, be applied in conjunction with the opposite maxim that the ordained supreme leader is always right. But the maxim that authority must always be kept in check does not conflict with the different maxim that lawful acts of authority warrant compliance. Furthermore, the value of freedom and the maxim of checked authority jointly affect the practical alternatives on the level of institutional arrangements. Both value and maxim jointly sustain a division of authority into separate branches, legislative, executive, and judicial. Both reject as incompatible a structure of authority combining these three powers into one political organ. On the other hand, the institutional arrangement of divided powers may be combined with arrangements for needed cooperation beween the different political organs.

Role of Ideology. The interrelated values and maxims of political theory lend a strong weight of justification and propriety to the political institutions they support. Political institutions so supported acquire self-evident merit in the eyes of those who are consciously or unconsciously permeated by those same underlying values and maxims. Simultaneously, however, political theory also provides standards of general accountability for institutional performance. For example, an American newspaper editorial, say, may blast a legislature for giving consideration to an undemocratic measure. Even if practicable in a narrow sense, the measure would still be open to attack as being in conflict with democratic political theory. In the British phrase, such a proposal is something that politically "isn't done." Conversely, criticism may be aimed at the failure of a governmental agency to do what on grounds of ideology it is under an obligation to do. A constitution, or its integral political institutions, may become lifeless unless constantly animated by its spirit—the ideas that gave it rise and give it meaning.

It is thus only too plain that no political system can afford to be indifferent toward its own ideology. Nor can it safely be casual about emerging challenges, whether these challenges come to the fore in the guise of ideas or of realities. Yet ideologies differ in their methods of meeting such challenges. An ideology that is in effect a secular religion will claim the right to respond with repressive countermeasures. This claim may go so far as to entail a police system of thought control. Another ideology will accept the challenge and gain from it an incentive to increase the effectiveness of institutional performance.

Ideological Deception. Of course, one must not leave out of account man's innate capacity for illusion. Political theory may hand him rose-colored glasses, and he may grow so fond of the pretty picture they present that he forgets the lessons of his drab day-by-day experience.

An ideology may, for example, promote the belief that anyone through just hard work can reach the highest rungs of the social ladder, thus assigning to government a generally passive role. The illusion of unobstructed opportunity is not necessarily harmed by dry statistics to the contrary. Yet there is such a thing as a law of diminishing ideological returns—at least in the longer run.

In the longer run, disparity between the assertion and the reality is likely to cast doubts upon the ideology itself. Advocates of political change have therefore always faced an ugly dilemma. If they boldly conjured up an idealized goal, its inspirational appeal might provide a powerful initial boost, but the discrepancy between it and hard facts would later cause trouble. On the other hand, a sober statement of realistically defined objectives, though more easily attainable in the light of experience, would fail to stir up mass emotion. The art of statesmanship consists in striking the best balance possible between the two.

Adaptation of Ideology. All ideology has its own propaganda, acknowledged or unacknowledged. The basic political values are deliberately taught —in the schools, in the press, over the radio, in youth organizations, in political parties—by all forms of government. At the same time, such changes as stem from the dynamics of social or economic development have continuously to be accommodated in the given ideological framework. Ability to accomplish such accommodation is perhaps the cardinal test in the survival of an ideology.

This last point brings up the question of who is to function as the caretaker of the ideology. One could think of different possibilities—a designated body, a recognized elite, a formal majority, a continuing consensus freely sought. Once more, in the choice among these alternatives, one is made aware of a sharp distinction between different systems of government. Democratic government would reject as incompatible with itself any form of minority control over its ideology. It would hesitate to take too great stock in a formal majority—except in an exceedingly stable one. Democratic government would accomplish ideological adaptation in the gradual consolidation of a popular consensus. In direct contrast, totalitarianism settles such problems by pronouncement of the leader.

The Ideological Trap. Authority can be claimed in the name of democracy for a popular consensus only when its development is free, when no coercion stifles individual expression of conviction. Coercion may have different origins. Legislative and administrative measures may aim to make it dangerous or highly unprofitable for individuals to express certain opinions, or to volunteer opinions generally unless these be commonplace. Government officials may deem it their business to tell the public what "good citizens" do, thus building up pressure against other conceptions of proper civic action. Organized groups outside government may undertake to discourage, by word or deed, the open expression of minority views. Ingrained habits of thought as well as settled prejudices may operate as factors of coercion, too. Above all, the contagion of fear may become a powerful source of coercion by rushing the large body of people into conclusions that would not stand up to calm inquiry.

In a sense, no doubt, the free development of a popular consensus is hampered by the modern nation-state itself, in part because its mighty machinery is always available for the conscious promotion of a consensus in support of given public policies, in part because in an age of crisis the nation-state has little patience with processes that take time. Yet adaptation of ideology under democratic auspices does take time. It is a matter of growth of public understanding, of understanding widely shared; and it requires conditions conducive to the kind of unforced growth that sinks each root deeply.

Democratic ideology, by its very nature, is a living thing, forever engaged in winning a reception in individual minds and individual hearts. It is a guide to each citizen's personal responsibility, and it therefore implies man's ability and willingness to assume such responsibility. It does not say, as does totalitarianism: "Here is the Word. It is your duty to take it and to live by it. You are not free to reject it for you would thus reject yourself." Democracy has no use for this ideological trap. For the definiteness of a secular gospel, at once assuring and enslaving, and for the self-appointed guardians of the right line, enforced as the higher law, democracy substitutes a greater aspiration. Its aspiration is to attain, through each individual's contribution, a political order whose highest dogma is the worth of man.

CHAPTER 2

ALTERNATIVES OF IDEOLOGY

1. The Basic Themes

Individuality and Community. As a social being, man is drawn in two opposite directions at once. Because, on the one hand, he seeks to be himself, his concern is with his own individuality; because, on the other, he seeks association with his kind, his concern is with various social groupings. This intricate duality of concern, part and parcel of man's social nature, introduces into political thought a difference of emphasis more marked than any other. To put it very simply, the aim of political theory may be seen either as the defense of the individual against the community or as the guarding of the common good against harm by individual self-interest.

Fundamental though this distinction seems to be, one should not forget that ultimately it turns into a difference of emphasis. The difference, however, is far from slight. Americans have long valued an ideology that supplied the ramparts behind which man's individuality could find protection against the inroads of political power, including that wielded by the politically organized community. This theme, as a matter of fact, represents the dominant undercurrent of political thought in the Western world, especially in the theory of constitutional government. On the other hand, influential political theorists have heralded the organized community as social man's most important achievement and as the most direct fulfillment of his needs. In this perspective the political community is seen as man's better self, his individuality finding its worthiest expression in participation in the functions of the community. Man's dedication to the attainment of common ends thus becomes at the same time the consummation of his noblest individual aspirations. Here, then, is a countertheme to the fundamental individualism that is woven into the Western constitutional ideal.

Collectivist Variations. Theme and countertheme have sometimes drawn together temporarily, but generally each has pursued its separate course. The countertheme, which lends great weight to collective needs, has exerted a passing influence upon Western constitutionalism in times of stress, most conspicuously in support of sweeping governmental action under emergency conditions. But it is more sharply evident in the body of ideas mustered on behalf of the collective state proper—particularly those that have given rise to the different types of totalitarianism, whether its proletarian form, as adopted under Soviet auspices, or the bourgeois variety championed by Hitler and Mussolini. Yet one should not identify the collectivist branch of political theory with modern totalitarian regimes alone, inasmuch as it has played an important part in the development of political institutions throughout history, especially in the ancient Eastern world—with effects quite different from those produced by totalitarianism.

Perhaps the finest example of this development is China's Confucian tradition. If proof were needed, the beneficial working of the Confucian ideology in China's past would go far to demonstrate that a political theory focusing attention on the community does not deny the individual. It does not compel the latter to surrender himself body and soul to the state.

Synthesis of Values. On reflection, of course, this conclusion is hardly surprising. Whether, as a general proposition, one attaches the greater value to the community or to the individual, the paramount problem is always that of the relationships between the two. Man must relate his individuality to the needs of his social nature. The community must relate its social contributions to the needs of individual self-expression and participation.

The creative potentialities in these delicate relationships are lost when either the individual interest or the collective interest, overrunning its proper bounds in the social context, seeks a ruthless triumph over the other. This disruption occurs when man, in pathological travesty of individualism, sees himself only and refuses to see the community. It also occurs when the collective impulse of the community is corrupted into a quest of power for power's sake. Much of the significance of the ideological system ascribed to Confucius lies in its character as a productive synthesis of man's individual and collective interests. Conversely, it illuminates the folly of drawing too categorical a contrast between the individual and the community. Each, of necessity, is in some way part of the other.

2. The Confucian Tradition

Distinguishing Features. In comparing the Confucian system with modern constitutionalism, one finds it marked by four distinguishing features. In the first place, the role of the primary regulatory agency in the Confucian tradition was played not by government, but by a body of doctrine. Second, this body of doctrine addressed itself to all human relations, private and public, thus providing a comprehensive code of righteous conduct. Third, compliance with the code was insured by making it the most important subject of all education. And fourth, a scholar-officialdom, trained to interpret the code wisely, was charged with the dual task of acting as living examples of righteous behavior and of guiding government along the path of justice and welfare.

In all four respects the Confucian tradition absorbed into itself much that was not specifically present in the teachings of its originator, K'ung Fu-tzu, or Master K'ung, westernized as Confucius (551-479 B.C.). But this development led to no sacrifice of basic continuity and consistency. Confucius centered his attention on man's character as a social being. In his explicit social orientation he proceeded by a road independent of religious faith and so escaped a later conflict with the message of Buddhism. Nor did he find satisfaction in the metaphysical and mystical appeal to man's inner self that signified the essence of Taoism, as elaborated by Lao Tzu. Confucius articulated the inherited values of the Chinese way in order to arrive at an enduring prescription for the good society. He allied himself with the best of the past in order to give it a controlling effect in the present and the future. His social doctrine thus developed as a force at once of enlightenment and of conservatism.

Place of Government. The Confucian ideology, uniting a system of values and a body of social rules in a doctrine of cooperative living, reached from the immediacy of family relations to increasingly wider circles—neighborhood, village, guild, and district. The widest circle, relatively remote from the individual, was that of the highest authority. This authority was government, central or provincial. Government might visit punishment on offenders, but usually it did not give orders to the people. The standards of propriety pervading each of the successive circles of relationships needed little formal enforcement, because these standards were accepted as having universal validity. They shaped human behavior more intimately than could the impersonal commands of a legal order.

In the general context of social relations, government had only a limited sphere of influence. Chiefly, it helped to maintain the code of righteous living through the personal conduct of its scholar-bureaucrats. The role of the latter, who spent much of their time studying the great writings, was to inspire needed reforms and to hold even the Emperor to faithful observance of the common morality. Although government carried on few administrative activities, its functions extended to defining the range of legitimate private gain—as, for example, by price control. Such determinations called for the kind of insight into the common interest that only knowledge based on study and reflection was supposed to bring.

Education for Righteous Living. Although convinced of the need for scholar-guardians, Confucius did not recognize distinctions of privilege among social classes. Education was not to be reserved merely for a well-to-do minority. The public service, accessible through examinations, was to be recruited from among all those of talent. Learning, being directed primarily toward the art of cooperative living, was to enhance the learner's understanding of the common weal. This understanding, founded on disciplined judgment, was considered the highest qualification for governmental responsibility. As one of the Confucian texts explains:

An educated man, familiar both with the appropriate steps toward the attainment of learning and the standards of sound discrimination, is capable of insight. Having acquired insight he can indeed be a teacher. When he can be a teacher, he is qualified for high government office.   Being qualified for high government office he is able to be the ruler.   Hence it is from the teacher that one learns to be a ruler, and the choice of a teacher must be considered of greatest importance.   As it is said in the Record, 'The three kings and the four dynasties were what they were by their teachers.' [1]

With devout learning as the mediator between them, ruler and ruled were guided by the same unwritten constitution of ideological tenets.   This constitution interlaced civic virtue, official duty, and social ethics.   Individual freedom was confined to the choice between moral equivalents.   No one living by the common doctrine could claim the freedom to reject its guidance.   If a ruler proved bad, he forsook his moral title and marked himself for expulsion—if necessary, by popular revolt.   The recurrence of peasant uprisings in ancient and medieval China suggests the difference between actual conditions and the Confucian ideal, but the very acknowledgment of the difference shows that the ideology stayed alive.

Doctrinal Adjustments.   True enough, as centuries passed, shifts occurred in some of the characteristics of Confucian teaching.   Ultimately, the philosophers of the Sung period (960-1279) gave birth to Neo-Confucianism.   The idea of filial deference to the parent—a pivotal feature of the ethics of Confucius—was consciously extended to the governmental sphere, giving rise to the principle that the Emperor could do no wrong.   The support lent by Neo-Confucianism to the supremacy of the Emperor explains in part why the alien Manchu dynasty (1643-1911) made no effort to weaken or destroy the Confucian heritage.   Yet the unaccountability of the ruler was not intended to lessen the moral responsibility of his officials to keep government on the course of righteousness.

After the establishment of the republic in 1912, its most distinguished leader, Sun Yat-sen (1866-1925), set out to draw Confucianism into the service of a new era.   To this end he tried to infuse the old doctrine with Western concepts, especially with those of nationalism and democracy—a move not of abrogation but of conservation.   It is significant that in the final definition of Sun's position, in his *San Min Chu I,* the strength of the Confucian tradition as a doctrinal approach to effective community life is plainly in evidence.[2]

3. Foundations of Western Political Thought

Early Variety of Political Experience.   If the Confucian ideology appears predominantly community-centered, in contrast the most conspicuous strand in Western political thought is properly labeled individualism.   To be sure, there is in Western civilization no dearth of ideas linking the dignity of man with a constructive role in common affairs.   Such views are especially per-

[1] *Li Chi,* XVI, 16.   The translation given here differs somewhat from the standard one by James Legge.
[2] For a thoughtful presentation of Sun's position, see P. M. A. Linebarger, *The Political Doctrines of Sun Yat-sen* (Baltimore, 1937).

suasive when the community is regarded as the small-scale reflection of a higher order, of a purposeful universe. But they have never displaced the lingering fear that a closely organized body politic might easily become a barbed-wire enclosure of serfdom. The claims of individuality, voiced in the battle cry of freedom, have been the most compelling influence in the political evolution of the Western world.

Before the advent of the Hellenic age, however, divine and secular authority remained so intimately associated that man's individuality could not emerge as a separate thing. Controlled by the universal order, life moved along a predestined cycle. Man as an individual was not yet born. Much that is known about political thought among the Egyptians, Mesopotamians, and Hebrews illustrates this general dependence of humanity on an ordained pattern of expectancies.[3] In many ways the pattern parallels—though with considerable modifications—the broad outline of moral values and canons of conduct that one finds in Confucianism. But theoretical elaboration was not lacking. It is on earlier thought that Greek political philosophy relied in its classification of types of government as monarchy, aristocracy, and democracy, with their corruptions into tyranny, oligarchy, and mob rule, respectively.[4]

From the wide familiarity enjoyed by this classification before the time when Athens, in its political decline, became the capital of Western learning, one thing is clear—the variety of experience with different forms of governmental organization. The Confucian tradition, with its immutable verities, discouraged such variety. In Greece, absence of the constricting influence of a single ideological formula left ample range for political inventiveness and organic growth. The most significant product of both in combination was Athenian democracy. In the height of democratic development, during the Periclean period, the citizen of Athens had reason to regard himself as an equally competent manager of his private affairs and those of the state. His freedom, though not a matter of express legal guaranties, was his own personal accomplishment as a politically active man. It rested on a free community, governed by the many, and supported by the sense of ease that prevailed throughout the city-state. To the Athenian, civic indifference on the part of one who shared in the glory of the good society had the implication of moral failure.

Government Built on Knowledge. The shock of military defeat and the ensuing internal strife too soon deflated the proud self-assurance of Athens. Plato (427-347 B.C.) impressed upon his students in the Academy only the ineptness and subversions of democracy. When, in *The Republic,* he tried to define the best kind of government, he made it very plain that the citizen's

---

[3] An illuminating treatment, pieced together from scattered sources, is to be found in H. Frankfort and Others, *The Intellectual Adventure of Ancient Man: An Essay on Speculative Thought in the Ancient Near East* (Chicago, 1946).

[4] For the purpose of this chapter, it is not necessary to refer the reader to any of the standard treatises on political theory. It is to be hoped that Eric Voegelin's massive history of political ideas will soon be available to stimulate fresh evaluations.

amateurish dabbling in public business and the politician's shortsighted or selfish ministrations would never do. This appraisal was not simply an intellectual's gesture of contempt for ordinary people or self-made leaders. To Plato it was a conclusion arrived at in the discipline of abstract reasoning. Like Confucius, he held that the good, and hence the common good, can be recognized by superior knowledge; that the capacity for acquiring such knowledge can be identified reliably only by the test of educational achievement; and that the affairs of government can be managed for the true good of all only by one who has attained the highest knowledge—in other words, by the philosopher-king, aided by his scholar-peers of the guardian class.

Plato did not think it possible for these servants of the state to give unqualified devotion to their duties if they remained exposed to the seductions of personal interest. He therefore denied them property and family—though not offspring, because such offspring would ordinarily prove an asset to the community. The withholding of property and family gave rise to the mistaken idea that Plato stood for a communist society where women were held in common, a misconception since nowhere does he put forth such a view. He was, however, unconventional enough to scandalize his contemporaries by deeming qualified women eligible for guardian service.

All this was related to Plato's idea of justice. According to him, the key to justice was to be found in the balance of natural capacities and aptitudes. He was sure that, in a normal distribution of abilities, each member of the community would be best placed and therefore happiest in the kind of business for which he had the greatest talent. As a result, the guardian would stay guardian, in spite of the sacrifices associated with his role. And the ordinary citizen, knowing himself well governed, would confine his interests to his craft or trade. But Plato—again in the line of Confucian thought—fully appreciated the mind-molding importance of an ideology. Inviting though his general scheme of things might look, he knew that it would not work save for the affirmation given it by a political faith firmly implanted in the hearts of the people. Significantly, Plato saw with great acuteness that such a faith might effectively proclaim as true what science knew to be unverified or even false.

Government Built on Constitutional Rule. Plato's great disciple, Aristotle (384-322 B.C.), dismissed his master's search for the best kind of government as a dubious adventure. He objected to it because to him it represented a running away from both the facts of life and the scientific method. Pure logic needed the steadying hand of observation.[5] A political system so precariously poised on the ruler's superior insight into the common good, where no one was in a position to take issue with him, would lack all defense against a clever tyrant. This danger had come to bother Plato, too, and in his later writings he had tried to combine his original idea of government by the wisest

---

[5] For Aristotle's general contribution to empirical political science, see above, chap. 1, "Man and the State," sec. 2, "The Value of Comparison."

with the quite different idea of government according to law. But the effort
was a halfhearted one; it mainly served to illustrate the possibility of combining in one political structure organizational features borrowed selectively
from monarchy, aristocracy, and democracy—in other words, the principle of
the mixed state, with its system of checks and balances. Aristotle, who shared
Plato's distrust of democracy, employed this principle as the most convenient
means of substituting for the daydream of the best kind of government a practicable kind of good government.

Aristotle's theory, sketched in his *Politics,* aimed at creating a less exalted
ruler and a more elevated citizen. The force designated to establish a basic
moral equality between the two was law. And law, in turn, was recognized
as the foundation of constitutional rule. But law, in Aristotle's general meaning, was neither the edict nor the statute. Rather, it was the geological
deposit of social experience, the norms of custom and tradition in which is
recorded the common sense of the community. Correspondingly, constitutional rule did not assume the existence of a formal constitution. It did sig-
nify government limited and guided by the common sense, and thus the consensus, of the community; government in the general interest as contrasted
to class rule; government never divorced from the citizenry.

Under constitutional rule, as Aristotle conceived it, the economic pattern
within the state could hardly fail to affect the character of government.
Plato's corps of guardians, being devoid of property entanglements, was presumed to pursue the general welfare in public-spirited neutrality toward the
economic interests represented in the community. This ideal condition Aristotle considered impossible. But he fully agreed with Plato's regretful
admission that even the smallest state was divided into two—one of the poor
and one of the rich. Too marked inequalities in the property system, obviously, would destroy the foundations of a general consensus, and hence of constitutional rule. Awareness of this peril made Aristotle a warm supporter of
the middle class, in which he saw the chief bulwark of political stability and
strength, especially in a community that cherished freedom. Generally speaking, Greek political theory viewed with equal disfavor excessive wealth and
excessive poverty. But neither Aristotle nor Plato had much confidence in
attaining redress by formal legislation, such as the agrarian law by which Harrington (1611-77), in his *Oceana,* proposed to correct undue concentration
of landed wealth.

Individuality and the Higher Law. The Greek ideal of the citizen who
earned his security and freedom by being an actively participating member of
the community passed into history with the disappearance of the city-state.
The new empires that engulfed man left him politically dissociated and
highly insecure. Taking a new and desperate interest in his individuality, he
soon discovered that in his changed political condition a foundation for
human values could be found only in the universal order itself. The law of
nature, constructed from reason and pronouncing the perennial rules of

reason as a higher law, above all man-made legislation, was one answer to this need. The spiritual universality of Christianity was another.[6]

The fame won by Cicero (106-43 B.C.) was in the main a tribute to his eloquence in restating the doctrine of natural law as developed by the Stoics in the intellectual climate of Greece. Through most of the centuries that followed, the law of nature barked at the heels of those in power, reminding them of the elementary respect that reason reserved for all human beings. From the premises of natural law, a direct line of thought, reinforced by the individualist tendencies of the Reformation, reaches all the way to John Locke (1632-1704) and his espousal of man's inalienable rights. Locke declared the rights of life, liberty, and property to be an attribute of personality, not the fruit of political bargaining. To make these rights secure, Montesquieu (1689-1755) argued the case for a separation of powers in which the plenary authority of the ruler would be divided into three distinct departments, the legislative, the executive, and the judicial. The Founding Fathers of this country, when framing the constitution for a more perfect union, struck upon the principle of federalism to carry the system of checks and balances one long step farther yet.[7]

Christianity, viewing man as the child of God, directed his soul to a fountain of morality wholly outside the political area. To the Christian, the law of reason was necessarily the law of God. Hence, it was doubly evident that the precepts of this law towered above the cunning and frailty both of those wielding power and those living under it. Moreover, as a spiritual force, Christianity could not be satisfied with declaring political affairs outside its jurisdiction. Once the spiritual and secular spheres were seen as linked, it was possible to conceive the God-governed cosmic community as a single legal order, reaching from the highest principle to the smallest regulation. The grand design for such a unification of God, man, and nature was drawn up in the work of Thomas Aquinas (1225-74). By building a bridge from eternal law to human law, he related all of man's concerns to one embracing universality of inspired reason. A lawless or arbitrary ruler thus was more than a despot; he was guilty of offending God.

Although this bold cosmic synthesis never conquered reality, the effects of Christian ethics and natural law went far to keep absolute power on the defensive. The principle of the divine right of kings was not supposed to lend sanction to brutal force. Jean Bodin (1530-96), the most articulate exponent of sovereign monarchy, assumed as a matter of course that every act of the ruler in the exercise of his sovereignty must conform to the higher law. In a different way, Thomas Hobbes (1588-1679), perhaps the ablest apologist

[6] This general theme is consistently developed by Arnold J. Toynbee, *A Study of History*, which the reader can now conveniently consult in the abridgment by D. C. Somervell (New York, 1947). In this context, reference should also be made to F. S. C. Northrop, *The Meeting of East and West: An Inquiry Concerning World Understanding* (New York, 1947).

[7] For the most comprehensive work on American political thinking, see V. L. Parrington, *Main Currents in American Thought* (New York, 1927-30).

for absolutism, responded to the individualist legacy of natural law. In his *Leviathan,* he justified authority as the source of order indispensable to man in his quest of the good life.

Lure of Nationhood. Locke's accent on man's inalienable rights reversed the position considered self-evident by Greek political thought. The natural thing now was not the living community, but the satisfaction of man's self-interest. This emphasis, in the last analysis, was a socially disorganizing tendency, even though it opened wide avenues for the kind of creative self-expression that was to usher in an age of striking scientific and technological advance. In so far as the idea of the political community was restored to importance, history had replaced the Greek *polis* with the rising nation-state. But the national community proved a vastly different thing.

In view of the new lure of nationhood, it is an arresting irony that Niccolò Machiavelli (1469-1527) should have been goaded by love of his native Italy to provide European statecraft with so cold-blooded a manual of power politics as that offered in *The Prince.* Here was a precise indication of how tyrannical and immoral a course a sincere republican might advocate in order to save his fatherland—at least in the face of such a national emergency as caused Machiavelli to fear for Italy's life. But the full meaning of nationhood remained unexplored until Jean Jacques Rousseau (1712-78). Although himself much less susceptible to the magic of nationality than Machiavelli, Rousseau conferred upon the nation-state the splendor of a higher purpose. This new grandeur was the result of the theory, propounded in his *Social Contract,* that the political community is possessed of a general will of its own, distinguishable from the individual wills of its citizens.

Glorification of the Nation-State. In one sense, Rousseau's concept of the general will resembled a solemn and irrevocable commitment of the state to direct its collective energies toward goals commonly beneficial, and therefore of equal benefit to every citizen. In another sense, the general will could be conceived to be the custodian of the common good, imposing due restraint upon the citizen's pursuit of his individual interests. By arming itself with the superiority derived from moral validity, the general will gained the stature of an unalterable though unwritten constitution. This rudimentary constitution defined the boundaries, however vague, within which the citizenry could exercise free choice in directing the affairs of government on the basis of popular sovereignty. The political community, as envisaged by Rousseau, thus was governed under the general will. The people was sovereign, but in the exercise of its sovereignty it was bound by the moral imperatives of an unalterable collective purpose.

The next milestone in the advance of the national idea is represented by Hegel (1770-1831). Because to him the nation-state was the essential manifestation of nationhood, Hegel did not hesitate to treat the state as an incorporation of the paramount ethical values in human affairs. From this angle, man's civic duty to the state was not only a moral necessity but also a means of individual self-development. The same conclusion applied to the monarch. As an organ of the state, like officialdom itself, he was morally accountable in the light of the state's supreme mission, though only in his own conscience. This enthronement of the body national brought with it a proportionate demotion of the individual. Both Hegel and Rousseau in effect so adjusted the balance of values that man's civic contribution to the ends of the nation-state became the ultimate test of public virtue.

Seen in the long perspective of national life, state and nation overshadowed any living generation. For all practical purposes, this vision of perpetuity meant a conscious deference to the past and to the future. No nation could think of itself as living aimlessly in the present moment only; it had a higher task. There was need for the state to preserve the identity of the national character; to husband the political genius of the nation imprinted in its history; and to acknowledge the deeper significance of existing national institutions. One version of this ideological outlook gained expression in the reverence for national tradition that Edmund Burke (1729-97) impressed upon the political temper of both England and the United States.

Nationalism and Totalitarianism. Nationalism entered the arena of history as a popular force, allied with the mounting pressure for *liberté, egalité, fraternité.* The era of national sovereignty, with its high-powered political organization, gradually converted nationalism into something different. The new nationalist doctrine prompted aggressiveness sustained by militarism, and played into the hands of conservatism and reaction within the borders of the nation. It was usually the roots of nationalism that fed the tree of empire, with imperialism as its poisonous fruit. More recently, nationalism became the handmaiden of middle-class totalitarianism.

Mussolini made the promise of a new Rome the mainstay of the Fascist creed. Hitler employed the emotional appeal of national superiority by dedicating the Third Reich to the cultivation of a repulsive parody of German *Volkstum.* In a peculiar blend of native tendency and Western inspiration, Shintoism in Japan preached the gospel of national honor and national duty. In these extremes, nationalism produced the optical illusion of an unbroken column of generations, past and present, marching toward one and the same goal—national destiny. There is no doubt that the patriotism of the modern era owed its militancy to the spiritual nationalization of the individual. It has carried him along like a mighty wave.

Liberalism and Progress. Nationalism has become an integral part of the nation-state. In different degrees, it is today present in every country's political life. Its effects are minimized, however, where there are healthy ideological crosscurrents. One body of political ideas that has tended to constrain nationalism, especially in the English-speaking countries, is liberalism. Liberal theory owes much to the utilitarian dogma of Jeremy Bentham (1748-1832) and his companions-at-arms; it achieved a significant elaboration in the writings of John Stuart Mill (1806-73), above all in the celebrated essay

On Liberty; and it was ultimately brought to a somewhat bizarre apotheosis by Herbert Spencer (1820-1903).

A doctrine of political, economic, and social reform, liberalism allied itself with different humanitarian causes. In the nineteenth century it had extraordinary effect as the voice of progress. It was particularly successful as a middle-class movement in England, where it overran and destroyed the strongholds of the landed gentry. Originally by no means hostile to resourceful government as a factor of reform, liberal theory urged uncurtailed freedom both of economic initiative and individual thought. The postulate of free enterprise was advanced in the name of an industrial system that was assumed to maintain itself in automatic balance through the play of its natural laws. Untrammeled competition among individuals as well as among all parts of society was thought to prod man to achieve an ever higher level of self-fulfillment, prosperity, and comfort. Spencer's more extreme position led him to denounce every kind of public regulation as so many shackles upon man's creative spirit. It was thus natural for him to inveigh against all governmental authority, not excepting what he cursed as the tyranny of majorities.

Freedom under Law. Such overstatements caused little immediate damage to the liberal creed in the capitalist upsurge of the nineteenth century. A change of public mood took place only when it became painfully clear that the supposedly automatic forces of the free economy failed to provide either balance or stability. Under the blows of periodic economic crises, liberalism slowly abandoned as an article of faith its professed preference for a night-watchman type of government. It came to support the idea of positive government, popularly controlled, as the ultimate guarantor of man's freedom—political, economic, and social.

In place of Spencer's strident antigovernmentalism, a fresh understanding developed of the essential role of government under constitutional rule.[8] Instead of being as fearful of democracy as were the spokesmen of reaction, the new liberals reaffirmed their confidence in freedom under law. Freedom under law implied regulation democratically arrived at. It implied a system of government that would safeguard equal opportunity in the general determination of the common good by democratic action.

4. The Marxist Challenge

Call for Revolution. A hundred years ago, amidst Europe's revolutionary uprisings of 1848, two well-educated sons of well-to-do fathers, Karl Marx (1818-83) and Friedrich Engels (1820-95), published a spirited tract intended for a popular audience. This leaflet, the *Communist Manifesto,* opened with the ominous assertion that Europe was being haunted by the specter of com-

---

[8] For a thoughtful exposition of basic aspects of democratic theory, see A. D. Lindsay, *The Modern Democratic State,* I (New York, 1947).

munism. To dubious contemporary readers, this assertion might have seemed a ludicrous exaggeration. Today the specter of communism is haunting the world, and very few people fail to see it.

The *Communist Manifesto* made the disquieting forecast, dressed up as a scientific conclusion, that capitalism would soon have dug its own grave. The toiling masses were assured that in due time they would inherit the earth —and a godless heaven as well. All they had to do was to understand their historic opportunity, seize power by revolutionary means, eradicate every remnant of the existing class structure, and so inaugurate the classless society as the ideal order of mankind. The *Communist Manifesto* was not the scientific analysis it claimed to be. What gave the tract its long lease on life was the fact that its authors supplied such analysis to bolster it in a shelf of other writings, most famous of which was Marx's *Capital*.

Socialism, Old and New. Neither Marx nor Engels was the first to spot the flaws in a capitalist economy geared to mass production. Earlier exponents of socialist theories, such as Fourier (1772-1837), had ventured some very acute observations about the troublesome problems the future appeared to hold in store for industrial society. By its appearance, the *Communist Manifesto* did not sweep away older branches of socialist thought founded on different hypotheses. These continued their doctrinal development in relative independence, as did certain later offshoots.

From such independent socialist thought, for example, came the intellectual impulse for a state socialism of governmentally owned and managed economic undertakings. Indeed, despite Marx and Engels, many socialists felt certain that universal suffrage would bring about government control by the laboring masses as the result of the gradual but irresistible process of evolution, without a shot being fired. This view became the working doctrine of Social Democracy, which for many decades numerically dominated European labor movements. The British Fabians adopted a similar outlook. Orthodox Marxism, by contrast, considered decisive change attainable only by revolutionary upheaval. It launched vitriolic attacks on those who thought it possible to displace capitalism without resort to violence.

Class and Class Conflict. To Marx, the structure of political control had neither substance nor meaning when considered apart from the economic structure.[9] The history of government, and with it the changing share of different groups in the exercise of political power, was simply a reflection of shifts in the organization and methods of production. In the case of industrial capitalism, owners, managers, and investors stood divided from the army of workers, who, by their underpaid labor, created the goods of manufacture

---

[9] Of course, one need not be a Marxist to recognize the close relations between economic and political factors, as the famous tenth paper of the *Federalist* shows. For Greek political thinking on this point, see above in the preceding section. For an able discussion of the whole subject, see C. A. Beard, *The Economic Basis of Politics* (rev. ed., New York, 1945).

for profitable disposition by those in control of the means of production. Because of their diametrically opposite economic positions, the exploiters and the exploited, according to Marx, were virtually different breeds of man. Each breed was given its identity by what held it together—the bond of class.

The national idea, then, was just a crude fake. So, too, were the fine words about individual liberty and popular rule. The controlling factor, Marx insisted, was the unity of class interest, not the unity of the national interest. The formal system of government in the capitalist economy made no difference to the proletarian. Whatever the empty rationalizations of political theory, in one way or another the exploiting class would see to it that ultimate power remained in its hands.

The practical operation of the capitalist system, so Marx predicted, would sharpen rather than allay the fundamental conflict of class interests. The natural drive toward monopoly would cause wealth to be concentrated in the hands of an ever smaller oligarchy. This oligarchy, in turn, could ensure its own safety only by keeping the working people enslaved to it. Profit, in any event, was in the main legalized theft—theft by the factory owner, who took from the worker, upon payment of a low wage rate, all the value of labor expended upon a product. In order to keep profits high and production costs low—that is, in order to have ample and cheap labor—the capitalist would have to do his best so to depress the wage level as to hold it near that of starvation. In the end—and Marx assumed a rather early end—this condition would resolve itself by the irrepressible upsurge of the masses.

Marxist Dialectic—Reason and History. In trying to clinch his main points, Marx made skilled use of a methodological device he appropriated from Hegel—the dialectical approach. Hegel, in his study of the past, had persuaded himself that to understand history, one would have to accept a particular concept of development—that of a permanent and repeated sequence of three stages. The first stage would be completed with the consolidation of current factors and forces into a basic historic theme, or *thesis.* The very appearance of this thesis would exert pressure to effect a grouping of opposite factors and forces into an *antithesis.* Thesis and antithesis would next, as a natural development, engage each other to bring forth a *synthesis.* Thereafter, in due time, as synthesis narrowed down to produce a new thesis, the three-step sequence of thesis, antithesis, and synthesis would be repeated to bring forth still another order of things, and so on.

Marx took over this dialectic, not only as a way of understanding history, but as an inner law of history itself. His dialectical reasoning therefore made it possible for him, assuming that it was correct, to project developments into the future. As the standard-bearers of liberalism had had their enthusiasm kindled by the wishful thought of social progress, so Marx employed the dialectical method to nail down as scientifically established what he said would happen to capitalism. He thus could proclaim the inevitability of the classless society, revolutionary seizure of power by the proletariat being not a mere possibility, but the necessary effect of the internal contradictions of capitalism.

Proletarian Dictatorship and Classless Society. Once recognized, the dialectic of historical materialism could not fail to apply also to the succession of steps by which the classless society would come into being. As soon as industrialization had run its course far enough, the class-conscious masses would rise and take command of the machinery of power. The revolution would be followed by a second phase, the dictatorship of the proletariat. This phase would require the fullest use of every ounce of governmental power, including organized terror, to annihilate the inherited class structure. The third phase, initiation of the classless society, would not be a matter of revolutionary action. It would occur as a natural consequence of the elimination of all remnants of class.

As this stage was reached, the state would "wither away," as Engels put it. For organized government and governmental authority there would be substituted a collective type of management of common affairs, especially of the process of production. Man's mastery of Marxism, as a comprehensive scientific system of social thought and action, would enable him to play his proper part in sensitive awareness of the needs of a collective society and, therefore, in freedom from the compulsion of force. Only in the classless society, in the final consummation of communism, could man hope to be really free. Up to this point, both under capitalism and during the transitional dictatorship of the proletariat, he would remain subject to the machinery of power.

Evolution of Marxism. The intellectual estate of Marxism, after vicious battles among various contenders, was eventually claimed, with considerable success, by a Russian disciple now everywhere known by his underground name, Lenin (1870-1924). It was he who undertook to give Marxism its twentieth-century form. Long an exile, Lenin prepared himself and his small band for the Russian Revolution of 1917 by holding the Bolshevist party with iron determination to the teachings of Marxism as construed by him. His criticism of those Social Democrats who expected to achieve their ends in czarist Russia by relying on the tactics of trade unionism was biting; he was equally sharp in denouncing as pointless the disconnected acts of assassination plotted by terrorists. Time and again he advised those willing to listen that revolution, from the Marxist point of view, was a professional business requiring men and women clear in their minds about the correct interpretation of Marxist doctrine.

Lenin's most important contribution to the evolution of Marxism stemmed from his keen appreciation of the need for redefining the orthodox position in the light of fresh experience. He combined the mentality of a theorist with the practical sense of a man of action. This combination made him ideally suited to give Marxism an elasticity of strategic and tactical freedom quite at variance with the dogmatism of many of the faithful. His achievement is well conveyed in the introduction to the revised edition of the official *History of the Communist Party of the Soviet Union*:

The Marxist-Leninist theory is the science of the development of society, the science of the proletarian revolution, the science of the building of the Communist society. And as a science it does not and cannot stand still, but develops and perfects itself. Clearly, in its development it is bound to become enriched by new experience and new knowledge, and some of its propositions and conclusions are bound to change in the course of time, are bound to be replaced by new conclusions and propositions corresponding to the new historical conditions. . . .

And just because Lenin and the Leninists have advanced the Marxist theory, Leninism is a further development of Marxism; it is Marxism in the new conditions of the class struggle of the proletariat, Marxism of the epoch of imperialism and proletarian revolutions, Marxism of the epoch of the victory of socialism on one-sixth of the earth's surface.[10]

Bourgeois totalitarianism, both in its Fascist and its Nazi variants, assembled its creed from sundry sources. At no time did it display as much concern with points of doctrine as did Lenin. For its own working theory of planned violence and mass action, it remained under a heavy debt to Lenin and the sporadic but incisive writings he scattered through the first two decades of our century. Neither Mussolini nor Hitler, however, was able to point to an ultimate aim as tempting as the Marxist utopia of the classless society.

The rising generation in Italy and Germany was carefully groomed in a new psychology of robot response. But the response was blind, unenlightened by a dialectic or by a time-honored literature. By way of contrast, under the auspices of Marxist ideology, the man with a new psychology became a different standard product. The dialectic told him scientifically that his leaders were right and that he was right in following his leaders. He could nurture his zest on a body of classics that left the man of faith under no necessity for wasteful conjecture. He knew that there were no unmarked forks in the road, and that a brisk pace would lead him faster to his destination.

But when man's responsibility is reduced to keeping his place in the columns of the toiling masses; when he owes it himself to maintain a supreme confidence in the genius of *the* leader; and when the leader, far away from the masses, has only the advice of his lieutenants—in these circumstances the risk of fateful blunders at the top becomes appalling.

---

[10] Control Commission of the Communist Party of the Soviet Union (Bolsheviks), *History of the Communist Party of the Soviet Union* (Moscow, 1945). For another authentic appraisal of Marxism today, see *Century of Marxism*, a special number of *Science and Society*, 12, No. 1 (1947).

PART II

CONSTITUTIONAL GOVERNMENT:
THE BRITISH WAY

CHAPTER 3

ENGLAND'S CONSTITUTIONAL TRADITION

1. Constitutionalism without a Constitution

Power as Force and Authority. In present-day Britain, there are certain things that are not done.[1] Men who want to take over the government, for instance, do not hire a gang of thugs and pay them to murder those in power. People who are obnoxious to the government do not just disappear. But many acts of force that are considered improper today were considered right in seventeenth-century Britain. The rules of the political game as it is now played in Britain thus are not only distinctly British; they are also distinctly modern. The things that are done have hardened into well-established customs and institutions; the things that are not done have become taboo. Generally, the former are constitutional, the latter unconstitutional.

Government in Britain, as in every country, employs force, including the policeman's nightstick. But the government has a monopoly of force. Where force is eliminated is not in the use of governmental power, but in the ways in which this power is acquired and retained. The right to use force is obtained without using force. In Britain, moreover, such force is kept in the background. Although available for use, it is seldom used. Primarily, British government substitutes moral authority for physical force. The very fact that power is acquired without violence helps the government to command a respect that makes force largely unnecessary. Then, too, the processes through which government exercises its authority are grounded in custom. Because people are used to these processes, what is done through them commands a high degree of acceptance.

Basically, the respect of the British people is not for the government of the day so much as for those familiar institutions through which government

---

[1] A selective listing of material pertinent to this chapter would include: W. I. Jennings, *The British Constitution* (Cambridge, 1945); W. A. Robson, *The British System of Government* (London, 1940); H. R. G. Greaves, *British Constitution* (New York, 1938); Ramsay Muir, *How Britain Is Governed* (New York, 1930); A. L. Lowell, *The Government of England* (New York, 1908); S. J. M. Low, *Governance of England* (rev. ed., New York, 1914); Walter Bagehot, *The English Constitution* (New York, 1901); E. C. Thomas, ed., *Leading Cases in Constitutional Law* (8th ed., London, 1947); A. V. Dicey, *Introduction to the Study of the Law of the Constitution* (9th ed., London, 1939); W. I. Jennings, *Law and the Constitution* (rev. ed., London, 1938); A. B. Keith, *Constitution of England from Queen Victoria to George VI* (Toronto, 1940); E. C. S. Wade and G. G. Phillips, *Constitutional Law* (London, 1946). For special bibliography, see British Council, *British Civilization and Institutions* (Chicago, 1946). An indispensable periodical is *Political Quarterly* (London).

acquires and exercises authority. Everybody, including the government, abides by these institutions and works through the processes they support. In this sense, Britain has a constitutional government. The British constitution may be described as those well-known and well-understood ways and means by which governmental power is acquired and exercised.

Continuity and Change. In order to command respect, these institutions and processes must undergo a gradual change. Change they must, for if they cease to be in harmony with the needs of the age, they will cease to command respect. Yet they must not change too rapidly, or they will lose their sanctity. British constitutionalism thus involves a cult of continuity—of continuous growth, adjustment, and adaptation. The evolutionary nature of the British constitution is universally recognized. Social evolution is taken for granted, and the gradual evolution of government is assumed to be an essential part of the evolution of society. The "inevitability of gradualness" is a phrase in which the British Fabian thinkers Sidney and Beatrice Webb summed up this attitude of mind.

In the Britain of 1776, political parties were exclusive clubs. The King chose the Prime Minister to manage his business. The Prime Minister held together a majority of the King's servants in Parliament by influence and patronage. No government was ever defeated at the polls. Seats in the House of Commons were sold in the open market. There was no uniform franchise. The majority of men had no vote. Civil service jobs were rewards for the clients of aristocratic patrons. The hereditary landed aristocracy was the most powerful force in politics. Local government was in the hands of closed municipal corporations and a hereditary rural squiredom. Moreover, the group that governed Britain made laws for her colonies without consulting them.

Today, in almost every respect that matters, British government is fundamentally different from that against which the American colonies revolted. From a common English seventeenth-century trunk, American government has grown in one direction and British in another. Both, it is true, have become democratic, and both have had to be adapted to the rise of mass parties and broadly formed interest-groups. But in other respects they have grown increasingly dissimilar. Many American concepts are foreign to British ways of thinking. The sharp distinction between legislature, executive, and judiciary, for example, has long since faded in Britain. There the separation of powers, as understood in the United States, is unknown. Checks and balances are not heard of. Bicameralism no longer means two equal houses. Diffusion of parliamentary responsibility among many strong committees does not exist. Judicial review presents no challenge to acts of Parliament. And federalism has been rejected as a means of maintaining the unity of the Empire.

Government and the Social Pattern. One notable aspect of the strength of British political life is to be found in the exceptional degree of correlation existing between society and government. The constitution of society and the constitution of government are in Britain about the same. The classes that set the tone in society tend to be the same classes that set the tone in government. The civil service, for example, with its wide spread of salary and education, is itself a reproduction of society; its top group, the administrative grade, is socially on a par with the Cabinet ministers. The two main political parties, though both representative of a cross section of society, are socially weighted in their leadership and following, each in a different direction.

The British constitution, then, is not a bundle of legal clauses, techniques or recipes that can be torn from their social environment. On the contrary, it is an essential part of the whole texture and pattern of British society. To understand British government, one must understand the society with which it is intertwined.

2. *His Majesty's Government*

The Prime Minister—Background and Status. In British usage, "the government" means the group of high officeholders who rule the United Kingdom. The head of the government, for the past two hundred and fifty years, has been the Prime Minister. The title originated in France; in England it was first used in derision, being applied to Godolphin and Walpole when they ruled on behalf, respectively, of Queen Anne and King George I. The essence of the office of prime minister lay in the full confidence and responsibility vested by the King as head of the state in the Prime Minister as head of the government with full authority to manage the nation's business. The practice originated as a convenience to the King, who thus shifted to another some part of the work and the blame. Because a prime minister who had outlived his usefulness could be got rid of more easily than a king, the office gradually commended itself to the people; today, the entrusting of the whole business of government to a prime minister is an essential part of the British constitution.

But official recognition of the office was long in coming; until well into the present century, the Prime Minister's official title was that of First Lord of the Treasury, the title bestowed upon him when, in 1714, the office of Lord High Treasurer having been abolished, the Treasury was put into commission, and the Prime Minister became the chairman of "my lords commissioners of the Treasury," a commission that never met. It was as First Lord of the Treasury that the Prime Minister drew his salary and occupied a small house at No. 10 Downing Street, London.

In 1905, the position and title of Prime Minister were recognized by a royal warrant of King Edward VII, assigning to the holder of the office a definite place in the order of precedence, and by an act of Parliament of 1917 giving him free use of a country house, Chequers. His present annual salary is £10,000 before payment of income tax; and upon retirement he is eligible for a pension. The country house and the pension are a boon to men without private fortunes; the present century has seen a number of such men rise to the premiership—H. H. Asquith (1908-16); David Lloyd George (1916-22); and Ramsay MacDonald (1924, 1929-33).

Selecting the Prime Minister. During all these two hundred and fifty years, the one indispensable requirement for prime minister has been the ability to hold together a majority in the House of Commons. Unless the Commons voted the taxes and appropriations that were needed, "the King's government" could not have been carried on. Above all, the Prime Minister was the manager of the King's business in Parliament.

With the establishment of strong parties solidly organized under recognized leaders, the range of the King's discretion in picking the Prime Minister almost disappeared. Now if one party has a majority in the House of Commons, and if this party has chosen a leader, the King has no choice but to make him Prime Minister. If no party has a majority—as happened in 1924 and again in 1929—the obvious choice for Prime Minister is the leader who stands most chance of winning both the support of his own party and enough other votes to give him a reasonable hope for a majority. In both 1924 and 1929, the leader of the Labor party was appointed; although his party did not have a majority, it seemed likely that the Liberal party would tend to vote with Labor against the Conservatives, thus providing a majority, even if not a very dependable one.

If the King is not to have much discretion, it is essential that each party make it clear who its leader is. If a party in opposition loses its leader, it usually has time to choose a new one. On the other hand, if the party in power loses its Prime Minister, whether through death or infirmity, it may not be able to choose another leader on short notice. In this case, the King would have to choose—as Victoria, in 1894, chose Lord Rosebery rather than Harcourt; and as George V, in 1923, chose Baldwin rather than Lord Curzon. Then the party might find itself saddled with a leader whom it would not itself have chosen.

Originally, there was nothing to prevent a Prime Minister's being selected from the House of Lords, provided that this would not stand in the way of his forming and holding a majority in Commons. In the eighteenth and nineteenth century, about half the Prime Ministers were chosen from the House of Lords. In the present century a new situation arose, consequent upon the fact that the Labor party was practically without representation in the House of Lords. Since the official leader of the Labor party, then, could be found only in the House of Commons, it became necessary for the Conservative party to find its national leader there as well.

Term of Office. A fixed term of office for the Prime Minister is inconceivable. His tenure has always been dependent upon two factors—his party's ability to maintain a majority in the House of Commons and his own ability to retain the leadership of his party. No Prime Minister since Liverpool (1812-27) has stayed in office more than eight years at one stretch; the last who survived so long was Asquith (1908-16). Several, however, have held office more than once—Gladstone having been Prime Minister four times (1868-74, 1880-85, 1886, 1892-94) and Baldwin three (1923, 1924-29, 1933-37).

Ministers—Role and Choice. The Prime Minister has always shared power with a number of colleagues.[2] The term "the government" is plural, or collegial. Policy is decided not by the Prime Minister alone, but by a group of ministers. His single vote cannot override theirs. He can interpret the consensus of opinion; if in doubt, he can poll each minister. But once they have made a decision, both he and they are bound by it. In public no minister will ever speak or vote against the decision reached by his colleagues except with their permission, a permission seldom given. On the contrary, he is expected to speak and vote publicly in support of the government's decision, even though in the privacy of the Cabinet room he may have spoken and voted against it. If his conscience rebels against this discipline, he is free to resign. But so long as he stays in the team, he must play its game, not his own.

The Prime Minister chooses his colleagues and can, if need be, have them dismissed. In selecting them he has some, but not much, freedom of choice. The objects of his choice must be or become members of Parliament and should show strength in Parliament. One who would be dangerous to the government if left out must be brought into it. Ministers should represent all shades of feeling in the party. They should be a representative team, holding together the government's majority in Commons.

Dismissal and Resignation. For the Prime Minister to have a colleague dismissed is always possible but seldom necessary. It happened once a hundred years ago, when Lord John Russell as Prime Minister had Palmerston ousted from the Foreign Office for pursuing a foreign policy of his own. Usually, however, the Prime Minister requests and gets a resignation. Some Prime Ministers are even said to have requested submission of undated resignations upon appointment, to be used whenever necessary. Most ministers who feel that they are out of harmony with the government usually resign without being asked to do so, but it is the Prime Minister who decides whether or not to accept their resignations. A resignation may be accepted not only for the sake of dropping some minister, but also in order to reshuffle a number of ministerial posts. Such reshufflings are frequent; consequently, many ministers acquire some familiarity with a number of administrative departments without, as a rule, becoming closely identified with the viewpoint of any one of them. Hence, ministers tend to keep their ability to see

---

[2] Cf. generally W. I. Jennings, *Cabinet Government* (rev. ed., Cambridge, 1951); M. P. A. H. Hankey, *Government Control in War* (Cambridge, 1945) and *Diplomacy by Conference* (New York, 1946); K. C. Wheare, *The Machinery of Government* (Oxford, 1945); John Anderson, "Machinery of Government," *Public Administration*, 24 (1946), 147 ff.; W. A. Robson, "The Machinery of Government," *Political Quarterly*, 19 (1948), 1 ff.; F. G. Lee and Roger Stevens, "Coordinating Policies and Operations in the Government of the United Kingdom," *Public Administration Review*, 6 (1946), 354 ff.

government policy as one whole. Only in foreign affairs and in finance is it usual to leave a minister in the same ministry for several years.

On one unparalleled occasion, in 1931, a Labor Prime Minister (Ramsay MacDonald) handed in the resignation of his entire Cabinet, and then proceeded to pick a new Cabinet, composed for the most part of his former political opponents from the Conservative party. On this party he relied to win an election and secure a majority in the House of Commons.

Cabinet Organization and Procedure. The Prime Minister and a roomful of his colleagues have met together as a "Cabinet" for more than two centuries. There have always been some grounds for indecision as to which of the ministers in charge of departments should be called to Cabinet meetings and which are the ministers whose regular attendance would be less useful for determining general policy. Each Prime Minister, therefore, determines the composition of his own Cabinet. In 1950, for example, there were eighteen Cabinet members. Fifteen other ministers of Cabinet rank were summoned to the weekly Cabinet meetings whenever the agenda made their participation especially desirable.

Cabinet meetings in the past were informal, in that no record of them was kept beyond a four-page letter from the Prime Minister to the monarch.[3] Sometimes the meetings carried informality to the point of being merely Cabinet dinners, in order to avoid the need for any record whatever. Each minister was expected to make notes on decisions concerning his own department. Not until the middle of World War I did it become normal to have a secretary draw up an agenda and keep minutes of decisions. But since then the Cabinet secretariat has become an important unit. For a few years the experiment was also tried of recording the way in which ministers spoke and voted, but the natural reluctance of the latter to make their most personal views a matter of public record ended the attempt.

Inner Cabinet. It is not always possible or feasible to call together the usual members of the Cabinet. A sudden crisis may not find all of them in London —some may be scattered all over the country, campaigning in a general election; some may be abroad. In a drawn-out emergency, they may be reluctant to spare the time to meet together as frequently as is necessary. Consequently, there is a constant tendency for an informal inner cabinet to emerge.

For example, the decision to implement the understanding with France in 1906 by permitting talks between the military leaders of the two powers was made by the Prime Minister and the three ministers in charge of the Treasury, the Foreign Office, and the War Office, without consultation with the rest of the Cabinet. In both World Wars, the inner Cabinet crystallized

---

[3] It is said that these "Cabinet letters" were invented by Lord Melbourne soon after Victoria's accession. They seem to have been an aspect of the rise of the Prime Minister to a position of leadership in the Cabinet. In the eighteenth century, Cabinet meetings seem to have been called by any Cabinet member who had business to lay before his colleagues. A formal "Cabinet minute" was then made by the minister who called the Cabinet, using the formula, "Agreed to recommend to His Majesty . . . ."

temporarily into a formal War Cabinet, small enough to meet at least daily.[4] At the close of hostilities in 1945, Winston Churchill's War Cabinet had eight members. No less than thirty-three other ministers of Cabinet rank were outside the regular circle of the War Cabinet.

Junior Ministers. In addition to the thirty to forty ministers of Cabinet rank, who may or may not be regular members of the Cabinet, there are as many ministers again who are not of Cabinet rank—the "junior ministers." Most of these are parliamentary secretaries and under-secretaries of departments—posts that are either rewards to members of Parliament for long and loyal service to their party or opportunities for younger members to distinguish themselves. When, in addition to these, certain parliamentary private secretaryships and a few jobs in the royal household given to the government whips are considered, it will be seen that ministerial posts thus add up to a total of about one hundred, held by members of Parliament at salaries ranging from £1,500 to £5,000 a year.

Cabinet and Its Committees. Altogether then, as the following sketch shows, there may be said to be four concentric circles of ministerial responsibility: first, the informal inner Cabinet of four to five ministers; second, the formal Cabinet of fifteen to twenty ministers; third, ministers of Cabinet rank in charge of departments, totaling thirty to forty; and fourth, the ministry in general of eighty to one hundred members, including junior ministers. The collective responsibility of members is clearest at the center, where they actively participate in shaping top policy. It is haziest on the circumference.

Cutting across the three innermost of these circles are the Cabinet committees that have evolved during the past fifty years. Many of these are *ad hoc,* for special and temporary purposes; others are more permanent. Of the permanent committees, the most important are the Prime Minister's committee on economic policy, the Lord President's legislation committee, and the defense committee presided over by the Minister of Defense as deputy for the Prime Minister. Most ministerial committees contain members of Cabinet rank other than regular members of the Cabinet. Some include permanent officials; others have subcommittees made up of permanent officials. To one committee—the defense committee and its subcommittees—the Prime Minister has sometimes invited ranking leaders of the opposition, in order to keep them informed and to gain the benefit of their advice. In general, more and more questions are referred to ministerial committees before being laid before the full Cabinet for formal decision; in this procedure the Cabinet secretariat plays a very useful role.

---

[4] This procedure was adopted after the rejection of two other possibilities. One alternative (tried by Asquith, 1914-16) was to have the defense committee (under various, changing wartime names) submit its plans to the full Cabinet for approval or possible rejection. Another alternative (advocated by Lloyd George and Maurice Hankey, 1916) was to have the defense committee run the war without referring matters back to the Cabinet. See David Lloyd George, *War Memoirs* (New York, 1933), II, 369, and M. P. A. H. Hankey, *Diplomacy by Conference,* cited above, note 2, p. 54.

Trends in Cabinet Operation. Several problems are posed by these trends in Cabinet operation. One is the question of the kind of ministers in whom, collectively, the highest responsibility shall be lodged. There is a tendency

STRUCTURE OF THE BRITISH CABINET

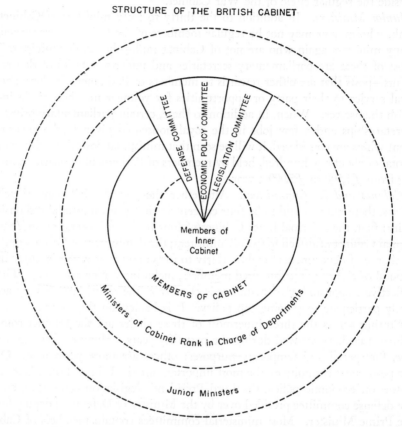

to use for this purpose certain ministers of state with honorific but meaningless historic titles, such as the Lord President of the Council and the Lord Privy Seal, who have no administrative responsibilities. These may form the inner Cabinet and preside over Cabinet committees. This is about what happened in World War I, when Lloyd George's War Cabinet consisted almost entirely of ministers without portfolio. The alternative is to recognize the ministers in charge of certain key departments as being of cardinal importance. Thus, in World War II, Winston Churchill preferred a War Cabinet most of whose members carried departmental responsibilities.

Another problem is that of the relationship between the few ministers at the center of power and the many that are not regularly called to Cabinet meetings. Ever since World War I, there has been a stream of proposals for the grouping of departments and ministers into a small number of super-departments. These would be presided over by supervising ministers forming a Cabinet of reduced size that would make an inner cabinet superfluous. Such a plan is akin to Léon Blum's proposals for France. Perhaps from experience with Cabinet committees, a clearer relationship between the Cabinet and the other ministers in charge of departments may be developed. Of this the first and only example is the relationship between the Minister of Defense, who is in the Cabinet, and the First Lord of the Admiralty and the Secretaries of State for War and Air, who are not in the Cabinet but are members of its defense committee.

One virtue claimed for this possible development is that it would offer leeway to the increase in the number of departments that may be made necessary by nationalization. It is assumed that the supervising ministers would have no power of command over the departments grouped under them, but would act solely as coordinators. They would be responsible for taking part of the Cabinet's load by working toward the definition of policy in terms not of the vested interests of this department or of that, but of the general national interest. Such an organizational pattern would correspond with the obvious fact that no one responsible minister can achieve intimate familiarity with the affairs of more than a handful of his colleagues.[5]

Ministerial Division of Labor. The function of a minister is to help achieve correlation between the policy of his department and that of the government as a whole; he is a link. To be effective, he must gain enough familiarity with the work of his own department to enable him to interpret its outlook to his Cabinet colleagues, to Parliament, and to the public. He need not be especially competent as an administrator, nor is he likely to stay so long with one department that he becomes an expert in its affairs to the exclusion of those of the government as a whole.

What the minister lacks in departmental experience is supplied by the permanent head of each department. A department thus has two heads—one "political" and the other "permanent." If the political head's title is "the Minister of ——," that of the permanent head is "the permanent Secretary of ——." If the political head is "Secretary of State for ——," the permanent head is "Under-Secretary for ——." It is on the permanent head that prime responsibility for the administration of the department falls. This responsibility may include the educating of a succession of ministers, so that they may go out and fight the department's battles.

Cabinet Secretariat. Even the Prime Minister has recently acquired a permanent opposite number. Since 1904 he has had, as chairman of the defense committee, a permanent defense secretariat; in 1916 this body became the

---

[5] The principle involved here is one of span of attention, not of span of command. No minister—not even the Prime Minister—may command his colleagues, except, perhaps, in wartime. This top level of government is deliberative rather than operational. In order to understand the working of Prime Minister and Cabinet, it is necessary to banish from one's mind the concept of a chief executive as administrative manager.

secretariat of the War Cabinet.[6] With the restoration of the peacetime Cabinet after 1919, the secretary of the defense committee remained as secretary of the Cabinet. In 1938, when the first secretary of the Cabinet retired, his post was linked with that of the permanent Under-Secretary of the Treasury, popularly known as "head of the civil service," but this fusion did not last.

Beginning in World War II, the Cabinet secretariat has been more adequately staffed, not only for defense planning, but also in order that it may supply information as a basis upon which the Cabinet may decide general policy. The secretariat now includes a central statistical office, which has contributed essential data, published each year in a pioneer statement of national income and outgo. The secretariat also contains an economic section for the analysis of the probable results of alternative policies. Political responsibility, of course, remains with the Cabinet. All that the secretariat can do is to help the Cabinet reach its decisions with more facts at its disposal than it would otherwise have had, facts that are relevant to the general interest rather than to the desires of particular departments.

3. Cabinet and Parliament

Responsibility versus Separation of Powers. Mutual responsibility of Cabinet and Parliament is the most distinctive trait of the British type of government.[7] Cabinet and Parliament are dependent upon each other for their survival. The Cabinet, on the one side, may use the power of the Crown to dissolve Parliament. Parliament, on the other, by indicating lack of confidence, can force a Cabinet to resign. Neither Cabinet nor Parliament has a fixed term; either can put an end to the tenure of the other. On the other hand, there may not be an interval of more than five years between general elections, unless Parliament decides otherwise, by agreement between both major political parties.

In two ways, then, the separation of powers as applied in the United States is unknown in Britain. Executive and legislature are not so independent of each other that in the event of deadlock neither can throw the other out. Moreover, the British type of Cabinet is in essence a committee of Parliament, not a separate body. Yet, if the doctrine of separation of powers be restored to the meaning it had in Montesquieu's day, Britain was and is as good an example as can be found of a country that owes its freedom to the separation of powers. The whole power of government does not rest in any one agency, but is divided between two—Cabinet and Parliament. Nor is one at the mercy of the other; rather, each depends upon the other.

Mutual Responsibility. The system of mutual responsibility arose in eighteenth-century Britain. It attracted little notice in other countries un-

---

[6] This side of British government is of wider significance, in that the secretariat of the Cabinet's defense committee became the nucleus of the secretariat of the Inter-Allied Supreme War Council (1917), and therefore a model for the Secretariat of the League of Nations (1919). See also Joseph Davies, *The Prime Minister's Secretariat, 1916-20* (Newport, 1952).

[7] See W. I. Jennings, *Parliament* (Cambridge, 1940), and the writings cited in note 2, page 41.

til it caught the attention of French refugees in Britain during the French Revolution who carried it with them when they returned home. From France the idea spread to Belgium in 1830 and from there to the Netherlands, the Scandinavian countries, and Italy. It was also adopted by the self-governing colonies, later dominions. Thus, today, more than a dozen countries employ variants of the British system of a Cabinet and Parliament mutually responsible.

This mutual responsibility resulted from two practices that have evolved simultaneously. One is Cabinet leadership. The other is parliamentary checks upon the Cabinet.

Cabinet Leadership. Leadership of Parliament by the Cabinet began in the eighteenth century. At first it consisted in the "management" of Parliament by systematic distribution of patronage. This management was effected not from the outside, as is presidential management of patronage in the United States, but by the Cabinet, an inside group. The fact that leadership was concentrated inside Parliament, rather than being located outside, made possible a change in the nature of Cabinet leadership when the franchise was democratized and mass parties arose in the nineteenth century. Instead of being the "managers" of Parliament, the Cabinet became the policy or steering committee of the majority party. At the same time, various techniques and procedures were developed through which this leadership could be made effective.

When Jefferson, as Vice President, drew up a manual of procedure for the Senate, it was not easy to know the rules of the British Parliament. Since 1810, however, the standing orders of the House of Commons have been reissued annually; they have also been revised frequently in the interest of the government. Gradually, they have become an instrument for the transaction of government business rather than for the protection of the members of Parliament. This fact shows itself in the control of the parliamentary timetable. In the eighteenth century, the House of Commons supposedly controlled its own business, but, being "managed" by the Cabinet, it made a certain amount of time available to the government as a matter of courtesy. By the beginning of the nineteenth century, one day a week was reserved for the government. At the present time it amounts, during much of the session, to four days in the five-day week. Since 1853, the government has determined the order in which government business shall be taken up. The power wielded in the United States by rules committees is in Britain exercised by the Cabinet.

The government's estimates for financial outlay are invariably accepted by Parliament. Proposals for taxation also come without exception from the Cabinet, as part of its budget. In consequence of its initiative in proposing both expenditure and revenue, a British Cabinet is in a good position to balance income and outgo. Finally, nearly all bills passed by Parliament are "government bills"—that is, bills that are initiated by the Cabinet. Thus, one might say that, whereas in the United States legislative leadership is diffused among many committees, in the United Kingdom this leadership is concentrated in a single committee of the legislature—the Cabinet. This same committee also functions as policy committee for the majority party. In addition, it is the executive power.

Parliamentary Checks. Although the Cabinet leads Parliament, it certainly does not control it. The possibility of revolt has always to be borne in mind by the Cabinet, and parliamentary objections have to be anticipated. A Cabinet composed of experienced parliamentarians is well qualified to know how far Parliament will go without balking. The latter's check on the Cabinet thus arises in large measure from the mutual dependence of the two bodies.

Parliament may show its mood in the ostentatious actions of influential members, sometimes carried to the extent of refusing to yield to the party's whip. Parliamentary unrest may show itself also in a disruptive campaign by a group of the government's supporters, such as that directed against Ernest Bevin's foreign policy in 1946-47 by the more anti-American and pro-Soviet members of the Labor party. Such a campaign may be carried into the meetings of the parliamentary party and into the national party conference. Faced with this situation, a government has but two alternatives: either to let its party be disrupted and its majority destroyed, or to adapt its policy to meet the rebels at least halfway.

Channels of Influence. To help manage its relations with its majority, the government has whips—a chief whip, who is paid as parliamentary secretary to the Treasury, and four junior whips, who are paid as officers of the royal household. Looked at from one point of view, the whips are a channel through which the desires of the Cabinet are transmitted to the majority; hence, the office of whip is an organ of the Cabinet's leadership of Parliament. Looked at from another viewpoint, however, the whips provide a channel through which the doubts, difficulties, hesitations, and outbursts of the backbenchers are transmitted to the Cabinet. Thus the office of whip is also an organ through which the parliamentary check on the Cabinet becomes invisibly effective.

It is usually in such informal ways—and even by absenteeism and abstention—that the majority in Parliament exercises a powerful check upon its leaders. It insists on being led, not driven. Sensitivity to parliamentary feeling is all-important; in recent times it has largely taken the place of formal votes of nonconfidence. Normally, this subtle flexibility, adaptability, and responsiveness in the relations between Cabinet and Parliament is what matters. Only if the government does not have an assured majority, but must depend upon the uncertain loyalty of a third party (such as the Liberal party in 1924 and 1929-31), can a formal motion of nonconfidence win a majority.

In addition to indicating a general lack of confidence, a government's supporters can amend its legislative proposals in detail in committee. Or, just as effectively, remarks made by them either in open debate or in private discussion may induce the government to present amendments itself—in committee or at the report stage.

4. The Opposition

Institutional Recognition. "His Majesty's opposition" is a phrase that came into use around 1820. In earlier days, opposition to the government had been regarded as disloyal. Eighteenth-century Tories were suspected of drinking to "the King over the water," rather than to the other King whom the Whigs had seated on the throne. The Whigs of the 1790's had similarly been regarded as disloyal for their opposition to Pitt's holy war against the French Revolution. But a generation later, there was no doubt that the Whig opposition was as loyal as the Tory government.

Just as the government majority has its policy committee—the Cabinet headed by the Prime Minister—so the opposition must have its rival policy committee, a shadow cabinet headed by the leader of the opposition. If the Conservatives are in opposition, it is their leader who chooses the shadow ministers to form his shadow cabinet. If the Labor party is in opposition, it is the Labor party meeting that elects both the leader and the other occupants of the opposition's front bench. The loyal opposition is so much a part of the British system of government that, in gauging the temper of the nation, one must take into account the views of the opposition, not just those of the party in power. Since 1936 the opposition leader may apply for a public salary of £2,000, provision for which is included in each year's appropriations.

Procedural Devices. The role of the opposition in parliamentary practice is well recognized by custom, although it has not been embodied in any standing order. During the annual review of general policy to which the government's presentation of appropriation estimates gives rise each spring, the opposition is allowed to choose the order in which the estimates shall be called up and the parts of them that shall be subjected to discussion. When the minister in charge of a bill moves "that the bill be now read a second time," the opposition may propose postponement—either by moving the previous question ("that the question be *not* now put"); or by moving to substitute some other date for "now"; or by moving to omit all words after "that" and substituting for them a statement of disapproval. At the opening of the session, when a five-day debate is held on the government's policy as outlined in the King's speech, it is the opposition that moves amendments to the vote of thanks.[8] Moreover, whenever the opposition wishes to move a vote of censure, the government accepts the challenge and provides time for a full-dress debate.

---

[8] By abandoning the "address to the President" thanking him for his annual message on the state of the Union, the United States lost a parallel opportunity to force the opposition party to take responsibility for stating its own policy.

In the seventeenth century, when Parliament struggled against the King, it developed many procedures for giving voice to grievances that have now redounded to the advantage of the opposition. Then it was the function of Parliament to oppose; now it is the function of the opposition.

Responsible Opposition. An opposition, of course, is less responsible than a government; it does not have to face the immediate consequences of the policies it advocates. On one occasion, the opposition in Britain has condoned a general strike against the government. On another, it has condoned preparation for armed opposition to the law of the land. On the whole, however, the opposition is restrained by the fact that it is an alternative government. It is also restrained by the responsibility it shares with the government for the use of parliamentary time—an arrangement for which "the usual channels" are the government and opposition whips. The opposition will sometimes carry restraint so far as to avoid asking questions that might embarrass the government in the field of foreign policy.

The British parliamentary system is geared to enable the opposition to have its say. The latter is free to make its appeal to the public, with an eye to the next general election. For the moment, however, it stands next to no chance of having its way, except in the unusual circumstance of a revolt either by the government's own supporters or by a third party holding the balance of power. The opposition must therefore work for the future. It can do this more effectively by a discriminating opposition in Parliament than by nonattendance and agitation outside Parliament. By choosing parliamentary channels for agitation, the opposition makes itself, together with the government, the joint guardian of the British tradition of constitutionalism.

Wartime Record. In both World Wars, the opposition began by agreeing not to oppose; a year or two later, it agreed to share responsibility by joining in a coalition government. For the duration, there was no opposition. And, if there was no alternative government, why hold a general election? It therefore became natural for Parliament to pass laws extending its life by postponing a general election for the duration. In both instances, the coalition broke up at the end of the war, thus presenting the electorate with the possibility of an alternative government at the first postwar general election.

During periods of wartime coalition, British parliamentarism undergoes a considerable change.[9] The only way of bringing about a change of government in such periods is to reshuffle ministers, drop some of them, and bring in a few others. In World War I, the struggle between government and opposition was replaced by a struggle among groups and cliques within the Cabinet itself. Only the greater gravity of the situation in World War II prevented the recurrence of such strife. At the same time, the backbencher felt freed from restraint; since the government was no longer in any danger

---

[9] Cf. the long series of articles begun by W. I. Jennings and continued by H. R. G. Greaves, "Parliament in Wartime," *Political Quarterly,* 1939 and later.

of being beaten by the opposition—for there was none—he became more independent in his questions, his speeches, and his votes.

5. The House of Commons

Dual Role. To speak of the House of Commons—or of Parliament as a whole—as a legislature would be incorrect. It is both more and less than that; less, because most legislation emanates from the Cabinet and is implemented by the administrative process; more, because one of the principal functions of a representative assembly under responsible government is to maintain a constant check on the policy pursued by the Cabinet.

The functions of the House of Commons may then be described as two: policy control and lawmaking.[10] Each function takes approximately half of its time—some 75 out of 150 days in an average peacetime session lasting 30 weeks. To equip the Commons for their dual role, a series of fourteen select committees on procedure presented reports between 1837 and 1946. It is in the light of their suggestions that successive Cabinets have taken responsibility for initiating procedural reforms.

Policy Control. Policy control is bound up with the reciprocal responsibility of Cabinet and Commons compelling them to work together. All policy, both domestic and foreign, has financial implications. It is therefore in connection with finance that the influence of the House of Commons over policy is most manifest. For this purpose, two "committees of the whole" are all-important—the Committee of Supply and the Committee of Ways and Means. To the House, sitting as a Committee of Supply, the Cabinet presents its estimates for the fiscal year beginning April 1. These estimates have been given in considerable detail for the Army since the Revolution of 1688 and for the Navy and the civilian agencies since the early nineteenth century. Discussion in the Commons runs for some thirty days every spring.

Inasmuch as the Cabinet is, in effect, a committee of Parliament, the Commons felt able, in 1706, soon after the system of parliamentary appropriation was invented, to leave to the Cabinet the right to initiate expenditures. The only formal amendment that can be made is to reduce the estimate by some token sum, but such an amendment would stand practically no chance of being passed. The control of the House of Commons over expenditure is thus to be found simply and solely in the influence of publicity. It is not only what is said that has a restraining influence on government; it is also the fear

[10] Many of the most authoritative books on British parliamentary procedure have been written by men who have worked as "clerk of the House of Commons." See, for example, Sir Gilbert Campion's *Introduction to the Proceedings of the House of Commons* (rev. ed., London, 1947) and Sir T. Erskine May's *Treatise on the Law, Privileges, Proceedings and Usage of Parliament* (1st ed., London, 1844; 14th ed., 1946). In British usage, it is not possible to equate policy-making with legislation. Policy-making is a more general term and includes many aspects of foreign and colonial policy for which little parliamentary action is needed except annual consideration of estimated expenditure. Legislation is a narrower term and implies the implementation of government policy by specific changes in statute law.

of what might conceivably be said.   It is the same with the raising of revenue. Here, too, the House has yielded the initiative to the Cabinet.   It is the Chancellor of the Exchequer who, in one of the most important speeches of the year, at the beginning of April "opens the budget" to the Commons sitting as a Committee of Ways and Means.   The most that is permitted by way of amendment is to modify the proposed tax schedules in some minor way; even this occurs very seldom, since the government usually senses the opinion of the House in time to introduce changes itself.

Owing to the virtual certainty that the Cabinet's expenditure estimates and revenue proposals will be accepted by the Commons, it is normal to discuss both in Committee of the Whole after the fiscal year has already begun.   It is also normal to put both into effect without waiting for the committee debates to be completed.   Thus, a portion of the estimates for the coming fiscal year is voted "on account," and a Consolidated Fund (No. 1) Bill is passed at the end of March as an interim measure, although the Consolidated Fund (Appropriation) Bill for the whole fiscal year may not be passed until the beginning of August.   Similarly, a Ways and Means Resolution passed immediately after the presentation of the budget permits changes in the raising of revenue, without waiting for the eventual passage of the Finance Bill for the year.[11]

Review of Administration.   An important but limited role has been found for two committees of the House of Commons.   One, the Committee of Public Accounts, has, ever since the 1850's, examined the regularity of the "appropriation accounts" with a view to checking their conformity to the appropriations voted.   This committee is aided by the Comptroller and Auditor General and his staff.   A channel has thus been provided for keeping a number of members of Parliament informed regarding the appropriation audit, so that their findings may help to hold the government responsible. Because this committee is an instrument for implementing Cabinet responsibility to Parliament, the Comptroller and Auditor General has not been empowered to relieve ministers of their responsibility by himself disallowing expenditures before the accounts are settled.   A recommendation from this committee is needed before a departmental commitment in excess of appropriations may be met.   Usually, the committee has a chairman and other members drawn from the opposition.   It has the power—unusual for British parliamentary committees—of taking evidence from civil servants, whose care in administering appropriations is thereby enhanced by the risk of questioning.

The other similar group is the Select Committee on Estimates, known in

---

[11] If the Cabinet fails to take the lead in initiating fiscal policy, the only possible alternative is for some outside body to do so.   On two interwar occasions, the Cabinet allowed leadership in "economy drives" to slip out of its hands into those of departmental committees that it had appointed for the express purpose of wielding the axe, under the chairmanship of Eric Geddes (1922) and George May (1931).   For the committee reports, see Cmd. 1581 (1922) and Cmd. 3920 (1931).

wartime as the Select Committee on National Expenditure. Its duty is to inquire into the government's estimates of expenditure and to report to the House on the effectiveness with which the policy to which the House has agreed is being carried out. The committee is not broken down into sub-committees. Nor—unlike the public accounts committee—does it have the benefit of a full-time salaried staff upon whom to call for help.[12] Some members of Parliament have begun to feel that these two committees might be fused.

Parliamentary Questions. Lastly, the House of Commons can indicate its feelings by asking questions. From the time the first question was printed in 1835, use of this procedure has grown enormously. Today, an average of some 100 questions a day is "starred" for oral answer, with the peak demand reaching 150, although the most that can be answered in an hour is about 70. Time for questions had to be limited to one hour (1902); and the number for each member to be starred for oral answer restricted to three a day (1920).

In order that questions may serve as liaison between Cabinet and Parliament, any question that is not addressed to a minister or other member actually in charge of official business is out of order; questions may not be addressed to private members or to former ministers as such. Some questions are no doubt suggested by ministers themselves as a convenient way of imparting information to Parliament and the public. Others are the work of critics bent on picking holes in a none too consistent policy, or even on harrying a minister out of office. Still others are merely the transmission of a constituent's complaints; and in these cases oral answers might be less sought after if written answers came more rapidly or if members' letters to departments were answered more promptly. The departments have only twenty-four hours in which to prepare oral answers to members' questions. This necessity for always being ready to explain one's actions has a powerful effect on permanent officials as well as on ministers.

Parliament and Legislation. The other principal function of the House of Commons is legislation. Just as the proportion of the national income needed by government has increased gigantically with the general expansion of government's role in society, so also has the quantity of statutory law enacted by Parliament. The average number of pages of new law added to the statute book each peacetime year has increased nearly threefold since before World War I.

In its passage through the House of Commons, a bill goes through four principal stages subsequent to introduction (first reading) and prior to transmittal to the "other House": (1) "second reading," when the government explains its proposed legislation, the opposition has an opportunity to impede the bill's moving to the next stage, and the majority approves the bill in prin-

---

[12] Cf. L. M. Short, "Administrative Management in Great Britain," *Public Administration Review,* 3 (1943), 273 ff.

ciple; (2) "committee stage," when the bill is gone over word by word and
verbal amendments are made; (3) "report stage," when the House decides
whether to accept the amendments proposed in committee; and (4) "third
reading," which provides the last chance to make amendments before the bill
goes to the Lords.

Committee Procedure. Of the four stages, the one that attracts most public
attention is the debate on second reading; the most time-consuming, however,
is the committee stage. Until 1882, the committee on all bills was the Committee of the Whole House. At that time the standing orders were changed
so as to retain the Committee of the Whole only for finance bills and bills that
the House considered to be of highest constitutional importance. Most other
bills thereafter were sent "upstairs" to one or another of the new standing
committees. These have now been named "A," "B," "C," "D," "E," and
"Scottish bills." Unlike the French or American type of parliamentary committee, they have not been functional committees, each of which specializes
in a particular field. Each committee (except the one on Scottish bills) consists of a nucleus of twenty members (quorum is fifteen), to whom are added
up to thirty other interested members for consideration of each particular
bill.

The committee is able to make only amendments, because the vote at the
report stage is on the motion "that the amendments proposed in committee be accepted," which wording has always been assumed to exclude all
possibility of a committee's substitution of a new bill of its own. Minutes
of the proceedings of the standing committees are printed, in order that the
amendments may be publicly recorded. But there is no incentive to any
member to court publicity; the committee is a workplace for the improvement of bills.

In order to handle the heavy postwar legislative program, changes have
been proposed in the committee system: that there be seven instead of five
committees; that they meet three times a week instead of twice; that they sit
for more than the customary two hours; that whenever the congestion is
very bad, the House be adjourned after questions in order to permit committees to meet in the afternoon; above all, that the "guillotine" type of closure
be introduced into the committees, fixing both the total time that might be
spent on one bill and the time to be spent on each part of it. This last suggestion was recently accepted by the Cabinet and the House.

Delegation of Powers. The other principal method of relieving parliamentary congestion and increasing legislative productivity is "delegated
legislation." In Britain it is considered constitutional for Parliament to
delegate legislative powers to responsible ministers; and the activity of government departments under these grants is frankly called "legislative," not
"quasi-legislative." The administrative regulations made under an act of
Parliament are now known as "statutory instruments." They numbered
1,661 in 1938 and 2,467 in 1949.

The only control that Parliament has over four fifths of the statutory instruments is its general control over policy. Under responsible government, this control is very important. Over the remaining one fifth, Parliament has an additional check, in that each is subject to parliamentary confirmation or annulment. In order to make this check effective, a Select Committee on Statutory Instruments was established in 1944, consisting of a dozen members of Parliament. The committee meets every few weeks to determine whether the special attention of the House should be drawn to a statutory instrument on any of the following grounds: (1) that it imposes a charge on public revenue or requires payments to be made to the government or a public authority for license or service; (2) that it is made in pursuance of an act specifically excluding it from challenge in the courts (which is discussed in the next chapter); (3) that it appears to make unusual or unexpected use of the powers conferred; (4) that there appears to have been unjustifiable delay in its publication; and (5) that for any reason it calls for elucidation.[13] Before reporting to the House, the committee is obliged to afford the department concerned an opportunity to furnish explanations.

The principal importance of such a check lies not in the number of statutory instruments it draws to the attention of the House, but rather in its deterrent effect on the departments. It is bound to make them more careful not to misuse the delegated legislative powers. It also helps to create an informed opinion among members of Parliament, thus strengthening the general control of Parliament over policy.

Concentration of Parliamentary Leadership. In discharging its two essential functions of policy control and lawmaking, the House of Commons is so organized that its leadership stems primarily from two centers—the government and the opposition. This fact is both symbolized and aided by the arrangement of the chamber. With considerably more members than the United States House of Representatives, the House of Commons has only one quarter of the floor space. Government and opposition face each other across a table. Each side has seats for its leaders on the "front bench," with the Prime Minister on Mr. Speaker's right and the leader of the opposition on his left; the nonministerial supporters sit on the "back benches" behind their leaders.

Only for ministers, the leader of the opposition, and the party whips is there any office accommodation. For the "backbencher" there are no reserved seats, nor a table on which to lay his papers or rest his feet. Nor is the "private member"—one who does not hold ministerial office—given free secretarial service. For him, there is only the library in which to read his papers and write his letters. This distinction between officeholders and private

---

[13] The select committee prints reports, proceedings, and minutes of evidence. For its appointment, see *Parliamentary Debates, House of Commons,* May 17, 1944. On delegated legislation, see Lord Chancellor's Committee on Ministers' Powers, *Report* (Cmd. 4060 [1932]); and C. T. Carr, *Concerning English Administrative Law* (New York, 1941).

members is also reflected in the salaries paid to members of Parliament. Until 1911, a member of Parliament as such received no salary. A minister, officer of the House, or officer of the royal household whose office pays £5,000 or more continues to receive no salary as member of Parliament. If his office pays less than £5,000, he receives an additional salary of £500 as member of Parliament; and the same thing holds true for the leader of the opposition and anyone who draws a pension as a former Prime Minister. Other members of Parliament get a salary of £1,000, of which a minimum of £100 is assumed for income-tax deduction purposes to go for expenses.

Distribution of Influence. Of the one hundred and fifty days that make up a parliamentary session, all except twenty have been at the government's disposal ever since, in 1902, the Balfour Cabinet took the lead in persuading the House to change its standing orders. Of these twenty "private members' days," about one third are for motions on Wednesdays between November and Easter; two thirds are for bills on Fridays—when the sitting is exceptionally short and ill attended—between November and Whitsun. Private members in search of publicity for themselves or their ideas may draw lots for a place on the timetable. Some of this limited private members' time is taken up by members of the opposition to advocate the principles and policies for which they stand, although they have plenty of other opportunities for doing so. The remainder proves useful when some exceptionally persistent and resourceful private member grasps a nettle that is too hot for party leaders to handle, or that is outside the main paths of party policy. Between the wars, an average of ten private bills was passed each session.[14] One of these was A. P. Herbert's Matrimonial Causes Act, which modernized the law of divorce without forcing either political party to antagonize the Catholic vote. The introduction of a "fair wages clause" into government contracts also stemmed from private members' motions.

For committees, as for private members, only a limited role is reserved. Since no committee except the Cabinet has any power of legislative initiative, committee hearings are not needed as a means of eliciting facts and opinions on which to base legislation; they have no place in the work of standing committees. Hearings are restricted to two purposes. They occur when the committees on accounts, estimates, or statutory instruments wish to take evidence from civil servants and others in holding the government responsible for the use of its powers. They also occur when a committee wishes to take evidence on a request to have some privilege granted or some wrong righted by means of a private or local act of Parliament. In both cases, a judicial procedure is followed, with formal cross-examination of witnesses by counsel, to determine the facts at issue.

---

[14] Private members' acts are the only British statutes that commonly bear the name of the member who introduces them. Other historic examples are Fox's Libel Act (1792) and Plimsoll's Merchant Shipping Act (1876). Private members' bills were used to promote such ideas as votes for women and meals for schoolchildren, thus preparing the way for government bills on these subjects.

Impartiality of the Speaker.   The role of Mr. Speaker is also a limited one. In the fifteenth and sixteenth centuries he had managed the Commons on behalf of the King.   In the midseventeenth century, he became the spokesman of the House against the King, and as such, for a while, the leader of the House.   With the rise of Cabinet leadership in the eighteenth century, this practice ceased, although the Speaker still attended Cabinet meetings and even stepped from his office to that of Prime Minister.   With the full recognition in the 1820's of the loyalty of the opposition, and of the leadership of the House by the Prime Minister or his deputy, Mr. Speaker retired into the position of an impartial presiding officer.

When a new speaker is elected by the House, it is normal for the election to be moved from the government side and supported from the opposition side.   When the opposition becomes the government, there is usually no change of speaker.   When Mr. Speaker stands for re-election, it is unusual for a candidate to be run against him; it would be improper of him to conduct a party campaign against an opposing candidate.   Recognizing members about to speak; ruling on procedural questions, including the interpretation of standing orders and precedents recorded in the *Journals* of the House; admonishing, reprimanding, or imprisoning for "breach of privilege" any persons who obstruct the House in its work; and determining which bills are "money bills" within the meaning of the Parliament Act of 1911—these and similar functions have given to the bewigged British Speaker an almost judicial air.

The "Other House."   Ever since the function both of government and opposition came to be centered in the Commons, the House of Lords has steadily declined in importance.   In one sense, the Parliament of the United Kingdom—like the national parliaments of all British countries—is bicameral. That is, it has a second house, in which questions may be asked, amendments proposed, and hearings conducted on private bills.   Under a system of government by discussion, it is undoubtedly advantageous to have a second house in which additional opportunities for discussion are available.   On the other hand, the Parliament of the United Kingdom does not consist of two equal houses.   The primacy of the Commons in financial matters, and therefore in the general control of governmental policy, has been gradually strengthened, until by the Parliament Act of 1911 it became absolute.   For financial purposes, the United Kingdom is now virtually unicameral.

For legislative purposes, the Parliament remains bicameral.   Even here, however, the House of Lords has only a suspensive veto, since any bill passed by the Commons in two consecutive sessions becomes law in spite of rejection by the Lords.   Thus far, the House of Lords has four times persisted in using its suspensive veto.   It failed to block the Welsh Church Act in 1914, and the Parliament and Iron and Steel Acts in 1949, and it delayed the passage of the Government of Ireland Act of 1914 until changing circumstances made it improbable that the act could be carried out peaceably.

Under the Labor government carried into power in 1945, the House of Lords contented itself with proposing many amendments to some of the government's nationalization bills. Some of these amendments were accepted by the government, but the more far-reaching ones were rejected by the Commons and not persisted in by the Lords, except that in the iron and steel nationalization, the "vesting date" was set after the general election of 1949, so that the Conservatives could repeal the act if they won the election. A new custom may be developing, under which the House of Lords refrains from exercising its suspensive veto during at least the first two or three years after a general election, thus recognizing the all-important relationship between Cabinet, Commons, and electorate in legislation as well as in policy control.

6. Crown and Sovereign

Symbol of Unity. The operation of a system of government depends as much on unwritten attitudes as on written laws. It is a matter of mental outlook as much as of administrative machinery. These attitudes must be explained psychologically rather than logically. They are historically conditioned and hard to communicate to the outsider. They are focused on symbols. Such, in some countries, are the flag and the constitution, as emotive representations of the unity and historic continuity of the nation. Such in Britain is the Crown.[15]

The idea, for example, that government is based on the consent of the governed is expressed in the coronation oath prescribed by the Act of Parliament of 1689, sworn with high religious pomp and ceremony by incoming kings, who promise to govern "according to the statutes in Parliament agreed on," and according to the laws and customs of the people. Parliament, too, does not simply begin its session on some appointed day, but is ceremoniously opened by the King. The government's policy and legislative program for the session are not simply printed as an agenda, but are embodied by the Cabinet in a "King's speech" or "speech from the Throne," delivered in the House of Lords, as the original House of Parliament, with the Commons standing at the bar. All bills, when passed by Parliament, receive the royal assent. In ways such as these, the historic institution of the Crown is intimately associated with the equally historic institution of Parliament—a link as strong in the day of Elizabeth II as it ever was.

Fountain of Honors. In most countries, there are also ways in which honor and recognition can be given those who have rendered outstanding public service. Some ways are formal, whereas others are informal. Formally, in Britain the Crown is the "fountain of honors," the source from which titles and distinctions flow.

New forms of distinction are continually being invented, from that of the

---

[15] Parliamentary appropriations to meet the cost of the ceremonial headship of the state are included in the "civil list" and do not come up for annual vote.

Knights of the Garter or the Bath in the late Middle Ages to the Order of the British Empire in the First World War or the George Cross for civilian bravery in the Second. Some distinctions, such as the two last, are available without limit as to number of recipients; others, such as the two former and the Order of Merit, are limited in that respect. Most of these honors are for life. Most of them are simply so many letters after a name. Knighthoods, however, carry with them the life title "sir," placed before the name; for women who are to be honored with a title in their own right, the life title "dame" was adopted during World War I. Other titles are hereditary. Such is the baronetcy, conferring a "sir" before the name and a "bart." after it. Such also are the four kinds of peerage—barony, viscounty, earldom, and marquisate— that are still granted to subjects of the Crown and that usually carry with them the privilege of a hereditary seat in the House of Lords.

It must be recognized that the fountain of honors may become polluted, public service being interpreted as large contributions to the Conservative party or, formerly, to the Liberal party. Thus, until World War I, it was the chief whips of those parties who were responsible both for collecting party funds and for drawing up the list of new public-service peerages for transmittal by the Prime Minister to the King. Since 1922 it has been a criminal offense to buy or sell a peerage. The Prime Minister must now accompany his proposals with signed statements about the source from which each proposal has come. His proposals are reviewed by a special statutory committee of the Privy Council, appointed by him and composed of members of his party. Labor governments have been unwilling to confer peerages on men who have heirs.

Royal Prerogative. The Crown may also be regarded as a reserve of legal powers. The "prerogative," evolved by lawyers, might be defined as all those common-law powers of the sovereign that have neither died out nor been modified by statute. It is, for example, the King who grants titles and appoints ministers, including the Prime Minister. It is the King who dissolves Parliament, proclaiming at the same time the date when the next Parliament will assemble. It is the King who closes Parliament, stating at the same time the date when the next session will begin. It is he who annexes territory, grants dependencies their constitutions, declares war, and ratifies treaties. None of these powers has been conferred on the King by act of Parliament. They are historically part of the royal office. Parliament may, of course, supersede the prerogative. It is, moreover, becoming a common but not invariable practice to submit treaties to Parliament for approval before royal ratification, although any government would probably feel free to have a treaty ratified if the Lords withheld their consent. It is also customary to ask parliamentary approval before giving away territory subject to the British Crown.

The King, in exercising his prerogative, is in the habit of asking advice of his Prime Minister, the only important exception being the choice of the

Prime Minister himself on certain rare occasions when the King has no prior advice to guide him. Anything that the King can do by virtue of his prerogative he is also free to refuse to do; and there have been occasions when he has posed conditions before complying with advice to use the prerogative. For instance, Edward VII declined to swamp the House of Lords with new peers unless the Prime Minister could win two general elections. The Crown has even refused to follow the advice given, as when Victoria declined to appoint a republican as minister of the Crown. At the same time, there are certain uses of the prerogative that have died out. Thus, no king has dismissed a cabinet since 1834, or withheld assent from a statute since 1707. Certain other uses of the prerogative have been abolished by statute, especially the suspension of acts of Parliament, which was declared illegal in 1688.

For his exercise of the prerogative, there is no way of holding the King responsible. He may not be held responsible in a court of law, for "the King can do no wrong." Nor can he be held politically responsible, for there is no easy method of getting rid of him without his own consent. For these reasons, he is always deemed to have acted under advice, as he does for all practical purposes; and the Prime Minister regularly accepts full political responsibility for every use of the prerogative.

Royal Succession. The decision who shall exercise these royal powers is made partly by act of Parliament and partly by common law. By the Act of Settlement of 1701, the Crown was settled on a particular family. Within that family, marriage is regulated by a special law and requires formal consent by the King in council—that is, on the advice of his ministers in the Privy Council—if the would-be spouse is under twenty-five; the right to disapprove the marriage is reserved to Parliament if the person in question is over twenty-five. Within the appointed family, again, succession is by the ordinary rules of the English common law concerning the inheritance of intestate landed property. Parliament, of course, is constitutionally free, subject only to the formality of royal assent, to pass an act locating the Crown in any hands it likes.

In a crowned republic such as Britain, the sovereign is not the King but the King in Parliament. It is to Parliament that the King owes his throne. By statute the prerogative is limited and superseded. By statute the terms on which the King takes office are prescribed. King, Lords, and Commons together make up the Parliament; and it is by act of Parliament that the tenure and powers of each of these three "estates of the realm" are defined.

Sovereignty and Law. In the United Kingdom, no law is more fundamental than an act of Parliament. Parliament, then, is sovereign. No distinction is drawn between constitutional law and statute law. If a change is to be made in the British constitution, all that is needed is a simple majority of members present and voting for the change in two Houses of Parliament— or, under the Parliament Acts of 1911 and 1949, in the Commons alone, if they vote so in two consecutive sessions. To a statute lawfully passed the King always assents.

British courts are free to interpret all statute law in the light of what they regard as basic principles of common law and equity. By interpretation they may give the statute a meaning that Parliament never intended. In order to prevent the courts from following such a precedent in future cases, it may therefore be necessary for the supreme law of the land to be declared by some higher authority. In Britain this authority is Parliament itself.[16]

It follows that the courts may not declare statute law null and void for non-compliance with what the courts think is meant by the written or unwritten constitution. Judicial review in the United Kingdom does not extend to acts of Parliament, but is confined to ensuring the compliance of delegated legislation with the statutes under which it purports to be issued. Judicial review may thus be a means of reinforcing parliamentary sovereignty, but it cannot for long obstruct or impede its exercise. It is "the high court of Parliament" that under popular control is the final judge of whether a proposed law is or is not in accordance with the basic principles of the British constitution.

---

[16] On the "reversal" of the Taff Vale decision (1901) by the Trade Disputes Act of 1906, see Sidney and Beatrice Webb, *History of Trade Unionism* (rev. ed., New York, 1920), pp. 600 ff.

CHAPTER 4

GOVERNMENT BY CONSENT AND DISCUSSION

1. Political Parties

Historic and Geographic Bases. Although of strong national cohesion, for more than three hundred years Britons have been accustomed to being divided into two different political camps. It is to the civil wars of the seventeenth century that this two-party cleavage is usually traced. In the armed conflicts that were then fought, some Englishmen sided with the King and others with Parliament; some were attached to the established church, while others preferred religious nonconformity. Each acquired a nickname from its opponent. Those who favored King and church were branded Tories, meaning Irish papists; those who favored Parliament and nonconformity were labeled Whigs, meaning Scottish Presbyterians. The former were stronger in rural counties, where most country gentlemen were of this way of thinking. The latter were more numerous in the urban centers. These lines of division survived into the nineteenth century. They did not become completely outmoded until the interwar years of the twentieth, by which time the remaining rivalry of King and Parliament, "church" and "chapel," rural gentry and urban middle class had been definitely replaced by new groupings, owing to the rise of organized labor and the spread of socialist theory. Thus, the habit of having two parties is ten generations old, though the actual contestants of today have been fighting each other for only one generation.

Between the two principal parties of today, there are no noticeable religious differences. Constitutionally, the only important difference is that Conservatives have a respect for the House of Lords that is lacking in the Labor party. Ideologically, the distinction is that Conservatives extend public ownership with reluctance, whereas Labor extends it with conviction. Socially, the Conservatives find their following among the gentry and the professional and upper middle classes; Labor finds its supporters in the families of organized workers in both the "wage-earning" class and, since World War II, in the "salaried" lower middle class. Geographically, the Conservatives look to the agricultural counties, the more fashionable quarters of the greater cities, and the resort towns; Labor looks to the coal-mining counties and the general run of urban centers.

Meanwhile, a steady evolution has taken place in the structure of parties. In the first phase (the seventeenth century), the opposing factions settled their differences by armed conflict. In the next phase (the eighteenth century), armed conflict was abandoned, the rival parties centered around rival clubs in London, and party rivalry found its first theoretical defender in Edmund Burke. In the third phase (1832-67), the statutory introduction of official registers of qualified voters led to the spread of local registration associations; for this purpose local "agents" began to be hired, and party organization came to be as much a matter of local associations as of fashionable London clubs. Finally, during the current phase (since 1867), the great extension of the franchise has necessitated a series of experiments in the welding together of central leadership and local support. To this problem both the Conservative party and the Labor party have found solutions, though very different ones. The collapse of the Liberal party was largely due to its inability to solve its organizational problems.

The Conservative Party. The Conservative party is built around its leader. This position is normally held by the Prime Minister if the latter is a Conservative. If such a prime minister happens to have been picked by the King, the party acquires a leader whom it has not chosen. If the party goes into opposition, its leader normally exchanges the post of Prime Minister and leader of the Commons for that of leader of the opposition, while retaining the party leadership. Only if a change of leader becomes necessary when the party is in opposition does the party itself choose its leader. Then the choice is normally made by the retiring leader and those who stand close to him, to be confirmed by the party conference.

The leader issues the party's election platform, in the form of a circular letter addressed either to his own constituents or to his fellow candidates. If his party is in opposition, the leader decides which parliamentary colleagues shall sit with him on the opposition's front bench and be the ghost ministers in his shadow cabinet. Above all, the leader controls the Conservative Central Office. Established by Benjamin Disraeli in 1870, this agency receives voluntary contributions; accepts offers of service from would-be parliamentary candidates; suggests candidates to local associations; makes grants to local associations toward election expenses; and denies the leader's endorsement and the Central Office's financial support to any candidature that it disapproves, thus virtually exercising control over the choice of parliamentary candidates. Management of party finance is delegated by the leader to a Central Office treasurer, by whom large contributions are collected from rich individuals and corporations and who is presumed to invest the party's capital profitably.

In addition, there is a National Union of Conservative Associations, also established originally by Disraeli. It holds an annual conference in a resort town during the summer recess, as a means of giving local agents and volunteer workers a feeling of participation, crystallizing their support behind the leader's program, winning their approval for a new leader or for the leader's destined successor, and reaching the great mass of the party's support-

ers by being in the news. The National Union is in no sense a policy-initi-
ating body, although it is commonly utilized as a policy-endorsing organ.

Conservative Auxiliary Organizations. To keep its hold over its supporters between one election and the next, the Conservative party has a number
of auxiliary agencies. Each has an elaborate organization of its own, with
officers, dues, national conferences, local chapters, and periodical publications.
Oldest are the Conservative Workingmen's Clubs, with billiard tables, bowl-
ing alleys, and liquor licenses. Next comes the Primrose League, named
for what Disraeli is said to have said was his favorite flower and providing an
array of genteel attractions, from dancing classes for "primrose buds" to
bridge parties for adults, with a fair seasoning of social snobbery and political
propaganda thrown in. Similarly constituted is the Imperial League and its
"Junior Imps."

In such ways as these, besides political conviction, the active participation
of thousands of volunteer workers is assured and their ability as organizers
is constantly tested. They are available as a permanent trained reserve to be
drawn upon at election time. These networks of primary groups also provide highly personalized media for the steady cultivation of enduring attitudes, as well as for the rapid circulation of the password of the moment.

The Labor Party. The Labor party has no leader and no Central Office.
Authority within it is more widely diffused.[1] In the Labor party it is easier
for pressures to work their way up from the bottom. At the center, since
1920, has been the National Council of Labor, a joint coordinating body composed of the chairmen and the executive committees of the National Labor
party, the Parliamentary Labor party, and the Trades Union Congress. The
Parliamentary Labor party, composed of all members of Parliament who recognize the Labor whip, elects its own chairman. He becomes Prime Minister or leader of the opposition, as the case may be; and, if in opposition, it
chooses the Labor members who are to sit with him on the front bench.
From 1929 to 1946, the Parliamentary Labor party's "standing orders" denied
the Labor label to any member in Parliament who voted against the decision
of a majority in a party meeting.

The National Labor party, at its annual conference in a resort town, elects
its executive committee, its chairman for the coming year (a different one
each year, and never the chairman of the Parliamentary party), and its full-
time executive secretary (who conducts its business from national headquarters at Transport House in London). The national conference formulates
the party platform in the form of a lengthy pamphlet.

National-Local Relations. The composition of the annual conference of
the National Labor party is obviously of great importance. Originally, as
constructed by Keir Hardie in 1899-1900, the party represented an alliance between a number of trade unions and a few socialist societies. Each delegate

---

[1] Cf. especially the *Labour Yearbook* (London, annually). Cf. Herbert Tracey, ed., *The British Labour Party* (London, 1948), 3 vols.

to the national conference cast as many votes as there were members in the organization he represented.   To these two original kinds of group members —trade unions and socialist societies—a third kind was added under the secretaryship of Arthur Henderson in 1918.   The latter provided for local organizations with individual membership as a means of attracting support from housewives, the self-employed, the retired, and others who were not necessarily members of either trade unions or socialist societies.   This move undoubtedly helped the Labor party to take its present place as rallying point for the opposition to Conservatism and to think of itself as the heir to the traditions of the Whigs and the Liberal party.

The trade-union delegates have preponderant weight in the national conference.   But this fact is somewhat compensated for by the election to the executive committee of men and women from the socialist societies.   Socialists have also helped indirectly to mold Labor's policy through staff work on the very influential research and publications offices both of the Labor party and of the Fabian Socialist Society.   In local constituencies a similar organization prevails.   The local unit is composed of representatives both of local chapters of trade unions and of individual party members.   It is normally the local Labor parties that choose the parliamentary candidates, the national secretary confining himself to help and advice and a possible veto.

Relations with Labor parties in other British countries are carefully cultivated.   Conferences of the Labor parties within the Commonwealth are held from time to time.   These parties are also loosely associated with the Socialist parties of other countries, especially in Western Europe, but stand in opposition to parties of the extreme left.

Exclusion of Communists.   Communists are barred from individual membership in the Labor party by requiring from each member a signed declaration that he is not a member of another party and by disaffiliating any local Labor party that breaks this rule.   The Communist party has also been refused affiliation with the Labor party as a socialist society.

The only way in which Communists have been able to bore into the Labor party has therefore been through some trade unions.   Hence, the reserve powers in the hands of the national secretary and the executive committee to withdraw recognition from any local party, organization, candidate, or member of Parliament that does not abide by the declared policies of the party.   Party discipline is thus comparatively strict and has been consistently used to prevent Communists from capturing any part of the party machine.

Party Finance.   The chief source of income for the Labor party is derived from membership dues, which have run about one shilling a year each member.   The collection of these dues by trade unions has been governed by what is practically the only intervention of the law in British party organization.   The development has passed through five phases.

At first it was assumed that trade unions were free to collect dues for any lawful purpose.   Next the courts ruled that trade unions were exceeding their lawful powers if they collected dues for a purpose other than one explicitly permitted them by law. In the third phase (1911-26), thanks to an electoral alliance between the then rising Labor party and the Liberal party, trade unions were permitted by the Trade Union Act of 1913 to collect dues for any purpose not illegal, including political representation; but any trade unionist might "contract out" by signing a statement that he did not wish to pay dues through his union to the Labor party. In the fourth phase (1927-45), the Conservative party used its parliamentary majority to allow the Labor party union dues only from those trade unionists who "contracted in" by signing a statement that they wished to pay dues; in the same law, trade unions were forbidden to collect political dues from government employees or to affiliate with the Labor party if they were unions of such employees. In the fifth phase, the Labor party used *its* majority to put the law back to where it was during the third phase—one of the very few examples in British politics of legislation passed by one party being undone by the other.

Bases of Labor Support. The Conservative party relies greatly on social activities to keep its hold on its workers and supporters. The Labor party relies mainly on the economic activities of the trade unions and the intellectual activities of the socialist societies. As the range of union organization has extended from industry to commerce, the hold of the Labor party has expanded from the working-class to the lower-middle-class constituencies. When full employment boosts the number of trade-union members, the Labor party is more successful than when unemployment brings disorganization.

The socialist societies have provided a path into the Labor party for many members of the professions. The Fabian Society, established in 1884, has been especially effective. Its members included at one time or another such outstanding British writers as George Bernard Shaw, Sidney and Beatrice Webb, H. G. Wells, R. H. Tawney, H. J. Laski, and G. D. H. Cole.[2]

Party Characteristics. No British party is merely a loose alliance of local or regional organizations. Every British party is thoroughly national in leadership, organization, and platform. None is based upon patronage. Each stands for policy, or at least for an attitude of mind. Stress on policy and attitude necessitates a considerable printed output, with the Labor party setting the pace in both the quantity and the quality of its publications. Party workers have to be indoctrinated, the doubtful have to be persuaded, and the young have to be called to service. British parties are thus engaged in a continuing task of civic education.

Party is unknown to British law. A British political party is as much a private association as is a football club. No law defines the organization of a party, the choice of its officers, the management of its funds, or the way in which it presents candidates for nomination. Membership in a party is based on payment of contributions or dues; the official registers of voters do not

---

[2] The pamphlets prepared for the Fabian Research Bureau are indispensable for the understanding of contemporary Britain.

record a voter's party allegiance. There is no restriction on the sources from which parties may get funds, apart from the statutory clause under which a trade unionist may "contract out" of contributing to his union's political activities. Every British party is thus master in its own house.

2. The Electoral Process

Constituencies. Britain has no national plebiscites and no national referenda. No question is ever referred by Parliament to the voters. Nor do the voters initiate any legislation through the ballot. "Direct democracy" is almost unknown in Britain, except for local affairs in the smallest rural parishes. Instead, Britain is a land of "representative democracy." Decisions are made, not directly by the people, but by the people's elected representatives. These representatives are not chosen at large by any method that will make the number elected for each party proportional to the number of votes cast for that party by its supporters. Instead, representatives are elected from constituencies.[3]

This process is an age-long English tradition. "House of Commons" means "house of communities"—a house whose members sit by virtue of election as representatives from specific communities. From the thirteenth to the nineteenth century, these communities were rural counties or urban boroughs. Their representatives were "knights of the shire" (county members) or "burgesses" (borough members); and every such county or borough, whether large or small, returned the same number of members of Parliament —two from each community. A mathematical conception of representation led, in the nineteenth century, to some modifications in this ancient tradition. From time to time, an act for the "redistribution of seats" or the "representation of the people" would be passed to make the constituencies approximately equal in population.[4]

Equal representation of unequal communities has thus been abandoned in Britain. The parliamentary constituency survives, however, as the basic unit of representation, in the form of the single-member electoral district. Equalizing the population of constituencies is regarded as a matter to be settled by all-party commissions, presided over by Mr. Speaker, rather than by a party majority in Parliament. Nor is there any effort to prevent redistribution of seats on grounds of local interest. This attitude is helped by the fact that a candidate is under no obligation—either legal or customary—to reside in his constituency. Election of nonresident candidates has been normal for the past four hundred years.

Winning Constituencies. Above all, a Briton knows, when he elects his member of Parliament, that he is really engaged in choosing a government.

---

[3] J. K. Pollock, *Money and Politics Abroad* (New York, 1932) provides an exceptionally able introduction to British electoral traditions.

[4] Today, there is approximately one member of Parliament for every 70,000 of the population; in Northern Ireland, 43,000. On members' backgrounds see "Honourable Members," *Economist*, 162, No. 5657 (Jan. 26, 1952), 194 ff.

It is on this that his attention is riveted.   He does not have to think also of
electing executive officers or members of another house, even at several levels
of government, or of voting on referenda.   The ballot is short; its purpose is
in most places to elect one candidate only.   It is so easy for a British voter
to get to know his candidates' names that it is not necessary for the ballot to
carry party labels.   Since only one candidate is elected at a time, the question
whether to vote a straight or a split ticket cannot arise.   No voting machines
are needed to handle so simple a ballot.

Whereas, in any election, the British voter in his constituency is thinking
mainly of the government that may emerge from his vote, the national party
organizers are thinking not so much of winning votes as of winning constituencies.   To win a majority of seats it is not necessary to win a majority of
votes.   The two usually go together, but not necessarily.   The Conservative party, for example, won a majority of seats on five occasions between the
two World Wars, and again in 1951, but only twice obtained a majority of
votes.   More than one third of the constituencies must be considered "doubtful"—a switch of a few thousand votes will transfer victory from one side to
the other.   On these doubtful constituencies both parties concentrate their
organizing ability, their popular speakers, and their literature.   The resulting
shifts may be great, as the accompanying table shows.

PARTY STRENGTH IN SEATS WON AT GENERAL ELECTIONS TO THE HOUSE OF COMMONS
1918–1951

Year	Labor Party	Conservative Party and Electoral Allies	Others
1951	295	321	9
1950	315	299	11
1945	394	216	30
1935	156	419	40
1931	52	521	42
1929	287	260	68
1924	151	412	49
1923	191	258	166
1922	142	405	64
1918	61	509	31

In addition to efforts to win a general election by winning the doubtful
constituencies, a principal concern of the national party machines is to test
popular sentiment by contesting so-called by-elections.   Whenever a seat becomes vacant through the death or resignation of its incumbent, both parties
descend upon it with their biggest guns, in the hope of demonstrating that
there has or has not been any significant change in voters' attitudes since the
general election.

Electioneering Expenses.   For at least four hundred years, a seat in Parliament has been so highly prized that men of means have willingly spent large
sums to stand for election.   As the franchise was extended in the nineteenth

century, candidates were faced with the prospect of evergrowing costs. In 1883, Parliament passed the Corrupt and Illegal Practices Prevention Act. This act placed full responsibility for election expenses on the candidate's election agent, freeing the candidate from any obligation to meet unauthorized expenditures. To authorized expenditures a legal limit was set, which now stands on the average at about £1,250 in a county or £1,000 in a borough. Moreover, none of this money may be spent on "treating" voters or on hiring vehicles to transport voters. Only a limited sum may be spent to hire workers, and the agent's fee is fixed at £75 in a county or £50 in a borough. Accounts have to be filed immediately after the election. The unsuccessful candidate may then institute prosecution for breach of the law, seeking to have the election voided—provided he is able and willing to deposit £1,000 to cover legal expenses.[5]

Apart from some unauthorized expenditures by individual supporters of a candidate, some occasional illegal expenditures, and some doctoring of election accounts so as to charge some election expenses to running the machine between elections, the statutory restrictions would seem to have been effective in keeping down costs. The rise of the Labor party may have done even more toward that end, since most of its candidates have spent less than half of the legal maximum. The net result is that a general election now represents a total outlay of some £1 million for individual candidates, in addition to central outlays on behalf of the party as a whole—which is probably less than was expended a hundred years ago. Some reduction in election expenditures has also been caused by free postal distribution of one 2-ounce package of mail to each voter in a constituency from each candidate.

Selection of Candidates. For the official nomination of candidates, only eight petitioners' signatures are needed, although it is common practice for a party to demonstrate its candidate's popularity among different groups of voters by having him nominated on several petitions. So that ease of nomination will not result in too many candidates, a candidate is required to deposit £150; this deposit is forfeited unless he polls one eighth of the votes cast in the district. Nomination petitions, like ballots, bear no party label. If a Fascist or Communist candidate wishes to run the risk of being beaten and losing his deposit, there is no legal impediment to his doing so. The only adult citizens who are not permitted to be candidates are peers, bankrupts, idiots, lunatics, and clergymen of the Churches of England, Scotland, and Rome.[6]

Behind the official party nomination lies the adoption of the candidate by the local organization. Behind that, in most places, lie many years of a candidate's "nursing" of the constituency. These primary stages in the process of

---

[5] The intervention of unauthorized bodies—such as the brewing industry—on behalf of a candidate's election has also been regarded as corrupt since 1918.

[6] Irish peers may be elected to the House of Commons, unless they have been elected to the House of Lords by the other Irish peers.

selecting a candidate are—like all other aspects of the internal organization of British parties—entirely unregulated by law.

Third Parties. Apart from expense, the principal obstacle to the rise of new parties is psychological. The British voter votes for a supporter of either the government or the opposition. He does not want to "throw away his vote," as he expresses it, on a party that stands no chance of winning an election and forming a government. These psychological factors undoubtedly contributed to the decline of the Liberal party between the World Wars. Third parties in Britain during the last hundred years have had electoral success only when based on a group loyalty so strong as to overcome both the financial and the psychological obstacles to the election of their candidates.

The first great example was the Irish Nationalist party, which captured nine tenths of the constituencies in Ireland in 1886 and held them until 1918. Profiting from an overrepresentation of the Irish population in the Commons, it was able to hold the balance between the Liberal government and the Conservative opposition in 1886, 1892-95, and 1910-16. This Irish Nationalist party made its support of Liberal governments conditional on their support of Irish home rule. The granting of self-government to Ireland in 1921 eliminated this third party from British political hazards.

The other great example is the Labor party. By 1910 it had won so much of the trade-union vote that the Liberal party refrained from fighting it in working-class constituencies in the hope of its general support against the Conservative opposition (1910-16, until the wartime coalition). With the breakup of the Liberal party, the Labor party was able to present itself to the anti-Conservative voter as an alternative. By refusing to have its policy as a government dictated by the Liberals, although they held the balance (1924, 1929-31), the Labor party concentrated attention on its own relative importance. By refusing electoral pacts with the Liberals, it obliged them to engage in "three-corner fights" or not to fight at all. One result of the simultaneous rise of the Labor party and the disruption of the Liberal party was that certainly no general election between 1910 and 1945 led to a parliamentary majority for any one anti-Conservative party, while probably the Conservatives obtained a parliamentary majority more frequently than they would otherwise have done.

3. Group Influence

Discussion and Consent. Political parties aim at capturing the power of the state. The electoral process is the constitutional way of deciding which party shall have the next turn at exercising this power and which shall take a turn at having the lesser influence of the opposition. Government by consent is thus assured. But in the constitutional form in which it is practiced in Britain, it implies more than mere consent. Consent in some countries is manufactured more easily by suppressing the opposition. Indeed, although nearly all government in the modern world is based upon consent, governments differ fundamentally in the manner by which consent is obtained. British government is not only government by consent, but also government by discussion.[7]

Government by discussion implies an atmosphere in which it is taken for granted that every individual or group is free to contribute to the common good. The war of words between two or more contending parties is an essential part of this unceasing discussion, for it helps to guarantee a climate of opinion that is favorable to discussion by all manner of groups. This, to a Briton, is democracy; it is a pattern of free political influence by groups that are not primarily political. But the rank and file of members of Parliament have so little initiative that it is not so much these individual members as it is the Cabinet that needs to be influenced. Influence has to be aimed much more at persuading the Cabinet that it may lose the general election than at persuading the individual member of Parliament that he may not be renominated.

The groups by which Cabinet policy has been most notably influenced in recent years are of two principal kinds. For convenience they may be called general-interest groups and special-interest groups.

General-Interest Groups. The general-interest groups are really disinterested special-purpose associations. These believe that it would be in the public interest for a particular policy to be adopted. They would hope to share as citizens in the public benefits that would result, but no other advantage would accrue to them as individuals or as groups.

For example, the Council for the Preservation of Rural England did much to convert town planning into town-and-country planning. A committee for raising the school age did much to write this particular reform into the Education Act of 1944. The Howard League for Penal Reform has supported the abolition of local jails, the extension of probation, and the general substitution of re-education for punishment. Eleanor Rathbone's League for the Endowment of Motherhood prepared the way for family allowances, much as Charles Booth's Old Age Pension League had done for old-age assistance a generation earlier. Other groups fight for government support of birth control, eugenic sterilization, or voluntary euthanasia. The Society for the Abolition of Slavery is still active on behalf of the peoples of dependent territories. The League of Nations Union, by organizing a "peace ballot," was largely responsible for the government's reversal of policy in the Italo-Ethiopian war, a reversal from partitioning the victim to sanctions against the aggressor. The first and greatest of all such groups was the Anti-Corn Law League, through whose activity the tariff was abolished in 1846 and free trade in essential foods assured.

Groups of this general-interest kind have relied entirely on awakening the public, including the Cabinet, to the true public interest. Animated by a

---

[7] For the political theory of British democracy, see A. D. Lindsay (now Lord Lindsay), *Essentials of Democracy* (Philadelphia, 1929), being lectures given at Swarthmore College.

strong sense of vocation, they have sought to educate the Cabinet if possible and the people as well if necessary.

Special-Interest Groups. Special-interest groups are associations formed for the direct advantage of their supporters, which advantage they seek by various means, one being political influence. Some of these groups are economic, such as the trade unions, the Federation of British Industries, the National Union of Farmers, the Cooperative Union, and special-purpose groups sponsored by special interests such as the brewers. Others represent professional interests, such as the doctors, the teachers, and the clergy of various denominations. Economic and professional groups of this kind commonly identify their own special interest with the general interest of the nation at large. It is therefore hard for a government to adopt their viewpoint and still try to serve the mass of the people. Yet the government may be dependent upon such groups in various ways. It therefore will want to work with them rather than against them and to legislate with them rather than for them.

It is hence normal for a department to consult with these special-interest groups when planning its program. For example, the recent nationalization of air lines, inland transportation, and coal was planned in consultation with the operators and workers concerned. The Education Act of 1944 was similarly planned in consultation with the established church of England, to such an extent that a member of Parliament called it a concordat between the church and the Board of Education. The Industrial Injuries Act of 1945 likewise was planned in consultation with the trade unions, which wished to find a way of avoiding the heavy litigation expenses in workmen's compensation cases. There has been some protest in Parliament against the extent to which recent legislation is based upon understandings between the government and the interest concerned. Such understandings make it morally difficult for the government to accept amendments as the bill goes through Parliament.

In certain ways, the government needs the help of the special-interest group as much as the special-interest group needs the support of the government— and sometimes more. The interest group is therefore able to obstruct legislation by refusing to be consulted. For instance, it was the intention of the British Medical Association not to consult with the government on the setting up of a national health service, until a referendum of its members indicated considerable general willingness to do so. In instances such as this, interest groups have drawn a line between consultation on bills and cooperation in subsequent administration of the law. Opposition to the former has not meant opposition to the latter. The British Medical Association thus has shrunk from calling a doctors' strike against either the National Health Insurance Act of 1911 or the National Health Service Act of 1947.

Relations Between Parties and Interest Groups. The relationship between economic special-interest groups and political parties is everywhere very important. In Britain it has three noteworthy aspects. First, the trade unions are organically linked with the Labor party and business is financially linked with the Conservative party. The spokesmen for organized labor and for organized business are therefore to be found on the benches of the Commons rather than in the lobbies, especially since there is nothing to prevent a member of Parliament from drawing an income from an outside source. And spokesmen for either organized business or organized labor, though never for both at once, are to be found in the Cabinet.[8]

Second, members of Parliament are loyal party adherents, whose parties are clearly aligned with one or the other of the great rival interests in modern Britain. They stand or fall with their national party. They are not lone wolves whose fortunes can be made or marred by sectional economic interests. Nor can they be grouped into economic blocs regardless of party: the Labor party is *ipso facto* a labor bloc, the Conservative party is *ipso facto* a business bloc, and there is no farm bloc.

Third, the civic education or propaganda that in some countries is mainly the work of special-interest groups is concentrated in Britain in the political parties.

Extraconstitutional Action. Actions speak louder than words. Groups sometimes express themselves in ways that are barely constitutional. Non-conformist free-churchmen have gone to prison in protest against tax support for parochial schools. Women suffragists have burnt churches in order to attract attention. Ulstermen have threatened rebellion in the name of the King, rather than submit to an act of Parliament subjecting them to a parliament at Dublin. Army officers have resigned in mass rather than enforce such a law. The Trades Union Congress threatened a general strike in 1921 against war with Russia and in 1925 against a worsening of working conditions in the coal industry; in 1926 it carried out its threat. The financial policy that wrecked the Labor Cabinet in 1931 was said by the Chancellor of the Exchequer to have been arranged between the Governor of the Bank of England and the Governor of the Federal Reserve Bank of New York.[9]

Pressures of this kind are part of the political life of any free country. One of the tests of statesmanship is ability to keep open constitutional channels so that resort to "direct action," passive disobedience, active resistance, obstructive noncooperation, nonviolent obstruction, physical violence, and economic force remain the exception rather than become the rule.

4. Communication Media

Old and New. Government by consent and discussion implies the availability of media for the two-way communication of ideas. Until the eight-

---

[8] On the open question of the extent to which business has "dictated" recent Conservative policy, see Ramsay Muir, *How Britain Is Governed* (New York, 1930), pp. 132 ff.; Pollock, *op. cit.* above, note 3, pp. 112 ff.; Brian Barker, *Labour in London* (London, 1946), pp. 52 ff.

[9] P. Snowden, *Autobiography* (London, 1934), II, 947.

eenth century, personal contact in small primary groups was virtually the only method by which the government's viewpoint could be communicated to the people or the people's to the government. Ministers spoke in Parliament. Members of Parliament talked to their friends and neighbors back home. Clergymen expressed what their parishioners expected of the government or—in the established church—what the government expected of parishioners. Justices riding circuit made speeches on the state of the nation when opening assizes and reported back on the state of the provinces when they returned to Westminster.

These older forms of personal contact were supplemented in the earlier nineteenth century by the introduction of the mass meeting, made common with the massing of people into cities. It was by means of the "platform" (a word whose new application was invented in 1819) that democratic and liberal doctrines were spread. British municipalities, from the middle of the nineteenth century, helped in this development by building public auditoriums as part of their town halls and by setting aside space in their parks and on their commons for open-air meetings. From 1878 on, the leader of the opposition deigned to address mass meetings, and a few years later the Prime Minister followed his example.

The Press. The platform in its turn was supplemented by the press, which grew into a vast estate. Beginning in the First World War, the government bestowed on the "barons of Fleet Street" peerages for public service. Nowhere else do so few newspapers serve so many people. On the eve of World War II, out of 12 million copies sold daily by morning newspapers throughout the country, 10 million were sold by eight London dailies; and by the end of the war, these same eight dailies were selling 15 million copies each morning. In no other country of equal or greater population does the national press so far outweigh the local.[10]

Of the eight national dailies, four are popular. Lord Beaverbrook's *Daily Express* leads with a circulation of 3.7 million daily, followed by three papers that cluster around the 2-million mark: Lord Southwood's *Daily Herald,* Lord Rothermere's *Daily Mail,* and Mr. Cadbury's *News Chronicle.* Two national dailies are tabloids and have a combined circulation of 4 million, mainly among women: Lord Rothermere's popular *Daily Mirror* and Lord Kemsley's classy *Daily Graphic.* The two remaining dailies cater to the employing class, with a combined circulation that has risen above the 1-million mark: Lord Camrose's *Daily Telegraph* and Major Astor's *The Times.*

Political Leanings. Of the eight newspapers, all but two are Conservative. The *Daily Herald* is tied to the Labor party by a contractual obligation to follow the policy of the National Labor party's annual conference and by the fact that the General Council of the Trades Union Congress holds 49 per cent

---

[10] The most thorough surveys are *The British Press,* published by Political and Economic Planning (London, 1939), and Royal Commission on the Press, *Report* (Cmd. 7700 [1949]).

of its stock and chooses four of its directors. The *News Chronicle* is an amalgamation of a number of former Liberal organs. Of the six that are Conservative, the *Daily Telegraph* enjoys the reputation of standing nearest to the party leadership. The others indulge in various degrees of "independence."

All the national newspapers are business concerns whose ownership changes by purchase or inheritance. But the stock of The Times Holding Company, Ltd., may not be sold without the consent of a trust composed of the Lord Chief Justice, the Warden of All Souls' College, the Governor of the Bank of England, the President of the Institute of Chartered Accountants, and the President of the Royal Society. This provision is for the purpose of keeping *The Times* a "national institution." A few of the surviving provincial dailies retain a tradition of independence that gives them a reputation out of all relation to their circulation. Such are the Liberal *Manchester Guardian,* in the hands of the Scott family, and the Conservative *Yorkshire Post,* connected with Anthony Eden.

Sunday papers in Britain are operated as distinct entities, and no dailies appear on Sundays. But the Sunday papers are almost as highly concentrated as the dailies, with the late Lord Riddell's *News of the World* purveying entertainment to more than 7 million homes, Lord Southwood's *People* to over 4 million, and Lord Rothermere's *Sunday Pictorial* to about the same number. The Labor party is dependent upon the ownership of *Reynolds' News* by the consumers' cooperative movement. Lord Astor's *Observer* and Lord Kemsley's *Sunday Times* look to the upper class for support. Evening papers are more numerous. Many a provincial town has its own. But most of them form parts of three chains that have apparently divided the country among them, under the control of the Berry family (Lords Camrose and Kemsley), the Harmsworth family (especially Lord Rothermere), and a group of Liberals including the Pearson (Lord Cowdray) and Rowntree families.

Quality of Information. The press oligopoly is formally organized in two cooperatives, linked together by a joint subsidiary. The two are the provincial Press Association for cooperative purchase of telegraph facilities and the national Newspaper Proprietors' Association for cooperative purchase of railway transportation facilities. Their link is Reuter's, for collecting and disseminating news abroad in cooperation with foreign news agencies. Any newspaper proprietor who breaks his understandings with his competitors can be expelled from these organizations. One, for example, was expelled before World War II for announcing broadcasts by a foreign radio station that competed with the British newspapers' advertising monopoly by beaming advertisements at the British public.

The extent to which the British public is kept informed of its problems both at home and abroad depends in large measure on a very small group of newspaper magnates. In domestic matters, the readers probably have enough experience to enable them to judge many matters for themselves and reach conclusions the reverse of those of most of the press, as they showed by returning a Labor majority in 1945. In international matters, newspaper readers have less of a basis of experience, and comparatively little is done to enlighten them. The better side of the British press is that its financial success removes it from all temptation to sell itself to foreign powers.

Newspapers, of course, are only part of the press. Political weeklies have played an important part in British life ever since *Cobbett's Weekly Political Register* got around the newspaper stamp duty by printing editorial comment without news. At the present time, the leading political weeklies are the Labor *New Statesman,* the Conservative *Spectator,* and—though it is less "political"—the Liberal *Economist.* All these are believed to have circulations just about big enough to enable them to pay their way.

The Radio. The radio has supplemented the press since 1923 in Britain.[11] It is largely to this supplementation—as well as to the older media of the platform and the pulpit—that must be ascribed the failure of an overwhelmingly Conservative press to keep the people from voting Labor.

The British telegraph has been a post-office monopoly since 1869. The courts held that telephones were a form of telegraphy, and radio communication was assumed to be a form of telephony. A sender's license from the post office was therefore required when, in 1922, six business concerns that wished to manufacture radio sets established the British Broadcasting Company. At the same time, these concerns arranged for the post office to sell receiving licenses to listeners for each radio set owned, the receipts to be shared between the post office and the BBC. The company's dividends were limited to 7½ per cent, because its stockholders hoped to make their profit, not out of broadcasting, but from the sale of radio sets. This arrangement was regarded as experimental. To help elaborate a long-term policy, the government set up a departmental committee, which reported in 1925 that "the broadcasting service should be conducted by a public corporation acting as trustee for the national interest." It added that a corporation would be preferable to direct ministerial control as a means of allowing the fullest possible liberty, enterprise, and initiative.

The government therefore chartered a second BBC, with a Crown-appointed general director and a salaried board of governors. To the new BBC the post office issued a sender's license that stipulated the ratio of listeners' license receipts (now 7½ per cent) to be retained by the post office to meet expenses, leaving the rest for possible appropriation to the BBC. Twelve million listeners now buy £1 licenses; to this must be added £1 million in profits from publications and concerts and a £4 million subsidy for foreign broadcasts. The country's size—with an area only one thirtieth that of the United States—has made it possible to achieve national coverage

---

[11] See Broadcasting Committee, *Report* (Cmd. 8116 [1951]).

with the help of only a few regional stations, without a network of small local stations.

Political Impartiality. Nationalization did not affect the relationship between radio and the press. The newspapers, in particular, were not deprived of their lucrative advertising monopoly. On the other hand, British radio had already established the tradition of adding to its revenues by publishing radio magazines, some of which have since achieved circulations of several million.[12] British radio has also developed its own news-gathering service and prides itself on its broadcasting of straight news at certain hours of the day and night. By stimulating interest in the news, the radio seems to have contributed to the growth of newspaper circulation, thus adding to the newspapers' success as advertising media. At the same time it has emancipated its listeners from dependence on the newspaper for news and opinions.

Any radio system tends to give more opportunity to established institutions than to others. British radio, however, has tended to keep the balance reasonably even among the principal parties, especially at election time. Its chief problem in the distribution of time has arisen from the existence of Liberals and others who do not fit into the symmetrical two-party pattern.

Criticism of the BBC has concentrated on its reluctance to organize much friendly competition within itself; its failure to cultivate community stations; and its dislike of spontaneity. Its compensating advantages are that it is not dominated by advertising concerns or by newspapers; does not sell time to political parties, churches, or other groups; has no editorializing commentators expounding special viewpoints; avoids promotionalism; and, in general, takes very seriously its educational mission.

Films. The production and exhibition of films in Britain pose some peculiar problems. The motion-picture industry is operated for profit; ownership and management both of studios and of theaters is largely American. The government's interest in the industry therefore forms part of its international trade policy. One tendency is for the government to protect British producers and exhibitors from the pressure of larger-scale American operators by compelling British theaters to show a certain quota of British films. This tendency, however, has had the effect of inducing American producers to produce films in British studios. In order to reduce the drain on Britain's dollars to pay for American films, an agreement was negotiated in 1948 between the British Board of Trade and the American Film Producers Association, under which only a limited sum of dollars may be taken out of Britain each year by the American film industry.

Although the economic aspect of the film industry is the first to necessitate governmental regulation, it is by no means the only one of political importance. The film has become one of the principal media for communicating standards of conduct and systems of social values and for modifying the mo-

---

[12] The weekly *Listener* is particularly valuable for its reproduction of radio talks on all subjects, both political and cultural.

tivations of men and women as members of the community. To ensure the
embodiment of British rather than American ideals in films produced in Britain by Americans, the government relies mainly on informal consultation
with American producers.

Governmental Public Relations. The British government, like every
other, has to take special steps to inform and influence the public. It cannot
leave the performance of either of these functions to the newspaper chains,
and it does not wish the BBC to become suspect as a propaganda organ.

Under cabinet government, departments have to be careful to say nothing
that may undermine or circumvent the Cabinet's relations with Parliament.
The Cabinet is responsible to the people through the House of Commons,
not through the press. Ministers have to refrain from giving information to
the press before it is given to Parliament, except perhaps during a parliamentary recess. Contact between departments and newspapers therefore has two
principal purposes. It may be to give lead to editorial comment, especially
on foreign policy. It is generally accepted, for example, that "in diplomatic
circles" means "according to a permanent official of the foreign office," while
"it is understood that" means "according to the Foreign Secretary." Alter-
natively, the purpose of contact between departments and newspapers may be
to win interest in the services rendered by government. For this purpose an
administrative agency attempts not only to inform editorial policy through
press conferences, but also to demonstrate its work on the spot to visiting
journalists. On the eve of World War II, moreover, the Treasury began to
consent to public advertising by departments. British war-bond advertising
was paid for by the government, not by private advertisers.

If the government wants to put a serious study of some problem before the
public, the usual way is to present a "white paper" to Parliament and to dis-
tribute it cheaply through His Majesty's Stationery Office. HMSO is at once
a publishing concern and a retail bookstore, with sales offices in all the principal cities. Finally, if the government wants to give anything that it is doing
the greatest possible prestige, it can have the King publicly display his interest
in it and commend it to all sections of the people, regardless of their party
preference.

5. Civic Participation

Electoral Participation. To participate in a British election is to help
choose the governing body, whether of the nation or of a locality. Many factors combine to bring out a heavy vote. A national election does not come
around by clockwork every two or four years. Instead, it is timed for effect
and is fought upon a comparatively clear issue. The attitudes that the parties
express are differentiated and have been well publicized by debates in the
Commons, policy resolutions passed by the parties' annual conferences, and a
steady stream of printed matter published during the preceding years. The
dramatic quality of a contest between two well-known teams is still further

enhanced by the fact that in Britain the teams are believed to stand for something more than the great prize of office.

Moreover, participation in an election is made extremely simple for the British voter, who is faced with one choice only. He does not even have to go to any trouble to get registered. The keeping of the register and its revision twice a year are the responsibility of the registering officer, not of the voter. The latter is encouraged to vote. The registering officer calling at his door to make sure that he has neither died nor moved away and the postman bringing a free delivery of election mail from each of the candidates both help to create the feeling that everyone eligible votes. Nor is it hard for an adult citizen to qualify for the franchise. He does not have to prove his ability to read and interpret the law of the land or to present a tax receipt. All that is required of him is that he reside in a constituency at the time the register is brought up to date.[13]

Participation in voting is consequently high. At the general election of 1951, there were nearly 28 million voters in an electorate of 34 million, or a participation of nearly 83 per cent. One consequence of a heavy vote is that many voters go to the polls who have no well-established party allegiance or whose interest in politics may be confined to election time. These "independent voters" seem to number about one tenth of the total. It is they who "swing the pendulum." It is therefore to them that much campaign oratory and literature is addressed.

The Volunteer and the Conscript. Voluntary agencies are often used by government and are sometimes subsidized for this purpose. Youth groups for adolescents' leisure-time activities, rural community councils operating village centers, and welfare associations to provide pastime occupations for persons too old or too handicapped to work—these are examples of voluntary welfare agencies doing work that otherwise government itself might have to do. Participation of voluntary associations in public activities is valued in Britain, not only because of the satisfaction that comes from it, but also because of the advantages of introducing a human touch into administration and providing the social services with lay supporters able to interpret them to the public.[14]

Tens of thousands of spare-time volunteers are enlisted in emergencies, especially as special constables, air-raid wardens, and members of county war agricultural executive committees.[15] At other times the volunteer is less used in an official capacity. In London most social casework for school chil-

---

[13] Until 1948, some 225,000 university graduates also had a second vote exercisable in one of the seven "university constituencies"; and some 75,000 voters were registered for a second vote as "occupiers of business premises."

[14] Cooperation of public and voluntary agencies for social work is analyzed in Elizabeth Macadam, *New Philanthropy* (London, 1934) and H. A. Mess, *Voluntary Social Service* (London, 1947).

[15] Cf. D. E. Vandepeer, "County War Agricultural Executive Committees," *Public Administration,* 24 (1946), 14 ff.

dren is done by volunteers under the guidance of professional social workers. The "hue and cry" of the law-abiding as part of the *posse comitatus* remains as little more than a tradition. Jury service is of declining importance; and the grand jury has been abolished.

Compulsion to be educated, compulsion to be healthy, compulsion to pay taxes, compulsion to serve one's country in time of emergency—these are the great compulsions of the modern state. In World War II, compulsion was applied to essential work and civil defense as well as to military service. Workers could not quit or be discharged in breach of essential-work orders. Conscripts were ordered to hew coal instead of fighting the enemy. Conscientious objectors were directed into approved work. Women as well as men were drafted. "Manpower budgets" were prepared and enforced by the Ministry of Labor and National Service; for Britain recognizes the implications of total war by combining all aspects of manpower control in a single ministry.

Local Administrative Discretion. Responsibility for exercising discretion in making administrative decisions is by no means confined to paid officials, but is delegated to tens of thousands of unpaid citizens. The offices held by many of these are elective; for every unit of local government has its elective governing body, which so arranges its local work as to require only the part-time—and in most cases only the leisure-time—service of its elective members. No full-time or salaried local officials are chosen by election in Britain.

Election, however, is not the only means of becoming a member of a British governing body. "Co-optation" is almost as important. On a borough council, the elected councilors co-opt the aldermen. A local education authority is a statutory committee composed partly of elected members of the local council, but partly also of citizens co-opted on the grounds of their special interest in education. Thus, the qualifications of particular individuals, including nonpartisans, can be utilized. Spokesmen of special interests can be put in a position that calls for a more broadly public viewpoint; a representative of a local teachers' union, for example, can be co-opted to the local education committee. A well-known author has been chairman of his borough library committee without having been first elected to the borough council.

Central appointment of local bodies has also been widely used as a means of obtaining local administration of central legislation. Large numbers of trade unionists and employers, for example, have been familiarized with the social insurance system by being appointed to tripartite tribunals of referees to review complaints and give fair hearings.

Local Advisory Bodies. Local advisory committees without powers of administrative decision have been appointed centrally in accordance with statute. Such are the local employment and juvenile advisory committees of the Ministry of Labor and the local advisory committees of the National Assistance Board. Such also are the regional transport users consultative committees appointed by the Minister of Transport since 1947, after consultation with bodies representing the interests of agriculture, commerce, industry, shipping, labor, and local government. Such too are the area consultative councils appointed by the Minister of Fuel since 1947 from among representatives of local authorities and consumers of electric power.

Small as has been the legal power of these advisory groups, it would seem that they have had considerable influence in bringing central administration and local opinion into harmony, thus helping to attain flexibility in detail along with easier acceptance of general principles.[16]

National Policy Formation. Selected citizens can play a significant part in policy formation without being elected to Parliament, without acting as spokesmen of an interest group, and without being civil servants. This situation is possible because an important channel exists for utilizing the service of experts who count in their own fields—the consultative committee in its many forms.

The most important present-day type of consultative body is the departmental committee, so called because it is a minister who appoints the chairman and members of the committee and gives them their terms of reference. These are nearly always "to inquire . . . and to advise. . . ." Their inquiries are normally conducted by means of research, interview, and the receipt of memoranda from departments and interested groups. As a general rule, a "white paper" prepared by a departmental committee and presented to Parliament by the government is the first step toward important legislation. Two recent examples were the great wartime recommendations for postwar reform—the Beveridge report on *Social Insurance and Allied Services* (1942), which became the starting point for the general overhaul of the British social security system in 1945-1948,[17] and the Uthwatt report on *Compensation and Betterment* (1942), which opened the way to the Town and Country Planning Act of 1947.[18]

An older method, now less often used, is the royal commission. It collects much of its evidence by the less scientific method of examining witnesses in public and publishes a verbatim report of the evidence, although it cannot subpoena either witnesses or documents without statutory authorization. It is commonly composed not of experts, but of celebrities or a balanced assortment of specialists representing rival interest groups. It is frequently more in the nature of a fishing expedition than of a next step in policy determination. And many royal commissions have presented sharply differing majority and minority reports. Among the more important royal commissions of the present century may be cited the poor-law commission

---

[16] Local advisory committees are usually credited with the success of the Assistance Board in eventually winning public confidence, especially by adapting rent allowances to local standards. The inadequacy of the juvenile employment service has been attributed to the reluctance of the Ministry of Labor to set up juvenile advisory committees.

[17] Cmd. 6404 with Cmd. 6405 (1942).

[18] Ministry of Works and Planning's Expert Committee, *Final Report* (Cmd. 6386 [1942]).

(1909), whose minority report became the foundation for the abolition of the poor law; the Peel commission (1939), whose report recommended the partitioning of Palestine; and the Barlow commission (1940), whose majority and minority reports prepared the way for the Distribution of Industry and New Towns Acts of 1945. The parliamentary select committee has been almost entirely superseded by the royal commission and the departmental committee.

Counseling the Departments. Policy may be within the administrative powers bestowed by Parliament upon a minister. In such conditions, it is easy to make a strong case for obliging the minister to consult with a standing advisory body.[19] For example, the suggestions of the Ministry of Education to the local education authorities to which it also distributes grants in aid are of great importance in deciding what they shall do. Experience having taught that this ministerial discretion did provoke resentment, a permanent consultative committee was established. Its Hadow report on *Education of the Adolescent* (1926) became the basis for the introduction of a break between primary and secondary education at the age of eleven and for the first steps toward "secondary education for all."

Many of the permanent consultative committee's other reports were similarly influential. The Education Act of 1944 therefore replaced it with three permanent "councils of education" for England, Scotland, and Wales and extended their duties from "consultative" to "advisory"—from the giving of advice when requested by the ministry to the offering of advice without waiting to be asked.

6. Hereditary Participants

House of Lords. There are two hereditary elements with official status in British political life—the aristocracy and the monarchy. Both have been so reduced in power that they are no longer an obstacle to government by consent and discussion. Instead, they make notable contributions to these processes. The House of Lords, with some 1,000 members, is regularly attended by not many more than 50. It includes 2 archbishops, 24 bishops, some law lords, and about 100 peers created in the recent past, as well as over 800 "hereditary legislators." It is from among its nonhereditary members that most of the regular participants are drawn. Most of these are men who have distinguished themselves in public life, either as politicians, officials, or officers, or as men who have made a contribution by their scientific, artistic, or business achievements, but who might never have entered public life through the process of election.

The principal value of the House of Lords is as another place for serious discussion, with the government obliged to submit to criticism and to the need for explaining its actions and its views. This discussion is all the more

---

[19] For a detailed and authoritative prewar study, see R. V. Vernon, ed., *Advisory Bodies* (London, 1940).

free because of the impossibility of overthrowing a government by an adverse vote in the House of Lords. The furthest that the Lords can go in opposing a government is in delaying passage of legislation for one year. The problem that this suspensory veto poses is whether it stands in the way of government by consent and discussion. Certainly, the suspension of the Irish home rule bill by the House of Lords in 1912-14 provided an opportunity for armed resistance as the result of which the Irish problem was settled by physical force. The aim of the Lords, however, was to induce the government to dissolve Parliament and fight a general election on the Irish issue. Similarly in 1947, the Conservative threat to have the House of Lords suspend a bill for nationalization of the iron and steel industry was coupled with the hope for an election on the issue. Here the government accepted the challenge, but only after enactment of a bill for shortening the suspensory veto from two years to one.

The House of Lords does not claim the right to defeat the will of the people. All that it claims is the right to find out what is the feeling of the people on a particular question; and since the referendum is not practiced in Britain, the only way to do this is to precipitate a general election on the issue. The objections to this procedure are two. One is that in accordance with the spirit of the constitution, a government with a majority in the Commons does not expect to fight an election on any issues other than the ones it itself poses. The other objection is that the power to precipitate a general election by opposition in the House of Lords belongs only to the Conservative party, because of its permanent and hereditary majority in that House. The claims of the Lords have never been advanced against a Conservative government and have always been rejected by Liberal and Labor governments.

Reforming the Lords. Reform of the House of Lords has been much discussed for several generations. It has two principal aspects—membership and power. As to membership, the leaders of all three parties agreed in 1948 that they would have no objection to drawing a sharper distinction between "peers of the realm" and "lords of Parliament." The peerage might remain hereditary, but should be shorn of the hereditary right to counsel the Crown in Parliament. Membership of the House of Lords, on the other hand, should rest on royal summons for life only, with safeguards against one-party majority.

As to powers, it was agreed that such a reformed House should retain a suspensory veto. If this veto were to be applied during the last year of the life of a House of Commons, it should not be overridden until after a general election. Where agreement failed was on what should happen if the Lords applied their veto during the year preceding the last year. The Conservative party was against overriding the Lords until after a general election, whereas the Labor party favored overriding them.

The King. The monarchy has come to play a somewhat similar though less obviously partisan role, not obstructing changes but insisting on full discussion and clear expression of the people's consent. In the constitutional crisis of 1909-11, for example, when the House of Lords was deprived entirely of its veto power over money bills and obliged to be content with a suspensory veto over other legislation, Edward VII played an important part in setting the rules by which this great decision was effected. His cooperation was needed. Without it the government could not have threatened to flood the House of Lords with new peers; and this was the only way of causing the Lords to acquiesce in the statutory curtailment of their own powers. In consultation with the government, the King posed the condition that the government demonstrate the support of the people by winning two general elections—which it proceeded to do in 1910. The King, that is to say, did not obstruct the government's program, but insisted on making sure that this constitutional change was discussed at length and that the government really did have the people's consent.

Again, at the height of the controversy over the Lords' suspension of the Irish home rule bill, George V brought together spokesmen for all the groups involved in a series of special conferences at Buckingham Palace—for which Asquith as Prime Minister accepted responsibility. This, too, was not an attempt by the King to promote a policy of his own, for he had none. It was simply an endeavor—though in vain—to arrive at a policy by discussion and consent, without resort to physical force.

Information and Confidence. Above all, the King claims the right to be informed by his ministers about the affairs of the individual departments of which they have charge. Informing the King of Cabinet decisions was long the principal assurance that the Cabinet would reach clear decisions and that ministers would abide by them. Action by a minister contrary to Cabinet decisions was thus a breach of his respect toward the King as well as of his loyalty to his colleagues and to their majority in the Commons. By training and long experience, moreover, the King is assumed to become a useful adviser to his own ministers. His term of office is normally so much longer than theirs that he tends to become not only a symbol of continuity, but also perhaps a repository of valuable knowledge and of experienced common sense.

If an inheritor of the royal title does not earn this kind of confidence from his ministers; if he does not respect their position as the responsible spokesmen of the parliamentary majority and therefore of the people; if he shows signs of not understanding the limitations attaching to hereditary office in a crowned republic; and if there is a conviction among ministers that he cannot be relied upon to comply with accepted standards of constitutional or social behavior—then even a Conservative Cabinet prefers to have the King abdicate and has Parliament pass an abdication act to that effect.

CHAPTER 5

THE STRUCTURE OF PUBLIC ADMINISTRATION

1. Administrative Policy-making

Formation of Policy. Nearly all British legislation is introduced by a minister with the approval of the Cabinet. This phrase means that it has been drafted by the department of which he is the temporary political head. The inspiration for the bill may have come from him, but the details that go into the bill will certainly come from his permanent civil servants. Toward the "bureaucracy" there is therefore a feeling of mingled confidence and helplessness, for the ministers—and hence Parliament—are entirely dependent upon it. By the Conservatives this relationship is taken for granted. Their ministers and the higher permanent civil servants have for the most part been members of the same social class and products of the same schools and universities. By the Labor party, and especially by Fabian socialists, the expert as such is respected as a craftsman with rare skills.

In the 1930's it was even said—perhaps half-humorously—that Cabinet policy was as good as formed when there was agreement between the permanent Secretary of the Treasury, the permanent Under-Secretary of the Foreign Office, and the Secretary of the Committee of Imperial Defense (who was then also secretary of the Cabinet).[1] The cardinal importance of these top officials has made it inevitable that public attention be attracted toward them. The anonymity that is supposed to attach to British permanent officials has become hard to preserve while they are still in service and impossible to maintain after their retirement.[2]

From the evidence available, it is clear that politicians and permanent officials are partners in the shaping of British policy. Except in individual cases, it would be quite wrong to think of the Cabinet as making policy which the officials then carry out.

Preparatory Work. The definitive formulation of policy may require decision by the Cabinet and approval by Parliament. Yet its formation is a long process of which these formal acts are but the culmination. Preparatory work is the task of the departments.[3] Nor is it their work alone, for they

---

[1] W. Y. Elliott in H. M. Stout, *Public Service in Great Britain* (Chapel Hill, 1938), p. xix, referring respectively to Sir Warren Fisher, Sir Alexander Cadogan, and Sir Maurice Hankey.

[2] For evidence, see the anti-German pamphlets of Lord Vansittart, former permanent Under-Secretary for Foreign Affairs, and the anti-internationalist lectures of Lord Hankey.

[3] Cf. C. K. Allen, *Law in the Making* (rev. ed., Oxford, 1930).

prepare the way for policy developments and new programs by long and often arduous consultation with organized interests.

There is also a marked tendency to associate permanent advisory committees with a department, or to have the department utilize temporary departmental committees to inquire into some large problem. These, too, become means by which the department plays a major—but not unassisted—role in the shaping of policy. Only after the permanent civil servants have thus prepared the ground, with the help of their minister, is the time ripe for the Cabinet to consider assuming political responsibility for the measures that are proposed.

Implementation of Policy. When a minister transmits the government's decision to the permanent head of his department, it becomes the duty of the permanent officials to see that the policy is faithfully carried out, even if it is not exactly what they have urged. There is little evidence in Britain of civil servants sabotaging the policy of the responsible political head of their department.

Most modern British statutes are "skeleton legislation." They need filling in by departments before they are workable. The preparation of masses of administrative regulations is therefore unavoidable and is expressly provided for by statute. These "statutory instruments" are so numerous that ever since 1890 Parliament has provided for the publication of an annual volume of "statutory rules and orders." Of recent years, one considerable criticism of such "delegated legislation" has been directed against a clause, occasionally inserted into statutes since the end of the nineteenth century, that empowers the minister to modify the act of Parliament if in any detail it should prove unworkable. One hundred years ago, criticism was also directed against the delegation of legislative powers to autonomous commissions; but this practice has now been virtually abandoned, so that almost all delegated legislation is issued over the signature of politically responsible ministers.

Over delegated legislation, the principal British check is the responsibility of ministers to Parliament; and it is presumably on account of this tradition that there has been so little reluctance to delegate very broad legislative powers to ministers. The check has been reinforced to some extent by putting on certain ministries an obligation to lay draft regulations on certain subjects on the tables of both Houses of Parliament for a certain number of days. In order to make the check more effective, the Lord Chancellor's departmental committee on ministers' powers recommended in 1932 that a special standing select committee be established; this select committee on statutory instruments has been in operation since 1944.[4]

Quasi-judicial Determinations. Some administrative policy-making takes a quasi-judicial form. For example, the Minister of Town and Country Planning is empowered to decide what "development charge" shall be levied

---

[4] See above, chap. 3, "England's Constitutional Tradition," sec. 5, "The House of Commons."

on land developers and where a new town shall be located. The President
of the Board of Trade is empowered to determine what regions of the country shall be declared "development areas," in which industry will be financially encouraged to locate. Decisions of this kind are not truly judicial;
they involve the weighing of advantages against disadvantages, rather than
the determination of legal rights. They are, however, an extremely important means by which administrators make policy and shape the nation's future, within the framework of powers agreed to by Parliament.

2. Government Departments

Organic Principles. British government departments differ from those of
other countries in the principles on which their organization is based and
in their relations to a nuclear Treasury. The British preference is for departments discharging a particular function, such as education or health, not
for departments serving a particular clientele, such as veterans, women, children, labor, or agriculture. This preference was clearly stated in a classic report on administrative organization prepared toward the close of World War
I.[5] In addition to the functional, the only other important basis for departmental organization in Britain is the geographical. Thus, there are Secretaries of State for Foreign Affairs, Commonwealth Affairs, Colonies, and
Scotland; and formerly there were similar ministers for Ireland (until 1921)
and India (until 1947). Autonomous commissions have now almost disappeared.[6] The logic of the British system of government makes for a close
knitting-together of all its organs, with the line of responsibility running
clearly through Cabinet to Parliament.

The independent regulatory commission has likewise disappeared from
British political and economic life, its place being taken by the government-
owned corporation. This development is natural in a country in which government ownership and operation of business with monopolistic tendencies
is preferred to a combination of public regulation with private ownership.
Government-owned business corporations, however, are not fully autonomous
bodies. The members of their boards of directors are appointed and dismissed by the responsible minister. Questions may be asked, but not on
operating details. The House may debate the policies and management of
the corporation. And policy directions may be given by the minister to the
corporation, provided these are included in the next annual report to Parlia-

---

[5] Minister of Reconstruction's Departmental Committee (chairman, Lord Haldane) on Machinery of Government, *Report* (Cmd. 9230 [1918]).

[6] The Cabinet tried in 1935 to divest itself of responsibility for administrative regulations
concerning assistance to the unemployed by setting up an autonomous Unemployment Assistance
Board. The political storm aroused in 1936 by the board's regulations obliged the Cabinet to
consent to the submission of all future regulations to Parliament for its approval or rejection.
Bipartisan bodies with overlapping terms have now been practically eliminated; and nearly all
such boards and commissions as remain are responsible to a responsible minister, entitled to
dismiss as well as appoint their members. The latter hold office "at pleasure," not "during
good behavior."

ment. The independence of the corporation is therefore limited to the everyday business management of the enterprise, and its responsiveness to Cabinet and Parliament is assured.

Departments need to be reorganized from time to time and functions transferred from one department to another. The manner of achieving such regroupings is not a matter of controversy in the United Kingdom. In some instances they are effected by executive action—occasionally by use of the royal prerogative, more often by virtue of powers of reorganization granted by Parliament, or by the inclusion of a new office in the annual financial estimates. More usually, however, agencies are set up by Parliament; and in that case they can be abolished or consolidated only by virtue of powers granted by Parliament. In either case, it is the Cabinet that is responsible for the reorganization.

Treasury Control. Among the departments, one has a well-recognized primacy. This department is the Treasury. Its importance does not lie in the collection of revenue, which is mainly the work of two subordinate agencies for inland revenue and for customs and excise. Instead, the Treasury is the agency responsible for planning the government's budgetary and fiscal policy. No department may request Cabinet approval of any policy involving additional outlay without first clearing the project with the Treasury. The annual estimates of departmental outlay are also worked out during the latter half of each calendar year in consultation between the Treasury and each department. The Treasury has a reputation for adopting a negative approach to all proposals for additional outlay.

Whereas the Cabinet secretariat's economic section and central statistical office think in terms of *national* income and outgo, the Treasury has thought in terms of *government* revenue and expenditure. One of the biggest open questions today is whether the recent union of office between the Cabinet secretary and the permanent Under-Secretary of the Treasury lasted long enough to help the Treasury to take a broader, more positive and more constructive view of its responsibilities. Statutory creation in 1947 of the post of economic under-secretary—in addition to the time-honored post of financial under-secretary—in the Treasury, and Cripps' assumption of responsibility for general economic policy as well as for the budget, may have hastened the trend in this direction.[7] The emphasis on frugality and retrenchment was appropriate to an age of peace and *laissez-faire;* it may have ceased to be appropriate in an age of total war and of economic planning.

The Treasury also exercises close control over personnel management and over organization and methods work within each department. In these ways, too, the economy and efficiency of each agency is the Treasury's con-

---

[7] The Treasury is represented in the House of Commons by one Cabinet minister (the Chancellor of the Exchequer) and by three junior ministers: the parliamentary under-secretary, who is chief whip; the financial under-secretary; and the new economic under-secretary.

cern. During and since World War II, it has built up a staff of experts in administrative management and procedure, who devote the whole of their time to reviewing organization and methods both in the central services and in the field offices.[8] Because of its indispensable functions, the Treasury has become the most influential of all government departments.

3. The Civil Service

Scope and Status. When a Briton talks of civil service, he thinks of the permanent officials of the national government.[9] On the eve of World War II these numbered 100,000 in the other departments and 250,000 in the post office.[10] Among the civil servants are the permanent heads of all the ministries, who serve as general managers of their departments whatever the political color of the minister temporarily in charge. For these top civil servants (who have no equivalent in the United States) the salary ceiling is not the salary of a member of Parliament who holds no office, but that of a Cabinet minister; their salaries go up to £4,000 ($11,000) in most ministries, or £5,000 ($14,000) for the permanent head of the Treasury. The nonpecuniary rewards—in influence, prestige, and honors—are also very great. For anyone of public spirit, public administration thus provides great incentives for a satisfying career.

Although earlier an object of personal patronage, civil service jobs in Britain have at no time been distributed as party spoils, with consequent high turnover, insecurity, and instability. Instead, Britain has long had a tradition of political neutrality in the service, with permanence and security of tenure. From 1782 to 1867, civil servants were not allowed to vote. Today they have to resign on becoming candidates for parliamentary election. The higher the rank of the civil servant, the more necessary is it that he be free to advise his minister on policy without being himself committed to the platform of either party. And the more direct the power a civil servant wields, the more important is it that he should not be suspected of playing political favorites. It is therefore only in the lower grades, and only in certain of the departments, that civil servants are allowed to be active in party organizations or run for local office.

To this day a British civil servant's tenure rests on custom, not law. And

[8] House of Commons Select Committee on Estimates, *Report on Organization and Methods and Its Effect on the Staffing of Government Departments* (1947).

[9] For pertinent writings, see Stout, *op. cit.* above, note 1; Harvey Walker, *Training Public Employees in Great Britain* (New York, 1935); L. D. White, *Whitley Councils in the British Civil Service* (Chicago, 1933); Herman Finer, *The British Civil Service* (London, 1947); W. A. Robson and Others, *The British Civil Servant* (London, 1937); N. E. Mustoe, *Law and Organization of the British Civil Service* (London, 1932); H. R. G. Greaves, *The Civil Servant in the Changing State* (London, 1947); Royal Commission on the Civil Service (chairman, Lord Tomlin), *Report* (Cmd. 3309 [1931]); and several articles in *Political Quarterly*, 15 (1944).

[10] In January 1947, civil servants numbered 450,000 in other departments and 250,000 in the post office.

his retirement pension is also a matter of customary royal grace, which he has not insured by any contributions. Since 1948 ministers responsible to Parliament are empowered to transfer or suspend Communist civil servants on the advice of a committee of retired civil servants before whom the suspected Communist is entitled to a hearing.

Entrance Examinations. Entrance examinations as a method of testing an applicant's merit were gradually introduced by executive action, first in one department and then in another, between 1848 and 1870.[11] A Civil Service Commission was set up by order in council in 1855; it has acted solely as an examining body, thus having less resemblance to a tool of administrative management than to a tribunal admitting practitioners to a profession. The written examinations were at first confined to candidates nominated by patrons. From 1870 they have been open to all who could satisfy the educational requirements, pay the examination fees, and meet the cost of taking the examination, which for certain grades has been held only in London.

The written examination has been closely geared to educational qualifications. As it was practiced between the two World Wars, it was geared to three classes of candidates, who had completed university, secondary, or elementary education at the age of 21, 18, or 15, respectively, and who should therefore be admitted to the administrative, or the executive, or the clerical grades of the civil service. For each grade the examination has been basically academic. It was assumed not that a candidate had practical experience elsewhere, but that he came straight from school into the civil service, with the intention of making this his life's work.

In addition to holding written examinations, the Civil Service Commission set up selection boards to hold oral examinations in the form of interviews. In times of exceptional pressure for recruitment, and also for certain technical skills, the written examination was dropped, but the oral interview was retained.

Recruitment Methods. Much criticism has turned on the method of recruiting British civil servants. Although it is generally assumed that the examiner is preferable to patronage, it has been widely felt that a Civil Service Commission could do better in devising examinations. For example, during most of the interwar years, the written part of the examination for university graduates who tried to enter the administrative grade covered not only general knowledge but also a range of subject matter roughly equivalent to a major in two particular fields. Few graduates therefore felt able to compete unless they could afford special coaching. In 1937 the commission increased the weight given the oral examination. Few procedures could have been more controversial than the interview by the selection board. Its defenders stressed its freedom from partisan political bias. Its critics stressed its proneness to social bias and its preference for candidates who made a pleas-

---

[11] The initiative for this reform seems to have come from a civil servant, Charles Trevelyan, then Assistant Secretary of the Treasury, and brother-in-law of Lord Macaulay.

ant impression on first meeting rather than for those distinguished by vigor, initiative, and imagination.

It was widely believed that a decline occurred between the wars in the caliber of graduates recruited for the administrative grade. Some observers attributed this decline to the interview by the selection board. Others regarded it as part of a general social change, which in an age of high taxation led men combining intelligence with affluence to maintain their family fortune on the stock exchange, rather than run the risk of working under others whose intelligence was not accompanied by inherited wealth. Although the top tenth of each year's intake into the administrative grade was able and sometimes brilliant, the rest tended toward mediocrity.[12]

Since World War II, the Civil Service Commission has begun to experiment with new techniques for selecting administrators, with one eye on the inappropriateness of the academic type of examination when testing veterans and the other on the methods used during the war for selecting candidates for officers' training. The most important innovation is the insertion of several days of group living and of observation by psychologists at a country house between the initial screening of educational qualifications and the written examination (which was temporarily confined to English and intelligence). The interview by a selection board still remains as a hurdle.[13]

Specialists and Generalists. Professional and technical specialists have gradually become ten times as numerous as the presumed generalists of the administrative grade. They have been recruited a few years later in life, so as to allow time for some graduate study and some practical experience.

The nineteenth-century distinction between these specialists and the hierarchy of "government clerks" topped by the administrative grade has made it difficult to use professional men with graduate training as administrators, except in wartime. This difficulty may have deprived the civil service of administrative talent.[14]

Treasury Personnel Management. The Civil Service Commission has no responsibility for the careers of civil servants after their entry into the service. Their two-year probation, their promotion, their transfer, their salaries, their termination, and their pensions are all the concern of the Treasury. It may well be that lack of responsibility for the consequences of its decisions has been one reason for the commission's inadequate responsiveness to the needs of the service. For personnel management within the service, the Treasury has a permanent under-secretary in charge of "establishments," and within each ministry there is an "establishments division" to maintain liaison with

---

[12] The shortcomings of recruitment became even more marked in the Indian and Colonial civil services, where the "competitive interview" was used in the 1930's to admit candidates who could probably not have entered by written examination.

[13] Cf. F. W. Holden, "Administrative Reconstruction Examination," *Political Quarterly,* 18 (1947), 137 ff.; Arthur H. M. Hillis, "The British Civil Servant of Tomorrow," *Public Administration Review,* 11 (1951), 173 ff.

[14] Promotion to the permanent headship of a department may also have become difficult for any civil servant who has not shared the outlook of the Treasury.

the Treasury. Treasury personnel management has been criticized in the past on the ground that the Treasury has been traditionally more interested in economy than in efficiency or initiative.

One aspect of Treasury personnel management, however, is generally rated as a great success. This aspect is the development of machinery for collective bargaining and the settlement of disputes in the service. For most ministries individually and for the civil service as a whole, joint councils have been set up, composed of representatives of top management and of the lower ranks. They are known as Whitley Councils. It is through these channels that decisions have usually been reached on such matters as hours, pay, and holidays. For arbitral awards, appeal goes to the Industrial Court, which sits for this purpose with assessors drawn from both the managerial and the employee sides.

This organization for conciliation and arbitration, worked out at the close of World War I, has necessitated the development of strong employee associations. Most of the associations are trade unions. The close ties between British trade unions and the Labor party have inevitably called in question the political neutrality of the subordinate personnel. Indeed, between 1927 and 1946, recognition was denied by statute to civil service unions affiliated indirectly as well as directly with a political party. The more than 2 million employees of government-owned corporations are not civil servants. They have their own rules of employment and are outside the jurisdictions of the Civil Service Commission, the Treasury, and the National Joint Civil Service Council. The same thing is true of local government service.

4. Field Administration

Principal Ways. There are two principal ways in which government can carry its services to the ordinary citizen. Either the central government has its own appointive agents scattered throughout the land or it calls upon elective units of local government to do the work. Both methods are used in Britain; both are deeply rooted in history.

Whichever method it chooses, the central government is not merely providing for the administration of services. It is also educating the people to the significance and implications of the services it is receiving.

National Administration of National Services. On the whole, it may be said that economic services tend to be administered by the national government itself. These include the regulation of business, which in Britain is seldom a local function, and the provision of a national minimum of social security.[15] The agents of the central government have not all been civil servants. Some have been local citizens appointed by the central govern-

---

[15] This long-term tendency toward national administration of economic policy began with the rise of mercantilism around 1400. It has been somewhat obscured by the breakdown in central control over the central government's own local agents from the midseventeenth to the midnineteenth century, owing to civil war and revolution followed by the control of the central government by the local aristocracy and squirearchy.

ment to do its work in their spare time. Such is the sheriff of an English county, who is "pricked" by the King to hold office for one year at his own expense and is never elected. Such also are the justices of the peace, "the great unpaid," who are appointed by the Lord Chancellor to hold office at the pleasure of the Crown. Before 1888, the justices of the peace administered highways and bridges. Before 1834, they did much administering of poor relief. These magistrates still administer liquor licensing and share in police administration.[16]

To these historic part-time appointive agents brought into existence by royal prerogative, others have been added by parliamentary enactments of recent years. Such are the regional hospital boards set up since 1946. They must include members with experience in hospital management, and they must not be predominantly composed of persons associated with any one type of hospitals. To these statutory boards, responsibility is delegated for deciding the function of every hospital within the region. The medical practitioner service established since 1946 has similarly been placed under local executive councils, composed half of medical practitioners and half of lay persons, including members drawn from local authorities. These statutory councils are empowered to nominate new entrants into general practice and to discipline medical practitioners for improper administration of medical care—all questions about medical practice being initiated by a subcommittee consisting entirely of doctors.[17]

Similar, again, are the local unemployment insurance tribunals set up since 1946, not only to hear appeals, but also to decide what to do for each unemployed worker when he has exhausted his half-year's benefit rights. In the light of their familiarity with the local economic structure, these tribunals are intended to determine whether the applicant shall be continued indefinitely in full benefit, or whether continuance in benefit shall be made conditional upon his availability for some other kind of work.[18] Members of the tribunals are drawn equally from employer associations and trade unions on a rotating panel basis. As another example, the Agricultural Act of 1947 largely depends for good estate management and good husbandry on the work of county agricultural executive committees.

Powers and Control. In such instances, important discretionary powers are delegated to appointive regional and local bodies. These powers are in some instances so broad as to permit a large measure of subordinate policymaking. The principal means by which the responsible ministry can obtain

---

[16] Such, too, are Crown-appointed and unpaid "commissioners of sewers" (later called "drainage commissioners") and "navigation conservancy boards," which date back at least to Henry VIII.

[17] These local executive councils are the successors of local health insurance committees established in 1911.

[18] This local discretion was temporarily superseded under the Control of Engagement Order of October 6, 1947; an unemployed worker who refuses voluntary engagement in an essential occupation may be "directed" by the Ministry of Labor.

the adoption of a uniform national policy is to educate its local tribunals, councils, boards, and similar bodies to its own point of view.

The principal difference between the new administrative bodies and the justices of the peace appointed for the past six hundred years is that the new bodies have been created for special functions instead of general purposes. They are agents of particular ministries rather than of the central government in general.

Regional Coordination. Whether administering a service directly through their own salaried permanent officials or indirectly through appointive local bodies, most British ministries have found it convenient to organize their field administration on a regional basis. Services such as the post office, coal, electricity, gas, and hospitals are said to have gained by regionalization in flexibility, awareness of need, and opportunity to experiment. In Britain, nationalization is something of an umbrella for regionalization. Decentralization has become as normal in the management of the nation's business enterprises as in the management of privately owned undertakings. Whether regionalism is as successful in the administration of regulatory controls is less certain; it may produce delays by interposing a bottleneck between the locality and Whitehall.

There has been much discussion of the possibility of coordinating the various services of the national government at the regional level. Any such coordination is made difficult by the fact that British administration is primarily functional and only secondarily regional. Thus, each department divides the country into regions suited to its own convenience, regardless of the regional divisions that may seem better suited to some other ministry. Nor is there any regional coordinator of all central services, like a prefect in European continental countries or a provincial administrator in South Africa. Regional defense commissioners existed from 1940 to 1945 to undertake this role in case the island should be invaded and each region compelled to fend for itself. The nearest that Britain has yet come to peacetime regional coordination has been in the organization in 1945 of regional boards of industry to bring together the senior regional officials of various departments, as well as representatives of management and labor. One purpose of these boards is coordinated action with a view to stimulating or deterring the location of industry within the region.

National Supervision of Locally Administered Services. Although itself administering many national services, the British government has also long been accustomed to devolving many responsibilities upon elective local authorities or units of local government. This fact, however, does not mean that the central government has surrendered all responsibility for the particular services. On the contrary, the department concerned maintains a strict watch over the local authority's discharge of its responsibilities. The department's administrative controls are of two principal kinds—negative and positive.

Negatively, a department may send around its district auditors to inspect the accounts of local authorities in order to make sure that they have spent public money only on purposes authorized by law. A local authority has no inherent powers, but only such rights and duties as may be conferred upon it by statute or by administrative regulation made pursuant to statute. Any expense incurred outside the strict limits of its mandatory duties and its permissive rights is *ultra vires;* and, not being chargeable to the corporate body, such expense is "surcharged" to the members of the local body as private individuals. Members of local authorities that engage in experiments have therefore to be prepared to face serious financial consequences.[19] On one occasion, for example, upon appeal to the courts a large part of London's educational program was declared illegal. So was the payment by a local authority of what it considered to be a living wage, when this was higher than the prevailing rate of wages.

Positively, a department may buy the adherence of a local authority to departmental policy by granting aid on certain specified conditions. Of this conditional help the most important form is the grant in aid. Apart from a few amenities provided by the smallest local authorities, there is in Britain very little local outlay that is wholly locally financed. The great expansion of local government activity since about 1870 has been financed jointly by the national government and the local authorities. To some extent, joint financing has taken the form of a sharing of certain taxes and their devotion to specific purposes. On the whole, however, this form has not found favor, since it proportions a local authority's revenues to some variable tax receipts instead of the authority's needs. Grants in aid out of the central government's consolidated fund have therefore been preferred.

Grants in Aid. Most grants in aid are allocated by specific ministries on behalf of specific services. In these cases, payment by results has long ago been abandoned. Instead, some simple basis of calculation is used, such as so much per capita. In addition, an important "block grant" has been developed by the Ministry of Health for general local government purposes, including health services. It has been granted from 1929 to 1947 on the basis of a formula under which population was taken as a base, but was weighted so as to grant greater aid to localities with a high proportion of children and young people or unemployed, with a sparse population, or with a low rateable value.

Although the formula was much criticized in detail and had to be modified from time to time to meet unforeseen contingencies, the general principle of a block grant based on a formula found acceptance among local authorities. After local government was relieved of responsibility for social security, hospitals, and medical care, the block grant was reduced and put on a new basis in 1947. It is now available only to those counties and county

---

[19] Since members of British local authorities are unpaid, it is not usual for them to give bond or to insure against the risk of surcharge for acting *ultra vires.*

boroughs whose per capita rateable value is below average, population being weighted for this purpose by counting twice all children under sixteen, and rateable value being assessed by the national instead of the local government. The function of the block grant is thus one of adjustment, compensation, or equalization on behalf of the poorer localities at the expense of the general taxpayer.

Inspection. In Britain it is regarded as axiomatic that any grant in aid shall be followed up with inspection. The inspector no longer wields a big stick by threatening to cut off a grant unless certain conditions are fulfilled. This power is, of course, kept in reserve; but it is very seldom used or even mentioned.

Instead, the inspector has become an adviser to the local authorities whose services he inspects—a new dual channel of communication by which high standards can be promulgated locally and pressing problems made known to the central departments. Moreover, increasing reliance upon positive administrative stimulation through grants in aid and inspection may lead to diminished emphasis on restrictive regulation and on auditors' surcharges.

Control of Local Borrowing. Meanwhile, another administrative control is gaining in importance—national control over local borrowing. This control has hitherto involved approval both by the department concerned and by the Treasury. In some instances, the government has also made funds available at lower interest rates than the local authority itself would have commanded.

Since 1946, all borrowing by local authorities has had to be channeled through the Treasury, which operates for this purpose through its Public Works Loan Board. The procedure enables the government to correlate capital outlay by local authorities to the plans for its own investment outlay or that of government-owned corporations, thus helping local government to play its part in stabilizing the nation's economic development.

Legislative Controls. Administrative controls are far more important in Britain than legislative controls in the whole field of relations between central government and local authorities. In this there is nothing altogether new, for borough charters have always been granted by the Crown and not by Parliament. Since 1834, however, charters have followed certain statutory forms, and it is not safe for any local authority to risk exceeding the powers provided for by Parliament. The time-honored way of modifying the powers or the area of a local authority is therefore to go to Parliament and petition for the passage of a private or local bill after expensive hearings.

This procedure is still necessary to some extent. To a larger extent, however, the various departments have been given statutory powers to issue "provisional orders," thus saving the local authorities most of the expense attaching to private bill procedure. Whenever convenient, a batch of these provisional orders is then submitted to Parliament for confirmation in what is virtually little more than a "third reading." Similarly with the area of local authorities: changes are normally made by boundary commissions and then require no act of Parliament.

5. Local Government

The Governmental Map. England is traditionally a land not of scattered homesteads, but of nucleated settlements. The smallest of these settlements are villages, which together with their surrounding countryside constitute parishes. A number of parishes form a market area, grouped around a small market town. This rural market area was constituted a poor-law union in 1834, and today is designated as a rural district. Throughout the centuries certain definitely urban settlements have been granted the privilege of being incorporated by charter as boroughs, both large and small. And many other places that grew urban, but had not been incorporated as boroughs, were constituted as sanitary districts in 1848 and today are designated as urban districts. English units of local government thus are not artificial creations, but have their roots in England's social evolution.[20]

The medieval custom has persisted of cutting an urban center off from the surrounding rural area. Up into the nineteenth century, this practice took the form of separation between borough and county. Since 1888 the distinction is between the county borough and the administrative county.

Toward Larger Units. Many modern governmental services can be efficiently organized and expertly staffed only if they are planned for a considerable population with adequate taxable wealth. There has therefore been a striking tendency in England since 1888 to concentrate all the newer and more specialized services in the largest units of local government. These are the 61 administrative counties and those 83 boroughs that have been considered big and strong enough to be given county status as county boroughs. Between the larger authorities and the lesser ones, three different arrangements have resulted, known as the one-tier, two-tier and three-tier patterns of local government, as shown below.

PATTERN OF UNITS OF ENGLISH LOCAL GOVERNMENT

One-tier	Two-tier	Three-tier
County Boroughs	Administrative Counties	
	Urban Districts Metropolitan Boroughs Municipal Boroughs	Rural Districts
		Parishes

[20] On British local government in general, see: Local Government Boundary Commission, *Second Annual Report* (London, 1948); K. B. Smellie, *History of Local Government* (London, 1946); W. A. Robson, *Government and Misgovernment of London* (London, 1939); E. D. Simon, *City Council from Within* (London, 1926); C. R. Attlee and W. A. Robson, *The Town Councillor* (London, 1925); J. H. Warren, *The English Local Governmental System* (London, 1946).

In the one-tier system, there is only one level of local government—the county borough. All the powers granted by the national government to local government are concentrated in this one authority. The county has no power over the county borough. Under the two-tier system, there are two levels—the administrative county and the county district. The administrative county is basically the historic county; but the county boroughs have been torn out of it, and four of the bigger counties have been split, each into two or three administrative counties. The county district is a self-governing subdivision of a county. It may be either a municipal borough, an urban district, or a metropolitan borough. A municipal borough is a town that is dignified with a mayor and aldermen under a charter of incorporation, but has been subordinated to the county within the last hundred years because it has not been considered sufficiently populous to be promoted to the rank of county borough. The urban district, set up since 1848 under general act of Parliament instead of by charter, has a mere chairman and council. A metropolitan borough is to be found only in the county of London, where it originated as a parish.

Under the three-tier system, one finds an additional level—the parish. Again, the administrative county is divided into county districts, but these are rural districts instead of urban. The parish is a subdivision of the rural district; it is mainly concerned with small-scale neighborhood affairs, such as the maintenance of the village green, the village graveyard, and footpaths.

Special-Purpose Units. All these units of local government are general-purpose authorities. Those that began as special-purpose authorities—like the urban districts, originally for sanitary purposes, and the rural districts, for poor relief—have now enlarged functions, general instead of special. Those units that have always served a variety of purposes, such as counties, boroughs (both county and municipal), and parishes, have swallowed up the former special-purpose authorities.

During the eighteenth and nineteenth centuries, special-purpose authorities abounded in Britain as in North America. Gradually, however, they have been superseded. School districts, for instance, established in 1870, were abolished in 1902, their functions being now exercised by counties and county boroughs. Poor-law unions were similarly abolished in 1929, their functions being merged with those of counties and county boroughs. The abolition of special-purpose authorities has had many advantages. Coordination of the various services has become easier. The building of schools, for example, could be linked to the provision for public recreation and to civic planning in general. At the same time, public attention was more easily focused to secure public control. The only serious disadvantage springing from the demise of special-purpose authorities has been the proportionate increase in time and effort required of councilors, especially of counties and county boroughs.

There are today only two forms in which the special-purpose unit survives.

The one is the indirectly elected joint authority, in which a number of local authorities join together to cooperate for some special purpose—water supply, town and country planning, or the control of river basins. The other type is the special-purpose unit elected and financed by its users or beneficiaries, as with drainage boards and some port authorities, including that of London.

Time Lag and the Governmental Map. In mapping local government areas, the biggest problem today is to bring units formed by past social history into harmony with present social needs. New methods of social surveying, developed in Britain by Sir Patrick Geddes and his followers, have been used as a basis for the physical reconstruction of British cities by Sir Patrick Abercrombie and other civic planners.[21] The social scientist of today thinks in terms of region, metropolis, community, and neighborhood, whereas the politician and administrator have to act through county and county borough, which as a rule coincide with the way of thinking and living of 1888 rather than of 1948.

To the modern British social scientist, the country falls naturally into a certain number of regions, each of which finds its cultural center in its regional metropolis. This concept has been adopted by the government; thus, the Ministry of Health has appointed regional hospital boards and the Board of Trade its regional councils of industry. Most nationalized industries have their regional offices, boards, and consultative councils. The Ministry of Local Government and Planning is empowered to draft master plans for each region. Moreover, Professor Abercrombie has pleaded for the incorporation of regional development authorities, each of which would be a multipurpose public-utility enterprise, responsible for carrying out the Cabinet's master plan for the region by purchasing land, building factories, homes, and community facilities, and seeking provision of highways, railways, recreational areas, and refuse disposal plants, in close cooperation with other public-utility enterprises. The region is not envisaged as a unit of local self-government, but as an area for national-regional administration.

The regional metropolis has spilled out over its boundaries as county borough into a suburban fringe. Annexation of the suburban fringe by the nuclear metropolis has been resisted by the surrounding counties. It has also been opposed by many in the new suburbs, especially if local government in the suburbs was under Conservative control, and in the older nucleus under that of Labor. Royal commissions have probed this problem for the London, Tyneside, and South Lancashire areas, without reaching any general agreement. Up to the present, there has been no instance in Britain of successful adaptation of a unit of metropolitan self-government so as to make it coextensive with the metropolis as it really is.

---

[21] Cf. L. P. Abercrombie, *Greater London Plan* (London, 1945); J. H. Forshaw and L. P. Abercrombie, *County of London Plan* (London, 1943); P. L. Boardman, *Patrick Geddes* (Chapel Hill, 1944).

Community and Neighborhood. At the same time, the community has been rescued from obliteration in the great metropolis. The metropolis itself has been envisaged as a "conurbation" of communities, each with its distinct history, character, and social center. Above all, every community, whether in the metropolis or elsewhere, has been redefined as a service area that is large enough to support every kind of secondary education and that therefore has some 50 to 60 thousand inhabitants. Accordingly, urban districts and municipal boroughs with less than this population have been deprived since 1944 of the right to administer education. The community concept also governs in reconstructing blitzed or blighted areas under the Planning Act of 1944. This rediscovery of the local community has important consequences for local government. It raises doubts about the wisdom of having only one level of local self-government in the county borough and suggests the advisability of making the wards coincide with communities as now defined.

Within the community, a smaller nucleus is identified as the neighborhood, or primary-school service area, with a population of some 5,000 and some of the intimacy of a rural parish, even when in the midst of a metropolitan community. This unit is another important concept for planning the location of government services, such as playgrounds, highways, and nurseries, and also for residential and industrial zoning. It has less use in the delimitation of local government areas.

Local Government Structure. In England it has been customary to draw a line of distinction between counties and boroughs. Until 1888, the county was administered by centrally appointed justices of the peace, whereas the borough was governed by its own locally chosen mayor and council. Only then was the principle of local self-government through an elected council extended from the borough to the county. The democratization of English boroughs is usually attributed to the Municipal Corporations Act of 1835. Before this reform, every borough had its own form of government in accordance with its charter. Many boroughs had previously been closed corporations, in which aldermen co-opted whom they pleased to fill vacancies, much like a board of trustees. This habit had to be taken into account when the principle was introduced of having the borough council elected by the whole body of burgesses and when this group was enlarged so as to enfranchise all occupiers of premises on which local taxes were paid.

The pattern of 1835 provided for one third of the borough councilors to be elected each year and for the councilors to co-opt aldermen to one third their number, the aldermen to sit for overlapping terms of six years. In this manner, sensitivity to changes in popular feeling has been combined with safeguards against sudden change. This pattern was copied, with minor modifications, in the county and district councils, which assumed their present form in 1888 and 1895, respectively. The pattern of 1835 provided also for the council annually to elect its chairman, to whom the title of mayor was given.[22] The chairman of county and district councils has no such title.

Whereas the leadership of Parliament has gravitated into the hands of the Cabinet, leadership of local councils has not become concentrated in a single all-purpose one-party committee. Instead, it has been diffused over a large number of functional all-party committees. These committees have grown accustomed to working with the respective permanent officials in the local departments. The permanent officials have become accustomed to checking with their committees before embarking on any program, policy, or expense. The always subtle distinction between policy-making and administration is thus not too sharply drawn. When a new permanent head of a local department is needed, the committee that will have to work with him plays a leading part in his selection. Decisions made by a committee are nearly always confirmed by the full council, unless there is a clash with the finance committee. The committee that has come nearest to being a steering committee is the "general purposes committee." In moments of emergency, such as the wartime blitz, councils have sometimes delegated their powers to the general purposes committee.

Local Management. The permanent official who may be compared to a general manager of the borough's business is the town clerk—called clerk to the council at other levels. He is essentially a legal counselor, able to keep members of the corporation from acting *ultra vires*. He has little responsibility for coordinating his fellow officials or even for providing housekeeping services for them. His lack of close familiarity with other-than-legal aspects of civic planning may have made him a less constructive adviser than he might otherwise have been. Permanent officials are men with appropriate professional qualifications. They do not have to be local residents before appointment. There is thus a national market for local government officials. Town clerks, borough engineers, medical officers, and education directors have commonly moved round the country as they have risen in their professions. Party patronage has been virtually unknown, although personal influence and social bias have not been excluded. In the whole of English local government, there is no such thing as a popularly elected administrator, except for borough auditors.

Among the committees are some that a council is compelled to have—the statutory committees; and for Parliament to compel a council to have particular committees is one way of making it face up to a problem without exactly telling it what to do. Among the statutory committees are some that have been established as a substitute for abolished special-purpose authorities. Such are the education committees set up in 1902 and commonly referred to as local education authorities. Usually statutory provision is made for co-

[22] Lord Mayor in most places where the crown has accorded the borough the honorific title of "city."

optation, which in general is permissible for most local committees and required for some.

A considerable proportion of members of Parliament of all parties, especially of the Labor party, has had experience in local government. To this experience they owe much of their knowledge of the practical problems of government, and in particular the administration of services such as health, education, housing, and child welfare.

Local Finance. The financing of English local government, including education, rests almost equally on two sources—national grants in aid and local rates. From each nearly £250 million is derived annually. Rates are local taxes. Like the American property tax, they originated in the poor rate of the sixteenth century. In the course of time, however, their base has been narrowed. In a land where tenancy has always been more common than freeholding, rates have fallen not on the real-estate owner as such, but on the occupier. Unoccupied land or premises have been free of rates. Being an occupancy tax, rates have come to fall on "annual value" rather than "capital value," because it is much easier to find out for how much property rents than for how much it could be replaced; nor is there so big a variation in rents as in building costs or sale prices. English rates are therefore expressed as so many "pennies in the pound" on annual value.

A local authority will reckon that a "penny rate" will bring in a certain sum. Thus, the rateable value of England and Wales in 1945 was £320 million, and the product of a penny rate was £1,250,000. If the proceeds of a penny rate fell below a certain level, central departments or boundary commissions might argue that so poor an authority is unable to afford the more expensive duties of modern government.

English rates fall on occupiers of all property, including churches, schools, and government agencies. The only exemption is a three-quarter one for occupation of agricultural premises since 1896 and of industrial property since 1929. It was largely to compensate for this "derating" that the national government developed its system of block grants. These grants may thus be regarded as an indirect subsidy to British production.

6. *Judicial Administration*

Decline of Local Courts. Justice in England is highly centralized. England has no local courts, in the sense that no courts are locally elected. It is centrally that the "common law"—one law and one procedure for all England—came to be evolved.[23] In this long process, many local courts were beaten down, and there have been times when it was difficult for Englishmen to go to court without going to London.

Take the recovery of small debts. By an act of 1285, the county courts, which freeholders had been accustomed to attend for many centuries, were

---

[23] See especially R. C. K. Ensor, *Courts and Judges in France, Germany, and England* (Oxford, 1933); R. M. Jackson, *Machinery of Justice in England* (Cambridge, 1940).

debarred from handling cases where an object of more than 40 shillings was at issue. Where larger sums were at stake, action was to lie only in the King's courts. As the value of money declined, so did the role of the free-holders' county courts. Only since 1846 have judges been appointed for a new system of county courts to hear civil cases involving small sums. Above the legal limit, which now stands at £200, there are many comparatively small disputes that must go to London. Or take certain equitable remedies, such as the injunction. It was originally obtainable only from the Lord Chancellor's court of chancery, one for the whole kingdom. Since the fusion of chancery matters with the superior courts of common law in 1873, injunctions have been obtainable only from the judges of the High Court of Justice. In short, no strenuous efforts have been made to give every Englishman his "day in court." Litigation has tended to be something for the comparatively well-to-do.

Judicial Reforms. Criminal justice, on the other hand, has been adequately provided for. For many hundreds of years, the more serious offenses have been tried in the counties with the help of juries—by the county bench of Crown-appointed justices of the peace in quarter sessions; or by the paid urban equivalent, usually a borough recorder; or by itinerant commissioners on assize sent out from the central High Court. The less serious offenses, which are ten times as numerous, have been tried summarily, without juries, by justices of the peace in petty sessions or their urban counterpart, often a stipendiary police magistrate, centrally appointed but locally paid. In one or other of these ways, the courts have helped in the rigorous repression of breaches of the "King's peace."

Under the inspiration of Jeremy Bentham, many great reforms have been effected in the administration of both civil and criminal justice, beginning about 1822 and continuing to the present time.[24] One is the reform of procedure so as to lessen delays, widen the range of proper evidence, and remove the danger of justice being prevented by technicalities. Another is the unification of courts so that litigants may obtain every available remedy in whatever court they happen to find themselves. Another, again, has been to bring within everybody's reach a low-priced but well-staffed court, competent to handle all manner of small civil cases. This reform was begun with the establishment of the new county courts, which now handle up to 250,000 cases a year.

Yet another reform has been the overhaul of the jury system. The picking of trial juries was reorganized in the 1820's, so as to prevent jury-packing and remove the need for juror-challenging. During World War II, jury trial in civil cases was curtailed, a jury—reduced to seven persons—being henceforward available only with the consent of the judge.

---

[24] On these reforms, see A. V. Dicey, *Lectures on the Relation Between Law and Public Opinion in England During the Nineteenth Century* (held at Harvard, 1898; rev. ed., Toronto, 1905), especially pp. 204 ff.; C. H. S. Fifoot, *English Law and Its Background* (London, 1932).

Criminal Prosecution. Initiation of criminal proceedings has been radically changed as public authorities have assumed responsibility for prosecutions. This change was effected through the coming into being of a director of public prosecutions in the Home Office, with the duty since 1879 not only of instituting and conducting criminal proceedings but also of advising law-enforcement officers. Being under the civil service, the public prosecutor's office enforces the law with strict impartiality and in closest cooperation with the police. It proved so successful that after sixty years of growing public confidence indictment by grand juries was abolished in favor of information filed by the public prosecutor's office. One advantage is that a civil service prosecutor is not at the mercy of local political machines, as could easily happen if he were locally elected. The absence of any tie-up between politics and racketeering may be attributed mainly to the method of placing responsibility for conducting public prosecutions. Since police officers have confidence in the public prosecutor and can rely on his cooperation, they seldom rely on "third degree" methods of discovering clues.[25]

Cost of Justice. One problem that has not been solved is that of expense, which remains very high. In one way it has even been heightened by the multiplication of appeals, which may now go from the courts of first instance up through the Court of Appeal (established 1873) or through the Court of Criminal Appeal (established 1907) to the House of Lords. The expensiveness of justice led the British Labor movement in 1945 to secure a transfer of workmen's compensation for industrial injuries from the ordinary courts to inexpensive administrative tribunals.

A related problem is that of the local magistracy. England's 20,000 justices of the peace are unpaid and untrained. They have to rely on the clerks of their courts. Yet they are responsible for trying a very large part of the offenses committed in breach of law and for settling an equally large portion of the domestic and matrimonial cases. Their unreliability, to a large extent, made it seem desirable to create the new county courts.

Judicial Tenure. There is one beneficial characteristic of British justice that antedates the law reforms of recent generations. This characteristic is the tenure of judges. Ever since 1714 they have enjoyed what is virtually life tenure. Technically, their tenure is said to depend on "good behavior" (*quamdiu se bene gesserint*); they may be deprived of their offices only on request of both Houses of Parliament or after conviction by a court. No British judge is elected. Once he is appointed, he can be completely independent of partisan pressure.

Judicial appointments are made on the advice of the Lord Chancellor. He is a lawyer of judicial stature, chosen by the Prime Minister as being acceptable to the higher justices. He is a member of the Cabinet and the presiding officer of the House of Lords—both as a parliamentary chamber in the afternoon and when it sits of a morning as the highest court of appeal.

[25] Cf. P. Howard, *Criminal Justice in England* (New York, 1931).

In England, the road to the bench is the bar. It is almost unknown for a man to become a judge who has not attained distinction as a barrister in private practice. He does not rise to the bench by way of service as a public prosecutor, as may happen on the European continent. To his distinction at the bar, however, he may have added political activity. At its highest, this activity may take him from the post of Attorney General to a high court, from which he may move back into the fringes of politics as Lord Chancellor. It is, nevertheless, not regarded as unjudicial to preside over a royal commission or departmental committee of inquiry or to serve on a statutory compensation tribunal.[26]

Impact of the Judiciary. No judiciary is so independent as one appointed for life.[27] The disadvantage of so independent a judiciary is that in its basic attitudes it may be inadequately responsive to social change. This danger, however, is much less in Britain than in those English-speaking countries that have written constitutions.

British judges, like all others, make law by interpreting it. The general principle of judicial review enables them to declare any action—public or private—contrary to the law of the land. But in Britain the supreme law of the land is an act of Parliament. An act of Parliament thus cannot be unconstitutional; the most that judges can do is to interpret it away. If they do, it is possible by act of Parliament to override or reverse a judicial interpretation—that is to say, to lay down as a future guide for the courts a principle different from the one they have undertaken to follow.

---

[26] Normal British practice is for recorders, stipendiaries, and justices of the peace to be in politics, and for justices of the higher courts and judges of county courts to stay out of politics. Controversy has centered around the role of law lords in the House of Lords.

[27] In the whole of England, there are fewer judges than in the state of New York. In proportion to the population, there are four times as many judges in New York as in England.

CHAPTER 6

LIBERTY AND OPPORTUNITY

1. Civil Liberties

Personal Freedom. Far from being mere abstractions, the ancient "rights of Englishmen" are those for whose enforcement concrete procedures were developed in the seventeenth century. Some of these procedures are judicial elaborations of the common law. Others are laid down by statute. In Britain it has been recognized that measures for safeguarding the survival of the state have to be accompanied by measures for safeguarding the rights of the citizens if the survival of the state is to appear justifiable to its citizens.[1] Personal liberty has been traditionally protected by the right of anyone in England to a writ of *habeas corpus*. This instrument is a means of ensuring his release on bail if he is charged with a misdemeanor; or his speedy trial if charged with treason or felony; or his speedy release if he is neither charged with any offense nor confined by order of a court or Parliament. The famous Habeas Corpus Act of 1679 provided effective methods for enforcing this common-law right.

From time to time, some clause of crisis legislation permits a minister to confine individuals on certain specified grounds and obliges the courts to accept the minister's allegations as proper cause for the confinement. Moreover, in case anyone is wrongly confined through misinterpretation of such emergency legislation, an indemnity act is usually passed after the emergency is over, so as to free the offending officials from any penalties to which they might otherwise be subject under the act of 1679 and similar laws. This double method of circumventing habeas corpus by emergency and indemnity legislation—though not by royal prerogative—is popularly known as "suspension of habeas corpus." It has long been common practice in combating illegality in Ireland.[2] In Britain, the Defense of the Realm Act (DORA, 1914-20) permitted the issuance of administrative regulations, some of which empowered the Home Secretary to detain indefinitely without trial persons suspected of "hostile origin or associations." Similarly, the

---

[1] On this subject in general, see A. V. Dicey, *Introduction to the Study of the Law of the Constitution* (many editions since 1885); O. and I. Cruchley, *Freedom in Our Time* (London, 1937); National Council for Civil Liberties' news sheet, *Civil Liberty* (from 1939); C. T. Carr, "Crisis Legislation," in his *Concerning English Administrative Law* (New York, 1941).

[2] There it survived in the special powers given the Minister for Home Affairs in Northern Ireland in 1922 to order anyone detained indefinitely whom he suspects of acting in a manner prejudicial to the maintenance of peace and order.

Emergency Powers (Defense) Act (1939-47) authorized the issuance by order-in-council of Regulation 18B(c), under which the Home Secretary was allowed to detain anyone on the same grounds; but one so detained could lodge objections before an advisory committee, and the minister had to make a monthly report to Parliament showing both the numbers of detained persons and of instances in which he had not followed the committee's advice.[3] In spite of the greater peril, personal liberty thus was better protected in the Second World War than in the First.[4]

Freedom of the Press. Freedom of the press consists essentially of the absence of censorship prior to publication, since the last licensing act was allowed by Parliament to expire in 1695.[5] Only in World War I has censorship again been applied to the press. There are, however, a number of other ways in which the press may be deterred from certain kinds of publication. One is the passage of a series of acts on official secrets beginning in 1889, making it an offense to receive or publish confidential data. This prohibition has been used to prevent statesmen from including unpublished documentation in their memoirs; to prevent newspapers from reporting certain government activities; to punish a scientist for giving away atomic information; and to impose comparatively petty restrictions. Another deterrent is the risk of prosecution under the Incitement to Mutiny Act of 1797, for tending to seduce a member of the armed forces from his duty *and* allegiance; or under the Incitement to Disaffection Act of 1934, for possessing documents that might tend to seduce a member of the armed forces from his duty *or* allegiance. The former act has been used to punish syndicalists and Communists, but not Ulster unionists. The latter has made it hard to find printers and publishers for pacifist writings.

There is a possibility of police seizure of sexy literature under the Obscene Publications Act of 1857, which has enabled the Home Office to suppress some controversial novels. There is also a possibility that the post office will refuse to carry what it considers indecent, including products of other countries. Criticizing a judge has been construed as contempt of court; it is considered unwise to publish anything in a report of judicial proceedings if the judge does not wish it published. Moreover, the Judicial Proceedings (Reg-

[3] As originally phrased in a great hurry on the outbreak of war, the regulations did not contain these safeguards of individual liberty. They were inserted by the government only after two months of public protest, culminating in a motion in the Commons to annul some of the regulations. The Emergency Powers (Defense) Act of 1939 contained this improvement over DORA, that it provided for possible parliamentary annulment. See House of Commons, *Debates,* October 31, 1939.

[4] Other inroads into habeas corpus have been made by extradition acts and by acts for discretionary deportation and detention of foreigners; also by the Public Order Act of 1936 and the Prevention of Violence Act of 1939 permitting detention for a few days while the government decided whether or not to prosecute for wearing political uniforms or committing acts of terrorism, respectively.

[5] See especially Political and Economic Planning, *Report on the British Press* (London, 1938), particularly chap. 9; and W. H. Wickwar, *The Struggle for the Freedom of the Press* (London, 1928).

ulation of Reports) Act of 1926 expressly forbids the reporting of "human interest" details concerning divorce and matrimonial cases, except in so far as the judge makes some concluding observations. "Privilege"—immunity from prosecution—was extended to the reporting of parliamentary and judicial proceedings in the midnineteenth century, but does not extend to the reporting of local government business.

The biggest legal restriction on the freedom of the press comes not from modern statutory legislation, but from the common law of civil libel. Libel law enables gold-diggers to hold up newspapers for ransom and makes it particularly unwise to say anything about anyone who might feel that his interests could thereby be in any way injured. Libel actions may be brought only in the High Court. It is doubtful whether this fact is much of a protection to the press, since it increases the risk of heavy legal costs and therefore the pressure to settle out of court. Prosecution for criminal libel—seditious, blasphemous, obscene, and defamatory—has ceased to be a danger to the press; for the government in the midnineteenth century adopted the policy of not enforcing this part of the common law.[6]

Other Liberties. The right of public meeting, like the freedom of the press, is enjoyed by virtue of the very limited number of ways of interfering with its exercise. A public meeting or procession may be prevented by the police if it obstructs the highway, which by British definition is a place to "move along" in. A meeting may also be prevented by breach of the peace on the part of those provoked by it; and it may then be the duty of the police to restore order by dispersing the meeting. When Fascist anti-Semitism became provocative and uniformed Fascists tried to expel from their meetings those who attended only to be provoked, an act on public order was passed in 1934. This act empowered the police to take the names and addresses of hecklers and hand them to the chairman of the meeting in case he should wish to initiate a prosecution. More usefully, the act empowered the police to fix the routes of processions to avoid clashes and to ban the procession entirely, with the consent of the Home Secretary and the local authority.[7]

Lastly, the British civilian is subject only to civil jurisdiction. Parliament

---

[6] Nothing except common sense prevents emergency regulations from being used to impede the free expression of ideas. In World War I, in particular, there were many police raids and prosecutions against advocates of conscientious objection and of a negotiated peace, on the ground that they impeded recruitment, demoralized the armed forces, or might encourage the enemy. For a good account, see P. Snowden, "Free Speech in Wartime," in his *Autobiography* (London, 1934) I, 414 ff. Other media of communication are subject to the same possibilities of administrative and judicial action, especially in times of crisis. In addition, drama is subject to prior censorship by the Lord Chamberlain; the present law dates from 1843. Movie theaters are subject to licensing by local authorities. Radio scripts have to pass the British Broadcasting Corporation.

[7] Under the Emergency Powers (Defense) Act of 1939, Regulation 39E empowered the Home Secretary to prohibit in advance any meeting or procession on the ground that it would be likely to cause disorder or disaffection; but the local police were not permitted to ban meetings without express written authorization from the Home Secretary, unless they alleged that air raids made it unsafe to hold them.

has never put him under military tribunals. In this sense, "state of siege" is no part of the British constitution. In so far, however, as constitutional government breaks down and force is used against force, as happened in the civil war in Ireland, there is nothing to prevent martial law from being brought into play by the military. To obviate this possibility in the event of "recent or immediately apprehended enemy action," the Emergency Powers (Defense) Act (No. 2) of 1940 authorized the establishment of civilian war-zone courts, capable of administering criminal justice more speedily than would be practical in the ordinary courts.

Britain has no written code of liberty it depends upon the courts to enforce. Instead, dependence is upon the reluctance of Parliament to acquiesce in repressive legislation and the strong criticism that arises in informed circles whenever there is danger of a repressive use of the necessary powers of government.

2. Changing Concepts of Human Rights

Removal of Governmental Interference. During the past few generations, a great change has occurred in British concepts of personal freedom. This change corresponds broadly with recent American tendencies to supplement freedom *of* speech or *of* religion with freedom *from* "want and fear." The earlier viewpoint demands limits to governmental regulation; the later requires an expansion of governmental services.

Governmental interference with personal freedom, except in times of emergency, was limited by procedures. Interference with the press has now been narrowed to a number of defined points, none of which is likely to prevent the press from criticizing the government of the day. Nor are these forms of interference likely to prevent ridicule of any established institutions, except war. Reasoned criticism is permissible. Pleas for reform are permissible. Even advocacy of revolution is permissible, provided it is not focused on inciting disaffection among the armed forces and the police. Obstacles to public meetings are exceptionally few. And practically no obstacles to free association have remained since the government ceased to prosecute under the common law of conspiracy.

Yet the removal of obstacles to freedom has not stopped with the removal of governmental obstacles. There are other obstacles, social in nature, that only government can remove. Such are the various hurdles that stand in the way of access to the possible benefits of our civilization.

Establishment of Governmental Responsibility. A man's ability to find satisfying social relationships depends to a large extent on education. Access to a suitable education is one of the cardinal rights of the modern Briton. The Education Act of 1944, in broad and general terms, places on the Minister of Education the duty of *"promoting the education of the people of England and Wales and the progressive development of institutions devoted to that purpose,* and of securing the effective execution by local education authorities, under his control and direction, of *the national policy in providing a varied and comprehensive educational service in every area.*" Much the same goes for an opportunity to do one's share of the world's work and support one's family during the working years of life. But the "right to work" is not something that can be enforced at law. Its realization depends to a large extent upon governmental policy aimed at providing work opportunities for all who are capable of meeting them. This policy has been laid down in a famous wartime "white paper," which said: "The government accept as one of their primary aims and responsibilities *the maintenance of a high and stable level of employment* after the war." The Commons, under the leadership of the wartime all-party coalition, voted "that this house welcomes the statement of His Majesty's government." The organization of the Cabinet secretariat is now largely geared to this end.[8]

The right to have enough to live on implies adequate wages. Minimum wages have gradually been assured by administrative action, in establishing "trade boards" for ill-paid occupations and encouraging collective bargaining in ill-organized trades. This thirty-year process was virtually completed during World War II with the extension of coverage, by Ernest Bevin as Minister of Labor, to workers in retail stores.[9] The right to have enough to live on implies also "income security" for those who are too young, too old, or too infirm to support themselves and for workers who pass through an interval of unemployment. The goal, as stated by Lord Beveridge, is to "abolish want by ensuring that every citizen willing to serve according to his powers has at all times an income sufficient to meet his responsibilities." [10] This goal has been approached by the national insurance and children's allowance laws of 1945-46.

Another basic interest is good health. Yet it can be thwarted by maldistribution and unavailability of medical services, both preventive and restorative. Much loss of life and health has already been prevented by public medicine in Britain. Restoration to health also is a goal that is being made more accessible by the national health service available to all since 1948.

In all these instances—education, employment, income, and health— the freedom sought is not freedom *from* government, but freedom *through* government. The rights are secured not by absence of laws or of law enforcement, but by passage and administration of laws. These laws are enforced not through law courts, but through administrative agencies. These,

---

[8] Ministry of Reconstruction, *Employment Policy* (Cmd. 6527 [1944]); House of Commons, *Debates,* June 23, 1944; W. H. Wickwar, "British Plans," in a symposium on "Maintaining High-Level Production and Employment," ed. F. Morstein Marx, *American Political Science Review,* 39 (1945), 1137 ff.

[9] This move may have been partly responsible for the swing of doubtful lower-middle-class constituencies to the Labor column in 1945.

[10] William Beveridge, *Social Insurance and Allied Services: Report* (Cmd. 6404 [1942]), par. 444.

like other and older rights, are claims of the individual against society. But the claim is a positive one, for service, instead of a negative one, for avoidance of harm.

3. Groups and the State

Group Liberties. There has been a marked tendency for the rights of the modern Briton to be realized by public policy rather than private individual action; there has also been a tendency for the most important liberties to be liberties of groups rather than liberties of individuals, like the right of association in self-governing groups of many kinds. In this development, there is nothing intrinsically new. Medieval liberties were group liberties—liberties accorded to the church, to a borough, to a feudal fief, to a manor, to a guild, to a court, or to Parliament. England's Bill of Rights (1688) stressed the rights of Parliament, the courts, and the established church, rather than the rights of the individual. The latter's supreme right, in fact, is the right to be subject to Parliament and the courts rather than to an unlimited, absolute, and arbitrary personal sovereign.

Only for a relatively brief period after the breakdown of some of these older groups was British thinking in terms of individual rather than group rights and of the state as the only "body politic." Yet such abstract individualism was less widely cultivated than in most other Western countries. Among the economists, for example, John Stuart Mill, in his *Principles of Political Economy* (1848), envisaged an ideal capitalism in which social cooperation would be more valued than competition among individuals. Among the legal theorists, similarly, Jeremy Bentham rejected the doctrine of natural rights focused on the individual, according supreme value to the social institutions that would contribute most to the greatest happiness of the greatest number. Conservative theorists, both Whig and Tory, went even farther. A long line of writers, from Southey to Disraeli, stressed social solidarity rather than individual self-seeking. The dominant trend in the Conservative party has been one of "Tory democracy," advocating collective action for the general welfare.

Political Pluralism. British political theorists of the twentieth century have all been group theorists. They have stressed the fact that the state, although the most important of all social groups, is nonetheless only one among many. Lord Acton, teaching the dependence of liberty on other organizations besides the state; J. N. Figgis, preaching the rights of churches; G. D. H. Cole, advocating "guild socialism"; Harold J. Laski, recognizing the inevitability of "political pluralism"; R. H. Tawney, attacking "individual acquisitiveness"; F. W. Maitland, translating Gierke and Althusius; Graham Wallas, suggesting that the House of Lords be reformed to represent organized groups; the neo-Hegelians, searching for "group persons" and the "group mind"; and A. D. Lindsay, showing that the essence of democracy is not consent but group discussion—one and all, these theorists have been more concerned with the role of groups within the state than with any other problem.

Yet the primacy of the state in Britain is never forgotten. The state is never resolved into a mere assemblage of groups. Government is not merely a regulator of group relations. Nor is policy-making reduced to working out intergroup compromises. For the state is looked upon as serving the basic moral and material needs of its members by general policies.

Groups and Sovereignty. Between group liberties and state sovereignty, modern British thought has held an uneasy balance. G. D. H. Cole, for example, moved from guild socialism to Fabian socialism, and Laski, similarly, from emphasis on the group to stress on state sovereignty. These changes and uncertainties are but evidence that here is one of the dominant problems of present-day British politics.

Moreover, the groups to which attention has been given in Britain are not envisaged primarily as associations that are struggling for their own material advantage or survival. Rather, they represent long-continuing attitudes of mind, each cherishing its own scale of values.

4. Religious Liberty

Structure of the Established Church. England and Scotland have established churches; Wales and Northern Ireland have not. The Anglican church, as by law established, claims to be the national church of England, in almost unbroken continuity from the first gains of Christianity in the seventh century right down to the present day. Its bishops have always been nominated by the Crown and elected by the cathedral chapters; and since the Reformation, it has been a penal offense for a cathedral chapter not to elect the royal nominee. The church considers itself bound by the decisions of oecumenical councils only in so far as it consents to them. It has not accepted the jurisdiction or doctrine of any authority outside England since it rejected the claims of the Pope in Rome in the sixteenth century. In this sense, it is "Protestant Episcopal," like its sister church in the United States; but it never uses this expression, preferring to stress its continuity with its past, rather than the changes it underwent with the Reformation.

Bishops, being royal nominees, are actually chosen on the advice of the Prime Minister. Since they are selected by laymen, their choice faithfully reflects the movement of lay thought. They represent so wide a range of opinion on all matters, both social and philosophical, that there have always been some among them whose views have been regarded as heretical by their colleagues. As a result of lay selection of bishops, the Anglican church has ceased to have any distinctive doctrine, except the doctrine that, being national, the church has no one standard of orthodoxy.

The parish clergy is appointed to its livings by whoever has each living in his gift. This person may be the bishop of the diocese. More often, he is a lay patron or the Crown, having inherited the right from distant days. A considerable number of church livings is in the gift of the Crown; for the exercise of ecclesiastical patronage, the Lord Chancellor is responsible. Twenty-four senior diocesan bishops—including always Canterbury, York, London, Winchester, and Durham—have seats in the House of Lords. The parish clergy are regarded as public officials, in being under a legal obligation to marry couples; a marriage so registered is equal to one in the civil register. The form of worship contained in the church's Book of Common Prayer has been prescribed by Parliament. The ritual of the Church of England is that used on all state occasions.

Political Role of the Church of England. The established church receives no financial assistance from the state and is not even tax-exempt. From the past, however, it has inherited two considerable sources of income— its landed property and other endowments, and tithe. Its property has been managed since 1834 by the Ecclesiastical Commissioners, a lay body appointed by and responsible to the government of the day. A large part of this property is urban land, which has increased greatly in value during the past century. Like most property in England, much of it has been rented on 99-year lease. It has hence tended to pass through the usual decline into slum conditions toward the end of the lease, followed by slum clearance afterwards. Tithe was a rent-charge paid by owners of any land on which it had not been commuted by a lump-sum settlement. The last remains of tithe have now been finally commuted by the government's paying to the church a capital sum and then collecting from owners of titheable land, for a term of years, smaller charges than the interminable ones they would otherwise have had to pay.

During the past century, the Church of England has become aware that it is no longer the national church in the old sense. Since the 1820's, for example, Protestant Nonconformists and Roman Catholics have been allowed to become members of Parliament, thus giving them a voice in the control over the church. All public offices except the kingship have gradually ceased to be reserved for those who practice at least "occasional conformity." Since 1880, Protestant Nonconformists have been admitted to the Cabinet. Of a population of over 40 million, only 2 million are Easter communicants of the Church of England. It has thus become obvious that church and state are not identical. In order to preserve its own identity, the Church of England has come to stress its canons. On the part of some of its clergy, this spirit has shown itself in disobedience to the law of the land in the name of a higher law. They have refused, for example, to marry persons who have been divorced or have not been baptized; or they have administered sacraments in ways other than those prescribed by Parliament in the Book of Common Prayer.

For such ecclesiastical liberty, a lawful channel had to be found. Under the Church of England Act of 1919, there now meets annually a Church

Assembly composed of three houses—bishops, clergy, and laity.[11] By this act, the assembly is empowered to pass "measures" for the good government of the established church, to be approved by Parliament in a kind of third reading. It may therefore be said that today the Church of England has the benefits both of establishment and of liberty.

The Scottish Kirk. The Scottish kirk is in a somewhat similar position. Its links with the state are even slimmer. Being presbyterian in organization, it has no bishops to be appointed by the government or to sit in the House of Lords. Without a prayer book, its forms of worship are less subject to ultimate determination by Parliament. Because they do not regard marriage as a sacrament, its ministers have come into less conflict with the civil law.

The annual Kirk Assembly at Edinburgh is welcomed and dismissed by a lay commissioner selected by the Crown for the occasion, but he has no power. The patronage formerly used by Scottish lairds in favor of "moderate" ministers provoked a revolt of "evangelical" parishes; and in the 1830's, when the assembly proved legally powerless to remove the cause of this disruption, parliamentary enactment became necessary to abolish patronage and substitute election of ministers by the congregation.

Other Churches. The Protestant Episcopal churches of Ireland and Wales were disestablished by Parliament in 1868 and 1914, respectively, on the ground that they were in no sense national churches. Their bishops ceased to be chosen by the government and to sit in Parliament. Their property was assigned by Parliament, some to ecclesiastical purposes, but some to charitable and educational uses. In this limited sense, they were "disendowed" as well as disestablished.

In all parts of the United Kingdom, there are "Protestant free churches"—religious organizations outside the established churches. Protestant Episcopalians are in fact "Nonconformists" in Scotland, as Presbyterians are in England. Toleration for Protestant dissenters has been permitted in England since 1689. Public offices were opened to them in the eighteenth century by the practice of "occasional conformity," and by indemnity acts that removed the penalties for any who had held office without passing the religious "test"; this test was abolished in 1828. The Baptist, Congregational, Methodist, Presbyterian, and Unitarian churches, the Salvation Army, and the Society of Friends (Quakers) have nearly all found it convenient to have their basic forms of government embodied in acts of Parliament. Then they cannot make fundamental changes in their organization without going to Parliament. With this exception, however, they are free and independent churches.

The Roman Catholic church was illegal until 1791; its members were excluded from Parliament until 1829 and were subject to other disabilities un-

---

[11] The election of a house of laity has made it necessary for the first time to lay down criteria of active membership in the Church of England.

til 1846. Roman Catholic dioceses are not allowed to assume the same historic titles as Anglican bishoprics. Legal barriers still exist to a Roman Catholic's becoming King, Queen, or Lord Chancellor. On the other side, religious freedom is not confined to ecclesiastical liberty, but extends also to the right to be a member of no religious body. Many freethinkers and agnostics have felt a need for corporate expression through such organizations as the positivist Ethical church and the Rationalist Press Association. The common law of blasphemy is not enforced; and an act of Parliament of 1888 permits those who have no religion to make a declaration instead of taking an oath.

Churches and Education. One field in which no government can avoid defining its relations with the churches—whether established or free—is that of tax support for education in cases in which the school is provided, not by local government, but by a religious body. The English rule is that public money, both national and local, is available for all schools for which there is a demonstrable need, if they meet certain conditions. But distinction is drawn between "provision" and current "maintenance" of education. Today, under the Education Act of 1944, managers of schools of the Church of England transfer their financial responsibilities to the local education authority, which will provide the building as well as an "agreed syllabus," but the Anglican managers reserve a veto on the appointment of the head teacher and of those teachers who give denominational instruction. This arrangement applies to what are known as "controlled voluntary schools." Managers of Roman Catholic schools, not being able to adopt an "agreed syllabus" for religious education, remain responsible for providing the building. But they are relieved of the cost of maintaining instruction, provided that they give the local education authority a veto over their appointment of teachers and permit any child whose parents so desire to have religious instruction based on the "agreed syllabus." These schools are known as "aided voluntary schools." An "agreed syllabus" is one agreed upon between the Church of England, the Protestant free churches, and the teaching profession; it is used in publicly provided and controlled schools. In all publicly provided schools, the first or last period every day must be devoted to nondenominational religious instruction; but a "conscience clause" in the act permits any parent who so desires to withdraw his child from this instruction.

At least as important as provision of schools is provision of teachers' training colleges. Most of the older ones were provided by the Church of England. Only in the twentieth century have the universities begun to eclipse the church as trainers of teachers. The church and the universities thus appear as rival contenders for the favor of the Ministry of Education, as the authority for both fixing standards of teacher certification and giving grants in aid of teacher training.

5. Occupational Groups

Employer Associations. Associations of business concerns engaged in the same kind of enterprise have long been common. The "merchant adventurers" trading between England and the Low Countries and the "Turkey merchants" trading between England and the Levant were important examples. Each firm traded on its own account, but all who engaged in the trade were expected to join a "company," which by Crown charter regulated the commerce and represented the interests of the members in negotiating with governments abroad. This kind of national company for foreign trade died out in the eighteenth century. So did most of the local guilds that were chartered to regulate the commerce of their members within some particular city. The idea of a chartered company or guild survived, however, and as late as 1871, the London underwriters of marine insurance were chartered as "Lloyds."

Between the World Wars, a great revival of this kind of "industrial self-government" occurred, as every hard-hit industry asked for legal power to legislate for its members. For instance, the shrinking export industries were forced to seek government help. In addition to public subsidies, and indeed as a condition for receiving them, they asked and were granted the privilege of restraining cutthroat competition and so fixing prices as to ensure enough income to continue to attract capital and labor into the industry. During this phase, public aid to private enterprise thus consisted as much in conferring "industrial self-government" as in what critics called "putting capitalism on the dole."

Combination to restrict competition was unlawful at common law. In 1871, however, Parliament had narrowed such combination by declaring that it should not be indictable as a criminal conspiracy. The Trade Union Act of 1876 expressly forbade the courts to entertain any legal proceeding for enforcing agreements about conditions on which members should transact business. There is in Britain thus nothing unlawful about a voluntary cartel. It is well known that shipping lines on all oceans except the North Atlantic have been controlled by "conferences" since the late nineteenth century. But legislation is needed before cartelization can be enforced against reluctant businesses.

Forms of Organization. Such legislation was advocated by the Royal Commission on the Coal Industry, which reported in 1926. After some voluntary experimentation under a permissive act, cartelization was made mandatory by the Coal Mines Act of 1930. Thenceforth, quarterly quotas were assigned to each district, and monthly quotas to each mine, with penalties for overproduction and bonuses for underproduction. Minimum prices were fixed, and cooperative marketing introduced. The whole organization for these purposes was entrusted to representatives of the colliery owners, subject to the approval of the Board of Trade. Free competition among collieries had therefore ceased half a generation before the industry was nationalized in 1946. One reason for nationalization was that, while enjoying the privilege of noncompetition, the colliery owners had failed to reorganize the industry with a view to greater efficiency and productivity.

The Cotton Spinning Act of 1936 set up a "spindles board" and empowered it to collect a levy on every spindle for the next fifteen years, with which to compensate mill owners for surplus spindles eliminated during the next three years. The Cotton Industry (Reorganization) Act of 1939 extended this set-up to all sections of the cotton industry and provided also for price-fixing by a cotton industry board appointed by the Board of Trade to represent management and labor. Similarly, a governing committee of the shipbuilding industry was empowered to levy dues on members for the elimination of surplus shipyard capacity. And tramp shipping after 1935 benefited by "a scrap and build" subsidy administered by a committee of tramp owners. Agriculture also has had its marketing boards since 1930, elected by farmers and empowered to regulate the marketing of agricultural produce. The trend between the wars was thus for the British government under either party to permit producers in selected industries to restrict production and raise prices.[12]

At the end of World War II, the climate of opinion called for increased rather than restricted productivity. Similar means were now used for a different end. "Working parties," representing management, labor, and the public, were established for eighteen industries by Sir Stafford Cripps as President of the Board of Trade. In their reports, these parties suggested ways in which the productivity and selling power of particular industries could be increased. On the basis of these reports, policies have been agreed upon between the government and the various industries. The Industrial Reorganization Act of 1947 established a procedure for setting up tripartite industrial development councils, which have authority to finance industrial research by means of a compulsory levy on member firms, subject to ministerial approval. Since this procedure involves an important delegation of part of Parliament's taxing powers, it is provided that any order issued for this purpose by a department is subject to affirmation by both houses of Parliament.

Trade Unions. The liberties enjoyed by trade unions have been granted by Parliament in the course of less than one hundred years, in the teeth of constant opposition from the law courts. Welfare funds are among the oldest ways in which British trade unions have endeavored to help their members, death benefits being particularly widespread. As far back as 1855, Parliament provided for voluntary registration of trade unions, not merely for the sake of auditing them, but in order to give them the benefits accorded

---

[12] Competition was similarly restricted among motor-bus proprietors from 1930 and among truck owners from 1933; but this restriction was accomplished by a system of government licensing, although the government was under strong pressure from the transportation industry to give a "fair deal" by handing over its regulatory powers to the railways and road haulers conjointly, until it nationalized them all in 1947.

any "friendly society" (fraternal order) of protecting their funds by access to the summary jurisdiction of local magistrates. Participation of trade unionism in politics is also an old thing. To promote favorable legislation, unions have joined together in local "trades councils" since about 1855, and in a national Trades Union Congress since 1868. After the affiliation of trade unions with the Labor party, the courts enjoined them from collecting political dues, but Parliament in 1913 legalized this activity, provided that political funds were kept separate from others and that any member who wished could "contract out."

Collective bargaining originally was obstructed in various ways, until Parliament in 1906 declared that no civil action would lie against a "trade combination" for any act done by it or its agents in pursuance of a trade dispute. The trade-union law applies equally to all "trade combinations," whether of management or of labor. An employer association or voluntary cartel thus comes under the trade-union law; it has been exempt from criminal prosecution since 1876 and from civil action since 1908, and it is eligible for registration and protection of its funds as if it were a friendly society. Because British trade unions are not corporate bodies, they can sue like a friendly society but cannot be sued like a business corporation. In the Taff Vale case (1901), it was held that a trade union was suable as if it were a corporation; and in the Osborne case (1909), it was held that a trade union's lawful purposes were limited to those mentioned in the act of 1876, which did not list political action. These judicial decisions were reversed by Parliament in the Trades Disputes Act of 1906 and the Trade Union Act of 1913, respectively, which thus restored the original law.

Jurisdictional disputes between unions are settled, not by the government, but by the General Council of the Trades Union Congress. The procedure worked out by the unions in 1923-24 calls for all such disputes to be submitted to the council's "disputes committee" for settlement, in consultation with an advisory council composed of all unions engaged in each particular industry. Any union that fails to abide by this procedure is subject to risk of suspension or disaffiliation.

Record of Unionism. The legal implications of any widespread sympathetic strike or of any action bordering on a general strike are somewhat uncertain. It is doubtful whether such a strike is protected as a trade dispute; and, if called by a union's officers in breach of the union's registered rules, it may expose them personally to damage suits. No case involving a general strike, however, has yet been appealed to the House of Lords. For twenty years (1927-46) an act was on the statute book declaring illegal any strike with an object other than a trade dispute within the trade or industry in which the strikers were engaged, or calculated to coerce the government either directly or indirectly by inflicting hardship on the public. But this legislation has been repealed. There remains an emergency powers act of 1920 that permits the government to safeguard vital services for a short time whenever a strike is threatened "of such a nature and on so extensive a scale as to be calculated, by interfering with the supply and distribution of food, water, fuel, or light, or with the means of locomotion, to deprive the community or any substantial portion of the community of the essentials of life." This power has been used in several emergencies.

The union shop, under which certain categories of worker are expected to join a union after obtaining a job, is common practice in some British industries. In publicly owned trading enterprises, the union shop is normal, but it does not apply to other kinds of government work. The closed shop, in which certain categories of worker are recruited only from among trade-union members, is common only among those skilled craftsmen who run their own hiring halls, such as printers. Use of the union shop or the closed shop is entirely a matter of custom or agreement; it is enforced by the sanction of the strike. There are no laws upon the subject, nor any declarations of public policy, except in so far as the government is itself an employer.

For the prevention of industrial disputes, "joint councils" of management and labor were promoted by Mr. Speaker Whitley during World War I. An industrial court was established by statute in 1919 to give nonobligatory awards in disputes voluntarily submitted to it.

Current Problems. The strongest stress in present-day Britain is neither on the granting of liberties and privileges to unions, nor on the curbing of their power, but on the opening of more and bigger opportunities for them to participate in the raising of industrial productivity. Production committees with union representation have become usual in every pit, yard, or shop. Union representatives are always appointed to governmental "working parties," and union representation on industrial boards and councils has been insisted upon by statute for the past twenty years. The unions as such have no place in the management of nationalized industries, but many trade-union officials have been appointed to the boards of directors of these industries. Moreover, constant consultation as well as collective bargaining is the accepted practice. During World War II, a National Joint Advisory Committee, composed of equal numbers of representatives of management and labor, was set up by the Ministry of Labor to consult with it upon all administrative regulations on conditions of employment. This body proved so useful that it has been carried over into peacetime.

Most British trade unions have regarded Communists as a "disruptive element" and since about 1927 have barred them from official posts or from appointment as delegates to the Trades Union Congress. The principal exceptions are the South Wales coal miners and the East London furniture makers, in whose unions Communists have continued to hold high office. There are no laws against Communist leadership of unions. In every respect, British trade unions are trusted to govern themselves and are encouraged to participate responsibly in carrying on the nation's business.

Professional Bodies: Lawyers. Many privileges have been granted to an increasing number of professions, such as law, medicine, and teaching.[13] The legal profession is divided in England into two branches—barristers and solicitors. The former monopolize the right to appear as advocates before the highest courts, and the latter monopolize the right to deal directly with litigants and clients; the two together have a duopoly in the drafting of legal documents for a fee.

Barristers are admitted to practice by the so-called benchers of one of the four inns of court in London. These are clubs six hundred years old, whose benchers lay down the qualifications for admission to their bars, administer their rules, disbar those whose conduct lets down the profession, and promote to benchers those whose conduct does it honor. The ethics and etiquette of the inns rest largely on immemorial custom; such, for example, is the rule that a barrister able to confine himself to advocacy may apply to the Lord Chancellor for recognition as a "King's Counsel" (KC). When the government wishes to consult with the bar, it approaches it through the Bar Council, organized in 1894 and elected by members of the profession.

Solicitors are the lineal descendants of attorneys at common law and solicitors at equity. To them is open the Law Society, a voluntary body on which Parliament has conferred the power to administer the statutory rules for the admission of solicitors. The society makes regulations about law examinations (subject to veto by a committee of judges), keeps a register of all who are admitted to practice, and shares responsibility with the judges for setting scales of solicitors' fees. Misconduct may cause a fine or erasure from the register, inflicted by a committee of the Law Society judicially appointed.

Physicians. Doctors may join the British Medical Association, a voluntary body incorporated as a "limited company not for profit" under the Companies Act. It has no legal powers over the profession. Its first achievement was the passage of the Medical Act of 1858, under which a General Medical Council and a general register to cover all medical practitioners were set up. Registration was made conditional on the practitioner's being licensed by a professional corporation or university that met the educational standards approved by the General Medical Council. The council is a mixed body, representing the registered practitioners, the Crown, the old professional corporations, and the new university medical schools. Any practitioner may be deregistered by the council who is convicted by a court of a crime or by the council of "infamous conduct in any professional respect." The chartered professional corporations (Royal College of Physicians, 1518; Royal College of Surgeons, 1745; Society of Apothecaries, 1617) survived as licensing authorities, empowered also to build up the prestige of leading licentiates by granting them membership.

Another achievement of the British Medical Association, in addition to

[13] See especially A. M. Carr-Saunders and P. A. Wilson, *The Professions* (Oxford, 1933).

raising the status of all practitioners, has been its championship of those many doctors who work for public authorities. The association prevents the advertising in the medical press of vacant positions for which the salary is below its standard scale. It warns applicants against authorities paying less than the scale. And it negotiates with the government on the fees to be paid to "panel doctors" under the national health service laws, reinforcing its negotiations with threats by the doctors not to cooperate in the scheme unless the terms granted are acceptable to the association.

Teachers. Teachers began as salaried employees dependent on a denominational or a local education body. The recent improvement in their status is due to the pressure of a number of voluntary associations, among which the biggest is the National Union of Teachers, an unincorporated association dating from 1870, not registered as a trade union. These associations have obtained for teachers the right to be co-opted to local education authorities. They have freed them from the more humiliating aspects of dependence on the employing body and especially have obtained for women the right to continue their professional work after marriage. Above all, in 1919 the associations obtained the establishment of a standing committee of representatives of teachers' organizations and local authorities. This committee has now laid down a national standard scale of teachers' salaries, enforced by local teachers' strikes and by threats of the Ministry of Education to reduce its grants.

These professions are examples of the British practice of utilizing the voluntary organizations of professional men and women as useful instruments of responsible self-government, even to the extent of conferring on them a measure of jurisdiction over fellow members of their profession.

6. Universities

Bases of Academic Freedom. As training places for civil servants and statesmen, British universities have a high importance. It is all the greater in view of their selective character and the comparatively small proportion of the population that goes to the universities.[14] Their freedom as self-governing corporations and the freedom of their students and staffs are also of constitutional significance.[15] This freedom owes much to several facts.

---

[14] "Higher education" does not mean quite the same thing in different countries. Comparative figures may therefore be misleading. It is usually reckoned that in the United States, before World War II, one in every 250 of the population was at college or the university; on the European continent or in Scotland, one in 500; in Wales, one in 750; and in England, one in 1,000.

[15] On British universities, see Abraham Flexner, *Universities, American, English, German* (Oxford, 1931); F. H. Swift, *European Policies of Financing Public Educational Institutions* (Berkeley, 1939); J. H. Goldthorpe, "British Universities and the Government," *American Association of University Professors Bulletin*, 30 (1947), 474 ff.; Lord President of the Council's Committee on Scientific Manpower (chairman, A. Barlow), *Report* (Cmd. 6824 [1946]); Committee on Provision for Social and Economic Research (chairman, J. Clapham), *Report* (Cmd. 6868 [1946]).

One is that there are so few universities—eleven in England, four in Scotland, and one each in Wales and Northern Ireland—that it is comparatively easy for them to be adequately financed. No charter is granted without an endowment of £1 million. British universities are therefore relatively free from pressure by big money, and they never have fund-raising campaigns. The principal pressure is that of local industries eager to see an expansion of technological research and training in directions of their special interest. Pressure to influence the political and economic attitudes of the universities is less apparent; lack of adaptability to new ideas on their part arises mainly from their deep-seated conservatism.

In order that a small number of strong universities may be built up, rather than a large number of weak ones, the government never charters more than one university in any one city. As far as possible, it avoids having more than one university in the same region. No charter is granted for a denominational university. The formerly Anglican universities of Oxford, Cambridge, and Durham have been compelled by Parliament to abolish all religious tests for both staff and students; the newer universities never had any such tests. Nor is there any distinction between state and private universities. Every university has its own endowments and also receives public funds from both local government and the Treasury. The broad basis of this financial support—public and private, religious and secular, national and local—is one of the guarantees of independence.

Another factor that has aided in this development is the English distinction between a *university* for examining students and granting degrees and a *college* as a place of learning and teaching, with the examining university envisaged as a federation of teaching colleges. Oxford and Cambridge became loose federations of teaching colleges in the seventeenth century. London evolved into a similar federation of nonresidential schools and colleges by 1898, and Wales by 1893.

Security and Stability. Although there are no legal guarantees of tenure in a British university, it is a well-established custom that anyone who has survived an initial term appointment may regard his position as a kind of "parson's freehold," held during "good behavior" and not at the pleasure of any individual or governing body. The academic opportunities for intolerance in Britain lie less in defective tenure than in defective recruitment. Co-optation is the usual method of selection; it inevitably tends to make every college and university into a self-perpetuating closed corporation.

Academic freedom in Britain does not include the right of everyone who can pass certain tests to hang out his shingle and offer courses. One consequence is a remarkable hesitancy to open up new fields of study. In all England, for example, there are less than half a dozen chairs of political science; the same thing is true of sociology. In many teaching colleges, including some of the largest, liberal arts faculties include no specialists in social sciences other than history, philosophy, and, in some cases, psychology. Only

Oxford has developed an effective major in this whole field of the social sciences. Many of the shortcomings as well as the merits of civil service recruitment thus spring from the nature of the British universities.

Governmental Influence. The sovereignty of Parliament is called into play from time to time to effect reforms that the universities seem incapable of achieving themselves; for in Britain there are no constitutional obstacles to statutory revision of charters. Oxford was thus reformed in 1854-71—ecclesiastical privileges being abolished and scholarships opened to competition instead of being reserved for members of specific localities or particular families. The way to statutory reform is usually paved with inquiry and report by a royal commission. The other principal method of governmental influence is through financial aid. This aid has become necessary only with the rise of natural science and technology and the consequent need for constant and heavy capital outlay on new and expensive equipment. In order the better to maintain their liberty, British universities have insisted on receiving their grants not through the Ministry of Education, with its tradition of close regulation and supervision of all recipients of grants, but directly from the Treasury. Allocation of the grants among recipients is entrusted by the Treasury to a university grants committee composed of representatives of the universities themselves.

These grants are now rising sharply. Recurring grants are to average £10 million each year during the quinquennium 1947-52, and capital grants are also to be made. The grants committee is ceasing to be merely the recipient of requests; it is becoming for the first time an instrument for implementing certain aspects of governmental policy, such as an increase in the numbers of medical practitioners and of students of underdeveloped areas of the world. In short, British universities are strongholds of corporate liberty, of high status and considerable dignity, commanding the respect of the government as of the people. They need the occasional intervention of the state in order to keep them in step with the evolution of society, but tend on the whole toward increasing cooperation with the state in the implementation of its policies.

7. Four Countries in One

The United Kingdom. The United Kingdom of Great Britain and Northern Ireland was formed by the gradual merging of four countries under the sovereignty of one King and one Parliament. Whether it is a one-nation state (as France claims to be) or a multinational state (as Switzerland takes pride in being) is a problem of nomenclature that is never raised. Patriotism has in it nothing exclusive; it is possible to love Scotland as well as England, Northern Ireland as well as Wales.

The people in one of these four countries—England—outnumber the inhabitants of the three others by six to one. This fact, however, has not prevented official recognition of difference. In one case—Scotland—this national difference was recognized in a freely negotiated Act of Union (1707). In both other cases—Wales and Northern Ireland—it has been conceded in the twentieth century as a step of political expediency. In all cases, such recognition has involved territorial organization.

The United Kingdom, from 1801 to 1921, was a unitary state; and for the most part it still is. Recognition of nationality has been a form of decentralization. Authority that could have been exercised by the central government has been devolved upon regional bodies, with the region defined in these three instances on historic grounds, in every case tallying with significant differences of culture pattern and social attitude. The degree of devolution varies greatly. It goes furthest in Northern Ireland, less far in Scotland, and least far in Wales.

Northern Ireland. Northern Ireland has had its own Cabinet, Parliament, and civil service since 1921. To Cabinet and Parliament many responsibilities have been devolved in practice. Yet Northern Ireland is still represented at Westminster and is part of the United Kingdom so far as customs duties, postal communications, defense, and foreign policy are concerned. It may legislate for itself—and, if it so pleases, consult with Eire— on its public utilities, its social services, and its agriculture. Its legislation, however, may be overridden by that of the United Kingdom, which is in all respects paramount. The relationship between Northern Ireland and the United Kingdom somewhat resembles a federal relationship in fact—though not in law; but no other part of the British Isles has a comparable link with the central government. Under the Government of Ireland Act of 1920, Southern Ireland had been intended to occupy a similar position, yet chose in 1921 to abandon its link with Westminster.[16]

The six counties that were selected to be joined together as Northern Ireland have many characteristics that set them apart from the remaining counties. In politics, they have a slight unionist majority. In religion, they have a slight Presbyterian majority, descended from seventeenth-century Scottish colonists. In economic life, they have a highly developed manufacturing industry, based on coal from near-by Scotland. In social structure, they have a large and wealthy urban middle class, and considerable labor organization.

At the same time, Northern Ireland has many of the characteristics of the South. In particular, it has a large minority of political nationalists and religious Catholics, whose attitude toward Eire is one of irredentism. Northern Ireland is in fact the meeting place of two national minorities—the Presbyterian and unionist Ulstermen, who feel themselves a minority in relation to the Catholic, nationalist, and republican majority of Irishmen; and the Catholic nationalists and republicans, who feel themselves a minority in

---

[16] "Home rule"—in the British sense—applies to either of these forms of self-government: a subordinate quasi-federal relationship, such as was granted Northern Ireland in 1921, or dominion status, such as Southern Ireland achieved 1922-49.

Northern Ireland and in the United Kingdom. Of these two minorities, the Protestant unionist Ulstermen have a permanent majority in Northern Ireland, thanks to the careful inclusion of only six of the eight counties of Ulster and the careful districting of the six into parliamentary constituencies. Only a more rapid increase in the Roman Catholic than in the Presbyterian population would be likely to upset this unionist majority.

Scotland. Scotland gave up its own parliament in 1707. Since 1881, it has had in the House of Commons its own standing committee on Scottish bills, on which all members from Scotland sit, and which consequently may well have a majority opposed to the government of the day. Administration is concentrated in a Scottish Office, located in Edinburgh, staffed by Scots, and represented in the Cabinet by a Scotsman as Secretary of State for Scotland. Here is a perfect example of what the French would call "administrative autonomy." It has for Scotsmen the advantage that when they have business with a central department they have only to go to Edinburgh. Nor is governmental machinery the only institution that makes Scotland different. Its established church is presbyterian. The royal family, when in Scotland, conforms to what is there the church by law established.

Thanks to the influence of the kirk, education has long been more widespread in Scotland than in England; and, in Scotland as in the United States, it does not hurt a man in his career to have been at a publicly provided school. In law also, Scotland differs somewhat from England. Instead of coming under the influence of the English common law, it "received" the Roman law from the Continent in the fifteenth century. It still cherishes its own procedures, principles, terminology, courts, and bar. Many laws have to be separately enacted to make them apply to Scottish conditions; special care has always to be taken to have at least one Scot as a law lord. Indeed, the principal reason for retaining the appellate jurisdiction of the House of Lords is that this body is the only common tribunal for the whole of the United Kingdom.

Scotland is a poor country, with bad housing, high mortality, high illegitimacy, and a high emigration rate. Such industry and commerce as it has, it owes largely to the right to trade with the English empire after 1707; Glasgow, for example, was built on Virginia tobacco and Sea Island cotton. Scottish nationalism has therefore never been able to blame the English for Scottish poverty. Ever since the time of Robert Burns, Sir Walter Scott, and Robert Chalmers, nationalism has concentrated on a romantic attachment to Scotland's historic institutions, rather than on any demand for separation from England. What Scotland needs is not home rule but a TVA; it has now found one in the North of Scotland Hydroelectric Board, established in 1944 and financed by Scottish banks to redevelop the highlands by selling power to the lowlands.

Wales. Wales is a problem for which it has proved less easy to devise a political solution. Half of its two million people speak Welsh. Welsh is the language of instruction in many publicly provided schools in Wales, because any local education authority is free to use a language other than English. Wales is a land of scattered hamlets rather than of nucleated villages. In religion, it is a land of evangelical chapels rather than of parish churches. The Anglican church failed to keep the loyalty of the Welsh people and was disestablished in 1914. Lack of old educational endowments made it necessary to provide secondary schools at public expense a generation earlier than in England. Politically, Wales became first a stronghold of the Liberal party and then of Labor—the former because its farmers were freeholders instead of tenants like the English, and the latter because of the industries of South Wales.

Yet Wales is not geographically a unity. Instead of being united by central lowlands as Scotland is, it is cut in two by its central mountains. It has no city to which all roads lead easily. It has no historic capital. When the United Kingdom is marked out into regions, whether for electric power or for hospitals, the temptation is to center North Wales on Liverpool and South Wales on Bristol, neither of which is in Wales. In education, Wales now has its own permanent advisory council; but in most respects it has not lent itself to regional administration. It has neither home rule, like Northern Ireland, nor administrative autonomy, like Scotland. It has neither its own national church nor its own national law. It does have its annual cultural assembly, the Eisteddfod, but this owes nothing to government.

When a bill before the House relates exclusively to Wales, the standing committee to which it is referred is reinforced with all the members of Parliament for Welsh constituencies. A Council for Wales, representing management and labor, central and local government, the University of Wales and the Eisteddfod, meets quarterly to review the impact of administrative action on Welsh welfare.

Diversity in Unity. The British Isles include not only the two principal islands of Great Britain and Ireland, with all the former and part of the latter joined together politically in the United Kingdom, but also a number of smaller islands, not all of which are part either of the United Kingdom or of Eire. The Isle of Man, for example, has been ruled ever since Norse days by its House of Keys and was not subjected to the rule of Parliament at Westminster until World War II. The Channel Islands are all that remained to the Kings of England when they lost their duchy of Normandy in the thirteenth century. These are a few disconnected self-governing islands, with their own laws and their own taxes—the only part of the British Empire to be occupied by the German invaders (1940-44).

The British Isles thus are not a single political unit any more than the United Kingdom is a melting pot. Cultural diversity is deliberately and consciously cultivated, and governmental machinery is correspondingly diversified. Multiformity rather than uniformity is characteristic of the United Kingdom. Small wonder that Britons have been successful in devising political structures enabling British and French to live together in Canada and British and Afrikaner in South Africa. It was in the British Isles themselves that they learned to find practical solutions to the psychological problem of national feeling.

Two things symbolize this diversity in unity. The one is the national flag—the Union Jack, compounded of the crosses of St. George of England, St. Andrew of Scotland (since 1707), and St. Patrick of Ireland (since 1801). The other is the lack of a national holiday both for the United Kingdom as a whole and for its component parts. St. George's, St. Andrew's, St. David's, St. Patrick's, and Orange days are occasions for unofficial celebration in all parts of the world, but not for official celebration in the countries of origin.

CHAPTER 7

MAIN FUNCTIONS OF GOVERNMENT

1. Economic Planning

Rise of Planning. In modern times, one of the chief characteristics of Western countries has been governmental responsibility for the "regulation of commerce." Government is expected to pursue a policy favorable to economic enterprise. Government and business together can thus work for the strength of the state and the wealth of the nation. As eighteenth-century utilitarians would have put it, government policy must be directed toward making the general interest of the country coincide with the particular interests of its inhabitants.

In pursuit of this end, government in Britain has followed different policies, and has therefore needed different organs, in different epochs. From about 1390 to about 1820, the general policy was that known as mercantilism. Its net effect was to sweep away all internal barriers to the movement of goods and persons within the British Isles and to direct British capital to the development of sea transport, the planting of colonies, and the exploitation of the East Indies.[1] From about 1820 to about 1930, the general policy was that known as *laissez faire.* Its net effect was to make it easy for business concerns to decide for themselves whether or not to compete, and to open British ports to the ships and products of all nations in order that Britain's manufacturing industries might be aided by cheap food, cheap raw material, and cheap transportation.[2] Since about 1930, Britain has become a "planning state," in which once again the government is expected to supply the general framework for economic enterprise—not by regulation as in the epoch of mercantilism, nor by nonregulation as in the epoch of *laissez faire,* but principally by provision of essential services.[3]

In planning its economic services, present-day Britain is especially conscious of two new needs: better location of industry and maintenance of a high and stable level of employment.

---

[1] For comparison of British with other kinds of mercantilism, see E. F. Heckscher, *Mercantilism* (London, 1935).

[2] The best studies of British *laissez faire* are A. V. Dicey, *Lectures on the Relations Between Law and Public Opinion in England* (rev. ed., Toronto, 1905); J. H. Clapham, *Economic History of Britain* (rev. ed., Toronto, 1938); and Elie Halévy, *History of the English People* (New York, 1938). In contrast, see D. N. Chester, ed., *Lessons of the British War Economy* (Cambridge, 1951).

[3] See W. H. Wickwar, *Social Services* (rev. ed., London, 1949), *Public Services* (London, 1938), and "Social Democracy in the British Commonwealth," *Journal of Politics,* 9 (1947), 239 ff.; also, United Nations, *Methods of Social Welfare Administration* (New York, 1950).

Location of Industry. The unplanned location of industry has resulted in what in Britain is regarded as maldistribution. Certain regions of the North and West have become dependent upon single industries, such as coal, cotton, or shipbuilding. The interwar decline in these export industries produced "depressed areas" whose population could not find employment without migrating. At the same time, London, the "home counties" (around London), and the Midlands (around Birmingham) attracted new light industries and an ever growing population.

For individual business concerns, there were economic gains in establishing themselves in the Southeast, especially in short hauls and nearness to customers. There were also social advantages for management, in offering labor nearness to more attractive living conditions. The country as a whole, however, suffered economic waste, in that capital outlay was required for new housing and community facilities in the Southeast at a time when the housing and community facilities of the North and West were being abandoned. The country also suffered social waste, in the breaking up of families by migration of young workers. Finally, there was military danger, owing to the concentration of vulnerability in the corner of the island nearest the Continent. Diversification and balance of industry therefore became the goal of national policy, upon recommendations from a royal commission in 1940 and by an act of Parliament passed by the wartime coalition in 1945.[4]

Securing Full Employment. Maintenance of a high and stable level of employment has commended itself to Britain no less than to all other countries that experienced the great depression of 1929-33. In the United Kingdom, cyclical unemployment coincided with severe "structural unemployment," owing to changes in the economy and, especially, to the contraction of some of the stable export industries. Thus, the problem of high and stable employment overlapped that of distribution of industry. To solve the problem of cyclical fluctuations, additional measures were needed.

These, as analyzed in the "white paper" on employment policy in 1944, were envisaged primarily as government action, in peacetime as in wartime, to ensure the stable expansion of national income and outgo. National outlay on consumer goods was held to be comparatively easy to stabilize, by such measures as social security and tax variation. The principal difficulties were seen in the stabilization of investment in new capital and the stabilization of markets in raw-material and food-producing countries.[5]

Land-use Planning. To promote the government's new economic and social ends, several new governmental means have been devised. One of these is positive land-use planning. The negative or regulatory form of

[4] Cf. Royal Commision on Distribution of Industry (chairman, Sir M. Barlow), *Report* (Cmd. 6153 [1940]).

[5] See above, chap. 6, "Liberty and Opportunity," sec. 2, "Changing Concepts of Human Rights." On such new machinery as the Economic Planning Board, see H. W. Davey, "The Experience of Other Countries," in a symposium on formulation of economic programs, *American Political Science Review*, 42 (1948), 297 ff.

land-use planning that consisted in zoning land for various kinds of use no longer appears adequate. It is supplemented by positive inducements to industry to locate in certain places rather than in others. One such inducement is the "trading estate"—a project operated by a government corporation offering favorable leases of factory space to new industrial concerns. Another is the "new town." This project is a complete new community, developed by a government corporation, with its own trading estate, housing projects, and community facilities. A third inducement is the utilization of the power of eminent domain to obtain sites for private manufacturing concerns. Still another is the opening in every region of information centers to help manufacturers locate their new factories.

All these facilities together are aimed at minimizing the location of new industry in London and maximizing its location in outlying parts of the metropolitan region or in formerly depressed "development areas." Creation of new towns is the responsibility of the Ministry of Local Government and Planning. All other aspects of government aid in the location of industry are operated by the Board of Trade.[6]

Capital Investment. Control of capital investment is also sought through other new forms of governmental action. One of these is the creation by statute of a number of "finance corporations"—whose very name is derived from such a body as the Reconstruction Finance Corporation in the United States. They use bank deposits as a means of financing new business ventures, both large and small, at low rates of interest. Although the corporations tend to be autonomous and are financed in some cases entirely from private sources, their boards of directors are selected in consultation with the government and contain many former government officials. A further means of controlling capital outlay has been developed in the power of particular ministers to give direction to an increasing number of nationalized industries, all of which are in great need of re-equipment. Then also, all borrowing on behalf of local authorities is now centralized under the Treasury. These several measures combine to give the government control over the timing of capital outlay in a large portion of the economy.

Certain more negative powers can be brought into play for the same purpose. Thus, the allocation of scarce materials may be directed toward one form of construction rather than another, with an eye to "social priorities" rather than to private profit. For example, preference is given to the building of factories for export over the building of houses, and to the building of houses over the building of theaters or commercial premises. The Capital Issues Committee of the Treasury—established originally in 1936 as a Foreign Transactions (Advisory) Committee—has some power to grant "posteriority" to the least desirable of big bank loans and big stock-exchange issues,

[6] For detailed analysis of procedures and agencies to encourage location of industry in development areas, see House of Commons, Select Committee on Estimates, *Administration of Development Areas* (May 1947).

both domestic and overseas.[7]   In case these controls are not altogether adequate, the Treasury has also set up an advisory committee on capital investment, composed of both private and governmental spokesmen.   By correlated operation of these devices, under Cabinet leadership, it is hoped to reverse the prewar tendency to deflate capital investment, both public and private, whenever national income shows signs of depression.   Under the Cabinet, major responsibility for the application of the novel stabilizing techniques rests with the Treasury.

Bulk Purchasing.   The new tools of economic planning include the "bulk purchasing agreement."   During World War II, various ministries entered into contractual arrangements with agencies in raw-material and food-producing countries overseas for the purchase of fixed quantities at a fixed price for a fixed number of years.   By this means, farmers overseas were encouraged to increase production.   Purchasing agreements between Britain and overseas countries thus played a role similar to the floor placed beneath crop prices in the United States, in helping to assure the farmer a parity of purchasing power with the industrial worker.

These agreements have been prolonged into the postwar period.   They promise to be a standard method in maintaining an "ever-normal granary" when more than one country is involved.   The principal countries covered by the agreements are, within the British Empire, Canada, New Zealand, South Africa, and the sugar colonies; and Eire, Argentina, and Denmark without it.   Responsibility for administering this policy rests with the various "purchasing ministries," which thus engage the British government in international commerce as a wholesale trader.   They may take a loss on any commodity, by selling it to the British people below cost.   Subsidization of imported food, as a technique, is made peculiarly simple by "bulking" procedure.   So is prevention of black markets in rationed goods.

Support by Economic Theory.   For these new services by government to the economy, the climate of opinion had been well prepared by a long line of British economists.   John Stuart Mill had early preached the social utility of a spirit of cooperation.   J. A. Hobson, in a long series of works (1895-1940), had enlarged on the failure of competition to meet man's basic needs.   A. C. Pigou had pointed the way toward the economics of welfare.   Above all, J. M. (later Lord) Keynes, in his *General Theory of Employment, Interest, and Money* (1936), had woven together the various threads into a full-fledged theory of an expanding yet stable economy, provided that government play its part in so planning its outlay as to stabilize the expansion of the national income.   Keynes's position became in Britain a new standard of economic orthodoxy.   "Full employment," regarded by him as an attainable and desirable goal, became an article of common agreement in the platforms of all parties.   When governmental outlay brought full employment

[7] Cf. Chancellor of the Exchequer, *Capital Issues Control* (Cmd. 6645 [1945]).

in World War II for almost the first time in twenty years, it seemed as though the Keynesian doctrines had been demonstrated and that what had been done in wartime could be done also in peacetime and by the same agency—government.

The test of this policy will come not during the immediate postwar years, when there is an abundance of jobs that need doing, but during the subsequent period when deflation and depression again become a possibility. Such a possibility, according to British economic thinking, can be avoided by governmental planning of the size of the national income and the direction of its use.

2. Nationalization

Monopoly and Public Control.   In every land of free enterprise, certain sectors of the economy exist that are so vital to all other sectors that they are regarded as being "affected with a public interest." In the United States, such undertakings as transportation, communication, and electric power are normally subject to a dual control, in which private ownership and management are combined with public regulation.   In the United Kingdom, it is considered economically sounder and more efficient to subject these same sectors of the economy to a unified control.   Since this control cannot be private, it must be public.[8]   It is an old doctrine among British economists, and one propounded in particular by the younger Mill, that a monopoly, when more useful than competition, should be under public control; and that it is simpler and cheaper to achieve such control by concentrating full responsibility in the public as owners than by dividing managerial responsibility between private managers and public regulators.

British economic historians also stress the rise during the past generation of the monster corporation with millions of stockholders.   Most of these do not directly participate in the choice of directors or the determination of policy, but leave effective control in the hands of a self-perpetuating managerial nucleus.   From such combination of diffused ownership and concentrated managerial direction, it is but a step to the still wider diffusion of ownership in the public at large as citizens.   At the same time, through the political process, a chain of responsibility of management to the public is forged by public ownership.

These historical interpretations and economic theories are so widely held that public ownership has been advanced by each political party, Conservative, Labor, and Liberal.   The only significant debate concerns the size of the economic sector to which this policy shall be applied.   Until 1949 it covered only those essential service industries that usually are or ought to be monopolies.   It did not extend to industries that manufacture for general public use, however monopolistic they may be, and whether they contribute mainly to the production of capital goods (as with steel) or to that of

---

[8] Cf. W. A. Robson, ed., *Public Enterprise* (London, 1937), and references above, note 3.

consumer goods (as with chemicals). Political discussion, however, has since shifted to this field, with the completion of the long process of subjecting essential service industries to public ownership and control.

National versus Local Control. At one time there was not much controversy about the level at which public ownership and control should be achieved. Fabian socialists even made a point of stressing the value of municipalization, rather than nationalization. They had their eye mainly on municipal utilities such as gas, electricity, water, and transit; and they were willing to demonstrate the success of municipalization before proceeding to nationalization. Three factors, however, have now swung the balance the other way.

One is the obvious inadequacy of operating on a merely local scale, especially when every municipality has spilled over into suburbia. Another is the Keynesian emphasis on the need for controlling national outgo in general and capital outlay in particular; this control obviously needs to be nationwide in order to be effective. A third factor, one that has been present all the time, is the legal principle that a business concern may not secure a franchise or the right of eminent domain, nor a local authority the right to expropriate such an undertaking, except by act of Parliament. Hence, all policy concerning business affected with a public interest must be made at the national level.[9] For these reasons, less is heard today about public ownership in general and more about nationalization in particular.

Nationalization Procedure. The industries thus far nationalized are: the telegraph (1868); the telephone (trunk 1892, local 1911); electricity (wholesale 1926, retail 1947); radio (1927); London passenger transport (1933); coal (mineral rights 1938, mining 1946); civil aviation (1929-46); central banking (1946); cables and wireless (1946); railways, road haulage, canals, and docks (1947); gas (1948); and iron and steel (1950). Most of these service industries were subject to public regulation before being transferred to public ownership. Some were also dependent upon public financing, either by Treasury guarantees for their borrowing or by outright subsidies. In every case, the private enterprises had enjoyed publicly conferred privileges that in one way or another limited the entry of competitors into the industry. In none of these cases can it be fairly said that free competitive enterprise was any longer a practicable alternative to nationalization.

In almost every instance, nationalization has been effected by statute. The procedure by which compensation is to be awarded to former owners has also been fixed by statute; and no court has any right or power to say that anyone is being deprived of property without due process of law, so long as the ex-

---

[9] Two procedures have been used: (1) Parliament has laid down general principles in a public general act known as a "clauses act"; each individual case has then been provided for by a special or local act, with the private bill committee to report on compliance with the general law. (2) Parliament has laid down general principles in a public general act delegating powers to a central department; each individual case has then been provided for by provisional order, wayleave, or license granted by the department.

propriation is in accordance with act of Parliament. It would in fact be lawful for Parliament, in the exercise of its sovereignty, to take private property without any compensation at all. But this has never been done; it would be contrary to the principles of each of the parties as well as to the customs of the realm. There is, however, room for differences of procedure in determining what compensation to award. The cost of nationalization is shown in the accompanying table.

COST OF NATIONALIZATION TO THE BRITISH GOVERNMENT

Industry	Price Paid (£ millions)	Other Capital Immediately Invested (£ millions)
Telegraph, 1868	8.0	2.0
Telephone:		
Trunk, 1892	0.5	1.8
Local, 1911	12.0	100.0
Radio, 1927	0.07	1.0
Civil Aviation, 1939	3.2	——
Coal:		
Mineral, 1938	67.0	——
Collieries, 1946	165.0	150.0
Railways, 1947	900.0	250.0
Electricity, 1947	355.0	——
Gas, 1948	——	——
Iron and Steel, 1950	——	——

The first procedure, used when purchasing the telegraph in 1868, was the same as the one by which railway companies and other privately owned undertakings as a compulsory process acquired land for constructing their "public utilities." Each side appointed arbitrators, who appointed an umpire. The umpire calculated what the property was worth to the seller, then added a solatium to compensate him for being unwilling to sell, next made a further addition to compensate for the vanished hope of higher income in a rising market, and finally added an allowance to cover cost of finding another equally good investment. The next procedure, used when buying the telephone exchanges in 1911, was to have the seller's plant valued as it was; in this case the plant was all that the company had, as it had reached the end of its lease. A third procedure, used when purchasing the Bank of England, was to give to holders of stock the amount of government securities that would enable them to continue to receive exactly the same income. A fourth and very important procedure, used first when purchasing the mineral rights to coal and next when purchasing the coal mines, has been to set up a special arbitration tribunal. The tribunal determined the yearly income that the owners might reasonably expect ("net maintainable revenue") and then the number of "years' purchase" by which to multiply this figure in order to arrive at a capital value. A fifth procedure, used principally when purchasing the railways, power distributors, and iron and steel, has been to give government-guaranteed stock of a market value equal to the stock-market valuation of the seller's stock. A sixth, used with radio, civil aviation, and cables and wireless, has been to negotiate a settlement that is agreeable both to the seller and to the government.

Management of Nationalized Undertakings. More important is the organization for managing the nationalized undertakings. To this problem there have been two different approaches. Before the First World War, nationalized undertakings were merged in the post office and became the direct responsibility of the Postmaster General. The alternative method came with the invention of the government-owned corporation, with its government-appointed board of directors and its self-balancing financial structure.[10]

Use of the alternative method has raised important new problems of relationship between government corporations and the Cabinet. The principle generally accepted is that all government corporations come within the scope of one or another of the central departments, so that a minister is answerable in Parliament and in public for the corporation's policies, but not for details of day-by-day management, which is left to the corporation, subject to direction from the responsible minister on major matters of policy—such as the timing of capital outlay or measures to make coal mining less unattractive. The corporation's annual report is submitted to Parliament; it includes ministerial policy directives. Opportunities are provided for a discussion of the report, although no appropriation estimates are normally needed. Lastly, Cabinet approval is needed before the limits for Treasury-guaranteed borrowing can be hiked; these limits are usually somewhat narrowly drawn.

3. Social Services

The Economic Floor. In the early years of the twentieth century, Sidney and Beatrice Webb coined the phrase the "national minimum." The idea behind this phrase was that everyone who lived under a modern economy had a right to a minimum standard of living. The standard might cost a different amount in different localities, but in essence it would everywhere consist of the same opportunities. Instead of the state ensuring such a minimum only to convicts, soldiers, and sailors, it would ensure it to all its

---

[10] The British origin of this new type of governmental instrumentality is obscure. From the United States it seems to have been introduced into Britain by Conservatives in the 1920's. The only British antecedent would seem to be the regional board of commissioners, indirectly elected like the Metropolitan Water Board, or elected by a special constituency, as with the Port of London Authority. There is, however, considerable difference between a regional board of commissioners and a government corporation, in that the governing body of the former is elected from below, whereas that of the latter is appointed from above. In Britain, there seems to be some confusion between the two types, illustrated by use of different titles and by statutory commissioning of directors to exercise managerial functions individually as well as to determine policy collectively. British government corporations pay the same taxes as other corporations.

citizens. No one would be prevented from rising above this minimum; everyone would be prevented from falling below it. It would be a floor, not a ceiling.

This concept has appealed to men and women with a wide range of social attitudes. Those Conservatives who regard themselves as "Tory democrats" have attached great value to the re-creation of an atmosphere of social solidarity, which makes everyone feel that he has a place in the community. They expect the nation-state of today to mean as much to its members as the manorial village of the past. Liberals like Keynes and Beveridge have linked this attitude with their "full employment" economics, in which fear of poverty ceases to be a dominant economic drive. Socialists have viewed the socialization of income and the socialization of industry as equally integral parts of socialism.

The "floor beneath living standards" has a number of aspects. It includes income security, education, health, housing, and civic planning, all carried far enough to ensure "minimum adequacy." These governmental activities have been given the name "social services." [11]

Income Security. Income security is at present provided under a series of laws passed in 1945-48. It has two principal sides. For workers it means the assurance of minimum wages, whether through collective bargaining (applicable to about half the labor force) or by order of wage councils (for the other half). For those who are not at any given moment workers, it means the availability of family allowances, national insurance, and national assistance.

Family allowances are made half in cash, paid to the mother through the post office, and half in kind, in the form of school meals. The former is available on behalf of all children after the first; the latter, on behalf of children attending school. Family allowances are financed entirely out of national taxes. They are administered on behalf of children as children, without any investigation of means and needs.

National insurance is available at a flat rate of benefit to all who have qualified by payment of the requisite number of contributions. Insurance covers all instances in which earned income ceases by reason of temporary sickness, chronic invalidity, work injuries, retirement, old age, widowhood, orphanhood, or temporary unemployment, and is also paid on certain occasions of heavy expense, such as birth or death. Contributions, like benefits, are at flat rates, but are tripartite, being charged in approximately equal portions to employers, employees, and general taxation. National assistance means monetary aid to those who have not qualified for national insurance or whose national insurance benefits are inadequate to meet their needs. Some recip-

---

[11] The term "social services" has been used in Britain since 1913 by way of contrast with "debt services" and "defense services." It covers all benefactory services of direct assistance to individuals and has been contrasted since the 1930's with the "public services" (described in the preceding section), which are also benefactory, but assist the individual only indirectly.

ients are people who live in high-cost areas such as London.

Welfare Services. All income security having become a national responsibility, local poor-relief was finally abolished in 1948. Local authorities—counties and county boroughs—remain responsible for only those forms of assistance which do not involve the granting of money income. Residential accommodation is provided for the aged, infirm, and subnormal in homes or hostels as near to their former residences as possible. Home, board, and care are here available below cost at a standard rate, so fixed as to permit recipients of national insurance benefits and national assistance allowances to pay it and still retain some pocket money. Temporary accommodation is provided for persons whose family arrangements have broken down. Children deprived of normal home life are placed in foster families. Clubs may be provided for the aged, handicrafts for the infirm, sheltered workshops for the handicapped, and counseling on available services. In short, wherever the chief need is for guidance and neighborliness, local initiative is encouraged; but where the chief need is for distribution of spending power, national responsibility is recognized.

For the two different kinds of work—administering income security and providing welfare services—two different kinds of personnel are required. Adjudication of claims to family allowances, insurance benefits, and assistance allowances involves a comparatively simple determination of facts and a checking of these facts against the law. It is a kind of clerical and administrative work for which general education is useful but special training hardly necessary. On the other hand, provision of welfare services and maintenance of morale in special residential accommodations calls for the skill of trained professional social workers. Here each instance of need requires differentiated treatment, based on the particular situation.

All forms of income security are administered by the Ministry of National Insurance, which, in the case of national assistance, works through a subordinate operating body, the National Assistance Board. Initial decisions are made by officials of the ministry or the board; but appeals lie to tribunals of referees—usually three-member bodies appointed by the ministry, presided over by a solicitor and including one member drawn from a roster of workers' spokesmen. Welfare services, on the other hand, are locally administered under supervision of various ministries, through which grants in aid are available from the Treasury.

National Education. Education is at present provided within the framework of an education act passed under the Churchill coalition in 1944. This act divides the educational process into three phases, called primary, secondary, and further education. Primary education is compulsory from five to eleven. Most children avail themselves of publicly provided free education in what are popularly called council schools. A minority go to voluntary denominational schools, some of which are provided at public expense (subject to public control), whereas others receive public aid for maintenance only. A still smaller minority of children go to schools run for private profit but subject to public inspection and licensing.

Secondary education is compulsory from eleven to fifteen; the Ministry of Education is empowered to extend the compulsory limit to sixteen as soon as adequate facilities are available. Secondary schools fall into three educational types: modern, technical, and grammar. Modern schools are for the majority of children. Grammar schools—so called because they teach the ancient classical languages—carry up to the age of eighteen those who can qualify, preparing them for college entrance. There are four principal ways in which secondary schools of these various types are provided. Most of them are provided by the local education authority, in which case they are tuition-free. Some are provided by a religious denomination but maintained by the local education authority, in which case also they are free. Some are provided by an endowed foundation aided by a direct grant from the Ministry of Education; in these, at least one quarter of the places are free, but some places are filled by pupils who pay fees proportioned to their means. A few —mainly boarding schools—pay their own way without receiving public aid and please themselves as to what scholarships they give and what tuition fees they charge. These are as a rule proprietary "preparatory schools" (for boys and girls eleven to fourteen) and endowed "public schools" (for the ages fourteen to eighteen). Except in the case of the fee-paying minority of pupils, the decision as to which type of secondary education is appropriate to a particular child is made by examination. The examination is conducted by the local education authority on behalf of all schools that it provides or maintains, or by the school itself if it is not maintained by the local education authority.

Further education is for those who have completed their full-time schooling. It takes various forms, all of which all local education authorities are obliged to provide. One form is the young people's "county college," at which attendance one day a week is to be compulsory from school-leaving age (fifteen for most young people) to eighteen. This part-time education is regarded in Britain as a highly effective means of keeping the employment service, the health service, and the youth service in touch with the many adolescents who leave school early to go to work. A second form is vocational training, both day and evening. A third form is nonvocational adult education, which is very popular. It includes university extension lectures and "tutorial classes" sponsored by the Workers' Educational Association. A fourth form is the youth service, in which youth leaders and voluntary agencies (such as the Boy Scouts) provide for the leisure-time activities of young people (fifteen to twenty) who have left school. A fifth form is the provision of centers for leisure-time cultural training and recreation.

Special Problems of Education. Singularly complete provision is thus made for the principal phases of education, on behalf of the great mass of the British people. Responsibility for all three phases rests upon the local education authorities—counties and county boroughs—acting through their education committees. Within two years after the passage of the act of 1944, they had to submit "development plans" to the Ministry of Education, which on this basis issued orders binding on the local education authority. The kindergarten stage (two to five) has not been given the same recognition as the three later stages. Local education authorities are supposed to provide nursery schools whenever there is reasonable demand, but of such demand they are the judges.

The university stage is outside the purview of the Ministry of Education and the local education authorities. The ministry is concerned with the universities in only two ways. It provides several hundred high-value "state scholarships," covering both tuition and maintenance. It also encourages the training of teachers within the universities, rather than in small rural training colleges. The local education authorities are also concerned with the universities in but two ways. They likewise provide many scholarships to the universities. Some authorities make contributions to the general support of a regional university and thereby earn a seat on its governing board. On the whole, however, the universities and their constituent colleges preserve a jealous autonomy. When they need financial aid, they manage to get it directly from the Treasury.

Socialized Medicine. A national health service has been long advocated by the British Medical Association. It was finally brought into its own under an act of 1946, in operation since 1948. "Preventive medicine" or "public health" remains the responsibility of local health authorities, especially counties and county boroughs, each of which has its medical officer for the purpose. This responsibility is interpreted broadly and has come to include immunization, health education, and preventive treatment, as well as health visiting, home nursing, domestic help for the sick, maternal and infant welfare centers, and clinics for school children. At the request of the medical profession, the services are now being expanded to include health centers, in which general practitioners will be able to have offices and share X-ray and other diagnostic facilities.

A general practitioner service has been provided for insured wage earners since 1911. For school children, in respect to corrective treatment, such a service has existed in many localities since 1907. For mothers in childbirth, there has been a local midwifery service since 1936. These phases are now rounded out into a general practitioner service available to all without direct payment. Each local health authority has an executive council composed one half of local practitioners, one third of representatives of the local health authority, and one sixth of ministerial nominees. The executive councils act on the advice of wholly professional medical, dental, ophthalmic, and pharmaceutical committees. In admitting new doctors to practice in their locality, the councils are governed by the determination of a central medical practices committee, which thus has the power to direct new doctors to settle in neglected rather than in oversupplied regions. Remuneration—partly by salary, partly by capitation fee—is also centrally determined. The sale of public practices is forbidden; but the state pays compensation on death or retirement for loss of the right to sell. The health service is nationally financed, partly through national insurance contributions, but mainly out of taxes. Local health authorities contribute only the health centers. General practitioners are thus free from local pressures.

A hospital and specialist-consultant service has similarly been built from a number of existing pieces. The teaching hospitals are taken as nuclei around which the country is organized into fourteen hospital regions. Within each region, a regional hospital board allocates appropriate functions to each hospital and assures adequate specialist care to each patient—a procedure that was first improvised in the emergency of World War II. All hospitals and out-patient centers—whether municipal or voluntary in origin, including tuberculosis sanatoria, mental hospitals, and venereal disease clinics—are transferred to the administration of the regional hospital boards. But these leave the business management of each particular hospital to its own management committee.

Neighborhood and Community Planning. Two different techniques have hitherto been used in Britain for town and country planning. The one has been for some large-scale landowner—such as a noble family, the Ecclesiastical Commissioners, the Crown lands office, or a garden-city company —to develop or redevelop an estate with a view to building a neighborhood or community in which human beings will find satisfaction in living. The other has been for a local authority to regulate the enterprise of real-estate subdividers, speculative builders, and small owners, especially by zoning regulations, so as to limit the extent to which a neighborhood may be spoiled. Negative regulation having proved ineffective, the stress is now on positive planning, the more so since World War II made it necessary to think in terms of redevelopment of blitzed as well as blighted areas.

Under the town and country planning legislation, all local planning authorities are permitted to develop new communities, with all appropriate public services, amenities, and conveniences for the relocated industry and population, even though the new communities be outside their old borders. The authorities are also permitted to relocate public services and private business undertakings, so that in redeveloped communities the residential neighborhoods are not broken up by industrial sites and traffic ways. Under the New Towns Act of 1946, the Ministry of Local Government and Planning designates sites for new communities and establishes development corporations with capital adequate for providing all necessary services.

With land-use development guided into governmental channels, there is obviously diminished opportunity for private speculations in real estate. This opportunity is still further lessened by the prohibition of land development without permission of the ministry and the heavy taxation of increment value whenever development is permitted. Land-use development has thus been "socialized," in the belief that planned communities are economically more efficient and socially more beneficial to those who live and work in them.

A Nonequalitarian Society. The social services do not prevent inequality; they do lessen it. Setting a floor, they do not set a ceiling. Britons may have a higher income than the guaranteed minimum. They may purchase more expensive schooling and more expensive medical care than the government provides. They may spend as much on housing as they can afford. In all these forms of consumption, great differences exist in social standards, on the whole linked with differences in wealth and income.

Most of these class distinctions exist only in custom and usage. Some, however, are written into law. Such are the provisions that government-subsidized housing shall be for members of the working classes. Other distinctions are reinforced by law. Such is the permission given to "public schools" to stand aloof from the national educational system, neither accepting public aid nor granting a statutory proportion of free places. Such also is the permission given the medical profession to render a higher level of service in private practice than under the public health service. And such is the limitation of most professions to those who can afford an expensive education. Government policy is limited to abolishing extremes of wealth and poverty, lessening the distance between the rich and the poor, and bringing their consumption levels and living standards a little nearer together.

Fiscal policy in Britain has social as well as economic and financial aims. Ever since Gladstone's days in the Exchequer, it has been taken for granted that there should be no sales taxes or excise or customs duties on absolute necessities of life, but only on conventional necessities, such as beer, whiskey, tea, and tobacco. Bulk buying of foodstuffs and housing materials has aided in subsidizing absolute necessities. Provision of health and educational services out of taxes, and also the tax contribution toward social insurance, have been veritable transfers of means from the more fortunate to the less fortunate classes of society. Moreover, income tax has been graded so that earned income shall be tax-exempt up to twice the guaranteed minimum income, whereas one with an income of £10,000 retains only £3,500; and one with £50,000, only £5,000.

4. Defense Services

Sea Power and Air Power. The British attitude toward defense services is largely determined by geography. To block invasion by Continental armies, the first line of defense has long been the Royal Navy. It has prime responsibility for preventing contraband from reaching enemy countries and for ensuring that supplies of all kinds reach Britain and Britain's allies. It must seek to blockade the enemy and prevent the siege of Britain. Because "Britain's borders are the coasts of her enemies," the British Navy has long had the same importance as that given by Continental countries to their armies.

In the decade ending 1945, air power gained an importance similar to that of sea power. In the "Battle of Britain" (1940), defense by fighter aircraft checked the damage done to seaports, naval bases, and war plants; it lessened the danger of invasion; and it prevented the cutting of Britain's lifelines. A British-based strategic bombing offensive opened up a new chance of accelerating the process of attrition.

Use of the rocket near the end of World War II—long before the atomic bomb—revolutionized Britain's defense problems. The country became for the first time vulnerable to artillery, without compensating advantages. More importance than ever had to be attached to the control of bases across the Channel.

Role of the Army. The present century has seen a great increase in the importance of the Army, not for home defense, but for service on the Continent, including occupation of enemy territory in the zone nearest the British Isles. For this reason, the size as well as the quality of the Army is a matter of serious concern.

It has become necessary to increase both the number of men under arms in peacetime and the number of reserves for mobilization in wartime. Hence the revival of universal compulsory service in peacetime in 1938 and its retention after World War II. New circumstances have compelled Britain for the first time to become a land power as well as a sea power, at a time when it has neither men nor money nor materials to spare for this task.

Defense of the Empire. The test of atomic power in 1945 has made it obviously vital to Britain's survival that it prevent war, avoid involvement in war, and decentralize its industry in the United Kingdom, as well as, perhaps, relocate part of the Kingdom's population and industry throughout the scattered Commonwealth and Empire.

The increasing vulnerability of the United Kingdom makes it impossible to defend each and every piece of colonial territory. Reduction in overseas commitments is also necessitated by shortages of capital, labor, and foreign exchange. Britain has to choose which places and routes are primarily vital, in conversations and consultations with the other countries of the Commonwealth. The share of the United Kingdom in imperial and in world-wide defense is a policy-making responsibility of the Cabinet, advised by its Defense Committee. It is also an administrative responsibility of the Minister for Defense, the First Lord of the Admiralty, the Secretaries of State for War and Air, and the Minister of Supply.

For coordination of British defense with that of other countries, several experiments have been tried. In 1918, there was an Inter-Allied War Council with its own secretariat. After 1942, there was an Anglo-American board, the Combined Chiefs of Staff, each side of which had its own secretariat. Because lack of effective strength has increasingly limited Britain's capacity to pursue an independent foreign policy, experiments with new organs for the coordination of policy with that of other countries have commended themselves.

5. Foreign Affairs

Britain's Regional Interests. Much as the United States has its Monroe Doctrine, so Britain has acquired a special interest in certain regions. The countries across the Channel—France, the Low Countries (Belgium, the Netherlands, and Luxemburg), and Germany from the Lower Rhine to the Baltic—are such a region of vital interest. For nearly four hundred years it has been a settled British policy to oppose anyone trying to unite the region under the control of a single hostile power, whether Spain (about 1600), France (about 1700 and 1800), or Germany (1914-18, 1939-45). Britain's treaty of 1839 with France and Prussia guaranteeing the neutrality and integrity of Belgium was one expression of this lasting interest. Another manifestation of the same policy of "no unification without British participation" is the Western Union, discussed with the governments-in-exile at London toward the close of World War II and organized under the Pact of Brussels (1948). The pact makes provision for a consultative council, various committees of ministers, and a military staff committee in which Britain participates along with France, Belgium, the Netherlands, and Luxemburg.

The Mediterranean has been reckoned a British lake since 1706, the British being the dominant fleet in it and the two fortresses of Gibraltar and Malta being in British hands. The principal value of Mediterranean hegemony would seem to lie in setting a limit to the southward expansion of any power that might dominate the Continent. The Mediterranean is also a convenient though not indispensable route to the Middle East. Some recent tendency for the British hegemony to be shared with the United States has so far remained without any organic arrangement for full coordination of the policies of the two countries.

The Indian Ocean has been under the controlling naval power concentrated in British hands since 1802. Around it many British interests have arisen—gold mining in South Africa, white settlements on the plateaus of Eastern Africa, oil from the Persian Gulf, jute growing in Pakistan, tea plantations in Ceylon, rubber plantations in Malaya, sheep runs in Australia. Protection of these interests is vital, because from their returns, Britain obtains most of the means of buying the products of the Americas. The Arab countries are mainly important in that their control by a hostile power would menace the peace of the Indian Ocean. With some countries of the Middle East, then, Britain has developed special relationships. In the kingdoms of Egypt, Iraq, and Jordan—as also in the republic of Burma—Britain has the treaty right to bring in military advisers and troops and use bases. In two "mixed enterprises," the government of the United Kingdom is the biggest single stockholder. These enterprises are the French-registered Suez Canal

Company and the Anglo-Iranian Oil Company, Ltd.—the latter, in turn, is a large shareholder in the petroleum undertakings of Iraq and other Arab countries. Oil royalties are the principal source of revenue to the kings of the Middle East. These bilateral arrangements are often revised by negotiation. They may be unilaterally overturned, as when Iran nationalized its oil industry in 1951. They may be upheld by force, as at Suez in 1951-52. Or they may give way to multilateral arrangements.

In one other region Britain has a major interest—the North Atlantic. But this is the only region in which there is little danger to the British interest, whose security rests on two factors. The first is good understanding with the United States. Britain has relinquished to the United States complete control over the Caribbean approaches to the Panama Canal (1901) and granted 99-year leases of a string of naval bases from Newfoundland to Trinidad (1940). The second factor is the pacification of Ireland. In World War II, Eire was neutral and Northern Ireland was loyal, whereas in all previous great wars all Ireland had been hostile.

A difficult area of British policy centers around relations with the Soviet Union. The Foreign Office has found new grounds for its traditional fear of Russian expansion toward the Mediterranean, the Middle East, and the Indian Ocean. It is to some extent in order to compete with Soviet communism that the Labor government has made a virtue of necessity in granting full self-government to such former dependencies as Burma, India, Pakistan, Ceylon, Israel, and Jordan. Pressure from an expansive Soviet Union has helped to align Britain diplomatically with the United States in search for new forms of cooperation among non-Soviet countries.

The United States and Britain, on the other hand, are commercial rivals for the trade with underdeveloped continents because their products are not complementary. Bilateral trade between them thus is almost impossible to arrange, and the working of multilateral trade is almost unpredictable. The British Board of Trade does attach great importance to the revival of multilateral trade, especially to that "triangle of trade" that consists in British exports of manufactured goods to the lands around the Indian Ocean, the export from these countries of raw materials such as rubber and gold to the United States, and American export of machine tools to Britain. But the board also feels bound to do all it can to develop sources of supply outside the dollar area. It has thus been a duty of the Cabinet to seek a policy that might balance political sympathies with economic interests.

Participation in Regional Bodies. Britain occupies a middle position between the European continent and the other continents opened up by Europeans. Britain earns its living essentially by transoceanic multilateral trade; it would lose more than it would gain by staking its economic future on a European continental market area. This consideration has affected

British policy toward the organization of regional intergovernmental agencies.

The British government has been lukewarm toward organizations merely European in composition. Although joining in the purely deliberative Council of Europe, with its Strasbourg assembly and its committee of ministers, Britain has held aloof from efforts to turn this body into a European federal government, create a European army, and place the European steel industry under the control of a European supranational authority.

On the other hand, Britain has participated energetically in regional organs of cooperation between North America and Western Europe, bilaterally from 1942 and multilaterally since 1948. Through the Organization for European Economic Cooperation, Britain has joined with seventeen other European countries in planning and administering American economic aid. Through the North Atlantic Treaty Organization created in 1950, Britain and eleven other signatories placed their armed forces (including the Royal Navy) under an American commander. Unwritten understandings (*ententes cordiales*), gentlemen's agreements, and executive arrangements between Britain and its neighbors, across the Atlantic and the Channel, are thus giving place not only to formal alliances but also to formal organizations.

Participation in International Bodies. Politically, Britain is not strong enough to stand alone. Economically, it is too industrialized to be self-sufficient and has to aim at self-support by buying and selling on the world market. Isolation has become impossible for Britain. Its survival depends upon its relations with other countries. These relations fall to a great extent within the framework of three organized groups of countries—the British Commonwealth and Empire, the Western states, and the United Nations.

As the next chapter will show, consultation and conference, usually on particular practical issues, with the other British countries are an everyday habit. As for the countries of the Western world, they are bound together, not only by multilateral trading and international investment and by participation in new regional bodies, but also by membership in a number of specialized international agencies. These include the International Bank for Reconstruction and Development, the International Monetary Fund, the International Civil Aviation Organization, the Food and Agriculture Organization, the International Labor Organization, the World Health Organization, and the United Nations Educational, Scientific and Cultural Organization. All fit in with a British feeling that international organization ought to be "functional, not federal."

Britain is also a member of the United Nations, with a permanent seat on its Security Council and a veto over substantive resolutions by that body. It has thus far made full use of the machinery of the United Nations for settling political disputes, including submission to the Assembly of the Palestine problem in 1947 and to the World Court of the Iranian oil problem in 1951.

CHAPTER 8

FROM EMPIRE TO COMMONWEALTH

1. Colonial Status

Powers of the Mother Country. During the past four hundred years, more than a hundred colonies have been planted by people from the British Isles. Some of these have grown into the United States and into the British Commonwealth of Nations. Colonial status is thus important as the historic start for a number of countries that have now outgrown it, as well as for many others that are still in the colonial stage of constitutional development.[1] Colonial status has two sides: the powers retained by the mother country, and the privileges granted to the colony.

The mother country has retained responsibility for colonial administration, appointing the governor, the civil service, and the judges. So also the defense of the colonies is managed, the mother country deciding to what extent it will discharge this responsibility and to what extent it will enlist the help of the colonies in their own defense. The mother country thus implicates them in its wars. Its treaties and its laws are binding on their courts. They have no foreign policy apart from that of the central power. Its parliament claims the right to regulate commerce among the several parts of the Empire and with the aboriginal tribes. The constitutions of the colonies are charters or letters-patent granted by royal prerogative, or occasionally by act of the imperial parliament; and the power to grant includes the power to rescind.

Privileges of the Colonial Territory. On the other hand, the mother country has usually conferred upon its subjects, when planting colonies overseas, the privilege of building institutions that resemble those they have known at home. Thus, England has always allowed English colonists to elect legislative councils empowered to tax the inhabitants of the colony for colonial purposes. More than that, it has extended this privilege from Eng-

---

[1] See E. P. Chase, "Government by Consultation in the British Commonwealth," *Journal of Politics,* 9 (1947), 198 ff.; P. J. Baker, *Present Juridical Status of the British Dominions in International Law* (London, 1929); R. M. Dawson, *Development of Dominion Status* (Oxford, 1937); W. Y. Elliott and H. D. Hall, eds., *British Commonwealth at War* (New York, 1943); W. K. Hancock, *Survey of British Commonwealth Affairs* (Oxford, 1937); A. B. Keith, *The King and the Imperial Crown* (Toronto, 1936), and *Dominions as Sovereign States* (London, 1938); K. C. Wheare, *Statute of Westminster and Dominion Status* (Oxford, 1938); A. E. Zimmern, *Third British Empire* (Oxford, 1926); Arthur Willert and Others, *Empire in the World* (Oxford, 1937).

lish colonists to such other colonists of European origin as passed under its rule, from the Dutch of New York (1683) to the French Canadians (1791) and the Afrikanders of the Cape (1853).

Exactly how far this privilege extended became a matter of debate in the eighteenth century, with Parliament claiming to be an imperial body possessed with paramount legislative and taxing powers in the interest of imperial unity, and the colonial legislative councils claiming an exclusive right of taxation in the interest of colonial liberty. Thereafter, in all colonies that did not then join in the American Revolution, the constitutional principle of the legislative sovereignty of the imperial parliament and of the subordinate powers of the colonial legislative assemblies had to be accepted.

The privilege of electing a legislative council with taxing powers originally was not granted to inhabitants of the colonies who were of other than European origin. After the revolt of the thirteen American colonies, most of the remaining British dependencies were preponderantly non-European, and the number of tropical dependencies unsuitable for European settlement increased considerably during the following century. The problem of extending English parliamentary institutions to non-European peoples thus grew in importance. It was not so much the color of the non-Europeans that stood in the way of their enfranchisement as their culture patterns and social attitudes. In Barbados, the Cape of Good Hope, and New Zealand, colored people were admitted to the franchise in the nineteenth century, as soon as they, as individuals, met such legal qualifications as property, occupancy, residence, or literacy. But there was some tendency to cut back the powers of the legislative council and even to make it a predominantly appointive instead of an elective body, as in Jamaica. Only with the twentieth century has it become normal for the British government to aim consciously at the extension of parliamentary institutions to non-European peoples, as one of the better aspects of their inevitable assimilation to Western culture.

Relations between Colony and Mother Country. The problem of relations between the imperial parliament and the colonial legislative councils has always been difficult. In the absence of any provision for the colonies to elect members of Parliament, the most that eighteenth-century colonists could do was to send commissioners to be heard in the lobbies and at the bar of the Commons, and to select committees of correspondence to keep in touch with these commissioners. With the revolt of the American colonies, even this loose link apparently disappeared. The colonies that remained had for the most part even less of a share in the central government.

No British colony (except perhaps Gibraltar) lacks all self-government. Rather, a colony is not wholly self-governing. From complete absence of self-government to full self-government is a path that leads to a wide range of gradations. Somewhere in this process comes the passage from colonial to dominion status.

2. Dominion Status

Cabinet Responsibility. Into the self-government of British dependencies, a new element was injected in the nineteenth century. It arose from a sudden awareness that for the past hundred years the essential characteristic of the British form of government had been not only that it was representative, but also that it was responsible.

Apply this principle and the centrally chosen governor of a colony ceases to govern. Like the King in the United Kingdom, he leaves this to a cabinet of ministers responsible to the colonial legislative council. Imperial control over colonial administration being thus abandoned, what happens to imperial unity in defense, commerce, and foreign affairs? Only in an epoch of peace and *laissez faire* could this be abandoned; but such an epoch existed in the nineteenth century, when Britain was glad to be rid of responsibility for garrisoning colonies and to buy in the cheapest market, whether inside or outside the Empire.

Sent out as Governor General and High Commissioner after the Canadian rebellion of 1837, Lord Durham proposed a way to prevent further conflict between a colonially elected legislature and an imperially appointed executive. This way was to authorize the next governor general to call to his counsel men who should have the confidence of the inhabitants. The procedure was applied by Governor General Lord Elgin soon after taking office in Canada in 1847. Within the years 1847-57, the new technique of responsible government was extended to the Maritime Provinces and Newfoundland, the Australian colonies, and New Zealand; and by 1872 it had reached the Cape of Good Hope. From then on, the spread of British political institutions was to mean not only parliamentarism, but also the cabinet system. Britain was to be not only the "mother of parliaments," but also the mother of responsible cabinets. This development was the first stage in the emergence of dominion status.

Continental Union. A second aspect of the process emerged when neighboring colonies on a continental mainland or near-by island were linked together. This linking might be done by superimposing on them a federal parliament and cabinet. In such a way were brought into existence the Dominion of Canada (1867) and the Commonwealth of Australia (1900)—blending together the invention by the United States of federal union, widely copied after the Civil War, with the British invention of cabinet responsibility. A similar result might be achieved by abolishing the legislatures and cabinets of the constituent colonies and replacing them with a single parliament and cabinet, as in the Union of South Africa (1909)—a blending together of European continental traditions with those of Britain.

These new organic unions of several colonies were better able to cope with problems of continental development, especially the planning and financing of railways and harbors, the protection of infant industries, and the regulation of immigration. Once established, they have also shown the power of growth, by incorporation of colonial territory such as the Hudson Bay region, Southwest Africa, and Northern Australia.

Foreign Policy. The third and consummating stage in the emergence of dominion status came with international recognition of something approximating sovereign statehood.[2] Having freely contributed to victory in World War I, the dominions claimed, and were not denied, a voice in postwar international affairs. They signed with other nations the peace treaty of Versailles (1919). Territories conquered in the war were mandated to them. They became original members of the League of Nations, and later of the United Nations. They even won acceptance for the principle that in turn they ought always to have one of their number elected to the League Council (beginning with Canada, 1927), now to the Security Council of the United Nations.

The principle that a treaty negotiated by imperial plenipotentiaries could be specifically acceded to or withdrawn from by any particular British territory was elaborated so that it became normal by the end of the nineteenth century for dominion plenipotentiaries to do the actual negotiating of treaties concerning their own dominion. But the signature was still by the British Ambassador, and royal ratification was on the advice of the British Foreign Secretary. Canada insisted in 1923 on Canadian signature of its halibut fisheries treaty with the United States; and the subsequent Imperial Conference confirmed the propriety of a dominion's signing its own treaties. Canada next declined to be bound by the peace treaty of Lausanne with Turkey, on the ground that it had not participated in either the negotiating or the signing or the recommendation to ratify. Again, the Imperial Conference of 1926 confirmed the principle that a dominion could not be bound by a treaty that it had neither signed nor recommended for royal ratification. Dominions have thus insisted on the principle of "no obligation without participation."

Claims of Independence. Canada had a minister at Washington to act as deputy to the British Ambassador. Eire therefore claimed the right to have a minister too; but the United Kingdom did not want *him* as deputy to its ambassador. Once more, the Imperial Conference accepted the point—a dominion could freely choose its own diplomatic representation. By its Status of the Union Act (1934), South Africa transferred the King's prerogatives in foreign affairs to its own governor general. The Union of South Africa claimed, and Eire actually exercised, the right to declare its neutrality in World War II; Eire thereby forfeited charter membership of the United Nations. Finally, a dispute between India and South Africa was carried

[2] Certain colonies, such as Newfoundland and Southern Rhodesia, reached dominion status in the sense of responsible self-government but not in the sense of control over their own foreign policy. Newfoundland achieved a voice in foreign policy only by federation with the neighboring Dominion of Canada (1949).

before the United Nations Assembly in 1947, instead of being settled within the Commonwealth. In brief, some dominions have acted as though they were sovereign and independent states, whose relations among themselves were no different from those existing between any other independent countries.

In one hundred years, a tremendous advance has thus occurred from colonial to dominion status. The quarter of the world that was once the British Empire has become divided into the "commonwealth of self-governing nations" with dominion status and the "dependent empire" with colonial status. Nor is there any hard and fast line between them; for dominion status is a milestone, if not a goal, in evolution from dependent or colonial status. When "dominion status" was granted to Southern Ireland in 1921-22, it meant the same status as had been acquired by the premier dominion, Canada, and as was being enjoyed also by Australia, New Zealand, and South Africa. Since then, dominion status has continued to evolve. In 1947-48, dominion status in its more fully evolved form was conferred upon India, Pakistan, and Ceylon; India in 1950 declared itself a republic. Burma could have had dominion status, but chose that of an entirely independent republic. And discussions were initiated that pointed to the granting of dominion status perhaps to a Caribbean federation.

Today, the very term "dominion" is passing out of favor. It symbolizes a distinction not only between self-governing and colonial territories, but also between the United Kingdom and the other self-governing British countries. Such distinction does not jibe with the principle of their equality.

3. The Statute of Westminster

Equality of Status. In the years following World War I, when British statesmen became aware of dominion status as something new and distinctive in political evolution, it was constitutional equality with Britain—not independence from Britain—that was stressed. The cabinets of the dominions objected to being placed in a position that was constitutionally inferior to that of the Cabinet in the United Kingdom. They did not want their governors general to exercise a measure of discretion that the King himself had long allowed to fall into desuetude. Nor did they want to be committed to any course of action without their own consent. Equality of power with the United Kingdom they were unlikely to achieve. But so far as they were free agents, they wished for equal freedom with the mother country.

To this attitude official expression was given in a declaration by the Imperial Conference of 1926. It stated that the United Kingdom and the dominions were "autonomous communities within the British Empire, equal in status, in no way subordinate one to another in any aspect of their domestic or external affairs, though united by a common allegiance to the Crown, and freely associated as members of the British Commonwealth of

Nations." The legal implications of this declaration were embodied in the draft of a law that was approved by the Imperial Conference of 1930 and by all dominion parliaments. It was enacted by the imperial parliament in 1931,[3] and is known as the Statute of Westminster.

The preamble states: "Inasmuch as the Crown is the symbol of the free association of the members of the British Commonwealth of Nations, and as they are united by a common allegiance to the Crown, it would be in accord with the established constitutional position of all members of the Commonwealth in relation to one another that any alteration in the law touching the succession to the throne or the royal style and titles shall hereafter require the assent as well of the parliaments of all the dominions as of the parliament of the United Kingdom." The new procedure was followed when Edward VIII gave place to George VI and his heirs. The statute of the United Kingdom effecting the change was assented to by order in council—that is, Cabinet action—in some dominions, and by parallel enactment by Parliament in other dominions (including South Africa, where the new reign began one day later than elsewhere).

Powers of the Imperial Parliament. The rule of legislative supremacy grants a British parliament full power to repeal, amend, or supersede previous statute law, regulations, common law, and acts of the royal prerogative. This rule is extended so as to permit dominion parliaments to modify imperial law in so far as it is applicable to them. Exceptions are the federal constitutions of Canada and Australia, which may be modified only in accordance with their own distinctive procedures.

The legislative supremacy of the parliament at Westminster is in turn limited by the provision that "no act of Parliament of the United Kingdom passed after the commencement of this act shall extend or be deemed to extend to a dominion as part of the law of that dominion, unless it is expressly declared in that act that that dominion has requested and consented to the enactment thereof." The power of the imperial parliament to legislate extraterritorially is also extended to the dominion parliaments. They are no longer limited to legislating on matters occurring on their own soil, but may now define offenses and prescribe penalties in such matters as counterfeiting, bigamy, foreign enlistment, military discipline, and divulging official secrets, wherever committed.

Dominion parliaments are further empowered to abolish "reservation" by governors general of bills enacted by dominion legislatures. The new responsibility of the dominions in foreign affairs removed the need for the imperial government to veto "reserved" bills on the ground that they might imperil good relations with foreign powers. In their own interest, however,

---

[3] Australia and New Zealand approved this bill only on condition that its provisions should not apply in their own territories without adoption by their own parliaments; that is to say, they approved of it for the other dominions, but not for themselves.

the dominions have agreed to reserve to the parliament in the United Kingdom the right to override any dominion legislation that might imperil the listing of their bonds at London as "trustee securities."

Bill of Rights for the Dominions. If the Statute of Westminster is regarded as a written constitution, it may be open to the criticism that Lord Bryce leveled against the Golden Bull of Emperor Charles IV (1345): "He defined anarchy and called it a constitution." But the constitution of the commonwealth of self-governing nations, like that of Britain itself, is something bigger and more elusive than any statute. It consists in the main in institutional patterns of behavior.

It is on these institutions, rather than on any basic documents, that the unity of the Empire rests. The Statute of Westminster is not so much a constitution for the Commonwealth as it is a bill of rights for the dominions within the Commonwealth.

4. Commonwealth Unity

Common Citizenship. To answer the question of the links that remain between other Commonwealth countries and the United Kingdom, one must look both at the law and at custom. There are no sanctions behind the Statute of Westminster. It depends for its validity not on physical force, but on moral authority. It is freely consented to. All the surviving "bonds of empire" are thus spiritual bonds. They show themselves in the attitudes of men. But men respond to symbols.

In all member countries except India government is in the name of the King. It was decided at the Imperial Conference of 1926 that the governor general of a dominion should be regarded as the representative of the King rather than of the government of the United Kingdom. In 1930 it was agreed that this decision meant that the governor general should be nominated to the King by the King's ministers in the dominion concerned. The governor general thus has come to be selected by the dominion's parliamentary majority speaking through its Cabinet. Each dominion acquires what practically amounts to its own "head of state" for ceremonial purposes and as umpire for the working of its constitutional traditions. The power of the dominion government to select and remove the governor general is the best guarantee of the dominions against use of the reservation of dominion legislation and the royal veto. Yet, through the governor general, the Crown remains the symbol of historic continuity except, since 1950, in India.

Regardless of whether it is governed in the name of the King, every member country recognizes the Crown as a symbol of Commonwealth unity. To be a Commonwealth citizen and to be a subject of the Crown are synonymous expressions. Each member country has its own nationality law, under which a person is at the same time a citizen of his particular country and of the Commonwealth. Thus a quarter of the world's population now enjoys a large measure of more-than-national citizenship. Wherever they are, Commonwealth citizens may expect protection from Commonwealth authorities. They may freely enter and leave the United Kingdom; when resident there, they may vote or be elected or, if entitled, sit in the House of Lords. In no other part of the Commonwealth, however, do they have equal privilege. Canada, Australia, New Zealand, and South Africa have denied the rights of immigration, property, occupation, and election to Commonwealth citizens on such grounds as color.

If Canada desires to amend its federal constitution—the British North America Act of 1867—confirmation by the parliament at Westminster is still required for some purposes, to preserve the compact between the French-speaking and English-speaking provinces in the face of a linguistic majority. But the confirming statute must expressly declare that the dominion has requested and consented to the enactment. The power to initiate constitutional change thus rests exclusively with the dominions.

From the King's courts in the dominions, appeals have long lain to the King in council, acting since 1833 on the advice of the judicial committee of his Privy Council. The committee consists of approximately the same persons as sit in the House of Lords as law lords. Appeal from the highest Canadian courts, federal and provincial, to the judicial committee has been common practice, both on controverted cases and on advisory opinions; appeal has been abolished by the Canadian Parliament in criminal cases. From Australian courts, leave to appeal is seldom granted. From Irish and South African courts, appeal to the judicial committee has been abolished by the parliaments of those countries. Even when appeal is retained, the enforcement of the decision of the King in council usually depends upon the willing cooperation of the courts in the dominion from which appeal has gone.

According to law, dominion status is now identical with independence. Within the Commonwealth, sovereignty is no longer exercised by a common sovereign. Since India became a republic, it has no longer been possible to regard the Commonwealth as one state, with a single "head of the state" (the King) acting on the advice of a number of different governments in his different dominions, and calling into play different principles of international law in different dominions (for instance, when some are neutral while others are at war). Within the Commonwealth, the legal links have worn thin and are wearing thinner. More important are the practical aspects of "free association."

Reciprocal Aid. Among all the nations of the Commonwealth, there is an unusual measure of intimacy and confidence. The principle is well recognized that every member should be informed or consulted if likely to be affected by diplomatic or military steps taken by any other member. Although sometimes overlooked, this principle is generally considered to be morally binding as well as politically expedient. A government that omits this duty exposes itself to sharp questioning and criticism in its own parlia-

ment.   None considers itself bound to implement policies about which it was
not consulted in advance.

Mutual aid, both military and financial, has become normal among members of the Commonwealth.   Military aid was freely given by the dominions
in both World Wars, though each remained the judge of the extent and character of its own contribution.   Plants for producing war supplies have been
freely relocated among the British countries; this fact has helped greatly in
the development of shipbuilding in Canada and Australia, and of industrial
production in the latter.   Responsibility for exercising control over the sea
routes of the southern hemisphere is now being effectively transferred from
the United Kingdom to Australia, New Zealand, and South Africa.   Four
phases have characterized the military interrelations within the Commonwealth.   In the early nineteenth century, Britain garrisoned the territories of
the Empire, fought their native wars, and patrolled their sea routes.   In the
later nineteenth century, they were left to fend for themselves.   In the early
twentieth century, the dominions were invited voluntarily to support Britain's lead.   In the current phase of planned participation, they deliberately
and consciously share their power as they feel able.

When Britain found it difficult to finance its imports in the later part of
World War II, the dominions piled up large sterling balances in London, thus
effectively postponing repayment for their supplies until Britain should resume exports after the war.   They agreed that their sterling balances should
not be freely convertible into dollars; except for Canada, they pooled their
dollar earnings, thus forming a "sterling bloc."   More than this, the British countries made free gifts with which to cover part of Britain's purchases
in their markets—just as Britain gave them the services and locally available
supplies needed for their military establishments in Britain and its dependent
territories.   Like American lend-lease and its British counterpart, reverse
lend-lease, this arrangement served a double purpose of expanding overseas
business activity at a time when it might otherwise have contracted and also
of helping hold Britain as an advance base for all the allies.   Unlike lend-
lease, "reciprocal aid" did not have the adverse psychological connotations of
possible eventual bargaining about repayment or some political equivalent.

Commercial Regulation.   In their commercial intercourse, the British
nations have shown a marked tendency to work together.   The age when
the imperial parliament regulated the commerce of all British lands ended
during the nineteenth century in *laissez faire*—the principle that the most
effective regulation is nonregulation.   The late nineteenth and early twentieth centuries saw a divergence of policy.   The United Kingdom adhered to
free trade, whereas the dominions, led by Canada and Australia, emulated the
example set by the United States of restrictionism by high protective tariffs.

The current phase began with the abandonment of free trade by the United
Kingdom in 1931, in the hope for better bargaining with protectionist countries both in and out of the Empire.   This move had the effect of shifting

commercial regulation to a multilateral basis. Now it was possible for tariffs to be fixed by negotiation, instead of being determined by each country at its own sole pleasure. The new trend was inaugurated at a Commonwealth conference held at Ottawa in 1932, where a network of trade agreements among British countries was negotiated. Each country made concessions to all the others. But these concessions were not automatically extended to countries outside the Empire. For example, the United Kingdom agreed to retain wheat from British countries on the duty-free list, but levied a duty on all non-British wheat from 1932 until the United States negotiated trade agreements with the United Kingdom and Canada in 1938. It is figured that the general effect of imperial tariff preference was to set import duties among British countries about one tenth below the duties that they levied on imports from non-British countries. In the United Kingdom, for example, where duties range from a mandatory 10 per cent to a permissive $33\frac{1}{3}$ per cent on dutiable articles, they would normally be scaled down to 9 per cent to 30 per cent for Empire countries.[4] In addition, associations of producers in any British country were accorded the right to appear before the consultative tariff committees of other British countries.

New Regulatory Means. Meanwhile, tariffs have ceased to be the only or even the principal means of regulating commerce. Another important method since 1931 has been quantitative regulation by means of quotas, assuring a country an agreed share of imports of meat or some other commodity into another country. Here, too, because the quota system was extended to some non-British countries, priority in negotiation and preference in allocation of quotas was accorded by British countries to one another.

Another means is the bulk-purchasing agreement. Such agreements were originally developed between the Ministries of Food and Supply in the United Kingdom and the marketing ministries of other British countries during World War II. Subsequently, bulk purchasing extended to other countries that export primary products.

There has thus been a marked tendency for British countries to give prior consideration to one another when regulating commerce by means either of quotas, tariffs, or bulk buying. When negotiating with the United States and other foreign countries, the various British countries usually make common cause. It is therefore generally a necessity for the foreign country to negotiate with all if it wishes to reach agreement with any of them.

Nature of Relationship. The growing economic cohesion of British countries would probably not have found these recent political expressions if it had not been in conformity with the trend toward a community of economic interests. As the commerce of British countries has grown, a continually

---

[4] Preferential tariffs among non-British countries are confined to countries enjoying geographical propinquity, such as the United States and Cuba. British "imperial preference" can be regarded either as an example of "regional preference," interpreted in a cultural or sociological rather than a geographical sense, or as a survival from the concept of the Empire as a single state in the eyes of international law.

increasing proportion has been among themselves—rising from one quarter on the eve of World War I to one third on the eve of the great depression and to nearly one half today.[5]

This commerce has come to constitute one of the few stable and dependable factors in present-day world trade. Moreover, although the British countries are politically equal, their economic cohesion is due largely to the pull of the United Kingdom, which is the world's biggest buyer, its greatest consumer of imported primary products, and the banker for the Empire (though a debtor facing the dominions as creditor countries). The community of interests of the British countries makes it unrealistic to think of the United Kingdom as simply one among the countries of Western Europe.

Parallel Partnership. After Commonwealth-wide consultation at the end of World War II, agreement was reached on systems of coordinated air transport and telecommunications known as "parallel partnership." In civil aviation, each British country now has its own air-line corporation—either government-owned, like the British Overseas Airways Corporation, or a government-subsidized "chosen instrument" like Trans-Canada Airlines. Flights between any two British countries are scheduled by agreement.[6] Mail is flown by both post offices on the airliners of both countries. All these air lines may be directed by their own governments to fly unprofitable as well as profitable routes. As a channel for permanent consultation, a British Commonwealth Air Transport Council was set up in 1945.

A similar development has taken place in telecommunications. It was agreed in 1945 that each British country should have its own radio communications, operated as part of its own postal services and staffed by its own personnel. Hence the dissolution of the Empire-wide Cable and Wireless, Ltd., by a process of "parallel nationalization." It has also been agreed that a Commonwealth Telecommunications Board be created, both for consultation and for subsidizing the loss on cables out of the profit from radio.

Political Significance of the Commonwealth. Commonwealth experience in the past twenty years has reinforced the British attitude toward all intergovernmental cooperation both within and without the Empire. "Functionalism, not federalism" is standard practice of British countries in dealing with one another. Current British stress on consultation among all interested parties, as the very essence of democracy, is also reinforced by the experience of the Commonwealth, for this community of nations is based upon consensus, compromise, respect, and tolerance.

The greater the political and economic perils of our age of world wars and great depressions, the deeper the urge among British countries to hang to-

---

[5] Another quarter of this commerce today is with the United States, nearly half of whose total commerce is with British countries.

[6] A civil aviation agreement between Eire and the United Kingdom in 1946 gave the Irish line a monopoly across the Irish Channel on condition that British European Airways Corporation should have a monopoly across the English Channel.

gether rather than hang separately. It is conceivable, however, that in a world of universal peace, full employment, and economic and social progress, both Commonwealth and Empire might cease to be necessary.

Even as it is, and with their imperfect success, the League of Nations and the United Nations have hastened the transformation of the Empire. This process has been accomplished by according a large measure of equality internationally to the self-governing dominions; by communicating directly with the government of each separate British country; and by providing their delegations with an opportunity to take the initiative in seeking solutions to world problems.

5. The Dependent Empire

Diversity in the Tropics. The commonwealth of self-governing British nations is a kind of inner circle to which not all countries in the British Empire have yet been promoted. The self-governing dominions are for the most part in the temperate zone and have been largely settled by people of European culture. The dependent empire, on the other hand, is almost entirely tropical and is inhabited for the most part by people of African or Malaysian origin.[7]

The 80 million people who live in the self-governing countries of the commonwealth have some of the highest standards of living, some of the largest industrial production, and some of the biggest cities in the world. Their numbers are almost stable. The 60 million people who live in the colonial dependencies are overwhelmingly rural and agrarian. Their productivity and their consumption standards are low, whereas their numbers are increasing with great rapidity. The self-governing peoples of the Commonwealth have culture patterns that are variants of our common Euramerican culture. The peoples of the colonial dependencies have many fundamentally different culture patterns, which are being modified only slowly by contact with peoples of Euramerican background. There is thus more similarity among the various self-governing members of the Commonwealth than among the dependencies.

The extreme cultural diversity that exists in the dependent empire carries with it great diversity in forms of government. There are no two dependencies on which an exactly identical constitution has been bestowed. Lack of uniformity has been further enhanced by the British habit of treating a colonial governor as a gentleman. Once he is appointed, he is trusted to use his own best judgment in administering the colony. Certain main lines of policy are laid down by the Colonial Office, such as the principle that the welfare of the natives is paramount, or the more recent principle that mineral rights must not be granted to private interests. No man who did not accept these principles would be appointed governor. Each governor, however, as

---

[7] No attention is given here to military outposts such as Gibraltar or Malta. Pakistan and India are left for consideration in the next chapter.

"the man on the spot," is relied upon to apply basic principles in the way that seems most suited to the social pattern of his own particular colony.

Lack of uniformity is particularly noticeable in fiscal policy, where every individual colony balances its budget as best it can. This practice has made Empire-wide free trade impossible. The most that the colonies have been able to grant to one another and to other parts of the Empire is a small margin of "imperial preference." The fiscal unity of the Empire, after which Britain strove in vain under the spell of eighteenth-century mercantilism, was abandoned during the dominance of nineteenth-century ideas of *laissez faire*.

International Position of Dependencies. Even the status in international law of the various dependencies shows considerable diversity. Most of them are colonies over which the British government has full sovereignty. In the case of some colonies, this sovereignty has been limited by international agreement; in East and Central Africa, for example, the Congo basin agreements in the 1880's have forbidden military training of natives and also have interpreted the "open door" so broadly as to preclude even the smallest margin of imperial preference.[8]

Many dependencies are not technically colonies. Of these, some are protectorates, ruled by native rulers, over whose subjects Britain as protecting power has only so much jurisdiction as has been agreed to in treaties or agreements negotiated between Their Excellencies the Rulers and His Majesty the King; most of Malaya, Uganda, and Nigeria is in this group. Sudan is in the anomalous position of being a *condominium* under the joint sovereignty of two *condomini*—Britain and Egypt; it has a currency and customs union with Egypt, and its affairs are therefore handled by the Foreign Office instead of the Colonial Office. Other dependencies again were formerly under a mandate of the League of Nations, and are now under trusteeship of the United Nations; such is Tanganyika.

Economic Progress. In spite of these vast differences between the various dependencies, certain factors are at work that tend to mitigate the diversity. One of these factors is the deliberate stimulation of economic and social evolution, by means of a Colonial Development and Welfare Fund. The fund was contributed entirely by the United Kingdom, on the supposition that much of British wealth is of colonial origin, which grant has been rising steadily, increasing from £1 million each year in 1929 to an annual average of £10 million since 1945. The fund is a very important addition to the £30 million or so a year that the dependencies spend on economic development and social welfare out of their own revenue; it has made it possible for them to embark on ten-year plans of public investment.

---

[8] There is no evidence that such international agreements have had much effect on the share of the United Kingdom in a colony's trade. The flow of commerce has been affected more by social and economic ties than by legal and fiscal provisions. On the eve of the Second World War, half of Nigeria's foreign trade was with Britain, as against only one quarter of Malaya's, though the former was an open-door dependency, whereas the latter granted imperial preference.

The dependencies thus are not only being opened up by air transport, but also are being equipped for new community services such as water supply, epidemic control, rural education and research. An effort is being made to mold the social change that inevitably accompanies economic development—for instance, by sending out trade-union organizers, cooperative advisers, and social welfare officers, and by establishing regional universities.

Governmental Advance. Along with this emphasis on planning for economic development and social progress, a belief is growing widely prevalent both in Britain and the dependencies that an essential element in cultural evolution is movement toward the goal of responsible self-government of the kind achieved in the dominions. Colonial governments are therefore being remodeled so that they may approximate the British type as quickly as possible.

Another factor mitigating the diversity of the dependencies is the rising tendency to group them together regionally. Thus, the British West Indies have a single Comptroller for Development and Welfare; and they have agreed to take part in a conference to consider means of closer association. West Africa has a regional governors' conference with its secretariat, and a council as well as a court of appeals; during World War II, it had a "resident Cabinet minister." East Africa has a regional high commission composed of three governors; a central assembly representing three legislative assemblies, which controls utilities and customs; an intergovernmental airways corporation; and an agricultural research institute. Central Africa has its regional council. Singapore and Malaya are coordinated by a governor general. There may thus be some possibility not only of the dependent territories achieving self-government, but also of their doing so within a federal framework that would enable them to grow into sizable dominions.

Responsibility of the Colonies. To the question about the way in which the British type of government has been adapted to use in a dependent empire, half the answer is that adaptation takes the form of an attempt to grant the dependencies the nearest possible approximation to the British constitution. The approximation, however, is not complete, because for certain aspects of imperial government the line of responsibility runs back—through the governor, the Colonial Office, the Cabinet of the United Kingdom, and the imperial parliament—to the British electorate.

The constitution of a dependency takes a variety of forms. For most of the crown colonies, it is an order in council, issued and amendable by the Crown under the responsibility of the British Cabinet. For some of the West Indies, for historic reasons, it is an act of the imperial parliament, for whose introduction again the British Cabinet is responsible. For protectorates, such as most of Malaya, it is an agreement, for whose negotiation once more the British Cabinet is responsible and for whose amendment its consent is needed. In most of these cases, the contents of the order in council, statute, or agreement are the subject of consultation, discussion, and deliberation in

the country concerned and between that country's leaders and a representative
of the British government. In legal form and theory, however, the order in
council and the act of Parliament are of purely British origin.

The Colonial Governor. The permanent representative of the British
government in the dependency is the governor. Under the orders in council by which a crown colony gets its form of government, the governor
has some "reserved powers." These enable him to "certify" a bill as if it had
passed the legislative council even though in actual fact it had been rejected.
His, then, are supplementary powers of legislation and taxation, unlike those
of the governors of the American colonies in the eighteenth century. In the
West Indies, in order to establish these powers, it was necessary to curtail the
liberties of the local legislatures and increase the discretion of the governor
after the emancipation of the slaves. The crown colony, in the strict sense,
is thus a nineteenth-century invention. The orders in council limit the governor to using his power in the interest of "public order, public faith, or good
government." He may, for example, prevent the legislative majority from
discriminating against other sections of the people, or he may prohibit the
colony's destruction of its own credit by an attempt to default on its debt.

Each governor, at the time of his appointment, is also given royal instructions. These oblige him to "reserve" certain classes of bills for "the signifi-
cation of His Majesty's consent." The bill then needs the assent of the
Colonial Office besides that of the governor. It is normal to reserve bills
concerning defense, foreign relations, foreign trade, and currency. As a dependency moves toward self-government, the number of reservations is reduced, especially with the substitution of internal checks in the place of this
external one. The governor, moreover, has a veto power over bills passed by
the legislative council. The veto has not died out, as in Britain and the dominions, for the reason that its more smoothly working British substitute—
Cabinet leadership of Parliament—is being introduced only gradually into the
dependencies. The governor does not hesitate to use the veto.

Governors of dependencies are all drawn from the colonial service, made
up of civil servants recruited by "competitive interview." Recruitment is
regardless of race. Native West Africans are in the administrative grade of
the service; and one of the most distinguished of African governors was a
British West Indian. The interview takes place in London; a British university education is expected. The colonial service, unlike its counterpart
in the two Low Countries, is restricted to British subjects from Britain, the
dominions, and the colonies. "Protected persons" from protectorates—of
whom the number with suitable education has hitherto been small—have
not been eligible. Needed specialists who are not British subjects, including some American technical experts, are hired under contract, however.
On account of the tropical climate, colonial civil servants usually qualify for
pensions after some twenty-five years. Turnover is high; promotion tends

to be rapid. To compensate for residence overseas in a climate that was formerly considered unhealthy, pay is high. There is some question whether native members of the service should be paid the same rate as others—whether they should be paid according to a local standard or whether equal work necessitates equal pay.

Unsolved Problems of Government. The principal criticism leveled against the colonial service is lack of intellectual preparation. The time has gone by when all that needs to be asked of the colonial servant is that he be healthy and a born ruler of men. In an age when the dependencies are developing politically, economically, and socially with astounding rapidity, a training in the social sciences acquires greater utility than ever before. Thus far, however, no marked preference has been given to candidates who show some familiarity with social studies. This circumstance may necessitate their being supplemented with technical advisers brought in for temporary service, who therefore would not have to be British subjects.

The grosser forms of patronage have been absent from the colonial service for the past hundred years. Even governors are nonpolitical, in the sense that they do not come and go with the rise and fall of ministries. The permanence of the civil servant facilitates continuity, but there is room for doubt about the value of too much continuity and permanence in the upper reaches of colonial administration. Some new device may be needed to make the colonial service a little less immune to the great tides of political and social change that are sweeping over Britain.

Procedures for achieving responsibility to Britain's center—Cabinet, Parliament, and electorate—are rather weak. It may happen that colonial affairs are debated in Parliament only one day in the year—the day when the appropriation estimates for the Colonial Office come up for discussion. Moreover, the dependencies of today, unlike the American colonies of the eighteenth century, do not even have commissioners to speak for them at the bar of the Commons. Their only spokesmen are usually present and past colonial secretaries on the government and opposition front benches, and retired colonial administrators in the House of Lords. The majority of members of Parliament absent themselves from colonial debates. Nor has the electorate been interested in colonial problems. Pride of empire and a consciousness of the "white man's burden" are confined to a comparatively small minority even among politically minded Britons. The destinies of the dependencies still lie in a relatively small number of hands.

6. Self-Government in the Dependencies

Uncertainties of Approach. The English Parliament has long been a "mother of parliaments." The continental American and West Indian legislatures are its seventeenth-century children. The dominion parliaments are its nineteenth-century descendants. The legislative councils of most of the dependencies are its twentieth-century progeny; the English Parliament is their model. Now it is clear that the British type of parliamentarism is workable only as part of a certain social pattern.

If people live in big families or clans, support themselves without need of buying or selling, hiring or being hired—then obviously they will not be ready for the institutions that make up the British process of self-government. But suppose that a primitive culture has begun to break down, so that a small fraction of the colonial people has moved to the ports and become Europeanized—then this fraction of the population may demand self-government and may be ready to work it. Yet it would not follow that the minority would be representative of the mass of the people, or that it would understand their best interests, or that it would serve an interest other than its own.

Or suppose that Europeanization has gone a long way, but the prime loyalty of the politically conscious and technically competent minority is to different religions rather than to their country. Without basic change, there would be again hesitation on the part of the mother country to give up all control over the dependency.

Practical Examples. The problems that have to be faced may be illustrated by measures taken since World War II to develop self-government in the most valuable of Britain's tropical dependencies.[9] Malaya[10] is an exceptionally rich area, with a big foreign trade. It is therefore able to pay for its own government, its own program of public investment, and its own health, educational, and welfare services. Malaya was even rich enough to make a gift for the defense of the Empire—which then failed to defend it. On the other hand, the Moslem Malays of the peninsula are ruled by nine sultans, to whom prewar Britain was merely a protecting power. Under the treaties in force between Their Excellencies the Rulers and His Majesty the King, the former had full jurisdiction within their own territories (subject to advice by a British "resident"), while the latter managed their foreign affairs and defense. The economic opportunities presented by Malaya, moreover, had attracted a vast immigration, with more than half of the people in Malaya (and nearly all the people in the neighboring island of Singapore) being non-Malay. Some of these were Indian laborers who expected to return to their homes in India. Still more were Chinese merchants and clerks, whose generosity was directed to Chinese causes, whose schools were conducted in Chinese, and whose political interest was mainly in the future of the Chinese Republic. Prewar Malaya thus lacked the feeling that it was one country.

---

[9] See in general Malcolm Hailey, *Position of Colonies in a British Commonwealth of Nations* (London, 1941), and *Future of Colonial Peoples* (Princeton, 1944); W. E. Simmett, *British Colonial Empire* (London, 1942); Martin Wight, *Development of the Legislative Councils, 1606-1945* (London, 1946); series of handbooks on British dependencies (Longmans); W. K. Hancock, *Empire in the Changing World* (New York, 1943).

[10] Cf. Colonial Office, *Malaya Union and Singapore* (Cmd. 6724 and Cmd. 6749 [1946]), and *Federation of Malaya* (Cmd. 7171 [1947]).

It lacked all organs for mobilizing its inhabitants for a united and unified resistance to the Japanese.

Immediately after liberation, new agreements were therefore negotiated by the Colonial Office with the rulers of the nine states, under which they ceded "full power and jurisdiction" to the British Crown. This act cleared the way for two forward steps. One was the establishment of a strong central government. The other was the introduction of a common Malayan citizenship for all who "regarded Malaya as their home and the object of their loyalty." The first attempt in this direction aimed at a Malayan Union (1946-48); it antagonized influential Malays by leaving the sultans with only their religious authority over Moslems and making it comparatively easy for non-Malays to acquire citizenship. In separate negotiation with Malay leaders and non-Malay spokesmen, an alternative Malayan Federation was then brought into being.

Malayan Federation. Under the new agreement, a federal legislative council was established. It was given a long list of powers. Little, besides religion, was left for legislation by the state councils that the sultans agreed to set up. The federal legislative council was to consist of 14 officials, 11 members indirectly elected from the 9 state councils and the councils of two British colonial settlements, and fifty nonofficials, who would be appointed in the first instance to speak for various interests, but would, as soon as practicable, be elected. Here, then, was the first attempt at a unified legislature for a united Malaya. As initially constituted, it aimed at representativeness without direct election. Hence, at this stage, no provision was made for responsibility in the traditional British sense; the governor, called High Commissioner, retained all his powers.

Malayan citizenship by birth was conferred upon all who were Malays by religion and language or were subjects of a Malay ruler. For citizenship by naturalization, however, fifteen years of residence is needed; the non-Malay immigrant majority was thus converted into a political and electoral minority.[11] To confirm further the Malay character of the federation, Malay as well as English was made an official language of the federal legislative council. Power to block changes in immigration policy was conferred upon a federal conference of rulers jointly with the federal legislative council.

Indirect Rule in Africa. A further deviation from the British type of self-government is to be found in the African colonies and protectorates.[12] In Nigeria, on the eve of World War I, Governor Lugard found himself so short of civil servants that he had to rely on the tribal chiefs and clan headsmen to govern those parts of the population that had not yet lost their native culture

---

[11] A British subject who would qualify for Malayan naturalization would have dual citizenship. This would also be the case of British subjects born in the two colonial settlements on the Straits of Malacca.

[12] See especially Malcolm Hailey, *African Survey* (rev. ed., Oxford, 1945).

by contact with European ways. By his success and by his writings he made "indirect rule" into the normal type of self-government in the tribalized portions of British African dependencies.

Only in the Europeanized coast towns is the European form of self-government practiced, with popular suffrage and representation by election. To bring together these two culture areas into which each colony is divided, a legislative council has been or is being set up. In Nigeria, for example, it consists of representatives elected by three regional councils, to which in turn representatives are elected either by tribal chiefs or by coastal municipalities.

Other Areas. In the British West Indies the problem is different again.[13] Here the African culture of the majority of inhabitants was destroyed by slavery and the way opened for a new culture. East Indians and Chinese, though numerous, are nowhere a majority. The English settlers brought their parliamentary ways of taxation and lawmaking with them in the seventeenth century. Many seventeenth-century procedures are indeed still preserved in the West Indian legislative councils—such as the initiation of money bills by private members instead of by holders of executive office. All legislatures except those of the smallest islands have appointive as well as elective members; these sit bicamerally as a council and an assembly, respectively. Race discrimination is unknown to the law; Negroes and "colored" people (that is, light Negroes) are appointed to judgeships and elected to legislatures.

Until recently, all islands had a franchise restricted by property qualifications, and no island had responsible cabinet government. Recently, in the bigger islands, the franchise has been widened. Jamaica in 1944 and Trinidad in 1946 had their first elections by universal suffrage, with the result that popular parties are now arising on the basis of conflicting social and economic policies. This development would produce only friction and frustration, unless accompanied by responsibility. In Jamaica, therefore, a small beginning has been made by having half the members of the governor's executive council chosen from the House of Representatives.

Further advance toward responsibility awaits solution of the problem of closer association among the various islands and territories of the British West Indies. They have but little feeling of unity among themselves. Those with budgetary surpluses do not wish to share their plenty with those that have deficits. Yet most of them are so small that their legislatures have more resemblance to county councils than to parliaments. Administration will no doubt have to remain decentralized. Political attitudes may well remain centrifugal—with more attachment to London or Harlem

---

[13] Cf. Royal Commission on the West Indies, *Summary of Recommendations* (Cmd. 6174 [1940]), and *Report* (1945); Anglo-American Caribbean Commission, *Reports* (1942-45); Paul Blanchard, *Democracy and Empire in the Caribbean* (New York, 1947); T. R. Simey, *Development and Welfare in the West Indies* (Oxford, 1946).

than to the region. But a strong case can probably be made for common advisory services, processes for promoting parallel legislation, joint support for some undertakings of general utility (such as the new regional university opened in Jamaica in 1948), and perhaps even the subordination of the nine governors to a single governor general or to a responsible cabinet.

International Implications. Self-government would be an illusion if it resulted merely in the establishment of pygmy states, too weak to have much voice in their own economic destiny, too poor to provide their citizens with a high standard of services, and too small to offer adequate scope to the brilliant and the ambitious.

The rise of British colonies to full self-government has usually been preceded or accompanied by federation or unification. Most British tropical dependencies, however, are in regions in which a number of North Atlantic powers have long-standing interests and which are therefore only partly under British rule. Their political boundaries, moreover, do not coincide with cultural frontiers; they are incidental products of the history of the North Atlantic peoples, not of their own. The future of Malaya and Singapore is bound up with that of the rest of Indonesia, in which France, the Netherlands, and the United States (through the Philippines) are interested. The future of Britain's scattered West African dependencies is linked to that of French West Africa and Liberia (in which the United States is also interested). The future of the British West Indies is associated with that of the American, Dutch, and French possessions in the Caribbean, to say nothing of the tiny republics that are apt in that region to combine economic dependence with political independence. And the natural unity of the Pacific islands is broken by their being shared out between Australia, Britain, New Zealand, France, and the United States.

It would therefore seem possible that we may be entering into an epoch when the political, economic, and social development of dependencies could become a matter of international as well as of imperial concern. Three kinds of international organs are being developed with which to meet this problem—regional organs, such as the Caribbean Commission (with the United States, the United Kingdom, the Netherlands, and France as members), the South Pacific Commission, and the Commission for Technical Cooperation in Africa south of the Sahara; a central planning organ, the Overseas Territories Committee of the Organization for European Economic Cooperation; and a global organ, the United Nations, whose task extends to the collating of information on economic and social (though not necessarily political) developments in all territories that do not govern themselves.

CHAPTER 9

DOMINION GOVERNMENT

1. The Dominion of New Zealand

Inherited Common Features. All British countries have inherited certain common constitutional features, derived from British constitutionalism as it was practiced in the early Victorian epoch.[1] They all deny the need for a categorical separation of powers and instead carry on "responsible government" in the familiar sense. In brief, their executives—the Cabinets—are the steering committees of their legislatures, dependent upon legislative support for continuance in office. The so-called lower houses of the legislatures, with which alone the Cabinets have this relation of mutual responsibility, are popularly elected, representation being approximately proportionate to population. Upper houses, or "second chambers," have been preserved at the national level, but only as bodies of secondary deliberative importance to which the Cabinet is in no way responsible.

Political parties are well organized, and the trend toward unicameralism is strengthened by official recognition of a leader of the opposition in the lower house of Parliament. Administration is increasingly left to civil servants, selected on merit and engaged in public service as a dignified profession and a satisfying career. Every department has two heads; the political head changes with each change in Cabinet, the permanent one is selected from the professional civil service. Judges are never elected but always appointed for life, as the most effective means of guaranteeing their independence; but they are called upon to preside over official inquiries. Parliaments are trusted with sovereign power over the rights of subjects, unlimited by any fundamental declaration of rights or any other written form of "higher law." Everywhere there is a ceremonial head of the state, whose principal duty is to dissolve and summon Parliament on the advice of ministers whom he appoints and dismisses. It is his function, too, in general to preside as umpire over the working of these constitutional conventions.

On the other hand, some important deviations from this basic British pattern exist. One such deviation results from the impact of American federalism, with some consequent need for written constitutions. Another comes from a different attitude toward financial control—less Treasury control over personnel, less parliamentary discussion of estimates, less checking

---

[1] From the sending of the Durham royal commission to Canada in 1837 to the passage of the Colonial Laws Validity Act in 1865.

by the opposition of the auditor general's accounts, more parliamentary discussion of developmental capital outlay, and, in one country, the creation of a new supergovernmental organ to control capital development. Still another deviation stems from the prevalence in most dominions of people who have inherited a non-British culture and speak a language other than English. Not least important are divergences due to the different tasks incumbent upon government in countries as far apart geographically as the countries of the British Commonwealth.[2]

Social Laboratory. Of all the dominions, it is New Zealand that is constitutionally most British. From the first introduction of representation by election in 1852, it has evolved steadily—making its executive council responsible to its House of Representatives; reducing the term of members of its legislative council from life to seven years; extending the franchise for its House of Representatives to all resident adult citizens, male and female; and compelling all qualified voters to register. All this has been done without any attempt to lay down a fundamental framework of government in any written constitution, and without even formally adopting the Statute of Westminster.[3]

In size and climate, New Zealand is the only dominion that in any way resembles Britain. Moreover, it has been settled by a cross section of British social classes, religious denominations, and national groups, from the 1830's—when it was first planned by the New Zealand Company of the philosophic radicals—to the present day. Twice, however, in its history it has come under the rule of a political party with a clear-cut policy that has made New Zealand one of the world's most interesting social laboratories.

Businesslike Socialism. The first time was in 1891, when a Liberal government came into power. It changed the whole pattern of land use, from scattered settlement on vast sheep ranches to close settlement on family-type dairy farms. The shift was helped by the invention of the refrigerator ship, which made it possible to supply Britain with animal foods instead of wool. The Liberal government also set a pattern for industrial organization by establishing a court of conciliation and arbitration to settle labor disputes, available if both parties registered as "trade unions"—a great incentive to unionization of workers and association of employers. National responsibility was assumed for the full cost of free, compulsory, and secular education. Also, New Zealand came to lead the world in introducing a generous system of old-age pensions.

The second instance happened during the years since 1935, when Labor rose to power, like the Liberals, with a combination of both agrarian and urban

---

[2] See in general Alexander Brady, *Democracy in the Dominions* (Toronto, 1947), which has a useful bibliography; K. C. Wheare, *Federal Government* (Oxford, 1946); A. B. Keith's many works, including *Governments of the British Empire* (London, 1935); James Bryce, *Modern Democracies* (New York, 1921); W. H. Wickwar, "Social Democracy in the British Commonwealth," *Journal of Politics*, 9 (1947), 239 ff.

[3] Cf. J. C. Beaglehole, ed., *New Zealand and the Statute of Westminster* (Wellington, 1944).

support. In reaction against the deflation of the depression, a "new deal" attempted to raise domestic spending power and consumption standards. On behalf of the farmers, the Labor party erected a marketing department, which assured stable prices for primary products by export subsidies, trade agreements with Britain, and long-term bulk sales to the British government. On behalf of urban labor, the government made union membership obligatory before any dispute could qualify for settlement by the court of conciliation and arbitration. On behalf of all sections of the people, social security was put through on a new and inclusive basis by levying a social-security contribution (7½ per cent since 1946) on all income, whether personal or corporate, earned or unearned, and using this fund to finance old-age pensions, disability pensions, children's allowances, school meals, and a national health service. When newspapers gave more publicity to the opposition's criticism than to the government's policies, the government took to broadcasting parliamentary debates over the government-owned radio.

In a hardheaded, businesslike, and nondoctrinaire way, New Zealand has become the most socialistic democracy in the world. Capital outlay in developing the nation's assets is carefully planned. The state's economic undertakings, including social security, have to pay their way through self-balancing funds.[4] And for the administration of every such undertaking, a minister is responsible to Parliament.

Maori Representation. The indigenous Maoris constitute some 5 per cent of the nation's million and a half people. They have the same parliamentary representation as any other New Zealanders, four out of eighty constituencies being apportioned to them. Moreover, they normally have one representative in the Cabinet.

Maoris constitute the only example in the English-speaking world of a nonwhite indigenous population that is accorded complete equality with the white settlers.

2. The Commonwealth of Australia

Constitutional Growth. When the popularly elected Australasian national convention drafted a written federal constitution, there were already six states scattered around the coast of the island-continent.[5] Each of the six states had its own British-type constitution. Along lines laid down by immigrant philosophic radicals and Chartists, each state had contributed notable improvements to the mechanics of democracy, including the secret "Australian ballot," used in South Australia from 1856. Each state had developed its own port, its own railroads, and its own land tenure. Because

---

[4] On one such service, see N. S. Heaney, *Public Trusteeship* (Baltimore, 1942), pp. 14 ff.

[5] See especially F. A. Bland, ed., *Government in Australia: Selected Readings* (Sydney, 1944), and review by F. Morstein Marx in *Public Administration Review*, 4 (1944), 368 ff.; also E. R. Walker and E. J. B. Foxcroft, "War Administration in Australia," *Public Administration Review*, 3 (1943), 223 ff.

of low rainfall, each state had been settled sparsely in the interior, with its tremendous sheep ranches usually leased from the state government, and densely settled only in the raw-material exporting state capitals. Local self-government did not flourish under these conditions, so that many of the local functions were performed by the states. All schools were state schools. The gap left by lack of local poor-relief was filled partly by denominational residential institutions and partly—from 1901—by state pensions.

Nowhere have the members of a federal union been more important than in Australia. This importance they sought to safeguard when they framed their constitution according to a "states' rights" interpretation of the United States model.[6] The federal parliament was to have power to legislate only in explicitly enumerated fields, power over all other fields remaining with the state parliaments. The enumerated powers were likely to be as strictly interpreted as the provisions of any other British statute. Control over external affairs, for example, would not empower the federal government to implement international treaties and agreements by extending its legislation into fields reserved to the states.

The enumerated powers were like those of the United States constitution. The only significant additions in the Australian constitution were concurrent but paramount federal power over marriage and divorce; invalidity and old-age pensions; conciliation and arbitration in industrial disputes extending beyond the limits of any one state; and, since the constitutional amendment in 1946, "the provision of maternity allowances, widows' pensions, child endowment, pharmaceutical, sickness, and hospital benefits, medical and dental services, benefits to students, and family allowances." Against this slightly longer list of enumerated powers must be set the almost complete lack of implied powers. Thus, in Australia, federal power to regulate interstate commerce does not extend to intrastate collective bargaining, monopolies, railway rates, or agricultural marketing. Moreover, the explicit enumeration of industrial arbitration has had a limiting effect on federal labor legislation. On balance, it would seem that the federal parliament has inadequate power over the national economy in general, except in wartime, but adequate power to provide special phases of social security.

Adjusting the Federal Balance. Apart from defense, the principal means by which the federal parliament has been able to extend its powers without constitutional amendment is the spending of money "for purposes of the Commonwealth," as well as the borrowing of money. Conditions attached to the spending of money, of course, may become in effect regulatory. Such conditions have not found judicial support. Explicit amendment was therefore needed before the courts recognized the right of the federal parliament to pose the conditions on which medical service would be available to all Australians without payment of fees. Interpretation of the constitutional

---

[6] Australia's founding fathers seem to have been much influenced by James Bryce's *American Commonwealth.*

document, in order to determine the relative powers of the Commonwealth and the state governments, is by a federal supreme court. State governments, acting through their state Attorneys General, often take responsibility for challenging federal legislation. The court has sometimes been influenced by decisions of both the United States Supreme Court and the judicial committee of the Privy Council. But it has not allowed appeals to go from its decisions to the judicial committee in London.

The constitution includes several procedures for its own amendment. One is unanimous grant of powers by the states to the federal government. Another is a parliamentary resolution submitted to popular referendum and carried by a majority both of the voters and of the states—a double majority very hard to obtain.

Policy Councils. One very important constitutional amendment was approved in 1929 embodying a financial agreement of 1927 that had already been accepted by the federal parliament and all the state parliaments. This amendment established a new supreme organ for determining certain aspects of economic policy, the Australian Loan Council. It is composed of two representatives of the federal government and one from each of the six states. This body controls all foreign borrowing by either the federal government or the states. A National Works Council has been constituted along lines similar to those of the Loan Council. Under a coordinator general, and well staffed, it is to map out a public works program covering both nation and states, broken down into priorities and budgeted in labor as well as money.

Thus, an instrumentality originally designed to safeguard Australia's foreign credit is being converted into a means of stabilizing capital investment, and thereby stabilizing employment and the expansion of productivity.[7] Australia's chief handicap in pursuit of this policy is the refusal of a majority of the states to permit the federal parliament directly to control the marketing of primary products in peacetime. As a result, however, indirect and cooperative action by Commonwealth and states was encouraged, as the only means of putting a floor beneath the prices of primary products.

Aspects of Administration. The administrative system of the states and the Commonwealth has several notable features. One is the early establishment and general acceptance of "public service boards," recruiting civil servants on merit. A certain percentage of places in the career structure are reserved for college graduates; but, in obedience to the principle of equal opportunity, they have to begin at the bottom and work their way up. The functions of the public service boards usually include regulation of promotion and tenure, departmental organization, and administrative economy and efficiency in general. Remuneration and other conditions of employment,

---

[7] See Commonwealth of Australia, *Full Employment in Australia* (Canberra, 1945); R. I. Downing, "Planning of Public Investment in Australia," *International Labour Review,* 52 (1945), 352 ff.

however, are subject to determination by the industrial courts of conciliation and arbitration.

Publicly owned business undertakings are usually operated by autonomous boards of commissioners, in the hope that this will keep them out of politics. Working conditions are determined by industrial courts of conciliation and arbitration; but public service boards have little or no control over the organization and staffing of these autonomous bodies. Moreover, their capital investment is not controlled by the Loan Council.

The influence of public employees on government is inevitably great in Australia as it is in New Zealand. As voters, they choose their political employers. As supporters of the Labor party, they are committed to one potential employer rather than another. Australia, like New Zealand, thus shows some signs of becoming a land of "patronage in reverse," in which politicians owe their offices in considerable part to the vote of public jobholders, rather than jobholders theirs to politicians.

Labor's Strength. The line-up of political parties tends to be one of "the Labor party versus the rest." "The rest" are from time to time reinforced by dissidents from the Labor party. Such breaks arise from the Labor party's heavy emphasis on regularity, to the point of binding a member of Parliament by majority vote in the parliamentary caucus. They also result from divergencies between the Commonwealth and the state party organizations over such matters as external credit and defense. The voting strength of the Labor party appears to lie with the pastoral and metropolitan wage earners, who would drop below the desirable standard were it not for the social security and health service provided by the Commonwealth and the educational opportunities provided by the states.

To ease the task of getting out the vote, Australian political parties have introduced compulsory registration of voters and compulsory voting. The latter, in particular, probably does not warrant the importance accorded it in the theoretical writing on popular participation in the electoral process.

3. The Dominion of Canada

Federal Principles. Canada, being a federal union of ten provinces, needs a written constitution in order to define the principal relationships between the Dominion and the provincial governments.[8] The constitution was drafted by Canadians at the Quebec Conference of 1867 and enacted by the imperial parliament that same year as the British North America Act. Its purpose is in two ways more restricted than that of the constitution of the United States. It does not endeavor to define the separation of powers be-

---

[8] See especially Canada's Royal Commission on Dominion-Provincial Relations (chairmen, Rowell, Sirois), *Report* (Ottawa, 1940); H. M. Clokie, *Canadian Government and Politics* (Toronto, 1945); W. P. M. Kennedy, *Constitution of Canada* (Oxford, 1938); J. A. Maxwell, *Federal Subsidies to Provincial Governments* (Cambridge, Mass., 1937), and *Recent Developments in Dominion-Provincial Fiscal Relations in Canada* (New York, 1948).

tween legislature, executive, and judiciary, because Cabinet responsibility to Parliament is incompatible with any formal separation of powers. Nor does it proclaim the rights of the people against the government, because in British countries such rights are assumed to rest on the unwritten constitution, the prevalence of a spirit of toleration, and the availability of procedural remedies in case of abuse. Canada's written constitution, like that of Australia, is limited basically to relations between the Dominion and the provinces.

The Canadian constitution, moreover, is an act of Parliament of the United Kingdom. This fact affects both its formal amendment and its judicial interpretation. Since it contains no explicit provision for its own alteration, it is formally amended by petition from the Canadian Parliament to that of the United Kingdom, with or without prior consultation with the Canadian provinces, and without being referred back to the provinces for approval or disapproval. Interpretation of the constitution by the judicial committee of the Privy Council is literal rather than liberal, in the light of what the text says rather than of what its framers intended.

As with all federal constitutions, the boundary between central and provincial powers is an uncertain one, needing continual reinterpretation. Section 91 of the constitutional enactment empowers the Dominion Parliament "to make laws for the peace, order, and good government of Canada in relation to all matters not coming within the classes of subjects by this act assigned exclusively to the legislatures of the provinces; and, for greater certainty, but not so as to restrict the generality of the foregoing terms of this section, it is hereby declared that (notwithstanding anything in this act) the exclusive legislative authority of the Parliament of Canada extends to all matters coming within the classes of subjects next hereinafter enumerated." The enumerated powers include not only all those concerning national defense and national commerce, but also banking, marriage and divorce, and criminal law. In addition to these exclusive powers, the Dominion has paramount powers and the provinces have subordinate powers over agriculture. Moreover, it is plain that the residue of powers not enumerated rests with the Dominion. Section 92, on the other hand, gives to provinces exclusive legislative power over "property and civil rights," as well as over social services, judicial administration, and local and private matters.

Modification of Power Allocation. In weighing section 92 against section 91, the judicial committee of the Privy Council has made itself the protector of "provincial rights," thus throwing on the Canadian Parliament the onus of petitioning for an amendment of the constitution before using its residual powers in possible infringement of provincial control over "property and civil rights." The climax of restrictive judicial interpretation came when in 1937 the judicial committee annulled five pieces of Canadian "new deal" legislation enacted by a Conservative majority led by Prime Minister Bennett in 1935. One of these statutes found unconstitutional provided for national unemployment insurance, another for a national marketing board, and three for implementation of international labor agreements. Neither judicial interpretation, however, nor formal amendment is the only means by which the relative powers of the Dominion and the provincial governments have been modified. More important, indeed, have been the structure of the party machine and the power of the purse.

Political parties have evolved in Canada along American rather than British lines. Every party is a loose assortment of provincial and local party machines, which have to be kept in line by a discreet distribution of favors and judicious compromises in policy. Between the two principal parties there are no clear-cut differences of policy, principle, or ideology. Both alike have to respect provincial rights in order to win French Catholic votes in Quebec. Both alike have to advocate federal grants in aid in order to equalize opportunity in the poorer prairie and maritime provinces. Both alike have to be temperate in this advocacy in order not to frighten the taxpayers of Ontario. Seats in the Cabinet and on the Supreme Court are distributed with an eye to geographical representation. By an unwritten convention, identity of interest between provinces and Dominion is thus sought mainly through the working of party machinery, and especially through the selection of members of the Dominion Cabinet.

The development of relationships built on party politics has made for diminished reliance on legal powers. The constitutional document provides, for example, that the Dominion government should inherit the former imperial powers over the lieutenant governors of the provinces. It should hire and fire them. They might reserve their consent to provincial legislation until they had consulted the Dominion government; and the Dominion government might disallow the provincial legislation. The main weight of responsibility for checking provincial governments thus is on the Dominion Cabinet rather than the Supreme Court. But the close interaction of the provincial and Dominion party machines, together with the similarity and rivalry of the two principal parties, has led to a substitution of unobtrusive party consultation in place of frequent formal disallowance. The constitutional powers of Dominion control over provincial legislation are now kept in reserve and are used only when the nation's credit or foreign policy is menaced or when a third party is in control of a provincial government. Perhaps the interaction of provincial and Dominion party machines has also made for the absence of serious friction in the single system of judicial administration. Dominion laws are applied by provincial courts, except at the highest level.

Effects of Dominion Grants. A remarkable reallocation of functions has resulted from two complementary factors—the Dominion's plenitude of taxing powers, coupled with the impecuniousness of two thirds of the provinces. The Dominion government strives for a monopoly of those taxes that are of greatest economic significance, especially the income tax, both personal and corporate. Provinces that are none too well financed by levying these taxes are more than willing to give the federal government, on certain conditions, the sole right to collect them. In return, the provinces ask for unconditional federal block grants, intended to compensate them for the below-average showing of their taxing power. The provinces also expect the federal government to assume all heavy expenditures, such as debt charges and income security for unemployed wage earners, families with children, and old people. At the same time, the provinces want to keep untrammeled control over administration of all social services. They have therefore resisted cooperative federal-provincial administration and federal setting of standards by way of conditional grants in aid, such as have become normal in the United Kingdom and the United States.

These general principles, elaborated by a royal commission on Dominion-provincial relations in 1937-40, might be summed up as "separation of sources of revenue, and separation of governmental responsibilities." In their historic aspects, the principles were adopted by all provinces as a wartime expedient in the tax suspension agreements signed with seven of the nine provinces and approved by the Dominion Parliament in 1947.

In their current form, the principles have given a peculiar cast to the recent Canadian approach to social security. The Dominion has endeavored to confine itself to fiscal measures, leaving welfare services to the provinces.[9] Thus, the Family Allowance Act of 1944 is so calculated as to give low-income families a federal money grant roughly equivalent to the dependents' rebates they would have received had they been liable to federal income tax. On the other hand, health and welfare services for the recipients of these allowances are left strictly to the provinces. The Dominion has similarly proposed to institute unconditional old-age pensions for all Canadians seventy years old and above; old-age assistance for younger ones, on a basis of individually determined means and needs, would remain with the provinces.

Federal Policy-making. Conferences between the Prime Ministers, Dominion and provincial, are held from time to time as a matter of obvious political wisdom, especially whenever any constitutional issue is involved that is of direct concern to both levels of government. Such conferences are inevitably centrifugal in outlook. They have proved effective only as a means of demonstrating which national policies are politically inexpedient in a land of extreme provincial diversity.

The Dominion Parliament at Ottawa is bicameral.[10] But in practice the Cabinet is responsible only to the House of Commons; it is represented in

---

[9] This division of responsibility is akin to the one emerging in the United Kingdom, where income security as an element in a policy of economic stabilization has become a national responsibility, whereas much provision of educational, health, and welfare services is left to the local communities.

[10] The provincial legislatures are unicameral, except in Quebec, and are subject to dissolution and re-election at request of the provincial Premier and Cabinet, with consent of the lieutenant governor appointed by the Dominion.

the Senate by a single minister without portfolio. The Senate consists of life members, twenty-four each from Quebec, Ontario, the four western provinces together, the three eastern provinces together, and six from Newfoundland. Most of the nominees are reputed to be heavy contributors to party funds, or men who have otherwise served their party well. The reputation and influence of the Senate have not stood high. In the written constitution, the Senate is the equal of the House of Commons; in the unwritten constitution, it is distinctly inferior. Dissolution of the Dominion Parliament and the calling of a general election are theoretically at the discretion of the governor general. But, like the King in the United Kingdom, he has learned to use his discretion discreetly.

The political parties have well-recognized leaders. It was Canada, in fact, that started the custom of paying a salary to the leader of the opposition in its House of Commons. Party leadership may last a very long time. One of the dominant differences between the Liberal and the Conservative parties is that the Liberals have had only two leaders, Wilfred Laurier and MacKenzie King, in all the sixty years 1887-1948. By contrast, the Conservatives have had a succession of leaders, not one of whom has achieved the success of the Liberal leaders in holding the party together and winning elections over a long period of time.

Other Characteristics of Political Life. Political activity is inevitably divided between Ottawa and the provincial capitals. Inevitably, therefore, the parliament at Ottawa is less important as a focus for Canadian political opinion than the parliament at Westminster is for British political opinion. Moreover, its sessions are shorter, so as to allow its members to carry on their ordinary vocations back home in the provinces; few members of the House of Commons can therefore be regarded as professional politicians. Nor is the Dominion Cabinet subject to such thorough questioning as is the British Cabinet, remaining immune from parliamentary criticism during the greater part of the year.

The civil service was long subject to patronage distributed on the basis of party spoils. It might indeed be said that one of the motives in establishing responsible government was to transfer patronage from British-appointed governors to Canadian-elected politicians. Certainly, one of the bases on which nation-wide political parties were developed was the sharing-out of jobs. Only since World War I has the merit rule been substituted for spoils. In making this substitution, however, care has been taken to make the permanent civil service an attractive career, leading right up to the post of permanent head of a government department, with the title of deputy minister. In Canada, as in the United Kingdom, these top permanent posts are regarded as "policy-making" in nature. As in all British countries, the judiciary is appointed for life and thereby achieves a position of great independence and high respect. Judges are regarded as available to serve on royal commissions, including commissions to investigate matters that may later come before a court for trial, such as the disclosure of atomic secrets to a foreign power. They are also called upon for advisory opinions.

In the field of civil liberties, much less attention is paid to individual rights than to the corporate rights of churches and provinces—and especially to the liberties of the Roman Catholic church and of the province of Quebec. It was to ensure these liberties that a federal union was substituted for a unitary state in 1867. In most of the fields left to it as a province, Quebec has preserved and developed its own distinct culture pattern, with the Roman Catholic church assuming responsibility for many of the functions that are elsewhere discharged by government. Quebec has also had its own particularist French-Canadian nationalism, often of excessive intensity, in addition to the all-Canadian nationalism fostered by the major political parties.

4. The Union of South Africa

Diversity of Population. The Union of South Africa is a self-governing country the majority of whose inhabitants are not self-governing.[11] The ethnic composition of the population is a matter not only of political interest, but also of legal discrimination. It is approximately: European, 2,000,000; colored (light Negro), 750,000; East Indian, 250,000; detribalized natives, 3,000,000; and tribal natives, 3,000,000. On the assumption that these different sections of the citizenry are at different stages of development, segregation laws are strictly enforced. A native may not move about without a pass. He may not ride the same bus or street car as Europeans, except in Cape Province. He may not possess firearms or liquor or have sexual intercourse with one of another race.

His lack of liberty and equality, however, does not mean total neglect. The Europeans, it has been said, are too humane to deny the non-European all rights and too human to grant him full rights. Of native children of school age, one out of three gets some schooling, as against one in ten in the most progressive of British dependencies. State-supported universities do not exclude native students and are beginning to produce a native professional class. Municipal housing for detribalized natives is becoming common. Trade-union organization is allowed them, but does not have the protection of the law. Old-age, invalidity, widows and orphans pensions are available to detribalized natives as well as to Europeans, though at a much lower rate.

Enforcement of Inferior Status. The inferior status of the non-European is written into law, which is rigorously enforced by the police. It is not based on unwritten custom, enforced by lynch mobs; the Union of South Africa is a land of legalized discrimination. The presence of a large number of

---

[11] Cf. C. W. de Kiewiet, *History of South Africa* (Oxford, 1941); Roderick Peattie, *Struggle on the Veld* (New York, 1947); J. H. Hofmeyr, *South Africa* (London, 1931); B. Williams and Others, *The Selborne Memorandum* (London, 1925); A. P. Newton, *Select Documents Relating to the Unification of South Africa* (London, 1924); Julius Lewin, *Studies in African Native Law* (Philadelphia, 1947).

colored (lighter-skinned) people helps to make the color bar less sharp in
Cape Province than in other provinces. Some colored are of semi-Malaysian
origin and of Moslem religion. All colored are regarded by the law as a
distinct group, subject to lesser disabilities.

The Indians of Natal, also partly Moslem, who immigrated in the midnineteenth century and have never been granted the equal status they had
been promised, form another group apart. But some of them have grown
sufficiently wealthy to foster a powerful protest movement. Indians are forbidden to settle outside the province of Natal or to enter skilled trades. In
support of their agitation, India in 1946 broke off commercial relations with
the Union and invited the United Nations Assembly to intervene in this
South African affair.

The South Africa Act of 1909 provided that an otherwise uniform franchise might not be used to disenfranchise on grounds of race or color any class
of persons hitherto entitled to vote in the Cape Province; and the letter of
the law has thus far been respected. But the franchise has been extended
to European women, while remaining restricted to men among non-Europeans in the Cape. Native males in the Cape have been allowed to retain the
franchise, but have been put on separate electoral registers and grouped in
separate electoral districts. They have thereby been separated from the Cape
colored people, who have been left on the same register and in the same districts as the Europeans. Only Europeans may sit in Parliament. Among
the 150 members of the Assembly, the three representatives of the male Cape
natives thus have to be Europeans. The Senate includes four Europeans
indirectly elected by natives in four native areas, and two Europeans—one
elected and one appointed—to represent East Indians. The Natal Indians,
however, have introduced Mohandas Gandhi's tactic of noncooperation and
passive resistance.

Origins of Racial Inequality. There are several reasons why South Africa
adopted the attitudes it now displays toward race relations. One is a matter
of legal system. The Anglo-American common law blurs the distinction
between law and custom and operates through procedures that make it almost impossible to enforce the law when it is contrary to local custom. The
Roman-Dutch law of South Africa, on the other hand, is more self-contained
and less flexible. Secondly, Roman-Dutch law has always allowed much
place to differences of ethnic origin and stage of civilization. Thirdly, the
Afrikander Boers were untouched by the eighteenth-century creed of reason,
natural rights, and human equality. Their legal thinking, therefore, was
not refashioned in an equalitarian mold.

Nor is this stress on ethnic diversity restricted to relations between Europeans and non-Europeans. It pervades the relations among Europeans themselves, to such an extent that Afrikaans-speaking families are compelled
to send their children to Afrikaans-speaking schools, and English-speaking
families their children to English-speaking schools, even though both kinds

of schools are publicly provided. Similarly, some kinds of social assistance for Afrikanders—and most "poor whites" are Afrikanders—are distributed through tax-subsidized voluntary welfare agencies attached to the Dutch Reformed church, to which nearly all Afrikanders belong. Some years ago, a book was even published denying that there are South Africans.[12] Its point was that the various groups of British subjects in South Africa thought of themselves as Afrikander, British, colored, Indian, or native, rather than as South African. The country thus presents one of the very few examples in the modern world of a "plural society" whose cultural and ethnic pluralism is embodied in the law of the land.

But its pluralism is not territorial. The native does not stay on his reservation, but goes to work on an Afrikander farm or in an English city. The Afrikander no longer stays on his farm; beginning in the First World War, he has been drifting to the city. It is therefore impossible to envisage the Union as a confederated body of ethnically distinct cantons, like Switzerland, or as a federal union balancing culturally distinct provinces, like Canada. Segregation is primarily in different quarters on the farm, and in different neighborhoods in the metropolis; it is only secondarily and incompletely in different parts of the country. The ever-present problem of racial diversity is thus the bond of union that makes South Africa one country. It is competition for native labor, and therefore the development of rival native policies, that provides the two poles—the Afrikander farm and the British gold mine—on which the political parties turn. Moreover, it is from the revenue contributed by the British gold mines on the Rand that government supports services to the Afrikander on the Veld.

A Unitary State. South Africa is, next to New Zealand, the smallest of the "white" dominions overseas and the most densely populated, although reliance on cheap labor rather than mechanical skill has made it a land of lower productivity and consumption than any other dominion. Relatively small and fairly crowded, the Union of South Africa was planned by the national convention of 1908-09 as a unitary state. The unitary constitution was approved by the parliaments of the Cape, Orange Free State, and Transvaal, and by the voters of Natal. It was embodied in the South Africa Act of 1909.

The Union government is fully sovereign. The Crown in whose name foreign policy is conducted is the Crown of South Africa. The sovereign Parliament is entitled to amend the South Africa Act, though this was not foreseen in that act; but there seems to be a constitutional custom that that act be regarded as a fundamental and supreme law.

The procedure of the Union Parliament is distinctive; thus, native policy is apt to be handled as a nonparty matter, in which the Cabinet turns over the leadership to a select committee before the second reading. As for the role of the Cabinet in general, the Status of the Union Act of 1934 says ex-

---

[12] G. H. Calpin, *There Are No South Africans* (Toronto, 1941).

plicitly that reference to the King "shall be deemed to be a reference to the King acting on the advice of his ministers of state for the Union." The Governor General has refused a dissolution of Parliament at the request of the Prime Minister alone, as in the United Kingdom, insisting instead on a request backed by a majority of ministers in the Cabinet. Above all, the unitary state shows itself in the fact that provincial ordinances need the consent of the Union government and can be overridden by Union legislation. As another aspect, the provincial councils may be abolished by Union legislation.

Provinces and Metropoles. The most important units of local government are the four provinces, whose councils are elected for a fixed term. Their executive committees consist of four members elected by the councils and an administrator on term appointment by the central government. Constitutional custom has done away with certain powers of the provinces, leaving the Union with full responsibility qualified only by the approval of a Provincial Consultative Committee. Thus far, this process has occurred in respect of social assistance and other social welfare services, the Union having assumed the entire responsibility for the raising of basic consumption standards, except for emergency poor-relief in Natal.[13] The Union has also become fully responsible for vocational education.

The provinces, on the other hand, have been allowed to retain responsibility for elementary education and for roads. At least half the provincial expenditures are met by the central government, with supplementary equalization grants to the more rural provinces. Much of the remaining outlay is met by provincial surcharges on Union taxes collected by the Union. All borrowing for the provinces is done by the central government. Moreover, the provinces and the Union have a single unified civil service.

Apart from the provinces, the only important units of local self-government are the big metropolitan areas. They are responsible primarily for control of environmental development, land-use planning, public utility undertakings, and housing. City limits have been drawn with extreme generosity, and much land ownership has been vested in the municipal government. A considerable portion of municipal revenue is derived from the sale of real estate and services.

5. Ireland

Political Individuality. The self-governing British dominions fall chronologically into three groups. First came the four countries of European settlement overseas: New Zealand, Australia, Canada, and South Africa. Next came Ireland, or Eire, which achieved dominion status after World War I by a revolt of European natives against European settlers. Third and last

---

[13] South Africa, like Australia and New Zealand, prefers noncontributory assistance to contributory insurance; but all its assistance grants are conditional on investigation of means and needs. Three distinct budget scales are used: (*a*) European, (*b*) Indian and colored, and (*c*) native, in a ratio of 4:3:2, respectively.

came the tropical countries around the Indian Ocean, led by India, Pakistan, and Ceylon, which have achieved dominion status since World War II by concession to peoples of non-European culture by the previous European rulers. Although different in origin from the first four, Ireland thus represented an important transition between them and the later comers.[14]

Ireland is different from Britain. This characteristic did not have to await dominion status before it obtained official recognition. The Irish system of land tenure has never been the same as the one dominant in Britain. This social fact was acknowledged in two ways. First, landlords in Ireland were deprived by statute of the right to fix rents, evict tenants, and profit from the permanent improvements made by them. Second, the government forcibly purchased the landlords' land in order to resell it to the Irish tenants at a lower annual charge than the rent they had previously been paying. A written constitution interpreted judicially might have prevented such statutory interferences with the sanctity of contract and property. But the unlimited sovereignty of the parliament of the United Kingdom allowed it to effect this radical and revolutionary social change. The laws transformed Ireland from a land of rack-rented leasehold peasants into one of freeholding farmers —at the very time when Britain was becoming one vast urban market for the products of Ireland's new cooperative creameries and bacon factories.

As with land tenure, so it was with religion. When the younger Pitt effected the parliamentary union of Ireland with Great Britain in 1801, only fear of George III's insanity prevented the experiment of "parallel establishment" of the principal churches in Ireland, including the Roman Catholic. During the next generation, state aid was granted to Roman Catholic parochial schools and non-Protestant higher education, the foundation thus being laid for the present National University of Ireland. In 1869 the churches were put on a footing of equality by the disestablishment of the Protestant Episcopal church of Ireland and the diversion to Irish education and social welfare of those of its endowments that dated from the Middle Ages.

Toward Independence. In politics, the same process was at work. The extension of the franchise in 1884 to nearly all adult males, regardless of their property status, made it possible for the Irish Nationalist party to sweep twenty-six of the island's thirty-two counties. Thus, it was able to hold the balance in the House of Commons at Westminster and to oblige the British parties to follow an Irish line, with the Liberals emphasizing "home rule" and the Conservatives "union." The establishment of elective county councils after 1888 gave Irish farmers and merchants a big measure of local self-government, which they used in a practical and constructive manner.

The republican uprising extended from the American-financed and German-armed Easter Rebellion of 1916 to the "treaty" with the United Kingdom

---

[14] The Irish constitution of 1938 is reprinted in *International Conciliation*, 343 (1938), 352 ff. See also A. W. and M. C. Bromage, "Vocational Senate in Ireland," *American Political Science Review*, 34 (1940), 519 ff.

of December 6, 1921. The subsequent achievement of dominion status was essentially the culmination of a longer-range process of national reconstruction. Irish self-government was in fact completed when the Irish republican members of Parliament, elected under the law of the United Kingdom at the general elections of 1918 and 1921, assembled at Dublin instead of going to Westminster; when local officials all over Ireland recognized this self-constituted elective body as their rightful government; when ministers of the United Kingdom entered into negotiation with the rebels; and when the parliament of the United Kingdom regularized the secession by giving it statutory recognition.

National Self-rule. From 1921 to 1948, the majority of Irish republicans, led by Eamon de Valera—born an American citizen—strove through the Fianna Fail party to give the finishing touches to the symbolism of national self-rule. Meanwhile, a number of smaller parties, rallying around the republican minority in the Fine Gael party, have devoted their attention to practical problems rather than ideology and symbols.

Of this symbolism, one aspect is language. The almost extinct Gaelic language is being artificially revived. All school teachers and all pupils have to learn it. Every institution is decked with an Irish name. Ireland is Eire, its Parliament is the Oireachtas, its House of Commons is Dail Eireann, its Senate is Seaned Eireann; and every politician respells his name in Gaelic style.

The principal symbol of national self-rule is the constitution of 1937. Initiated by the de Valera Cabinet, passed by Eire's Parliament, and approved by the voters in a referendum, this basic law is the only example in the world of a written constitution interpreted judicially, supreme over statute law in a unitary state. In all other unitary countries, such as the United Kingdom, New Zealand, and South Africa, there is either no such fundamental law or, if there is, as in France, it is not subject to judicial interpretation, especially in the sense that it cannot be used as a weapon for annulling statutes.

Framework of the Constitution. The constitution begins with a preamble, "In the name of the Most Holy Trinity, from Whom is all authority." It lists certain fundamental rights—collective rather than individual—repugnancy to which would void a statute. Such are recognition of the family as the fundamental social group and of marriage as the fundamental institution; recognition of existing religious denominations and particularly of the special position of the Catholic church as the guardian of the faith professed by the majority; and recognition of the right to form associations and unions. The constitution also lays down some principles of social policy for the guidance of Parliament, and perhaps also for the guidance of the courts when interpreting the law. Such are distribution of property and regulation of credit for the common good rather than for individual gain; assurance to all citizens of adequate means of livelihood; establishment of families in economic security on the land; and safeguards to the interests of widows and orphans, the aged, and the infirm. Amendments to the constitution must be passed by Parliament and approved by the voters in a referendum.

The name Ireland (Eire) indicates a claim to the whole island, including the six counties of Northern Ireland which have chosen through their Parliament to remain part of the United Kingdom.

Organs of Government. The relationship between Cabinet and Parliament is slightly different in Eire from that which prevails in other British countries. The Prime Minister is elected by the House of Commons, by which also his choice of ministers is formally confirmed. These provisions were made originally in 1922 in the expectation that there would be a number of small parties, no one of which would command a majority. The Senate is one of the weakest anywhere. It is merely a deliberative body with a ninety-day suspensory veto. Of its sixty members, six are elected by university constituencies; eleven are appointed by the Prime Minister; and forty-three are elected indirectly, by members of Parliament and representatives of county councils, from among candidates nominated on vocational panels.

The titular head of the state, originally (1922-37) a governor general in the name of the King, is now a president elected by the people for a seven-year term. In selecting a prime minister and other ministers, he is completely governed by the advice of the House. Before signing a bill passed by Parliament, the President in council may consult the Supreme Court on the bill's constitutionality and may submit it to referendum if so requested by a certain number of members of Parliament.

In local government, two significant deviations from the British pattern have occurred. One is an attempt to prevent interference in administrative detail by committees composed of elective councilors. The first means tried was appointment of central commissioners in place of locally elected councilors. Then, in 1927, an alternative method was adopted—mandatory appointment of full-time professional managers. Thus, the four county boroughs, twenty-seven administrative counties, and fifty-eight urban sanitary districts now have managers, removable only with the consent of the central government, as well as elective councils—an interesting compromise between the American council-manager system and the German burgomaster system. At the same time, the central government set up a Local Appointments Commission to prepare a panel of qualified managerial and professional personnel and submit suitable candidates to the selection boards of local councils.

Political Problems. Eire has assumed positive responsibility for national economic development, in the hope of lessening its dependence on the British market; reducing the need for Irish wage earners to emigrate in search of employment; increasing the productivity of Irish agriculture; and adding to the amenities of both rural and urban living. Hydroelectric power, especially from the Atlantic tides; beet sugar and industrial alcohol; credit facilities and insurance; shipping and civil aviation—these interests all have received government help, usually in the form of state subscription for shares in the stock of a mixed enterprise.

Economically, Eire cannot do without the British market. On the monetary side, the Irish pound is tied to the pound sterling, with the government-owned Central Bank for Ireland as an agency for freely converting the notes of the one country into those of the other.

During World War II, the country preserved a benevolent neutrality. The anomalous status of the country has been summed up by its Prime Minister in the frequently repeated phrase, "an independent republic, associated as a matter of external policy with the states of the British Commonwealth." [15] Since April 18, 1949, the Republic of Ireland has ceased to be part of "His Majesty's dominions," and its citizens have ceased to be *ipso facto* citizens of the Commonwealth. Yet under the laws of the United Kingdom, Ireland has not thereby become a foreign country, nor have its citizens become aliens. Those of its nationals who have close ties with the United Kingdom are permitted to be at the same time citizens of both countries. The representative of Ireland at London, although called Ambassador, has the same legal status as the High Commissioner of a Commonwealth country.

6. *India and Pakistan*

Non-European Dominions. The Indian Independence Act of 1947 permitted the establishment in Asia of two fully self-governing dominions— India and Pakistan—on the second anniversary of the surrender of Japan.[16] Here, for the first time, dominion status was conferred upon a land of non-European culture (though of Indo-European language). Here, for the first time, the very title of an act passed by the parliament of the United Kingdom conceded that dominion status was tantamount to independence, including the right of the dominion to choose for itself any form of government and any form of relationship with the British Crown that it might desire. At a time when neither the French nor the Dutch had found a way of handling their postwar colonial problems without fighting, the British had at hand a tried political technique that they used with effectiveness to liquidate their imperial liabilities peacefully, in the hope of leaving behind a heritage of good will and a reputation for constructive achievement.

India is an area as small and as hot as the Caribbean in which more people are massed together than live in all the Americas. The "communities" to which most of them are devoted, and by whose symbols they can be aroused, are not political but religious. They are the two great religions brought into India by former conquerors from the northwest—Hinduism, with its Aryan scriptures, its polytheism, its belief in reincarnation, its pacifist and vegetar-

---

[15] E. de Valera, on several occasions, more recently in Dail, *Debates,* June 19, 1946.

[16] Cf. M. A. Jinnah, *Pakistan* (New York, 1940); J. Nehru, *Toward Freedom* (New York, 1941); R. W. Coupland, *The Cripps Mission* (Oxford, 1942).

ian leanings, its caste system, and its outcasts; and Islam, with its Semitic scriptures, its monotheism, its militancy, and its equalitarianism. The former has planted itself, from the first millennium before Christ, the whole length of the peninsula, from the Himalayas in the north, through the sacred valley of the Ganges, to the plateau of the Deccan in the south, until its adherents now number nearly 300 million. The latter has planted itself principally at the northwestern and northeastern landgates to India, in two widely separated areas, whose inhabitants are rising toward 100 million.

Impact of the Foreigner. The British, coming by sea, to trade and not to settle, were less successful than these former conquerors in substituting new religious attitudes for old. They allowed the Hindu and Moslem ways of living and thinking to persist without frontal attack. What they did, however, was to add to them many elements of Western culture.

In the realm of material civilization, they developed overseas trade, substituting interdependence for self-sufficiency, promoting a money economy, outcompeting village handicrafts, investing capital in large-scale enterprises, developing seaports, building railways, alleviating famine, lessening disease, postponing death, and permitting population to rise faster than productivity. In this clash of cultures, there was but little conscious planning. The final result had both its good and its bad sides, both equally unintended. Mechanical transportation and communication gave the peninsula a bigger measure of unity than it had ever known before and opened the way to common action on the part of leaders in different places. At the same time, a feeling developed among the people of India that their poverty was being intensified by the unplanned economic and demographic changes.

New institutions and new attitudes were also built up during the two hundred years of the British "raj." Among these was a whole network of governmental institutions, which have left India and Pakistan better organized politically than most self-governing countries in Asia. Among them also was an educational system, which, though reaching only a minority, fostered the spread of a Western outlook. Not least were Western concepts such as social progress, economic well-being, rising living standards, self-government, nationalism, liberty, and democracy. Although the old institutions and attitudes were left carefully alone, they have thus been exposed to many forces that have profoundly modified them.

Ways of Government. Thus, on coming into existence in August 1947, India and Pakistan inherited an institutional structure that, on its religious side, was Aryan and Arabic, but, on its political as on its economic side, was British. When the Mogul empire broke down in the eighteenth century and the British East India Company intervened in the resulting civil strife in order to be able to carry on its business, two different types of government were established. Half of what is now India, and nearly all of what is now Pakistan, became "provinces" under the direct rule and absolute sovereignty of the central government. The other half of India remained as "states" under hereditary rulers who agreed in treaties to accept the "paramountcy" of the imperial Crown. This agreement meant that they would take on British advisers and no others, and that they would have no foreign relations but those of the imperial Crown. When the new dominions were constituted in 1947, one of the first problems to be settled was therefore that of the accession of the states to one or the other of the dominions. The next problem was the status of the states as self-governing units side by side with the provinces in what was bound to become some type of federal union.

An Indian civil service, with entry by competitive examination, was built up beginning in 1833—a generation earlier than that in the United Kingdom. Examinations for top posts were originally held only at London; between the World Wars, however, they came to be held simultaneously at London and Delhi, thus increasing the chances of Indians being able to compete. On the eve of independence, more than half of the top thousand officials were Indian, as were nearly all intermediate and subordinate officials. As in all British countries, many of the attitudes of the British civil servant were carried over, including the expectation that he would find in the service a rewarding life career, with access to the very highest posts, and with inflexible standards of integrity and nonpartisanship expected of at least the holders of top positions. So important had the civil service become that it was often charged with perverting Indian education by providing an incentive to the development of an irrelevant, verbalistic, English-language kind of instruction, and one leaving the civil service with a less practical outlook than it needed.

India's international status was staked out when, like any dominion, it became one of the original members, first of the League of Nations, and then of the United Nations. The government of India, composed largely of British civil servants, was consulted on matters concerning it as much as a dominion.

Political Agitation. A domestic press was permitted to develop and to go to great lengths—though not so far as it would have liked—in rousing public criticism of governmental action and contempt for the existing political system. Political parties were also allowed to develop. These aimed both against the British and against one another. Their activities were restricted, and their leaders detained or imprisoned when they obstructed government or defense by fostering mass noncooperation or sabotage. For other purposes the parties operated freely; along with the press, they gave the country the first beginning of political consciousness.

To provide an outlet for the rising national feeling, the British tried to introduce some measure of parliamentary representation and ministerial responsibility by two acts passed in 1919 and 1935. Under a system of "dyarchy," however, these acts permitted transfer only of certain functions to responsible Indian ministers, while reserving to governors and civil servants all other functions, as well as safeguards in respect of transferred ones. The granting of full self-government was made conditional on prior agreement among the principal organized groups in India as to the kind of constitution under which they would be prepared to operate. Such agreement could not be reached, either between provinces and states or between Hindu and Moslem.

The dominant party was the Indian National Congress, which sought to create an all-India patriotism that would transcend religious diversity. Its leaders, however, were Hindu. In opposition, there arose a Moslem League, convinced that the only way to prevent the tyranny of a permanent Hindu majority over a permanent Moslem minority was to create a counterbalancing sovereign state of Pakistan ("the land of the pure") in which the Moslems would be in a majority. Party rivalry thus became exacerbated by communal feeling in the religious sense and by territorial regionalism.

Collapse of Unity. During World War II, the governor general prepared the way for an all-Indian Cabinet. He created a Cabinet secretariat on the British model and invited Indian leaders to join his executive council on an individual basis as ministers responsible for liaison with the permanent secretaries who headed the various departments. In May 1946, a British Cabinet mission to India arranged for the executive council to become an interim government, presided over by the leader of the leading Indian party and composed of spokesmen for the various parties; this was to be the first step toward an elected constituent assembly.[17] The interim government was joined first by the Congress party, headed by Pandit Nehru, and later by the Moslem League, headed by Mr. Jinnah. Only the Congress party participated in the constituent assembly, however; the League abstained. By "direct action" in the form of communal rioting, it made plain that an all-India constitution would meet with active resistance in the predominantly Moslem regions.

In these circumstances, full agreement was reached at last in June 1947 between Governor General Lord Mountbatten, the Indian party leaders, the British Cabinet, and the British opposition. The agreement provided for a procedural plan by which any province that did not wish to abide by the constitution then being drafted in the All-Indian Constituent Assembly might join another constituent assembly; the plan also allowed the Moslem portions of the provinces of Bengal and the Punjab to exercise a similar option. In addition, the agreement provided that full dominion powers of self-government and self-determination should be conferred on August 15, 1947, upon both India and Pakistan. They would then elaborate their constitutions by virtue of dominion status, instead of as a condition for achieving that status.[18]

Relations between the two new dominions became their own responsibility. Cooperation was needed in the dividing of their assets and liabilities and

---

[17] Cf. Cmd. 6821 and Cmd. 6835 (1946).
[18] House of Commons, *Debates*, June 3, 1947.

in providing for the exchange of twelve million refugees. Rivalry was inevitable in winning the accession of states ruled by princes. Since 1948, one such dispute has been before the United Nations.

The Republic of India. By 1950 the constituent assembly at Delhi had completed the transformation of the Government of India Act of 1935 into the Constitution of the Republic of India—the longest of all written constitutions, but one that can be amended by a two-thirds majority in both houses.

India is a federal union in which the balance of power is sharply tilted toward the center. The constitutions of the component states are embodied in the national constitution; the states therefore have home rule in the British but not the American sense. The governors are appointed by the Union government, much as in Canada, and have to consult that government before signifying their assent to state legislation that may impinge on national policy. Certain enumerated fields, such as local government, health, relief, and cooperatives, are reserved to the states. Many other fields, including economic and social planning, social security, and employment, are under concurrent jurisdiction, with preponderance to Union legislation. Residual powers belong to the Union. State governments get most of their revenues from the Union. In an emergency the Union government may suspend state governments.

At each level a Council of Ministers is responsible to an elective parliament. The Union Parliament is virtually unicameral for money bills but bicameral for other matters, as in Britain. The House of the People is directly elected by universal suffrage, with one member for every 500,000-750,000 of the population, without a literacy test. The Council of States is for the most part elected by the state legislatures. The House of the People, like the British House of Commons, lasts five years, but can be dissolved sooner. The Council of States, like the American Senate, is renewed one-third every two years. If the two houses sitting separately do not pass a bill in a form satisfactory to the government, the government may have them dispose of it in joint session.

For protection against the tyranny of religious and linguistic "communities," much reliance is placed by the constitution on a Bill of Rights and on recruitment of civil servants by Public Service Commissions, state boundaries based on accidents of history rather than on a dominant language, and retention of English for legal and other official purposes. The way these safeguards will work out may depend on the kind of party system that emerges.

The Republic of India—with the consent of the Conference of Commonwealth Prime Ministers, and after consultation with the Republic of Ireland —has chosen to remain a member of the Commonwealth. Her citizens are Commonwealth citizens. Her Parliament presumably retains a voice in the succession to the Crown as the symbolic headship of the Commonwealth.

7. Ceylon

Problems of Representation. The Independence of Ceylon Act of 1947 completed the long process by which that prosperous little tropical island and useful naval base in the Indian Ocean evolved gradually and peacefully from the status of a crown colony to that of a dominion.[19]   In consultation with Ceylonese political leaders, the United Kingdom had already granted to Ceylon by order in council a constitution intended to be adequate for self-government.   In framing this constitution, two problems had to be wrestled with.   The one was how to make the legislative council representative.   The other has been how to make it responsible.

To make representative the present House of Representatives, principal reliance has been placed on a careful delimitation of electoral districts so as to make them communally homogeneous.   This process is a kind of gerrymander in reverse; it is aimed at preventing the Buddhist Singhalese majority from depriving the Hindu Tamil minority of representation.   To strengthen the minority further, the delimitation takes account of area as well as population, since the minority's density of population happens to be lower than that of the majority.   Even so, a few places had to be reserved for "nominating" (that is, appointing) representatives for small but important minorities that are too widely scattered to be provided with territorial districts.   Such are the Europeans (British), Burghers (Dutch), Moors (Arabs), and Malays.   In case this is not enough for proper balance, a Senate had also been added, half of whose thirty members are elected by the House of Representatives whereas the other half are appointed.   Appointment is to secure representation for individuals who have served Ceylon with distinction in their professions or in some way other than by getting elected to office. There is also an unwritten understanding that minorities be represented in the Cabinet as well as in Parliament.

The franchise was formerly limited by property and literacy tests.   Universal manhood suffrage was introduced in 1931, followed by universal adult suffrage in 1947.   The step was taken with the intention of obliging politicians to consider the welfare of the masses—which, indeed, they have done by a considerable extension of rural education, school lunches, water supply, and relief for those not able-bodied.

Securing Responsibility. Responsibility, in the British way of governing, is as essential as representativeness.   As soon as those not officials outnumbered the officials, the majority in the legislative council could be counted upon to become a permanent opposition. Friction between governor and

---

[19] Colonial Office, Committee on Constitutional Reform in Ceylon (chairman, Soulsbury), *Report* (Cmd. 6677 [1945]); *Proposals for Conferring on Ceylon Full Responsible Status within the British Commonwealth of Nations* (Cmd. 7257 [1947]).   W. I. Jennings, *The Commonwealth in Asia* (Oxford, 1951).

legislative council then became inevitable; but the two sides were in totally different situations. The governor as an administrator had to face the practical consequences of his acts, whereas the legislative majority did not. The British formula for avoiding this impasse prescribed the handing over of the government to a cabinet of ministers responsible to a parliament. The step, however, seemed a very big one to take all at once. In Ceylon, it was therefore broken down into two steps.

Of these, the first was embodied in the "Donoughmore constitution" of 1931—so called because it was proposed to the Secretary of State for the Colonies (Sidney Webb, Lord Passfield) by a special commission of inquiry presided over by Lord Donoughmore. It set up a board of ministers, three of whom were still to be members of the governor's staff; the remaining seven were to be chosen from the legislative council, now rechristened a council of state. The board of ministers fell short of being a true British-type cabinet, in that it was not homogeneous in institutional composition and therefore could not be collectively responsible to the council. An interesting experiment was therefore tried of splitting the council into seven executive committees, like those of a British county council, and having each committee elect its chairman, who thereupon became the minister in charge of a group of departments. It was hoped that in this way more members of the council would acquire a sense of executive responsibility and that the experience would be shared by both the Singhalese majority and the Tamil minority. In this first stage of responsibility, of course, the divergence from the British model was quite serious. Ministers felt free to oppose one another's policies in public and even to criticize the policies voted for their own departments by the majority of their fellow committee members.

The next stage toward full responsibility for internal self-government was to introduce a cabinet true to type. This stage was accomplished when the ministers drafted a constitution which came into effect in 1947. It was hoped that the process of selecting a prime minister and having him choose his cabinet colleagues would produce a politically homogeneous and collectively responsible cabinet. It was also expected that cabinet government would stimulate the formation of two parties, the one in support and the other in opposition. Each party, moreover, would be in such need of the support by the minority groups that these would be politically certain to receive seats in the cabinet.

Achievement of Dominion Status. In taking this step toward responsibility, Ceylon ceased to be a dependency in the technical sense and thereby ceased to be eligible for grants from the Colonial Development and Welfare Fund. It had to assume responsibility for its own development.

In three crucial ways, however, Ceylon had then not yet reached dominion status. It was not yet responsible for its own defense and foreign policy. Instead of choosing a governor general, it still had a governor picked by the

Colonial Office and endowed with some reserve powers.   And it was not yet free to modify its own constitution.

With the removal of these restrictions by act of Parliament of the United Kingdom, the island of Ceylon became a fully self-governing dominion.[20]

---

[20] See also Charles Collins, *Public Administration in Ceylon* (London, 1951).

PART III

CONSTITUTIONAL GOVERNMENT: FRANCE AND ITALY

CHAPTER 10

DEMOCRATIC AND AUTHORITARIAN TENDENCIES IN FRANCE

1. Historic Background

French citizens created the Fourth French Republic in 1946. They built it out of the ruins of war and the ravages of four years of the German occupation of World War II. But the foundations of the Fourth French Republic go back at least to the great French Revolution of 1789, a revolution which, in turn, sprang from years of authoritarian misgovernment. Several times since then the French people have lived under authoritarian rule— where the ordinary citizen was the object of government but did not take part in it. These experiences are woven into the historical background of the Fourth Republic. But even as authoritarian traditions have played their role, so have democratic traditions. To understand the constitution of the Fourth French Republic, we must first trace the course of these conflicting traditions.

Effects of the French Revolution. The heritage of the great revolution, one of the building blocks of the present French government, is a mixed heritage. On the one hand, it provided precedent for overthrowing any government not momentarily supported by Parisian mobs. The French historian Lamartine wrote in 1847:

I scarcely exceed the middle age of man, yet I have already lived under ten dominations, or ten different governments, in France. Between infancy and maturity I have witnessed ten revolutions—ten cataracts, by which the spirit of modern liberty and the stationary or obstructive spirit have endeavored by turns to descend or to remount the declivity of revolutions.[1]

If he had lived until now, he could have added more revolutions and forms of government to his account.

On the other hand, the great revolution provided Frenchmen with an enduring political ideal, the ideal of "liberty, equality, and fraternity."[2] The concrete application of this ideal was written into the *Declaration of the Rights of Man,* one of the first enactments of the revolutionary National

---

[1] Quoted in Charles K. Adams, *Democracy and Monarchy in France* (New York, 1874), 4.

[2] For an interesting eyewitness account of some of the events of the French Revolution, see Arthur Young, *Travels in France and Italy during the Years 1787, 1788 and 1789* (ed. Ernest Rhys, New York, 1942).

Assembly. Founded on the philosophical ideas of Voltaire, Montesquieu, and Rousseau, its phrases are noble:

Men are born free and remain free and equal in rights. . . . The aim of all political organization is the conservation of the natural and imprescriptible rights of man. . . . The foundation of all sovereignty rests essentially in the Nation; no agency, or individual can exercise authority except such as comes expressly from the Nation. . . . Liberty consists in the ability to do all things which do not do damage to others . . . these limits on liberty can only be determined by law. . . . Free communication of ideas and opinions is one of the most precious rights of man; all citizens may, therefore, freely speak, write, and print, being responsible only for the abuse of this liberty in cases determined by law.[3]

This same declaration was made a part of the preamble of the Constitution of the Fourth French Republic.

But the revolutionary leaders gave France more than noble documents. They also gave the nation some enduring institutions—for example, the present local government unit, the French department. It was set up first in November and December, 1789, in an effort to break down the ancient, deeply felt, provincial loyalties of French citizens. The revolutionists swept away the old French provinces, just as they had swept away many other evidences of the privileged *ancien régime* of Louis XVI and his predecessors. The departments created were named mostly from geographical features of the landscape.

The departments were retained in the organization provided by the moderate Constitution of 1791. But other institutions of the revolution quickly passed away as leader after leader won the temporary support of the revolutionary masses. Some leaders slaughtered their opponents, and were in turn slaughtered. Many of the changes of leadership were reflected in French constitutions. The limited monarchy established by the Constitution of 1791, for instance, was supposed to be replaced by the republican, Girondist constitution of 1793. However, this draft constitution was never put into effect; it disappeared with the fall of the *Gironde* and the momentary rise of Robespierre. Nor was the *Montagnard* constitution of 1793 put into operation. It was superseded by the Constitution of the Year III (1795), the constitution of the Directory. The five directors were the executive authority under this constitution. They paid little attention to their legislature, no matter what the constitution provided. In many ways they were utterly dictatorial. In the end they were the victims of their spectacularly successful general, Napoleon Bonaparte.

Napoleonic Contributions. Napoleon has been called the preserver of the ideals of the French Revolution. This is true to the extent that he made last-

---

[3] Author's translation, from *Archives Parlementaires,* 1st ser., 9 (Paris, 1877), 236 ff.

ing contributions in administration and law. His work in governmental innovation began with his first constitution, that of the Year VIII (1799), the constitution of the Consulate. By its terms Napoleon gave himself, as first consul, all the real executive power, including the power of proposing laws, selecting administrative advisers, and naming ministers, ambassadors, officers of the army and navy, and members of the local administrations. Much of Napoleon's sweeping executive power was exercised under his direction by his major administrative advisers. These were organized by the constitution of 1799 into a Council of State, which became the center of the Napoleonic administrative system. The Council was divided into various sections: legislative, interior, financial, war, navy, and commercial.[4] It wrote projects of laws and also drafted orders for enforcing the laws. It helped to perpetuate the ideas of the revolution by translating some of the theoretical objectives of the revolution into precise rules and orders that the French people had to obey. This organization still operates in the Fourth Republic, although some of its functions are somewhat changed.

Under Napoleon the Council of State had another important function. It had the power to decide controversies ensuing from actions of civil servants in the official performance of their duty. French citizens were thereby given a method of protesting against illegal actions of their civil servants. Likewise, the Council laid the foundations of French administrative law and separated this law from the ordinary civil and criminal law.

This Council of State continued to operate in 1802 when Napoleon, after a popular vote, made himself Consul for life. In 1804 Napoleon had himself proclaimed Emperor of the French; further, he made the office hereditary in his family.

Napoleon made still other administrative contributions. For example, he centralized local government under the prefect. This official was appointed at first by the First Consul, later by the Emperor. Each department had its prefect. He was the agent of the central government and enforced its orders. Under Napoleon, also, the departments lost their elective governing councils that had existed since the revolution. The council's powers were given to the prefect and his assistants, who were responsible to the Minister of the Interior. Thus Napoleon centralized French local government.

He left his mark also on the legal system. Of this he was especially proud. He said once that, more than all of his battles, his glory was the Napoleonic code. Actually, before Napoleon, as early as 1791, in the first stages of the revolution, some efforts had been made to collect all of the criminal and civil laws into comprehensive codes, but little was done to carry out the undertaking. Napoleon provided the driving force. He turned the routine work over to skilled lawyers, but he himself, at the head of his Council of State, supervised their work and often made personal decisions. With some

---

[4] This last section was added in the constitutional law of 28 Floréal, Year XII (May 18, 1804).

modernizations and changes, these codes are still the bases for the French legal system. As H. A. L. Fisher says, the codes "preserve the essential conquests of the revolutionary spirit—civil equality, religious toleration, the emancipation of land, public trial, the jury of judgment."[5]

French Experience in Constitution-making. Although Napoleon, falling from dizzying heights of power to die on the island of St. Helena, was repudiated by his people and defeated by a great European alliance, his administrative system continued to operate. It worked effectively throughout many changes in the form of French government during the 19th century. It gave the Bourbon kings, restored to the French throne in 1815, a weapon for administrative centralization, although they greatly reduced its importance as a political instrument. It continued in effect when the Bourbon Charles X, too anxious to restore the *ancien régime,* was forced to flee from France in 1830, and also during the Orleanist regime, from 1830 to 1848, under Louis-Philippe, the "citizen-king." It was used to even better advantage after the revolution of 1848, which brought the Second Republic into being. Perhaps the man who made best use of it was the first president of this Republic, Louis Napoleon, a nephew of Napoleon Bonaparte. He incorporated the system in the Constitution of 1852, under which he became President for ten years. This constitution was a faithful copy of that of his uncle's consulate. The similarity did not end there: a few months later Louis Napoleon, after a plebiscite, made himself Emperor.

For each of these changes of regime, a constitution was drafted. Thus the French, at the fall of the Second Empire in 1870, had had much experience in constitution writing—for republics, monarchies, and empires, with any number of different legislative bodies and executive structures. Through all of these constitutions, however, the ordinary citizens followed the principles set down in the Napoleonic codes, with relatively little change.

2. The Third Republic

Beginnings of the Republic. Meanwhile France was transformed from a quiet agricultural country into a modern industrial power. It was this modernized France that fought, in 1870, with a modernized Prussia—and lost. The Franco-Prussian cataclysm led to the setting up of the Third French Republic, a form of government that endured longer—from 1870 to 1940—than any other since the time of the French Revolution. This Third French Republic is important also as the model for the Fourth French Republic. Indeed, it would be hard to understand the machinery of government of the Fourth Republic without knowing something of the structure, functioning, and political problems of the Third Republic.[6]

---

[5] In *Cambridge Modern History* (Cambridge, 1907), Vol. 9, 179.

[6] For a detailed discussion of the political history of the Third Republic, see Denis W. Brogan, *France under the Republic* (New York, 1940); also David Thomson, *Democracy in France* (London, 1946). For analysis of the government and politics of the Third Republic, see R. K.

The Third French Republic, paradoxically, was shaped by men who represented a minority of the French voters. The majority preferred a monarchy. Only later did the minority view become that of the majority. At the time of its founding, the republic was established almost by default.

As the Franco-Prussian war ended, the Napoleonic empire was in collapse. Louis Napoleon (Napoleon III) himself was taken prisoner at Sedan. When this news reached Paris, the legislative body under the empire debated the foundation of some sort of a provisional government. While it was debating, the Prussian army was about to storm Paris. Because the debates led to no action, mobs invaded the assembly hall. Under the leadership of Gambetta, a fiery republican, they approved a Government of National Defense on September 4, 1870. This government, in spite of its name, was unable to improvise a defense strong enough to defeat the Prussian army. The spirited defense of the homeland by irregular troops could not substitute for the power of a disciplined, trained army. Thus, eventually, the Government of National Defense had to ask for an armistice. During the three-week armistice period it hastily called for the election of a regularly constituted, representative body to decide the question of peace or war.

The election for the National Assembly took place on February 8, 1871. Delegates were elected by universal manhood suffrage, following the liberal suffrage rules of 1849, hurriedly revived. The election returns showed that approximately 400 of the 630 seats of the National Assembly had gone to the monarchists.[7] The monarchists, however, were almost equally split between two contending groups: Bourbon and Orleans. The Assembly also contained about 30 Bonapartists. The remaining members—about 200—were republicans of one shade or another.

The first major task of the Assembly was to provide France with a government. This it did by naming Adolphe Thiers "Chief of the Executive Power of the French Republic." Thiers, as several French newspapers said, was the man of the moment. Part of his popularity was due to the tour of the western countries he had made during the time of the heaviest German attacks, when he had tried unsuccessfully to get assistance for France. Twenty-six different departments had elected him as their delegate to the Assembly. He was, furthermore, a distinguished historian, and he seemed to be capable of putting aside party connections. It was his unhappy job to accept his country's defeat. The monarchist deputies were willing enough that the terms of victorious Germany should be accepted by the head of a

Gooch, "The Government and Politics of France," in J. T. Shotwell, ed., *Governments of Continental Europe* (New York, 1940); Edward M. Sait, *Government and Politics of France* (Yonkers-on-Hudson, 1926); Walter R. Sharp, *The Government of the French Republic* (New York, 1938); and Robert Valeur, "French Government and Politics," in Raymond L. Buell, ed., *Democratic Governments in Europe* (New York, 1935).

[7] The Assembly was to have 768 members, but different districts could select the same man. Thus the actual membership was 630.

republican government. Some of them hoped that the defeat of France would in later years be blamed on the republican cause.

Under the leadership of Thiers, peace with Germany was concluded. When the peace terms were decided and payments for a large indemnity by France to Germany were begun, the National Assembly turned to the problem of the future government of France. Some republican members objected, saying that the assembly was usurping power. It had been elected, they said, to make peace, not to build a constitution. French constitutional lawyers are not agreed about this issue even today. Whatever its original powers, the National Assembly began to make a constitution. It appointed a committee of its members to draw up constitutional proposals.

The Commune. But a dramatic incident preceded the selection of the committee. It was touched off when the National Assembly was forced to attend to events in the city of Paris. By the peace terms the city was partially occupied by German troops. To some Parisians this was grossly tragic—it showed that the provinces were willing to degrade the city for their own convenience. The government of Thiers approved even more indignities than this. For instance, it put the seat of the National Assembly at Versailles instead of at Paris. Still more annoying, it ordered the collection of rent and debt payments that had been suspended during the siege of Paris. These offenses, to the Paris revolutionaries, were evidences that the monarchists of the National Assembly had little respect for the republicanism of Paris—a republicanism that had flared into open revolt periodically since 1789.

On March 18, 1871, fighting began in Paris. The revolutionaries set up their *Commune*—a model, by the way, discussed by Karl Marx and much studied by revolutionaries in Tsarist Russia. Communal government became a reality in Paris, although elsewhere in the country it was non-existent. Paris was again besieged, but this time by French troops. Ultimately the government army won, but the struggle was bitter.

Republic or Monarchy? After the communard interlude, once more the constitutional problem came before the National Assembly, and once more the thorny choice between monarchy and republic became paramount. The monarchists tried to bring together the two pretenders to the French throne: the Comte de Chambord, of the legitimate Bourbon line, and the Comte de Paris, a grandson of Louis-Philippe of the Orleanist line. If this could have been done, the republic might have been abandoned and a monarchy restored; but just as things seemed to be going along well, the Comte de Chambord threw them into complete confusion by his proclamation of July 5, 1871, saying that above all he must come to the throne under the white flag of the Bourbons. In his words, "Henry V cannot abandon the white flag of Henry IV." Yet even a majority of the monarchists knew that the tricolor flag of the revolution would have to remain; the clock could not be put back 80 years to the *ancien régime.* While negotiations with the Comte de Chambord were going on, elections were being held in many parts of the country to fill vacancies in seats to the National Assembly, mostly caused by resignations. More than 110 seats were to be filled; the number was this large because under the earlier election rules one man's resignation might affect several districts. In the elections of July 2, 1871, 100 republicans won.

These two situations—the insistence of the Comte de Chambord on the use of the Bourbon flag and the election victories of the republicans—led some republican members of the National Assembly to try to make the government somewhat less temporary. The result was the Rivet law of August 31, 1871. By it Thiers became President of the French Republic. In addition, the office was to last as long as the National Assembly was performing its functions. It also gave the President the power of appointing and dismissing ministers, the heads of the executive departments. The ministers, according to the law, were responsible to the National Assembly. All of the acts of the President must be countersigned by a minister. By this law, for the duration of the National Assembly, France was almost made into a parliamentary republic. At least the central feature of the parliamentary form was provided—that is, responsibility of ministers to the National Assembly. Ministers would be expected to resign if they were not supported by the votes of a majority of the National Assembly.

But the Rivet law left the government still provisional. Thiers' position was not completely defined. Was he a ceremonial chief of state? Did he have only the appearance of power but not its reality? It could be so argued: his acts had to be countersigned by a minister. On the other hand, the Rivet law made no provision for a prime minister. On this basis it could be said that Thiers ran the government, as in fact he did.

Nor was the question of republic or monarchy yet definitively settled. In this matter the National Assembly, in spite of the new elections, was still monarchist. At the same time the position of Thiers became more difficult. Originally an Orleanist, he had convinced himself that restoration of the monarchy was almost impossible. He therefore spoke in favor of a conservative republic; but in so doing he alienated the monarchist majority of the assembly, yet did not gain the support of the republicans, most of whom favored a more radical republic. Ultimately, on May 24, 1873, the National Assembly voted lack of confidence in Thiers. He resigned, and with his resignation his quasipersonal and quasiparliamentary government came to an end.

His successor was Marshal MacMahon, the Duc de Magenta, a distinguished soldier and a monarchist, who felt responsible to the monarchist majority in the National Assembly. It was hoped that he would remain President of the Republic until a monarchy could be established. To accomplish this, however, the old problem had to be solved whether the reigning house was to be Bourbon or Orleanist. Another attempt was made to settle the question during the summer of 1873. The Comte de Paris was willing that the Comte de Chambord should take the throne if, at the end of the reign of the latter, the throne should go to the Comte de Paris, since De Chambord was childless. It appeared that this compromise would solve the problem, but it did not. The heraldic scruples of the Bourbon Count remained uppermost: he would not support the tricolor of the revolution. To yield on this question, he argued, would be to begin a reign to restore the country by an act of weakness.

Consolidation of Republican Form. With the blasting of the monarchists' hopes, it became possible to give the government a more regular form. This was done by the passage of the Septennate Act in November, 1873, which provided that the powers of Marshal MacMahon as President should last for seven years, and that a commission of thirty should study drafts for a more permanent constitution.

Two more years passed before the Third Republic was anything but temporary. Finally, by indirection, in January, 1875, the Third Republic was given a full lease on life. This miracle was accomplished by the passage of the Wallon amendment, by the narrow margin of 353 to 352, in the National Assembly. In essence, the amendment provided that the President of the Republic should be elected every seven years.

With the question of monarchy or republic momentarily resolved in favor of the latter, the National Assembly quickly completed the drafting of the constitutional laws of the Third Republic.[8] Except for a few unimportant amendments, these constitutional laws lasted until the fall of the Third Republic in 1940. Taken together, they made up its constitution. They are relatively simple and brief.

Organization of Powers. The principal constitutional law was that of February 25, 1875, on the organization of public powers. It described the legislature, consisting of a popularly elected Chamber of Deputies and an indirectly elected Senate. It also provided that the President of the Republic should be elected by a majority of both houses of the legislature, that his term be seven years, and that he be eligible to succeed himself. He was given the usual executive powers: to propose bills to the legislature; exercise the right of pardon; command the armed forces; select high civil and military officers; send and receive ambassadors; and promulgate laws passed by both houses. The President also had another important power: the authority to dissolve the Chamber of Deputies and order a new election, but only with the consent of the Senate. This was done once, in 1877, with such an ill effect upon the political fortunes of the President that the power was never used again.

The seemingly sweeping powers of the President were limited by the provision that for their exercise, the countersignature of a minister was required. This made the President almost a figurehead, because his powers were exercised for him by his ministers.

According to the same law on the organization of public powers, the

---

[8] Translated in Lionel H. Laing and Others, *Source Book in European Governments* (New York, 1950), 81 ff.

ministers were collectively and individually responsible to both chambers. Thus a vote against a proposal made by a minister in either the Chamber of Deputies or the Senate might result in the minister's resignation.

The law also described the amending process, which was exceedingly simple. First, the two houses meeting separately were to decide that the constitution needed to be amended. Then the members of the Chamber and the Senate met together as the National Assembly, to pass the amendment by a majority vote of all the members. This simple amending procedure was later used to kill the Third Republic.

The Senate. Another major constitutional act was that of February 24, 1875. It dealt with the composition of the Senate. This body was to have 300 members, of which 225 were to be selected by electoral colleges formed in each department. The colleges were composed of (1) the deputies of the department, (2) the members of the elected departmental general council, (3) the elected councillors of the *arrondissement* (a division of the department), and (4) one delegate from each of the many communes (municipalities) in the department. The colleges elected senators to serve for nine years. One third of the senators thus elected were to retire every three years. The 75 remaining senators were named for life by the National Assembly; they could be replaced by the Senate itself.

The senators, like the deputies, could initiate legislation, and they must pass on bills that came from the Chamber. On financial legislation the Senate could act only after the Chamber had initiated the bill and passed it. In addition to these legislative powers, the Senate had the judicial function of impeaching the President and the ministers.

Relations of Powers. The third constitutional law was that of July 16, 1875. It dealt with the relationship between the President and the legislature. It provided for regular annual sessions of the legislature, with the President entitled to call special sessions. It provided also that the President could communicate with the chambers by means of messages. He was required to promulgate within one month the laws the chambers passed and sent to him, except that if the chambers termed the legislation urgent, promulgation must take place within three days. The President, however, had a suspensive veto. He could send a bill back for reconsideration, provided the period for promulgation had not expired. This power, of course, required ministerial countersignature for its use. Should the chambers pass such a bill again, it became law. Other relationships between the President and the chambers were clarified by the same law. For example, although the President, through his ministers, was responsible for conducting foreign affairs, he could not declare war without the consent of both houses; nor was he authorized to ratify treaties of peace or of commerce or those involving the finances of the state or property rights of Frenchmen overseas without the consent of the chambers.

These three constitutional laws were supplemented by two organic acts.

One of them, of August 2, 1875, added further details on the election of senators. The second organic act, of November 30, 1875, provided for the election
of members of the Chamber of Deputies. They were elected for terms of
four years from single-member districts based on the *arrondissements*. If no
candidate received a majority of the votes cast in his district, and if no one's
vote was more than one quarter of the registered voters in his area, a second,
or run-off, election had to be held. In this second election, the man with the
plurality won.

The three constitutional acts were amended only three times. The first
amendment, in 1879, removed the seat of the government from Versailles;
subsequently it was placed in Paris. The second, in 1884, accomplished
several ends: it speeded the electoral process, declared the republican form of
government unchangeable, made members of former ruling families of
France ineligible to be President, and subjected the constitutional law on the
election of senators to change by ordinary legislation. The third amendment, in 1926, dealt with some minor details of finance.[9]

Omissions in the Constitution of 1875. This basic legislation formed the
constitutional structure of the Third Republic. It was fragmentary. It did
not set up a judiciary. It said nothing about a bill of rights, nor did it describe the powers of local governments. That these important matters
were omitted, however, does not mean that they were neglected.

The judiciary was already regulated by an ordinary law. The bill of
rights had already been written in the revolutionary *Declaration of the
Rights of Man,* and had been carried over into the Napoleonic Code. Similarly, institutions of local government had been provided by law at least
since the time of Napoleon. The constitutional laws were thus the irre-
ducible minimum of agreement between the contending factions of the
National Assembly—the Bourbons, Orleanists, Bonapartists, and conservative
and radical republicans. These laws provided a framework within which
a government could operate. They almost proved the old French adage that
it is only the provisional that endures.

The Problem of Executive Leadership. At the outset it was clear that the
President of the Republic was not the real executive. This was made clear
by the actions of the first President, Marshal MacMahon. He tried, in the
famous crisis of May 16, 1877, to assert the President's power, but the upshot
was that both his power and that of the Senate were discredited. The effect
of the atrophy of the power of dissolution on the position of the Chamber of
Deputies was enormous. It meant that deputies, elected for four years, need
not worry about having to fight another election campaign during their term,
no matter what their actions in the Chamber might be. They therefore
could upset cabinets with impunity—and did so. The effect of the crisis of
1877 was even greater on the position of the President.

The background of the crisis was the election of 1876, the first under the

---

[9] The amendments of 1879, 1884, and 1926 are translated in Laing and Others, *op. cit.* above,
note 8, 87 ff.

new constitution. The indirect election of senators resulted in a majority of the right over the republicans—132 against 93. The balance was still in favor of the right when the nominated senators—those selected for life by the National Assembly—were included, although a good many of these were republicans. The elections for the Chamber of Deputies, on the other hand, had resulted in a republican victory. There were approximately 340 republicans to 195 representatives of the right. The President was monarchist. This distribution of sentiment—the Senate conservative, the Chamber republican, and the President monarchist—made legislation very difficult.

At the time of the crisis, Jules Simon, a republican member of the Chamber, was Premier. On May 16 he received a letter from the President reproaching him for not having enough influence over the Chamber of Deputies to make the views of the government prevail. The President was concerned about two minor pieces of legislation: a bill on the press and another on public sessions for municipal councils. The Premier felt that the only reply to the letter could be his resignation. The President then appointed as Premier the Duc de Broglie, an ardent conservative, though clearly De Broglie could not get a majority vote in the republican Chamber of Deputies. To most republicans the Marshal's action was a last-ditch attempt to rule against the expressed wishes of the voters. Certainly the Marshal himself, in an address to the chambers, accepted personal responsibility. He said that he did not care to associate even distantly with the ideas of the radicals, and that the country would agree with him.

Thus the President took a definite political stand. He was not playing the role of a ceremonial, nonpolitical executive, but, instead, that of an active protagonist of a cause. De Broglie declared in the Chamber that this was properly the role of the President, that indeed he should not be the blind and passive agent of the majority. But the Chamber voted against De Broglie. The Senate, by a slim majority, agreed with the position taken by the President and De Broglie. The Chamber of Deputies was dissolved.

In the subsequent election campaign the republicans united against what they thought was an attack on the Third Republic itself. The position of the President was intensively debated. The President himself was an active campaigner, delivering speeches, sending out manifestoes, and traveling through the country. The result of the election was a republican victory, 325 to 207. As Gambetta, the republican leader, had said, the President would have to give in or get out. He gave in. The election settled the question of the position of the president in French politics. He became virtually a figurehead.

Presidents of the Republic, after MacMahon, mostly played a role of impartiality and dignity, but not of power. Jules Grévy, the immediate successor of MacMahon, said in his opening message to the chambers that he would never enter into a struggle against the popular will as expressed by constitutional organs. Of course, presidents did not lack all influence on politics, though their influence was not often seen in public. Behind the scenes, they contributed their often rich political experience. But if their judgment was respected, it was not because it was necessary to show such respect, but because the opinions themselves were worthy of respect. The limitations of the position tended to prevent brilliant political figures from becoming President. One president, Casimir Perier, was so disturbed by his lack of real power that he resigned after a few months in office. Certainly, then, the President did not exercise the real executive power of the French Republic.

Such executive power as existed was exercised by the President of the Council of Ministers, or the Premier, as he is sometimes popularly called in France. Even the Premier was not a strong executive because he depended on majority support in a chamber in which in fact no party had a majority. He presented the program of his government to the legislature and worked to have it translated into action. This program was put into effect not only by the legislature but also by the ministers, appointed by the President at the request of the Premier. As heads of the executive departments, they directed the work of public administration. The two houses could question occasionally the regulations signed by the ministers, but day-to-day direction of the administrative machinery was the function of the Premier and his ministers.

Legislative Supremacy. Many times it has been said that French government is really government by the legislature rather than by the executive. Certainly this was true of the Third Republic. The main reason for this was the multi-party system, under which no party had a majority of the seats of the legislature—indeed, usually no party even came close to having a majority. Consequently the majority of votes needed to pass laws could be obtained only by coalitions of parties, and the coalitions were not stable. Thus the cabinets based on these coalitions were equally unstable, falling often, as the coalitions formed and dissolved.

A minister would introduce a piece of proposed legislation. One party of the governmental majority would object to the legislation and vote against it. Then the defeated minister would often resign. Cabinets therefore did not last long; the average life of cabinets during the Third Republic was a little less than eight months. Upsetting the Cabinet was not a dangerous procedure; it did not bring on a dissolution of the Chamber, causing the deputies to worry about fighting another election. "Fishing in the troubled waters," therefore, was a popular practice. This meant that a cabinet would be lightly upset in the hope that the party doing the upsetting might gain more posts in the next. Dissension between members of a cabinet also caused many a crisis.

Yet this instability was greater on the surface than it was in fact.[10] Very

---

[10] For a discussion see A. Soulier, *L'Instabilité ministérielle sous la troisième république* (Paris, 1939); Carl J. Friedrich, *Constitutional Government and Democracy* (rev. ed., Boston, 1950), 365 ff.; and John G. Heinberg, "The Personnel Structure of French Cabinets," *American Political Science Review*, 33 (1939), 267 ff.

often in the reshuffles the same ministers would be reappointed. Many individual ministers, therefore, served much longer than eight months. They provided continuity in spite of the appearance of discontinuity. Aristide Briand, for example, had been in 17 ministries and was Minister of Foreign Affairs in 14 cabinets, for a period of nearly seven years.[11] There are many other ministers whose careers were not unlike that of Briand.

The Third Republic, for all its provisional beginning, the weakness of the executive, and the lack of strong direction from Parliament, endured many crises. It weathered the Boulanger affair of 1889, when Boulanger, a "man on horseback," the youngest general in the French army, almost accomplished a *coup d'état*. It surmounted the Panama scandal of 1892, when it was rumored that 104 deputies had been bribed to vote to subsidize the Panama Company, mired in debt and wasted by extravagance. The Third Republic also withstood the Dreyfus affair, when highly placed figures were implicated in a conspiracy to convict an innocent Jewish officer of selling state secrets rather than to expose the defection of a high army officer. It also endured the long years of World War I, and emerged in good working order. It triumphed over the Stavisky scandal of 1934, when police and other officials were thought to be involved in a plot to fleece the government.

Death of the Third Republic. The Third Republic did not live through World War II. In fact, it collapsed after eight weeks of fighting in 1940. This unexpected and total military defeat was partly caused by the ineffectiveness and indecisiveness of the government—a state reflecting the attitude of French citizens. Some were deeply devoted to French democracy. Others argued, however, that France was much too democratic for her own good; that strong central control was needed; that Hitler's principle of a governing elite was sound; and that a dictatorship was superior to a democracy.

This attitude of indecision was likewise reflected in the legislature. In 1934, 1935, 1937, 1938, and 1939 it passed decree laws, for example, giving the Cabinet the power to legislate in certain areas, without additional parliamentary consent.[12] Yet the governments holding these decree powers were not certain what should be done with them.

3. Vichy Interlude

The Third Republic died quickly,[13] and the dictatorship that took its place was established just as quickly. At the time of the defeat in 1940, the government fled first to Tours, then to Bordeaux, and finally to Vichy. The wartime Premier, Paul Reynaud, resigned when a slender majority of his

---

[11] Joseph-Barthélemy, *Le gouvernement de la France* (rev. ed., Paris, 1939), 121.

[12] See Otto Kirchheimer, "Decree Powers and Constitutional Law in France under the Third Republic," *American Political Science Review*, 34 (1940), 1104 ff.

[13] See Karl Loewenstein, "The Demise of the French Constitution of 1875," *American Political Science Review*, 34 (1940), 867 ff.; Hamilton F. Armstrong, *Chronology of Failure* (New York, 1940); Pertinax, *Les Fossoyeurs* (New York, 1943).

Cabinet voted to sign a separate peace with Germany. He was succeeded by Marshal Henri-Philippe Pétain, victor at Verdun in World War I, then an octogenarian, and a man who had many times demonstrated a lack of patience with the behavior of democracies. In the armistice with Germany, conducted under his auspices, France was divided into an occupied and an unoccupied zone. The occupied zone included the west and north of France. The French government in Vichy, though in the unoccupied zone, was in no way free from German influence. Marshal Pétain himself said that he did not pretend that his government was free.

Amending the Constitution. It was at Vichy, under the guidance of Marshal Pétain, that the Third Republic was finally killed. The deed was done by applying the amending process of the constitution, almost to the letter. The Chamber of Deputies and the Senate met separately and decided on the need for revision of the constitution. On July 9, 1940, the Chamber voted 393 to 3, and the Senate 225 to 1, to call a National Assembly to revise the constitution. The total number of deputies was 618, and that of senators 314. The National Assembly met the next day in the theater of the Casino in Vichy, and passed the following constitutional law by a vote of 569 to 80:

The National Assembly gives full power to the Government of the Republic, under the authority and signature of Marshal Pétain, to promulgate, in one or several acts, a new constitution for the French state. This Constitution must guarantee the rights of work, of the family, and of the native land. It will be ratified by the nation and applied by the Assemblies that it will create.

Some French constitutional lawyers have argued that this act of the National Assembly was unconstitutional, on the ground that a constituent assembly could not grant its constituent power to any other agency. Others contend that the amendment was perfectly legal, because a constituent assembly can make whatever arrangements it wants to make.[14]

The Vichy Constitution. In any event, the Assembly gave Pétain full personal power to rewrite the constitution and to put in it the new virtues of "work," "family," and "native land." These virtues were to replace the outmoded ideas of "liberty, equality, and fraternity." The new ones were more in line with Hitler's preference for work, silence, and obedience as guides for the building of the new state. They pointed the way to the "national revolution," as Pierre Laval said, when he introduced the amendment to the National Assembly. By this revolution, he declared, France would again become a peasant land.

The national revolution was obviously to be guided directly by the government and not by the legislature. This was evident in the first two constitutional acts promulgated by Marshal Pétain on the day after the National Assembly had given him full powers. The first act made Pétain Chief of

---

[14] For an extended discussion, see Loewenstein, *loc. cit.* above, note 13.

the French State. It also provided that thereafter the Chief of the French State would serve indefinitely, thereby abrogating the Wallon amendment of the constitution of 1875. The second act essentially set up a dictatorship in France; the democratic machinery was nearly destroyed and the legislature became all but unnecessary.

By this act Marshal Pétain, as Chief of the French State, gave himself the power to appoint and remove ministers, who were to be responsible only to him. Pending the creation of legislative assemblies, he and his ministers had the power of making laws; even if a legislature were in operation, he was entitled to legislate in an emergency without asking the consent of the legislature. Furthermore, he was the sole judge of the existence of an emergency. He also could control the budget by decree; and, as has so often been said, he who controls the purse strings controls the government. In addition, the act gave the Chief of State the usual executive powers: to promulgate laws, supervise their execution, send and receive ambassadors, appoint civil and military officers, command the armed forces, and grant pardons and amnesties. All of these powers, unlike those of the President under the Third Republic, were exercised without the need for counter-signature by a minister. They rested only on the authority of the Chief of State.[15]

Twelve additional constitutional acts were promulgated by the Chief of State under the Vichy regime. None of them, in spite of the requirement fixed by the National Assembly in its constitutional amendment, was ever ratified by the nation. These succeeding acts filled in some of the details of the dictatorship. One provided that the legislature should be adjourned until it was called back into session by the Chief of State. It was never called back. Another named Pierre Laval and Admiral Darlan as successors to the Chief of State in the event of Pétain's incapacity or death. The last group of constitutional acts, promulgated in April and November of 1942, made a considerable change in the governmental structure. Under them the position of Chief of the Government was created; in reality this meant that Pétain's powers as Chief of the French State were greatly diluted, while Laval, as Chief of the Government, became a virtual dictator.

Spirit of Vichy. The underlying idea of this so-called "national revolution" was the replacement by authoritarianism of the "outmoded" democratic system—outmoded because it was founded on individualism. As Pétain wrote, "Individualism never was creative. . . . The individualist receives everything from society and gives nothing back. . . . Nature did not create society separate from individuals; she created individuals as a part of society."[16] This society was embodied in Pétain as Chief of State. His position was to be like that of Hitler, who claimed to embody the German

---

[15] Translated in Laing and Others, *op. cit.* above, note 8, 88-90.
[16] As quoted in Marcel Prélot, *Précis de droit constitutionnel* (Paris, 1950), 264.

nation. Political power was designed to increase the stature of Pétain as the embodiment of the French nation. All political power was supposed to flow from him.

As a matter of fact, however, no one individual in France could use such enormous powers, least of all a man who was well into his eighties and under the thumb of the victor. The national revolution under Pétain's leadership was not much of a success. The government tried all sorts of pressure—increased police powers, prohibition of political party actions, punishment of unenthusiastic civil servants—but the national revolution did not win wide popular support.

As the Allied forces slowly recaptured French territory, the Vichy regime fell, but the very fact of its past existence has reminded French voters of the dangers of authoritarian government. It had been in the tradition of the *ancien régime,* of Napoleon and of Louis Napoleon. It was a modern demonstration of centralized power. The builders of the Fourth Republic heeded this lesson. They built, instead, on the democratic tradition of France.

CHAPTER 11

THE CONSTITUTION OF THE FOURTH FRENCH REPUBLIC

1. Reestablishment of Democracy

Record of Compromise. The constitution of the Fourth French Republic which went into effect in 1946 was little more than a new and slightly modernized edition of the constitution of the Third Republic. This was paradoxical, because in October 1945 over 96 per cent of the French electorate voted against restoring the constitutional laws of 1875. Yet the new document emerged from the parliamentary battles of two constituent assemblies as just such a revision. Using the old formula had at least one advantage—there was a backlog of 65 years of experience with the Third Republic. Thus its traditions and customs could be used as the solid underpinning of the Fourth Republic.

The idea of a new constitution was originally the object of great popular enthusiasm, engendered by the spectacular exploits of the French underground. A new spirit of unity in France replaced the divisions that had partly caused the disastrous defeat of 1940. Now France was coming alive again. This time, resistance leaders hoped, the revived and purified France would have the inspired constitution that she richly deserved.

However, once the constituent assemblies were elected and commenced the actual business of writing a constitution, much of the enthusiasm for a new France had evaporated. All of the old divisions of opinion and some new ones appeared; consequently the new constitution was filled with compromises. It was not completely satisfactory to any one group, but it could finally be accepted by most.

The actual writing of the constitution was the last phase of a long political development. Some of the early planning for a new constitution took place on French soil, some abroad. Yet neither the resistance leaders in France nor those overseas had a common program for reconstructing French government, in spite of their dreams of unity. General de Gaulle, spokesman for the French in exile, expressed only the vaguest ideas about the details of reconstruction. He did, however, try to rally underground and overseas French opinion to a National Assembly that would have full power to decide the country's destinies. Meanwhile, the big problem was not the future government of France; it was, instead, that of getting the Germans out of France and of defending French interests in the plans of the Allies fighting the war.

Interim Government: The French Committee of National Liberation.
From the point of view of the Allies, the reconquest of France involved a
highly political question. Who, in fact, could speak for the people of occupied and unoccupied France? The British inclined to listen to the voice
of General de Gaulle. The United States, on the other hand, perhaps dis-
trusting De Gaulle's austere mysticism, preferred to deal with General Henri
Honoré Giraud, recently escaped from a German prison camp. They hoped
that he could prevent Vichy troops in Algiers from attacking Allied landing
forces. Giraud, however, could not get the loyalty of the Vichy troops in
Algiers. Consequently, in the interests of military expediency, the Allies
dealt instead with Admiral Darlan, the Vichy heir apparent of Marshal
Pétain.[1] But before the political problem of unifying French support under
Darlan became pressing, Darlan was assassinated on December 24, 1942. He
had been in power only a few short weeks. Thereafter General Giraud was
back at the head of the French in Algiers.

French interests could not long be divided between De Gaulle and Giraud.
Four months after the Casablanca Conference of January, 1943, the two
generals were finally brought together. A Committee of National Liberation was set up representing both camps. Gradually De Gaulle emerged as
the dominant figure.

The Committee of National Liberation moved into France in the wake of
the Allied armies and became the provisional government of France, pending the call for a constituent assembly. For fourteen months De Gaulle
headed this government. He appointed its ministers, who were responsible
to him. Under his direction war-torn France was reconsolidated.

Preparation for the Constituent Assembly. One of the tasks of the government was to prepare for a constituent assembly. De Gaulle provided, by
decree, the electoral law for forming the Constituent Assembly. Selection
of delegates by proportional representation, with the department as the base,
would be, he thought, the fairest method of mirroring the political views of
the French voters. Elections were held on October 21, 1945. De Gaulle
immediately turned governmental power over to the newly elected body.
The Assembly gave the power back to him as President of the new Provisional Government. This government was organized according to a preliminary constitution approved by the voters at the same time they chose
the members of the Constituent Assembly. Under it the old offices of
President of the Republic and President of the Council of Ministers were
rolled into one. The President and his ministers were responsible to the
Constituent Assembly, but the President did not have to resign unless
the deputies had expressly voted a motion of censure against his regime;
the mere voting down of a proposal of his ministers did not bring on the
resignation of the government.

---

[1] This episode is fully described in William L. Langer, *Our Vichy Gamble* (New York, 1947).

The First Constituent Assembly. The first Constituent Assembly was by no means politically unified.[2] No one political party had won a majority. The Communists had a plurality of two seats over the Popular Republican Movement (MRP), which was thought to be the party closest to De Gaulle. The third major group was the Socialists, the party of elderly and distinguished Léon Blum, who had spent much time in the Buchenwald concentration camp during the war. Each of the three major parties had about 150 seats apiece. Scattered between these three major groups were many smaller parties holding a little less than 150 of the 586 seats.

In the actual drafting of the constitution, the Socialists held the balance of power. They usually voted with the MRP, but on several major features of the first constitution they agreed with the Communists. These features were the unicameral legislature, the weak ceremonial executive, and the process by which the legislature selected the Premier. The MRP and the Socialists agreed that there should be many limitations on the power of the one-house legislature. Most importantly, if the legislature overturned two cabinets, the legislature could be dissolved and new elections held.

While the Constituent Assembly was debating about the shape of the constitution, General de Gaulle suddenly resigned on January 20, 1946. His official reason was that the country was well on the road to recovery, but it was an open secret that he did not like the emerging shape of the new constitution. In his place the Assembly elected Félix Gouin, a Socialist. Gouin was more inclined to govern by persuasion and compromise than by issuing manifestoes.

Rejection of the First Constitution. Within the seven months fixed for its deliberations, the Constituent Assembly completed its work. The constitution was submitted to the voters on May 5, 1946. They rejected it by a vote of about 10½ million to 9½ million. In the campaign leading to this rejection, slogans were more important than discussion of the proposed governmental structure. The Communists enthusiastically supported the constitutional document. The MRP was its main opponent, calling it the path to dictatorship, on the ground that the unicameral National Assembly had too much power.

The Second Constituent Assembly. After the rejection of the first constitution, the voters had to select another constituent assembly. It was elected on June 2, 1946. Apparently the electorate had not greatly changed its mind: the second Constituent Assembly was not much different in party complexion from the first. This time the MRP had the plurality, having gained a million additional votes and 19 seats. The Socialists lost some seats, and the Communists lost a few too, but won more popular votes than they had had before.

---

[2] For a masterly account of the drafting of the French constitutions, see Gordon Wright, *The Reshaping of French Democracy* (New York, 1948); for a good shorter account, see Robert K. Gooch, "Recent Constitution-making in France," *American Political Science Review,* 41 (1947), 429 ff.

Indeed, three-quarters of the deputies of the first Constituent Assembly had been returned to the second.

In the new Constituent Assembly, MRP leaders held key positions—Georges Bidault was elected provisional President. The Assembly used the rejected constitution as a basis for its work. The major change was the creation of a two-house legislature, but the new upper house was explicitly forbidden to overthrow the Cabinet. Also, the position of the President of the Republic was slightly strengthened. There were few other changes.

The electoral campaign for the new constitutional draft was fought mainly between De Gaulle and his supporters on the one hand, and the major parties of the second Constituent Assembly on the other. The General vigorously opposed the weak executive provided in the new draft. In the voting on October 13, 1946, his opposition was not enough to wreck the draft, but he was credited with keeping a third of the voters away from the polls. The number of ballots was far fewer than in any of the previous elections since 1881. The result was that a little over one-third of the electorate accepted the new constitution, about one-third opposed it, and another third did not vote at all. So it was that the Fourth Republic began its life almost as uncertainly and as weakly supported as the young Third Republic.

2. The Constitution of 1946

The Bill of Rights. The civil rights of the French are briefly described in the preamble of the constitution of 1946. Because they are located in the preamble, the legislature is bound morally but not legally to respect these rights. The tendency is for the courts to consider themselves bound by them.[3]

The constitution begins by reaffirming the *Declaration of the Rights of Man* of 1789. Then it adds to these political rights a number of economic rights, among which are the right to employment, to trade union membership, to using the strike (in accordance with the law), and to collective bargaining. The moral obligation of the government to provide social security is stated in these words: "Every human being who, because of his age, his physical or mental condition, or because of the economic situation, finds himself unable to work, has the right to obtain from the community the means to lead a decent existence."[4] In addition to economic rights, the preamble deals with international affairs. It pronounces moral condemnation of wars of conquest and adds that the French Republic "will never use its arms against the freedom of any people." Concerning the French overseas areas, the preamble says that France "proposes to guide the peoples for whom she has assumed responsibility toward freedom to govern themselves and democratically to manage their own affairs."

---

[3] Marcel Prélot, *Précis de droit constitutionnel* (Paris, 1950), 335-336.

[4] This and other quotations from the constitution are taken from a translation by the Information Division of the French Embassy in New York City. See also Owen R. Taylor, *The Fourth Republic in France* (New York, 1951).

Judicial Guaranties of Civil Rights. Although the rights of French citizens are only briefly mentioned in the constitution, many of them are more explicitly described, and thus safeguarded, in codes of law. These codes are mainly enforced by the courts; French judges are therefore guarantors of civil rights. To free the judges from political pressures, various laws assure the independence of the judges.

The constitution itself says little about the judiciary. This is not unusual; the constitutional laws of 1875 did not mention the judiciary at all. The independent position of the judges is indirectly recognized in the constitution of 1946 in a section providing for the Superior Council of the Judiciary. This Council is headed by the President of the Republic; the Minister of Justice is its vice president. Six of its twelve other members are elected for six-year terms by the National Assembly by a two-thirds majority; these may not be members of the Assembly. In the first election of these six there were no opposition candidates. Of the other six members, four are judges selected by groups of judges; the other two are appointed by the President of the Republic from among the legal profession.

The groups of judges that elect the four members correspond to the major divisions of the French court system. One group is made up of justices of the peace, who deal with minor infractions of the law; their main job is to prevent cases from getting into court by bringing the parties together informally. A second group is made up of judges of courts of first instance—that is, courts in which the more important cases have their beginning. A third group is made up of judges in the courts of appeal. The fourth group consists of judges in the Court of Cassation; this is the court set up to unify the law all over France. Incidentally, this court does not substitute its decision for that of the lower court; it simply rescinds the lower court's decision and sends the case back to another court on the same level for a decision in harmony with the ruling of the Court of Cassation.

The Superior Council of the Judiciary has the power to submit names of prospective judges to the President of the Republic, who appoints them. It also has the power to discipline judges and is responsible for the administration of the courts. Finally, it makes recommendations to the President on his use of the power of pardon. Because of its powers, the Superior Council guarantees the independence of the judiciary. And the independence of the judiciary, in turn, safeguards the rights of Frenchmen.

The Sovereign Electorate. The first important articles of the constitution deal with sovereignty, an abstraction that has caused endless arguments among political theorists. In France, sovereignty belongs to the people. The voters exercise it in constitutional matters through their representatives or by referendum, and in all other matters through elected deputies in the National Assembly. The underlying principle in the exercise of this sovereignty is government of the people, by the people, and for the people. The writers of the constitution took these words directly from Abraham Lincoln's majestic Gettysburg address. The sovereign people the constitution describes thus: "All French citizens and nationals of both sexes, who are majors and enjoy civil and political rights, may vote under conditions determined by the law." Elections to the National Assembly are conducted by universal, equal, direct, and secret suffrage.

The details of the electoral system are not found in the constitution; they are set down instead in an ordinary law. These details are so important that it is not too much to say that the very existence of the Fourth Republic in its present shape depends upon them. A large body of voters oppose the present structure of the government, especially the Communists, who want a strong one-house legislature, and the De Gaullists, who want a strong executive. Thus the electoral law was drafted with the intent to minimize the votes of those who objected to the existing form of government.

Election of the National Assembly. Just before the elections to the National Assembly of June 17, 1951, the electoral law of October 5, 1946, was amended. By these much-debated amendments, most of the deputies to the National Assembly were chosen by a majority list system, based generally on the departments, with one balloting.[5] An exception was made for Paris and its suburbs; there a list system of proportional representation was used. Under the majority list system, each department sends as many deputies to the National Assembly as its population entitles it to. In each department in which a party wants to run candidates, it prepares a list of as many names as there are seats. Parties may declare electoral alliances in advance of the voting. On election day the voter casts his ballot for the list of candidates of the party he supports. If any party list in the department gets a majority of the votes cast in that department, then all of its candidates have been elected. On the other hand, and much more likely, if no party list has a majority, but two or more allied parties have a majority, the seats from that department are allotted on the basis of proportional representation between the allied groups. If no party or allied parties have a majority, then all of the seats are allotted by proportional representation.

One idea behind this proportional system of counting ballots and allotting seats is to make the number of seats each party wins in the legislature equal, or as nearly so as possible, to the percentage of the total vote the party won in the election. Thus, if a party had 40 per cent of the votes, it should win about 40 per cent of the seats. The French method of bringing this about is somewhat complicated.

Under the list system, the first seat in the department is given to the party with the highest number of votes. The second seat is allotted to that party whose remainder is highest after dividing its total vote by the number of seats it has already received plus one, unless another party's list has more votes. For example, let us assume that there are five seats to be allotted in

---

[5] The amendments are dated October 5, 1950, and May 9, 12, and 23, 1951. They are summarized in *Constitutional and Parliamentary Information,* 3rd series, No. 7 (1951), 139 ff.

a department, with the votes as follows: MRP, 60,000; Communist, 50,000; De Gaullist, 40,000; and Radical, 20,000. The seats will then be allotted this way. The first goes to the MRP list, because it has the highest number of votes. The second seat will go to the Communist list, as the next highest, because the remainder of the MRP's vote, after its total vote has been divided by 1 seat plus 1, is 30,000. The third seat will go to the De Gaullists, because their 40,000 vote is higher than the 30,000 remainder of the MRP and the 25,000 remainder of the Communists. The fourth seat will go to the MRP, because its remainder of 30,000 is now the highest figure. The fifth seat will go to the Communists, as the next highest group. Once the seats have been allotted to the party lists under this system, the candidates whose names are highest on the lists—in the order determined by the party—will be declared elected. Thus, in our example, the MRP winners will be the first two on the MRP's list of five candidates the party put up. If 50 per cent of the voters for any list show that they prefer an order of names other than that of the party, the seats are allotted so that the voters' preference is obeyed. This would practically require an organized understanding among the voters.

The consequences of this system of proportional representation are several. It gives the party considerable control over its candidates because it chooses the order of names on its list, and thus can place one candidate over another. The candidate who is first on the list naturally has the best chance of election. Further, in both the proportional list system used in Paris and the majority list system used in the rest of France, the parties have more control over their candidates because the voters have less. The voters in an area as large as a department have less contact with their deputies when there are several of them. For example, if there are five deputies from one department, the voters are likely to know their representatives less well than if there were only one deputy from a smaller electoral district. Thus the people's views about the parties are better reflected by the list system, but each elected deputy knows, and is known by, his electors less directly. It would be hard to say whether this list system is more or less democratic than the single-member district, for both appear democratic in different ways.

The clauses about electoral alliances in the law of 1951 were designed to influence the party complexion of the National Assembly, and they did. They were directed at the Communists and the De Gaullists. The center parties that supported these clauses in the National Assembly reasoned that no party of any size would pool its lists with the Communists; and the De Gaullists had said loudly that they wished to win power by themselves, so that it was unlikely that they would make many electoral bargains by pooling lists. Since most of the center parties were willing to pool their lists, they increased their chances of winning a good number of seats.

Another electoral detail that had real political effect was the use of proportional representation for Paris and environs. The Communists were strong in this area. If the majority list system were employed there, the

Communists might win a great many seats. Consequently, proportional representation was applied in order to minimize their votes.

In the election of June 17, 1951, estimates made by the center parties of the probable results were not far wrong. While there were not as many pooled lists as were expected, there were enough at least to keep the center parties in control.

Election of the Council of the Republic. The Council of the Republic and the National Assembly jointly form the French Parliament. Unlike the Assembly, the Council is chosen by indirect election. The system is described in the law of September 23, 1948. Under it, members of the Council of the Republic, like the senators of the Third Republic, are elected by a departmental electoral college made up of (1) the deputies elected to the National Assembly by the department, (2) the elected general councillors of the department, and (3) a variable number of municipal councillors and delegates, depending on the size of the municipalities. The authors of this law intended an overrepresentation of the small municipalities in the electoral college, in the hope that the Council of the Republic would thereby be made conservative.

Nevertheless, the political complexion of the Council of the Republic is by no means as important as that of the National Assembly, for the Assembly is by far the more powerful house. Unlike the Senate of the Third Republic, the Council of the Republic cannot overturn the government. On the other hand, the Council does take part in electing the President and concurs in the declaration of war. It also gives its opinion on proposed laws, but this opinion must be given in two months. For the budget the time is much less; here the Council may not take any more time than the National Assembly has taken. In addition, if the Assembly passes any bill by urgency procedure, which greatly reduces the time for discussion, the Council must give its opinion in the time allowed by the Assembly's own rule. If the Council takes longer than the prescribed time, the proposal becomes effective without its advice. If, on the other hand, the Council does not agree with the law as proposed by the Assembly, then the Assembly must reexamine the law. In the reexamination, if a majority of the members of the Council have agreed to amendments, a majority of all the members of the Assembly is required for their rejection. A united Council of the Republic could therefore block and perhaps veto the proposals of a divided National Assembly, but it is unlikely that the political complexion of the two houses could be so different that this would occur often.

The major function of the Council of the Republic is to give advice. In the few short years that the Council has been in existence, its advice has been accorded more and more respect, partly because its members are often well-informed spokesmen of small-town France, and partly because the advice is accepted on its intrinsic value by the National Assembly.[6]

---

[6] See Jean Bruyas, "L'évolution du Conseil de la République," *Revue du Droit Public,* 65 (1949), 541-582.

The Economic Council. Two other chambers created under the constitution of 1946 also give advice to the National Assembly. These are the Economic Council and the Assembly of the French Union. The Economic Council has existed in a somewhat different and less official form since 1925. Now its 154 members are chosen by various economic groups. The Economic Council usually meets twice a month while the National Assembly is in session, advising both the Assembly and the government. When the Council's advice is requested, it prepares a report that is sent to all members of Parliament. This report is read before there is general discussion of a particular matter in Parliament, and a member of the Council holds himself ready to explain the advice to the houses.

While the Council may give its advice either on its own initiative or on that of Parliament, it may take up only matters "within its purview."[7] These do not include the budget, nor do they include laws that only indirectly affect the economy. The Council concerns itself only with those matters that are essentially economic in nature.

The Economic Council is required by the constitution to give advice also at the request of the ministers. The Council of Ministers must consult it especially "concerning the establishment of a national economic plan for full employment and the rational utilization of . . . material resources." Indeed, most of the debates of the Economic Council have dealt with the economic plan.

While the Economic Council was quite influential in its early years, it has tended to lose power to the Council of the Republic. The ministers have made rather more use of the Economic Council than has the National Assembly, but even they have not asked its advice on some of the most important economic issues.

The Assembly of the French Union. Another organization that gives advice to Parliament is the Assembly of the French Union. The Union consists, on the one hand, "of the French Republic which comprises Metropolitan France and the overseas departments and territories, and, on the other hand, of the Associated Territories and States." This is the modern form of the French empire. In spite of the elaborate machinery of the French Union, however, the component states have about the same powers as they had formerly as parts of the empire.

The French Union has its own agencies. It is headed by the President of the French Union, who is the President of the French Republic. It has an advisory High Council, whose chairman is the President of the Union, and whose members are delegates of the French government and "the representatives that each associated State is permitted to accredit to the President of the Union." By the law of April 24, 1949, the French government's delegates are ministers, and the representatives of the states are those allowed by arrangements made between France and the state. The other major agency

[7] Organic law of October 27, 1946.

is the Assembly of the French Union. Half of its members are elected by the National Assembly and the Council of the Republic, and the other half are chosen by the overseas departments and territories and the associated states. How the representatives of all of the associated states will be chosen is not yet entirely clear, especially in areas where there are still debates about the tie between that area and the French government, such as in the case of Indo-China.

In its relationship with the National Assembly, the Assembly of the French Union is an advisory agency. Its advice may be given on its own initiative, but in such crucial areas as civil liberties and political and administrative organization in the overseas territories, final legislative power rests with Parliament.

The National Assembly, therefore, has several advisory groups on which it can draw: the Council of the Republic, the Economic Council, and the Assembly of the French Union. But the National Assembly alone adopts the laws. This is, of course, its most important work. Indeed, the National Assembly is the principal agency of government in France, and the Council of Ministers but its creature.

Organization of the National Assembly. The rules under which the National Assembly operates are of particular importance. In fact, one French writer has said that sometimes the rules of the Assembly are more important than the constitution.[8]

By these rules, under the constitution, the deputies in the National Assembly elect their own presiding officer by secret ballot. He is the President of the National Assembly, and has an honorific as well as an active position. Honorifically, he is the second citizen of the Republic, the first being the President of the Republic.

According to the constitution, the President of the Assembly serves in place of the President of the Republic if the latter has resigned or died, or for some other reason cannot serve; and if the National Assembly has been dissolved, he is the interim President of the Council of Ministers. He also promulgates the laws if the President of the Republic has not acted within the time allowed by the constitution, and he is invariably called in to give advice to the President of the Republic after the resignation of a cabinet. His regular job, however, is that of presiding over the National Assembly. He has to keep order, and in an assembly where temperaments often explode in fiery debates, this task requires finesse, calmness, and the ability to secure cooperation.

The President of the National Assembly is assisted by a bureau consisting of six vice presidents, fourteen secretaries, and three questors. These bureau members are elected by proportional representation from among the parliamentary groups. The vice presidents substitute as presiding offi-

---

[8] Eugène Pierre, *Traité de droit politique, électoral et parlementaire,* quoted in Prélot, *op. cit.* above, note 3, 400.

cers, usually during the less important debates and at less busy times. The secretaries supervise the preparation of the stenographic reports of the debates and act as tellers when votes are taken in the chamber. The questors look after the chamber's housekeeping functions—paying expenses, keeping up a library, keeping the furniture in order, provisioning the bar, and the like. The bureau may control the actions of the Cabinet when the National Assembly is not sitting by calling a meeting of Parliament. The bureau may also call meetings of Parliament at the request of one-third of the deputies, or of the President of the Council of Ministers.

Another agency of the National Assembly is the Commission of Presidents. It is made up of the President of the National Assembly, the vice presidents, the presidents of each of the permanent commissions, and the presidents of each of the party groups of fourteen members or more. This agency decides the agenda of the Assembly—what it will discuss and when it will discuss it. The Assembly itself finally approves its agenda, but normally it accepts the decisions made by the powerful Commission of Presidents.

The "group" is still another constitutional part of the organization of the National Assembly, and also of the Council of the Republic. Groups are made up of deputies who have some common degree of political agreement. They tend to divide along partisan lines closely parallel to those in the country. Thus the existence of political parties is recognized in the constitution through these groups. Although deputies do not have to belong to any group, the greatest number of them do; if they did not, they would have no voice in the selection of the bureau or, much more important, in the selection of the commissions. Each group of fourteen or more deputies is entitled to nominate members to each commission in proportion to its strength in the Assembly. There is a Communist group, an MRP group, a Socialist group, and several smaller groups. Groups are not supposed to be formed out of particular interests, professions, or localities, but a few such interest groups have formed indirectly under the name of study groups, such as one for tobacco and another for sugar beets. The groups, to the extent that they act as party organizations, have a great deal of control over the legislature and also over the government.

The spade work of legislation is done by another constitutional organization: the commission, whose members are selected by proportional representation from among the groups. The function of the various commissions, according to the constitution, is to aid the National Assembly in the study of proposed laws and bills. The general commissions are the most important; there are nearly twenty of them, each with 44 members. Each deals with a particular field, such as economic affairs, foreign affairs, agriculture, national defense, education, public health, finance, interior, justice and legislation, merchant marine and fisheries, communications and tourism, press, radio and cinema, universal suffrage, labor and social security, and so forth. In addition to these general commissions, special commissions may be formed to study particular problems. In general, the commissions prepare the legislation, have an eye on the government, and conduct inquiries. They are miniature legislatures; their decisions are most often approved by the Assembly as a whole.[9]

Assembly Business. Much of the policy made by the National Assembly, of course, takes the form of laws passed. Many of these are introduced by the President of the Council of Ministers, or by a minister singly. Ordinary members of the Assembly may also propose bills and amendments. Once a bill is proposed, it is referred immediately to the appropriate commission, which usually rewrites it, and sometimes even changes it so much that its original author disowns it.

The Assembly usually debates only the commission report, not the original proposal. First it discusses the general idea of the bill; if the Assembly approves it, then each article of the bill is discussed. Next the text is approved as a whole. At any stage, the proposal may be sent back to the commission for revision or other action. This somewhat lengthy process can be shortened by the urgency procedure. As a matter of fact, in recent years most of the laws discussed in the Assembly have been passed by this abbreviated procedure. Once the Assembly has passed the proposal, it is sent to the Council of the Republic, which can normally only force reconsideration of the proposal. Thereafter it is sent to the President of the Republic, who may ask the Assembly to reconsider it; if he does not, it will be promulgated within ten days.

Laws that change the constitution are in a special category. First, a majority of all the members of the National Assembly must pass a resolution in which the purpose of the amendment is stated. Three months later the same resolution is considered again by the National Assembly and must be approved by the same majority, unless the Council of the Republic has in the interim approved the resolution by a majority of its members. If the resolution passes these stages, the amendment itself is drafted and treated as an ordinary law by Parliament. If it passes both houses by majority, it is referred to the French voters for final action, but if two-thirds of the National Assembly or three-fifths of both houses pass the legislation, the referendum is not necessary.

The Constitutional Committee. A novel provision of the constitution deals with laws that have the effect of changing the constitution. This provision sets up a Constitutional Committee; headed by the President of the Republic, it has two other ex-officio members, the President of the National Assembly and the President of the Council of the Republic. In addition, the National Assembly annually chooses seven members and the Council of the Republic three, none of whom may be members of the chambers. These ten are chosen by proportional representation. The Committee de-

---

[9] For commissions as they were under the Third Republic, see Robert K. Gooch, *The French Parliamentary Committee System* (New York, 1935).

cides whether a law passed by the National Assembly implies an amendment of the constitution. If it is decided that such is the implication, the amending procedure must be followed.

Actually, the Committee is sharply limited in its powers. In the first place, it cannot deal with the preamble of the constitution, which contains the controversial material of civil rights. Secondly, it can act only at the request of the President of the Republic and of the President of the Council of the Republic, "the Council having decided the matter by an absolute majority of its members." Furthermore, the request must be made within the short period allowed for promulgating the law. If the Committee decides that the law does change the constitution, then it must try to bring about an agreement between the Council of the Republic and the National Assembly. If it fails in this, the amending procedure must be followed.

The Committee dealt with its first case on June 18, 1948. The case concerned an argument between the two chambers over the time limit on urgency legislation as provided in the constitution. The Constitutional Committee decided that the Council of the Republic should observe a time limit in which to consider bills passed under urgency procedure in the National Assembly. After consultation, the National Assembly agreed, establishing a three-day period. This decision, incidentally, considerably strengthened the position of the Council of the Republic, because the National Assembly had been trying to limit the power of the Council of the Republic by shortening the Council's discussion time to as few hours as the National Assembly had taken under the urgency procedure.[10]

Supervision of the Executive. The National Assembly is not only concerned with legislation; it also controls the Council of Ministers by accepting or rejecting the legislative proposals of the ministers. In addition, the constitution requires that the Assembly must approve of the President of the Council of Ministers before he is appointed. This is the central feature of the French parliamentary system. Thus, when the President of the Republic has designated his candidate for President of the Council of Ministers, the latter presents his program to the Assembly. If it supports his program, it approves his nomination, and the President of the Republic appoints him. This advance consent of the legislature was not required under the Third Republic. Under the Fourth Republic it has been one of the main stumbling blocks to the formation of cabinets. Yet it has also prevented the formation of cabinets that would have had only a slight chance of survival.

The National Assembly controls the President of the Council of Ministers also while he is in office. It can force him to resign by voting a motion of censure against him. On the other hand, the President of the Council of Ministers may ask for the support of the Assembly by requesting a motion

---

[10] See Auguste Soulier, "La Délibération du comité constitutionnel du 18 juin 1948," *Revue du Droit Public,* 65 (1949), 195.

of confidence. Before making such a request, he is required to consult his ministers, although sometimes that has not been done. If the Assembly votes against the motion, he must resign. Under the constitution a day must elapse before a motion either of censure or confidence may be voted on. This provides a cooling-off period. Furthermore, both kinds of motions must be voted on by roll call, and both require a majority vote of all the members of the Assembly for passage. Obviously, these articles were put in the constitution to make sure that a cabinet was not too easily overthrown.

The National Assembly has other controls over the government. Its members may ask ministers oral or written questions. These serve in France, as in England, as a device for checking on the actions of the ministers or their subordinates. The questions are usually quite detailed: one deputy may ask a minister, for example, why a civil servant in a certain place poured 100 gallons of good milk down the drain. In France questions are more often written than oral; yet one type of oral question is much used: the interpellation. Interpellations are proposed by a deputy. If the minister or the President of the Council of Ministers accepts the challenge of the interpellation, or if the Assembly so requires, he must explain his general political view with reference to a particular matter. Thus interpellations touch off a general debate about the policy of the government. They end with a vote of the Assembly to return to the normal order of the day's debate; in the motion to return, however, the government may be supported or attacked. Many cabinets in the Third Republic fell because of adverse votes at the end of the interpellation debates. In the Fourth French Republic the procedure has been less often used to upset cabinets, although the second Schuman Cabinet resigned on September 7, 1948, as a result of such a debate.

Although the government is a creature of the National Assembly, the Assembly is not itself fitted to exercise day-to-day control over governmental activities. This is the work of the executive: the President of the Republic, the President of the Council of Ministers, and the ministers themselves.

The President of the Republic. In the constitution of 1946, the President of the Republic, at first glance, seems to have considerable executive power. Most of this power is more apparent than real, however. The President is chosen by a joint meeting of both houses of Parliament. The first President under the new constitution, Vincent Auriol, was elected by a secret ballot with a majority of the votes, under a special arrangement of the Constituent Assembly. This procedure need not be followed in the future. Auriol, like his predecessors in the Third French Republic, had risen to the office after a parliamentary career. At the time of his election he was President of the National Assembly. Eight out of his twelve predecessors in the Third Republic had also been presiding officers of one chamber or the other.

The President serves for a seven-year term and may be reelected once.

During his tenure he is honored as the first citizen of the Republic. But his position is more than honorific. He has certain political functions to perform. Through the Council of Ministers he appoints a host of officials. He presides over many important governmental bodies: the Council of Ministers, the Committee of National Defense, the Superior Council of the Judiciary, and the Council of the French Union. When he actually presides, he is in a position to give advice, although his advice need not be taken. He also has the power to promulgate the laws, and to ask for reconsideration of a law that he does not approve. His request for reconsideration may not be refused. While this power was not used under the Third Republic, it has been used several times in the Fourth, not for the purpose of political obstruction but to correct errors and suggest improvements.

These powers are less great than they seem because all of the actions of the President must be countersigned by the President of the Council of Ministers and by an individual minister; many acts are countersigned as a matter of practice by several ministers. These signatures relieve the President of the Republic of political responsibility for the acts.

The President does have a few real political functions, aside from giving advice. He names the President of the Council of Ministers, subject to approval by the National Assembly. This gives him some power because there may well be several political figures who could form a cabinet that would win majority support in the Assembly. The choice among them is made by the President, without the requirement of another official's countersignature. The President and the Premier-designate both send letters to the Assembly announcing the designation. Of course, the President is limited here by the need to have the Assembly approve his nominee.

The President of the Council of Ministers. Although the President of the Republic has some limited power, the real executive is the President of the Council of Ministers, popularly called the Premier. His nomination requires much advance consultation. Before designating a Premier, the President of the Republic customarily calls in the presiding officer of the Assembly to ask his advice. He usually calls the heads of the various party groups in the Assembly, too. The man he tentatively decides upon as his choice for Premier then talks with the different party groups to see whether he can get their support. When finally the President is satisfied that his candidate can probably win a majority in the Assembly, he appoints him as Premier-designate, subject to approval by the Assembly.

When the Premier is approved and has selected the Cabinet, his problem is one of trying to keep the support of a majority of deputies. The constitution aids the Premier by making it somewhat harder to overthrow the Cabinet than it was under the Third Republic. Two minor obstacles have already been described: the provisions dealing with motions of censure and questions of confidence. The articles on dissolution in the constitution serve the same purpose, that of stabilizing the Cabinet. They provide that if two Councils of Ministers have fallen within eighteen months because of a motion of censure or a question of confidence, then the Council of Ministers, with the approval of the President of the Assembly, may decide to dissolve the Assembly and order new elections. Crises occurring within fifteen days after the formation of the new Cabinet do not count in application of this rule. The underlying idea was to strengthen the position of the Cabinet so that it could threaten the members of the Assembly with the expenses of another election campaign if they persisted in upsetting cabinets.

These rules were supposed to make the government more stable, but in the first few years of the Fourth Republic they did not always have that effect. Many cabinets fell, not on motions of censure or confidence, but either because there were disagreements within the cabinet or because the cabinet's measures were not supported by the Assembly. Some premiers handed in their resignations to avoid having to call for motions of confidence, and in turn avoiding the necessity for new elections. The effect of avoiding the confidence motion was to make cabinets under the Fourth Republic as unstable as those of the Third.

So long as a cabinet has the confidence of the Assembly, its head is in effect the chief executive. As such, he nominates ministers to direct the executive departments, though the President makes the formal appointment. Then, both the Premier and the ministers are responsible collectively to the Assembly for the general policy of the Cabinet, while ministers are individually responsible for their own actions. Collective responsibility operates when a whole cabinet resigns because one of its measures is not supported by the Assembly. Individual responsibility, on the other hand, operates when one minister resigns, either because the Cabinet will not support him or because he cannot agree with the views of the President of the Council of Ministers.

Although constitutionally the Premier has a free hand in naming his ministers, in fact he is limited by political realities: he must pick men who can get along together and who have political support in the Assembly. Sometimes there are statesmen so preeminent that they cannot be overlooked. Candidates also must usually have seats in the Assembly. All the usual political problems involved in getting a working governmental team have to be solved by the Premier.

Once the Premier has made his political bargains and chosen his ministers, these men become responsible, under him, for carrying out public policy and enforcing the laws. They do this as heads of administrative departments. As such, they speak for their departments from the floor of either house of the legislature. Under them, the work of their departments is done by civil servants.

The Civil Service. The body of civil servants provides some of the continuity that seems to be lacking in the cabinet, because while cabinets come and go, the civil servants go on continuously. Therefore the status of civil servants and the way they are selected, promoted, and retired, are important.

Under the Third Republic there was no general civil service law and no effective link between the different branches of the civil service; the departments were mostly laws unto themselves. Starting with De Gaulle's government in Algiers and continuing under the provisional government, efforts were made to tie the civil service together. To do this, a civil service agency was set up, first by an ordinance of October 9, 1945, made permanent later by the law of October 19, 1946. Now the French national civil service, under this agency, is more nearly a unit. Its members are classified into four groups: administrators, administrative secretaries, administrative clerks, and clerks and attendants. There are some exceptions: this law does not apply to the employees in nationalized industries, judges, or the military. The law provides for a uniform system of recruiting civil servants by examination. The examinations for entrance into the higher civil service are given through the National School of Administration, which trains aspirants and also gives courses for those already in the service.[11] In addition, a Superior Council of Civil Service was created. Half of its twenty-four members represent the civil service unions, the other half the government. This council gives advice on civil service matters. Now that the civil service is more unified than it used to be, a new *esprit de corps* may develop at the higher levels because of the intensified training program.

The Cabinet Secretariat. Another postwar innovation that adds to the better coordination of the French executive machinery is the General Secretariat of the President of the Council of Ministers. Before World War II, several premiers had tried to pull together the work of the different departments, and some of them had established temporary cabinet secretariats, none of which lasted very long. The premier had almost no assistance in coordinating the work of the different departments, and without it he lacked the political power that goes with centralized direction. To secure aid and to increase his political power, he used to take the office of Minister of the Interior as well as that of the President of the Council. The Minister of the Interior controlled the prefects, the most important administrators in the field, and hence he was particularly powerful.

After the war, building on the experience of the provisional government, a permanent cabinet secretariat was set up. It is headed by a senior civil servant, who attends the meetings of the Council of Ministers and takes notes on its decisions. This secretariat is a useful coordinating agency between the departments; all government bills, before being introduced in the legislature, must be referred to it. After it has cleared the bills with all interested departments, the secretariat sends them to the Council of State for further advice, and later presents them for the signature of the President of the

---

[11] See B. Mirkine-Guetzévitch, "The National School of Administration in France," *American Political Science Review*, 43 (1949), 1026 ff.; Jean Trouvé, "The French Civil Service Office," *Public Administration Review*, 11 (1951), 180 ff.

Council of Ministers; then they are introduced in the Assembly. Through this secretariat the premier now has a means of coordinating the work of the departments and of obtaining the technical assistance necessary for his work.[12]

Local Administration. One particularly important branch of administration in France deals with local government. For many years local government has been centrally controlled. Napoleon created the office of prefect to give himself control over the local areas; even earlier the kings had used *intendants* for much the same purpose. This centralization has continued until the present time. It was so great at times that a wit once said that French government suffered from paralysis at the extremes and apoplexy at the center.

The writers of the constitution of 1946 tried to introduce a balance between local government and central administration. They were particularly opposed to the power of the prefect; therefore they required that organic laws should "further extend the liberties" of the geographic departments and municipalities. They also provided that laws should determine the conditions under which field agencies of central administration were to function, "in order to bring the central administration closer to the people." These field agencies of central administration did not, under the Third Republic, work closely with the prefect. The new constitution provided that local units should be governed by elected councils as before, but added that their presiding officers should carry out their decisions, which formerly had been a function of the prefect. These provisions were meant to take power away from the prefect.

Pending the complete establishment of this new system, the constitution provided that temporarily most of the old machinery should continue to operate. The only exception was that the prefect, when acting as head of the geographic department instead of as central representative, was to be under the supervision of the president of the elected departmental council. In most respects, however, the prefect is still the most powerful administrator in his area. In this capacity he enforces the laws.

French Regionalism. For many years it has been said that France had too many prefects and too many geographic departments. With quick means of transportation and communication, the departments did not need to be so small. Consequently various attempts have been made to form larger area units. In the Vichy regime several departments were combined into a region because of the emergency. The men of Vichy could not depend on the old prefects to support them. In 1941, therefore, they created regional prefects to act as their eyes and ears in the country. The regions themselves were largely fictitious. They were not corporate areas; they had no budgets;

---

[12] See René Cassin, "Recent Reforms in the Government and Administration of France," *Public Administration*, 28 (1950), 179 ff.; Roy C. Macridis, "The Cabinet Secretariat in France," *Journal of Politics*, 13 (1951), 589 ff.

the services they furnished were not many; and the regional prefects were not given legal power over the departmental prefects. With the end of the Vichy regime, the regional prefects disappeared.

By the ordinance of January 10, 1944, the De Gaullist government put in the place of the regional prefects Commissioners of the Republic, who were given many powers over the police and other governmental agencies in the region. Their chief work was to keep order. This was no easy task while the land was being reconquered. In June 1945 the commissioners were given power to "stimulate, control, orient, and coordinate the activity of the prefects and of the chiefs of the regional services." [13] As peace and order were reestablished in France, the extraordinary powers of the commissioners became unnecessary. Their offices were abolished on March 26, 1946. Their secretariats, however, were kept in operation, mainly for keeping the police records that had accumulated.

In March 1948 another regional development took place—brought on, too, by an emergency. Political strikes had spread throughout the country; there were so many strikes in different places that the police could not always be concentrated sufficiently to keep order. To deal with the emergency, the Minister of the Interior delegated some of his powers to Inspectors General of Administration with Extraordinary Mission. The inspectors have power to deal with matters of public security; acting under the minister's orders, they may control military and police units. They meet monthly with the Minister of the Interior, and frequently, also, with all of the prefects in their region. Often, in fact, the prefect in the chief town of a region is also inspector general.

In addition to preserving public security, the inspectors have acted as coordinating agents in the field for several ministries. While they have no separate regional organization, the inspectors do provide the Minister of the Interior and other ministers with a means of dealing jointly with the interrelated problems of several departments.[14] Meanwhile, the traditional prefects remain the principal administrative officials in their departments.

---

[13] See Brian Chapman, "A Development in French Regional Administration," *Public Administration*, 28 (1950), 327 ff.

[14] See Roger S. Abbott and Roger Sicard, "A Postwar Development in French Regional Government: The *Super Préfet*,'" *American Political Science Review*, 44 (1950), 426 ff.

CHAPTER 12

THE STRUGGLE FOR CONTROL IN FRANCE

1. Main Currents of French Politics

In the past 150 years France has seen many different forms of government. Yet through it all runs a strong current of continuity, a current composed of differing but remarkably persistent ideas about what governments ought to do. Those who have differed about these ideas have never ceased to struggle with one another for the control of whatever government existed at the moment.

Equality versus Authority. In the *ancien régime* the authoritarians argued that the king's rights and privileges were of divine origin; only the king and his nobles ought to rule France. In the great revolution of 1789 most of the authoritarians fled for their lives and hence lived to fight again. Those who survived took their places in the National Assembly at the right of the chairman. From that day to this, there have been protagonists of the *Right* in France, and their views have remained authoritarian.

In the Third Republic, they were in favor of restoring the monarchy. When hope of a monarchy vanished, the authoritarians remained on the Right in the republican Chamber of Deputies, calling themselves conservatives instead of monarchists. They flourished in the Vichy regime. After the collapse of Vichy, a few rightists were shot as collaborators with Hitler's new order, and a few more were imprisoned. With the advent of the Fourth Republic, there were still authoritarians on the Right. They would be ready, again, to create a strong executive government to replace the present legislative type.

Equally, since the great revolution, many groups have argued that equalitarianism was the only salvation of France. Equalitarians wrote the *Declaration of the Rights of Man* in 1789, led the French Revolution, and thereafter were the strong defenders of the republic against the monarchy. They were at the *Left* in the early years of the Third Republic. "Liberty, equality, and fraternity" were their watchwords.

Church versus State. When the issue of republic versus monarchy seemed to be settled, a new issue divided the Left from the Right: the role of the church in the state. Those of the Right firmly defended the church. In their view, the union of church and state under the concordat of 1801 strengthened both. They supported the church partly, too, because they thought that it was authoritarian. Those of the republican Left, on the

228

other hand, became violently anticlerical. They contended that the church was antirepublican, that first it backed the monarchists and then the conservatives to weaken the republic.

The outburst over the Dreyfus affair that rocked the French government at the turn of the century was partly caused by this political division. It divided clericals from anticlericals still more sharply, even as it divided the republican leaders from the army. The church was thought to support the side of order and authority—that of the high army officers—against the equalitarian foes of privilege. This momentous issue was settled by a law in 1905 that separated church and state, yet clericalism versus anticlericalism, like the issue of monarchy versus republic, is still one basis for partisan argument in France.

Capitalism versus Socialism. With the republic established and the church separated from the state, other issues rose to divide the Right from the Left. One of the most stubborn concerned the amount of control the state should have in the economic life of the nation. The republican battle cry of the 1890's was "No enemies on the left." More and more the Left became socialist, inheritors of the ideas of the Commune of 1871. The parties of the Left, once united in their republicanism, began to divide over this issue. As industrialization increased in France, the breach widened. Then a split developed within the socialist Left between those who believed that socialism could be reached gradually and those who argued that revolution was essential.

Many of the bitter political arguments after World War I were between the economic Left and the economic Right: socialism against *laissez faire*. Throughout the years, France, like other European countries, had introduced many social and economic reforms, so that the *laissez faire* doctrine was never applied completely; but each step away from it touched off new controversy.

France on the Continent of Europe. In the early years of the Third Republic, foreign policy did not cause much partisan bickering. When, however, French hegemony over Europe—constructed by the treaty of Versailles in 1919—crumbled with the rise of Hitler, the parties differed widely with one another and within themselves. For example, some Socialists were pacifist, while others pleaded for the building of a strong France; some argued that salvation could only come from a European federation, others that appeasement of Hitler was the only solution. Some of the rightists argued that Catholic France should come to terms with the dictators of Catholic Italy and Catholic Spain, while others supported strong ties with the Soviet Union as a counterweight to the nearby dictatorships. There were those in the center who favored close working relations with other western democracies; others gloomily thought that Hitler was certain to control all of Europe, and that he had best be placated. On issues of foreign policy there was, therefore, much division, and these divisions prevented uniformity in the policy pursued.

Underlying the conflicts as to foreign and internal policies, there was always the heritage of the Revolution. In accord with its spirit, partisans could argue that governments did not have to be tolerated: they could be overthrown. This attitude was sometimes found on the extreme Right as well as on the extreme Left. The explosion accompanying the Stavisky scandal in 1934 was an example. When the smoke of battle cleared on the Place de la Concorde, seventeen people were found dead and hundreds wounded.

2. The Party System

Characteristics. André Siegfried, a sharp-witted, careful student of politics, once said that French political parties are as changing as the clouds. Certainly to those accustomed to thinking of parties as they exist in the United States and England, French parties scarcely seem to be parties at all. They do not have the large organizations, supported by large campaign chests, of American and British parties. Few of them have large paid office staffs or even regular organizational meetings. None of them has a majority of the voters back of it. Characteristically, as one expert puts it, they are "parties of opinion" rather than electoral machines for getting power irrespective of consistent doctrine.[1] In the United States the two major parties include many shades of political opinion from left to right. At the time of election these different opinions are momentarily glossed over in platforms that are so vague and general that there is little difference between the doctrines of the two main parties. There is a strong will on the part of the *ins* to stay in, and of the *outs* to get in.

In France, on the other hand, almost every shade of political opinion has its own party. Ideas rather than machinery hold the party together. The ideas are kept alive by party newspapers; in fact, in France today there are few newspapers that try impartially to describe the events of the world around them. The typical French newspaper is written from a strongly partisan point of view, and interpets the news rather than records it.[2]

Growing Strength of Party Organization. In the past, French party organization was weak. The socialists, in 1905, were among the first to form a regular party organization, and a few of the parties on the extreme right followed their example. Even though party machinery was set up to exact some sort of discipline from the party members, accomplishments were far short of expectations. In 1927, for example, when Daladier was elected to head the Radical party, he determined to introduce more discipline. Shortly after he had sent out his directives on unified voting, there was a vote in the Chamber on calling up the military reserves. He voted against it, the head of the Radical group in the Chamber voted for it, and another Radical at the head of the finance commission of the Chamber abstained

---

[1] Georges Burdeau, *Traité de science politique,* Vol. I (Paris, 1949), 448. See also Mario Einaudi, "The Crisis of Politics and Government in France," *World Politics,* 4 (1951), 64 ff.
[2] See the interesting article by A. J. Liebling, "La Presse capricieuse," *New Yorker,* 25 (March 19, 1949), 58, on coverage of news events by political newspapers.

from voting.[3] On another occasion, the executive committee of the Radical Socialist party decided that members should abstain from voting in the debate on the occupation of the Ruhr. But only 35 of the 84 members of the party did abstain; the rest voted.[4]

The tendency under the Fourth Republic has been toward stronger party organization. In fact, during the meetings of the two constituent assemblies in 1945-46, some political observers predicted that France would become a country of monolithic parties.[5] At that time the Communist party was strongly disciplined and rigidly organized, reaching into almost every village. The Socialists also were well organized, and so was the MRP. Each of these was becoming a mass party rather than a party of opinion. Each one had elaborate machinery for getting votes and for keeping its elected members in line in the constituent assemblies.

Mass Party Structure. The organizational pattern of these mass parties is pyramidal. At the base, in each local area in which there are enough enthusiasts, a section is set up with its president and executive committee. The sections are gathered together into regional federations. On the next level is the national council of the party, made up of an executive committee, heads of the different federations, and elected deputies of the party. The executive committee controls the day-to-day work of the party through its secretariat. Once or twice a year a congress of the party meets: it represents all of the party's branches and members, and makes the major decisions.

Although the large French parties have much the same outward structure, the relationship between the structural parts differs in each of them. In the Socialist party, for example, every major decision of its congress and executive committee must have been discussed earlier by the lower units of the party.[6] When the congress of the party meets, there are often vigorous arguments between delegates, and close votes decide the stand of the party. This is also true of the MRP. In the congress of the latter held just before the elections of June 1951, for instance, the young delegates continuously argued for stronger stands on various issues. The older and more experienced parliamentarians worked to restrain their young companions-at-arms. In fact, the views of the two groups were so different that the MRP platform became quite vague. In the Communist party congresses, on the other hand, decisions were not so much based on long argument and close votes as on central party instructions warmly supported.

Most of the present French political parties have lasted for years, and are backed by fairly stable groups of supporters in different parts of the country. For example, François Goguel, a careful student of political parties under the Third Republic, points out that one electoral division in the

---

[3] Georges Bourgin, Jean Carrère, and André Guerin, *Manuel des partis politiques en France* (2d ed., Paris, 1928), 24.

[4] *Ibid.*

[5] Gordon Wright, *The Reshaping of French Democracy* (New York, 1948), 64.

[6] Burdeau, *op. cit.* above, note 1, 463.

department of Ardèche voted down Louis Napoleon's plebiscite in 1851; in the elections of 1936 it voted *left* by almost the same number of votes. He gives many other examples of the same tendency.[7]

3. Major French Parties

The Communists. In three out of four elections after World War II, the Communist party has won more popular votes than any other in France. Its votes come mainly from those departments that have historically voted with the Left. The party itself has been operating in France since 1920, but its popularity was not great until after World War II. Indeed, early in the war, from 1939 to 1941, when the Soviet Union and Germany were allies, the party was dissolved, and its leader, Maurice Thorez, fled to Moscow as a military deserter. With the attack on the Soviet Union by Hitler, the Communists switched their views. The war ceased to be an imperialist adventure of greedy capitalists and became instead a crusade of democracy against fascism. Thereafter the Communists became leaders of French underground resistance to Hitler. They were fearless and daring. Thousands of them were shot for acting in support of their new line, sacrifices which won the party hundreds of thousands of French votes.

After the Vichy interlude, the Communists cooperated with the other parties in reestablishing French government. They were in De Gaulle's Cabinet in the early days of reconstruction; they loudly proclaimed their desire to rebuild democratic France. They helped in this effort by keeping the miners from striking, as well as by agreeing with the other major parties to support the Monnet plan of economic revival.

In May, 1947, they were ejected from the Ramadier Cabinet over the issue of wage stabilization. Thereafter they opposed almost every action of the coalition of the center and the Socialists. They became less stalwart defenders of the "little man" and more nearly a French branch of Stalin's orthodox Communist party. They even implied that if a war should break out between France and the Soviet Union, they would welcome Russian defenders of the people's democracy on French soil.

Their election manifesto in 1951 is a good example of Communist political aims. With respect to international affairs, it could well have been written in Moscow, so closely did it reflect the official Stalinist view. The Communists attacked the Marshall Plan and the North Atlantic Treaty as tools of Wall Street. The American billionaires, they said, were preparing to plunge all countries into a new world war; the Soviet peace plan was the only defense against this. The Communist party newspaper, *Humanité,* the day after the election, headlined the results as "Victory for the Party of Peace" and "Disaster for Truman."

Further, like their mentor in the Kremlin, they favored outright prohibition of the use of atomic bombs. They declared their belief in working for

[7] In his *La Politique des partis sous la IIIe République* (Paris, 1946).

a democratic peace through respect for the United Nations charter and by means of a pact among the Five Powers: the United States, Great Britain, France, the Soviet Union, and Communist China. They strongly opposed the French armed intervention in Indo-China, urging that Indo-China's complete independence be recognized.

The Communist domestic program looks much like that of any democratic party of the Left. Like the French Socialists, the Communists favor a sliding scale of wages tied to the cost of living. To please another segment of voters, they would pass laws insuring fair prices to French farmers. Having in mind the perennial complaint that taxes are too high, they would substantially reduce the cost of rearmament and police maintenance in order to apply some of the money to socially constructive purposes.

In the Parisian area they made platform promises that if they were elected in numbers, 100,000 houses would be built in five years; 15 high schools would be constructed in three years; a 1000-bed children's hospital would be erected; the underground railway would be extended into the suburbs; and for the convenience of the workers, the busses would run after 9 P.M. in the Paris area.[8]

For the small businessman, the party guaranteed to protect his property—the fruit of his labor and thrift—and to reduce his taxes. The budget would be balanced, nevertheless, because the very rich would pay higher taxes. In short, the Communist program was designed to attract working class, farmer, and lower middle-class votes. The problem of the French voters is to decide whether the Communist program is but a propaganda means toward attaining the goal of a Communist society built on Marxist-Leninist-Stalinist principles. If it is, the words of the program would have a different meaning afterward than they might now have in France.

The Socialists. The second largest party on the Left, but with consistently fewer votes than the Communists since World War II, is the Socialist party. Its official title is the French Section of the Worker's International (SFIO). In December 1920, the Socialist party split in two. The majority voted to accept the dictates of the Communist International. The minority set up another SFIO, independent of Moscow. The new Socialists refused to attack the national defense program, as the Communists ordered, and tried to keep the trade unions divorced from the political control of the Third International. Apart from this, they were Marxist. They believed that the regime of private property must ultimately give way to a regime of collective property. They considered this objective to be revolutionary, but to be achieved by a gradual democratic process. In their view, true revolution is not accomplished by the violent conquest of political power, but by the step-by-step transformation of the structure of society.

The SFIO program is based on the idea that social justice is essential to liberty. Both of these terms have a moral connotation and are not purely

---

[8] *Humanité,* June 8, 1951, 4.

materialistic in the Marxist sense. Yet the French Socialist does not reject materialism. He argues that neither social justice nor liberty can be safe-guarded unless the material standard of living of the masses is improved. To accomplish his moral objective, he does not use the methods of either the complete individualist or the complete collectivist. For the Socialist, the individual gains his liberty through society, but neither the individual nor society is completely sovereign.

The details of the party program are supposed to produce social justice. For example, in 1951 the party proposed the nationalization of the steel and chemical industries on the ground that these industries are too important to the public welfare to be managed by a few for their own private profit. The party would make other economic changes: gradually increase the role of the workers in the management of industry; peg wages to the cost of living and at the same time set up a system of price controls to keep the cost of living down; and increase the amounts of aid to needy people—aged workers and the economically weak. The increased cost would be met by a steep rise in the income and profits taxes, rather than by increasing hidden excise taxes paid by the majority of the people.

The foreign policy of the SFIO is western rather than eastern in its inter-nationalism. It believes in a well-organized Western Europe defense sys-tem, although it is not enthusiastic about rearming Germany. It strongly supported the Schuman Plan, by which the German and French iron and steel industries are to be operated by an international agency.[9] The plan was viewed as a first step in the direction of greater European unity, one of the Socialist goals.[10]

The Popular Republican Movement. Of the center parties one of the most important in the immediate postwar years was the Popular Republican Movement, the MRP. Under the Third Republic this party was called Christian Democratic. At that time it had few adherents, but during World War II Catholic leaders of the Left became prominent in the under-ground resistance. One of these leaders, Georges Bidault, a lycée professor of medieval history, was also president of the underground resistance council. Another, Maurice Schumann, was active in Free French circles in London and was a broadcaster on the Free French radio program.

Shortly after the liberation of France, the MRP became a mass party. It organized along Communist lines, using strongly centralized machinery, and it united many of the former resistance groups that, though neither Com-munist nor Socialist, still had a leftist tinge. The church gave no official support to the new organization. Great numbers of voters did, however, partly because De Gaulle, then at the height of his power, was thought to favor the MRP. To many, the party seemed to fill the gap between the

---

[9] *Le Monde,* May 17, 1951, 5.

[10] See Alexandre B. Zévaès, *Histoire du socialisme et du communisme en France de 1871 à 1947* (Paris, 1947).

Left and those of the old center and the Right that had been discredited by the capitulation of the Vichy regime. In the first postwar elections the MRP scored tremendous successes: in two, it nearly equaled the vote-getting power of the Communists, and in one, in June 1946, it beat the Communists. In 1951, however, it lost heavily.

The basic idea of the MRP and of the other Christian Democratic parties like it has been well stated by Professor Mario Einaudi. He wrote:

> The common guide . . . is a belief that the body of Christian doctrine has some principles to offer to the political life of countries that in recent times have refused to take them into account. The ideas of community, of the common good, of social solidarity, of the relationship between morality and politics—these are some of the political tenets derived from Christianity for application in the world of today.[11]

Such principles, as applied to industry, put the party midway between the Left and the Right. It agrees neither that the state should control major industries nor that the capitalist should have complete freedom from control. Both views take away freedom from the great majority, and it is freedom that the state exists to maintain. The party argues that the capitalist in the past has been free, but that now he must share his freedom with his workers; the workers must participate in the management of the enterprises. The state becomes the balance wheel—it coordinates, and controls only where absolutely necessary.

These general ideas were specifically applied in the 1951 platform of the MRP. The party demanded that labor-management committees be given real responsibility in plants, as a new deal for labor. With respect to the economy as a whole, the MRP asked the government to work out a new five-year plan to modernize industry. The party favored small and medium-sized industries, because industries in the modern world are much too strongly centralized. In its view such centralization reduces the freedom of the individual; decentralization would restore initiative to individuals caught in the meshes of giant industrial empires.

The party, in 1951, wanted to preserve and extend the social achievements of the Fourth Republic. It would, for example, tie the guaranteed minimum wage to an automatic sliding cost-of-living scale. It favored, too, an equalized family allowance so that large families would not be penalized by rising costs. It would offer price support to the farmer for the same reason —to keep up his purchasing power.

The MRP was especially concerned with the position of the denominational schools. It insisted that local educational authorities should be more independent so that they could be more generous to the denominational schools.

The Radicals. Another of the center parties is the Radical Socialist, the

---

[11] From the first edition of this book, 223.

party that controlled France during most of the life of the Third Republic. Founded in 1901, the party's point of view derives from the French Revolution. It firmly defends the political freedoms of the *Declaration of the Rights of Man*. In earlier days this meant that the party stood for the advancement of popular suffrage and for bringing the executive under the control of the legislature. Later, as these objectives were accomplished, the party further interpreted the *Declaration of the Rights of Man* to mean safeguards for the position of the individual against the church; anticlericalism is deeply imbedded in Radical Socialist thought. More recently the party has pressed for safeguards to individual liberty by extending the social services of the government in the form of social security. The same principle was applied to large industrial enterprises, which were to be limited in the interests of the majority of the people. Lately the party has contended that the all-powerful collective state would menace the individual's freedom. Consequently, the state should relinquish its overwhelming economic power.[12]

As the Radical Socialist party dominated the Third Republic, so it was charged with bringing the Third Republic to grief. Thus, many thought at the end of World War II that the party had had its day and was dying. The first postwar elections, in October 1945, seemed to substantiate this belief. The Radical Socialists received less than half as many votes as any other of the three large parties. However, many politicians of the center thought there was need for a larger and better organized grouping of the center, considering that the three mass parties were all leftist in outlook. This need led to the creation of the *Rassemblement des Gauches Républicaines* (RGR), a center grouping of republicans. The major party in the group was the Radical Socialist, but it included also the *Union Démocratique et Socialiste de la Résistance,* formed out of several splinter parties.

The detailed program of the Radical Socialists grows out of their defense of the liberty of the individual. They feel, for example, that the state has grown too powerful through the nationalizations already accomplished in France—notably of gas, electricity, coal, and aircraft. They would, therefore, not only halt any further nationalization but also reform the nationalized industries by giving private enterpreneurs more power. Like almost every other French party, they would try to equalize the income of the farmers and the industrialists. The Radical Socialists desire, too, the extension of social security to the classes not covered—the small employers, agricultural wage earners, and other independent workers.

The Radical Socialists also would like to see political reforms, especially a return to the single-member district election system. Under it, in the Third Republic, they had received a large vote, and there are still many local political machines that would work for them. Likewise, they favor a restoration of the powers of the old Senate. On this point they have traveled full circle. In the early days one of their major campaign planks was that

---

[12] Bourgin and Others, *op. cit.* above, note 3, 136 ff.

the Senate should have less power, but as the years went on, the Radical Socialists gained control of many seats in the Senate. Consequently they now favor increased power for the Council of the Republic.

The De Gaullists. Still further to the right is the *Rassemblement du Peuple Français,* the Rally of the French People (RPF). This group scarcely considers itself a party at all, but prefers to think of itself as a great bloc of all those whose prime interest is the restoration of the greatness of France. The RPF nevertheless has many of the characteristics of a political party; it behaved like one in the first national election in which it took part, in 1951.

General Charles de Gaulle heads the party; he is its guiding star and prophet. Its great electoral success can be traced partly to recollection of the General's heroic efforts during the dark days of World War II. And he again distinguished himself by heading the French government during the hectic period of reconstruction. Thereafter De Gaulle groomed himself for a position as leader in the reestablishment of a preeminent France. As a leader, he feels he must be apart from ordinary men. He must be a man, as De Gaulle himself wrote of the military commander, whose prestige is based on mystery, whose reserve of soul is coupled with that of his gestures and words, whose silence heightens his authority. This man of action will only achieve his objectives if he is equipped with egoism, pride, endurance, and guile. Yet his outward appearance and his actions must lead to great achievements, to splendid goals.[13]

Thus De Gaulle, surrounded by an aura of mystery, is the focal point of the RPF. Its political objective is revisionist. In the General's opinion, there must be profound changes in the constitution of 1946 to bring back the grandeur of France.[14] The constitution must be built on the principle of the separation of powers. To do this, the President must be freed from parliamentary control, yet he must not be popularly elected; instead he would be chosen by an elaborate electoral college. If the strong President disagrees with the action of the legislature, he would have the option either of referring the disagreement to the voters in a referendum or of dissolving the legislature. Another change in the constitution would strengthen the Council of the Republic so that it would be a counterweight to the National Assembly, where political parties exert too much power. Indeed, political parties are evil.

The economic program of the RPF would give the worker some responsibility in the conduct of the enterprise by the creation of associations for controlling industry, to consist of representatives of labor, capital, and management. In order that the laboring man feel to be a part of the enterprise, his wages would fluctuate with its profits.

Another strong tenet of the De Gaullists is their opposition to communism.

[13] Charles de Gaulle, *Le Fil de l'Épée* (2d ed., Paris, 1944), ch. 2.
[14] From a speech to the RPF conference, quoted in *Le Monde,* March 13, 1951, 5.

They consider communism an alien force, and refer to the Communists as the "separatists." They intend to eliminate the Communists from French political life if De Gaulle is returned to power.

These general objectives became still more general in the 1951 electoral platform of the party, which aimed to: (1) reestablish the French state, (2) build national unity, (3) reorganize national defense, (4) strengthen the leadership of France in the French Union, and (5) develop the French economy. In the campaign literature this program was called the "wave of the future." The General said that postwar France had been engulfed in a wave of mediocrity, but as it had not been too dangerous, he had not turned to a *coup d'état* to restore French unity. Now the wave of mediocrity was passing; the Rally of the French People would rise triumphant above party.

Is the RPF fascist? This question causes endless discussion in France, and elsewhere. The Communists call the General a fascist, but they use the term for almost any political opponent to the right of them. Yet it is true that the De Gaullist movement has some of the trappings of fascism. It has a *mystique;* it has a leader who considers himself the chosen instrument for rebuilding French greatness; it has the carefully organized and dramatically stage-managed political meetings; it also has some of the economic ideas of Mussolini's corporativism; above all, it regards itself as being above ordinary parties, as the wave of the future. On the other hand, the General himself was active in the restoration of the old multiparty system while he was Premier-President. He withdrew from political power in 1946 rather than undertake a *coup d'état.* His political actions have been within the framework of the constitution of 1946 even though he means to supplant it. Yet De Gaulle's program is vague. It offers a faith in great objectives, not in detailed platforms, and in that new myth, "the liberal hero." [15]

Other Rightist Parties. Many splinter parties on the right in France are not generally organized throughout the country, but have only a central nucleus for advancing their ideas. There have been a few exceptions: the well-organized *Action Française* of the Third Republic was one. It had its newspaper—widely read in Paris because of the challenging editorials of Charles Maurras—and its ardent followers. It preached the gospel of an Orleanist restoration, by violence if necessary, regarding majority opinion in a democracy as not to be trusted or valued. Once in power, it would have set up a government devoted to the public welfare, monarchist, hereditary, antiparliamentarian, and decentralized. Hence there would be authority at the top and liberty at the bottom. This group and its paper were proscribed by the Fourth Republic for their role in the Vichy interlude.

Some of the members of two of the Third Republic's rightist groups

---

[15] H. Stuart Hughes, "Gaullism: Retrospect and Prospect," in Edward Mead Earle, ed., *Modern France* (Princeton, 1951), 261. See also André Malraux and James Burnham, *The Case for De Gaulle* (New York, 1948).

were active in the resistance.   These groups were the Republican Federation, whose motto was "liberty, security, and property"; and the Democratic Alliance, whose slogan was "laity and economic liberty." [16]   These two became the nucleus of the present Republican Liberty party, the PRL.   Other small rightist groups are the Independent Republicans and the Peasant Action.   These last three parties worked together in the elections of 1951 as the Union of Independents, Peasants, and National Republicans.   In general they support free enterprise, private control of nationalized industries, abandonment of subsidies, reduction of government spending, and other steps to take the government out of business.   In international affairs they are strongly behind the Atlantic Pact and every step in the direction of European unity as well.   This group considers itself the Fourth Force in French politics—neither Communist or part of the Third Force of the Left nor De Gaullist, but middle-of-the-road conservative.   Its candidates received slightly more votes than the MRP in 1951, and half as many as the De Gaullists.

4. Present-day Political Problems

Party Alignments.   Since the establishment of the Fourth Republic, French politics has followed much the same outward pattern as under the Third.   In spite of constitutional limitations, cabinets fell as often as before. In the life of the first National Assembly there were eleven different cabinets, not to mention the four cabinets just after liberation.   Almost all of the postwar cabinets have been center coalitions of Socialists, MRP, and RGR, with a scattering of Right independents and unaffiliated deputies.   After May 1947, these cabinets had no Communist members, nor were there any De Gaullist members, because the party was not founded until after the election of November 1946.   The center parties in the Cabinet, the Third Force, have been losing power.   After the municipal elections of 1947, in which the De Gaullists won nearly 40 per cent of the votes, the Third Force represented only approximately one-third of the electorate.   The other two-thirds were divided almost equally between the Communists and the De Gaullists.

In the elections of 1951 the Third Force remained fully intact, but only slightly stronger.   The Communists were still the largest party, with 26.5 per cent of the popular vote, but with far fewer seats in the Assembly.   The De Gaullists were second with 21.7 per cent of the vote, but with more seats.   The Third Force parties—the Socialists, MRP, and RGR—won 38.3 per cent of the popular vote and 45.2 per cent of the seats.   To keep a governmental majority, they must work with some of the Fourth Force deputies—the conservative independents—with their popular vote of 13.1 per cent and 15.7 per cent of the seats.   The plight of the Third Force parties in

---

[16] These parties are described fully in Bourgin and Others, *op. cit.* above, note 3.

1951 is graphically shown in the table opposite on French election results. The table also shows the numerical strength of these and the other French parties in the elections of 1936 and 1946.

Following the elections of 1951, therefore, the formation of a governmental majority was even more difficult than it had been after the elections of 1946. Other things being equal, the life of the cabinet can scarcely be longer.

The Debate on the Constitution. A crucial problem in France is the very structure of the government. The two largest parties, with 48.2 per cent of the vote in 1951, object to the constitutional framework. These two parties have diametrically opposite views about the changes that should be made. The Communists favor a one-house legislature and a weak executive. The De Gaullists, on the other hand, want a two-house legislature and a strong president. The Third Force parties are in the middle, holding a precarious balance of power and defending the traditional definition of democracy in France. They stand for liberal democracy against two authoritarianisms: Communism and De Gaullism.

The Economic Battle. The cabinets of the Third Force or of any other coalition have to solve the immediate problems of running the country. While De Gaulle and Thorez argue about the future form of government, the premier and his ministers have to wrestle with economic problems. Because of wars and danger of wars, France, since 1900, has not had ten years of prosperity.[17] In World War II, French soil was again fought over and there was great destruction of manpower and property. France recovered from the holocaust with remarkable speed, but by 1951 she was producing in total not much more than in 1929. This level of production was sufficient to replace damaged resources, such as railway lines, rolling stock, and farms that could only gradually be put back into use. Very little of the production was left to increase the standard of living of the French people.

There were other reasons for the economic difficulties. By comparison with American workmen, the French were considerably less productive. In 1938, for example, an American worker produced three times as much as a French worker, and in 1949 four times as much, mainly because the equipment used by the French worker is much less modern. Higher productivity, and almost that alone, will raise the French standard of living. It must come principally from modernizing equipment. Yet many French workers resist modernization because they have been trained as skilled artisans, devoted to careful hand-workmanship instead of mass-production methods.

To raise the standard of living the government is trying to increase worker productivity. This is the purpose of the so-called Monnet Plan, evolved in 1946. Under the direction of Jean Monnet, a French businessman, French

[17] Richard Ruggles, "The French Investment Program and Its Relation to Resource Allocation," in Earle, *op. cit.* above, note 15, 370.

ELECTIONS TO THE FRENCH CHAMBER OF DEPUTIES AND NATIONAL ASSEMBLY, VOTES AND SEATS 1936, 1946, AND 1951
(*Votes in thousands*)

Parties	Chamber of Deputies 1936			National Assembly 1946				National Assembly 1951			
	Votes	Per Cent	Seats	Votes	Per Cent	Seats	Per Cent	Votes	Per Cent	Seats	Per Cent
De Gaullists (RPF)				313*	1.6	5	0.8	4,134	21.7	118	18.8
Right	3,752	40.2	199	2,465	12.8	73	11.8	2,496	13.1	98	15.7
Radical Socialists and Allied Groups	1,923	20.6	147	2,381	12.4	65	10.5	2,194	11.5	94	15.0
MRP and Allied Groups	450	4.8	23	5,058	26.4	166	26.9	2,353	12.3	85	13.6
Socialists	1,455	15.6	149	3,431	17.9	103	16.6	2,764	14.5	104	16.6
Communists	1,502	16.1	72	5,489	28.6	187	30.5	5,038	26.5	103	16.5
Others	249	2.7	18	62	0.3	18	2.9	74	0.4	25	3.8
Total	9,331		608	19,199		617		19,053		627	

Source: Based on table compiled by Mario Einaudi, first edition of this book (page 231), and French Embassy, Press and Information Service, Doc. No. 51 (July 16, 1951).

* Votes cast for Gaullist Union lists.

capabilities and resources were surveyed. Then a governmental investment program was mapped out, supported by tax money in part, and later
by Marshall Plan money provided by the United States. Under this program, steel, coal, and electricity production has risen considerably above
the figures for 1938; in fact, more steel was produced in 1950 than in the
peak year of 1929.[18]

French governments have had other economic battles to fight. One of
these is against inflation. Its extent is demonstrated by the government's
basic economic indexes. While production in 1950 was 132 per cent of
1938, retail prices were 2,055 per cent of those of 1938, and wholesale prices
were 2,304 per cent of 1938. Yet the wage index is only 1,050 per cent of
1938, although this figure does not include the social security benefits that
the workers now have, nor their benefits for large families.[19]

Such inflation, and the gap between the worker's income and what he has
to pay, creates political unrest. The government has tried to solve this
difficult problem by rigidly limiting governmental expenditures and by
manipulating internal and external trade. But in 1951 a new pressure developed: the cost of raw materials, priced on the world market, rose alarm-
ingly. Then the government allowed collective-wage control negotiators
to increase wages to meet the rising prices. In turn prices were raised, and
the vicious cycle began again. The government was caught in a spiral. It
had to pay more not only for the things it bought—armaments, for example
—but also to its employees, including the industrial workers in the nationalized industries.

The Nationalization Program. Nationalization in France was a matter
of doctrine rather than of necessity. The doctrine was much more warmly
supported in the first Constituent Assembly than later. The first Constituent Assembly, under the leadership of De Gaulle, passed the nationalization
laws by huge majorities (517 to 35 for nationalizing the banks, for instance).
The political argument advanced was that the private owners of such vast
enterprises as coal, gas, electricity, and banks were much too powerful;
through their control over the enterprises they could also control the government. Nationalization would free the government from control by a
wealthy minority.

France had had earlier experience with nationalizations. In 1936, the
principal munitions and aviation industries were taken over, and later the
railroads and the Bank of France were nationalized. In each of these
cases, the government indemnified the former owners for their losses; their
companies were normally not disbanded, but governmental agents controlled
a majority of the stock.

The nationalizations after liberation were more far-reaching, however.

---

[18] French Embassy in the United States, Press and Information Service, Document No. 35,
February 1951.

[19] *Ibid.,* Document No. 33, January 1951.

The old companies were dissolved and the stockholders paid off with government bonds. Many of these stockholders complained that they were not given a fair return on their investments,[20] because the government paid them on the basis of the low market value of their stocks caused by the threat of nationalization.

Under the nationalization laws of 1946 the government controls the Bank of France and the four largest private deposit banks, thirty-four of the largest insurance companies, and the electricity, gas, and coal industries.[21] It controls these through boards representing the state, the workers, and the consumers, appointed by the appropriate minister. As a rule, a director manages the enterprise, subject to policy controlled by the board. In principle, the boards were supposed to be largely independent of the state, but in fact they have not been. The first appointments were often heavily weighted in favor of labor. For example, the first Communist Minister of Industrial Production appointed a majority of coal board members from the Communist-dominated *Confédération Générale de Travail* (CGT). He said that the state, the worker, and the consumer could best be represented by CGT men. In the autumn of 1948, these CGT board members urged the miners working under them to take part in the strike that the Communist party and the union had called. In addition, the government has interfered with many details of administering the different industries. It has been unwilling, for instance, to let the coal board raise prices as high as costs; hence a deficit is inevitable. But the government regards this deficit as an indirect subsidy of the price of coal, and one way of keeping down the consumer's cost of living.

The balance sheet of the French nationalizations cannot yet be presented. Many charge that the government is by no means as efficient an operator as the private owners would have been, and many say that the internal administration of the enterprises is so complicated that it is difficult to get work done. At the same time, most of the industries have continued to produce at about the rate they had maintained under private management.

If the nationalized industries have not been able to keep up with demand, it is partly because after the war demand rose at a spectacular rate. For example, many more people want electric and gas service than can get it. Demand for coal and steel also increased, and with it inflationary pressure. The cost of building up French defenses has been enormous. Before the signing of the North Atlantic Pact in 1948, the military budget was 321 billion francs; before the pact's ratification in 1949, the cost was 388 billion francs; after ratification in 1950, the defense budget was 420 billion francs; and after the Korean war began, the defense budget for 1951 was put at 740 billion francs. This is inflationary pressure indeed.

[20] See *ibid.*, "A Study of the Nationalized Enterprises in France," translated from a series of articles in *Le Monde*, August 8, 15, and 22, and September 5 and 12, 1948.

[21] For an analysis of the operation of these enterprises, see David H. Pinkney, "The French Experiment in Nationalization, 1944-1950," in Earle, *op. cit.* above, note 15, ch. 20.

France in International Affairs. The international political situation greatly endangers French security. Three major areas are affected: European France, the Atlantic region, and overseas France. In all of these areas France remains the prey of her geographical position. Her own security rests in defending her exposed low-lying northeast and central-east frontier, over which for centuries conquerors have swarmed into France. The French also have hundreds of miles of seacoast on the Atlantic and the Mediterranean. These land and sea frontiers must be defended by a large land army and a sizable navy. Modern wars are also fought in the air. France is particularly susceptible to airborne destruction; in World War II her industrial plants and railway facilities were almost eliminated.

In any future total war the French expect that their country will again be a battlefield for land armies, and that it will be assailed from the sea and from the air. In any such total war the French military power is ultimately limited—there are roughly 40,000,000 Frenchmen, as compared with 70,000,000 Germans and 200,000,000 Russians. While the French industrial plant is in good working order, its capacity is limited. Germany and Russia have a greater industrial potential. French foreign policy, therefore, must be based on alliances with other like-minded countries; for France, isolationism is impossible. No more tolerable is perpetual enmity between her and Germany.

France in Europe. In Europe, then, France must look for allies. She has been a leader in developing a European organization that she hopes will some day have military as well as economic and political functions.

A step in this direction was the setting up of the Council of Europe, the statute of which was signed in London on May 5, 1949. It has a Committee of Ministers representing the different countries, and a Consultative Assembly selected by the home parliaments. Its first members were France, England, Italy, Belgium, Holland, Luxembourg, Sweden, Denmark, Norway, and Ireland, to which Greece, Turkey, and Iceland were later added. West Germany is an associate member. The organization's limited power is "to achieve a greater unity between its members for the purpose of safeguarding and realizing the ideals and principles which are their common heritage and facilitating their economic and social progress." This does not include national defense. But the organization has provided a meeting place where ministers and other representatives can discuss mutual problems, though the political integration of Europe under French leadership has not yet made much headway.

On the economic level, too, the French have been trying to build European unity, with the United States also furnishing a good deal of driving force by the conditions under which it has granted Marshall Plan funds. The French negotiated a far-reaching customs union with Italy in March 1949. However, the treaty ran into opposition from French workers and industrialists, who feared that cheap Italian labor would undercut French prices. Thereafter other less sweeping economic arrangements were made with Italy and with the so-called Benelux countries of Belgium, the Netherlands, and Luxembourg.

The Schuman Plan further shows that France wants to work toward closer European economic cooperation. Its main idea is for all coal and steel facilities in the cooperating countries to be put under an international coal and steel authority. Then there will be a common market with no tariff barriers or other restrictions. The plan is surrounded with difficulties because it involves changes in conceptions of national control over basic resources, but its international concept contributes to ultimate European unity.

These plans of economic and political cooperation in Europe do not remove one of France's major problems: Franco-German relations. Clearly, the French solution depends upon France's past experience. The French do not forget that they were overrun by German armies in 1870, in 1914, and in 1940. They also remember that German productive capacity is enormous, and that there are more Germans than there are French. The government, therefore, when dealing with Germany must look first to the security of France. It knows that if western Europe were to be involved in a war with the Soviet Union, the industrial and military might of Germany would be vitally necessary to the defense of the West; but it knows also that a German army might well fight to regain territories that once were German—Alsace, for example, to mention but one much fought-over area. The French, therefore, oppose the creation of a German army, though they are willing for small German units to be incorporated in a European army, on condition that no German general staff be created, that there be no Minister of Defense in Germany, and that the German units be so small as to prevent their leaders from secretly coming together to plan unified actions.

The French have tried in addition to safeguard their security by concluding military agreements with other European countries. One of these agreements was the 1947 Dunkirk treaty of alliance and mutual assistance with Great Britain.[22] It calls for each country's aiding the other with all military and other support in the event one is attacked by Germany or involved in hostilities because of Germany. Still more extensive is the military alliance concluded at Brussels on March 17, 1948, between France, Belgium, the Netherlands, Luxembourg, and Great Britain. It requires of them "all the military and other aid and assistance in their power" if any one of the signatories is attacked in Europe by force of arms.[23]

France in the Atlantic Pact. But French security cannot be fully safeguarded by friends in Europe. Europe is part of a world dominated by two magnetic poles—the United States and the Soviet Union. These two powers oppose each other in almost every part of the globe. Most nations have felt impelled to join one or the other of the giant adversaries. France has thrown in her lot with the United States and the other western countries.

[22] United Nations Treaty Series, 9 (1947), 187 ff.
[23] *Ibid.*, 19 (1948), 51 ff.

However, French party leaders still argue about the wisdom of the decision. The Communists, speaking for more than one quarter of the voters, attack the decision daily. A much smaller group, called the *neutralists,* argue that France can only live if she stays out of both international orbits. The bulk of the voters, however, Third Force and De Gaullists alike, agree that French security can only be protected, along with that of the West, by joining the Atlantic Pact.

The Atlantic Pact is the capstone of the French security arch. The pact countries[24] have pledged themselves to help each other with all the measures that each considers necessary if any one of them is attacked in the Atlantic area. Under the pact, military and economic machinery is being built. There are a Council of Deputies and a cluster of committees—for example, a military committee. The fundamental concept is that the European countries, and France particularly, will provide much of the manpower for the defensive forces. The United States, on the other hand, will furnish most of the heavy military equipment. By means of the Atlantic Pact most Frenchmen hope to gain greater security than before, provided that the United States upholds its commitment.

France Overseas. French obligations extend beyond the European area. Protecting the integrity of the French Union in Indo-China in 1951 cost one half of the military budget of France and tied up more than 150,000 men.

But Indo-China is only one part of the French Union; the rest of it stretches from the Atlantic to the Pacific, covering parts of five continents.[25] In this far-flung empire, native nationalism, coupled sometimes with communism, is a potent force. With this force rampant, France's problem is the defense of her interests in the empire, as well as the defense of the empire against outside pressures. Whether the French Union, with its elaborate machinery, will evolve into a French Commonwealth of Nations remains to be seen. Meanwhile, the French commit large forces to the preservation of the Union.

---

[24] Belgium, Canada, Denmark, France, Greece, Iceland, Italy, Luxembourg, the Netherlands, Norway, Portugal, Turkey, the United Kingdom, and the United States.

[25] See Ellen Hammer, "The French Empire Today," in Earle, *op. cit.* above, note 15, ch. 26.

CHAPTER 13

ITALY'S CONSTITUTIONAL MONARCHY
AND FASCISM

1. Liberal Constitutionalism

Tradition of Separateness. The traditions of Italian government are local and regional, not central; the modern centralized state of Italy has not yet lived one hundred years. Geography has played a large part in the history of modern Italy. The mountains that run the length of the Italian peninsula sharply isolate one part of the country from another. Even the Po valley, the rich agricultural and industrial heart of Italy, is separated by mountains from the rest of Italy. These mountains affect the Italian economy, just as they have influenced the cultural and governmental tradition of the people. They limit the extent of agricultural land, and because they are poor in natural resources, they also limit the industry of Italy. To exist, Italy has to import large quantities of raw materials, and even with these imports many Italians live not far above a subsistence level.

The differences between northern and southern Italy emphasize regionalism. The north, the region above Rome, is far richer than the south. It has the fertile lowlands of the Po; it has the industrial area of Milan and Turin; it has the thriving seaports of Genoa and Venice. As Count Sforza, great Italian, has said, after four or five centuries the people of the north have conquered and subdued their land; the people of the south have still to fight for it every day.[1] The problem of the south is heightened by absentee ownership of the vast tracts of poor land. There is some fertile land in the south, such as that around Naples and Palermo; but much more of it is either flooded by rains or parched by the sun. The harsh life generates harsh attitudes. It is not surprising, therefore, that bandits and guerillas have flourished in the south. The Sicilian bandit Giuliano, killed by the police in 1950, had resisted capture for seven years.

There are, of course, some elements of unity in Italy. Since the early Christian era, the Roman Catholic church has united Italy spiritually although not temporally. Another element of unity is the Italian language. Since the days of Dante it has provided a means of communication between isolated areas, and has helped to spread a common cultural heritage. Nevertheless, hundreds of thousands of small farmers in Italy still speak only a dialect. Yet another tradition of unity is the Roman Empire, and perhaps

---

[1] *Les Italiens tels qu'ils sont* (Montreal, 1941), 116.

247

even more significant is the remembrance of the common cultural glory of the Renaissance. In literature, sculpture, painting, and architecture the Italian cities provided a model for others to copy; Italy was *par excellence* the country of the Renaissance.

The Risorgimento. Political unity did not come to Italy until 1870, and only then because of the conquests of the kingdom of Piedmont and Sardinia. In a sense, Napoleon began the process of unifying Italy by reducing the great number of ancient principalities to a few kingdoms ruled by his relatives and trusted advisers. He demonstrated that there could be a united Italy. The Congress of Vienna took Italy apart again and put the lion's share under Austrian domination.

In the half century after the Congress of Vienna, a few cultural leaders in Italy began a movement for a national rebirth in Italy, a *risorgimento*. The agitation spread mainly from the north, but it gradually captured the imagination of leaders everywhere and in all walks of life. One of the most important was Giuseppe Mazzini, the founder of the Young Italy movement. While he was not a particularly successful revolutionary leader, he did contribute moral and religious fervor to the movement. Giuseppe Garibaldi was another of the heroes of the *Risorgimento*. A soldier of fortune, he offered his services wherever he thought the cause of freedom would be served. He led troops in South American rebellions before fighting in Italy. In 1860, at the head of a small force, he conquered the Kingdom of the Two Sicilies and led them to vote by plebiscite to join with the emerging Kingdom of Italy.

The third great figure of the *Risorgimento* was Count Cavour, a man who was a statesman and journalist and later became the trusted adviser and negotiator for King Victor Emmanuel II of Piedmont. By 1861, as a result of revolts, wars, and diplomatic maneuvering, the Kingdom of Italy was established under the leadership of Victor Emmanuel. But Italy was not yet unified, as Austria remained in possession of Venezia, and the Pope still held central Italy. Italian control of Venezia, excepting Trento and Trieste, was obtained at the end of the Austro-Prussian War. Napoleon III meanwhile stationed French troops in Rome to protect the Pope. When the Franco-Prussian War broke out in 1870, Victor Emmanuel took advantage of the preoccupation of France in order to march his armies into Rome. On September 20, 1870, the Italian flag floated from the ancient capital of Italy. At the same time the Pope immured himself in the Vatican, saying that he was a prisoner. Over his strenuous opposition the unified and larger Kingdom of Italy was finally created.

With the heroic days of unification over, the difficult task of welding the country into a nation remained. Provincial loyalties had to be reduced so that a national loyalty could develop. Appalling problems faced the government. Illiteracy was one of these; in 1870 more than half of the people could not read or write. There were diseases to conquer, malaria, for example, which regularly sapped the energy of thousands of people in the south. Roads, too, had to be built to tie the country together.

The Statute of 1848.   The form of government under which these problems were tackled was a constitutional monarchy,[2] founded on the statute granted by Charles Albert of Piedmont to his people in 1848. The Statute of 1848 was by no means a clear and unequivocal charter of liberties, yet its vagueness gave it flexibility. As Piedmont expanded its power, so the area governed under the Statute of 1848 expanded. It lasted until the end of parliamentary government in 1922; even later the Fascists argued that they had preserved the statute, merely taking away the customs that had debased it.

Under the Statute of 1848 the King alone had executive power. As the chief executive, he commanded the army and navy, declared war, and made treaties of peace and alliance. All treaties that imposed a charge on the state had to be approved by the legislature. In practice almost all treaties were interpreted to require legislative approval. The King also had the power of appointing many government officials, but this power was exercised on advice of his ministers. In addition, he signed laws and promulgated them; he had the right of pardon; and he had the important legislative power of dissolving the Chamber of Deputies and ordering new elections. The King was not to use this power for his own political advantage, but to end argument between the cabinet and the legislature.

As in other constitutional monarchies, the King's powers were exercised for him by the ministers whom he appointed. The ministers, in turn, exercised their authority as long as they had the confidence of parliament. If the ministers lost the support of a majority of the legislature, then the King had the option of asking the ministers to resign or of dissolving the Chamber of Deputies. In naming a new prime minister after a cabinet crisis or a new election, the King exercised some discretion, since there were usually several ministers who might be able to form a cabinet.

Legislation under the Statute of 1848 was passed by the King in Parliament. Parliament was made up of a senate and a chamber of deputies. The Senate was supposed to be composed of old and distinguished leaders in various fields. Senators were appointed by the King, on nomination of the cabinet, from twenty-one categories, such as archbishops and bishops, ministers of state, ambassadors, heads of different judicial bodies, generals and admirals, and members of the royal academy of science. Senators had to be forty years old; once appointed they held office for life.

The actual role of the Senate was limited, even though the Statute of 1848 only restricted the power of the Senate in financial matters. The limitations arose partly from the special method of selection, separated as it was from

---

[2] See Henry R. Spencer, *Government and Politics of Italy* (Yonkers, 1934); Arnold J. Zurcher, "The Government and Politics of Italy," in James T. Shotwell, ed., *Governments of Continental Europe* (rev. ed.; New York, 1952). For historical background, see Benedetto Croce, *A History of Italy* (Oxford, 1929), and Cecil J. S. Sprigge, *The Development of Modern Italy* (New Haven, 1944).

popular opinion, and partly from the fact that the first minister could, if need be, request the King to appoint enough senators to get legislation through. This was done even in the time of Cavour. In fact, two astute observers of Italian political history have written: "Of the Senate it is unnecessary to say much. It is a piece of almost unused machinery, neglected by everybody, and quite without influence on the national life."[3] The Senate contented itself with pointing out and rectifying apparent mistakes in legislation.

The most important legislative work was done by the Chamber of Deputies. Its members were elected from single-member districts for five-year terms, unless the Chamber were dissolved sooner. At first only a minority of Italians could vote, suffrage being limited to those who paid a minimum tax and to those recognized for their special cultural attainments. Gradually tax and educational requirements were dropped, until in 1919 universal manhood suffrage was the rule. Yet the elections were not always democratic in spirit. All sorts of pressures used to be put on voters in the single-member districts to vote for the candidates with official support. The prefect would, for example, warn school teachers, civil servants, and local employees that they must vote for the right man or lose their jobs. In the south the Maffia, an armed band of criminals, was sometimes hired to see that the right candidate was elected. If the prefect did not so use his power, he might be suspended from office. Consequently many deputies were tied to the government by personal rather than partisan links. To avoid these evils, proportional representation was enacted in 1919. Its effect was to increase the importance of those political parties that were well disciplined.

The Italian Chamber was organized very much like the French Chamber of Deputies. First a committee looked over proposed laws; then the Chamber discussed its contents; and finally, by a curious provision of the Statute of 1848, the Chamber voted by secret ballot. Until 1920, with a few exceptions, committees were made up by drawing lots; this meant that party responsibility did not exist. In 1920 specialized committees were set up, consisting of members chosen in proportion to party strength. In addition to legislating, the Chamber checked on the national administration by interpellation.

The Centralized Administrative System. Many other institutions of Italian constitutional government were much like those in France. The highly centralized administrative system was similar, for example, except that the power of administrators was made considerably greater in Italy than in France by exercise of the power to issue sweeping ordinances having the force of law. The Chamber of Deputies did not often object to this dilution of its law-making power. When the criminal code was being considered, the Chamber allowed the final text to be promulgated without

---

[3] Bolton King and Thomas Okey, *Italy Today* (2d edition, London, 1904), 26.

having seen it; the only requirement was that the text be in harmony with the discussions in the Chamber.[4]

Administrative courts were created to rescind illegal actions of overzealous or corrupt administrative officials, but these courts were themselves subject to pressure. Although the judges were not easily removed, they were often transferred from desirable to undesirable posts if their decisions were against the authorities. The same pressures were applied to ordinary courts.

Personal Politics. Because of the administrative centralization in Italy, the ministers had great power. This power was not seldom used for personal political advancement. The weakness of party organization contributed to an individual approach. Cabinet members did not always present a united front to the legislature, and in the Chamber of Deputies most members were loyal to individual ministers instead of to a party. The cabinet held together precariously and fell easily, but whereas in France this was partly due to the clash of strongly held political principles, in Italy it was more often caused by personal rivalries.

Thus Italy was governed by cliques rather than by parties, a state of affairs partially growing out of regionalism, which expressed itself strongly in the attitude of deputies even though the Statute of 1848 provided explicitly that "deputies represent the nation in general and not only the provinces in which they are elected. Their electors cannot give them imperative mandates." Nevertheless, the deputies behaved, above all, as agents for their districts, getting favors and giving them. It was the way to get elected. Likewise, a minister held his position in much the same way: by working for particular deputies and their districts.

The Italian parliamentary system was typified by what is called *trasformismo*. Depretis, a shrewd leader on the Left, was the first to use it. Although his Cabinet had been made up mostly of politicians of the Left, in 1883 he added a man of the Right in the hope that it would strengthen his position. In angry response, all of the other major leaders of the Left broke with him. But he remained in power. He simply "transformed" his Cabinet in the direction of the Right. Thereafter, until his death in 1887, he transformed his Cabinet from right to left or left to right as the sentiment in the Chamber of Deputies seemed to change. This policy, continued by his successors, was sometimes also called a *rimpasto*—a rekneading of the cabinet. In this process of rekneading, party programs or any other general lines of policy were lost sight of. Thus adverse votes in the Chamber of Deputies did not greatly change policy; they only changed the cabinet. The premier went on serenely, until another more skillful manipulator could detach enough of the premier's friends from the clique to upset him.

---

[4] A. Lawrence Lowell, *Governments and Parties in Continental Europe*, Vol. I (New York, 1896), 165.

The advantage of *trasformismo* was that the premier was likely to hold office for a relatively long time.

Economic Progress. In spite of deficiencies in Italian parliamentary government, it had some solid accomplishments to its credit. Although national poverty remained chronic, economic conditions were improved. New roads and telegraph lines welded the regions to the center; railways multiplied their mileage ten times between 1860 and 1914; and industries, such as silk and steel, improved the standard of living by greatly increased production. Some of the industrial gains were used to build up an army and a navy of considerable proportions.

In the field of public welfare, the government also made progress. Infant mortality was cut nearly in half. The number of public schools doubled, constituting a real attack on the vast problem of illiteracy. Finally, the government tried to bring law and order into the regions—and mainly succeeded, except in the south, where brigandage could not completely be wiped out.

The Church. One of the most stubborn of the government's problems was the relationship of the state to the church. The Pope long considered himself a prisoner in the Vatican. In 1871 the government guaranteed his position by law, safeguarding his person, offering him a large annual grant of money, and endowing him with the rights of a sovereign prince. The Pope, however, refused to recognize this law; he would not admit that the Italian state had the temporal power to pass any law regulating his position. He did more than object; he instructed the people of Italy, the majority of whom were devoted to the church, to take no part in this usurping government. His opposition to the regime was not entirely removed until after the coming of Mussolini. The Italian citizen was continually torn between two conflicting loyalties, one to his country and the other to his church.

Wealth from Colonies? Nor could the government solve the problem of the poverty of the Italian masses, rooted as it was in a lack of natural resources. An effort was made to provide an outlet for the excess population by colonial adventures in Tripolitania, Eritrea, and Somaliland. These ventures did not add luster to the government. In fact far more Italians left home for the United States than ever lived in Italian colonies. To make these colonies useful required far more capital investment than Italy could spare.

Furthermore, colonial ambitions received a body blow in Abyssinia. In 1896, when an effort was made to establish Italian power in that potentially rich land, some 80,000 Abyssinians at Adowa completely defeated 12,000 Italian soldiers. As another try, in 1912 Italy took the Dodecanese islands, off the western coast of Asia Minor, from a tired and weak Turkish government. In the long run, however, the colonial policy of the government did not contribute much either to Italy's glory or to her economic well-being.

2. The Fascist Regime

Rise of Fascism.   The aftermath of World War I brought the downfall of the Italian parliamentary constitutional monarchy and the rise of Fascism.[5] A contributing factor to this downfall was the political division of the country brought on by the war itself.   At the outbreak of the war, Italy was bound by an alliance to Germany and Austria, but only if they were attacked by other powers.   Italy therefore felt free to declare her neutrality. In May 1915, she went to war on the side of the Triple Entente, composed of England, France, and Russia.   The Entente had lured Italy into the war by promising her in the secret Treaty of London *Italia irridenta,* the provinces of the Trentino, Trieste, and the Dalmatian coast that had remained Austrian at the time of the unification of Italy.   Yet the Italian voters were undecided in their minds.   Some thought that Germany and Austria should have been supported; some favored the Entente; and still more favored neutrality.

Thus Italy entered the war with a divided electorate.   Her expenditure of lives and money was much resented by those who had not wanted war in the first place; they later contended that Italy had lost the peace, for, in the negotiations at Versailles, the pledges of the Treaty of London were not completely honored.   While Italy did receive the Trentino and the Istrian peninsula, the Dalmatian coast was given to the new state of Yugoslavia. Many Italians believed that Italy had won the war for the Allies, because in the battle of Vittorio Veneto in the Po valley in 1918 Italian soldiers had finally turned the Austrian tide, and thereafter the Austro-Hungarian empire had disintegrated.   The view took hold that Italy had lost the peace because of the ineffectiveness of the government.

The economic effect of the war on Italy was enormous.   It had cost untold sums of money and some 600,000 lives.   Economic dislocations after the war reflected these losses.   Currency was inflated and the price of bread rose. Wages did not rise as fast as the cost of living.   A wave of strikes resulted. Jobs were hard to get.   War factories closed down, adding to the number of unemployed.   At the same time two million soldiers were demobilized. There were no jobs for them either.   The soldiers, too, instead of being welcomed home as returning heroes, often rather were treated as dupes who had been caught in a stupid war.

Meanwhile the government was not functioning smoothly.   It failed to take the drastic steps needed to remedy the economic distress, nor could it

---

[5] See Giuseppe A. Borgese, *Goliath; The March of Fascism* (New York, 1937); William Ebenstein, *Fascist Italy* (New York, 1939); Herman Finer, *Mussolini's Italy* (New York, 1935); Gaetano Salvemini, *Under the Axe of Fascism* (New York, 1936); Herbert W. Schneider, *The Fascist Government of Italy* (New York, 1936); and H. Arthur Steiner, *Government in Fascist Italy* (New York, 1938).   For other details, see H. Arthur Steiner, "Italy," in William Anderson, ed., *Local Government in Europe* (New York, 1939), ch. 4; and G. Lowell Field, *The Syndical and Corporative Institutions of Italian Fascism* (New York, 1938).

always even preserve order. An outstanding example of its weakness was the d'Annunzio adventure in Fiume in September 1919. D'Annunzio, a fiery nationalist poet, in defiance of the government and in glorification of the memory of Garibaldi, led volunteers to Fiume, a part of *Italia irridenta*. The city was occupied for almost a year and a half before Italian troops drove him out. Only then did Fiume become a free city, as the Treaty of Versailles had provided.

Another sign of governmental weakness was the operation of the parliamentary system itself. Cabinet succeeded cabinet in even faster succession than before the war. In two elections in November 1919 and May 1921 new names and parties appeared while the old politicians were often beaten. Two new parties made spectacular progress: the Socialists, who obtained 156 seats out of 535, and the *Popolari,* who won 100. The Socialists were widely split within themselves over the doctrinal question of revolution or evolution. The *Popolari,* the Christian Democrats of their time, were new on the political scene. They hoped, now that the war was over and a new society was to be created, that the principles of Christianity would be used for a moral rebirth.

The Socialists opposed the government and encouraged strikes that led to lockouts all over the country. To prevent lockouts, some strikers simply refused to leave the factories; these were the first sitdown strikes. Some factory owners demanded that government troops should throw the strikers out, but few wanted this to begin with their own plants.[6] The government waited until the bitterness subsided; then peace was negotiated under official auspices. Yet the government lost many supporters because it had not been able to protect private property.

The Fasci. A new element of confusion was the growing Fascist movement. The first meeting of the *Fasci di Combattimento,* a league of former soldiers, took place in Milan on March 23, 1919. It was called by Benito Mussolini, formerly a revolutionary Socialist editor, now a wounded veteran and incendiary orator. He violently criticized the Socialists and *Popolari* and their leaders. Gradually the new league spread to include many other veteran groups that had sprung up over the country. Mussolini insistently urged the government to take strong measures to revive Italy, above all to save the country from the Bolshevik peril of Socialist-inspired sitdown strikes. He built up armed units in his organization which, more and more frequently, clashed with bands of Communists and Socialists. Sometimes army officers joined the fray on the Fascist side, and usually the police looked the other way. Meanwhile the government waited for the revolutionary ardor to exhaust itself.

The Fascists tried their hand at winning seats in parliament. In the elections of May 1921, they won only 35 seats. The Socialists lost a few seats, the Communists gained a few, and the *Popolari* won a few also. Once having a

---

[6] Finer, *op. cit.* above, note 5, 126.

wedge in the Chamber, Mussolini surprised his followers by making peace with the Socialists and the principal labor organization. For this he nearly lost his leadership. In November 1921, the Fascist movement transformed itself into a political party and at the same time disavowed the peace pact with the Socialists. Only then did the government try to break up the armed gangs of Fascists. In the provinces, however, neither the army nor the prefects and the police paid much attention to government orders; they were not anxious to get roughed up by the armed bands of Fascists that roamed about beating up political opponents.

Meanwhile the government was much divided. The Socialists were un-cooperative, and their labor movement broke into several dissident groups. The *Popolari* leaders had angered many of their supporters by favoring the division of large estates and collective bargaining for workers. Govern-mental coalitions remained extremely unstable. Nor could Mussolini keep his armed bands under control; they were continually expecting a *coup d'état* which never seemed to come off. Finally, in October 1922, at the time of the Fascist party congress, the die was cast. Mussolini and his lieutenants prepared for a march on Rome. Small numbers of his armed bands began to arrive in Rome. They took over many provincial councils. The government asked the King to declare a state of siege, but he refused, not being at all sure that the army would obey orders; the result might be civil war. Instead, the King accepted the resignation of the Cabinet and called Mussolini to form a new one. On October 29, 1922, Mussolini boarded the evening train in Milan and rode to Rome. This was the "March on Rome" and the beginning of dictatorship.

Theory of Fascism. At first the Fascists had no particular ideas about the sort of government they wanted to build, nor about the aims it ought to have. Unlike Lenin, Mussolini had not developed an elaborate doctrine before taking power. The original Fascist doctrine simply called for "action" to take over the state and to remedy the sickness of the old parliamentarism by removing it. This was what Mussolini called "surgical violence." Its roots were found in World War I. The veterans did not always make the moral transition from war to peace. Many followed Mussolini when he urged that the postwar hero should use violence to bring forth the new millennial state, the Fascist state. This enthusiasm for violence substituted for particu-lar political theories. As Mussolini said of this time, "I had no specific doctrinal attitude in my mind. . . . My own doctrine . . . had always been a doctrine of action."[7]

Although without constructive beliefs, the early Fascist movement had some negative ones. Fascism rose because of what it was against rather than what it was for. It was against pacifism. It argued that although the pacifists derided the returned veterans, it was the pacifists who should be

---

[7] Benito Mussolini, "The Political and Social Doctrine of Fascism," in *International Concili-ation*, No. 306 (January 1935), 5.

derided. Mussolini said, "War alone brings up to its highest tension all human energy and puts the stamp of nobility upon the peoples who have the courage to meet it. All other trials are substitutes, which never really put men into the position where they have to make the great decision—the alternative of life or death." [8] Fascism was also against socialism, against the materialist conception of history. Mussolini denied that material wealth produced happiness; instead he believed in "holiness and in heroism; that is to say, in actions influenced by no economic motive, direct or indirect." [9] Fascism was also against democracy because democracy was based on a theory of equality of man. Mussolini said that fascism "denies that numbers alone can govern by means of a periodical consultation, and it affirms the immutable, beneficial, and fruitful inequality of mankind, which can never be permanently leveled through the mere operation of a mechanical process such as universal suffrage." [10] Fascism also opposed liberalism; it was "decadent." Mussolini said that its religion of liberty had not created Italian unity, nor had it created German unity. These had been founded on force.

Fascism rose by negation, but it grew by the doctrines it created to support itself. The great object of fascism, said Mussolini, was the glory of the state. He said, "Fascism conceives of the State as an absolute, in comparison with which all individuals or groups are relative." [11] This state organized the nation. The individual had only such liberty as was necessary, and he was "deprived of all useless and possibly harmful freedom." Of course, the state decided what liberty was necessary. As organizer of society, the state also had power over economic life. The all-important spirit of the state was indicated by its growth. Said Mussolini, "The growth of empire, that is to say the expansion of the nation, is an essential manifestation of vitality, and its opposite a sign of decadence."

Consolidation of the Dictatorship. Although fascism was mainly negative in doctrine, it was positive in government. The essential power of government was obtained soon after the party had taken over the reins. On November 25, 1922, the Chamber of Deputies by an overwhelming vote gave Mussolini full power to run the government for one year. At this time, less than half of the ministers in Mussolini's coalition Cabinet were Fascist, but the coalition parties gradually withdrew from the regime as Fascist bands continued to attack them.

Mussolini was quick to transform the state. One of the first changes was wrought by the Acerbo election law of 1923. Under this curious law, the party that obtained the largest number of votes all over the country, provided that it had one-quarter of the total vote, got two-thirds of the seats in the Chamber of Deputies; the other parties were given the other third under

---

[8] *Ibid.,* 7-8.
[9] *Ibid.,* 9.
[10] *Ibid.*
[11] *Ibid.,* 13.

proportional representation. In the election of April 6, 1924, the Fascists and the candidates of the right who had joined them hardly needed the law. They won control of the Chamber with the enormous number of some 5,000,000 votes out of a total of 7,628,859. This victory was won partly by playing politics with the old-line bosses, partly by intimidating the voters.

Yet even with two-thirds of the seats of the Chamber, Mussolini could not eliminate opposition by the other one-third of the deputies. The most vocal opponent, the Socialist deputy Matteotti, was silenced by the gangster method of being taken for a ride; leading Fascists were implicated in his murder. Subsequently, many of the opposition deputies withdrew from Parliament as a protest, in what has been termed the "Aventine secession." The protest was ineffective; it simply deprived them of a forum for venting their opposition to the regime. Thereafter Mussolini stopped criticism in every way possible.

The press was put under rigid governmental control, first by a decree of July 15, 1923, and later by law. Under it any newspaper owner lost his plant if his paper hindered "the diplomatic action of the government by publishing false or tendentious news," if it damaged "the national credit either at home or abroad," or if it awakened "unjustified fears in the population" or troubled the public order.[12] Journalists could write only if they were inscribed on the professional roll, where only "reliable" journalists could be listed. Gradually other sources of criticism were also eliminated. For example, all opposition parties were forbidden. The state had indeed become Fascist.

Fascist Machinery of Government. The distinguishing feature of the new state was the close relationship of the Fascist party with the government. At first the government seemed only slightly different than before. The King was still on his throne and remained the theoretical source of the power of the state. Mussolini considered himself responsible to the King. There was no need to change the Senate, since it could always be packed with Fascists if necessary; in due time it was.

Other institutions, however, having more independence than the King and the Senate, were changed because they had more power to lose. The Chamber of Deputies was mutilated. The Acerbo election law assured the Fascists of a thumping majority; other equally sweeping electoral changes followed. By the law of May 17, 1928, the whole of Italy was made into one electoral district. Under it, 800 candidates were named by syndicates made up of employees and employers in various occupations, and the remaining 200 were nominated by other professional and public bodies. The Fascist Grand Council, a party organization, then selected 400 deputies, either from among the 1,000 submitted or from elsewhere. This list was submitted to the voters. In the election in 1929, over 98 per cent of the voters

---

[12] Text from Silvio Trentin, *Les Transformations récentes du droit public italien de la charte de Charles-Albert à la création de l'état fasciste* (Paris, 1929), 669 ff.

supported the official list; in the election of 1934, the vote was 99.84 per cent for the list.[13]

The Chamber of Deputies, in spite of its Fascist method of selection, was further reduced in its power. Nothing could appear on the agenda for discussion unless Mussolini had put it there. Even this limitation was not enough in the long run. On December 14, 1938, the Chamber voted itself out of existence and put in its place a new body made up of representatives of the Grand Council of Fascism, the National Council of the Fascist party, and the Council of Corporations. The new chamber was supposed to represent the virile forces in the nation—the party and the corporate groups—and not mere hordes of voters. Once a man was named to this chamber, he remained a member until he left the organization that named him to it. Thus elections were done away with and the legislature became a rubber stamp to perfection.

The executive machinery of the parliamentary regime was adapted to the new circumstances, too. The President of the Council of Ministers became the "Chief of Government." This, of course, was Mussolini's job. Under the law of December 24, 1925, the Chief of Government was responsible to the King for the general conduct of policy. He was assisted by ministers, appointed and dismissed by the King at his request. There was no pretense in this law that the Chief of Government and his ministers were responsible to the Chamber of Deputies and, through it, to the voters.

The Chief of Government was still further strengthened by being given the power to amend the penal codes, the civil code, and the judicial procedure. Mussolini's ministers were his subordinates in every sense of the word. They were changed rather frequently so that young men might have fresh administrative experience. Mussolini himself often took over several ministries, sometimes as many as six or eight at the same time.

The ordinary work of the ministries was not done by frequently changing ministers, but by the civil servants. Before Mussolini took power, the Italian civil service was gradually being made over into a merit service; many posts were filled by oral and written examinations. Afterward this was changed. The civil servants were "purified" by the decree of December 24, 1925, under which only Fascists were retained. Even earlier, candidates could only be accepted if they had proved good moral, civil, and political conduct, which meant that they must be Fascists. Apart from this system of political selection, the formal machinery of administration was not greatly changed.

The judiciary was also forced into the Fascist mold. This was done in two ways: by "purifying" the ordinary judicial system and by setting up a special judiciary to try crimes against the state. The ordinary judicial system was dealt with under the civil service laws; the legal codes were inculcated with the Fascist view of life; and a whole series of new political crimes was

---

[13] For an analysis of the chambers as elected in 1929 and 1934, see Schneider, *op. cit.* above, note 5, 55 ff.

added. Thus the ordinary judicial system could be depended upon to support the Fascist regime.

The extraordinary court was created in 1926. It was essentially a military court that took cases involving attacks on the life, the integrity, or the personal liberty of the King, the Queen, the Heir Apparent, or the Chief of Government. For this offense, the penalty was death. The court also tried many other political cases, such as the crime of reestablishing a dissolved political party, or criticizing the state in such a way that its credit or prestige abroad might be minimized.

Local government was brought more directly under the control of the Fascist government. Centralization was increased by augmenting the power of the prefect. Under the law of April 3, 1926, he became the highest authority of the state in his province and the agent of the Minister of the Interior—again, Mussolini. In the old days the elected municipal officials had had some independence, but in 1926 the locally elected councils were done away with. The medieval office of *podestà* was recreated; under the new law, he became the equivalent of the mayor of the municipality. The *podestà* was appointed by the government and could be removed any time at the request of the prefect. He was advised by a municipal council appointed by the prefect.

The Grand Council. In addition to remodeling the old institutions, the Fascists added some new ones. Most notable of these was the Grand Council of Fascism, unique because it was part of both the party and the government. The more usual arrangement in one-party states is to keep party agencies legally separate from the government, even though there is an interlocking directorate of party and government. Under Fascism it was different.

The Grand Council was incorporated into the governmental system by law of December 9, 1928, although the council had existed as a party organ since shortly after the March on Rome. According to this law, the council was to give advice on all national, political, economic, and social questions at the request of the Chief of Government, who convoked the council and fixed its agenda; the secretary of the Fascist party could call meetings if the Chief of Government was absent. In addition to the Chief of Government and the secretary of the party, there were three sorts of members: unlimited-term, ex-officio, and nominated members. The unlimited-term members included the living "quadrumvirs" of the March on Rome, Mussolini's chief aides in 1922, Bianchi, Balbo, De Vecchi, and De Bono; and also those members of the government who had served for at least three years as members of the Council. The second category, the ex-officio members, included the President of the Senate, the President of the Chamber of Deputies, the ministers, and others. The third category of members was nominated by the Chief of Government because of their great contributions to the nation and to the Fascist revolution.

For the party, the Grand Council made out the list of deputies to the legislature, and discussed party rules and high officials. For the government it gave advice on constitutional questions, such as the succession to the throne, the roles of the Senate and the Chamber of Deputies, and the attributes and prerogatives of the Chief of Government, the First Minister, and the Secretary of State, all offices held by Mussolini. The Council, too, was empowered to keep a list of successors to the Chief of Government on the recommendation of Mussolini.

The Grand Council was originally the very heart of the Fascist regime. While its discussions were secret, at least there were discussions. Apparently here was the place where the real decisions on party and governmental policy were thrashed out, and this was the agency, in the end, that supplanted Mussolini. The decisions of the Grand Council filtered down through the party agencies as well as through the government.

The party machinery was hierarchical, with responsibility flowing from bottom to top and authority moving from top to bottom. At the base of the pyramid were the *fasci,* the local organizations of the party; these were combined into provincial federations, which in turn reported to the national secretariat of the party. The local heads of the party, and all of the rest up the line, were appointed by their immediate superiors rather than elected. At the top of the pyramid was the *duce,* the leader of the party—Mussolini. His immediate assistant was the national secretary of the party. Mussolini was advised by the National Directorate, mainly on financial affairs. A larger group, the National Council, was made up of some central officials of the party and the heads of the provincial federations. This agency discussed party policy. None of the party agencies was as important as the Grand Council, however, for in the council general policy was discussed and not just methods of accomplishing policies already decided.

The Corporative State. The Fascists set up a most elaborate machinery for detailed control over economic and cultural life. The result was the *corporative state,* called by Fascists their supreme contribution to the world. Its cardinal conception was that organizations of employees and employers should work together for the benefit of the state. The basic organization was the syndicate, not unlike a labor union. Some of these had existed long before the Fascist revolution, though under other auspices; others were created after the Fascists had come to power. In the Pact of the Palazzo Vidoni, negotiated in October 1925 under government leadership, the existing worker syndicates and the privately formed employer syndicates were pressed to cooperate. The Fascist labor syndicates became the sole bargaining agents with the syndicates of employers. Shortly thereafter, in April 1926, syndical corporations were set up. These consisted of employer representatives and employee representatives, who agreed to bargain together. The new law also provided that there could be no strikes or lockouts. A series of labor courts was established to settle labor disputes.

At first the syndicates had an elaborate regional organization. After

1929, however, partly as a result of the world-wide depression, more and more employers asked the government for assistance with their economic problems. The government then decided that if it were to subsidize industries, it might as well control them. It did this through the corporations created in accordance with the law of February 5, 1934, under which 22 corporations were organized, covering such products as cereals, chemicals, fruits and flowers, and clothing. The corporations consisted of the syndical employee and employer organizations in the particular field, and a Fascist party representative speaking on behalf of the public. Each corporation was presided over by a minister or other high governmental official.[14] Under the guidance of these officials, the corporations became but one more arm of the Fascist octopus.

Mussolini's Policies—The Lateran Accord. One of the most important political actions of the Fascist regime was the settlement with the church. By the concordat of February 1929, the state guaranteed the free public exercise of the church's spiritual power and rites; and the state was given the power to approve nominations of coadjutors, bishops, and archbishops. Another part of the church settlement was a treaty between the Pope and Italy by which the Roman Catholic religion was recognized as the sole religion of the state. The Pope was acknowledged to have sovereign jurisdiction over the 100-acre Vatican city. In turn, he agreed to abstain from interfering in temporal affairs. The settlement further empowered the church to approve the teachers who gave religious instruction in both elementary and secondary grades, but after 1929 Mussolini limited this concession by prescribing the curriculum for this instruction. In a financial settlement, the state gave the church about two billion lira.

Most important of all, the Pope agreed that "the Roman question" had been settled. He recognized the existence of the temporal Kingdom of Italy, with Rome as its capital city and with the descendants of the House of Savoy as kings of Italy.

Foreign Policy. The Fascist regime, like every other regime before it, had to wrestle with Italy's basic economic problem—overpopulation and limited resources. One attempt at a solution was the swamp drainage program, under which several million acres were reclaimed, especially in the countryside around Rome. The government also launched other massive public works programs, particularly during the depression. The unemployment problem remained acute, however, and could not be solved either by public works or by increased social security. The solution came from the Ethiopian war.

Mussolini's foreign policy was in part the outgrowth of a difficult internal problem, but it also fitted in with the Fascist theory exalting war. The war was touched off by an incident at a water hole in disputed territory. In short order the lightly armed Ethiopians were beaten by Italians equipped

---

[14] See the official account by Benito Mussolini, *The Corporate State* (Florence, 1936).

with modern weapons. In May 1936, Ethiopia's capital city of Addis Ababa was occupied, and Italy proclaimed the annexation of the country. By this act, Mussolini said, the Adowa defeat of 1896 had been avenged. The war produced a reaction in the almost moribund League of Nations. With England and France assuming leadership, the League voted financial and economic sanctions against Italy. In response Italy withdrew from the League.

At this time Mussolini began looking around for allies. He found Hitler a sympathetic friend. Gradually the Rome-Berlin axis took shape; Italy and Germany joined to aid the insurgent General Franco in Spain in overthrowing the republican government. Shortly before Hitler's attack on Poland in September 1939, Hitler and Mussolini concluded a military agreement. With the outbreak of World War II, however, Mussolini declared that Italy would remain neutral. It was not until Hitler's sudden full-scale attack on France was evidently successful that Italy declared war on France. Even then some of Mussolini's henchmen were against it. Thereafter Mussolini became the junior partner and Italy fell under the domination of Hitler.

Some Italian industries languished because large numbers of Italian workers were shipped to Germany. Italian factories closed down because raw materials were going to the German war machine instead of to Italy. Italy's agricultural position was no better, for skilled farmers were drafted to work in German fields, and the farmers left at home found that they had little seed for planting and little fertilizer to bolster the poor Italian soil. Much of the food Italian farmers grew did not get to the big cities where it was needed, partly because Allied bombings were concentrated on rail lines and rolling stock, and partly because the Fascist bureaucrats were not as resourceful as they might have been. The result was extensive rationing, shortages, and black markets. This reflected most strongly on the Fascist party, which took over responsibility for food distribution.

Downfall of Fascism. At this time of unrest in Italy, the Allied troops landed in Sicily on July 10, 1943. On July 19 Mussolini journeyed to meet Hitler and sat silently while Hitler lectured him about how much Italian defenses needed strengthening. But Hitler offered no troops. Mussolini returned on July 24 to give an account of his visit to the Grand Council at its first meeting since December 1939. He was confronted with a resolution, signed by two-thirds of the members of the Council, inviting him as Chief of Government to beg the King to take over command of the armed forces and to assume the supreme initiative of decision.[15] The motion was finally passed by 19 to 7. Mussolini submitted his resignation to the King on July 25; as he left the King's office he was arrested by some army officers operating independently of the Grand Council. This was the end of the Fascist dictatorship for Italy.

---

[15] For a brief account of this period, see Muriel Grindrod, *The New Italy* (London, 1947).

But Italy's present republic was not yet so easily established; there were eighteen months more of storm and stress. Again Italy was divided in loyalty. Again Italy was a battleground, on which the Allies fought Germany, Germans fought Italians, and Italians fought Italians.

The Badoglio Regime. For about the first month, however, the change of regime seemed to work smoothly. On July 25 the King made Marshal Pietro Badoglio, a military hero of the Abyssinian campaign, the new prime minister. Badoglio formed his Cabinet from among the less enthusiastic supporters of the Fascist regime, but immediately announced that the war against the Allies must go on. He liquidated the Fascist party, the corporative Chamber, and the Fascist corporations. He tried unsuccessfully to suppress all the political parties that had sprung up overnight at the end of the Fascist regime. These parties put out manifesto after manifesto urging the ending of the war.

Ultimately, on September 3, 1943, Marshal Badoglio was forced to sign an armistice with the Allies. Allied troops were not immediately available to occupy the whole of Italy, so that German troops quickly marched in, taking Rome and the most important northern towns. The King and the Marshal moved their government to the south.

The Italian Social Republic. At the same time, German soldiers liberated Mussolini from prison. From Germany the reestablishment of the Fascist dictatorship was announced, under the leadership of the Republican Fascist party. Later, at Verona, this party met to declare that the monarchy was replaced by a social republic. All of Badoglio's supporters in northern Italy were replaced by Fascists, who were controlled more by Hitler than by Mussolini.

Mussolini's new social republic lost more and more territory to the Allied armies as they moved up the Italian boot. At the same time, resistance groups in the north harried the Fascists. On April 28, 1945, Mussolini and his mistress were captured and executed; their bodies were hung in a public square in Milan. By the end of May 1945, the new Fascist republic had vanished.

Meanwhile the royal government continued to function in Brindisi in the south. It became a cobelligerent with the Allies against Germany on October 13, 1943. Its governmental operations were limited. In the first place, it controlled little territory. As the Allied armies moved northward, the royal government only gradually exercised more control. Immediate power rested with the Allied military government. During this period the question of the kingship was being warmly debated. A majority of the resistance parties felt that the King had been too closely connected with the old Fascist regime to rally Italy. In the face of this sentiment, the King agreed to transfer his powers to his son, Crown Prince Umberto, under the title of Lieutenant General.

Accordingly, when Rome was occupied by the Allies, the King withdrew and Badoglio resigned as premier. The new prime minister was Ivanoe Bonomi, who remained in power until the reconquest of northern Italy. When Italy was finally freed of all German troops, Ferruccio Parri was named prime minister because he could gain the support of all the major resistance groups in the north and the south. His coalition Cabinet fell in November 1945, when one of the parties objected to the way he was running the purification program to get rid of former Fascists. The Crown Prince then consulted with the major parties and at their request appointed Alcide de Gasperi as prime minister. The latter's first cabinet was formed on December 9, 1945, and it was under his leadership that the new Italian republic was created.

CHAPTER 14

ITALY'S REPUBLICAN GOVERNMENT

1. Governmental Organization

The constitution of the Italian Republic went into effect on January 1, 1948, almost 100 years after the statute of Charles Albert had introduced a constitutional monarchy in Piedmont-Sardinia. Whereas the old constitution had been granted the people as a gift by a monarch, the new constitution was written by a constituent assembly elected by universal suffrage. Whereas the old document had been hurriedly drafted to keep peace by forestalling a possible revolution, the new one was formulated shortly after a world war into which Italy had been dragged by a Fascist dictator, who had been driven out by Allied troops slowly and painfully. The new constitution was thus a product of World War II.

The Constituent Assembly. The Constituent Assembly that gave birth to the new constitution was not entirely free to write what it liked. It was bound, in the first place, to create a republic instead of a monarchy; this requirement was laid down by the voters at the time the Assembly's members were elected. In the voting on June 2, 1946, the republic won by the narrow margin of 12,717,923 to 10,719,284. Other conditions set for the Constituent Assembly were less obvious, but nonetheless real; these conditions were fixed by the political composition of the Assembly itself.

The Constituent Assembly reflected fairly accurately the attitude of the great masses of Italian voters by virtue of the electoral law under which it was chosen. This law had been approved by the Consultative Assembly on February 23, 1946, and was promulgated by decree on March 10. This assembly, popularly called the *Consulta,* had been set up in September 1945, a few months after the execution of Mussolini and not long after Italy was freed from German troops. It was made up of representatives of all the major Italian parties, trade unions, and professional organizations. Its 429 members were selected by the government from the lists of candidates drawn up by these various bodies. The *Consulta* provided that the Constituent Assembly should be elected by proportional representation, and that it should act as the legislature of Italy until it had finished its work. Then the *Consulta* went out of existence.

In the elections of June 2, 1946, the Christian Democratic party won nearly twice as many seats as any other single party, but by no means a majority. It had 207 seats out of a total membership of 556. The Christian

Democratic party was rather like its predecessor, the *Popolari* of earlier days. Its political views were not unlike those of the MRP in France. The second largest party was the Socialist with 115 seats. The Socialist party soon divided into two; one wing allied itself closely with the Communists, while the other took an evolutionary attitude not greatly different from the SFIO in France. The third major party was the Communist with 104 seats. These three were the mass parties. Only a few of the many other parties had enough seats to influence close votes in the Constituent Assembly. One of these was the National Democratic Union, with 44 seats—a union of the Liberals and the Labor Democrats. The Liberals were one of the more conservative parties favoring, in general, a private enterprise system. The Labor Democrats were not much different from the Christian Democratic party, but they were mainly a personal group devoted to their leader, Bonomi. The other small party was the *Uomo Qualunque,* the Common Man party, with some 30 seats. Its name and its vague program exalting the state as the servant of the common man had a Fascist tinge.

Naturally the three major parties played the principal roles in the Constituent Assembly, yet the constitution was not the work of any one party. Many of the members of the Assembly were skilled statesmen—Bonomi, for example, who was named premier in two cabinets at the end of the war. Another was Benedetto Croce, eminent historian and philosopher. Vittorio Orlando, who had represented Italy at Versailles, was also present. There were many young men who had fought in the resistance movement, and who now hoped to build an enduring government for Italy. All in all, it was an unusually distinguished gathering.

As the interim legislature for Italy, the Constituent Assembly was the agency to which the government was responsible. The ceremonial Head of the State, elected by the Assembly, was Enrico de Nicola, a lawyer from Naples. The active executive power rested with the President of the Council of Ministers, Alcide de Gasperi, who was responsible to the Assembly.

The Constituent Assembly turned over the work of preparing a draft constitution to a committee of 75, selected by proportional representation. The committee, in turn, was divided into three groups for working out the details of the constitution. On January 31, 1947, the committee submitted its work to the Assembly. Thereafter, in 173 meetings, the Assembly discussed different sections of the draft, and finally approved the constitution on December 22, 1947, by the overwhelming vote of 453 to 82. The deputies of the Right had tried to convince the Assembly that the document should be submitted to the voters before it went into effect, but the law that created the Assembly had expressly provided that the constitution should become effective when approved by the Assembly. Consequently there was no popular vote on the constitution.

The constitution is very long. It has 139 articles, not to mention the several transitional articles tacked on at the end. This great length indicates that the Assembly tried to safeguard the democratic form of government by carefully regulating the way it would operate. This was different from the attitude of the founding fathers of the constitution of the United States, who in 1787 provided only the barest bones of government; to fill in the flesh was left to those who would have to govern. In the Italian constitution, however, few of the details of government were left to an uncertain future.

The constitution begins with a brief section on fundamental principles,[1] followed by a bill of rights divided into four major categories: civil relations—the constitutional liberties of the individual; ethical-social relations—the family and the school; economic relations—the rights of labor and of property; and political relations—the participation of the citizen in government. The second main section deals with the structure of government—Parliament, the President of the Republic, the government, the judiciary, local government, and constitutional guarantees. The third section, purely transitional, deals with putting the new government into operation.

The Bill of Rights. The new bill of rights is much more extensive than the bill of rights of the Statute of 1848; indeed, as Professor Einaudi points out, this section is about one-third of the entire constitution.[2] It not only defines the rights, but shows how the rights will be made effective by public policy. For example, the constitution provides that "all citizens have equal social dignity and are equal before the law . . . ." Then the direction of future policy is laid down: "It is the task of the Republic to remove the obstacles of an economic and social order which, limiting in fact the liberty and equality of citizens, prevent the full development of the human personality and the effective participation by all workers in the political, economic, and social organization of the country."[3] Other articles that follow have a similar approach.

Many political liberties and rights had already been established in the Statute of 1848. The new constitution extended these and added others. In both constitutions personal liberty is declared to be inviolable; however, the new constitution allows that in exceptional cases, as provided by law, the police may adopt provisional measures limiting personal liberty. These measures must be reported to the judiciary within 48 hours; if the court does not validate them, they fall. Both constitutions also made the citizen's home inviolable—searches can be made only according to law. Both constitutions protected freedom of the press, although the old statute permitted religious publication only after approval of a bishop. The new constitution is much more detailed in its protection of the press: "Everyone has the right

---

[1] The constitution is printed in translation in United States Department of State, *Documents and State Papers*, 1 (April 1948), 46 ff. For a careful analysis of the contents of the constitution, see Mario Einaudi, "The Constitution of the Italian Republic," *American Political Science Review*, 42 (1948), 661 ff.

[2] *Loc. cit.* above, note 1, 672.

[3] This quotation from the constitution and others that follow are taken from *Documents and State Papers, op. cit.*

freely to manifest his own thought by word, by writing, and by every other means of dissemination." Here again, however, the police may intervene, provided that the courts are asked within 48 hours to determine the case. The related freedom of assembly is also guaranteed in both constitutions; but under the new, secret associations and groups pursuing military ends by military methods are prohibited. This clause clearly reflects the experience with the armed bands of *fasci*.

Both constitutions, too, contain provisions on religious liberty; in the old, religions other than the Roman Catholic were tolerated according to law; in the new, the state and the Catholic church are declared to be independent and sovereign in their own order, in accordance with Mussolini's Lateran agreements. Also, in the new constitution, all citizens are given the right to profess their own religious faith, provided the rites are not contrary to morality. Thus, the ordinary civil liberties—freedom of speech, press, assembly, religion, and so forth—are protected. The only new aspect is the rather more complete definition of each right.

The new constitution, differing from the Statute of 1848, contains many new civil rights of an ethical-social, economic, and political nature. The ethical-social rights deal mainly with the family and education. For example, the constitution declares that "it is the duty of parents to support, instruct, and educate their children, even if born out of wedlock." It also declares that "elementary instruction, imparted for at least eight years, is obligatory and gratuitous." Other ethical-social guarantees include governmental protection: of the family, by economic and other means; of public health, including free care to the indigent; and of the freedom of art and science.

The economic rights are also new, compared with the Statute of 1848. Most of these have to do with labor and property. It is said, for example, that "the Republic protects labor in all its forms and applications." Each man has a right to a wage proportionate to the quantity and quality of his labor, and "in any case sufficient to assure him and his family a free and dignified existence." Labor is also protected by social insurance. Likewise, workers may form unions, provided that they are internally organized along democratic lines; and workers may strike, as provided by laws that regulate strikes. At the same time, private economic initiative is declared to be free, although such free initiative "may not develop in conflict with social utility or in such a manner as to cause damage to security, to liberty, or to human dignity." The constitution also guarantees private property, but property may be limited by the state in order to exploit the land rationally, or to provide essential public services, or to place certain monopolies under state control.

The political rights and duties include: equal, free, and secret elections participated in by men and women; the right to form parties for political competition by democratic methods; the right of petition; and the right to hold public office. The duties are equally clear. One of them is to defend the fatherland by obligatory military service; another to pay for public expenses in accordance with the individual's taxable means; still another is that citizens are "duty-bound to be faithful to the Republic and to observe its Constitution and laws."

These many rights and duties were written into the constitution to limit the power of the majority. The majority in a democracy does not need constitutional guarantees, because the mere fact that it is a majority gives it power to do as it likes. A major purpose of civil rights is to safeguard individual dignity and personality against an overriding majority. Vittorio Orlando once said, "The worst of all despotisms is a numerical majority."

The Constitutional Court. Merely writing civil liberties into a constitution is not enough; some agency has to enforce them. This vital function was given primarily to the Constitutional Court, an innovation of the Constituent Assembly. The court is made up of fifteen judges, one-third named by the President of the Republic, one-third by Parliament in joint session, and one-third by the judiciary. All of the members must be professional judges or professors of law, or lawyers of at least twenty years' practice. They serve a twelve-year term and are not immediately eligible for another.

The constitution gives this court the power to decide on the constitutionality of laws, a power meant to preserve civil rights as well as other provisions of the constitution. If, for example, a law were passed that seemed to take away a civil liberty guaranteed by the constitution, the court would have to decide whether the law was constitutional or not. If the law were not, it would cease "to have effect from the day following the publication of the decision." The court has other powers that will enable it to protect the constitution. It decides the constitutionality of administrative measures having the force of law. It settles conflicts about the powers given different agencies of the state and disputes between the central government and the regions, or between the regions. The court also acts on impeachments of the President of the Republic and of ministers.

According to the constitution, the conditions under which this court should operate were to be established by a constitutional law, which was passed on February 9, 1948. The constitution further provides that ordinary legislation shall regulate other details about the court. These details were completed by act of March 17, 1951, which, however, explicitly denied the court the right to consider political factors, or to supervise the use made by Parliament of its own discretionary powers.

The Amending Power. The Constitutional Court is not the only protection against violation of the constitution. Another is the amending procedure. If the constitution were easy to amend, the precious individual liberties might equally easily be taken away. Actually the amending process is involved. First, amendments must be considered twice by the legislature, with an interval of three months between considerations. On the second occasion, the vote must be by a majority of the members of each chamber.

Then the amendments may be submitted to the voters in a referendum if (1) one-fifth of the members of either chamber or (2) 500,000 voters or (3) five regional councils request the referendum within three months of the passage of the amendment. A referendum requires a majority for adoption. If, on the other hand, the amendment is passed by two-thirds of the members of both chambers, a referendum is not permitted.

The Judiciary. The ordinary courts also protect the individual citizen from losing his rights. As ordinary courts make the final decision in preserving personal liberty, so the same is true of the secrecy of correspondence and other communications, and also of freedom of the press.

To protect these vital freedoms from arbitrary police action, the court system is separated from the legislative and the executive departments. To insure this result, the recruiting and disciplining of judges are the work of the Superior Council of the Judiciary, presided over by the President of the Republic. The president and prosecutor of the highest court, the Court of Cassation, are also members. Other members are elected; two-thirds are chosen by regular judges, and one-third by Parliament from professors of law and practicing lawyers. The Superior Council, according to the constitution, deals with appointments, assignments, transfers, promotions, and disciplining of judges. In the first years of the new republic, however, the Superior Council was not put into operation; in the meantime the old laws on the judiciary were used.

The Italian judges, like their French counterparts, are civil servants. In fact, the Italian judiciary is much like the French. In Italy, except for the *conciliatore,* an unprofessional, unsalaried arbitrator, and the *praetor,* the lowest in the hierarchy of judges, cases are tried by a panel of judges. Next above the *praetor's* court are the tribunals, and from them cases may be brought before courts of appeals. The courts of appeals become courts of assize for handling criminal cases. The court of last resort, as in France, is the Court of Cassation. As its name suggests, it annuls decisions of lower courts that were erroneously decided and sends them back for a new decision in harmony with the highest court's view of the law. There are also special courts in Italy, such as the military courts.

Administrative and ordinary justice are separated in Italy just as they are in France. The most important of the Italian administrative courts is the Council of State, which, according to the constitution, is "an organ for safeguarding justice in administration." It also gives advice to the Cabinet. It safeguards justice in administration by hearing cases in which a civil servant has exceeded his legal authority or has abused it by making an unwarranted decision. Thus, although civil servants have great power in Italy, the citizen can protect himself if he thinks he has been wronged.

Another administrative agency, the Court of Accounts, has similar functions. In the words of the constitution it "exercises a preventive control to assure the legitimacy of acts of the Government." Its usual functions are those of an auditor—to see that money is spent by public officials in accordance with the law. This agency also sees to it that ministers do not exceed their legal powers.

Of the agencies set up by the Italian constitution to perform the major functions of government, one of the most important is the executive. As in France, executive power is exercised by the President of the Republic, the President of the Council of Ministers, and the ministers.

The President of the Republic. In general, the President of the Republic has more of a ceremonial position than executive authority, yet the Constituent Assembly intended to give him greater power than his French counterpart. He was to be the neutral intermediary between the ministers and the legislature. Whether or not the President becomes more than a ceremonial official, however, will depend upon the customs that grow up in Italy. Certainly the constitutional clauses do not give him a great deal of power.

The President is elected by the two houses of the legislature meeting together with three delegates from each of the regions into which Italy is to be divided.[4] The election is secret, and a two-thirds majority is needed, but after three ballots a simple majority is sufficient. As first President, a distinguished professor of economics and liberal leader, Luigi Einaudi, was elected on the fourth ballot by 451 votes out of a total of 871.

The constitution requires that the candidates for President be at least fifty years old. Once elected, the President serves for seven years. The constitution says nothing about the number of terms. It gives the President the usual executive powers. He is "the head of the state and represents the national unity." He sends messages to the legislature, announces dates of elections to the chambers, fixes the date of their first meeting, announces referendums, and "authorizes the presentation to the Chambers of bills initiated by the Government." Once laws are passed by the chambers, he promulgates them; he also issues decrees and regulations. Like the French President, he nominates many officials. He is concerned with foreign relations—accrediting and receiving diplomats and declaring the ratification of treaties with the consent of the chambers. He also has powers related to the defense of the country: he commands the armed forces and presides over the Supreme Council of Defense, and he declares war after the chambers have so decided. He has some judicial functions: he presides over the Superior Council of the Judiciary, and may grant pardons and commute sentences. He also decorates worthy citizens.

In an effort to make the President more powerful and also to prevent legislative-executive deadlocks, the Constituent Assembly gave the President the power to dissolve either or both chambers after he has heard their presidents, although the power cannot be used "within the last six months of his

---

[4] Except that the Valle d'Aosta sends only one. For the first election under the new constitution, the regional delegates were not required, for the country had not yet been divided into regions.

term." An eminent Italian professor of constitutional law, Franco Pieran-drei, points out that the existence of this power may make the President a mediator between the Cabinet and the legislature. The President would have two options: he could dissolve the chambers at the request of the Premier, or he could refuse this request. In the latter case, the Cabinet would probably resign,[5] although it could possibly argue that the President had acted unconstitutionally, for the constitution also provides that "no act of the President of the Republic is valid unless countersigned by the Ministers proposing it, who assume responsibility for it," and that the President "is not responsible for acts performed while exercising his functions, except high treason or offenses against the Constitution." Thus the powers of the President are really exercised for him by his ministers, an essential element of the parliamentary system.

The President may have some influence on the course of events even though he is politically not responsible. He is chairman of major govern-mental committees—the Supreme Council of Defense and the Superior Council of the Judiciary. Although his advice need not be taken, it may be if it seems sound. The President nominates the President of the Council of Ministers and the ministers, and within ten days the fully constituted Cabinet must present itself to the chambers and be approved, a procedure contrasting to that followed in France where the President cannot even appoint the Premier until the National Assembly has approved the nomina-tion, and the Cabinet is formed only afterward.

The President of the Council of Ministers. The everyday power of en-forcing the laws in Italy rests with the President of the Council of Ministers and his Cabinet rather than with the President of the Republic. The Premier is slightly stronger than the other ministers since it is he who recom-mends their appointment by the President. By the terms of the constitution the Premier "directs the general policy of the Government and is responsible for it. He maintains unity of political and administrative direction, and promotes and coordinates the activity of the Ministers." He is required to countersign all acts of the President having the force of law.

The President of the Council of Ministers depends on his ministers to supervise the national administration as heads of the central departments, such as Foreign Affairs, Interior, Justice, and Finance. The ministers in turn direct the civil servants in the application of the laws.

The Council of Ministers as a whole, as is normal in a parliamentary system, must have the confidence of the legislature. This is more difficult to attain than in France, because in Italy the Cabinet is responsible to both chambers, whereas in France the constitution explicitly makes the Cabinet responsible only to the lower house. In Italy responsibility is tested by vote of confidence, which must be obtained within ten days of the formation of the Cabinet. Thereafter, confidence motions are hedged with some restric-

---

[5] Emilio Crosa, ed., *La Constitution italienne de 1948* (Paris, 1950), 146.

tions, such as a three-day cooling-off period before a motion of lack of confidence can be debated and the requirement that one-tenth of the members of a chamber must sign the motion before it can be debated at all. The motion of lack of confidence must include a statement of reasons and can only be passed by roll call.

Caprice on the part of the legislature is further restricted in that even if one or both chambers vote against a government motion, the Cabinet need not resign. Yet if such a vote were carried, it could easily lead to a vote of no confidence after a lapse of the constitutional three days, and thus to the fall of the Cabinet. Actually cabinets during the first Chamber of Deputies under the new constitution usually resigned because of internal dissension and not because of votes of lack of confidence. The Christian Democratic party enjoyed unusual strength: a majority in the Chamber, and in the Senate only slightly less than that.

But the Cabinet cannot function without the confidence of the legislature. The legislature, a central organ of power, is made up of the Chamber of Deputies and the Senate. The Chamber is elected for a five-year term unless it is dissolved earlier; the senators serve for six years. This difference between terms might lead to the two chambers' getting out of step with each other politically. The solution to such a dilemma is the dissolution of either or both chambers. Presumably the President would dissolve the chamber that had been elected earlier.

Election of Deputies and Senators. Most of the election details for the Chamber are fixed by law and not by the constitution, although the constitution does require that deputies be elected by universal and direct suffrage, in the proportion of one deputy for 80,000 inhabitants or for fractions greater than 40,000. By decree-law of February 5, 1948, Italy has a list system of proportional representation, with the remainders of the vote used in a national pool. If deputies die or resign, a new election is not necessary; their places are filled by the next man in line on the party list of the district. The effect of this law was to favor the large parties over the small; for example, the Christian Democrats won 48 per cent of the popular vote in 1948, but 53 per cent of the seats in the Chamber.

Senators are elected by a single-member district system that also makes use of proportional representation. To vote for a senator, a citizen must be 25 years old, whereas he can vote for a deputy when of age. The constitution requires that candidates for the Senate must be forty years of age, whereas deputies need be only twenty-five. The hope was that increased wisdom comes with increased age.

The electoral area for the Senate is the region, which returns as many senators as it is entitled to by its population, on the basis of one senator for 200,000 inhabitants or fractions greater than 100,000. No region except the Valle d'Aosta may have less than six senators—a concession to the regional attitudes. Each region is divided into as many single-member districts as there are senators for that region; then each party nominates a candidate for each district in which it wants to compete. If a candidate wins 65 per cent of the vote in the district, he is declared elected. If no candidate gets this very considerable number in a multiparty system, the votes are distributed by proportional representation, using the unallotted seats and votes in the region as the basis of the calculation; the seats are allotted by the French highest-average system. In the 1948 elections, only fifteen of the total number of senators won 65 per cent of the vote in their districts.

Not all senators are elected by the voters. All former presidents may become senators for life, and the President may nominate five life senators from among those citizens who have brought fame to the country "by merits of the highest order in the social, scientific, artistic, or literary fields." This clause is all that is left in the constitution of the attempt by the Christian Democrats to make the Senate an interest-group body instead of a directly elected body. The Christian Democrats said that economic and other interest groups were so vital to modern society that they should be represented by one house. The majority of the Constituent Assembly did not agree; in their view an interest-group legislature was too much like the old corporative Chamber.

The Constituent Assembly seeming anxious to reward itself, the first Senate under the new constitution had a considerable number of nominated members in addition to those elected. Those nominated members who sat in the Constituent Assembly had special characteristics; for example, they had been presidents of the Council of Ministers or of legislative assemblies; or they had been members of the old Senate; or they had been elected three times. The addition of the nominated senators made the political complexion of the Senate more leftist than it would otherwise have been.

The Legislative Process. A distinguishing feature of the Italian legislature is that both houses have equal powers. This feature was violently criticized by the Left in the Constituent Assembly. When the Left failed to weaken the Senate, it tried to make sure the two houses were selected by essentially the same electorate. The only difference now is in the age of the voters. In the elections of 1948, each major party's votes varied by less than one per cent between the two houses.

The equality of the houses is emphasized in the constitution by providing that the legislative function is exercised collectively by the two chambers. Legislation can be initiated by members of either chamber, as well as by the Cabinet, the regions, or the National Council of Economy and Labor. Even the people may initiate legislative proposals; if 50,000 voters support a particular draft, it is introduced in the legislature.

Once a bill is initiated, the legislators handle it in much the same way as in France. A bill is first referred to a committee and then, after the committee has made its report, to the chamber, which debates the bill article by article, afterward acting on the whole bill.

The Italian legislature has an unusual system for passing less important bills. This procedure is described briefly in the constitution, and in more detail in the rules of the chambers. Under it, the committee passes the bill without referring it back to the chamber. The shortened procedure may not be used for bills dealing with the constitution and the electorate, or for those delegating the exercise of legislative power, or for approving the budget or expenditures, or for ratifying international treaties. Many other bills are passed this way, however.[6] To prevent abuse of this power, the constitution provides that committee action is not final if the Cabinet, or one-tenth of the members of a chamber, or one-fifth of the members of the committee request that the chamber be given a chance to vote on the bill.

Once a bill is passed in the same form by both houses, it is sent to the President to promulgate it. Within a month he may send it back, with reasoned objections, asking for reconsideration. This power is not likely to be much used except for small revisions. If there were major objections to the bill, the President could not send it back without raising the question of the Cabinet's responsibility to the legislature, because his action requires the countersignature of the Premier, on whose responsibility the action would be taken.

The legislative power of the two chambers may not be delegated to any other agency except for a limited time and for defined purposes. In an emergency the Cabinet may issue provisional orders, but these must be submitted to the chambers on the same day they are issued. If the chambers are not meeting, they must be called to meet in five days; if the chambers do not convert the provisional orders into law in sixty days, the orders lose their effect.

In addition to these powers, the chambers have the usual parliamentary controls over the national administration. Deputies and senators may ask questions of a minister or may present formal interpellations. They have the power to investigate matters of public interest through committees organized according to party strength; these committees have the same powers as the courts in taking evidence.

While legislative power is ordinarily exercised by the chambers, the constitution gives some legislative power to the people (for example, the initiative by which 50,000 voters may present a proposal to the legislature). The referendum in connection with constitutional amendments has been mentioned earlier. Another kind of referendum concerns the abrogation of laws already in effect. If 500,000 voters or five regional councils request a referendum on a particular law or part of a law, a popular vote is held. These referendums may not, however, deal with tax or budget laws, laws of amnesty or pardon, or laws authorizing the ratification of international

---

[6] Ubaldo Cosentino, "Legislative Powers of Committees in the Chamber of Deputies," *Constitutional and Parliamentary Information*, 3rd series, No. 2 (Geneva, 1950), 94 ff.

treaties. During the first few years of the new republic, no law was passed determining the details for carrying out this referendum.

The legislature, and the cabinet as well, may ask advice of the National Council of Economy and Labor. This body, yet to be set up by law, is to consist of experts and representatives of the "productive categories."

Local Government. The Italian constitution, like the French, makes innovations in the structure of local government. As in France, these have not yet been completely put into operation. The new feature in Italy is the *region,* consisting of several provinces. The provinces have existed for many years, and so also have their smaller divisions, the communes, or municipalities. Under Mussolini both the provinces and the communes lost such independence as they had. After World War II, the delegates to the Constituent Assembly planned to build up local autonomy by creating regions, and by giving them many powers formerly mainly exercised by the central government. Regionalism was not to divide the Italian state, but rather to strengthen it by recognizing the regional differences.

The constitution provided that regions were to be "autonomous bodies with their own powers and functions." Although the Italian state was still unitary and not federal, there was to be a good deal of decentralization. The regions were to have control over such matters as urban and rural local police, fairs and markets, training of artisans, professional instruction, and municipal matters, but these powers were not to be used "in conflict with the interest of the Nation or of other Regions."

Each region was to have a constitution to be passed by its own legislative body and approved by the national chambers. The regional government was to consist of a regional council with legislative power in its own particular field, an executive committee elected from the council, and a president of the executive committee, also elected from among the council members. The national government was to be represented in the region by an administrative supervisor, called commissioner, with power to coordinate state and regional activities. Laws passed by the regional council were to be promulgated by the commissioner, unless the central government should disapprove of them. If they were disapproved, they would be returned to the council. Should the regional council again pass the legislation, the issue could be taken by the central government either to the Constitutional Court or to the chambers. If the regional council performed acts contrary to the constitution or the laws, or disregarded legal requests of the government, it could be dissolved. The regional council could also be dissolved for reasons of national security.

In the first few years of the new republic, the legislature set up only a few regions, those where there were unusual problems. The constitution allowed special regional arrangements to be made for Sicily, Sardinia, the Trentino-Alto Adige, Friuli-Venezia Giulia, and the Valle d'Aosta. Excepting that part of Venezia Giulia controlled by Yugoslavia, constitutional laws in 1948 made provision for these areas, where regional councils, executive committees, and presiding officers have come to function. A considerable degree of regional autonomy exists in these areas; for example, in the Trentino-Alto Adige the use of the German language is guaranteed, while in the Valle d'Aosta French may be used.[7]

Apart from this regional innovation, the Constituent Assembly retained the old machinery of local government. It simply provided that the provinces and communes were "autonomous bodies within the scope of principles fixed by the general laws" which determined their functions. The provinces are organized rather like French geographic departments, headed by prefects who are the chief representatives of the central government and appointed by it. The provinces are divided into communes, each of which has a locally elected council for managing its affairs. It elects a mayor and an executive committee for the everyday supervision of local government. Apart from the planned regional decentralization, Italian local government is therefore quite centralized.

2. Political Parties

Party leaders and their followers often determine how well a bright new constitution will work and what it will be used for. Italian voters went to the polls in 1948 with the possibility of choosing among at least seventeen different parties; afterward Italy almost found herself with a two-party system. The Christian Democrats had won 48 per cent of the vote, and the Communists and their immediate allies 30.5 per cent. The rest of the votes were scattered from left to right among smaller parties. Cabinets have been made up of several parties rather than one, and each of these parties has had its own axe to grind.

The Christian Democrats. The strongest party in Italy in 1948 was the Christian Democratic party, the heir of Don Sturzo's *Popolari* of World War I. Its leader, Alcide de Gasperi, also once led the *Popolari*. The Christian Democratic doctrine stresses the supreme importance of the human being created in the image of God, a human being who cannot attain his ultimate supernatural objective without divine assistance. Thus the social order, laws, economics, and politics should be derived from the moral order of Christianity.

The party's practical program rests on this basic doctrine. For example, the educational system must be designed to teach man his inspired origin, the nobility of his nature, and his chance of eternal salvation. The actual form of the state is not as important as its Christian objectives. Thus, by its nature, the movement can appeal to all classes of people. Seeing that classes do exist, however, the Christian Democrat is willing that each class should be represented as such, which was the reason why the party tried to make the second chamber of the legislature into an interest-group agency. The Christian Democrats consider the workers deserving of the support of the

---

[7] See "Regionalism in Italy," *The World Today,* new series, 5 (1949), 81 ff.

state, because by working, man creates, thus partly atoning for his sinfulness; and in creating, he transcends the limits of mortal life. The state, therefore, must assure social justice to the working man and maintain the rights of property because property is a part of the divine plan of the world. Those who have property have also the duty to be charitable.[8]

The Communists. The Communist party was the next largest in Italy in 1948. It has been extremely well organized under its leader, Palmiro Togliatti, once an official of the Communist International in Moscow. Under his guidance the party appealed to the landless peasants in the south by promising land. It appealed to the middle classes who had lost their savings in inflation by offering them security by state action. It also appealed to the large industrial proletariat in the north. Young intellectuals throughout Italy were attracted by the idealism the party professed.

The fundamental doctrine of the Italian Communist party, like that of Communist parties elsewhere, was stated in the *Communist Manifesto* of Marx and Engels in 1848: through inevitable class warfare, the bourgeois state would ultimately collapse. The strategy and tactics for assisting the collapse were worked out by Lenin. Essentially, the proletarians would be liberated under the dictatorship of their most class-conscious vanguard, the Communist party.

The program of the Italian Communists has certain local aspects. In 1944 Togliatti said that his party favored the creation of a liberal and democratic regime. According to Togliatti, the Communists had joined the other parties, both left and center, in the early days of the Italian republic, in the various Committees of National Liberation, to make sure that the elementary economic needs of the masses would be satisfied by preventing the owner class from putting its interests above those of the nation.[9]

In 1947 the Communist Party ceased to cooperate with the major parties and moved into the opposition. Thereafter, the Communists attacked the government as a capitalist conspiracy that stirred up new Fascist movements and strengthened the reactionary apparatus of the state—the police, the army, and the courts. Furthermore, they insisted, as a tool of the billionaire American imperialists, the Italian government would be dragged into a war against the truly democratic peoples of the world. As an alternative, the Communists offered the Italian people peace, to be attained by joining in the great crusade of the invincible Soviet Union, the new people's democracies, and the working forces of the entire world.[10]

The Left-wing Socialists. One of the larger parties in Italy is the left-wing Socialist, a remnant of the Socialist party that was the largest party in the Chamber immediately after World War I. Shortly before the rise of

---

[8] See Giovanni Gambarin, ed., *I Partiti dell'Italia Nuova* (Venezia, 1945), 85 ff.

[9] *Ibid.*, 67 ff.

[10] See the platform of the VIth Congress of the Italian Communist party in Lionel H. Laing and Others, *Source Book in European Governments* (New York, 1950), 202-207.

Mussolini, the party had split. One part became the Communist. Another part, the Maximalist Socialists, followed the doctrines of Marx and approved the Bolshevik experiment in Russia, but refused to follow the orders of Moscow. The third part, the Unitary Socialists, stood for gradual achievement of socialism and were willing to cooperate with any party that would assist them to accomplish their program.

At the end of World War II, the two Socialist wings of the old party united briefly, but split again over the question of following the Communist line or joining the Christian Democrats in a Cabinet without the Communists. The left-wing Socialists (PSI), under Pietro Nenni, joined a popular front with the Communists. They followed most of the policies of the Communists but did not unite with them.

The Right-wing Socialists. The right-wing Socialists, under Giuseppe Saragat, formed the Socialist Party of Italian Workers (PSLI) after the Rome congress of the Socialist party in January 1947. This party believes in obtaining the liberty of the individual through social and economic reforms. It vigorously opposes the Communists, pointing out that communism exalts the state over the individual, and that thereby the individual loses his liberty.

The PSLI favors a redistribution of land in order to create more work for farm laborers and more food for the hungry millions in Italy. It believes that greater production will reduce manufacturing cost and raise the standard of living. It would reduce the number of civil servants. These major objectives the party hopes to accomplish by working with the government instead of by joining what it calls the antidemocratic opposition.[11] It is, therefore, essentially a gradualist party. In the elections of 1948, the PSLI emerged as the third party in strength, but far less strong than the Christian Democrats or the Popular Front, the latter consisting of the Communists and the Nenni Socialists.

Still another division occurred in the Italian socialist movement in December 1949. The plan was that the PSLI and the right-wing members of the PSI would try again to form a larger group. At the last minute, however, Saragat refused to participate in the proposed congress. It met, nevertheless, in December 1949, and from it emerged the United Socialist party— (PSU). This party, apart from objecting to the division of Italian socialism, was based mainly on opposition to the approval of the Atlantic Pact by the PSLI.

The Liberals. Among the right-center parties of Italy is the Liberal group, which stems from the *Risorgimento* and takes Cavour as its hero. It defends a liberty which is not license but which respects the rights of others.

The party believes that classes will struggle with each other, but it does not make this the basis of its doctrine. Conflicting class interests, as well as other

---

[11] See Giuseppe Saragat, "Italian Democracy in Crisis," *Foreign Affairs,* 28 (1949-50), 615 ff.

ELECTIONS TO THE ITALIAN CHAMBER OF DEPUTIES, VOTES AND SEATS, 1921, 1946, AND 1948*

(*Votes in thousands*)

Parties	1921				1946				1948†			
	Votes	Per Cent	Seats	Per Cent	Votes	Per Cent	Seats	Per Cent	Votes	Per Cent	Seats	Per Cent
Right...............	1,290	19.6	107	20.0	2,626	11.4	66	11.9	1,934	7.4	32	5.6
Liberal Center......	1,712	25.9	157	29.3	2,287	10.0	55	9.9	1,215	4.6	19	3.3
Christian Democrats...	1,347	20.4	108	20.1	8,083	35.2	207	37.2	12,752	48.7	307	53.5
Socialists..........	1,631	24.7	123	22.9	4,745	20.7	115	20.7	4,739	18.4	81	14.1
Communists........	305	4.7	15	2.8	4,343	18.9	104	18.7	4,886	18.5	132	23.0
Others.............	323	4.7	25	4.9	869	3.8	9	1.6	638	2.4	3	0.5
Total..........	6,608		535		22,953		556		26,164		574	

Source: Compiled by Mario Einaudi for the first edition of this book (page 233).

* Constituent Assembly in 1946.

† The figures for the elections of 1948 have been rearranged so as to make them comparable with previous returns. Chiefly, this has meant the distribution of the "popular front" vote, which, as such, amounted to 30.5 per cent of the total, among its component elements, as follows: Communists, 18.5 per cent; Socialists, 11 per cent (this vote was added to the Independent Socialist vote of 7.4 per cent to make the 18.4 per cent reported in the table); other "popular front" groups, 1 per cent (added to "other" category). This distribution is naturally only the result of a number of guesses. The distribution of the votes among "right" and "liberal center" parties, given their elusive nature, is also only approximate.

conflicts, must be harmonized by the government; to protect the individual against arbitrary use of power is the function of law. A liberal government might intervene in economic affairs, but only to protect the individual's liberty. The majority would be restrained by bills of rights. With regard to religion, the Liberals defend the policy of Cavour: "A free church in a free state." Among the outstanding members of this party are Luigi Einaudi, the President of the Republic, and Benedetto Croce. The party has cooperated in the government as a member of many recent coalitions.

The Republicans. Another of the right-center parties is the Republican party (PRI). It also stems from the *Risorgimento,* but takes its inspiration from Giuseppe Mazzini. It emphasizes the political and moral goals of the French Revolution. It reminds the voters that Cavour placed the Piedmontese monarchy over a free Italy, while the Republican party was the real defender of a unified Italy, in which liberty and social and economic justice would flourish.

In the monarchical period, the Republican party agitated for universal suffrage, for free popular education, and for better land use. It bitterly opposed the ill-starred colonial adventures at the turn of the century. At the end of the Fascist regime, the Republican party was reborn; it worked to supplant the monarchy, as it had in earlier days. It was so opposed to monarchy, in fact, that it would not work in the Committees of National Liberation, nor would it join the government coalition until the monarchy was ended by plebiscite. The settling of this question removed one of the main props of the Republican platform, so that it had to develop others.

The right-wing of the party attacks the growing power of the government in economic affairs and urges political regionalism. In the economic field, the majority of the party, regarding both capital and labor as essentially despotic, seems to prefer a solution that would prevent any private interest from towering over the country. Ultimately both capital and labor should be eliminated as classes, and their place be taken by a class of free producers. Some of the left-wing members of the party are for socialization of the large and middle-sized industries and for cooperative management of the small ones.

Other Parties. On the right there are a few parties whose names and leaders change, but whose ideas are essentially similar in that they favor some form of authoritarianism. There are a few monarchists in the legislature, but they want a strong constitutional monarchy rather than an absolute one. There are very few deputies of the Common Man party, under the leadership of the colorful Guglielmo Giannini. His party, like the Fascists of former years, opposed more than it favored. It began as a by-product of the great popular success of a weekly satirical political journal published by Giannini with the slogan "We were better off when we were worse off." After the Communists withdrew from the coalition, his party worked with the Liberals; in the elections of 1948 it pooled its candidates with those of the latter. Its parliamentary representation very nearly vanished in 1948.

The Italian Social Movement—(MSI) advances not a few of the ideas of the Fascists, and like them believes in using force to achieve political ends. It has been involved in a good many pitched battles with the Communists; its offices have been bombed and its meetings forcibly broken up. In the elections of 1948 it made a poor showing; since then it has been both vocal and violent.

3. Problems Facing the Government

Balance of Coalition. The Italian government, under the new constitution, has substantially been a center coalition based on the massive bloc of Christian Democratic legislators, to which other parties have been added from time to time. Usually the governmental coalitions have included the right-wing Socialists, the Liberals, and the Republicans. The opposition bloc has been made up of the Communist deputies and their allies, the left-wing Socialists. The strength of the various party groups is shown in the preceding table on elections to the Chamber of Deputies.

The coalition governments, under the leadership of Premier Alcide de Gasperi since December 1945, have been constantly confronted with thorny problems. One of the earliest concerned the monarchy.

Launching the Republic. Many of the leaders of the liberation opposed the continuation of the monarchy in the belief that the King had been too easily convinced of the inevitability of Fascism in 1922. But it was also argued, on the other hand, that the monarchy would provide an element of continuity in the difficult period of reconstruction; the Allied occupation authorities early favored this view.

After a long struggle, the King withdrew from public life in June 1944, leaving his son as Lieutenant General. The Bonomi Cabinet at that time agreed to postpone the settlement of the monarchical question until the calling of the Constituent Assembly. At the same time that the Assembly was elected, the voters decided in favor of a republic.

But there was strain in getting the new form of government to work. Meanwhile, the Cabinet attacked other pressing problems: reconstruction after the disastrous war, "purification" of the state by driving out the most conspicuous Fascist sympathizers, and finding food, shelter, and work for the people of overpopulated Italy.

Other Problems. Another major problem was the peace treaty between Italy and the Allies at the end of World War II. In the treaty, Italy, as an enemy country and later a cobelligerent permitted to "work her passage home," lost four small areas to France and the Dodecanese Islands to Greece. She renounced her right to her African colonies. The bitterest pill was the setting up of the free city of Trieste and the gift of most of Venezia Giulia to Yugoslavia.

The government also had to face economic problems. The basic difficulty was that if Italy were to pay her way by exports, she needed to import raw materials and some partly finished products; yet she could not import because she had no money from exports with which to pay for imports. The Marshall Plan broke this vicious circle by providing credits for imports so that Italy could get her economy back into running order. The Marshall Plan has also influenced Italy's international orientation. Under Christian Democratic leadership, this orientation has consistently been toward the Western democracies; yet a large portion of the population consistently votes Communist and follows the Communist line. Communism in Italy as well as elsewhere thrives on economic distress. Thus the Marshall Plan, by helping to save the Italian economy, helps also in the government's campaign against the Communists.

The government has made a tentative—probably too tentative—approach to another of Italy's economic problems: the poor use made of the land by the absentee landlords in the south. Italy's land problem is not yet solved, nor is Italy's economy stable. The very existence of democracy in Italy depends upon the republican government's ability to meet these troublesome problems.

PART IV

CONSTITUTIONAL GOVERNMENT:
THE SCANDINAVIAN TRADITION

CHAPTER 15

CONSTITUTIONAL MONARCHY AND SOCIAL DEMOCRACY

1. The General Background

Common Characteristics. Small in population, unimposing in military power, and none too rich in natural resources, the Scandinavian peoples have become renowned for democratic government. Monarchical in form and loyal to their ruling houses, they have tended toward social democracy in politics. Established traditions of political liberty are strengthened by tested systems of adult education available to all; and economic cooperatives that compete freely and on equal terms with publicly and individually owned enterprises contribute to high standards of living. Geographically close to areas of totalitarian contagion, past or present, these three countries continue to uphold freedom of research and learning, of speech and the press, and respect for human beings regardless of race or political conviction.

Among themselves, the three countries—Denmark, Norway, and Sweden —enjoy a striking degree of homogeneity. All are constitutional monarchies. Their languages are so similar that any native of one of the countries can enjoy the literature of the other two with little difficulty. In all three, the vast majority are members of the established Evangelical Lutheran church. Complete religious toleration exists. Only the three Kings are required to be Lutheran. The late King Christian X of Denmark and King Haakon VII of Norway were brothers; their mother was a first cousin of Sweden's late King Gustaf V. The Scandinavians are Teutons, with the exception of several thousand Lapps in the arctic region, who are encouraged by the Swedish government to live in their traditional manner.

These common factors have made for close cooperation among the three countries. There are, for instance, uniform laws in various fields. In that of social legislation, the citizen of one country living in another is entitled to the relief benefits of a citizen of the latter. Yet, in spite of the strong habit of cooperation, the countries have no desire for political union. Although they have not been at war with one another for over a century and a quarter, and although current fears of Soviet intentions are drawing them together, all three countries show some tendencies toward nationalism. These have induced the Norwegians, for instance, to develop a distinct spelling for the written language they have shared for centuries with the Danes. The name of their capital was changed in recent times from Christiania to Oslo, substituting a Norwegian name for one of Danish origin.

Lands and Peoples. Denmark is a small country, somewhat larger than Switzerland. The peninsula of Jutland constitutes most of its area; the remainder consists of some five hundred islands. The capital, Copenhagen, is located on the largest island. Denmark has a population of about 4 million with a good half of it in urban areas, and almost a fourth in and around Copenhagen, the only large city. Denmark supports her dense population in the main by exports of processed agricultural goods and by shipping and trading around the globe. Soil is her only natural resource, and three fourths of the land is arable. But by imports of raw materials, Denmark employs a considerable majority of the people in industry, commerce, shipping, and finance, rather than in agriculture. In normal times, family incomes are high.

Norway is eight times as large as Denmark, but has a somewhat smaller population, being one of the most sparsely settled countries. The bulk of the people is concentrated in the South, where Oslo is located. Half of the country is covered with bare mountains, and one fourth is forest; only 3 per cent is cultivated. Norway exports much lumber, wood pulp, and dried fish. There is practically no iron and no coal, but waterfalls provide an unlimited supply of electric power. Almost a third of the people are farmers, with about another 10 per cent making their living as fishermen and whalers, and larger numbers in forestry. One third of the workers are engaged in industry, especially shipbuilding. The Norwegian merchant marine, before World War II, was the fourth largest in the world, following those of England, Germany, and the United States. Over 10 per cent of Norway's manpower was engaged in overseas shipping, a higher percentage than in any other nation.

Sweden is over ten times as large as Denmark, and only slightly smaller than Germany, but her population is no more than 7,000,000. As in Norway, population density is largest in the South with its cities, including Stockholm, the capital. Sweden's southern ports, like those of Norway, are ice-free. The country is rich in waterpower and furnishes 90 per cent of the high-grade iron ore in Europe, which facts also favor the development of her own industries. Only 9 per cent of the land is arable, but it supports one-third of the population. Immense forests greatly contribute to Sweden's exports.

From Absolutism to Constitutional Government. Generally speaking, each of the Scandinavian countries has gone through its own political and constitutional development.[1] From about 1500 to 1814, Norway was united

---

[1] Cf. Ben A. Arneson, *The Democratic Monarchies of Scandinavia* (2nd ed., New York, 1949), an indispensable, all-round treatment; Nils Herlitz, *Sweden: A Modern Democracy on Ancient Foundations* (Minneapolis, 1939); Margaret Cole and Charles Smith, eds., *Democratic Sweden* (studies prepared by members of the New Fabian Research Bureau, London, 1938); Josephine Goldmark and A. H. Hollman, *Democracy in Denmark* (Washington, 1936); Roy V. Peel, "Scandinavian Political and Constitutional Development," in James K. Pollock, ed., *Change and Crisis in European Government* (New York, 1947); Halvdan Koht and Sigmund Skard, *The Voice of Norway* (New York, 1944); Peter Manniche, *Denmark: A Social Laboratory*

with Denmark; and from 1814 to 1905, Norway and Sweden constituted a so-called personal union, as independent nations under the same King. For almost two hundred years (1660-1849), Denmark was an absolute monarchy, based explicitly upon a constitutional document that was adopted by an assembly of representatives of the country's university, the Lutheran clergy, and the burghers, over the protest of the nobility. Under this regime, Denmark became highly centralized, losing much of her earlier local self-government. Only in 1849 did a freely elected national assembly adopt a liberal constitution providing for manhood suffrage without property qualifications. Between that date and 1866, Denmark had no less than six different constitutions, primarily because of the problems growing out of her complicated relationship to the duchies of Schleswig and Holstein. The constitution of 1866 was less liberal than that of 1849, a loss that was not made up until the adoption of the constitution of 1915. During the intervening decades, the suffrage was widened to include by 1915 all men and women twenty-five years of age. The Cabinet is now responsible to the lower house of the legislature, and since 1849 the King's actions have been valid only with ministerial countersignature.

Norway was united with Sweden in 1814 at the decree of the European concert of powers without consultation of the Norwegian people, who fought but lost a brief war with Sweden for their independence. Just before this forced union, a constitutional assembly had been called by the last Danish Viceroy of Norway. Although the delegates had been chosen by the church congregations and by the Army and Navy, the constitution they adopted in effect provided for a limited constitutional monarchy. The King had merely a suspensive veto—a thorn in the flesh of the Swedish monarch. The Norwegian Parliament was able to uphold this fundamental provision when it abolished the country's hereditary nobility, in spite of the strenuous objections of the Swedish King. In 1907, Norway was the first country to extend the suffrage to women, though temporarily upon a limited basis. Two years earlier, the Norwegians had voted overwhelmingly for national independence, to which the Swedish King and Parliament wisely agreed. By popular vote, Prince Karl of Denmark was invited to become King of Norway; as Haakon VII, he has gained the affectionate loyalty of the Norwegian people.

Sweden has long been a unified monarchy, in which parliamentary government developed gradually. The *Riksdag* (Parliament) goes back to 1435, but until 1866 it consisted of four separate estates. After a violent period

(London, 1939); Bertil Ohlin, ed., "Social Problems and Policies in Sweden," *Annals of the American Academy of Political and Social Science,* 197 (1938); Richard C. Spencer, "Party Government and the Swedish Riksdag," *American Political Science Review,* 39 (1945), 437 ff.; Eric C. Bellquist and Wendell C. Schaeffer, "Inter-Scandinavian Economic Cooperation," *Foreign Policy Reports* (May 15, 1948), pp. 63 ff; Henning Friis, *Scandinavia between East and West* (Ithaca, N. Y., 1950); Franklin D. Scott, *The United States and Scandinavia* (Cambridge, Mass., 1950). See the *American-Scandinavian Review* for current developments. Appreciation is due Dr. Gustaf Petren, University of Stockholm, for criticism of this chapter.

of party strife, the four estates of the Riksdag in 1809 adopted a new constitution that was accepted by the King. With that of the United States, it is one of the oldest written constitutions still in effect. It had strong parliamentary features, making the King's orders dependent on the countersignature of a new Council of State, appointed by him but responsible to the Riksdag. When the royal family died out, Napoleon's brilliant field commander, Marshal Bernadotte, became king (1818). He was an outstanding statesman who did much for Sweden, even though for years he shared the reactionary sentiments of his time. In 1866, the Riksdag reformed itself by replacing the four estates with a bicameral legislature. This law, together with the constitution of 1809, and two other constitutional laws concerning the succession to the throne (1810) and freedom of the press (1812, reworded in 1949), constitute Sweden's written constitution. It can be amended by a simple majority vote of each house of Parliament on two consecutive occasions, the second following an intervening election to the lower house. The King has a veto power that he has rarely used since 1866. In Sweden, as in Norway and Denmark, the evolutionary democratization of public life was backed by a high degree of political education on the part of the voters, who recognized the democratic essence beneath the monarchical form. Scandinavians also have a high esteem for expert knowledge and administrative competence; their governmental activities are closely tied up with their limited natural resources and a general demand for social democracy.

2. Structure of Government

Parliamentary Government. The similarities of parliamentary government in the three countries are more numerous and basic than the differences. All three are hereditary constitutional monarchies, in which the executive power is vested in the King, but is exercised through a responsible Cabinet. The latter, in turn, is responsible to the legislature. In Norway, the King has a suspensive veto over ordinary legislation, but none over constitutional measures; in Sweden, the King has an absolute veto, which is no longer used. In Denmark, the King has not exercised his power of veto since 1865. It may be said that the Scandinavian Kings have little more power over legislation than has the King of England.

Cabinets are dependent upon the confidence of Parliament, but they are not ousted with French frequency. In Denmark and Sweden the executive may dissolve Parliament. This happened in Denmark in 1920, 1926, 1929, 1939, and 1951, but is a rare occurrence in Sweden. In Denmark and Sweden, Cabinet members are usually members of Parliament, but in Norway they are not allowed to be members of Parliament.

In Denmark and Norway, the Cabinet may pass provisional laws while Parliament is not in session. Such laws are subject to repeal by the next session of the legislature. This power has been more important in Denmark.

Each of the constitutions provides for annual budgets and full parliamentary control over them.

Legislative Control. Denmark and Sweden have bicameral legislatures, but only in Sweden are the two houses practically equal in power. Sweden, however, has a constitutionally anchored system of joint standing committees, which tends to coordinate the work of both chambers. When they disagree on matters of finance and taxation, they vote jointly. At that time, the larger number of votes of the popular chamber may decide the issue, provided it is united in its viewpoint, which is not always the case. The joint vote is not frequent. In Denmark, the popular house (*Folksting*) is somewhat more powerful than the upper house (*Landsting*). In spite of a strong demand for its abolition, the latter has remained as a check upon legislation. In Norway, the Parliament (*Storting*) is a one-house legislature that organizes into two divisions after election. The Storting selects one fourth of its membership to constitute the *Lagting;* the remainder forms the *Odelsting.* They are in effect large committees of Parliament, especially when one considers that the qualifications and length of term are the same for all members. Most committees represent the Storting and not one of the two sections. All laws except those on finance must be considered in the sections, but a bill may be enacted by the Storting as a whole even if it fails to be passed in each section. In addition, all financial bills and proposed constitutional amendments are considered by the Storting as a whole, not in sections.

In Sweden, the lower house consists of 230 members, elected for a four-year term on the basis of universal suffrage. The members of the upper chamber are chosen indirectly for eight-year terms by county councils and especially appointed electors, with one-eighth of them elected every year. Eligibility for membership in the upper chamber requires an age of thirty-five. Every successive Riksdag appoints two nonmembers as supervisory officials over civil (including judicial) and military affairs, respectively. Citizens can take complaints of maladministration and official misconduct to them for investigation. All three governments are subject to the fiscal scrutiny of a board of auditors chosen by Parliament, usually from its membership, whose duty it is to probe into the revenues and expenditures of the Treasury each year. The reports of the auditors also assist Parliament in the preparation of the new budget.

All the legislatures begin with a ceremonial opening, at which the King delivers a speech from the throne and the Prime Minister discusses important developments since the last session. Legislators possess the usual parliamentary immunities. The Scandinavian countries were leaders in the fight for woman suffrage; women hold some 10 per cent of the parliamentary seats. There is much similarity among the countries in the occupational grouping of members of Parliament. One finds large numbers of farmers, small businessmen, public officials, and journalists. Since re-election is common, the number of members with no legislative experience is small. Brilliant oratory is unusual, and matter-of-fact debate common.

The Executive Structure. Each country has about a dozen central departments, usually headed by Cabinet members. Particular Scandinavian concerns are reflected by department names like those of Ecclesiastical Affairs or Social Affairs. Since the Lutheran church is a state church in these countries, its general affairs and the training of the clergy are supervised by the government, although considerable local autonomy exists in the choice of ministers and bishops, who legally are appointed by the Cabinet. The Department of Social Affairs is in charge of various kinds of social insurance so prominently associated with Scandinavian life, and usually such matters as child welfare and the care of the blind, deaf, and feeble-minded. The Department of Public Works normally includes the postal service as well as the management or control of railways, communications, highways, dikes, and harbors. In the three countries most of the railroads are owned by the state, which may also have a large financial interest in privately owned corporations. The telegraph and telephone systems are usually state-owned, and state-operated.

The Ministry of Justice usually controls the state police and, depending on the laws, may also supervise local police administration. In Sweden and Norway, waterpower is considered a national resource; it is under the government's control and largely owned by either central or local governments. The national banks of issue, which may be publicly or privately owned, are closely controlled by the government. There are also various governmental banks set up to aid agriculture, home owners, wage earners, fishermen, and municipalities. Sweden's two parliamentary supervisors for civil and military affairs are directly responsible to Parliament, as is the board of auditors. Swedish government departments allow much internal independence to individual officials and administrative boards within their fields of action, an independence exercised without specific direction by the department head.

The civil service, in all the countries, has earned high public esteem and is characterized by merit rule and security of tenure. On the whole, the civil services are both efficient and democratic. Their members may hold elective office, and many of them are in Parliament while on official leave.

Administration of Justice. The Scandinavian court systems are nationally integrated. Judges are appointed by the Cabinet for life, subject to retirement at certain ages. In Norway, civil cases are not taken into court until after they have been before local conciliation councils that try to settle them. The councils have the right to give judgments in minor cases, where parties to a dispute agree, or when one party fails to appear. In Swedish cities, the presiding judge of the local court is the mayor, who is required to have legal training.

In Norway, lay judges are used to assist the permanent judges in cases involving technical or specialized knowledge of a nonlegal nature. In Swedish local courts, the judge is aided by a committee of twelve unpaid citizens chosen at public elections for six-year terms. Together with the judge, they pass on questions of evidence and of law. If they disagree, the decision lies with the judge; but their unanimous vote can overrule him.

Denmark and Norway both have the jury system. In Sweden, juries are used only in cases involving freedom of the press. The constitutional law guaranteeing freedom of the press, reworded in 1949, forbids all advance censorship, although it makes writers or publishers liable for damages and punishable for slander, blasphemy, or indecency. These cases are decided by a jury of nine, which attempts to balance the interests of free communication and protection of individual privacy.

Judicial Review and Personal Rights. There is no general system of judicial review of the constitutionality of legislation in Sweden, but the Riksdag has a strong tradition of strict observance of constitutional provisions. A Law Council, consisting of three judges of the Supreme Court and one judge of the Supreme Administrative Court, acts as an advisory body on such questions. Although its opinion is not binding on the Riksdag, it does exert considerable influence on the legislature. In Denmark, the courts do not exercise the power of judicial review, and Norwegian courts use it most sparingly. Citizens depend for protection of their civil and political rights primarily upon public opinion and Parliament, both of which are equally constitution-minded. The Storting consults the Attorney General in case of constitutional doubt, and rarely acts contrary to his advice. The Norwegian constitution specifically prohibits certain types of legislation—for instance, retroactive laws. In a case of this kind, Norwegian courts do not enter a formal decision declaring the law void, but simply refrain from applying it in situations where the rights of individuals would be affected retroactively. In effect, this is a form of judicial review.

Each country has specific constitutional provisions establishing individual rights. In the case of Denmark, for instance, they are religious liberty, freedom of the press, freedom of assembly and association, the right to engage in economic activities, prohibition of unreasonable search and seizure, the right of the accused to a court hearing, and the right of appeal. Only Sweden has a separate system of administrative justice, headed by a Supreme Administrative Court, to handle actions brought by individuals against decisions of governmental agencies. The constitution provides that the members of the Supreme Administrative Court must have held administrative posts in the government, but only two thirds of them need to possess the qualifications prescribed for judges. This court also decides contested elections, to state and local offices and to the Quinquennial Ecclesiastical Assembly.

Provincial and Local Government.[2] Each of the countries is divided into

---

[2] Cf. Roy V. Peel, "Local Government in Scandinavia," *National Municipal Review*, 25 (1936), 528 ff.; and Peel, "Lessons from Scandinavian Cities," *Public Management*, 18 (1936), 102 ff.

provinces or counties, headed by a prefect or governor, who is appointed by the central government and assisted by an official staff. The prefect sees to it that national laws are properly administered by the county, and also acts as the chief executive of the county as a self-governing unit. In Denmark and Norway, cities are not under the jurisdiction of the counties; in Sweden, only some of the larger cities have a separate status. Only Swedish cities have an ancient tradition of home rule; in Denmark and Norway, local self-government is only about a hundred years old. Perhaps "local administration" is a better term than local self-government, because the units of local government are extensively employed as administrative areas for the execution of national policies and laws. All units of local government elect their own legislative bodies, on the basis of proportional representation and along party lines. It is a matter of general interest that in the Scandinavian countries proportional representation in the form in which it has been employed has not demonstrated the disadvantages so frequently complained of in certain other countries of Western Europe. In Denmark and Norway, city councils elect the mayors, but in Sweden, they are appointed by the central government from among the three candidates favored most by popular vote. Copenhagen and Stockholm have a somewhat different government of their own because of their size and importance.

Municipal ownership is general. It normally includes water, gas, electricity, streetcars and buses, as well as beaches and housing. In Denmark, most of the larger movie theaters are municipally owned, and in Sweden, market halls and sometimes laundries as well. State supervision of local government, exercised through the county officers, extends to financial measures and disposition of municipal property, and includes the right to suspend or annul unconstitutional acts or acts in violation of private rights, as well as the power to withhold state subsidies.

3. The General Welfare

Social Welfare. All Scandinavian governments have gone a long way in promoting the general welfare through legislation, grants, and loans, and also through a helpful interest in cooperative efforts toward raising the standard of living. All three have to their credit outstanding accomplishments benefiting large numbers of the population from childhood to old age. The general features of this governmental interest show remarkable similarities from country to country.

Child welfare is administered locally, but on a national plan. Most of the cost is borne by the municipalities. Denmark has an intermunicipal fund to which both rich and poor municipalities contribute on the basis of financial ability and from which they draw according to their needs in child welfare. At the other end of the scale, systems of old-age pensions have long been prevalent, and in the course of years have become widely inclusive. In Denmark, all people over sixty are entitled to a pension, its size varying according to the pensioner's other income, marital status, and geographic location, with its differing cost of living. In Norway,[3] there exists a long-standing tradition of private old-age insurance paid for by employers, for which reason a general old-age pension law was not passed until 1936. The law includes fishermen, agricultural workers, woodsmen, and small farmers, who had not profited by earlier private insurance systems. In Sweden, old-age and disability insurance is compulsory for the entire population from eighteen to sixty-five; it is based on contributions by the insured, according to property and income. This provision differs from the systems in Denmark and Norway, where all payments are met by taxation.

Health insurance systems are strong, too. In Denmark, the system takes the form of so-called sick clubs that are aided by the state. Membership is compulsory for everyone from twenty-one to sixty years of age. The government exercises careful supervision over these clubs. In Norway, health insurance is compulsory for employees between fifteen and seventy years of age who make less than a certain amount of money. Sixty per cent of the contribution comes from the insured, 10 per cent from the employer, 20 per cent from the national government, and 10 per cent from the local government. Unlike Denmark and Sweden, Norway has no general system of disability insurance. The health insurance system of Sweden is voluntary. It is based on a system of private but state-subsidized benefit societies, the benefits to be paid constituting two thirds of the cost of medical care, free hospital service, and an allowance for working time lost.

Labor Security. Workmen's compensation is compulsory, but less inclusive in Norway than in Denmark and Sweden. The Danish law compels all employers to carry liability insurance in government-approved companies. If the employer is negligent and does not take out insurance, he becomes personally liable. If he is unable to meet the expense, the liability is transferred to the government-approved accident insurance companies, which are thereby induced to make sure that all employers take out liability insurance. Unemployment insurance is general. The governments give grants to approved unemployment benefit societies that were started many years ago by trade unions. The remainder of the funds comes from contributions by members and municipalities. Benefits are not paid to strikers or anyone unreasonably refusing a job.

Different governmental agencies deal with the settlement of industrial disputes. In general, one and the same procedure is followed. Organized labor has long been strongly established in these countries, and the right of collective bargaining is recognized. In cases where arbitration tribunals have jurisdiction, both unions and employers are responsible for damages deriving from failure to observe the decision. Mediation boards have the task of bringing the parties together and helping them to come to an agree-

---

[3] Cf. John E. Nordskog, *Social Reform in Norway: A Study of Nationalism and Social Democracy* (Los Angeles, 1935), chaps. 5 and 6.

ment, a job in which they are very successful. Special labor courts exist to interpret and enforce agreements between management and employees. Norway has experimented with compulsory arbitration, but the opposition of both the right and the left has prevented it from becoming a permanent institution. Labor courts and mediation boards, on the other hand, have met everywhere with general satisfaction. In Norway, the members of the labor courts are appointed by the government; in Denmark, half of them are chosen by management and half by labor. In Sweden, the chairman and two members represent the general public, and two each speak for labor and industry. Strikes in the Scandinavian countries are almost unknown.

In times of depression, unemployment relief is supplied in the form of work relief, in preference to payments without a contribution in labor. Sweden especially resorts to a public works program for this purpose, providing for projects under local initiative but approved and subsidized by the national government. Additional projects are of national scope; still others are purely municipal, without national aid. Such projects include the building of roads and bridges, forest work, and the construction of athletic fields, inland waterways, harbors, and water-supply and drainage systems.

Aid to Agriculture. Since agriculture plays an important part in Scandinavian countries, much governmental attention is given to the problem of effective aid. The percentage of tenant farmers is low, and strenuous efforts are made to help tenants or farm workers to become landowners with the help of loans.

In Norway, the government is subsidizing a private reclamation and homesteading movement, which has for its purpose a much-needed increase in arable land. Loans—for the first five years without interest and later at a low rate—help settlers to clear the land, put up buildings, and install drainage systems. In all these countries, farmers threatened by debts are aided by governmental mortgage banks. The government also concerns itself with agricultural education and farm advisory service.

Aid to Housing. The Scandinavian countries have long been engaged in extensive aid to housing by granting subsidies or loans at low interest rates, whether the purpose has been to build individual homes or apartment houses. Danish municipalities have also furnished aid through tax exemptions for new homes and housing projects. About one fifth of the population of Copenhagen live in homes owned by the government or by cooperative associations. In Oslo the percentage is about 90 per cent. In the interwar period, only Vienna equalled Oslo in regard to its record in municipal housing. Other Norwegian cities have shown a similar interest.

A comparable program in Sweden has been used partly as a remedy against social ills. Housing cooperatives and public loans are prominent. The main criticism of Swedish housing projects has aimed at the extremely small size of the modern apartments as a contributory factor to the very low birth rate. The "garden cities" of the three capitals and other urban centers are settlements on municipally owned land, where low-cost houses are built for workers, either by the municipality itself or by subsidized cooperative societies. Each family has a plot of land for gardening purposes.

Scope of the Cooperative Movement. Scandinavian cooperatives, famous for their achievements, are private organizations for buying and selling, or even for producing quality goods for consumers at the lowest price.[4] Considerable savings are achieved by the elimination of the middleman wherever possible and by turning unallocated profits back into the pockets of the customer-owners. In Denmark, the stress is on agricultural producer cooperatives, which enable the farmers to buy feed, fertilizer, and machinery cheaply through purchase in wholesale lots and to market milk and milk products, eggs, cattle, and pigs at good prices. An outstanding feature of the Danish producer cooperative is the high quality standard that has made Danish agricultural products widely known throughout Europe and salable at high prices. The essential methods of cooperation are taught in Danish folk and agricultural schools. Cooperative associations furnish expert advice to farmers on the handling of milk, on feeding, and the like, stimulating keen competition by the award of prizes. Three fourths of the Danish "bacon factories," or pork packing plants, are owned by cooperatives.

In Norway and Sweden, more stress is laid on consumer cooperatives, with workingmen's families making up the bulk of the membership, although Norway has also been successful in cooperative farmer associations. The national milk-producing association, organized into eight cooperative district milk pools, equalizes the price paid to producers for milk in such a way that the higher price received for fluid milk in the cities is used to help increase the income of the more distant rural farmers, who ordinarily would get lower prices for milk furnished to creameries and cheese factories. The milk-producing association and its milk pools are recognized by the government and allowed price-fixing powers, provided, however, that most producers in a given district choose to become members. Egg prices are fixed by regional committees of seven members made up of an equal number of representatives of the cooperatives and other egg producers, with the chairman representing the government. Norway's consumer cooperatives not only sell commodities in their own stores, but, as in Sweden, these cooperatives own factories producing shoes, soap, flour, electric light bulbs, and other goods. In all three countries, and especially in Sweden, cooperatives also grant agricultural credit.

It is an essential aspect of Scandinavian cooperatives that they exist side by side with other private and also publicly owned enterprises. None of them enjoys a monopoly. All compete keenly with one another, with re-

---

[4] See Frederic C. Howe, *Denmark: The Cooperative Way* (New York, 1936), chaps. 7-14; Marquis W. Childs, *Sweden: The Middle Way* (New Haven, 1936), chaps. 1-4; Roy V. Peel, "Consumers' Cooperatives in Scandinavian Countries," *Annals of the American Academy of Political and Social Science*, 191 (1937), 165 ff.

sulting benefits in the form of moderate prices, better quality, and able management alert to the needs and desires of a critical public.

4. Interplay of Political Forces

Party System. Owing to common economic and social factors, party life shows many parallels in the three Scandinavian countries.[5] Modern parties go back to about 1830 in Denmark and Norway and to the 1860's in Sweden. On the right, each country has a Conservative party that in the past strongly opposed the development toward parliamentary government, but is now entirely loyal to it. The party stands for nationalism and is opposed to socialization. It is backed by the upper classes and well-to-do farmers, and also by many civil servants. In line with the generally moderate temper of Scandinavian politics, the party can hardly be called reactionary. In Sweden, the Conservatives are a group of several right-wing organizations rather than a single party, though they are closely associated in intention and action. Each country has a broadly liberal party—named the Left in Denmark, the Liberals in Norway, and the People's party in Sweden. This party used to be the moving force toward parliamentary government. With achievement of its end, it has moved to the right, especially in Denmark and perhaps least in Sweden. Now it does not show marked differences from the conservative alternative. Norway and Sweden also have agrarian parties, and in Denmark agrarian influences are very strong in the conservative Left. Although the Danish and Swedish agrarians tend to be conservative, they have in recent years joined coalition cabinets with the Social Democrats, in which they have pulled toward a middle-of-the-road position.

The Social Democratic party in each country enjoyed a rapid growth in recent decades, with Social Democratic prime ministers in all three governments in the 1930's and again after 1947, although several Social Democratic cabinets were not based upon majority control in Parliament. Scandinavian socialism is moderate; even the Norwegian Labor party, formerly far to the left, has become less radical. Each Social Democratic party is firmly associated with the trade unions, but in no case is the party's influence confined to the urban centers. Many small landowners and agricultural laborers tend to support its program.

The Communists are active, but their numbers and influence are small and have been decreasing in the past few years. Fascist or Nazi parties were noisy in prewar days in all three countries, but have been unsuccessful politically. They are now, of course, suffering from the stigma of collaboration with the German invader, for which the leader of the Norwegian Nazis, Major Vidkun Quisling, was executed after the war. Several additional small parties complete the picture of an active party life. They include, for

---

[5] Cf. Eric C. Bellquist, "Government and Politics in Northern Europe," in David Fellman, ed., *Post-War Governments of Europe* (Gainesville, 1946), pp. 365 ff., and Bellquist, *op. cit.* above, note 1; Walter Galenson, *Labor in Norway* (Cambridge, Mass., 1949); John T. Bernhard, "Empirical Collectivism in Denmark," *Journal of Politics*, 13 (1951), 623 ff.

instance, a Henry George Justice Union in Denmark and the Christian People's party of Norway, a Protestant counterpart to the Catholic parties of Central Europe, standing for the application of Christian principles to party politics.

Party Organization and Elections. Parties are efficiently organized, with national, district, and local committees, strong leadership exerted by national headquarters, and a host of influential party newspapers, as well as women's auxiliaries and youth organizations. The voting age is now twenty-one in all of the countries of Scandinavia. Elections are usually fought with gusto, but over short periods of time. The voters have a good many parties to choose from in expressing their particular shade of political preference, and most elections have presented issues that gave meaning to the contests. The multiparty system, in general, has not weakened either the principle of party responsibility or the stability of government.

The percentage of eligible voters who exercise their civic right is much higher than in the United States. Each country uses the list system of proportional representation, but throws in some technical complications that make the determination of the election a more elaborate process than in other Continental countries. Norway has a nice little scheme of its own for making nominating conventions more attractive by paying the expenses of delegates from government funds.

Denmark's Wartime Fate. Little Denmark, located next door to Germany, wide-open and practically unarmed, made no attempt at resistance when the country was overrun by the German army in April 1940. Occupation methods were less severe than in any other country until August 1943, when the Germans declared martial law and tightened their control. Then the Danes organized a well-functioning resistance movement that contributed its full share to the Allied war effort. Following the German occupation, Prime Minister Thorwald Stauning's coalition government of the Social Democrats and the Radical Left was expanded into a Cabinet representing all the four main parties. After the declaration of martial law by the Germans, secret plans were made for a new government that went into office at the time of the liberation. It represented all parties, including the Communists and the resistance movement.

The election of 1943 was free, except that the Communist ticket was not allowed and opportunities for campaigning and publicity were limited. As an obvious protest move, 97.8 per cent of the voters supported anti-Nazi parties in the heaviest vote cast in Danish history.

Norway's Defense and Aftermath. The German occupation of Norway found strong military resistance, which for obvious reasons could last but a few months. The Social Democratic government that had been in office for over four years accompanied the King to London, where Trygve Lie, later Secretary General of the United Nations, became its Foreign Minister. The government-in-exile put the large Norwegian merchant fleet at the disposal of the Allied powers, trained its air and ground forces in Britain and Canada, and maintained close contact with the Norwegian underground. In Norway, however, Major Vidkun Quisling announced the formation of a pro-Nazi government on the day of the German invasion, without receiving popular support. Hitler suppressed all political parties except Quisling's *Nasjonal Samling,* which had existed for several years but had never been able to elect a single member to the Storting. The Germans attempted to "coordinate" Norwegian government and life along Nazi lines and to overcome strenuous opposition by arrests and imprisonments, confiscation of property, and even executions. The Norwegian underground, in turn, answered with effective acts of sabotage.

In May 1945, the government-in-exile returned to Norway. It was replaced by a temporary Cabinet, intended to stay in office until new elections were held and headed by a young Social Democrat who had been in a Nazi concentration camp. Although its majority consisted of members of the resistance movement, it also represented the various parties, including the Communists. For the first time, a woman became a member of a Norwegian Cabinet.

Sweden's Neutrality. By "luck and geography," Sweden escaped invasion and managed to preserve her neutral status, even though it was at times heavily dented. The policy of neutrality, together with strong armaments, was supported by all parties, while both the government and private citizens engaged in relief activities for Finns and Norwegians. After the Soviet attack on Finland, the four principal parties joined a coalition government headed by Per Albin Hanson, Prime Minister of the previous Social Democratic government. In spite of her precarious international situation, Sweden kept government on a democratic basis, with a minimum of interference with individual liberty and a strong showing of national unity.

Sweden held three wartime elections, two to the lower house in 1940 and 1944, and municipal and county elections in 1942. Up to 1942, the Social Democratic party gained, achieving a substantial majority of 134 out of 230 seats in the lower house. In 1944, however, it won only 115 seats, or exactly one half of the membership. With the exception of the election of 1920, this was the first time that the Social Democratic party had lost rather than gained votes in comparison with earlier polls. The Communist vote tripled in 1944, its percentage rising to 10.3 of the total, and membership in the lower house from 3 to 15 seats. In part, the advance of the Communists was due to their attacks on the Social Democrats for the freezing of wages. Sweden's first postwar elections, in September 1948, resulted in a loss of only 3 seats for the Social Democrats, who had been under fire for their trade and financial policies, giving them 112 out of 230 seats in the lower house. The Liberal party succeeded in increasing its representation heavily, from 39 to 57 seats, while the Conservatives dropped from 39 to only 22 deputies. Communist strength declined severely—from 15 to 9 seats. Nazi groups had existed in Sweden in the early 1920's, but had not polled much more than 1 per cent of the total vote even in 1936. This figure was roughly the proportion of the prewar Quislingists in Norway and never sufficed to elect a single candidate. A few Nazis, elected as Conservatives, sat in the Riksdag and in provincial bodies, but they had disappeared by 1942. Apparently, the political climate was not propitious for them in time of either war or peace.

Danish Postwar Politics. Contrary to the postwar situation in other Scandinavian countries, the elections of 1945, 1947, and 1950 in Denmark resulted in middle-class majorities. In other respects, the elections were so indecisive that they were followed by a conservative Liberal government in 1945, backed directly by only 38 of the 149 deputies in the lower house, and by a Social Democratic Cabinet in 1947, which could count on the support of no more than the 57 Social Democrats. In both cases, the minority Cabinet was able to remain in office only because some parties were willing to support it on specific issues, without being willing to tie themselves to a coalition program; and others were unwilling to overthrow the government and take over the reins themselves. The defeat of the first of these minority governments in October 1947 after a fifteen-hour debate was the result of the increasing seriousness of the economic situation, and particularly of a vote of nonconfidence against the Prime Minister because of his attitude on the South Schleswig question.[6] The Cabinet declared its solidarity with him and resigned.

The election results in 1947 differed from those in 1945 primarily in that the vote of the Communists and of the extreme nationalist *Dansk Samling* party fell off greatly, while the agrarian elements, the conservative Liberals, and the Social Democrats gained considerably, thereby continuing a political trend that had been apparent earlier. The campaign lasted only twenty-four days; popular participation was about the same in 1945, though far behind the percentage of 1943 when everyone went to the polls as a silent protest against the presence of the German Army. In 1950, the Socialists gained slightly and the Conservatives sharply, who assumed partial responsibility for a coalition minority Cabinet, which, incidentally, included Miss Helga Petersen as Denmark's first woman Minister of Justice.

Norway's Reconsolidation. When King Haakon VII of Norway celebrated his seventy-fifth birthday in August 1947, the "people's King" received a tremendous ovation. Like his late brother, King Christian of Denmark, he had become the popular symbol of resistance against the foreign oppressor. At the age of sixty-seven, he had shown courageous dignity

---

[6] The problem concerns the method of safeguarding the right of self-determination of the Danish minority in South Schleswig, which belongs to Germany. Prime Minister Knud Kristensen had advocated the inclusion of a provision in the future peace treaty between the Allied powers and Germany granting South Schleswig the possibility of a plebiscite on the question of union with Denmark. The majority of Parliament opposed any governmental initiative in the question, preferring the cautious attitude previously agreed upon by Parliament and Cabinet.

and power of determination in the face of the invasion. The Nazi demand for recognition of the Quisling government he answered by a call to the people of Norway to resist with arms. On his birthday, Prime Minister Einar Gerhardsen of the left-wing government read an address of appreciation. The Social Democratic president of the city council of Oslo said on the same occasion, "The King is the best democrat among us."

A strong feeling of national solidarity, born of war experience, has aided in the task of Norwegian reconstruction. Five months after liberation, elections were held in a rather apathetic atmosphere. The Labor party won 76 of the 150 seats in the Storting, though no majority of the popular vote— the party's first parliamentary majority. The Communist vote jumped very high, above the vote for the Agrarians. The popularity of the Communists was due in part to their active role in the resistance movement, after 1941. Because of the Labor party's parliamentary majority, the ten Communist deputies did not become the balance wheel. A greater surprise of the election was the success of the Christian People's party. With little experienced party organization and small financial means, it won seven seats. It is especially strong in the rural and religious areas of western Norway. The municipal elections in 1947 showed a slight shift to the right and some losses for the Communists. The bourgeois parties took 52.6 per cent of the municipal council seats, with the remainder going to the Labor and Communist parties—which is an exact reversal of the previous situation.

Prime Minister Einar Gerhardsen's Labor Cabinet took office in 1945. It did not claim a mandate from the voters to go ahead with general socialization; for instance, it has returned merchant shipping to the private owners since the war. But it made long strides toward a planned economy, with government controls on manpower, prices and profits, wages and production. Through the purchase of stock, it has extended government part-ownership of industrial enterprises.

In 1949, the Socialists increased their parliamentary strength from 76 to 85—out of 150 seats—though their popular vote was only 46 per cent of the total. The Communists lost all of their 11 seats, their percentage of votes decreasing from 11.9 to less than 6 per cent. The changes in the strength of the other parties were minor.

Sweden's Reorientation. In Sweden, King Gustaf V celebrated the fortieth anniversary of his succession to the throne in December 1947. A nonagenarian, he was then the oldest reigning monarch in Europe. He had often exercised personal influence on Swedish Cabinets, which recognized him as an expert adviser. In times of international strain, he made pointed public statements in support of the government's policy. He claimed the right to speak freely, especially in favor of maintaining the country's policy of neutrality. He was always a strong friend of persecuted people—especially Norwegian, Danish, and Hungarian Jews, and some 30,000 refugees from the Baltic countries. During his long reign, he gained the deep respect of his people. After his death, in 1950, he was succeeded by his son who, at the age of 67, ascended the throne as Gustav VI.

Concurrent with the presence of a strong King who has been able to exercise considerable influence on the government, there has been an intermittent series of Social Democratic cabinets. The elections to the lower house of 1944 gave the Social Democratic party 46.6 per cent of the total vote and 115 seats or exactly half of the membership. In the upper house, its majority was slightly larger. The Conservatives, Agrarians, and Liberals polled from 13 to 16 per cent of the vote each. In 1945, a Social Democratic Cabinet was formed, including a woman Minister of Education, Hildut Nygren. Local and provincial elections in September 1946 showed slight changes, mostly in favor of the Liberals, who took the place of the Conservatives as the country's second largest party. The Communists advanced to 11 per cent of the total vote. The Social Democrats gained slightly, but their percentage was below their maximum strength of 50.3 in 1942. At that, the Social Democratic party is almost three times the size of any other.

The government has been on the defensive, largely because the economic situation of the country has deteriorated to a marked degree. Sweden suffered a grave loss through the death in 1946 of Prime Minister Per Albin Hanson, the country's Social Democratic leader for two decades. His successor, Tage Erlander, is stressing a program of state control of economic life that has led to intense public debate throughout the country.

Scandinavia between East and West. Historically, culturally, and in their way of life, the Scandinavian countries are Western. Their political philosphy is like that of France, Switzerland, the Low Countries, and the Anglo-Saxon nations; nothing is further from their aims and preferences than Nazi or Soviet totalitarianism.[7] The Communist element ranges from 4.6 per cent of the total vote cast in the latest Danish elections to 6 and 11 in Norway and Sweden, respectively. It does not constitute a political threat, except as a fifth column in time of danger. Although there is no expectation of a *coup* of the Czechoslovakian variety, Sweden and Denmark are now strengthening their internal structure by excluding Communists from important positions in the armed forces and the police.

The hard facts of geography create special and serious problems for these small countries, and they disagree as to the best course of foreign policy. Norway, looking upon the Atlantic as her economic lifeline and traditionally close to Britain, goes furthest in the desire for a Western orientation. Both she and Denmark are ardent members of the North Atlantic Treaty Organization (NATO). Sweden, having not been involved in war for 135 years, is strongly tempted again to anchor her hopes on a policy of "balanced behavior" toward potential combatants—a policy in which she succeeded toward Germany when Norway and Denmark both failed. She prefers international cooperation for the furtherance of peace through membership

---

[7] Cf. Erik Seidenfaden, "Scandinavia Charts a Course," *Foreign Affairs,* 26 (1948), 653 ff.

in the United Nations and the Council of Europe. But at the same time, she insists on absolute military independence, which has resulted, for instance, in her unwillingness to acquire membership in NATO.

If peace were safeguarded by a strong international organization, the Scandinavian states would continue to make their contributions to the world's progress in a position of democratic leadership. In an era when the United Nations shows cracks and weaknesses, the three peoples are conscious of their exposed position. So far, their search has not led to Scandinavian solidarity in foreign policy, but under the pressure of events, especially from the East, each has progressed farther Westward than in the past. Through whole-hearted cooperation in the Marshall Plan, these countries have approached the position of partners of the West in the present diplomatic struggle. If their policies vary in degree, they are one in basic goals. The most heartening aspect of the Scandinavian North is each country's traditional and firm insistence on democratic processes and a stable political situation, in sharp contrast to most of Europe.

PART V

FEDERAL GOVERNMENT: THE CENTRAL
EUROPEAN RECORD

CHAPTER 16

THE GERMAN EMPIRE AND THE WEIMAR REPUBLIC

1. National Unification

Germany's Legacy of Contradictions. Ever since her belated unification in 1871, and in a sense because of it, Germany has been in the foreground of political interest. At times, the world watched apprehensively the military prowess and diplomatic clumsiness—even delinquency—of the growing contender among industrial nations. At other times, it admired early German leadership in fields such as public administration, local self-government, social insurance, and industrial organization. There was the lure of the political and economic experiments associated with the democracy of the Weimar Republic. There was also the shock of the dictatorship of nazism. Its abominations dragged the German name to the nadir of its historic reputation. This German eminence in opposites of political thought and action makes it both difficult and fruitful to ponder the lessons of the rise and fall of an important nation.

Germany, located in Europe's geographic center, is thus destined to be a pivotal state. Lack of natural borders, with few exceptions, has served to increase Prussian and later German emphasis on military strength, which turned easily into militarism. Even before World War I, Germany was smaller in area than Texas, but among European countries second only to Russia in size and population. As the result of her rapid industrialization after 1871, Germany became a densely populated country, even though she did not reach the degree of density characteristic of Britain and Belgium. The Empire included in its population some 3 million Poles, besides other smaller national minorities. After Germany's defeat in World War I, most foreign minorities were absorbed by their respective fatherlands in 1919.

Vastly more important, under the peace treaty of Versailles, Germany lost much territory—aside from her overseas colonies—and 6 million of her population to Poland, France, Denmark, and Lithuania; moreover, a smaller area was separated from her and set up with an independent status as the Free City of Danzig. Germany's loss of raw materials, however, was of a still greater importance than her decrease in size. Altogether, the Reich surrendered 65 per cent of her iron ore reserves, 15 per cent of her coal deposits, 72 per cent of her zinc ore, and 57 per cent of her lead ore, in addition to the 12 to 15 per cent of her principal agricultural products and about 12

per cent of her manufacturing establishments. Western and central Germany are predominantly industrial, as is Upper Silesia in her former southeast. Generally, the country is highly industrialized.[1] Before the last war,
only 21 per cent of the working population was employed in agriculture and
forestry. Germany's agriculture is characterized by intense production
methods and consequent high yields in large parts of the country.

Regional Differences. Germany is roughly divided into three main geographic sections. First, there is the north German plain, which is a continuation of the vast low-level lands of Poland, Russia, and Asia, extending in
the west into the Netherlands and Belgium. The central and southern up-
land area constitutes as large a part of the Reich. Nature has here acted as
a barrier to communication while fostering autonomous development of
small areas, giving them cultural individuality but making political unity
more difficult. These two areas are the economic backbone of the country;
the third region—the Alps and their foothills in the far south—is less important to national production. Germany is a country of regional diversity
also in regard to population characteristics, which have long ceased to coincide with political borders. For instance, both the lighthearted Rhinelander
and the stolid Pomeranian are Prussians. Certain pronounced regional
sentiments have had strong effects on party politics or the problem of federalism. Moreover, the Reformation brought about a religious schism that became a pronounced cultural and regional factor, with important political
consequences. The so-called Protestant North contains strong Catholic
population centers in the northwest, whereas in the so-called Catholic South,
Protestants outnumber Catholics in Württemberg.

In part as a consequence of the factors making for her diversity, Germany
is not a full-fledged family member of Western civilization. At various periods of her history, she has been influenced deeply by the constitutional
currents of the West and the autocratic tendencies of the East. Her landed
nobility (the *Junker* class), the Army, and the higher civil service for long
times formed a ruling element, which not only imposed its standards, but
was often imitated in its ways of thinking by the middle class and even by
large segments of the working class. Many Germans were fond of considering themselves superior not only to the East, but also to what they charged
was the predominantly materialistic culture of the West. Much of German
objection to democratic practices was tied up with resistance to the impor-
tation of Western ideas. This confluence of Eastern and Western tendencies
produced very uneven results, causing eastern Germany to take on some of
the character of a civilization different from that of the remainder of the
country.

It is therefore not surprising that the question of national unity has been

---

[1] Cf. Paul Kosok, *Modern Germany* (Chicago, 1933), pp. 3 ff.; Eugen Diesel, *Germany and
the Germans* (New York, 1931), pp. 173 ff. On regional factors, see Arnold Brecht, *Federalism
and Regionalism in Germany* (New York, 1945), chap. 5.

and is one of the strongest factors in German political life. The medieval
Holy Roman Empire of the German Nation, reaching from the shores of the
Baltic and the North Sea to the Mediterranean, included all German-lan-
guage areas and many non-German territories as well. It was a loose association of independent states, principalities, and free cities, rather than a
closely knit empire. When it collapsed under the impact of Napoleon's assault, what is now considered Germany consisted of more than three hundred independent territories, all jealous and suspicious of one another.
Upon this unhappy state of disunity, modern Germans look back with a
combination of sorrow, contempt, and fear of possible recurrence.

Road toward National Unity. From this plethora of states, Prussia rose
as the predominant power. Once contemptuously known as the "sandbox
of the Holy Roman Empire" in the center of the future Germany, the small
electorate of Brandenburg became the kingdom of Prussia, developing into
one of the great powers of Europe. Through conquest, marriage, and diplomacy, it expanded its territory. Frederick William I (1713-40) had forged
the Prussian Army into a powerful weapon that he used for holding down
the centrifugal power of the landed nobility and the urban patricians, making
himself an absolute ruler. His successor, Frederick II or the Great (1740-86),
reassured Prussia's hegemony in warfare and cemented the Prussian monarchy and nobility into a close unit. With Bismarck at the helm, Prussian
aggression against Denmark (1864) and Austria (1866) led to further aggrandizement. Under his leadership, the North German Confederation,
established in 1867, became a stepping stone toward the strong federal union
of Germany that came out of the Franco-Prussian War (1870-71), including
the southern states but not Austria.

Most Germans contrast favorably this process of German unification by
"blood and iron" with the abortive attempts of liberal movements to
achieve a unified Germany. The French Revolution had sent a gust of
fresh thought into western Germany. In 1848, a new revolutionary movement spread in Germany, attempting to achieve the twofold purpose of establishing liberal constitutional government and bringing about national
unity. *Deutschland über Alles* in those days was the battlesong of the liberals against the petty princes. But when the National Assembly at Frank-
fort-on-the-Main offered the imperial crown to the King of Prussia, it was
peremptorily rejected by the monarch, who abhorred the idea of receiving
such a gift from such hands. Another King of Prussia accepted the position
of Emperor of Germany only when it was offered him by his fellow-mon-
archs after the defeat of France in 1871, under the prodding of Bismarck,
who had just succeeded in checking the liberal trend of Prussia's political
life.

A Strong National Executive. Under the imperial constitution, drafted
by Bismarck, the structure of the Reich government included the Federal
Council (*Bundesrat*) representing the member states, the Emperor (*Kaiser*)

as the chief executive together with the Reich Chancellor (*Reichskanzler*), and the Federal Parliament (*Reichstag*) representing the voters and sharing legislative functions with the Federal Council and the Emperor.[2] The role of the Emperor was unique, in that he exercised much of his great power as King of Prussia, who by constitutional provision was always the Kaiser. As Emperor, he had no power to veto federal laws, but as King of Prussia, he could go far to effect a veto through his control of the votes of Prussia in the Federal Council. As chief executive, he represented the Reich in foreign affairs and shared in the treaty-making power of the legislature. He also appointed the Reich Chancellor and the Reich officials. As Commander-in-Chief, he exercised great political and psychological influence. The Kaiser was responsible only to his conscience, but he was restricted by the fact that none of his orders were valid unless countersigned by the Chancellor. It was necessary for these two men to work hand in hand, as was the case between William I (1871-88) and Bismarck, whereas the talented but impulsive William II easily quarreled with the policy of such a strong but able Chancellor as Bismarck.

The Chancellor was the personal and exclusive choice of the monarch, to whom alone he was responsible—with neither of them subject to control by Parliament except for its budgetary powers, which served as a limiting influence. As head of the imperial administrative system, the Chancellor had under him a number of ministers appointed by him as his subordinates, solely responsible to him. Normally, he was also Prime Minister of Prussia. As Chancellor, he was the presiding officer of the Federal Council, and as Prussian Prime Minister, he controlled the policies of the predominant state in the federal union.

Exercise of the Legislative Power. The Empire had a bicameral legislature, but its upper chamber, the Federal Council, held a position of overpowering influence. Each of the twenty-five German states was allotted a certain number of votes in the Council. Even the smallest had one vote, but Prussia, with more than half the whole population, had only seventeen votes out of fifty-eight. The votes were cast as blocks by instructed state officials. The allocation of votes was arranged in such a way that either Prussia alone, or the three southern kingdoms together, or even an aggregation of smaller states could prevent an amendment to the constitution. The meetings of the Council were secret, but it largely determined the character of legislation. Most business transacted by the Council was submitted by the Chancellor or the state governments. It was a hard-working body operating through committees, preparing—as well as being the first to adopt—all legislation, including the budget. It also was empowered to issue administrative

---

[2] Cf. Herman Finer, *Theory and Practice of Modern Government* (London, 1932), I, chap. 9; F. Morstein Marx, *Government in the Third Reich* (rev. ed., New York, 1937), chap. 1. The text of the constitution is found in Walter F. Dodd, ed., *Modern Constitutions* (Chicago, 1909), I.

ordinances for the enforcement of federal laws, to share in the power of appointment, and to audit accounts. It further served as a court of final appeal in disputes between the states or between the federal government and states. Finally, it shared in the powers of treaty-making and declaration of war.

The Federal Parliament—the popular chamber—was democratic in that every male German citizen twenty-five years of age or over was able to vote or be elected a deputy. The vote was direct and secret, cast in single-member constituencies every five years, unless the Reichstag was dissolved earlier. The number of deputies remained fixed at 397, with no redistribution of electoral districts, in spite of the rapid industrialization of the country, which drew the people from agricultural areas. For that reason, the conservative rural districts were greatly overrepresented, a handicap to the Socialist and Liberal parties, whose strength lay in the urban centers. Election procedures were traditionally honest.

The Reichstag shared the lawmaking power with the Council and the Emperor. It was able to initiate bills, although the practical advantage lay with legislative proposals originating either with the Chancellor or with the Council. The Reichstag had the power to examine and pass the annual budget and similar aspects of federal fiscal policy and shared in the conclusion of treaties. Deputies enjoyed the ordinary parliamentary privileges, such as freedom of speech and freedom from arrest while attending sessions. The so-called right of interpellation served not merely to elicit information from the government on its actions and policies, but also to express parliamentary criticism of the government.

Reich-State Relations. Federal laws, as a rule, were administered by the states rather than by federal agencies. The national government administered directly only most of the postal service, the Navy, and the *Reichsbank* —with Bavaria and Württemberg running their own postal systems. Even the federal customs duties were collected by state employees, for whose services the states kept a percentage of the revenue. The Supreme Court decided important cases on final appeal and had charge of high treason under its original jurisdiction. But the states provided all the other courts, appointing the judges, district attorneys, and police officers. Even military administration was federal only in wartime. In this way, Germany avoided the problem of duplication of government functions and jurisdictional disputes in a federal structure.

Prussia occupied a position of unchallenged primacy in the Empire. Her prestige and her large size made her what President Lowell of Harvard called "a lion among half a dozen foxes and a score of mice." The close relationship between the Reich and Prussia introduced many Prussian officials and much of the traditional spirit of Prussian bureaucracy into the Reich service. Prussia's seventeen votes on the Federal Council could be used as an obstacle to federal legislation. Generally speaking, her primacy in the federal system retarded the liberal and democratic development of the country.

Under the imperial constitution, the national government exercised enumerated powers, the states being left with the residual powers. The national government had exclusive and explicit legislative power over citizenship, the Navy (and, in times of war, the Army), trade, industry, insurance, currency and banking, post and telegraph, railroads and waterways, the merchant marine, customs and other Reich revenue, patents and copyrights, the press and associations, and civil and criminal law. In the course of time, the problems of modern industrial society led to a great increase in federal legislation in these fields. Eventually, a special system of federal taxation was set up, which made the government independent of the original scheme of financial contributions furnished by the states. Federal laws were not subject to judicial review with respect to their constitutionality, but in cases of conflict automatically replaced divergent state laws.

Political Parties. Germany has never had a two-party system, but rather five or six major political parties, with a number of so-called splinter parties in addition. The Conservatives had their strongholds in the agricultural areas, particularly in the East, but were also supported by a sizable sprinkling of voters in other population groups. The Conservatives ranged from a reactionary wing to the Free Conservatives, who finally founded a small party of their own. By means of an archaic three-class voting system, the Conservatives controlled Prussia until 1918, and they strongly resisted any constitutional change toward liberalism.

The Center party was almost wholly Roman Catholic, formed for the protection of religious rights and freedom against encroachments by the state. It was a truly national party in the sense that it found the stable support of every element of the population, ranging from members of the Catholic nobility and industrial barons to workingmen in town and village. Its unique social composition kept it from being a party of either the left or the right. It was conservative on some measures, but very liberal on others—for instance, on social welfare, where it was deeply influenced by the teachings of the papal encyclicals. The party was a strong opponent of Marxian socialism, which had been condemned by the Popes as being incompatible with the Catholic faith.

The National Liberals, influenced by industrialists but enjoying a large middle-class following, stood for a program of political change. They favored abolition of the Prussian class system of voting, reapportionment of electoral districts, and restriction of the influence of the nobility in government and Army. The Progressives were related to the National Liberals both in social composition and program, but they further demanded free trade and a parliamentary system that would control the government in both the Reich and the states. By contrast, the Social Democrats began as a Marxian party, but later took a "revisionist" turn when they insisted that all their economic and social aims be accomplished by the ballot rather than by revolutionary means. Their insistence on political democracy saved Germany in 1918 from the path of communism. The Social Democrats were largely a workingmen's party, with little support from other groups, except a number of intellectuals.

Political Issues. The powerful National Liberal party supported Bismarck for almost a decade, finding him a congenial ally against the Center party.[3] By compromising with Bismarck in 1874 on the size of the Army, it succeeded in limiting the formerly exclusive control of the King over the Prussian Army. It is to the credit of the National Liberals and Bismarck that they sponsored jointly the reform legislation of the 1870's, which created economic and civic equality. When Bismarck came out in favor of protective tariffs in 1878, he lost the backing of the Liberals and gained the support of the Conservatives and the Center party. Bismarck's Anti-Socialist Act of 1878 outlawed the Social Democratic party, but the party enjoyed a continuous increase in votes and again became legal in 1890; by 1912 it was the strongest party, holding 110 Reichstag seats out of 397.

A series of laws sponsored by Bismarck were aimed at strict supervision, if not control, over the Catholic church by the state. The Protestant middle classes, which supported Bismarck, declared that they were fighting a *Kulturkampf,* or struggle for civilization. But Bismarck realized within a few years that he had made a mistake in trying to coerce the Catholic church, and he brought about the gradual abrogation of the restrictive legislation. The Catholic church came out of the struggle with greater strength and prestige. The fight accentuated the religious schism in the country, but the growth of the Center party was able to counteract concealed governmental discrimination against Catholics.

Record of the Empire. National unity under the Empire grew in a number of ways. All Germans enjoyed an equal suffrage in the Reichstag elections, as well as a uniform civil status, which brooked no discrimination against out-of-state residents. In the economic field, the constitution provided for a Reich-wide customs system, integrated railway, postal and telegraph administrations, and the consolidation of the armed forces. The codification of civil and criminal law on a national basis was a large achievement, and the Supreme Court guaranteed uniform administration of justice. Nation-wide political parties increased the national consciousness of the average German. Still, sectional individuality continued to flourish, whether it was in separate states, such as the kingdom of Bavaria or the city republic of Hamburg, or even in individual provinces of Prussia, which were by no means uniform in cultural outlook or political character.

The German constitution of 1871 had no bill of rights, but various state constitutions did. Just as important, however, to the average German was the system of administrative justice that effectively protected the citizen against arbitrary action by government officials, providing him with a pro-

---

[3] Cf. Karl Loewenstein, "Germany," in James T. Shotwell, ed., *Governments of Continental Europe* (New York, 1940), pp. 327 ff.

cedure designed to check the abuse of governmental power. The idea of lawful administration ranked high within Germany's able civil service, which could trace its traditions to the days of the Great Elector of Brandenburg and his grandson, Frederick William I of Prussia. Under the Empire, the principle of life tenure was embodied in law, as a guarantee of the administrative independence and the nonpartisan character of the public service.

One of Baron vom Stein's great reforms after Prussa's defeat by Napoleon was the Municipality Act of 1808, which provided for local self-government subject only to a reasonable measure of state supervision. Similar laws were soon passed in the other German states, so that German municipalities generally began to manage their own affairs with much freedom. The citizens were thereby initiated into the sharing of governmental responsibility long before all states had received their first constitutions.[4] Viewed in general, the German Empire developed into a prosperous country with high standards of living and with liberal social-security protection against sickness, invalidity, and old age. The German level of education was high; in many fields of research, German universities were unexcelled. Science made great contributions to public welfare and industrial progress. The lack of parliamentary control seemed of little importance when affairs went well.

Wartime Changes. When World War I broke out, the Germans rallied around the government in a common demonstration of patriotism, which included the Social Democrats, long in opposition. Wartime unity was soon disrupted by left-wing Independent Socialists. Among other parties, there developed a strong movement for an early negotiated peace, in opposition to the annexation plans favored by certain industrial and nationalist groups. In the summer of 1917, the Reichstag actually voted in favor of such a peace, but was unable to force the government into taking action. At the same time, the question of constitutional reform was receiving favorable public attention.

When the military situation was approaching disaster in the fall of 1918, the Kaiser promised to liberalize the suffrage in Prussia. He also appointed Prince Max von Baden the first head of a parliamentary government, in which Social Democrats and Liberals were represented. To the general public, the November Revolution was as sudden and unexpected as the military defeat,[5] although there had been unrest among the working classes in the latter part of the war, as well as political strikes and revolutionary propaganda, especially after the Russian Revolution of 1917. There was also much suffering as a result of the poor food situation. When the sailors of the Grand Fleet mutinied at the end of October 1918, their action proved

---

[4] Cf. Roger H. Wells, *German Cities* (Princeton, 1932); F. Morstein Marx, "Civil Service in Germany," in Leonard D. White and Others, *Civil Service Abroad: Great Britain, Canada, France, Germany* (New York, 1935), pp. 161 ff.; and Morstein Marx, "Germany," in William Anderson, ed., *Local Government in Europe* (New York, 1939).

[5] Ralph H. Lutz, *Causes of the German Collapse* (Palo Alto, 1934).

contagious. The Emperor abdicated and sought security in Holland. The Social Democratic leader Friedrich Ebert formed a provisional republican government.

2. Advent of the Republic

Ascendancy of the Social Democrats. Ebert's government was composed of three Social Democrats and three left-wing Independent Socialists. The new government called itself a people's council, as a concession to the Independent Socialists and the revolutionary councils of workers and soldiers. But under the unwavering leadership of Ebert, a one-time saddlemaker, Germany escaped Communist domination and instead was directed into the channels of a parliamentary democracy. In January 1919, elections were held for a constituent assembly.

Ebert induced the civil servants to continue in office for the sake of law and order, and he secured similar cooperation from the high command of the Army. The demobilization of millions of soldiers was accomplished with relatively little disorder. The government obtained cooperation between the trade unions and the industrialists in speedy resumption of production.

Revolutionary and Counterrevolutionary Movements. The left-wing Socialists and Communists were horrified as they felt their hold on the government weakening. They sought direct action. To meet such action, the government appointed a Social Democratic leader, Gustav Noske, commander-in-chief of the loyal troops. He asked for additional volunteers, who formed the so-called free corps. In the course of time, most of these became the core of counterrevolutionary movements. During the spring of 1919, Communist revolts were crushed by government troops and free corps in Hamburg, Bremen, and Leipzig, in the Ruhr, and in central Germany.

Soon the councils of workers and soldiers were only shadows of their former revolutionary power. A revolt in Bavaria had been able to attain temporary success by declaring a Soviet Republic, but the Reich government sent in volunteers who freed Munich from the Communist regime. Bavaria thereafter became the strongest source of reactionary movements and finally the birthplace of nazism.

In 1920, a nationalist *putsch* was attempted against the Reich under the leadership of Herr von Kapp, a former government official. A combination of regular troops and free corps actually took control of Berlin, but were defeated in three days' time by a general strike called by the government. Various members and units of the free corps committed acts of murderous brutality without precedent in German history. That nationalism and political partisanship should take on such criminal forms in a country known for its obedience to law was indicative of a profoundly unsettled state that bode ill for the future.

The Complexion of the Constituent Assembly. Considering the general conditions, it was remarkable that the elections of January 1919 were held without disturbances. More than 30 million people went to the polls—83 per cent of the eligible voters. Only 2,300,000 voted for the revolutionary Independent Socialists, against 11,500,000 for the moderate Social Democrats. Fully 16 million voters expressed a non-Socialist preference, electing 89 deputies of the Center party, 74 Democrats, 42 Nationalists, and 22 deputies of the People's party. Four small parties divided among them 9 additional seats. Women voted for the first time, with the voting age for both sexes lowered from twenty-five to twenty years. In this as in later elections, women as a whole tended to express preference for parties that stressed patriotic and religious appeals rather than for the parties toward the left to whose insistence they owed the right to vote.

The constituent assembly met in Weimar, the city of Goethe and Schiller, to avoid the mass pressure and the Prussian atmosphere of the capital city. The assembly included a large number of workers who had long been active in the trade-union movement, as well as many writers and journalists, a fair sprinkling of university professors, and relatively few jurists.

Spirit of the New Constitution. Within a few days, the assembly adopted a law that made the provisional government responsible to the assembly. After electing Ebert the first President of the new Republic, the assembly proceeded to its main task of adopting a constitution, under the intellectual leadership of Hugo Preuss, a leading liberal professor of constitutional law. After a few months of efficient committee work and much public discussion, it was adopted August 11, 1919. The new constitution drew heavily on Western political experience, adopting features of the American, Swiss, and French systems of government. It was a remarkable document: in its first and institutional part an example of precise and realistic drafting, whereas the second part, the bill of rights, was an ineffectual compromise of liberal and socialistic ideas.

The document was of extraordinary length, partly because it dealt with the complicated relationships between the Reich and the state governments, partly because the parties of the left insisted on the inclusion of many novel economic as well as political provisions. Characteristically, many matters were referred to as being subject to future legislation, and many individual rights were granted subject to possible modification by law. Fully forty-two articles were devoted to the "fundamental rights and duties of Germans." In common with other European postwar constitutions, much was said on socialization, the status of labor, and plans for economic councils. Private property was guaranteed, subject to socially desirable use. Actually, little was done later along anticapitalistic lines, and few if any decisive changes were made in the basic economic life.

3. The Constitutional System

Status of the President. Any German citizen thirty-five years of age could be elected for a seven-year term, with the possibility of re-election.[6] A majority of the votes cast was required. If a runoff election was necessary, a plurality of votes was sufficient. A unique feature of the runoff election was that it was not limited to the two highest candidates, but was open even to newcomers. The constitution provided for a possible recall before the expiration of the term by popular vote, upon the request of two thirds of the Reichstag. Since the President was elected directly by the people, he was expected to have a corresponding prestige that would serve as a stabilizing element in the midst of political strife. But exercise of the powers of the President required countersignature by the Reich Chancellor or a minister. In that way, the Chancellor became responsible to the Reichstag for the actions of the President.

Friedrich Ebert, who with his political friends had guarded Germany from communism, did not serve long as the first President. After his early death, Marshal Paul von Hindenburg was elected in the runoff election of April 1925. He was re-elected in 1932, again only upon the second try, with Hitler trailing him by a wide margin. Ebert had been both able and well versed in party politics, to which Hindenburg was a stranger. The aged soldier had been Germany's most popular wartime army leader, and many Germans were grateful to him when he succeeded in orderly demobilization through the force of personality and prestige. In spite of his monarchical convictions, he sought to be loyal to his oath and to the Republic, but with increasing age fell a victim to the intrigues of false friends who played into the hands of reaction and nazism.

Regular and Emergency Powers. Aside from representing the Reich internationally, the President was also Commander-in-Chief of the armed forces, subject to parliamentary control. He had the power to appoint and dismiss the Reich Chancellor and, on his advice, the members of the Cabinet. No single German party ever held a majority in the Reichstag, so it was necessary for Cabinets to be backed by coalitions. Since coalitions would not always be formed by the same parties, it was possible for both Ebert and Hindenburg to exercise considerable choice in the selection of a Chancellor and thereby exercise much influence on government policies.

The President, further, had the important power of dissolving the Reichs-

---

[6] On this section, see Finer, *op. cit.* above, note 2; Frederick F. Blachly and Miriam E. Oatman, *The Government and Administration of Germany* (Baltimore, 1928), which contains the text of the Weimar constitution; Rupert Emerson, *State and Sovereignty in Modern Germany* (London, 1928); Arnold J. Zurcher, *The Experiment with Democracy in Central Europe* (New York, 1933); Harlow J. Heneman, *The Growth of the Executive Power in Germany: A Study of the German Presidency* (Minneapolis, 1934). For a review of various problems encountered by the German government from the beginning to the end of the Republic, see Arnold Brecht, *Prelude to Silence: The End of the German Republic* (New York, 1944).

tag under two conditions. Normally, it could be dissolved in order to give the voters a chance to express their opinion on government policies. If their verdict was negative, the government had to resign. It was also possible for the President to compel the resignation of the Cabinet and decree the dissolution of the Reichstag if he believed that Parliament, although still giving its confidence to the Cabinet, no longer represented the popular majority. This power made it possible for him under exceptional circumstances to dismiss a Chancellor whom he disliked and to appoint in his place a man of his personal preference, in spite of the fact that the dismissed Chancellor still enjoyed parliamentary support. Hindenburg used this power in 1932 to fire Brüning and install von Papen and von Schleicher.

Under article 48 of the constitution, the Reich government was empowered to take any steps necessary to meet emergencies by emergency decree, affecting even fundamental constitutional guarantees of civil rights. After 1930, the gravity of the domestic situation caused the emergency powers to be interpreted so broadly as to furnish the basis for a "constitutional dictatorship." Now article 48 was used to put into effect government policies dealing with finances, labor situations, or even changes in civil and criminal law, which the Reichstag failed to adopt as ordinary legislation. This article further provided that measures taken under it should be limited to the actual emergency period, but that proviso came to mean little with the emergency dragging on. The Reichstag had the constitutional power to demand a repeal of emergency decrees, even in opposition to the Cabinet and the President. It was incapable, however, of exercising this power effectively, as it was no more able to unite on revoking emergency decrees than it was capable of forming workable coalition majorities. The situation became so serious that in 1932 more than ten times as many emergency decrees were issued by the President, at the request of the Chancellor, as laws were passed by the Reichstag.

Chancellor and Cabinet. The Chancellor and the ministers constituted the Cabinet. The Chancellor was its head and had the power and duty to "determine the principal lines of policy" for which he was responsible to the Reichstag, as article 56 put it. Although bound to follow the policies laid down by the Chancellor, the ministers were not his subordinates as they had been under Bismarck. When voting on Cabinet resolutions, each minister had one vote, and the majority decided. When governments were formed, the parties would lay claim to a number of Cabinet posts corresponding to their parliamentary strength, and often to specific ministries of importance. Selecting Cabinet members therefore became a process of balancing the demands of parties for representation, leaving but little individual choice to the Chancellor.

The number of Cabinet members varied, but did not exceed a dozen. In most cases, they were members of the Reichstag, but some were outside specialists. All were responsible to the Reichstag for the administration of their departments, and all needed its confidence. Government under the Weimar Republic was therefore of the parliamentary type, but it was gradually qualified by a tendency for the Chancellor also to be in need of the confidence of the President. In times of deep internal disagreement and violent party strife, this tendency resulted in deadlock, with consequences fatal to the democratic system of government.

At the first election under the Weimar Republic, the Social Democrats polled 45 per cent of the votes; at the last election the Nazis had 44 per cent. The multiplicity of parties in Germany always necessitated a combination of several of them to support a Cabinet. The composition of coalitions differed. The Center party belonged to every one of them, the Democrats participated in thirteen, the People's party in eleven, the Social Democrats in nine, and the Nationalists in only three. Prior to the period of emergency decrees at the turn of the twenties, German government was based on a combination of the more or less liberal bourgeoisie, which until 1923 was joined by the Social Democrats; between 1924 and 1930, it was joined three times by the Nationalists and only once by the former. At times, the Chancellor was agreed upon in advance by the coalition parties, and his name would merely be ratified by the President. More often, the President would choose his candidate for Chancellor, in the hope that he would prove acceptable to prospective coalition parties.

Relations with the Länder. The powers of the Reich were much larger under the Weimar Republic than before.[7] They included exclusive legislative authority over foreign affairs, citizenship, national defense, currency, customs, immigration and emigration, and postal, telegraph, and telephone communications. In addition, the Reich had unrestricted power to legislate on civil rights, civil and criminal law, public health, trade and industry, railways, and other matters. On these subjects, the states—now known as *Länder,* to indicate their lesser status—were free to legislate only when the Reich did not; Reich legislation overrode state laws. The Reich also had additional powers of taxation, subject only to the requirement of due consideration of the financial situation of the Länder as a result of revenue losses. Of great importance was the additional power of the Reich to establish "fundamental principles" on taxation, education, religious affairs, and other subjects for the guidance of the states.

Aside from setting up its own administration in the fields of federal taxation and railroads, the Reich continued the old system of using the governmental machinery of the Länder for administering national laws, subject to its control and supervision. Disputes between state and federal authorities were submitted to the new Constitutional Court, whose decisions were enforceable by the national government through financial sanctions or even through armed force. The constitution provided for judicial review of state

---

[7] Cf. Brecht, *op. cit.* above, note 1, chaps. 3, 7, 8-13.

laws. The Supreme Court assumed a similar right in regard to the constitutionality of national laws as early as 1925.[8]

The Länder were not secure in their territorial size or even existence, since
state boundaries could be changed by constitutional amendment. In 1920,
a new Land, Thuringia, was established through the consolidation of several
small states. Other small states went out of existence by joining other
Länder, so that the total was finally reduced to seventeen. Under the constitution, the states were compelled to have a republican constitution and a
parliamentary form of government. Most of them had unicameral legislatures and no state president.

Politics and the Civil Service. The Empire's efficient civil service was
taken over intact by the Weimar Republic, which tried to instill into it a
democratic spirit. It was made possible for the ablest lower-grade officials
to advance to the high positions formerly restricted to candidates with advanced university education and an extended period of unsalaried probationary service. The constitution declared the civil service open to all citizens "without distinction," according to their capabilities and achievements.

Participation in strikes or revolutionary movements was forbidden. On
the other hand, the established service rights to life appointment, salary, and
pension were protected by the constitution. But when after 1924 salaries
were cut and government employees were dismissed or pensioned against
their will, the loyalty of civil servants to the new regime suffered.

Civil servants were given the constitutional freedom of political self-expression (except along extremist lines) and great leeway in active party
work. They were even granted leaves of absence from their duties to serve
as members of the Reichstag or in other legislative bodies. Necessarily, the
civil service was thus affected by party politics.

Structure and Procedure of the Reichstag. Participation in voting had
always been high in Germany. In spite of the political impotence of the
Reichstag under the Empire, from 60 to 85 per cent of the eligible voters had
participated in its election. Under the Weimar Republic, participation
hovered around 75 to 84 per cent. Voters absent from home on election
day were able to vote anywhere within the country with the help of a special
election certificate.

Reichstag membership included few lawyers but many government officials and representatives of agriculture, industry, and commerce—often employees of their respective trade organizations. A good many deputies were
journalists or free-lance authors. Many more were trade-union officials. A
large percentage of the membership had seen service in the old Reichstag,
which had not provided them with a real apprenticeship in political responsibility. Many had received good civic training in local self-governing

---

[8] Cf. Johannes Mattern, *Principles of Constitutional Jurisprudence of the German National
Republic* (Baltimore, 1928), pp. 570 ff.; Carl J. Friedrich, "The Issue of Judicial Review in Germany," *Political Science Quarterly*, 43 (1928), 188 ff.

authorities. Although the constitution provided that each member should be "subject to his own conscience" and not be bound by instructions, the rule of the caucus dominated the votes. Too many Reichstag members were older men, except in the Communist and Nazi parties.

So-called "minor questions" and more important interpellations provided vehicles for criticism of the government. These had to be in writing and signed by at least fifteen and thirty members, respectively. The government's answer to questions could not be debated, and replies to interpellations could be debated only if fifty members demanded it. They were not occasions for votes of nonconfidence. For most of its work, the Reichstag relied on committees. The constitution provided for two special committees. One, on foreign relations, functioned between sessions and even between parliaments, as a restraint on secret diplomacy. The other had the task of safeguarding the rights of the Reichstag when it was not in session or actually dissolved. On committees a party was represented in proportion to its numerical strength. The most important chairmanships went to the largest, others to the second largest party, and so on, providing some chairmanship even for the small parties. At the demand of one fifth of the Reichstag membership, special committees could be set up to undertake inquiries into legislative or other problems, such as the war-guilt question. Civil service experts aided the committee deliberations. As in other parliaments, committee consideration of bills was usually much more important than debate on the floor of the house.

Functions of the Reichsrat. The *Reichsrat,* or National Council, was composed of appointed representatives of the Länder, each of which possessed at least one vote and an additional one for every 700,000 of its population. As an intentional check on Prussia's preponderance, no state was allowed more than two fifths of the total vote. The Reichsrat was very influential through its informed scrutiny of Reichstag bills, over which it had a suspensive veto that could be overridden only by a two-thirds majority of the Reichstag or a popular referendum. Such scrutiny resulted in many compromises through mutual concessions.

The Reichsrat, too, could question Cabinet members on their administrative actions; but as it usually worked closely with the government, it did not constitute a federal check on the Cabinet's power. Differences with any Land were usually composed in conferences between Reich ministers and prime ministers of the Länder. The Reichsrat also had a part in framing ordinances relating to the administration of Reich affairs by the state governments. Reichsrat delegates were usually permanent officials whose positions were not affected by changes in Cabinet coalitions. They were experienced in dealing with complex problems, doing their work both in public meetings and through standing committees.

Judicial Independence. The various courts[9] were maintained by the Län-

[9] See R. C. K. Ensor, *Courts and Judges in France, Germany and England* (London, 1933).

der on a uniform basis determined by national law, which also prescribed their powers and procedure. The Supreme Court in Leipzig was the one federal court, as well as the highest court of appeal. It was divided into seven civil and five criminal chambers, each sitting with a prescribed number of judges. Its total membership was ninety-one judges. All other judges were appointed by the state governments.

The independence of the courts and judges was guaranteed by the constitution, under both the monarchy and the republic. It was fully respected in practice. The judges had life tenure and could be removed only by court decisions. Their professional preparation included three years of practical probationary training in various courts and offices of prosecuting attorneys after graduation from the standard university study of law, jurisprudence, and related fields of knowledge.

Like other Continental countries, especially France, Germany provided independent administrative courts for adjudging private grievances caused by administrative acts. Their setup differed in particulars from state to state. They were supplemented by courts specializing in certain types of cases, such as patents or war injuries. A long-standing demand for establishment of an organizationally unified system of administrative courts was never fulfilled, although the constitution had promised the creation of one single Reich supreme administrative court.

4. Contest of Political Forces

Parties of the Right. The German National People's party was the successor of the old Conservative party and related groups. Like its predecessor, it represented primarily agricultural interests and drew support and leadership from the landed estates of eastern Germany. Its devotion to the monarchy and outspoken hostility to socialism attracted many followers among army officers, old-time civil servants, and well-to-do businessmen, as well as the middle classes in general, which were afraid of the rising swell of socialism. The party also appealed strongly to religiously inclined Protestants. It even included antisocialist trade unionists. It favored protective tariffs, especially for agriculture; stronger national defense; revision of the peace treaty of Versailles; and opposition to the League of Nations. In the middle twenties, the party participated in several coalition governments, but under the reactionary leadership of Alfred Hugenberg, a big industrialist and owner of a large chain of newspapers, it came to stress its stand against the Weimar Republic. The Nationalists increased their parliamentary strength from 42 seats in 1919 to 111 in 1924; they later split into several groups with a total membership of only 81.

The German People's party stemmed from the conservative wing of the old National Liberal party. Under marked influence of business and industry, it favored a gradual decrease of wartime economic controls and a strengthening of governmental centralization, opposing clerical claims in the field of education. Originally monarchical, it turned more and more republican, and was represented in all Reich Cabinets between 1923 and 1930. In the field of foreign affairs, it favored German membership in the League of Nations, while insisting on a peaceful revision of the Treaty of Versailles—as did the Center party and the Democrats. After its leader Gustav Stresemann died in 1930, it lost much of its parliamentary strength.

Parties of the Middle. The Center party had grown strong in resisting the anti-Catholic policies of Bismarck. Aside from its religious interests, it remained a heterogeneous but stable group of voters from poor to rich, peasant to landed nobility, and laborer to industrialist, with an admixture of Catholic clergy. A truly national party, it did not favor any one class or region. Together with the Social Democrats and Democrats, it molded the character of the republican constitution, often through compromises. It was represented in every Cabinet prior to Hitler and furnished more than half of the Chancellors.

As it tended to favor centralizing measures, its Bavarian followers separated and formed the Bavarian People's party, stressing states' rights and favoring more conservative policies, but agreeing with the Center party in regard to religious education, social justice, government aid to agriculture, and foreign affairs. Eventually, the Center party turned strongly against the Social Democrats, to whom it had been politically close in the earlier years of the Republic.

The Democratic party attracted the left wing of the old National Liberal party under able intellectual leadership. With seventy-five seats in the constituent assembly, it began as the third strongest party, with the apparent prospect of becoming the great nonsocialist republican party of the future. But its hopes were dashed as early as 1920, when it lost more than a third of its seats. Under the influence of big-scale finance and commerce, the party became increasingly hostile toward the Social Democrats. Being essentially moderate and progressive in its aims, it suffered from the growing tendency of voters to turn to the left or right. Its ultimate demise and rebirth as the State party with a more conservative program failed to give it new life.

Parties of the Left. The Social Democratic party was the party of workers and employees, together with other large sections of the lower middle class. Its reformist group had such leaders as Otto Braun, for fourteen years Prime Minister of Prussia. Its left wing included a number of former Independents, closely tied up with labor unions, while in between there was a group that was more suspicious of the bourgeoisie than were the friends of Braun. Up to nearly the end of the Weimar Republic, when Hitler's Nazis seized the lead from the Social Democratic party, this party was the largest, with almost a million dues-paying members and a solid following among the majority of 8 million workers organized in socialist trade unions.

It exerted great influence on the making of the constitution and was the first to seize the presidency. Whereas it participated in a number of coalitions and furnished the Chancellor for a number of years, it was strongest in Prussia, where it had a chance to show its political and administrative mettle. Although it ceased to be a mere class party, the bulk of its parliamentary representatives were trade-union officials, party functionaries, or journalists working for the extensive press of the party and trade unions. It was strongly opposed to communism and outright in its stand for democratic government. It favored centralization and advanced social legislation, without stressing socialization as much as might be expected. It resisted militarism and ecclesiastical control over education. Internationally, it urged revision of the Treaty of Versailles; it supported the League of Nations and disarmament.

The Marxist revolutionary elements of 1918 merged into the Communist party. It was as hostile to the Social Democrats, whom it accused of treason against the working class, as it was to capitalism and democratic government. It took orders from Moscow and profited greatly by the economic distress of the depression years, until in November 1932 it polled 6 million votes and elected 100 deputies to the Reichstag. It opposed the peace treaty as capitalistic imperialism and praised the aims and achievements of the Soviet Union. The Communists did not hesitate to help the Nazis kill German democracy, in the optimistic belief that Nazi power would be temporary, lead to chaos, and prepare the way for a Communist regime. As millions finally voted the Communist ticket, the fear of Moscow was a prompting factor to drive other millions into the arms of the Nazis. Hitler's National Socialist party, with its very small beginnings, grew to be at last the strongest single party under the Republic.

Party Organization and Methods. Parties were thoroughly organized and strictly disciplined, with definite programs binding upon individual members as well as upon the national organization, the deputies in Parliament, and the members in the Cabinet. In this respect, German parties differed from those in most western European countries, where political individualism plays a greater role. Great political personalities were rare in Germany and when found had greater difficulty opposing the party machine. Parties were organized not only vertically—on a national, state, district, and local basis, reaching down into villages—but also horizontally, providing special representation for organized groups of women, youth, and the like.

All parties were continuously active, issuing propaganda and holding meetings of party members and followers, especially during electoral campaigns. Each party owned or controlled its own daily press—the Center party, for instance, could count on the support of some three hundred Catholic dailies. The press organs of the socialist and Christian trade unions tended to support the Social Democrats and the Center party, respectively. Every major party issued special periodicals addressed to its main supporters —whether women, university students, youth, farmers, or workers—not to speak of pamphlets, posters, and even books. Party activities were financed by membership dues, especially in the case of the left and the Nazis, and campaign contributions by friends of the party or special interests, with no legal limit to either contributions or campaign expenditures.[10] Candidates were selected by the party, which used this power to reward loyalty, to discipline or punish insurgence, and to attract the financial and propagandistic support of large organizations, whose representatives often received preferential places on the ticket.

Elections were hotly contested affairs, limited to a few weeks of intense effort. Numerous meetings were held, open to all. Opponents of the party as well as followers were permitted freedom of discussion following the main speech. Heckling was not uncommon. The frequency of calls to the polls —eight national elections in thirteen years—tended to wear out the voters. The results too often were inconclusive, necessitating, for instance, dissolutions of the Reichstag and new elections at an early date. Both in 1924 and 1932, two national elections were held in the same year.

Proportional Representation. Elections were held on the list system of proportional representation, which at Weimar in 1919 was considered by many the last word in democratic government.[11] Under the German system, the country was divided into thirty-five electoral districts, averaging about 1,700,000 inhabitants. Candidates stood for election not as individuals, but rather as names on a party list. For every fixed number of votes cast for a party in a district, one deputy of that party was elected, from the top of its list down. Votes of less than the fixed number were not lost, but could be utilized in one of two optional ways. A party could put up a "union list" for two or three electoral districts and use the leftover votes of each district for the election of one or more candidates on the "union list." Or the leftover votes from all electoral districts could be turned into a national pool for the same purpose.

The voter had no choice but to vote a straight ticket. He had no influence on the selection of candidates, who were picked by the party machine or forced upon it by special interests. Because of the large size of the districts, the candidates had little direct contact with their voters. When a deputy died or resigned, the candidate next on the list automatically moved in. But the list system made it possible to elect candidates who were desirable because of their personal or expert qualifications, regardless of any lack of vote-getting ability. It also resulted in the election of a much larger number of women than is found in the legislatures of Great Britain or the United States, where party organizations hesitate to entrust the fate of single-member dis-

---

[10] See James K. Pollock, *Money and Politics Abroad* (New York, 1932), chaps. 12-16, and also Pollock's *German Election Administration* (New York, 1934); Harold F. Gosnell, *Why Europe Votes* (Chicago, 1930); John Brown Mason, "How German Catholics Vote," *Commonweal*, Oct. 8, 1930.

[11] See Ferdinand A. Hermens, *Democracy or Anarchy? A Study of Proportional Representation* (Notre Dame, 1941).

tricts to women candidates. On the other hand, the list system also made possible the election of many who were merely pushed by special interests. The most serious harm was done by allowing the mathematically democratic representation of relatively small clusters of voters anywhere to undermine the stability of the government by encouraging the existence of a great many parties.

State within a State: The Army. The Treaty of Versailles forced Germany to have an army of not more than 100,000 officers and men.[12] In order to prevent a repetition of the device that Prussia had used against Napoleon in her hour of defeat, German soldiers were not allowed to be discharged after short periods of training, but had to serve for twelve years. This requirement made them professionals and set them aside from the population. Few workers enlisted, since the leftist element was antimilitarist and even pacifist. While great efforts were made by the early army command, especially its able organizer, General von Seeckt, to overcome hostility to the Republic by stressing loyalty to state and country, many officers found it hard to warm up to the new political institutions. The Army abhorred the peace treaty, which cut German strength to an extreme—with Poland having an army several times as large as Germany's.

Recruits were chosen on the basis of intelligence tests and qualities of potential leadership; they were trained in effect for future service as commissioned officers. The Army and Navy also engaged to some degree in concealed rearmament. Both managed to keep secret some of their activities and to hold off any parliamentary investigation. The Army considered the political left treasonable when it refused credits for the new "pocket" battleship that Germany was permitted to build under the Treaty of Versailles. The parties of the right, and later on the Nazis, strongly favored the largest possible expenditures for the armed forces—a fact that was bound to attract favorable notice among generals and admirals.

Death of the Republic. It was the tragedy of German democracy that it was not the fruit of slow growth over centuries, but the result of defeat. The young Republic became associated in the public mind with Germany's downfall. Having been born prematurely of exhaustion and revolution and reared in privation, it did not achieve normal strength. Meanwhile, the political and military forces responsible for the disaster of 1918 were allowed to withdraw into the background instead of being forced to accept their full responsibility.[13]

Germany's historic lack of nation-wide democratic experience was a serious handicap, while doctrinaire attitudes and constitutional deadlocks prepared the way for the death of the Republic. Allied statesmen denied the Republic adjustments in the field of foreign relations that Hitler later easily secured unresisted by force.

---

[12] See Herbert Rosinski, *The German Army* (London, 1939).

[13] Cf. Sigmund Neumann, *The Future in Perspective* (New York, 1946), pp. 91 ff.

CHAPTER 17

THE HITLER NIGHTMARE AND POSTWAR RECONSTRUCTION

1. The Rise of Totalitarianism

Hitler: Man and Movement. Few names in modern times have been cursed by so many as has Hitler's. His early life was characterized by frustration. A strong nationalist since his school days, he was born outside the Reich, in the Hapsburg monarchy that included more Slavs than Germans. As a would-be artist he was a failure; dire poverty haunted his early manhood. The outbreak of World War I found him in Munich, and the thrill of German unity in those days was one of the first great joys of his life. As a volunteer in the German Army, he was decorated for bravery. At the end of the war he was in a military hospital, disabled by poison gas, but he suffered more from German defeat and humiliation than from his own pains.

Amid the unsettled political atmosphere of postwar Munich, he found early contact with men of similarly violent nationalistic and antidemocratic convictions. Rising to leadership through his magnetic appeal as an orator, he built a large movement. When his National Socialist party first attempted a grab for power in the unsuccessful *putsch* of November 1923, it was badly defeated, and Hitler himself was imprisoned in a fortress. Although his movement was crushed and outlawed, he never lost his fanatical belief in its final success and in himself as its leader, or *Führer*.[1] While locked up, he had leisure to dictate to his devoted follower, Rudolf Hess, the long and cumbrous pages of *Mein Kampf,* which after his release became the bible of his revived movement. Hitler not only was a full-fledged demagogue, but also was both a genius and a victim of political intuition, one who knew the weakness and strength of the German character and proceeded to exploit both.

The growth of the National Socialist party was not rapid or even in its early years, but over a decade it was phenomenal. Following Hitler's example, it laid much stress on oratory, hammering into public consciousness slogans and principles that, through constant repetition, became pillars of belief in a world of uncertainty. Like other parties, nazism made promises to all, unmindful of contradictions and impossibilities. But where other

[1] See Konrad Heiden, *Der Führer* (Boston, 1944); Rudolf Olden, *Hitler* (New York, 1936); Frederic L. Schuman, *The Nazi Dictatorship* (rev. ed., New York, 1936); Hans Gerth, "The Nazi Party: Its Leadership and Composition," *American Journal of Sociology,* 40 (1940), 517 ff.; John Brown Mason, "The Judicial System of the Nazi Party," *American Political Science Review,* 38 (1944), 96 ff.

parties appealed primarily to desires for gain, Hitler also asked unhesitatingly for sacrifices in the name of patriotism, in this way attracting idealists to the movement. Oratory was supported by an extensive organization that reached the voters throughout the Reich. In contrast to the generally austere Republic, which provided little colorful display, the Nazis used pageantry with flags, martial music, uniforms, and parades, all so dear to Germans. Resort to violence became increasingly frequent. It was coupled with strong appeals to popular prejudices and common fears, especially toward Marxism and the Jews, and with appeals to national pride. In spite of their scorn of democracy, the Nazis—like the Communists—used the ballot in order to achieve power in a "legal" manner so as to win all the Germans accustomed to law and order.

Retention of Power. Hitler managed to retain his hold by a combination of force and persuasion. Knowing the importance of an oath in the German mind, he assured himself of the continued backing of the Army by having each officer and man swear an oath of loyalty to the person of the Führer. He used the same method with the civil service. He also employed his own cohorts to the fullest. During the early years of his struggle, Hitler had built up a private party army, known as the SA (*Sturmabteilung*). These brownshirted shock troops had first been used to howl and beat down public meetings of the opposition, especially of the Communists and Social Democrats and to "protect" Nazi meetings. The growing influence of the SA and its rapidly increasing numbers were balanced by the SS (*Schutzstaffel*) under the command of Heinrich Himmler. The black-uniformed SS elite guards were used not only against opponents of nazism, but also, if need be, with great violence against the SA. For instance, during the purge of 1934, Hitler ordered the execution without trial of Brownshirt leaders like Captain Röhm, whom he now feared. The ordinary role of the SS was to ferret out and destroy all opposition. For that purpose, it was closely tied up with the *Gestapo,* or secret police, which arrested suspected opponents at its wholly free discretion and placed them in concentration camps. In addition, all but Nazi organizations were suppressed or subjected to a process of "coordination" (*Gleichschaltung*).

The Nazi party itself was held in check by an elaborate system of party courts that were to be the "iron clasps of the movement which hold together the proud structure of the party," in the words of the Chief Party Justice. They had the double task of adjusting differences and friction among party members and party leaders and of preserving the prestige of the movement by punishing members who had committed crimes, failed in their obligations to the party, or otherwise become a liability. Party judges were outside the law and "bound only by their National Socialist conscience," considering Hitler's word their supreme law. Their most severe sentence was expulsion from the party, which had grave consequences. The SA and SS had similar courts of their own.

Nazi methods of persuasion were not limited to speech-making, but permeated press, movies, radio, and schools.[2] Newspapers and periodicals with well-established reputations were forced to publish camouflaged Nazi propaganda. In that way, publications of a religious, artistic, or professional character influenced the minds of those who were suspicious of authentic Nazi writings.

Articles of Faith. The Nazis held that the nation was a "community of blood," *ipso facto* excluding all "non-German"—that is, Jewish—elements. Much stress was put on the dogma of the inequality of individuals, nations, and races. Racial intolerance was a logical outgrowth of the belief in racial superiority, and "Aryans" were considered superior to all others. Germany was assigned a role of overlordship, and among the Germans themselves a Nazi elite was destined to lead and rule. The "leadership principle" reached its natural peak in the Führer, who was responsible to no one and destined to lead his people to national glory. So-called bloodless intellect and reason were rejected in favor of "feeling with your blood," a process of rationalizing one's prejudices. "National vitality" was to guide the people to growth and inevitable territorial expansion.

International law was soon decried, since it was a block in the way of Nazi expansionist aims. Violence and injustice were considered justifiable in both domestic and foreign affairs if they led to the defeat of opponents of party and state and to the aggrandizement of the Third Reich.

Structure and Task of the Nazi Party. The Nazi party dominated public and private life in every respect.[3] According to Hitler's pronouncement at the party convention in 1935, the party represented "the political attitude, the political conscience, and the political will of Germany." It covered the nation with a close network of regions (*Gaue*), districts, local groups, and cells, down to the city bloc. The head of each party organization acted as the watchdog in his area of responsibility, observing the party members and ordinary citizens. Periodically, these agents conducted an opinion poll, which kept the leadership informed of popular reactions. The organization also promoted and enforced attendance at party rallies and parades, and collected money for its vast expenditures. Party leaders were appointed to high administrative positions in the government service, thereby insuring Nazi control of all of its branches. The influence of the party was also exerted through its domination of affiliated organizations, mostly professional or functional associations of teachers, lawyers, judges, and the like.

Through its system of "total penetration" the party controlled and super-

---

[2] Cf. William Ebenstein, *The Nazi State* (New York, 1943), chap. 6; F. Morstein Marx, *Government in the Third Reich* (rev. ed., New York, 1937), pp. 92 ff.

[3] See Ebenstein, *op. cit.* above, note 2, chap. 4; James K. Pollock, *The Government of Greater Germany* (New York, 1940), pp. 53 ff.; Karl Loewenstein, "Germany," in James T. Shotwell, ed., *Governments of Continental Europe* (New York, 1940), chap. 26; James K. Pollock and Harlow J. Heneman, *The Hitler Decrees* (Ann Arbor, 1934).

vised practically everyone. The purpose was to get a spiritual grip on each citizen, not merely to make him afraid of opposing nazism, but preferably to mold him into a fanatical follower of the Führer, one who would obey blindly and accept none but official reasoning. The Nazi party had the job of dominating, supervising, and controlling everyone, and also of indoctrinating all with Nazi ideology.

Demise of Democratic Government. The amazing advent of the Nazis to power is best understood on review of the two years of parliamentary sterility and confusion that preceded it. When Dr. Heinrich Brüning of the Center party undertook to form a Cabinet in 1930 without majority backing, he began to fight the rapidly deteriorating conditions by use of the power of emergency decree. Beginning with stringent and unpopular financial measures, he issued almost a hundred of these decrees in two years' time, acquiesced in by the Reichstag only because its internal division made it impossible for it to pass legislation of its own. In 1932, it actually adopted only five laws, contrasting with five dozen decrees issued that year.

The entire period was characterized by tension and uncertainty. In September 1930, elections indicated a rapidly growing radicalism. Bolstered by the economic depression, the Nazis experienced a spectacular increase in the popular vote, winning 107 seats in the Reichstag, against their former 12. The Communist vote had also increased heavily. In 1932, just as conditions showed some improvement, the oncoming presidential elections threw the country into a turmoil. Hindenburg—now deserted by the Nationalists and supported by his former opponents, the Social Democratic and Center parties—won the runoff against the votes scored by Hitler and a Communist.

Even though the Chancellor had just obtained a vote of confidence in the Reichstag by a small margin, Hindenburg was induced by the intriguer Franz von Papen to force Brüning's resignation over a proposal for land reform in East Prussia, which was long overdue but fiercely resisted by the Junker element. The new Cabinet was headed by von Papen, who staged a *coup d'état* in Prussia by forcing the Social Democrats out of ministerial office. With organized labor weak because of the depression and with leadership dispersed, all democratic forces lay low, letting power slip from their hands. Yet, despite two successive dissolutions of the Reichstag, the government found no parliamentary foundation. Hindenburg had to accept von Papen's resignation. There was some hope that the new Chancellor, General von Schleicher, with his contacts with organized labor and strong Army support, might save the country, but he too fell victim to the game of intrigues and the opposition of Hindenburg's reactionary friends.

Hitler's Entry upon the Chancellorship. On January 30, 1933, Adolf Hitler was appointed Reich Chancellor. Once more the Reichstag was dissolved and elections set for March 5. The new government openly abetted violence by its followers. Shortly before election day, a sudden fire in the

Reichstag provided the occasion for a sweeping decree directed especially against the parties of the left. The Germans were told that the fire was part of a Communist plot. In an atmosphere of dread and oppression, they went to the polls. Even under these adverse conditions for free political expression, the Nazis polled only 44 per cent of the total vote, in an election in which 89 per cent of the electorate participated. But together with his Nationalist allies in the Cabinet, Hitler secured a small parliamentary majority.

Acting illegally, the Nazis excluded the 81 elected Communists from the Reichstag, as well as one fourth of the 125 Social Democrats. In a violent speech, Hitler demanded the passage of a temporary enabling act that actually went far to abrogate the constitution. By a vote of 444 to 94, it became law— a majority meeting the requirements for constitutional amendment. The Social Democrats had the courage to oppose it; the Communists had no chance to vote. The Center party voted for the act, in spite of its doubts and suspicions, believing Hitler's promise to use the well-nigh absolute powers granted him for four years without threatening the existence of either the Reichstag or the Reichsrat, diminishing the position and rights of the President, doing away with the Länder, or lessening the rights of the churches. Time was to show that he was willing to violate all these promises. Within a few months, he ordered the dissolution of all parties other than his own, including even the Nationalist, and put all power into his own hands as the Führer.

2. The Führerstaat

Position of the Führer. Hitler's magnetism, his uncanny ability to recognize weakness in his opponents, his sharp sense of timing, and his amazing early successes did much to lend a mystic aura to his person. The fullest popular belief in his "mission" became established, and his utterances took on the appearance of infallibility. On the one hand, they called for ready obedience, and, on the other, they lulled the people into a feeling of safety.[4]

Hitler's legal power knew no limits. His judgment was beyond question or error and embodied the will of the nation: Führer and state were one and inseparable. Such a conception left no space for a separation of powers. Instead, there was a trinity of people, movement, and state, personified by Hitler as the leader of people and party and as head of state and government. After Hindenburg's death in August 1934, Hitler combined the office of President with that of Chancellor. He abolished the presidential title and decreed that he was to be known as "Führer and Reich Chancellor." In 1939, he shortened this title to simply "Der Führer." Much earlier, he had appointed Rudolf Hess deputy leader of the Nazi party, leaving the designation of a general deputy leader and his successor for a later date.

---

[4] See Stephen H. Roberts, *The House that Hitler Built* (New York, 1938); Loewenstein, *op. cit.* above, note 3; Franz B. Neumann, *Behemoth: The Structure and Practice of National Socialism* (New York, 1942), pp. 3 ff.

Executive Structure. The members of the Cabinet, who were also the heads of their departments, were Hitler's personal choice. Usually, they were "old fighters," who had risen with the Nazi movement; a few were highly qualified civil servants, taken over from the previous Cabinet because of their professional qualifications. All Cabinet members were responsible to the Führer only, who had the power to dismiss them at any time. They were the subordinates of the Chancellor as they had been under Bismarck, rather than his colleagues as under the Weimar Republic. Their cosignature with Hitler's on government decrees only signified their personal responsibility to him. Department heads were independent in their affairs, subject only to the orders of Hitler, except where party questions were involved, on which they had to defer to Hess. Cabinet meetings were infrequent and often replaced by audiences of individual Cabinet members with Hitler, who had the last word on any differences of opinion.

Hitler's government was divided into about fifteen departments, some of which were newly created to deal with functions peculiar to its unitary character and previously handled by the Länder governments, such as Science and Education, and Church Affairs. The Ministry of Propaganda and Public Enlightenment was indicative of the totalitarian character of the regime, and such ministries as those of Air and, after 1940, Arms and Munitions revealed the stress on armaments. Six additional Cabinet members were ministers without portfolio, including Hess, Dr. H. H. Lammers, and Dr. Hugo Meissner, the last two—both career men—as heads of the Reich Chancellery and the Presidential Chancellery, respectively. Originally, the chief of staff of the SA held a Cabinet position, which was eliminated after its incumbent, Captain Röhm, was killed in the purge of 1934. Heads of other powerful organizations, such as Himmler, leader of the SS and the *Gestapo,* and Dr. Robert Ley, head of the Labor Front, would participate in Cabinet meetings as they involved their particular responsibilities.

There was little turnover in the Cabinet, with the exception of the Ministry of Economics. One Cabinet member (Röhm) was murdered by the SS, Vice Chancellor von Papen was soon demoted, and two ministers were able to resign. A few others were shifted to new positions of importance. Some of the top Nazis, including Göring, Frick, and Goebbels, were undoubtedly very able men, however offensive their political role. They were helped beyond measure by such extremely capable men as Count von Schwerin-Krosigk, whom Hitler had taken over as Reich Minister of Finance, and Lammers and Meissner, equally competent, who had served under the Weimar regime in corresponding capacities. Perhaps indeed the civil servants in high positions who presumed to serve Hitler on a purely professional basis were more responsible for his initial success than the fanatical Nazi leaders who were competing for power and his favor.

Lawmaking by Decree. In the Nazi state, dominated by the leadership principle, legislation was the expression of the political will of the Führer.

It therefore normally took the form of government decree. Only some seven laws were passed by the Reichstag, always in the form proposed by the Cabinet and enacted without amendment and discussion. The Succession Act of 1934, by which Hitler combined the functions of the President and Chancellor, was the only law submitted to a popular plebiscite. It had gone into effect before the people had a chance to vote on it, but it drew enough opposition to mark the plebiscite on laws a dubious experiment. It was never applied again to the legislative process.

Under the Enabling Act of 1933, the government was empowered to amend the Weimar constitution by decree, aside from certain limitations applying to the "institutions" of the Reichstag and the Federal Council and to the powers of the President. The Reconstruction Act of 1934, passed by the first all-Nazi Reichstag elected in November 1933, gave the government the power to enact "new constitutional law." From then on, there was no distinction between constitutional amendments and ordinary legislation. The Cabinet, at Hitler's indication, initiated all legislation, preparing drafts in broad outline for the Führer's approval and enactment. Often a law merely stated its general purposes and conferred sweeping powers on department heads, enabling them to issue all necessary orders and regulations. An outstanding example was the Four Year Plan of 1936, which made Göring, as commissioner for the plan, economic dictator of the country for the purpose of achieving economic self-sufficiency for Germany.

Creation of the Unitary State. Within less than a year's time, Hitler succeeded in abolishing all legal vestiges of German federalism and in creating a highly centralized unitary state.[5] Under the Reich Governors Act of 1935, the national governors, appointed by the Führer, became the permanent representatives of the Reich in the Länder (and later also in Austria and the Sudetenland). The governors were charged with the duty of enforcing national policy. They received instructions from the various Reich Ministers in their respective fields. Hitler reserved for himself the position of national governor of Prussia, but delegated all functions of the office to Göring, Prussia's Prime Minister. Most governors again were "old fighters," who received the considerable prestige and emoluments of their offices as rewards for faithful party service. They often were party heads for the same area, and sometimes also heads of the Länder governments, as in Saxony, Hesse, and Hamburg.

The Länder governments remained in operation—except for some changes resulting from territorial mergers—but as executive organs of the Reich, rather than of the Land. State cabinets were appointed and dismissed by Hitler. With the permission of a Reich minister, a Land might actually pass its own legislation, restricted to the state area, in such fields as mining or agriculture. Reich legislation expanded rapidly and took over all fields

---

[5] Arnold Brecht, *Federalism and Regionalism in Germany* (New York, 1945), chap. 15.

previously reserved to the states. Prussia was completely subordinated to the Reich. In Prussia, the functions that the Reich governors exercised in other states were put into the hands of the provincial presidents, who were designated as representatives of the governor. Provinces in Prussia were therefore on the same level from the administrative point of view as states like Bavaria or Saxony.

Before coming into power, the Nazis had created some thirty party regions—often coextensive with the election districts of the Republic. The number was later increased by ten additional districts, set up in annexed territory during the war. In 1942, the so-called national defense regions were made coextensive with the party regions. At the same time, thirty economic regions were established for all of Germany and the annexed territories, corresponding with either one or more party regions. They constituted the administrative subdivisions in the economic fields and for the geographic and functional organizations of commerce and industry. In some respects the final regional structure could, therefore, be considered a forerunner of the territorial reforms that the Nazis planned but never fully accomplished. As the states and provinces continued to exist, with often overlapping areas, the governmental map was often confusing.

Status of the Party. After Hitler had persuaded most of the parties to pass the Enabling Act and thereby grant him four years of almost absolute power, he suppressed the Social Democratic party and induced all others to dissolve themselves "voluntarily." Then he forged a handy weapon against all political opposition in the Law on the Formation of New Political Parties.[6] It established his as the only political party and provided heavy penalties for any activity intended to continue old political organizations or form new ones. Even discussion of such plans was treated as attempted treason. The law declared that the party was "the bearer of the state idea," which meant simply that it controlled the state and its principles. The party was thus placed by law above the law, controlling the state by the union of party and government offices. The supreme directorate of the party consisted of some twenty to thirty top Nazis under Hitler, constituting the actual government of Germany and using the Cabinet as a front for the execution of policies.

Only a few members of the directorate held high government positions—for instance, Hess, Göring, Goebbels, Frick, Darré, and Ley. There was always considerable rivalry and bitterness between Nazi leaders, some of which was public knowledge, like the feud between Göring and Goebbels. Most of them did not hesitate to denounce one another, which enabled Hitler to balance one against the other.

Echo of the People. During a large part of the republican era, the Reichstag had been a sickly institution with powers beyond its capacity to use effectively. Under Hitler, it had only nominal legislative functions.

---

[6] Cf. Alfred V. Boerner, Jr., "The Position of the NSDAP in the German Constitutional Order," *American Political Science Review,* 32 (1938), 1059 ff.

Its real role was to provide a platform for Hitler's more important speeches, as did the annual party congress, and to serve as a well-paid cheering section. The world soon formed the habit, as did the Germans, of listening carefully when the Führer addressed the Reichstag.

Under Hitler, there were three Reichstag elections. Their main purpose was to provide occasions for concentrated waves of Nazi propaganda, drumming the self-appraised achievements of the regime into the ears of the public. Since the Nazi party was the only legal one, its candidates were sure to be elected. Any opposition to the regime could be expressed only by leaving ballots blank instead of marking them with a cross. The Nazis exercised enormous pressure to bring out the vote, often parading prospective nonvoters through the streets with posters on their backs referring to them as traitors. After the reunion of the Saar with Germany and the annexation of Austria, the Sudetenland, and Memel, the size of the Reichstag was pushed up to the unprecedented figure of 862 deputies. The voting age remained at twenty, but Jews were disfranchised, as they were slowly and brutally pressed against the wall in every respect. Women could vote, but could not become candidates. All Nazi leaders were members of the Reichstag. Hitler usually headed the ticket in all thirty-five election districts.

There were also four so-called plebiscites, providing additional occasions for Goebbels' propaganda machine to do its efficient work. Hitler was skillful in timing his plebiscites and in tying them up with popular actions in the international field, for which he was bound to receive overwhelming approval. In November 1933, he asked the Germans to vote in favor of Germany's withdrawal from the League of Nations. In March 1936, he requested them to express their approval of the repudiation of the Treaty of Locarno, including its prohibition of the militarization of the Rhineland. And in April 1938, he wanted them to approve the union of Germany and Austria that had taken place a month earlier. In these plebiscites, the government received a favorable vote of 95.1, 98.8, and 98.9, respectively. Only when Hitler asked the Germans in 1934 to assent to the Succession Act was there any degree of outright opposition. Even then the percentage of favorable votes was 89.9. At least, these were the published figures. In 1936 and 1938, the voters marked only one ballot, which counted both as their affirmation of Hitler's foreign policy and their vote for the Nazi ticket.

Politically Guided Justice. The German courts, ordinary and administrative, as well as the law of procedure, had early established Prussia's and later Germany's reputation as a "state of law" (*Rechtsstaat*). To be sure, there had been complaints under the Empire of class justice, and under the Republic of the unwillingness of the courts to punish reactionary enemies of democracy. But on the whole, a German had always felt safe in his legal rights. This situation was reversed by the Nazis.[7] The administration of

[7] See Ernst Fraenkel, *The Dual State* (New York, 1941).

justice was now but one more means of political power. The Führer's will became the source of law, and independence of courts and judges disappeared. As the Nazis put it, "law is what is useful to the German nation." All Jewish or "politically unreliable" judges were removed in a purge of the judiciary in 1933. Judges and district attorneys now followed ideological hints in cases with a political connotation, especially in criminal matters. Civil cases tended to be decided on a basis of justice, unless Jews or Nazi party members were involved. The old legal principle of *nullum crimen sine lege* (no crime except by legal definition) was replaced by *nullum crimen sine poena* (no crime without punishment). Courts now inflicted punishment for any act that was considered in conflict with the "healthy sentiment of the people," even if no law was violated. "Preventive custody" came to cover the utter lawlessness of the concentration camps. The Ministry of Justice decreed that "persons inimical to the state, after having served their sentence or after acquittal (*sic*) by the court, are to be placed in the hands of the secret police for reforming them further in concentration camps."

As the list of political crimes expanded, tens of thousands of people fell into the hands of the secret police for their opposition to nazism. Soon special courts were set up to handle so-called attacks on the regime and treasonable activities, including offenses against the party. The People's Court, established in 1936, earned a gruesome reputation by severe punishments handed out in secret sessions in which the accused was granted few if any rights of defense. Dark red posters on public bulletin boards announced later that certain persons "convicted of treason" had been beheaded. The secrecy of proceedings and the severity of punishment succeeded in terrorizing the general public, but were unable to prevent new plots against the regime.

The administration of justice under the Republic had been noted for its stress on the reform aspects of punishment. This modern concept was abolished by the Nazis in favor of the principles of revenge by the state and harsh treatment of convicts as deterrents of crime. "Habitual criminals" became subject to internment in concentration camps and compulsory sterilization in addition to their regular sentences.

3. Administrative Transformations

Making the Civil Service Politically Reliable. Hitler found that only a small percentage of German civil servants had joined his party by 1933, compared with the many who had become members of other parties—except the Communist. Although the civil service as a whole was therefore suspected in the new regime, Hitler realized keenly that a modern state could not be run without trained and experienced personnel, no matter what its ideology. The bulk of the civil servants were for that reason taken over and fully utilized, while kept under political pressure and personal observation. All Jewish or partly Jewish civil servants were dismissed outright or marked for gradual elimination, as well as many Social Democrats, Liberals, Catholics, and others considered "politically unreliable." Some of the dismissed officials were granted full or part pensions. It is noteworthy that despite earlier Nazi claims, few of the victims were officials appointed during the Republic on a purely political basis. In the course of time, the Nazis filled more and more top positions with their own followers. By 1937, there were fully 356 Nazi party members among 438 holders of high positions in Prussia, 208 of them having joined the party before 1933.

In the course of time, the government returned to the merit system for new appointments, since many aspirants had found it convenient to join the SA or SS since 1933. The new Civil Service Act of 1937 restored a degree of professional stability. It applied to all civil servants, whether employed by the Reich, the former state governments, local governments, the Reichsbank, the railway administration, and other public corporations. The act refers to the civil service as a "pillar of the National Socialist State," placing it in certain respects on a level with the Army and party. The civil servants were bound to give allegiance to "Führer and Reich," owing unconditional obedience and unreserved discharge of their duties in return for permanent tenure. They were to remain faithful to the Führer "to the last breath." As a general rule, the merit system was expressly continued. But the act also created a new category of civil servants without professional training, eligible for permanent tenure after a minimum of six years in office.

Even under the impact of the Nazi revolution, the civil service showed a surprising strength and resiliency, enabling it to preserve many of its essential professional characteristics. Naturally, the numerous new Nazi officials objected to being assimilated as "outsiders" and considered it their mission to color the traditional professional spirit with party enthusiasm. The old-timers knew that they were continuously spied upon and that their professional status was politically uncertain.

Abolition of Local Self-Government. Next to administrative efficiency, local self-government of a high order had been one of Germany's cherished accomplishments, under both the Empire and the Republic.[8] Elected city councils established many economic enterprises on a sound financial basis, especially public utilities and urban transportation systems. Local governments generously supported cultural agencies such as stage and opera, libraries and museums.

Under the Local Government Act of January 1935, the Hitler regime subjected all municipalities (except Berlin) to uniform nation-wide legislation. The actual scope of local government remained almost the same, but elective offices were no longer. Moreover, administrative supervision was now integrated under the Reich Ministry of the Interior. Generally, standards of administrative efficiency remained rather high, though they suffered from

[8] See F. Morstein Marx, "Germany," in William Anderson, ed., *Local Government in Europe* (New York, 1939); Roger H. Wells, "Municipal Government in National Socialist Germany," *American Political Science Review*, 29 (1935), 652 ff.

Nazi interference. In each community, a party delegate, usually the head of the regional, district, or local organization, served as the political watchdog. Hitler reserved for himself this role for Munich, the "capital of the movement." The party delegate prepared a list of eligible candidates for the posts of mayor and heads of municipal departments, from which appointments were made by national authorities. Salaried positions to be filled were advertised and applications invited. The leadership principle was expressed in the concentration of all responsibility in the mayor, subject only to the superior authorities. The party delegate, in agreement with the mayor, appointed a group of unpaid municipal councilors for a six-year term. They did not have the right to vote, but the mayor was obliged to discuss important municipal affairs with them.

As a capital city and industrial center of some 4 million inhabitants, spreading over an unusually large area, and important enough to form both an economic and a defense region of its own, Berlin called for some special adaptation of the general municipal law to its special needs. Under the Republic, Berlin had made some progress in area consolidation and the development of a coordinated system of central and district government. The Local Government Act of 1935 was applied to the metropolis under the special provisions of the Berlin Act of 1936. The mayors of the twenty administrative districts created in 1920 were now given complete powers, subject to the general direction of the chief mayor of Greater Berlin, appointed by the Führer. Dr. Joseph Goebbels, as district leader of the party, became the party delegate for Berlin and was thereby placed in a position to exercise municipal functions that were not always in line with the policy of the Minister of the Interior.

Changes in Administrative Law. The principles and practices of administrative law led an uncertain life until they finally disappeared. The totalitarian state found it inadvisable to allow protection of the individual against illegal government action, which for decades had been the function of administrative courts. The emphasis was now on duties, not on rights. The Secret Police Act did not allow a court review of measures taken under its provisions. They were clearly "political acts" of the omnipotent state, not subject to challenge. The traditional concept of government of laws, however, was so deeply entrenched in the public mind that temporary compromises were made. Administrative courts were not allowed to interfere in decisions made by the political leadership, nor could they resolve controversies between local governments and supervisory authorities. But for a while citizens were able to take specific grievances caused by administrative acts to the proper tribunals for review.

In August 1939, as if to herald the outbreak of war, appeals to administrative courts were abolished, except in a few limited cases. In November, all lower administrative tribunals were ended. A new federal administrative tribunal was set up in April 1941, merging several administrative courts, but it was not given independent status, in keeping with the axioms of the totalitarian state.

4. Total Control

Control of the Economy. It is inherent in any totalitarian system of government that economics are absolutely subordinated to politics and that the state assumes the task of directing all phases of economic life.[9] The Nazis exercised total control through economic and cultural "estates." Nazi doctrine propounded a "German socialism" that assigned to labor a place of honor, emphasized the importance of the soil—the base and root of the farmer—and deprived capital of its preoccupation with profits, while regimenting the worker, farmer, businessman, and consumer for the "good of the state."

Practically every German was a member in one or more of the estates—Agriculture, Trade and Industry, Handicrafts, the Chamber of Culture, or the Labor Front. All these organizations were under government control, set up to channel occupational interests into common endeavors and subordinate special interests to the common weal, as defined by the state. In practice, this meant that the businessman headed an enterprise as directed by the state. The latter managed the currency, controlled bank credit, decreed types and amounts of production, set prices and wages, assigned labor to specific localities or types of employment, rationed food and raw materials, and directed investments.

Control of Labor. In many respects, the Labor Front[10] was the most important of these estates. Originally, it had only the task of replacing the suppressed trade unions and coordinating labor with the state. Gradually, the Labor Front included and controlled employers as well. It became an enormous organization of some 30 million members, grouped into industrial divisions with territorial subdivisions. It inherited the sizable confiscated properties of the old-time labor unions, and proceeded to accumulate great wealth from compulsory contributions. Its main job was to imbue its members with the principles of nazism and to check the class struggle that hurt the state's interests. Strikes and lockouts were punishable. Through the medium of the Labor Front, employers and workers were made to cooperate for the good of the state, which in turn took a paternal interest in their welfare.

The Labor Front did not confine its propaganda to mass meetings and publicity. It appealed to workers by stressing the "dignity of labor," and insisted on the beautification of plants and shops and on sanitary conditions.

---

[9] See Robert A. Brady, *The Spirit and Structure of German Fascism* (New York, 1937); Neumann, *op. cit.* above, note 4, pp. 221 ff.

[10] Cf. Taylor Cole, "The Evolution of the German Labor Front," *Political Science Quarterly,* 52 (1937), 532 ff.

A subsidiary of the Labor Front, called Strength Through Joy, had the double task of providing low-cost recreation and entertainment for the worker and his family and keeping a watchful eye on him during his leisure time. Cheap vacations in the mountains or at the seashore, to the distant fjords of Norway or the sunny shores of Portugal and Italy, were now for the first time possible for tens of thousands of workers, especially politically deserving ones.

On the other side, the Nazi regime compelled every young German between eighteen and twenty-five to serve six months in the labor service. Foreign visitors often admired the spectacle of young men draining swamps, building roads, erecting bridges, or helping farmers. Hundreds of thousands of girls likewise served in farm homes as helpers to mothers with large families of children, giving these women hitherto unknown vacations or assistance in their heavy tasks. But the visitors were less aware that the young men engaged also in intense premilitary training and that both men and women were subject to fanatical indoctrination. Away from their homes and other traditional influences, they were immersed in nazism at an impressionable age. The concept of labor service predated the Hitler government as a voluntary institution to aid unemployed young people. In the Third Reich it became compulsory and a medium of Nazi propaganda.

Control of Culture. Since cultural activities lend themselves easily to the shaping of public attitudes, totalitarian systems are anxious to control and direct them. As early as 1933, the Nazis set up the Reich Chamber of Culture, another of the estates. Its subdivisions included all professional associations of authors, journalists, editors, musicians, actors, singers, other artists, and radio personnel. Membership in the chamber was a prerequisite for exercising any of these professions. Expulsion for professional misconduct, usually indicating actual or suspected anti-Nazi convictions, meant professional death.

These silent methods of intellectual strangulation were effective, quickly superseding the earlier method of removing individuals from positions of influence, which was more noticeable abroad. "Coordination" of the written and spoken word and all forms of artistic expression soon was complete; but the level of the cultural media sank both as propaganda thickened and as certain great men chose emigration or silence rather than cultural prostitution. The number and total circulation of newspapers decreased heavily, owing to the monotony of official opinion that had superseded the traditional variety of party views. The Nazis recognized the propagandistic value of the radio by manufacturing cheap small sets that enabled large numbers of people to hear domestic stations but not foreign senders.

Nazification of Schools. The Nazis recognized clearly that the future lay with those who could win and hold the youth. They dismissed all teachers they considered undesirable, either racially or politically, and forced the remainder into a process of educational "overhauling," which impressed upon them the desirability of Nazi enthusiasm if not convictions. Textbooks were rewritten; educational films were utilized to an extent previously unknown anywhere. Many remained on an objective level, but others emphasized the "right" way of thinking.

Since there were many teachers who were Nazis by coordination rather than conviction and many parents unreconciled to the regime, large numbers of children, especially from big cities, were sent to Land Year Homes in the country for one-year periods, where work and play in a healthful environment were mixed with training in Nazi ideology by carefully selected leaders. Mail from home was examined.

Transformation of Universities. The German university, with its traditional freedom of teaching and research, had been a pride of Empire and Republic, indeed of the scholarly world. The Nazis destroyed this freedom, too, by dismissing some 1,100 university teachers for racial or political reasons and "transferring" hundreds of others to unwanted posts.[11] The Minister of Education, Bernhard Rust, head of the university system, declared frankly at the University of Heidelberg Jubilee in 1936: "National Socialism is justly described as unfriendly to science if its appraiser assumes that independence of presuppositions and freedom from bias are the essential characteristics of scientific inquiry. . . . there never can be a genuine contradiction between the aims of science and the purposes of the National Socialist State; for the latter have grown out of the practical understanding of the immanent laws of nature and history." Therefore, it was in line with good official reasoning that Phillip Lenard, a Nobel prize winner in physics, published a four-volume work, *Deutsche Physik,* stating in the preface that "Science, like every other human product, is racial and conditioned by blood."

As usual, the Nazis were not satisfied with negative control, but took positive measures to push their concepts of scholarship. In the field of history, for instance, they established the Reich Institution for the History of the New Germany, providing it with large appropriations. They set its members to work on rewriting history. History now had to be studied in the pan-German sense, as the spiritual expression of the Nazi revolution and the new order, and written to mold a new generation of intellectual leaders. The new Institute scorned the faith of the older historians in scholarly objectivity and demanded an objectivity that was "correctly interpreted." The physical sciences were not exposed to so much sniping; there progress was steady, and often amazing, under the impetus of German military preparations.

Struggle with the Protestant Church. Since their totalitarianism could

[11] See Edward Y. Hartshorne, *The German Universities and National Socialism* (Cambridge, Mass., 1937); John Brown Mason, "Academic Freedom under Nazism," *Social Science,* 15 (1940), 388 ff., and Mason, "Nazi Concepts of History," *Review of Politics,* 2 (1940), 180 ff.

not tolerate any freedom of the individual, even in religious belief, the Nazis waged a relentless war against the Christian churches.[12]   Their fight was aided by two historic facts: the traditional connection between throne and (Protestant) altar, and political Catholicism.

In the Empire, German Protestantism had been organized into thirty-four state-wide established churches.   A few were Reformed, a larger number Lutheran, but most were Evangelical.   All of them received financial assistance from the state and in return were subject to its supervision in matters of organization, personnel, property, and finance.   As a rule, the head of the state—for instance, the King of Prussia—was also head bishop.   The Roman Catholic church also received financial assistance, but was not an established church.   Only the so-called free churches, such as the Methodist and the Baptist, were supported entirely by voluntary contributions and without state supervision, but they were insignificant in numbers.   The republican constitution abolished state churches, but did not provide for separation of church and state as we know it in the United States.   The churches now had greater freedom, but continued to receive financial support, subject to limited state supervision.   German Lutheranism had no traditional belief that the state should be democratic, or that church members should feel free to criticize the state or its institutions.   Instead, it tended to encourage uncritical obedience and allowed many workers to become hostile to the Protestant churches because of their conservative and even reactionary associations.

When the Nazis came into power, they forced the Protestant churches to merge, but pushed the freely elected Reich bishop out of office because of his nonpartisanship.   New church elections were held in July 1933, in which the German Christians of Nazi vintage had a monopoly on press and radio. Under heavy government and party pressure, the result was a landslide for the German Christians.   A Nazi chaplain, Ludwig Müller, was made the Reich bishop.   All ministers of Jewish descent were dismissed.   In protest against violations of religious freedom, several thousand clergymen organized the Pastors' Emergency League.   When it was disbanded by the Nazis, the Confessional church replaced it.   Yet, by September 1935, Hitler had definitely placed the unified Protestant church under state control, subject to the orders of the newly established Reich Department for Church Affairs.

Opposition by the Catholic Church.   The Catholic church represented a minority of about one third of the population, with a lively memory of the struggle between the church and Bismarck, and of certain state-imposed disabilities and discriminations that were not abolished until 1919.   It had the

---

[12] Cf. Waldemar Gurian, *Hitler and the Christians* (New York, 1936); Nathaniel Micklem, *National Socialism and the Roman Catholic Church* (London, 1939); George N. Shuster, *Like a Mighty Army: Hitler Versus Established Religion* (New York, 1935); John Brown Mason, *Hitler's First Foes: A Study in Religion and Politics* (Minneapolis, 1936), and Mason, "Christianity Faces Caesarism," *Sewanee Review*, 47 (1939), 1 ff.; Paul F. Douglass, *God Among the Germans* (Philadelphia, 1935); Roger H. Wells, "The Financial Relations of Church and State in Germany, 1919-1937," *Political Science Quarterly*, 53 (1938), 36 ff.

strong support of a tightly woven net of church-sponsored organizations, some three hundred daily and many weekly papers or other periodicals, and its characteristic religious discipline. The existence of the strong Center party, which represented the church in the political arena, and the presence of many priests among the party's leaders, brought forth the Nazi charge of "political Catholicism."

The Catholic bishops had unanimously condemned a part of the Nazi program as early as 1930, because it contained heresies, and warned the faithful against joining the party. During several national election campaigns, the bishops publicly warned Catholic voters against supporting nazism. These ecclesiastical pronouncements helped the Center party to maintain its strength when other parties went to pieces under the drain of Hitler's vote-getting power. After his seizure of the Reich, the Catholic church accepted at face value his promise that the new Reich would be built on the basis of Christianity and concluded a concordat with Nazi Germany to insure its sphere of religious influence. The church thereby provided Hitler with his first success in the diplomatic field, only to find within a short time that he was more interested in violating the concordat than in observing it.

Although the two churches usually fought separately against Nazi encroachments, they stood for the same fundamental principles and suffered from the same use of force against them. Many ministers and priests alike were deprived of their positions, thrown into jails and concentration camps, and mistreated physically to the point of murder. Both churches were denied freedom to speak, write, and maintain independent organizations.

Ideological Eugenics. When the late Justice Oliver Wendell Holmes climaxed a United States Supreme Court decision in favor of the constitutionality of the Virginia sterilization law with the ringing words, "Three generations of imbeciles are enough," he did not dream that Nazi Germany would quote him in justification of its large-scale sterilization program.[13] While serving his early sentence, Hitler became convinced through the reading of writings on eugenics that sterilization could serve as a means of national regeneration. A law passed in 1934 provided for the compulsory sterilization of persons of either sex afflicted with one of eight hereditary diseases or with severe alcoholism. A nation-wide system of 1,700 eugenics courts, consisting of both judges and physicians, examined uncounted cases in secret sessions.

An official publicity campaign acquainted the population with the announced purposes and the provisions of the law, attempting to overcome widespread opposition to it. At first, the government made certain concessions to the Catholic church, which forbids eugenic sterilization, such as the substitution of institutional confinement. Eventually, this agreement also was violated.

---

[13] John Brown Mason, "Germany Tries Sterilization," *Social Science,* 13 (1938), 303 ff.

Hitler's Foreign Policy. Hitler first firmly embraced but soon abandoned the revisionist line of the Republic's foreign policy. The Nazis substituted a doctrine of force or threats of force and open violation of treaty obligations. Hitler rearmed Germany with increasing speed, yanked her out of the League, blasted international conferences, denounced Locarno, and stressed bilateral treaties, where he found it easier to hoodwink or high-pressure the other party. He used disunity among Italy, France, and Britain to win Mussolini's support in putting Franco in the saddle in Spain. He detached Poland from the French system of guaranties through a ten-year nonaggression pact and strengthened his relations with Hungary and Bulgaria, two other defeated and strongly revisionist powers, as well as Greece, then under a military dictatorship.

When Hitler was allowed to annex Austria without reaping a storm, he accomplished the semi-encirclement of Czechoslovakia and gained direct contact with Italy and the Balkans. After probing Western diplomatic strength, he developed the strategy of terror to a fine art, culminating in appeasement at Munich, where Czechoslovakia's Sudetenland was handed him on a platter. But Hitler's success went to his head. After maintaining for years that he wanted no more than the inclusion of all German-speaking people in the Reich—a demand bearing some resemblance to the democratic principle of self-determination—he put an end to Czechoslovakia's existence as an independent state. No one could now doubt that Hitler was bent upon conquest. By his surprising nonaggression pact of August 1939 with the Soviet Union, Hitler was able to buy her initial neutrality for a planned attack on Poland. But he fatally erred when he gambled that Britain would fail to honor her guaranty of Polish independence. Upon his invasion of Poland, both Britain and France declared war against Germany—the beginning of a drawn-out struggle that ended in the total destruction of the Third Reich.

5. Germany in the Postwar Period

Reich in Shambles. If the physical destruction wrought upon Germany was enormous, the Germans' mental and spiritual condition seemed even worse.[14] They were wholly exhausted and utterly confused by the sudden realization that they "had been fed a pack of lies." Youth as well as elders found their pillars of faith shattered, with no props to take their place. As happened after 1918, a period of national defeat and dishonor coincided with economic despair and the demands of foreign victors for Germany's conversion to democracy.

Hitler and every little Führer were gone, but the few living democratic

---

[14] Cf. James K. Pollock, *What Shall Be Done With Germany* (Northfield, 1944); Sidney L. W. Mellen, "The German People and the Postwar World," *American Political Science Review,* 37 (1943), 601 ff.; Ferdinand A. Hermens, *The Tyrants' War and the People's Peace* (Chicago, 1944).

leaders were unable to fill the entire vacuum. The underground opposition to Hitler had been led by a heterogeneous but growing group of men and
women from the right and the left. From 1938 on, elements of these had
plotted conspiracies culminating in the attempt of July 1944 on Hitler's life.
Its failure brought death to thousands, depriving the country of leaders badly
needed in the task of constructing a new Germany, at once democratic and
peaceful. The depletion of the ranks of aggressive anti-Nazism left Germany with a dearth of leadership more disastrous than her physical destruction.

Allied Military Government. After the unconditional surrender of the
German high command, the Allied powers divided Germany into four zones
of occupation: The eastern or Russian zone, embracing 18 million people
(part of East Prussia was annexed by the Soviets and large slices of eastern
territory by Poland); the northwestern or British zone, with 23 million inhabitants; the southern or American zone, with more than 16 million; and
the southwestern or French zone, with 6 million people.[15] An Allied control
authority was set up in Berlin, consisting of the four military zone commanders, who met monthly and passed legislation on matters "affecting Germany
as a whole," a phrase that was never clearly defined. Since its actions
required unanimity, the authority was unable to make decisions on many
important questions. The Potsdam protocol, signed in August 1945 by
Truman, Stalin, and Attlee, formulated these objectives of political reconstruction under Allied occupation: complete disarmanent and demilitarization, dissolution of the Nazi party and affiliated organizations, decentralization of government, and punishment of war criminals.

Even though two general directives laid down principles applicable to all
occupied Germany for the destruction of the Nazi party and its influence, the
actual process of denazification was handled differently in each zone. The
Potsdam agreement had further provided for the establishment of some central German agencies to act on a nation-wide basis. But they were never set
up, because of objections on the part of the Soviet Union, which disagreed
with the Western powers on policies toward Germany, and on the part of
France, which considered any degree of German centralization a menace to
her security. As it proved impossible for the four powers to deal with
Germany as an economic unit, the United States and Britain agreed on an
economic merger of their two zones.

Occupation Statute. Issued by the military governors in April 1949, the

[15] See Harold Zink, *American Military Government in Germany* (New York, 1947); James K.
Pollock, ed., *Change and Crisis in European Government* (New York, 1947), chaps. 3 and 4;
W. Friedmann, *The Allied Military Government of Germany* (New York, 1947); Carl J. Friedrich and Others, *American Experiences in Military Government in World War II* (New York,
1948); James K. Pollock, James H. Meisel and Henry L. Bretton, *Germany under Occupation—
Illustrative Materials and Documents* (rev. ed., Ann Arbor, 1949); Sidney Connor and Carl J.
Friedrich, *Military Government,* Annals of the American Academy of Political and Social Science,
267 (January 1950). Appreciation is due Dr. George Fleischer, of the United States High Commissioner's Office in Germany, for a critical reading of the following sections.

Occupation Statute expressly reserved "supreme authority" in the three Western zones to the governments of the United States, Great Britain, and France in matters of disarmament, demilitarization including related fields of scientific research, protection of allied forces, industrial development, displaced persons and refugees, restitution of former Jewish property, reparations, decartelization, trade discrimination, controls in regard to the industrial Ruhr area, foreign affairs, foreign trade and exchange, and observance of the basic law and the Länder constitutions.   In addition, the occupying authorities kept the right to exercise full authority to preserve security and democratic government in Germany.   In spite of the formidable list of reserved powers, the subsequent adoption of a federal constitution resulted in a considerable increase in German autonomy.   All German legislation became effective automatically 21 days after submission to the occupation authorities unless previously disapproved by them, which happened in only a few cases. Even in the reserved fields, the Germans were allowed to legislate and act "after due notification to the occupation authorities," unless they were directed otherwise or were acting in conflict with directives.   Only amendments to the constitution required previous approval.

A provisional peace settlement was negotiated in 1952, based on two agreements with the German government.   One ended the regime of the Allied High Commission but reserved some veto powers to an Allied Council of Ambassadors.   At the same time, a pact was concluded under which the Western powers guaranteed German security, while Germany specified her contribution to the defense forces of the North Atlantic Treaty Organization (NATO) under General Eisenhower.   Germany also accepted associate membership in the Council of Europe in 1950.   Opinion in the new federal republic has been strongly divided on the question of German rearmament, but Germany appears on the way to making a military contribution to her own defense.   One problem is to convince the western Germans that the establishment of a German element in an European army is in their own national interest but to prevent this element from becoming a threat either to democracy within the country or to peace in Europe.

Political Parties.   Of the two strongest postwar parties,[16] the Social Democrats form a moderate group resembling the British Labor party; the Christian Democratic Union has grown out of the old Center party.   The Free Democrats are an anti-Marxist liberal group of the middle classes.   The Communists as such are represented in the Western zones only.

The Socialist Unity Party is a forced merger of the Social Democratic and Communist parties in the Russian zone, where the former has been suppressed.   In the Western zones, the Social Democrats were free to reject the Communist tactics of the Trojan horse with poor results for the Communists, in spite of the substantial financial backing they appear to have everywhere.

[16] Robert G. Neumann, "The New Political Parties in Germany," *American Political Science Review*, 40 (1946), 749 ff.

The Social Democrats, naturally, are strongest in the urban and industrial regions. The party line-up has not changed much from the days of the Weimar Republic, including the old German tendency toward formation of splinter parties.

Bonn Constitution. Acting in agreement with the military governors, the heads of the 11 Western Länder called a meeting of constitutional experts to draft a constitution, to be submitted to a constituent assembly, which met in Bonn on September 1, 1948. This provisional constitution, called the Basic Law, was adopted on May 8, 1949, the fourth anniversary of the unconditional surrender of Nazi Germany. The military governors, with whom the assembly had been in constant consultation, approved the constitution within four days, subject to the Occupation Statute and other reservations.[17]

The two legislative chambers consist of a popularly elected Federal Diet (*Bundestag*), and a Federal Council (*Bundesrat*) representing the governments of the 11 Western Länder roughly according to population. The Council enjoys a suspensive veto over Diet bills, which may be overruled by the Diet if a conference between the two chambers is unsuccessful. All bills affecting the status or powers of the Länder, however, require approval by a majority of the Council. Constitutional amendments must be adopted by a two-thirds majority in both chambers. The 43 members of the Council are chosen by the respective Land cabinets, of which they must be members. Their votes are cast as a block. Under the electoral law of 1949, 60 per cent of the members of the Diet were elected in each Land in single-member districts, with 40 per cent of the seats distributed under the list system of proportional representation.[18]

The President is elected by a special convention composed of all members of the Federal Diet and an equal number of delegates selected by the Länder diets. Absolute majority is called for only on the first two ballots; on the third, plurality is sufficient. The term of office is five years, and tenure is restricted to two terms. The first President, Professor Theodor Heuss, was elected on the second ballot with 416 votes, against 312 votes cast for the Social Democratic leader, Dr. Kurt Schumacher. The President, as in France, occupies a weak position, while the Chancellor's status is one of definite leadership, like that of the Prime Minister in Great Britain. The Chancellor is elected by the Diet, which votes first on the candidate nominated by the President but may elect any other candidate. Dr. Konrad Adenauer, a Catholic leader of the Weimar period, was elected the first

---

[17] See Arnold Brecht, "Re-establishing German Government," in Connor and Friedrich, *op. cit.,* and "The New German Constitution," *Social Research,* 16 (1949), 425 ff.; Carl J. Friedrich, "Rebuilding the German Constitution," *American Political Science Review,* 43 (1949), 461 ff., 704 ff. See also Robert G. Neumann, "New Constitutions in Germany," *American Political Science Review,* 42 (1948), 448 ff.

[18] For a discussion of proportional representation in Germany, see F. A. Hermens, *Democracy or Anarchy* (Notre Dame, 1941), or its up-to-date edition, *Democratie oder Anarchie* (Frankfurt, 1951).

Chancellor on the first ballot. He headed a coalition government of the Christian Democratic Union (139 deputies), the Free Democratic party (52), and the German party (17), with the Social Democratic party (131) forming the main opposition.

The Chancellor can be forced to resign only if the Diet agrees to the election of a new Chancellor by an absolute majority. This so-called "constructive vote of lack of confidence" prevents a heterogeneous combination of opposition parties from overthrowing the Cabinet—as did the combined Nazis and Communists in the Weimar period—without being able to agree on another one. The Chancellor's position is further strengthened by the constitutional provision that the Cabinet must approve all decisions of the Diet which provide for increased expenditures.

The legislative powers of the federal government are broader than those in the United States, but the administrative powers are narrower than in the Weimar period. A Federal Constitutional Court decides on the constitutionality of federal and Land laws. The basic rights of Germans are pronounced as binding on the legislature, the executive, and the judiciary. While several exceptions are authorized, the principles involved are an unalterable part of the constitution and are not subject to amendment. Constitutional protection is withdrawn from those who would act against the constitutional order or the idea of international understanding.

The New Federalism. The constitution is federal, providing for a division of legislative competence between the Bund and the Länder.[19] While the Federal Council, representing the Länder, enjoys only a suspensive veto, this right may weigh heavily on certain occasions, as it requires an absolute majority of the Diet to override the veto, and even a two-thirds majority if the vote of the Council was taken by a two-thirds majority. In certain cases, the Council's consent to federal laws and regulations is required, thus changing the suspensive veto to an absolute one.

When the Western occupation authorities insisted on the territorial reorganization of Germany, they carved out 11 Länder roughly equal in size, without much regard for existing boundaries or economic and historical considerations. Some of the smaller Länder were abolished, while Prussia was broken up into several parts. Article 29 of the constitution on future territorial reorganization was suspended by the military governors until the time of the peace treaty, but the south-west area was expressly excepted from this delay.

Berlin. A new constitution, giving Berlin the legal status of a Land as well as of a city, was approved by the three commandants of West Berlin in 1950, replacing the provisional constitution of 1946. After the Communist-dominated Socialist Unity party had suffered a disastrous defeat in the city-wide elections in 1946, the Soviet authorities began a process of obstruction and

---

[19] See John B. Mason, "Federalism—The Bonn Model," in Arnold Zurcher, ed., *Constitutions and Constitutional Trends since World War II* (New York, 1951), 134 ff.

set up a Communist-dominated city government for East Berlin. In West Berlin, when elections resulted in a 65 per cent majority for the Social Democrats, Professor Ernst Reuter, a former Communist hated by the Soviet authorities because of his conversion, became mayor. The constitution of 1950, though making Berlin a Land, for international reasons suspended Berlin's inclusion in the Federal Republic. The elections of 1950 resulted in a shift to the right; for the first time since before World War I, Berlin lost its left-wing majority. In spite of his party's losses, Mayor Reuter was re-elected because of his prestige as a symbol of Berlin's courageous resistance to Communist threats.

Prospects for Germany. As European recovery and peace are irrevocably tied up with the German evolution, the growth of democratic institutions and attitudes in Germany is of primary importance.[20] Since the very beginning one of the major Western aims has been the development of the German people's political independence along democratic lines. It is too early to judge the depth and strength of democratic tendencies in Germany, but the prospects on the whole are encouraging.

The division of the country into two parts under Western and Soviet occupation has resulted in the existence of two areas that are not only separate but rigidly isolated from each other. While the present situation offers no early prospects for Germany's reunification, Soviet policy in the eastern zone results in a gradual but steady widening of the chasm.

6. German "Democracy" Soviet Style

East Germany's Constitution. The constitution of the part of Germany in the Soviet zone, which calls itself the German Democratic Republic (*Deutsche Demokratische Republik*), has the outward appearance of a democratic document.[21] In practice, however, it has lent itself to the establishment of a totalitarian police state. Under Soviet domination the government interprets democratic terms according to its own purposes, most often in opposition to the Western democracies.

The constitution came into being in a round-about and thoroughly undemocratic way. In 1948 the German People's Congress, formed by the officially sponsored Socialist Unity party and its satellite organizations but neither elected nor confirmed by the people, named a 400-member People's Council. This body set up a constitutional committee from among its own members to prepare a draft constitution. In 1949 the People's Council approved the draft—unanimously. A new People's Congress, elected on a single, Communist-sponsored "unity list," promptly confirmed the constitution and also named another People's Council. Next, the Council,

---

[20] See Gabriel O. Almond, ed., *The Struggle for Democracy in Germany* (Chapel Hill, 1949). The quarterly *Reports on Germany* published since 1950 by the United States High Commissioner in Germany are indispensable sources on current developments.

[21] See *Soviet Zone Constitution and Electoral Law,* prepared by the Office of the United States High Commissioner in Germany (Government Printing Office, Washington, 1951).

without benefit of elections, renamed itself the provisional People's Chamber provided for in the constitution as an elected parliament, promulgated the constitution, and set up the German Democratic Republic, which presumes to speak for all Germany, including the western zones.

These actions were not accompanied by public discussion. The slight murmurs of opposition from non-Communist party circles were effectively silenced by reminders about the need for "progressive thinking" and the shame of "undemocratic" behavior. Unlike the basic law of Western Germany, the constitution in the Soviet Zone was adopted almost in closed chambers. Public sessions such as took place in the Bonn Parliamentary Council were unknown. The net result was an interesting document of Soviet ideas set forth in democratic verbiage.

The constitution contains a Bill of Rights, but judges are specifically denied the power to examine the constitutionality of laws.

A Constitutional Committee is empowered to interpret the constitution and to adjudicate disagreements between the republic and the Länder. The committee consists of members of the People's Chamber elected in proportion to party strength, three members of the Supreme Court, and three professors of constitutional law. The constitution rejects the principle of a separation of powers. Constitutional amendments require a two-thirds majority in the People's Chamber, provided two-thirds of the membership are present, or a simple majority in a popular referendum.

The constitution declares propaganda for war and incitement of a "boycott of democratic organizations" to be criminal acts. It is, therefore, a crime to organize an independent trade union in competition with the German Trade Union Federation, dominated by the government. The constitution further provides for socialization and economic planning.

Branches of Government. The President is elected for a four-year term by a joint session of the two chambers of the legislature. He has representative functions only and can be removed from office by legislative action. The Cabinet is elected by the People's Chamber. Any political group represented in the People's Chamber by forty or more members can claim a seat in the Cabinet. The constitution requires that the Prime Minister be designated by the largest party, which means the Communist-controlled Socialist Unity Party (SED). In the face of a vote of non-confidence, the Cabinet or an individual minister must resign, but the Cabinet survives if its successor fails "to take office within twenty-one days after the motion of non-confidence has been carried," in which case "that motion shall become void." If the Prime Minister should resign, he would be succeeded by another member of the largest party.

The republic is granted a wide range of exclusive jurisdiction, augmented further by the priority it enjoys in other fields where it has concurrent jurisdiction with the Länder. It may also establish its own administrative system on all levels. Finally, the republic has the right to supervise both the administration of its laws by the Länder and the administrative functions which it delegates to them.

The legislature consists of two chambers, the People's Chamber (*Volks-kammer*) and the Länder Chamber. The former consists of 400 members, elected for four-year terms on the basis of proportional representation. The voting age is 18 years, but candidates for the legislature must be 21 years of age or older. Besides political parties, "democratic mass organizations" may put up candidates. The People's Chamber has a large legislative mandate, but laws may also be adopted by referendum.

The other chamber consists of representatives of the Länder selected according to party strength by their diets in proportion to the population of each Land—one for every 500,000 inhabitants, or a total of about 35. The Länder Chamber reviews legislation passed by the People's Chamber but may also initiate legislation by introducing bills in that house. It may reject laws passed by the People's Chamber. On the other hand, this veto can be overridden by the People's Chamber; if the veto receives a two-thirds majority, the same majority is needed in the People's Chamber to overcome the veto. Legislation having the effect of amending the constitution can be vetoed and the veto be overridden only by a two-thirds majority in each chamber.

The judges of the Supreme Court and the Prosecutor General are nominated by the Cabinet and elected by the People's Chamber, which may also recall them. All other judges are appointed by the government. The constitution lays down prerequisites concerning the political reliability of judges. It also establishes the principle of "lay judges" when it states: "Laymen are, as much as possible, to be used as judges. Laymen are elected, on the proposal of democratic parties and organizations, by the competent popular representative bodies." This provision has in practice become a constitutional sanction for the creation of "people's courts" to enforce the "right" way of thinking.

Political Parties. The Socialist Unity Party (*Sozialistische Einheitspartei,* or SED) was formed by the forced merger of the Social Democratic Party (SPD) with the Communist Party (KPD); thereafter the SPD was forbidden in the Soviet zone. The CDU (Christian Democratic Union) and LDP (Liberal Democratic Party) were allowed to continue in existence; but they have been progressively induced to make compromises in their party programs for the sake of greater political uniformity despite the nominal multi-party system.

In the legislative bodies in the Soviet zone, the SED insists on the concurrence of the CDU and LDP on all important measures. Seeming agreement is preferred over any expression of differences of opinion. By compelling the leaders of the CDU and LDP to compromise themselves through concessions, the SED sows uncertainty and cynicism among the non-Communist rank and file. Leaders of the CDU and LDP with any backbone have been removed from government and party offices and forced into oblivion. Some have fled to the Western zones for safety. The changes in party leadership tend to weaken the parties, cause distrust of the membership in the leaders, and deepen the feeling of futility about political activities outside the SED.

There also exist Communist-front parties which present themselves as spokesmen of those elements of the population that by tradition stand outside the SED. These include the National Democratic Party and the Democratic Farmers Party. Because of the rigid control of all media of information, the CDU and LDP are unable to unmask their competitors as Communist-front organizations.

Members of the SED receive preference in public employment, while other public employees have been dismissed in increasing numbers on the slightest excuse. The SED originally expanded rapidly to a total membership of 1,800,000, although many of them were only lukewarm members or even actual opponents. The party was later trimmed in size by repeated purges. Members have been subjected to a severe schedule of indoctrination courses in Marxism-Stalinism. The same systematic propaganda effort has also been forced on all public employees, including those in socialized industry.

The Elections of 1950. In October 1950, realizing that it could not win free elections after having remained subjected to its Soviet masters for four years while keeping German opposition down by intimidation, the government ran a sham election. In violation of the constitutional provision for election of members of the People's Chamber on a "universal, equal, direct, and secret ballot according to the principles of proportional representation," another "unity list" of candidates was forced upon the non-Communist parties. The SED allotted 70 per cent of the candidates to itself and "mass organizations" such as the Communist trade unions, and 15 per cent each to the Christian Democratic Union and the Liberal Democratic Party. But even the CDU and LDP candidates were usually named in "consultation" with the SED and were subject to its veto. No other names were allowed on the ballot; nor did it provide the voter with a "yes" or "no" alternative for indicating disagreement.

The election law itself explained the "unity list" as follows:

Motivated by a feeling of national responsibility and the desire to safeguard the constructive work of the Republic, the block of the anti-fascist democratic parties and organizations has made use of its constitutional right and resolved to conduct the elections on the basis of a joint platform and with joint lists of candidates of the "National Front of the Democratic Germany." Free of petty discord among egotistic interest groups, the elections of October 15, 1950, will thus become truly free elections of the people.

The government went still further in assuring docility on the part of the legislators by providing in the election law that deputies can lose their seats by vote of Parliament "if the requirements for a delegate's eligibility cease to apply" after his election—a phrase wide enough to allow for expulsion for even minor disagreement with official policy. To top it all, the same law provided: "Subject to his consent, a citizen may be admitted to a representative body by decision of the latter. He thereby acquires the same rights and duties as an elected delegate." This section allowed the Parliament to be packed with any number of the politically faithful.

The results in the diets and county assemblies to be elected on the same day were similarly predetermined. Voters were told that it was their duty "to pledge allegiance to the national program" and that there was no need for the election to take place within the secrecy of election booths. Thus it was made impossible for voters to register opposition by spoiling the ballot. The outcome was celebrated as a great victory for those in power.

The Police State. It is equally revealing that East Germany is blessed with a Ministry for State Security, on the Soviet pattern, which is in charge of the secret police. A State Control Commission supervises economic planning and what little is left of private enterprise; in addition, it combats "industrial sabotage." A Central Personnel Administration in the Department of the Interior checks the political records of all candidates for public employment, including those on the Land and local level. Political commissars, officially classified as assistants to public administrators but actually with power to give them orders, are attached to government offices on all levels. They constitute a "state within the state," concerning themselves with governmental, economic, cultural, and social affairs under strict control from above.

In one way or other, the government endeavors to regulate and control the life of every citizen, whether in his job or his leisure time. The churches are the last stronghold against this penetration. Schools and universities were among the earliest institutions to come under thought control, because of the emphasis which the regime places on capturing the youth. Proselytes are made among the young, intellectually through generous expenditures for sports and leisure-time activities, or economically through rewards in the form of important public positions.

The Free German Youth (*Freie Deutsche Jugend,* or FDJ), by promise or compulsion, seeks to take all young people into the Communist fold, while the Young Pioneers go after the children 6 to 14 years old. The so-called National Council—every one of its 65 members from the Soviet zone—cultivates the unquestioned acceptance of the aims and policies of the Soviet Union. It provides sponsorship of "enlightenment centers" in most communities, lectures at neighborhood meetings, and liberal distribution of literature. In addition, it organizes training for sabotage and for dissemination of scare rumors in western Germany, working often with individuals and groups that are not openly Communist or are even camouflaged along anti-Communist lines. Most of them share a violent anti-American attitude.

Some of these people are actually misguided idealists and utopian thinkers, often of pacifist persuasion.[22]

Berlin and the Eastern Zone. The hostility of the Soviet regime against western Berlin has resulted in repeated attempts to strangle that outpost of resistance by severe restrictions on traffic to and from the West and by other forms of economic, political, and psychological pressure. This is because western Berlin in the center of the Soviet zone constitutes a "show window" of the West which annually attracts uncounted visitors from eastern Germany. They cannot be isolated from the ways of the West so long as they have access to a free Berlin.

At the time of the elections of 1950 in the Soviet zone, this fact led to an impressive demonstration. The city government of western Berlin urged all Berliners living in the Soviet sector of the city who wished to protest in favor of free elections to mail the stubs of their ration cards to the West Berlin government. The result was the receipt of more than 400,000 stubs or letters stating that the stubs had already been destroyed. It should be added that East Berliners had to enter the western sectors in order to mail their stubs and letters. Moreover, the SED tried to stifle the informal referendum by announcing a special ration of clothing in exchange for the stubs.

---

[22] See in general J. P. Nettl, *The Eastern Zone and Soviet Policy in Germany, 1945-50* (Toronto, 1951).

CHAPTER 18

REPUBLICAN AUSTRIA

1. Political Evolution

Bridge or Buffer. Austria is a small country, but her political importance is out of proportion to her size. Located at the historic crossroads of central Europe, Austria is the meeting place of different peoples—Slavic, Magyar, Teutonic, and Latin. Hers is one of the oldest homes of European culture. Century-old ties with non-German neighbors and the ability to absorb alien contributions have made Austrian life a happy blend of native and foreign influences. Her leaders would prefer for her the role of a bridge between East and West, rather than that of a buffer wedged in between giant powers.

Austria is about twice the size of Switzerland, with a population of some 7 million. About half of the country's area consists of arable land and pastures, and the remainder of forests, mostly in mountainous regions. Industries include textiles in the western part, and steel or iron and steel products, including locomotives and machinery, in the central and especially the eastern sections. In a country with generally high standards of education, the industries employ a large percentage of skilled workers.

Dual Monarchy. In the course of centuries, Germanic Austria became the nucleus of a large polyglot empire. After 1867, its vast area, which came to sustain a population of some 50 million, was governed in the form of a dual monarchy. The ancient Hapsburg family furnished the Emperors of Austria, who were crowned in Budapest with the insignia of Hungary's sainted King Stephen. Only foreign relations and the armed forces, together with the financial support for both, were under joint Austro-Hungarian control.

The defeat of the Central Powers in World War I resulted in the speedy breakup of the dual monarchy.[1] From it, the states of Austria, Czechoslovakia, and Hungary were carved. States receiving large slices of territory included Poland, Yugoslavia, Rumania, and Italy.

Independent Austria. In the turmoil of political disintegration, the German deputies of the old Parliament constituted themselves as a national assembly, claiming independent statehood and the right of self-determination for German Austria. The German-Austrian Republic was proclaimed November 12, 1918, as a part of the German Reich. The victorious Allied powers, however, opposed the union with Germany.

---

[1] See Oscar Jászi, *The Dissolution of the Hapsburg Monarchy* (Chicago, 1929). Appreciation is due Dr. George Fleischer, United States High Commissioner's Office in Germany, for criticism.

355

The peace treaty of St. Germain of 1919 provided that Austria was not free to give up her independence except with the consent of the League of Nations —a round-about way of forbidding the *Anschluss* with Germany. The word "German" had to be dropped from the official name of the new republic.[2]

A Viable State? To the Austrians, the possibility of union with Germany was not merely a political question or the expression of preference by a small state largely surrounded by unfriendly neighbors. Economically, it appeared to be a question of life and death, the advantages being with Austria, rather than with Germany.

Vienna, the capital, had formerly served the needs of an empire. Now a state within the new federal union, its own population amounted to more than one fourth of the whole republic. Vienna had become an enormous "waterhead" on a dwarf body. Hunger stalked the streets of the metropolis as it went on to exist without most of its old hinterland, both a source of foodstuffs and an eager market for Vienna's manufactured products, as well as an outlet for its great experience in finance and trade.

2. Alternatives of Government

Constitution and Constitutional Change. The Austro-Hungarian monarchy had been a multinational state, held together by an imperial house that ruled largely by balancing one nationality group against another. The new Austria, by contrast, was predominantly German in population, without monarchical ties. Its internal divisions were along social, economic, and regional lines, rather than along racial ones. The new constitution was adopted by a constituent assembly, on October 1, 1920. The constituent Assembly, elected under a system of proportional representation, consisted of 72 Social Democrats, 69 members of the Christian Social Party, 26 German Nationalists, and a few others. Minor constitutional changes were adopted in 1925 in the direction of increased centralization. In part, they resulted from pressure by the Commissioner General of the League of Nations, in line with governmental reforms agreed to by Austria as the necessary price for foreign loans.

By 1929, there was much popular dissatisfaction, both on the right and the left, with the practical effects of the constitution. The domestic political and economic situation had steadily deteriorated. Since party strife and the weakness of the executive were given most of the blame, several constitutional amendments were adopted in order to strengthen the executive branch. The changes largely followed the German constitutional model. The President, who had been little more than a figurehead, was given greatly increased

---

[2] See M. Margaret Ball, *Post-War German Relations: The Anschluss Movement* (Palo Alto, 1937). On the Austrian Republic in general, see Charles A. Gulick, *Austria from Hapsburg to Hitler* (Berkeley, 1948), 2 vols.; Franz Borkenau, *Austria and After* (London, 1938); Mary MacDonald, *The Republic of Austria, 1918-1934: A Study in the Failure of Democratic Government* (London, 1946); G. E. R. Gedye, *Betrayal in Central Europe* (New York, 1939).

power, primarily at the expense of the National Council, the popular branch of the federal parliament. He was now to be elected directly by the people instead of being chosen by Parliament, and for a six-year rather than a four-year term. The Cabinet was to be appointed by the President instead of being elected by Parliament. The government still needed the confidence of the National Council, however. With the consent of the Cabinet, the President was enabled to dissolve the Council.

Governmental centralization increased once more—for instance, through the extension of powers of the federal police. The *Land* of Vienna, for example, had to abolish the special police force set up after the riots of 1927, which had been climaxed by the burning of the Palace of Justice. The federal government also gained additional powers over finance and education.

Rise of Dollfuss. Austria's two main parties, the Social Democrats and the Christian Social party, were almost evenly divided in strength. Generally, the Social Democrats stood further to the left than their German brethren. After an early period of understanding leading to the establishment of the Republic, the two parties became determined enemies. The left-wing riots of 1927 turned into one of the outstanding dates in Austrian history by deeply increasing the political bitterness. It was not eased when a move toward a customs union with Germany was defeated by France.

Chancellor Ignaz Seipel, an able Catholic clergyman, proceeded to draw the small Pan-German and Peasant parties into an antisocialist coalition led by his Christian Social party and to arm the semimilitary organization of the right, called the *Heimwehr* (Home Guard). By 1930, the Heimwehr men had sworn to seize power in the state, to reject democratic and parliamentary government, and to stand for the principle of leadership. The radical wing of this movement leaned more and more toward the Nazis, while the Christian Social party lost in popular strength. It endeavored to avoid threatening defeat by looking for a strong man, whom it found in Dr. Engelbert Dollfuss.[3] Appointed Chancellor in 1932, he tried to fight both the left and the Nazis with the help of emergency decrees. In the spring of 1933, he suspended Parliament and abolished freedom both of the press and of assembly. By June, the Nazi party was outlawed, and the Social Democratic *Schutzbund* (Protective Corps) and the Communist party were dissolved.

The Social Democrats were willing to join Dollfuss in the fight against nazism; but the Chancellor, under pressure from Mussolini, turned against them and favored the antidemocratic Heimwehr instead. On February 11, 1934, the remaining parties were dissolved. When, the next day, Social Democratic headquarters were raided by police and Heimwehr, fighting started, which in Vienna lasted for four days. The Government bombarded the worker's apartment blocks with artillery and succeeded in suppressing the Social Democrats. A number of their leaders were arrested and several

---

[3] See Malcolm Bullock, *Austria, 1918-38: A Study in Failure* (London, 1939), chaps. 10 and 11; Rudolf Schlesinger, *Federalism in Central and Eastern Europe* (New York, 1945), pp. 281 ff.

workers were hanged. Vienna now lost her self-government, which had resulted in sixteen years of Social Democratic rule.

Constitution of the Corporate State. Dollfuss decreed a new constitution, without providing for any popular control of government nor any participation by the people in state affairs. It was "approved" by a Parliament from which the Social Democrats and Communists had been expelled. The same body passed without debate a law approving 417 emergency decrees issued during the preceding fourteen months of dictatorship, including the new constitution. The entire business required ten minutes—fast even for a Hitler. Then Parliament adjourned *sine die*.

The constitution set up a so-called corporate state.[4] It provided for six deliberative bodies of a mostly decorative nature. Four of these were known as "advisory organs": (1) a council of state, appointed by the Cabinet and consisting chiefly of civil servants and political leaders agreeable to the government; (2) a council of culture, whose members represented the recognized churches and various organizations in the fields of the arts and sciences; (3) an economic council, representing the economic and professional "estates," such as agriculture and forestry, mining and industry, banking and insurance, trade and transport, the liberal professions, and the public services; and (4) a council of states, consisting of the governors and their chief financial officials. Legislative proposals, which could originate only with the Cabinet, were to be referred to one of these bodies for report and recommendation. A fifth organ of government, known as the Federal Diet, consisted of a smaller group, chosen from the other four bodies. The Diet, a ward of the Cabinet, had the power to approve or reject legislative proposals after they had been considered by one of the advisory councils. It was not allowed to propose amendments. In case the Diet opposed a proposal, it could be submitted to a popular referendum. The combined membership of all four advisory councils could meet for special purposes, such as the nomination of candidates for the presidency. This last and sixth body was known as the Federal Assembly.

The President was to be elected for a seven-year term by all the mayors of the country, from among three candidates chosen by the Federal Assembly. He had the right freely to appoint and dismiss the Chancellor, and other Cabinet members upon the latter's recommendation. The Chancellor and ministers had to countersign all presidential orders and decrees, but they were not subject to any parliamentary responsibility. The executive had extensive powers to issue emergency decrees, including, in certain cases, decrees amending the constitution. In addition, although the states, with the exception of Vienna, were granted wide powers, the federal government had authority to dissolve their diets as well as the municipal council of Vienna, to set aside state laws, and to remove the governors and the mayor of Vienna.

---

[4] See Arnold J. Zurcher, "Austria's Corporative Constitution," *American Political Science Review*, 28 (1934), 664 ff.

A Catholic State? Dollfuss and his political friends tried to revive the idea of a Catholic state. The Roman Catholic church was granted a favored status, although freedom of religion was granted to the other recognized churches as well. A concordat, dealing especially with matters of education and other important subjects, was concluded with the Vatican and given the status of constitutional law. Some enthusiasts, as well as equally thoughtless opponents, have claimed that the corporate state was based upon the principles of the famous papal encyclicals *Rerum Novarum* (1891) and *Quadragesimo Anno* (1931). These basic church documents, however, were not aimed at setting up a framework of government. Dollfuss' attempt to form a Catholic state, antisocialist, authoritarian, and quasi-fascistic, can best be characterized as "a pious illusion," to use Don Luigi Sturzo's words.[5]

Large parts of the new constitution actually never went into effect. What remained was a "nonpartisan," proclerical dictatorship based upon the so-called Fatherland Front, rather than a one-party state such as Nazi Germany or Fascist Italy was. Its harshness was mitigated in part by the fact that it was Austrian. Dollfuss was soon murdered by the Nazis, and some of the leading proponents of the corporate regime later died in Hitler's concentration camps, together with Socialists and Communists.

From Hitler's Rule to Liberation. In March 1938, Hitler, conniving with the Austrian Nazis, occupied Austria by military force and annexed the country. There was enthusiasm on public squares over the turn of developments, but how much was genuine is difficult to say. By Nazi decree, Austria lost her historic name and was now known as *Ostmark*, or Eastern Borderland. She was "coordinated" by imposition of Reich laws, which were enforced under strict German supervision in a country that had preferred a "leisurely efficiency." Nazi efforts were concentrated on *Gleichschaltung* of Austria's cultural as well as political and economic life. All of Austria became one German *Land* under a Reich commissioner. Within a year and a half, Austria entered World War II, by virtue of Hitler's decision.

The "declaration of independence" issued jointly on April 27, 1945, by the leaders of the Socialists, the People's party, and the Communists stated that "the Democratic Republic of Austria is restored and is to be organized in the spirit of the Constitution of 1920." The constitutional law of May 1, 1945— the first law of restored republican Austria—prescribed the re-enactment of the constitution as amended in 1929.[6] Postwar Austria thereby rejected the extreme parliamentary system of 1920 in favor of a stronger presidency. As Austria was occupied territory, the directives issued by the Allied council of the four occupying powers were still supreme, but the constitution gradually came to have more than *de facto* significance.

Austrian Federalism. In the old Austria-Hungary, federalist movements

---

[5] Luigi Sturzo, *Church and State* (New York, 1939), pp. 542-43.

[6] See Erich Hula, "Constitutional Developments in Austria," in James K. Pollock, ed., *Change and Crisis in European Government* (New York, 1947), pp. 62 ff.

had aimed at the problems of relations between the various nationalities. The republic that emerged at the end of World War I was homogeneous from a national point of view, but heterogeneous in social, economic, and sectional respects. If the country was to be governed democratically, decentralization was necessary to replace the former centralized structure. There had been antagonism of long standing between the strongly socialist elements in Vienna and in the industrial parts of Lower Austria on the one hand, and the conservative and rural-minded farmers of the Alpine regions on the other. Bridging this division became a cardinal task of federalism.

When Dollfuss proclaimed the corporate state, it was expressly declared to be federal. But the term referred to appearance rather than actuality. Since 1945, federalism has been honored again in practice.

Powers of the Federal Government. Under the constitution of 1920, the federal government was accorded exclusive legislative and executive powers in sixteen fields, of which the most important were foreign relations, military affairs, customs, currency, banking, trade and industry, transportation and communications, mining, civil and criminal law (with minor exceptions), justice, labor law (except in agriculture and forestry), and public health (excepting municipal functions). The federal government was also given extensive legislative and executive powers in the field of taxation, which to some extent it shared with the states.

In certain other fields, including citizenship, legislative power was vested in the federal government and administrative power in the states. When state officials acted in a federal capacity, appeals against their decisions could be addressed to the federal authorities. In still other areas of activity, the federal government possessed power, familiar from the Weimar constitution, to enact "principles," while the executive power was vested in the states. Among these subjects were the organization of state administration, poor relief, and care of mothers, infants, and children.

Development of the Presidency. The constitution of 1920 provided for the election of the President of the Republic by a simple majority of votes cast in the Federal Assembly—that is, in the two houses of Parliament sitting together. His term of office was four years, and his immediate re-election was permissible only once. Anyone eligible to vote for the National Council (the lower house) and thirty-five years old or older could be elected President, provided he was not a member of a ruling family, past or present.

The President had the usual duties and powers, such as representing the Republic in its external relations and appointing federal officials, including army officers. All acts of the President had to be countersigned by the Chancellor or another Cabinet member in his field of responsibility. Because under the constitution of 1920 the Cabinet was responsible to Parliament, the President was in no way independent. When progressive deterioration of conditions led to the constitutional changes of 1929, the power of the President was greatly increased at the expense of "almighty Parliament." He was to be elected by popular vote for six years. He now picked the Cabinet, though subject to the National Council's vote of confidence, and he also had the right to dissolve the Council.

Actually, no direct election of the President was held until 1951. Just prior to the time of the first scheduled popular vote in 1931, the political parties agreed on choosing the President once more in the old way, by vote of Parliament. When Austria was resurrected after World War II, the aged Social Democrat Dr. Karl Renner was unanimously elected President. After his death, his Socialist friend, 78-year-old Theodor Koerner, mayor of Vienna since 1945, was elected in 1951 in Austria's first direct presidential election.

A law passed in April 1948 under the impact of the Communist *coup* in Czechoslovakia provided that the functions of the President should pass to the Chancellor in case the former was prevented from exercising the functions of his office, and to the Principal Committee of the National Council in case the Chancellor was similarly handicapped. Only the Communist deputies opposed the law.[7]

Chancellor and Cabinet. The constitution of 1920 provided for a parliamentary system, in both the federal government and the states. The federal Cabinet, headed by a Chancellor, was elected by the National Council, on nomination of its principal committee. The constitutional amendments of 1929 terminated this power of the Council. The constitution provided further that Cabinet members had to be eligible for election to the National Council, but could not be members of that body. This departure from the ordinary features of parliamentary government followed the Swiss example.

The turnover among Chancellors was heavy, owing to the paralyzing difficulties of the sharp party division and the size of the country's inherent problems. Most of the Chancellors were Christian Social. The last parliamentary government, a coalition headed by Dollfuss in 1932, was supported by a majority of only one deputy.

After World War II, President Renner appointed a government headed by Chancellor Leopold Figl of the People's party, the successor to the Christian Social party. Socialist Adolf Schaerf became Vice Chancellor. The government was based upon a coalition of all three parties, including the few Communist deputies. Seats in the Cabinet were divided in proportion to the strength of the parties in the newly elected National Council, in which the People's party had 85 members, the Socialist 76, and the Communist 4 members. In the fall of 1947, the Communists resigned from the government over the issue of currency revaluation. When the People's party lost its majority in the elections of 1949, party representation in the Cabinet was redistributed virtually equally between the two large parties. Otherwise, the Cabinet has continued in office—with minor changes—longer than any other democratically constituted government of postwar Europe.

Bicameralism. The federal parliament consists of the *Nationalrat,* or

[7] *Neue Zürcher Zeitung,* April 25, 1948.

National Council, and the *Bundesrat,* or Federal Council, as the second chamber. When meeting together for certain purposes, they are known as the *Bundesversammlung,* or Federal Assembly; its main function, before the constitutional amendments of 1929, was the election of the President.

The National Council is elected for four years by universal suffrage of both men and women twenty years old or older on the basis of proportional representation. Candidates must be at least twenty-four years old. Elections are held on Sundays or other public holidays. The National Council adjourns only by its own decision, and its presiding officer has to summon it back into session immediately if one fourth of its members or the Cabinet request it. It is able to dissolve itself by law.

Composition of the Federal Council. The Federal Council constitutes the upper house, in which the states are represented in proportion to the size of their population, with slight adjustments, except that no state has more than twelve and less than three members. This arrangement works to the advantage of the rural states. The members are chosen by the state diets on the basis of proportional representation. As the leading members of the diets of the interwar period years were used to practical methods of collaboration in state government, they helped to mitigate the antagonism ordinarily prevalent on the national plane, especially in the years preceding the Dollfuss era.

Members of the Federal Council cannot be members of the diet electing them, but they have to be eligible for membership in it. Constitutional provisions regarding the Council may be amended only with the consent of the majority of the representatives of at least four states, in addition to the general requirements for constitutional change. The chairmanship of the Federal Council rotates among the states in an alphabetical order, in each instance going to the leading representative of the state for a period of six months. The chairman summons the Council; he must do it immediately on the request of one fourth of its members or of the government.

Federal Legislation. Bills may be introduced in the National Council by (1) its members, (2) the Cabinet, (3) the Federal Council, transmitting legislative proposals through the Cabinet, or (4) a popular initiative, in the form of a draft bill supported by the petition of 200,000 voters or one half the voters of three states. Bills passed by the National Council become law if agreed to unamended by the Federal Council. In case it raises opposition, the upper house enjoys only a suspensive veto, since the National Council may repass the bill, with at least one half of its membership present, whereupon the bill is promulgated as law. The Federal Council may not amend bills dealing with the rules of procedure of the National Council, the dissolution of that body, federal loans, or the administration of federal property. Every bill passed by the National Council shall be submitted to a referendum by the President, if this house so decides.

The postwar coalition parties have worked out a singular method of interparty agreement on common legislative programs that avoids an excess of public agitation and presents a picture of unity to the outside world, especially to the occupying powers. In the spring of 1948, specially appointed representatives of the People's party and the Socialists prepared a legislative program for both 1948 and 1949 under the leadership of Chancellor Figl and Vice Chancellor Schaerf. Such negotiations have tended to end with a gentlemen's agreement that is faithfully respected by the members of Parliament.

Federal and state powers are exercised subject to the authority of the Allied control council and the four High Commissioners of the occupying armies. Under the Interallied Agreement on Control Machinery of June 28, 1946, ordinary laws no longer require the unanimous assent of the control council before they become effective, a fact that has greatly increased the authority of the Austrian government. Constitutional laws, and laws containing provisions of a constitutional character, require a quorum in the National Council of at least one half of the members, and a two-thirds majority of the votes cast; such laws must be expressly designated. Every general revision of the constitution is subject to a referendum; on demand of one third of the members of the National Council or the Federal Council, a referendum is necessary also for every partial revision. A referendum is decided by an absolute majority of the votes cast.

Proportional Representation. The constitution provides for elections to the National Council and to the state diets on the basis of proportional representation. Electoral districts may not overlap state boundaries. Parliament adopted a list system, under which the voter had no opportunity to vote for individuals, but was limited to adopting or rejecting a list of candidates as a whole. In spite of the fact that as few as one hundred voters are able to make up a list of candidates and submit it to the electorate, Austria has not proved a fertile ground for the growth of splinter parties. The election law of 1949 liberalized the list system by allowing voters to change the order of names on the ballot.

Criticism in Austria has usually been directed against the results of the rigid list system. Primarily, it has had the effect that the party bureaucracy controlled the nominations, including the order in which the names of candidates appear on the list, which predetermines much of the chance of their election; that the list system favored "time-servers" in each party, rather than individuals with distinctive and independent views; and that there was little opportunity for the development of a personal relationship between the representative and his constituents.[8]

Judicial Review. The theory and practice of judicial examination of legislation on constitutional grounds reached notable development, in some ways different from those prevalent in the United States.[9] The constitution pro-

[8] See Arnold J. Zurcher, *The Experiment with Democracy in Central Europe* (New York, 1933), pp. 75-76.

[9] See J. A. C. Grant, "Judicial Review of Legislation under the Austrian Constitution of 1920," *American Political Science Review*, 28 (1934), 670 ff.; I. Seidl-Hohenvoldern, "Der Verfassungsdienst," *Oesterreichische Juristen-Zeitung*, No. 7 (1951), 160 ff.

vided specifically that the ordinary courts "may not inquire into the validity of any duly promulgated law," and instead set up a special constitutional court to fulfill this important function.   The court consists of fourteen regular and six alternate members, appointed by the President in three groups chosen from lists prepared by the Cabinet and the two houses of Parliament, respectively.   The judges have to possess previous training and experience in the fields of law and political science.

The constitutional court has power to annul an entire federal law or part of it.   It renders judgment upon the constitutionality of state laws at the request of the Cabinet, and of federal laws upon application by a state government.   The court may also on its own initiative decide the constitutionality of federal or state laws at the request of either the Supreme Court or the Supreme Administrative Court.   But no citizen on his own can take such a question to the constitutional court, except indirectly in civil liberty cases.

The court has the power to provide at its discretion that the annulment of a law found unconstitutional should become effective only after a certain period.   In this case, the legislature has an opportunity to substitute a new and valid law before the annulment becomes effective.   The period of grace might run for as long as a year.   A special government office devotes itself to examining the constitutionality of all federal bills before their submission to Parliament and of all proposed federal regulations in order to prevent the passing of unconstitutional measures and to avoid having them voided by the constitutional court.   Provincial bills are examined frequently for the same reason but only upon request by the individual provincial government.   This happens frequently as provincial governments wish to avoid federal objections to their laws.

3. State and Local Government

Powers of State Government.   The constitution of 1920 provided that all legislative and executive power not expressly vested in the federal government was left to the states.   In general, the Austrian states possessed more self-government than the German *Länder* under the Weimar constitution. If the legislative powers of the states were not particularly large, their share in administration was extensive, even in fields where the principles of action were laid down by federal statutes.   The states became, in fact, laboratories for social experimentation in a country where federal policy was blocked by an almost permanent deadlock between two bitterly antagonistic and almost equally strong parties.   The Dollfuss dictatorship destroyed in effect all state autonomy, but it was restored in 1945.

Because of its size and importance, and also because of the necessity for a political compromise between the Socialist and the Christian Social party, Vienna was assigned a special place in the federal structure.   The state diet of Lower Austria was divided into two assemblies, one representing the area outside Vienna, and the other, the municipal council, the federal capital. On matters of common concern, the two assemblies met together and passed legislation jointly. On matters not of common concern, each of the two divisions was deemed a state. In such matters, the municipal council, for instance, functioned as a state diet for Vienna.

The recognition of Vienna as a separate state was a great success of the Socialists in the framing of the constitution. It was made possible because it was also in the interests of the Christian Social party in Lower Austria. In Vienna, the Socialists had a permanent hold on 60 per cent of the voters; the Christian Social party was supported by about 50 per cent of the electorate in Lower Austria, where the Socialists at the most could poll much less. Consequently, Socialist rule was assured in Vienna and lasted until it was suppressed by brute force under Dollfuss.

Vienna's Economic and Social Policies. Since Vienna enjoyed the status of a state, its Socialist government was free to put into effect much of its economic and social program, which it was unable to push on a national scale. If it went to some extremes, causing hostility to the party in Vienna and throughout the country, it must also be recalled that Socialist welfare policies dealt a death blow to the Communist movement, which plagued so many other European countries, culminating in temporary Soviet republics in near-by Hungary and Bavaria. Vienna's most spectacular policy was its housing program. It was developed on a class basis, but for the class of people that needed it most, and it had the support of a two-thirds majority of the Viennese voters.

Various Austrian states undertook housing projects, financing them in accordance with their own political preferences. Vienna decided to use taxation for housing instead of loans. It was thereby enabled to keep rents low, since they were applied to current expenses only and not to the payment of loans or interest. In ten years' time, the Socialists built 60,000 workers' apartments, for more than 200,000 people or almost one eighth of the city's population. Between 1923 and 1930, Vienna spent thirteen times as much on municipal housing as all the other municipalities and states put together. Rents amounted to 4 to 19 schillings monthly, whereas in municipalities outside Vienna, rents in public housing projects based on loans were 12 to 25 and even up to 50 schillings for similar apartments. In a sense, these low rents were a subsidy to Vienna's industries, which could thus operate on a lower wage level.

Because federal unemployment insurance standards were low, Socialist Vienna spent heavily on public housing, partly to create jobs. Vienna's finances were sound during these years, with its budget either balanced or showing a surplus, at times of heavy federal deficits. This was true in spite of the fact that additional tens of millions were spent on improving various publicly owned utilities, and that municipal wages were about one third higher than those paid by the federal government for similar work. Other improvements included technical schools, psychiatric clinics, and cultural enterprises.

Local Self-Government. Austria's 4,973 communities enjoy a long tradition of self-government, expressed in the principle of the Provisional Municipality Law of 1849: "The foundation of the free state is the free community." The basic structure of local government is the same throughout the country for both large cities and small rural communities. All of them have a mayor, one or several deputy mayors, and a municipal council. In larger cities, the mayor is assisted by up to five city councilors elected by the municipal councils from among their own members. Councils are elected by the voters, and mayors and deputy mayors by the council.

The mayor, who is head of the local government, has a double or triple responsibility. He is responsible to the city council for all matters of local administration and to the federal authorities and the state governments for all federal and state matters administered by the communities. Larger communities employ a so-called director, who has a certain similarity to an American city manager, to serve as the top executive under the mayor. In communities of more than 10,000 inhabitants, the director is a university graduate who has passed the proper civil service examination. Permanent employees are usually subject to certain educational and professional standards set up by state legislation.

Local communities have the right of self-government within constitutional limits. This includes power to levy taxes; acquire, own, manage, or dispose of any kind of property; and carry on economic enterprises that they consider in the common interest of the community. The state government has the right and duty to remove the mayor from office if he fails in his functions as a representative of the provincial or federal administration. The city council may dismiss him on such grounds on its own initiative, or upon the request of the state authorities. The state also may dissolve the city council for neglecting its duties. Local self-government was drastically controlled under the Dollfuss regime.

4. Shifts of Political Orientation

Party Solidarity. Austria's political situation was and is typified by the predominance of two parties, the Christian Social party, now known as the People's party, and the Socialists, with the coexistence of a small Communist party and, at times, one or more minor bourgeois political parties. Since neither of the major parties tends to have a constant national majority, which would enable it to control the federal government over long periods of time, it normally becomes necessary to form coalition governments, with or without the Socialists. Because of this precarious equilibrium between the two main political forces, stalemates have been frequent in the federal government.

Both major parties are backed by strong economic organizations, such as trade unions or farmers' and small tradesmen's associations; and the Communist party has built up a system of factory cells. The two large parties own and control many newspapers of a strictly partisan nature and tend to train their followers intensively in the fields of politics and economics, from a partisan angle. There is also a strong tendency to use cultural and even recreational organizations to attract less politically minded citizens. The party organizations are highly centralized, and members of Parliament are subject to strict party discipline.

Dependence on their sectional, social, and cultural environment has caused most Austrians to be born into a political party—a situation that largely determines the size of either main party. The Socialists might make inroads among agricultural laborers, or the urban lower middle classes, but their chances of gaining any large number of new followers are slim. The postwar election figures indicate, however, a more even distribution than previously of party strength throughout Austria, suggesting perhaps a tendency toward national rather than regional parties.

Christian Social Attitudes. The Christian Social party, now the People's party, is one of the Catholic parties that are found in a good many European countries. Like the others, it aims to translate its Christian convictions into practical politics. Considering the ethical and theological demands of the church as basic to human life and values, the party naturally tends to espouse the right of the church to act freely and without government interference. Taking its clue from Catholic teachings, it opposes strongly all parties of Marxist materialism and at times others, such as that of nazism, when they encroach upon the freedom of the church.

When the Christian Social party came down to the grass roots of everyday economics and politics, it was capable of changing its specific demands and views from time to time, or of dividing into right and left factions. Prior to 1918, it had been a middle-class party with a strong anti-Semitic streak, but, after World War I, it turned into more of a general party, representing the middle and lower middle classes in the cities, and the farmers and even many agricultural workers in the country. In the state of Tyrol, it commanded a two-thirds majority. In Styria, it had a strong pro-Nazi faction under the leadership of Rintelen, who became the virtual leader of the Austrian Nazis by 1934. The party as a whole, however, turned strongly against nazism— a stand in which it was actively supported by the sharp condemnation by the Austrian Catholic bishops of certain tenets of the Nazi program as incompatible with the Catholic faith.[10] Under the leadership of Dollfuss and Schuschnigg, the party remained strongly anti-Nazi, but evolved an authoritarian system of its own, camouflaged with high-sounding religious phraseology.[11]

---

[10] See John Brown Mason, *Hitler's First Foes: A Study in Religion and Politics* (Minneapolis, 1936), pp. 1-2, 81-82.

[11] See Kurt Schuschnigg, *My Austria* (New York, 1938).

Pushed forward by Mussolini, the party suppressed eventually all democratic life, as the price demanded by Italy for support of Austria against Hitler. Christian Social opposition had long been firm against *Anschluss* with Germany, in large part because it would have weakened the position that the Catholic church enjoyed in Austria.

After World War II, the Austrian People's party was formed out of several old parties and politically active economic groups, of which the former Christian Social party formed the core. The People's party finds its most dependable support among loyal Catholics of all social groups and also among anti-Marxian elements, even if they are not religiously inclined. The party is also favored by the predominance of small shopkeepers and artisans over big entrepreneurs in commerce and industry. These small businessmen fear socialization and therefore seek political representation of their economic interests on the right. The farmers, constituting with their families and help a good third of the population, have similar economic interests and also strong religious sentiments. The party has a rather small following among urban workers. In 1945, it attracted many veterans and former Nazis. These two groups, however, seem likely to divide their future political support among all three parties. Apparently, the followers of the prewar bourgeois splinter parties tend to favor the People's party.

Socialism to the Left. When universal manhood suffrage was introduced in Austria-Hungary in 1907, the Social Democrats gained about one third of the total vote, but, because of discriminatory electoral provisions, only one sixth of the seats in Parliament. As elsewhere, the party worked hard for social legislation and democratic political principles. At the opening of World War I, it opposed Austria's declaration of war on Serbia, but decided in favor of defending Austria against Russian despotism, although an anti-war minority gradually increased in importance. In 1919, the Austrian workers failed to establish a dictatorship of the proletariat because of their party's belief in democratic principles. This stand gained them middle-class support in favor of social legislation. The Social Democrats favored municipal self-government, and opposed a strong Federal Council. The weakness of the upper house later made it easy for Dollfuss in 1934 to abandon all pretense of democratic government, in spite of vigorous opposition from the Social Democrats. Although strong in the state of Burgenland and in the industrial cities of the country, the Social Democrats failed to gain a majority in any state, except "red" Vienna, which they controlled and made the showplace of Socialist principles put into practice. Their strong hold over the trade unions gave them great extraparliamentary strength, since the workers were willing to strike in support of the social legislation of 1919, including the rent restriction law, and against any legislation curtailing their rights.

The generally agnostic Social Democrats were just as strongly anticlerical as the church was anti-Marxian. Originally, they had a clear majority in

Parliament and were able to give a strong Social Democratic flavor to the republican constitution. But when Austria hovered on the verge of economic collapse, they lost control of the government, except in Vienna, which accentuated the antagonism between the metropolis and the Catholic and generally conservative countryside. The Social Democrats were in favor of a union with Germany, partly because it would have strengthened the position of their party. Although the party used to be further to the left than its German counterpart, today it tends to come close in its ideology to the British Labor party.

The reborn party can rely on a large block of votes built up during long years through hard organizational and educational work. It attracts a large percentage of industrial workers, as well as anticlerical and antirightist factions. It also draws toward it the many people who today live in misery. In western Austria, the party now tends to be somewhat less antireligious; in Carinthia, for instance, it no longer promotes the freethinkers' movement. Such a change in attitude helps the party in the rural areas, where it has made some gains among agricultural laborers and small peasants.

Other Parties. Austria has demonstrated an amazing resistance to Communist promises and pressures. In the elections of 1945, the Communists polled 5.42 per cent of the total vote with 94 per cent popular participation, and in 1949, together with the Left Socialist splinter group, 5.45 per cent with 97 per cent participation. This is due largely to the religious beliefs of the strong Catholic element and to the anti-Communist convictions of the Socialist party and its leadership in the trade unions.

In 1950 an Independent party arose, appealing largely to former Nazis and others discontent with the "black-red" coalition. While polling an imposing 10 per cent of the ballots at its first try, it soon began to suffer from disunion in the rank and file.

The Communist party has been strengthened by the severe persecution it suffered at the hands of the Hitler regime, and by the desperate belief in early postwar days that the economic misery of the time called for radical action. From 80 to 100 per cent of the Communist voters are enrolled as party members, a fact that makes the organization a more potent force than election returns alone would indicate.

5. Austria—Free and Unfree

Division into Zones. At Moscow, the Allied statesmen declared Austria a "liberated" country rather than a conquered territory. But her present status has proved so costly that the man on the street is tempted to complain that the country could afford another war better than another liberation. Austria has been divided into four zones of occupation, like Germany, and Vienna even into five, an international zone being added to the other four. For two years the cost of occupation amounted to about a third of the Austrian federal budget; it still constitutes some 10 per cent. The United States now pays for its own occupation cost,[12] delivering to the Austrian government dollars for buildings, services, and the like needed by the United States forces.

The political, economic, and cultural consequences of Austria's division into zones with varying patterns of foreign supervision and direction, growing out of divergent and even conflicting aims, have had effects similar to those experienced in Germany. To some extent, the effects were mitigated by Austria's generally more favorable status and the early existence of a recognized Austrian government, which has been given large but still limited responsibilities by the occupation powers.

Economic Conditions. Austria cannot build up her place in the family of nations nor depend on normal political conditions at home unless her economic situation is put on a sounder basis. The country made great strides in 1947 over the previous years, especially in mining and in production of iron, steel, and electric power. Yet, in general, production totals still remain considerably under peacetime levels. The low productivity of workers is due to undernourishment, the transportation crisis, loss of machinery, and lack of tools. Badly needed increases in production require improvements in the food situation, regular supplies of raw materials, and additional machinery.

The food situation has improved, however. UNRRA furnished more calories in one year of postwar calamity than all of the country's agriculture put together. The American and British Armies added considerable amounts from their own imported supplies, while the Russians and French were living off the land. Private relief in appreciable volume came primarily from Switzerland, Sweden, Canada, and the United States. Because of the existing situation in agricultural eastern Europe, Austria remains dependent on American food.

The place of credit assistance under League of Nations auspices is now taken by the Marshall Plan, aided by small short-term import credits from Sweden, Brazil, and Egypt. Soviet exploitation of Austria's oil fields and of the production from Soviet-run Austrian factories constitute "the hole in the East." Through it flow the "silent reparations," which probably balance the current gifts from the West.

Political Resurgence. Austria's two major parties have a quasi-monopoly in the country's politics, partly because the occupying powers have refused approval to new parties. The People's party itself has its left and right wings, as well as some corners full of dissidents or temporary guests. So has

---

[12] In protesting strongly against the occupation costs, Chancellor Figl has said: "The continued occupation of Austria is based on grounds that are neither legal nor in the interests of Austria, nor in accord with the promotion of peace." See *The New York Times,* May 21, 1948, p. 5. Although the Austrians would love to be rid of the occupation, there is much fear of what would happen if the American troops would withdraw too far toward the distant Atlantic. See generally Winifred N. Hadsel, "Austria under Allied Occupation," *Foreign Policy Reports* (November 1, 1948).

the Socialist party, though probably to a lesser degree. There are under-currents of popular desire for one or more new parties, but their strength can be measured only at the polls. That opportunity will come only in the future.

More important has been the very continuation of the party system as known in Western democracies. On April 21, 1948, Parliament adopted a law for the protection of Austria "against events like those which recently have led to the formation of 'people's democracies' in various countries of Eastern Europe," passed by the vote of 161 Socialists and People's party members against the 4 Communists. The new law provides for the con-tingency that the members of Parliament cannot exercise their functions because of the use of force against them. Decisions of the President and the Chancellor may be declared null and void if made under pressure. So-cialist Vice Chancellor Schaerf, whose party proposed the bill, declared after the vote: "Now our defensive measures against any aggression from the East are complete. Austria has done everything in her power to protect democracy and put a stop to eastern totalitarianism." [13]

Pressure from the Soviets. Soviet power has been exercised in various ways, in addition to the presence of large occupation forces—larger than the three Western armies put together. Besides economic pressure, it con-sists of a long campaign of intimidation, including numerous arrests and deportations to unknown destinations and kidnappings of Austrians by Soviet forces. Similar to actions in Hungary and Czechoslovakia, the charge of "espionage" against the Soviet Union has also been used to send terror down the spines of more or less defenseless Austrians. The Western powers are directly drawn into this campaign of intimidation, since the acts of force have taken place in their own zones or in their own sectors of Vienna.

Austria's International Status. The Austrian government has been recog-nized by a number of countries and maintains legations in Washington, Mos-cow, London, Paris, and elsewhere. Austria has not yet been elected a member of the United Nations, because of Soviet opposition. As so often in the past, Austria now has only a limited chance to form her own future. After World War I, she was not allowed to unite with Germany, when she was too weak economically to stand on her own feet. Kept alive with loans granted her under the auspices of the League of Nations and spent under its strict control, she still never grew healthy economically. Threatened by Nazi annexation at a time when Austrian majority sentiment was against it, she became dependent on Mussolini. For the sake of her international independence, such as it was, Chancellor Dollfuss sold the country's de-mocracy down the Tiber. But Schuschnigg was forced to capitulate to Hitler after all.

Today, Austrian independence is still largely on paper. The Allied powers have been unable to agree on a treaty that would define the rights and obli-

---

[13] *Neue Zürcher Zeitung,* April 23, 1948.

gations of "liberated Austria," and in the cold war between East and West, Austria has become one more pawn. It is clear, on the other hand, that neither the Austrian people, with their strong opposition to communism, nor the Western democracies, faced with the strength of the Soviet bloc, can afford the type of liberation that would merely create a dangerous power vacuum. Unless there is, over the years, a relaxation of the tension between the East and the West, little opportunity exists for the genius of constructive statesmanship to give Austria both true national freedom and political security. *Austria infelix* may well continue to be an apt description.

CHAPTER 19

SWITZERLAND

1. The Constitutional Foundation

Special American Interest.[1] It is not surprising that American students of government have long shown a special interest in Swiss political institutions, for the influence of Switzerland and the United States on each other's government has been notable. When our country began its national life, it constituted a republican oasis amid an overwhelming number of monarchies; but Switzerland had known republican institutions for some five hundred years. Not a few Americans studied Swiss political experience intensively, hoping both for inspiration and practical lessons of history. Switzerland, in turn, took centuries to grow from a loose confederacy of almost sovereign cantons to a federal union, whereas this development in the American states was compressed into a few years. The mountain republic became a united state only by adoption of its federal constitution of 1848.[2]

This constitution adopted the bicameral legislature on the American model —contrary to Swiss traditions—because it promised to reconcile the conflicting claims to legislative power by the newly proposed federal government and the ancient cantons, corresponding to our states later.

Two Swiss institutions were transferred to the United States, when South Dakota, as the first state, adopted the initiative and referendum in 1898.

Linguistic and Religious Diversity. Switzerland possesses political and economic importance far out of proportion to the small size of her territory and her population of 4.7 million. One third the area of New York State and located in the high mountain ranges of west central Europe, she borders for over a thousand miles upon three large neighbors—Italy, Germany, and France—as well as on smaller Austria and tiny Liechtenstein. Since almost two thirds of Swiss territory is mountainous, large areas are unproductive. Most of the industrial and agricultural sections are in the plateau region between the Alps and the Jura mountains. Dairying and related industries—

---

[1] Appreciation is due to Professor Arnold J. Zurcher, of New York University, for a critical reading of this chapter.

[2] For standard treatises, see Robert C. Brooks, *Government and Politics of Switzerland* (Yonkers, 1918); Arnold J. Zurcher, "Switzerland," in James T. Shotwell, ed., *Governments of Continental Europe* (New York, 1940); William E. Rappard, *The Government of Switzerland* (New York, 1936); George Sauser-Hall, *The Political Institutions of Switzerland* (New York, 1946); André Siegfried, *Switzerland: A Democratic Way of Life* (New York, 1950). For current political and other problems, see *Die Schweiz,* an annual publication of the New Helvetic Society. For a comparative treatment, see K. C. Wheare, *Federal Government* (New York, 1947).

chocolate, condensed milk, and leather—furnish the chief agricultural products. Although Switzerland has to import nearly all her industrial raw materials, as well as much food, she is outstanding in the manufacture of machinery, electrotechnical supplies, watches, and textiles. By careful planning she has utilized her soil and rich waterpower resources, and the natural beauty of her landscape lures hundreds of thousands of foreign tourists, summer and winter.

Linguistically, Switzerland is heterogeneous. Almost three fourths of her people speak German, one fifth French, the remainder Italian, except for a few who speak Romansh, an ancient language of Latin origin. Since adoption of the constitution of 1848, the three main languages have been official languages of the confederation, with Italian in practice taking a less prominent place than German and French. The various cantons choose their own official language or languages.

Switzerland's religious diversity has presented some grave problems since the days of the Protestant leaders Zwingli in Zürich and Calvin in Geneva. In the past, religious schism has led to civil war and foreign strife. It is fortunate that the religious and linguistic areas do not coincide, but overlap. Protestants outnumber Catholics in nine cantons speaking German and in three speaking French, whereas the Catholics are stronger in seven cantons speaking German, in two speaking French, and in one speaking Italian. This geographic distribution has gradually made for mutual toleration, after political oppression on religious grounds had been common for three centuries in both Protestant and Catholic cantons. The population as a whole is 57 per cent Prostestant and 41 per cent Catholic.

Road toward National Unity. Switzerland's remarkable degree of national unity despite her pronounced linguistic and religious diversity has aroused the interest of many students of international affairs. They see in it hopeful evidence that a high degree of cooperation is possible between nations of widely divergent cultures and strong traditions of independence. It must be recalled, however, that Swiss unification was achieved only after six centuries, which included long periods of dissension and war. The spirit of unity and tolerance that is now so outstanding was not born overnight; its growth owes much to fear of foreign oppression, which has welded the people together. Its final attainment was made possible by the ingenious device of federation, which allowed for a combination of cantonal self-government and central authority with definite powers over the cantons as well as the citizens.

The history of Switzerland as such begins with the year 1291, when the three forest cantons of Uri, Schwyz, and Unterwalden concluded a perpetual league to safeguard their established liberties against the Hapsburg Dukes of Austria, then also Emperors of the Holy Roman Empire. During the next centuries, Swiss political development was characterized by numerous new covenants among the cantons, successful campaigns against foreign enemies, and the enlargement of the country partly by conquest and partly by the admission of independent cantons and of so-called allied countries. By 1573, the Swiss Confederacy numbered fifteen cantons, all German speaking. Six of them were democratic Alpine communities, four—including Bern—were urban aristocracies ruled by a few families. Zürich and two other cantons were oligarchies, where access to the privileged families of traders and manufacturers was easier. All three types of cantons, including the democracies, ruled over other territories subject to them.

Each of the cantons was sovereign. In the Diet, representing the cantons and allied countries, the rule of unanimity played havoc with the need for united action. As Professor Rappard has said: "When one considers the history of these five hundred years of strife and external intriguing, one cannot but be surprised at the survival of the Swiss nation as such." During the fifteenth and sixteenth centuries, Switzerland was a great military power, but in several decisive defeats she lost her winner's reputation. The "heroic period" of Swiss history was at an end, and the country gradually became a leader in peaceful efforts. The armies of the French Revolution foisted the Helvetian Republic (1798) upon the weak and disunited Confederacy, but the Swiss reacted so strongly against the French-imposed constitution that Napoleon was forced to restore the independence of the cantons by the Act of Mediation of 1803. Under this act, six new cantons were formed, chiefly out of allied and subject territories speaking French and Italian. After the downfall of Napoleon, the Helvetian Republic came to a quick end. In 1814, three western states were admitted as cantons, raising the total number to twenty-two. This was the last time territory was added to Switzerland, now a trilingual country. The Swiss Diet in 1815 adopted a new and less liberal constitution, but when the breath of freedom once more swept over Europe in 1830, all Swiss cantons became representative democracies.

Establishment of the Federal Union. It proved impossible to amend the Pact of 1815 in a constitutional manner, since some of the cantons prevented all revisions for fear of losing their sovereign and religious rights. In the brief civil war of 1847, the *Sonderbund* (Special League) of seven Catholic cantons was routed. A new constitution was drafted by the Diet and adopted by referendum.

This constitution of 1848 solved the old conflict between the large and the smaller cantons by the creation of a federal state, modeled upon the United States. The establishment of an effective federal government was accompanied by an immediate decline in party and religious strife, and steps were taken toward national unification. A federal postal service was set up; the telegraph was nationalized; and a uniform system of coins, weights, and measures was introduced. Roads, canals, and schools were improved on a nation-wide basis, and the military system was reformed.

Revised Constitution of 1874. In 1874, a strong movement toward further centralization, wider democracy, state socialism (or *étatisme,* as the Swiss call it), and anticlericalism led to the adoption, again by referendum, of a revised constitution that is still the basis of Swiss political life.[3] It is a rather lengthy document—much longer than the American constitution—and goes into a good many details, dealing with such matters as fishing and hunting, qualifications of members of the liberal professions, sickness and burial of the indigent, cattle diseases, gambling houses, and lotteries. Behind this plethora of detail is the desire for sharp delimitation of the respective competence of federal and cantonal powers.

Federal powers under this constitution are wider than under the American constitution. They include control over foreign relations, military affairs, the currency, civil and criminal law, communications and commerce, higher education, naturalization, conservation of natural resources, certain fiscal powers, child labor and social insurance, the settlement of disputes between cantons, and their defense against invasion and insurrection. All powers not expressly granted by the constitution to the Confederation are reserved to the cantons, an arrangement corresponding closely to the provisions of the tenth amendment to the American constitution.

Switzerland does not have judicial review of the constitutionality of *federal* legislation. Her legislative branch is supreme; its own interpretation of its constitutional powers is binding and final. Since the voters share in the legislative process through the referendum, they take part, one might say, in the interpretation of the constitution. The formal process of constitutional amendment requires a referendum. There have been some forty amendments since the total revision of the constitution in 1874. The constitution guarantees freedom of speech, press, petition, religious belief, and association; it also provides for equality before the law. Even the anticlerical constitutional provisions were intended by their proponents to contribute to individual freedom, although many Swiss are not convinced of the validity of the argument.

Expansion of Federal Power. In the course of time, the growth of federal power became more and more pronounced as the desire for national unity increased and as problems calling for government regulation or assistance overstepped cantonal boundaries and assumed nation-wide importance. Among these concerns were military training, banking, patents, transportation, traffic in arms and alcoholic beverages, production and marketing of grain, and railroads and radio, both of which were taken into government ownership. Agriculture, manufacturing, and the tourist traffic were subsidized; industry was protected; import quotas were fixed; unemployment relief and compulsory insurance were initiated. When the federal government resorted to direct taxation and excise duties, it offered the cantons a share in the new revenue that they had previously monopolized.

---

[3] The text is in the country's three official languages—each legally equal but "not always identical in wording or even meaning," according to Myron L. Tripp, *The Swiss and United States Federal Constitutional Systems* (Paris, 1940), p. 50. For an English translation, see William E. Rappard and Others, *Source Book on European Governments* (New York, 1937), pp. 19 ff.

During the two World Wars[4] and the economic depression, the federal government's scope of action was vastly increased. In 1914 and especially in 1939, Parliament granted the government exceptional and unlimited powers to protect the security, integrity, and neutrality of the country and to safeguard its credit, economic interests, and food supply. These plenary powers involved restrictions on the democratic rights of Swiss citizens; but they were readily accepted as necessary. Government actions included the outlawing of both the pro-Nazi National Movement and the Communist party. Since Swiss papers were willing to exercise self-censorship in line with governmental recommendations intended to safeguard the country's traditional policy of neutrality, freedom of the press technically was not abridged.

As the wartime emergency passed, the range of federal action decreased, but not to its former level. Swiss economic life, for instance, is today strictly controlled in its various aspects. As elsewhere, there is opposition in Switzerland to the growth of the federal bureaucracy and grumbling about its expense. Generally speaking, however, the Swiss—like other Europeans— put up with many regulations and restrictions the ordinary American has hardly heard of, because they are aware of the precarious state of their economic and political situation. They also note with satisfaction that large fields of governmental power still remain with the cantons, even if reduced in comparison with the past. In fact, parallel to the development in American states, cantonal powers have also been extended to new fields.

2. The Federal Government

Organization of the Executive. The framers of the constitution rejected the American precedent of a single elected exponent of the executive power as contrary to the ideas of the Swiss people, who were attached to government by councils and opposed to personal pre-eminence. Instead, they provided for a collegial body of seven members, known as the Federal Council (*Bundesrat, Conseil Fédéral*), to serve as the country's supreme executive. Its members are elected for four-year terms by the bicameral Federal Assembly, which meets in joint session shortly after the quadrennial elections. Any Swiss citizen who is eligible to the lower chamber can be elected a member of the Federal Council, but there may be no more than one member from any canton. By custom, one member comes from Zürich and one from Bern, the leading cantons historically and also the largest in population; one comes from Vaud, the largest French-speaking canton. Another tradition provides that not more than five members shall come from German-speaking cantons, allowing for the election of another councilor from a canton speaking French or Italian. Thus, a satisfactory regional and linguistic representation is assured. As far as social background is concerned, the large majority of the councilors elected since 1848 have come from old farm families.

The Federal Assembly annually elects the chairman and vice chairman of

[4] Cf. Ernest S. Hediger, "Switzerland in Wartime," *Foreign Policy Reports,* 18 (1943), no. 20.

the Federal Council for one-year terms, rotating the office on the basis of seniority. The chairman is known as the President of the Swiss Confederation, a position that involves presiding over the deliberations of the Federal Council and representing the Confederation on official occasions. As the office confers a more or less nominal honor, Swiss citizens are apt to forget who their President is "just now," although they are likely to know by name the majority of the members of the Federal Council.

All councilors are department heads in charge of the Political Department (Foreign Affairs), Interior, Justice and Police, Army, Finance and Customs, Public Economy (trade, agriculture, labor), or Posts and Railroads. They are therefore acting in a double capacity: as equal members of the Federal Council and as administrative heads of separate departments. In constitutional theory, they make all important decisions as a collegial body, but as a matter of fact many such decisions are made by individual councilors and accepted by their colleagues without formal joint action.

Powers of the Federal Council. The Federal Council conducts the foreign affairs of the country; guarantees the maintenance of domestic order—by military intervention in the cantons, if necessary; enforces all federal laws, ordinances, and court decisions; administers federal finances; supervises federal officials, including army officers; examines certain cantonal laws where they are subject to federal approval—for instance, when relating to the right to vote; guarantees the cantonal constitutions; and the like. In addition, the Council has the right to issue ordinances, often of the greatest importance, in the execution of federal laws. In some cases, the Council also settles appeals against administrative decisions taken by its subordinate organs. It has no power to veto laws. This diversity of functions obviously makes for a blurred rather than a clear-cut separation of powers.

The constitution provides that the Federal Council be dependent upon the Federal Assembly by which it is elected. The Assembly supervises the Council, and, often in the form of resolutions, it directs its executive functions. The Assembly authorizes or ratifies the Council's actions in the field of foreign relations, military affairs, or even ordinary matters of administration. At each session of Parliament, as well as upon request by either house, the Council furnishes detailed reports on how it administers governmental business. The councilors are also subject to questioning on the floor of each house.

Actual political practice has modified constitutional theory to a large extent. The Federal Council often suggests or denies the need or desirability of specific legislation and drafts the bills, whether the idea for them originates in the legislature or in the executive. Frequently, it guides the bills through Parliament, a councilor being present when the parliamentary committee studies the bill. He freely advocates the measure, on which he is likely to have considerable knowledge, bolstered by specialists on his staff; and finally he addresses the legislative bodies on the bill. Usually, he makes the most important speech on the subject. In fact, the committee reports, too, are often prepared with the assistance of government officials. The executive, then, is as influential as the legislature, concerned with lawmaking as well as executive and administrative functions.

Stability of the Executive. The members of the Federal Council cannot be turned out of office by Parliament before the expiration of their four-year term. Unlike American Cabinet members in relation to the chief executive, they may not be fired by the President of the Swiss Confederation, since they are his equals. In fact, a member of the Federal Council who disagrees with a proposed government measure may let his opposition become known publicly and still keep his position. In practice, however, such strong disagreement does not often occur; in a few cases, it has led to voluntary resignations.

The remarkable stability of the Swiss executive and its coherence on policy matters is based on a tradition of long standing taken over from cantonal government. It is aided by the lack of violent changes in the political climate of Switzerland. The membership of the Federal Council naturally reflects the political composition of the Assembly, but the continuity in party strength as well as established tradition makes for re-election of councilors. They are usually men with extended experience in the federal and cantonal legislatures and of mature age. As outstanding figures, if not party leaders, they represent the majority opinion of Parliament. As administrators of long tenure and consequent experience, they are able to lead the permanent civil servants, rather than be forced to depend on them helplessly in most matters.

Meetings of the Federal Council are not public, and no minutes are published of its proceedings. Knowing that all government measures presented to Parliament may be submitted to a popular referendum, the Council is acutely conscious of public reaction to any bill, a fact that has a strong influence on its sense of collective responsibility.[5]

Competence of the Civil Service. Switzerland has demonstrated that an efficient bureaucracy can be entirely responsible to democratic government.[6] Both her railroads and forests, for instance, which face exceptional difficulties because of the mountainous character of the country, are models of public administration.

Professor C. J. Friedrich, a special student of the subject, goes so far as to say of Switzerland: "Except to the extent to which she was helped by the example of France and Germany, she is full proof of the contention that a de-

---

[5] Federal Councilor Ernst Nobs, head of the Finance Department, was asked after his lecture before mayors of the canton of Zürich why he, the Social Democratic representative in the federal government, had not demanded a capital levy in line with the Social Democratic platform. In answer, he pointed to its likely defeat in a referendum. See "Probleme der Bundesfinanzreform," *Neue Zürcher Zeitung,* November 12, 1947, sec. 5.

[6] Cf. Carl J. Friedrich and Taylor Cole, *Responsible Bureaucracy: A Study of the Swiss Civil Service* (Cambridge, Mass., 1932); Robert C. Brooks, *Civic Training in Switzerland* (Chicago, 1930), chap. 6.

mocracy is able to do a better job, in fact, than other systems. For there can be little question that upon close scrutiny by an unbiased investigator the Swiss appear to have a more effective democratically responsive officialdom than any other country except Sweden (and Sweden also is very democratically governed)."[7] Naturally, even Swiss civil servants are not always perfect, nor is their competence justly appreciated at all times. Especially in periods of extensive federal controls, one can hear some good griping about *"Sankt Bürokratius"* and *"Monsieur le Bureau,"* and their manifold, complex, and bewildering activities.[8]

Powers of the Legislature. Contrary to practice in the United States, where the three branches of the federal government are coordinate and largely independent of one another, the Swiss Parliament is supreme. As it is expressed in the constitution, "subject to the rights of the people and of the cantons . . . the supreme authority of the Confederation is exercised by the Federal Assembly." The Assembly passes the laws, which may neither be vetoed by the President of the Confederation nor declared unconstitutional by the Supreme Court. Besides choosing the members of the executive—the Federal Council—the Assembly elects the judiciary, as well as the Chancellor, who is the permanent head of the civil service. There is no strict separation of powers and no system of checks and balances under the Swiss constitution as we know it in the United States. But the electorate has the right to veto all unpopular bills by defeating them in a referendum. The Federal Assembly may delegate large powers to the Federal Council in times of national peril, as it did particularly during both World Wars.

The Federal Assembly has the authority to declare war and to conclude peace, and, in certain cases, to sanction treaties made between cantons or between cantons and foreign states; to pass on the annual budget; to proclaim amnesties and to grant pardon in case of violations of federal laws; to examine and guarantee the cantonal constitutions; and to supervise the Army, the civil service, and the administration of justice. The Assembly also elects certain federal officials and, in case of war or threat of war, the Commander-in-Chief of the Army. It even has important judicial powers—namely, the right to decide appeals against certain administrative decisions of the Federal Council and to settle jurisdictional conflicts between federal authorities.

Procedure of the Federal Assembly. The Federal Assembly (*Bundesversammlung, Assemblée Fédérale*) is bicameral. The National Council

---

[7] From Carl J. Friedrich, *Constitutional Government and Democracy* (rev. ed., Boston, 1950), p. 394. Quoted by permission of the publisher, Ginn and Co.

[8] The number of federal officials and employees was 87,000 in 1947, against 63,000 in 1938. The cantons and communities employed another 140,000 either in administration or in their economic enterprises. Every ninth employed Swiss, therefore, in that year worked for the government or a publicly owned undertaking; see "Die Aufblähung des schweizerischen Beamtenapparates," *Amerikanische Schweizer Zeitung,* August 6, 1947. The tendency of "temporary" government offices to prolong their existence has been characterized by the saying: *"Ce n'est que le provisoire qui dure."*

represents the people, and the Council of States the cantons. The two houses have equal rights and powers. All legislative measures have to be approved by both; if no agreement can be reached through committee efforts, the bill is dropped—a rare event, since neither house tends to be uncompromising. No house enjoys priority—for instance, in regard to financial matters. Both houses have their committees, to which most measures are referred and on which all political parties are represented in proportion to their parliamentary strength. The committee reports are presented by special *rapporteurs* for the majority and the minority.

Both houses elect a president and vice president for one-year terms, with no possibility of immediate re-election. The presidents have no special privileges or powers, such as those of the Speaker of the American House of Representatives, except that both may cast the deciding vote in case of a tie. They enjoy a position of prominence and honor, however, and as a rule are elected on a basis of rotation, allowing periodic representation to various parties and cantons. The presidents usually agree early in each session on an apportionment between the houses of legislative tasks proposed by the Federal Council, in order that the time of each chamber be used effectively.

Legislative measures may be introduced by individual members of either house. If the house decides in favor of the practical value and the political desirability of the proposal, the Federal Council is asked to prepare detailed drafts. This practice further strengthens the influence of the Federal Council on legislation, supplementing its right of initiating and advocating legislation before the various committees and on the floor of each house. In turn, the members of each house have the right of interpellation, which compels the government to explain its actions and offers an opportunity to criticize them. Parliamentary criticism of the government, however, does not lead to resignation of the Federal Council or of any of its members, nor does it impair the stability of the government in any way. The two houses meet at the same time, at Bern. Ordinary sessions are convened at least once a year; extraordinary sessions may be called by the Federal Council at the request of one fourth of the membership of the National Council or five of the cantons. Decisions are made by an absolute majority. Only the "most important" speeches are published in the *Bulletin Stenographique Fédérale,* a practice differing pleasantly from that of the Congressional Record.

Composition of the Chambers. The National Council (*Nationalrat, Conseil National*) is elected for four-year terms by direct ballot of all male citizens who have reached the age of twenty and, since 1919, on the basis of proportional representation. The various cantons—or half-cantons—serve as separate constituencies. For each canton, the number of deputies is allocated on the basis of the population. Each of the cantons and half-cantons, however, is allowed at least one deputy, no matter how small its population. In the election of 1943, for instance, Bern, the canton with the largest population, elected 33 out of the 194 deputies, whereas four cantons were entitled to only one deputy each. All Swiss citizens eligible to vote in the elections to the National Council may be elected to its membership, unless they are clergymen. Members of the Council of States and the Federal Council or federal officials cannot become members of the National Council. If elected, they must resign one of the two offices. Members of the National Council receive no salaries, but only travel and subsistence allowances during their active legislative work.

The Council of States (*Ständerat, Conseil des États*) is made up of 44 members elected according to cantonal rather than federal law, since each canton is considered sovereign. In most cantons, election is at the polls, but the *Landsgemeinde*—the old open-air popular assembly of voters—makes the choice in four cantons and the cantonal legislature in four others. Each canton names two and each half-canton one representative. Terms of office are not uniform. In most cantons, it is four years, but in others it is three, and in some actually only one year. Although their emoluments are paid by the cantons, the representatives in the Council of States are not the official spokesmen for their cantons. They are forbidden by the federal constitution to vote on instructions from anyone, including their constituencies, as are the members of the National Council. Clergymen and federal officials may be elected to the Council of States, but not members of the Federal Council and federal judges.

Unity of Justice. The federal judicial systems of Switzerland and the United States offer striking contrasts. The Federal Supreme Court—the highest Swiss court—was established in its present form only by the constitution of 1874, replacing a part-time and anemic predecessor that was entirely subordinate to the legislative and executive branches of the government. Even the present court can hardly compare with the great power and influence of the United States Supreme Court. The Swiss Supreme Court does have original and final jurisdiction in all disputes between the Confederation and the cantons or between cantons; and also in suits, except over small amounts, against the Confederation or a canton. The Supreme Court also has appellate jurisdiction over civil cases coming up from cantonal supreme courts. Since there are no lower federal courts in Switzerland, the cantonal courts administer the federal law. The appellate jurisdiction of the Supreme Court assures uniformity of judicial decisions for the entire country, as its most important function. As a court of criminal justice, the Supreme Court —with the assistance of a jury—tries cases of high treason, revolt, political crimes and offenses connected with public disturbances, crimes against international law, and other crimes, such as counterfeiting.

The Supreme Court deals with violations of the constitutional rights of individuals and since 1929 has also decided cases in administrative law arising from decisions of federal departments and agencies. The court has no right to declare federal laws unconstitutional; this power was expressly and deliberately denied it by the makers of the constitution of 1874. The Federal Assembly alone has the right to interpret the federal constitution and to decide when a constitutional amendment is needed. In fact, as federal laws are subject to legislative referendum, a judicial decision declaring such a law unconstitutional would interfere with the cherished constitutional right of Swiss voters to accept or defeat legislation as they please. The Supreme Court does have a limited right of judicial review over cantonal constitutions and laws that violate the federal constitution or laws.

The seat of the Supreme Court is in Lausanne—a concession to the feelings of the French-speaking parts of the country. The number of judges has gradually increased from nine in 1874 to twenty-six at the present time. For judicial business, the court divides itself into a number of sections, with several judges each. The judges are elected for six-year terms by the Federal Assembly, which is required by the constitution to provide for representation of the three official languages in the membership of the court. By custom, cantons and political groups are represented as well. As it is also customary to re-elect the judges as long as they choose to serve, the independence of the judiciary is actually assured.

3. Cantonal and Local Government

Cantons and Their Powers. To many a Swiss, the canton or the local community seems more important than the Confederation, since they are closer to him and his affairs. He is a Swiss citizen by virtue of citizenship in a canton. The power of taxation by cantons and communities looms large; within these areas, elections of officeholders and popular votes on measures and appropriations are frequent and arouse much interest; and cantonal decisions may have a nation-wide effect on political parties and issues. Proposed political innovations—such as woman suffrage—are fought out on a cantonal basis before they reach the national arena. Like our American states, cantons serve in some measure as local and regional proving grounds. Their ancient and traditional importance is acknowledged in the constitution, which refers to the "sovereign cantons"—that is, "in so far as their sovereignty has not been limited by the federal constitution." They have retained their powers in the large fields not expressly reserved to the Confederation, such as maintenance of law and order, social welfare, local public works, highways, control of elections, public education, and control of local government.

The origin of the curious institution of a half-canton usually goes back to the simple fact that internal dissensions could not be settled except by territorial division. In one case, the split was an outcome of the Reformation, which resulted in a half-Catholic, half-Protestant canton. In the case of Basel, the division took place more than a hundred years ago over disagreements between the rural and urban elements, which a strong movement for reunion is now trying to overcome.

The twenty-five cantons and half-cantons have their own constitutions, which must comply with the provisions of the federal constitution.[9] The Confederation guarantees the cantonal constitutions on condition that they (*a*) do not contain anything contrary to the provisions of the federal constitution; (*b*) provide for the exercise of political rights in conformity with republican representative or democratic forms of government; and (*c*) have been accepted by the people and may be amended on the demand of the absolute majority of the citizens. Although the trend of modern times has led to a great increase in the functions of the federal government, the tasks of the cantons are also larger than in the past. Each canton has a complete system of government, with its executive, legislative, and judicial branches, and power of taxation to support them. Today's importance of cantonal and local government is indicated by the fact that their combined annual expenditures equal those of the national government.

Nature of the Landsgemeinde. One canton (Glarus) and four half-cantons elect their officials and pass legislation in annual open-air meetings. These are remnants of pure democracy, in that every voter has an opportunity to pass on all legislation directly, instead of through elected representatives. They differ from the old New England town meeting in that they deal with affairs of state—or canton—rather than with problems of local government.

These meetings, called *Landsgemeinden,* take place annually on a Sunday in April or May in the public square of the capital city or on a near-by meadow. They are presided over by the head of the cantonal government in an atmosphere marked by solemnity, prayers, hymns, and sometimes collective oaths. Although in past centuries turbulence was not unusual and electoral corruption not unknown, the meetings are now orderly and dignified affairs, witnessed by children from other parts of Switzerland.

Modern problems that have invaded even quiet valleys (one of the cantons, for instance, has become industrialized) necessitate as much careful preparation for this type of meeting as for ordinary legislative bodies. An elected advisory cantonal council prepares the agenda in cooperation with the cantonal executive officials; debates and votes at the meeting are confined to points listed on it. As the advisory councils discuss all proposed matters prior to the Landsgemeinde and report on them favorably or reject them, they exert much influence on the deliberations of the assembled voters, who have elected them as an act of confidence. All votes are taken by a show of hands. The powers of the Landsgemeinde differ from canton to canton under the cantonal constitutions. Generally, they include amendment of the constitution, adoption of laws, appropriations, taxation, and the like.

Cantonal Parliament. Pure democracy as expressed in the Landsgemeinde is obviously possible only in small cantons where the people can gather in one central location with relative ease. The large majority of

---

[9] For the text of the constitution of the canton of Bern, see Rappard and Others, *op. cit.* above, note 3, pp. 55 ff.

cantons have legislatures, which in part serve as training schools for national political leaders, as in the United States. All cantonal legislatures are unicameral, because of ancient tradition and also because the initiative and referendum provide for popular control over legislative measures, leaving little room for the check provided by a second chamber.

The membership of the cantonal legislature, usually known as the Great Council, tends to be large in comparison with the size of the population it represents. In some cantons, the number is fixed by constitutional provision, which in Zürich calls for as many as 180 representatives. In other cantons, the number varies, being a fixed proportion between the inhabitants and representatives, ranging from 1 to 250 to 1 to 4,000. The length of sessions also varies greatly among the cantons, but a session is called at least annually to pass on the budget. Cantonal legislators receive no salaries but only a nominal sum *per diem*. In most cantons, their terms run for four years; in the remainder, from one to six years. The tendency is toward longer terms, since the voters wish to cut down on the number of elections. In some cantons, the legislatures may be dissolved by popular vote, but in practice the initiative and referendum obviate any need for such action.

The powers of the cantonal legislature include control over the annual budget, loans, and taxation; control of the cantonal administration; power to declare a state of emergency and to call up cantonal troops if necessary; amnesty and pardons; ratification of intercantonal treaties; naturalization; election of higher judges in most of the cantons and of the members of cantonal authorities dealing with education, church affairs, and banking.

Cantonal Executive Power. Each canton is governed by a collegial executive body, known as the Government Council in German-speaking Switzerland and the Council of State in the French section. Numbering five to eleven members, these bodies serve from one to five years; in most cantons, the term is for four years. The executive bodies can be voted out of office by the legislature, and in four cantons also by the people, although this never happens because the voters exercise control through the initiative and referendum.

Members of the executive bodies are normally re-elected and often spend a lifetime in them. Geneva and Tessin are exceptions, because no party is certain of political control in those two cantons. The presidents of the executive bodies are rarely elected for more than one year, and are not immediately re-eligible. In some cantons, the presidents are elected by their colleagues, in others by the legislature, and in still others by the voters.

Cantonal Elections. Elections for the cantonal executive and legislative bodies are generally held at the same time or follow each other at short intervals.[10] The executive bodies are elected on the basis of proportional rep-

[10] For election statistics and related data, see Brooks, *op. cit.* above, note 6, chap. 5; Harold F. Gosnell, *Why Europe Votes* (Chicago, 1930), pp. 121 ff.; the Swiss variety of PR is described in Howard L. McBain and Lindsay Rogers, *New Constitutions of Europe* (Garden City, 1923), 109 ff.

resentation in two cantons only, but the majority of legislative bodies is so elected. Consequently, the executive and legislative bodies do not necessarily have the same majority. For instance, in the cantons of Basel City and Geneva, the Social Democratic governments had to work in recent years with unsympathetic majorities in the legislatures. The results made nobody happy. Most cantonal governments base their support upon coalitions, in the same way as in the federal government.

Cantonal elections sometimes exhibit a characteristically Swiss form of electoral compromise between opposing parties. For instance, in a canton that elects seven members of the Council of State, the majority party may include on its list of candidates one or more representatives of the minority parties. Or it may limit itself to nominating only four or five of its own candidates and leave one or more blank spaces on its list. In this case, the election contest often centers around one or a few candidates, while the others are certain of easy re-election. In the 1948 elections in the canton of St. Gallen, three party organizations agreed on the re-election of the seven incumbents—a decision confirmed by the voters, who gave practically equal support to the three Liberal, one Social Democratic, and three Conservative candidates. The lowest number of votes, incidentally, was cast for the man who during the war had been chief of the Department of Public Economy, the least enviable of government posts. It is also characteristic of Swiss political life that, with the exception of Tessin, members of the cantonal governments may also be members of either house of the Federal Assembly, although in seventeen cantons the number of such duplicate officeholders is limited by constitutional provision. Both houses of the Federal Assembly always include a fairly large percentage of cantonal officials. This custom makes for close contact between policy-makers, central and cantonal.

The functions of the cantonal governments are executive and administrative. As in the federal government, each councilor heads a department. The body as a whole appoints most of the officials and prepares all legislation to be discussed by cantonal parliaments. In most cantons, executive meetings are not public. The salary of the councilors varies; in small and poor cantons it may be so little that the officials are not expected to give their full time to governmental affairs.

Local Self-Government. There are 3,107 local communities in Switzerland. They have the right of self-government within constitutional and statutory limits, exercising authority delegated to them by the cantons. Local autonomy contributes to the interest of residents in public affairs and provides them with useful political training. The cantonal governments have the power to supervise the operation of local self-government to prevent abuses and excessive financial burdens.

The public services furnished by the local community resemble those supplied by the canton, including police; education; regulation of ecclesiastical affairs; maintenance or subsidization of museums, reading rooms, and

theaters; fire protection; welfare; and relief. Local governments have no
judicial powers. These various functions are exercised by a variety of local
bodies. Small-sized communities generally have only a municipal council
of three to nine members, directed by the mayor. The larger communities
have two councils. One constitutes a kind of municipal parliament; the
other is an executive organ. All councils are elected. The decisions of municipal parliaments are sometimes subject to referendum. Under the power
of taxation, some communities employ the personal services of their inhabitants. In such cases, inhabitants are called upon to assist in the repair and
maintenance of roads and bridges or in fighting fires or floods, in lieu of payment of taxes.

Swiss local government presents some features unknown elsewhere. Besides the so-called political commune, which takes in all inhabitants and provides such general public services as sanitation, water, and gas, there is in
addition in fourteen cantons the so-called citizen commune, which includes
only those formally enrolled as citizens. These citizens enjoy some exclusive rights, such as a share in certain community property and the right of
public assistance in case of need. Such rights are kept wherever the citizen
may actually reside, although his home community may require his return
if he applies for assistance. Other local units include the ecclesiastical districts in twenty-one cantons, consisting of all local inhabitants of the same
religious creed. They are in general charge of church affairs, including the
payment of salaries to the clergy. Most French cantons have integrated all
local units in the political commune, which exercises all local functions.

4. The Political Process

Organization of the Political Parties. The political parties exist on a cantonal rather than a national basis. Party preferences are expressed largely
on local grounds, and local elections and politics seem of primary importance.
Voters moving into another canton often change party affiliations—in fact,
party names often differ from canton to canton. Some deputies decide upon
their affiliation with a party in the Federal Assembly only after they have been
elected on a local political basis.

It should be remembered that Switzerland does not know nation-wide
elections for a national office, such as that of President. Elections to the
federal legislature have a strong local color. National party organizations
are maintained now, but they followed the establishment of cantonal parties
by several decades and still constitute mere alliances for common, nation-
wide purposes of otherwise independent cantonal parties. The Social Democratic party alone is an exception, in that it was founded in relatively recent
years on a nation-wide basis, with party subdivisions established in the various
cantons.

Conservative Parties. In general, Swiss parties may be divided into groups
showing either conservative or liberal (including Social Democratic) tend-

encies and the Communists. The Catholic Conservative party draws its strength primarily from the rural Catholic population. As the name indicates, the members have a common religious tie. They oppose certain provisions of the federal constitution that they regard as anti-Catholic or at least anticlerical. In line with the teachings of their church, they reject an all-powerful state and favor the rights of the individual in regard to family, school, and church. In general, this party is hostile to centralization. It first gained a seat in the Federal Council in 1891 and has held two since 1919. The Christian Social party, its left wing, emphasizes the improvement of the conditions of the working class.

The Liberal Conservative party finds support among a portion of the middle classes and some of the old patrician and Protestant families. It favors private enterprise, and cantonal autonomy as opposed to central power.

Liberal Parties. The Radical Liberal party historically is responsible for the union of Switzerland over the opposition of the Catholics. It has held a majority of the seats in the Federal Council continuously between 1848 and 1944, and it still holds three out of seven, the largest single group. Its strongholds are the rural Protestant areas and the urban middle classes. Through a political accident two of its present members in the Federal Council are from French-speaking Switzerland, although two thirds of its following is in the German cantons.

The party favors social legislation and a balance between the interests of producers and consumers. It stresses an individualist philosophy and therefore strongly supports personal liberties on the one hand and opposes excessive state regulation on the other. In religious affairs, it aims to keep the state free from ecclesiastical influence. It stands for a strong Confederation.

The Agrarian, Artisan and Middle Class party was founded in 1919 and is especially strong in the canton of Bern. It is interested in the welfare of the urban middle class as well as that of the farmers. It favors a high protective tariff on agricultural products. It has been represented on the Federal Council with one seat since 1929. A leftist offspring of the party was formed in 1935 as the Young Farmers party. It is much concerned with farm indebtedness. The Independent party, founded in the same year, is primarily interested in defense of the consumer; it also stresses opposition to state interference in economic matters. It is a curious party, in that it is built mainly around one person, Gottlieb Duttweiler, a businessman who became popular by his success in decreasing the cost of living in several large cities through a system of retail sales at wholesale prices.

The Social Democratic party is indebted to Karl Marx and his early followers, including many German intellectuals who found refuge in Switzerland in the late nineteenth century, and immigrant workers. The progressive industrialization of the country and the introduction of proportional representation in 1919 greatly increased the party's strength. It is now supported primarily by workers and many government employees. Like Socialist parties elsewhere, it stands for government ownership of the means of production. Originally antimilitarist to the extent of opposing appropriations for the Swiss Army, it changed its attitude in 1935, owing to the danger to Swiss national security from Italian fascism and German nazism. At present; the Social Democratic party is the strongest in the National Council, but it occupies only one seat in the government. Under the pressure of recent events, it has become more united in strong opposition to communism, over which some of its followers were once enthusiastic.[11]

The Communists and other Extremists. The Party of Labor is the Communist party. Prohibited by the government in 1940, it is again legal. It is strongest in the French cantons of Vaud and Geneva. In its international policies, it automatically sees eye to eye with the interests of the Soviet Union. Partly in reaction to communism and partly under the impact of nazism in neighboring Germany, several small parties sprang up after 1933 designated as "movements," "unions," or "fronts." The so-called National Front and the Swiss National Movement, especially Nazi in character, were dissolved by the government in 1940. A number of the followers of these totalitarian groups have since been sentenced to long terms of imprisonment after conviction on charges of treason.

Party Strength. The relative size of the various political parties as represented in the National Council is indicated in the table. Only few depu-

PARTY COMPOSITION IN THE SWISS NATIONAL COUNCIL, 1919–51[12]

Parties	1919	1931	1939	1943	1947	1951
Radical Liberal	59	52	50	47	52	51
Agrarian	31	30	22	22	21	23
Independent	—	—	9	6	8	10
Liberal Conservative	9	6	6	8	7	5
Catholic Conservative	41	44	43	43	44	48
Social Democratic	41	49	45	56	48	49
Communist	—	2	—	—	7	5
Democratic	4	2	4	6	5	4
Others	4	2	8	7	2	1

ties belong to no party. At present, the Radical Liberal party is the strongest group in the National Council—51 seats, with the Social Democratic party a close second, holding 49 seats. The Catholic Conservatives hold 48 seats and the Agrarians 23. The Communists have kept their representation to 5 deputies. Smaller parties account for the remaining members of

[11] Benedikt Kautsky, son of the famous German Socialist leader, the late Karl Kautsky, and resident of Switzerland after seven years in a Nazi concentration camp, exercises a strong intellectual influence along anti-Communist lines; see S. F., "Glossen zur Innenpolitik," *Neue Zürcher Zeitung,* August 24, 1947, p. 4.
[12] Table from Sauser-Hall, *op. cit.* above, note 2, pp. 171-72; data for 1947 from "Das Ergebnis der Nationalratswahlen 1947," *Neue Zürcher Zeitung,* October 31, 1947, p. 4.

the National Council. The shifts in party membership in 1947—the first elections after World War II—amounted to only one ninth of the total number of seats, giving another indication of Swiss political stability.

Conditions of Suffrage. Every male citizen has the right to vote in federal, cantonal, and local elections. When citizens move to another canton they may vote on federal matters immediately upon registration, and on other matters after three months of residence. But in community matters, they vote only on the affairs of the political commune, since they do not share in the educational, ecclesiastical, and other property of the other political subdivisions in most of the German cantons. The right to vote can be denied by the cantons to citizens who have been deprived of civil rights, or who are supported by public appropriations, or who are under guardianship, and also in certain cases of bankruptcy. Citizens may appeal against the denial of the right to vote to the Federal Council, whose decision is final.

Although Switzerland is considered one of the progressive democracies, it denies women the vote, except in some cantons on matters that relate to education, ecclesiastical affairs, public relief, or guardianship, or in the election of arbitration tribunals. Women may be elected to some of these public authorities. At the same time, all professions are open to women, and they may be appointed to administrative positions. Various cantonal referenda have rejected woman suffrage—the canton of Zürich as late as 1947—and in other cantons it has never been voted on. All kinds of arguments are being voiced against woman suffrage, including those of "biology," but the main reason is that Swiss men are opposed to it and Swiss women do not demand it with sufficient insistence.

Direct Democracy. The Swiss people cherish the conviction that they are sovereign—they are habitually referred to as such in newspaper editorials. To them it is natural to assert the right to take a direct part in the constitutional and legislative process. They have developed the referendum and the initiative to such an extent that both have become virtually Swiss institutions.

The power of the people may be exercised in different ways. In no case—neither in the Confederation nor in any canton—is the legislature entrusted with exclusive power over legislation, as in Great Britain. In the pure democracy of the Landsgemeinde, the voters legislate directly and exclusively. But the more common form of Swiss popular government is a type of "mixed democracy" wherein the legislative will of the people is expressed both through legislatures and through direct popular votes in the form of the referendum and the initiative.

Forms of the Referendum. The referendum enables the voters to act as the arbiter on the adoption or rejection of a constitutional amendment or a law. All amendments to the federal and cantonal constitutions are subject to the *obligatory constitutional referendum,* without which no constitutional change becomes final. In its specific form, it originated in the United States, where it was first applied in Massachusetts in 1778; it reached Switzerland by way of revolutionary France. Switzerland's constitution of 1848 and its revised form of 1874 were approved by this method, including the provision that cantonal constitutions must be similarly adopted in order to be guaranteed by the federal government. Proposed amendments to the federal constitution are usually passed first by the Federal Assembly in the same way as ordinary federal laws. They become valid, however, only after having been approved by a majority of the popular votes cast in a referendum and by a majority of the cantons. The vote of each canton or half-canton is determined by its popular vote.

The national *legislative referendum* is applicable to federal laws—except budgets and emergency decrees—and, since 1921, to international treaties concluded for an indeterminate period or for more than fifteen years. It is started off by a petition of at least 30,000 voters, presented within ninety days after the law or decree has been made public, or by eight cantonal governments. Only a popular majority is required for its adoption. All cantons except those retaining the Landsgemeinde provide for the legislative referendum. In some it is *obligatory,* in others *optional*—or depending upon a petition by specified numbers of citizens, the number varying from canton to canton. In still other cantons, the referendum is obligatory for important financial laws only and optional for others.

Between 1848 and 1942, the general voter rejected by this method forty-three and adopted forty-six constitutional amendments. During this same period, the legislative referendum resulted in the approval of sixteen federal bills and the rejection of thirty-one.

In 1947 the citizens by 854,000 votes to 216,000 voted themselves a "New Deal" in social security, and also approved a constitutional amendment giving the federal government the right to regulate the economy to overcome major economic upsets, an amendment previously twice rejected as going too far toward a planned economy.

Forms of the Initiative. By means of the initiative, the voter can make his influence felt in those cases where the legislature may not want to adopt a constitutional amendment or a law, or takes no steps to submit either to a referendum. The right of *constitutional initiative* exists in both the Confederation and all cantons. Under it a minimum of 50,000 voters may petition for an amendment to the federal constitution, either in the form of a request in general terms or as a definitely worded article embodying the proposal. If the Federal Assembly approves a proposal submitted in general terms, it submits a specific draft to the popular and cantonal vote. If, however, its two houses vote against the proposal or disagree, the petition as such is submitted to a popular vote. If it wins a majority, the Federal Assembly sees to it that an amendment is drafted in accordance with the petition, but the voters must again pass on it before it can become final. An unfavorable popular vote on the petition kills it.

If the initiative proposes a definitely worded amendment, it is immediately submitted to a popular vote, provided it has been accepted by at least one house of the Federal Assembly.   If both houses unite against the proposed amendment, they may either advise the voters to reject the initiative[13] or submit a counterproposal along with the original one.   Between 1874 and 1944, the federal constitutional initiative was successful in only seven cases out of thirty-five.   In seven other cases, the Federal Assembly offered substitute proposals, of which six were accepted.   It seems, therefore, that the Swiss voter tends to adopt those popularly proposed constitutional amendments that have found favor with the legislature.   The course of an initiative for total revision of the constitution is similar.   Upon the petition of 50,000 voters, the question of its desirability is submitted to popular vote.   If the vote is affirmative, parliamentary elections are held and the new Federal Assembly carries out the popular will.   Demands for amendments or total revision of the constitution may also originate with either of the two houses of the Federal Assembly, the Federal Council, or a canton.   If both houses of the Federal Assembly unite against such an initiative, the matter ends there; if they disagree on it, the question is submitted to a popular vote.   If this is affirmative, a newly elected Parliament provides for the constitutional revision.   None has taken place since 1874.

Since there is no federal *legislative initiative,* the constitutional initiative has been used to place all kinds of matters in the federal constitution; for instance, the prohibition against kosher slaughtering.   The constitutional initiative, on the other hand, has also been used for such politically significant purposes as the introduction of proportional representation and of the referendum on certain international treaties.

5. The Individual and the Nation

Tradition of Citizenship.   To the traveler and student visiting her after World War II, Switzerland appears to be a happy island in a sea of unrest. With the possible exception of the two Low Countries, she seems to have a monopoly of political stability among the nations of the Continent.

This situation is due to a combination of factors for which the Swiss deserve much civic credit.   They used to be as warlike as any power in Europe, but for centuries they have concentrated on domestic progress and international cooperation.   Having established a national union by firm action against dissident cantons, they cultivated cantonal autonomy.   In a country with great diversity in language, religion, and custom, their feeling of nationality is so strong as to allow every citizen the right to go his own way

---

[13] Early in 1948, the Federal Council recommended to the Federal Assembly that it vote adversely on a constitutional initiative entitled "Return to Direct Democracy," which would restrict drastically the power of the Federal Council to issue emergency decrees under article 89 of the constitution.   This proposed amendment had been supported by over 55,000 valid signatures.   See "Das Volksbegehren für die 'Rückkehr zur direkten Demokratie,'" *Neue Zürcher Zeitung,* February 28, 1948, sec. 6.

in cultural affairs. The German-speaking Swiss may fail to appreciate all the ways of his countrymen who speak French and Italian—and *vice versa* —but he insists on their right to be themselves and to cultivate their distinctive characteristics. This insistence is more than tolerance; it is a pride and conviction in the rights of the individual, basically unaffected by temporary antagonisms.

The stability of political institutions and processes, so typical of the country, is rooted in the ancient origins of Swiss democracy and aided by progressive adaptation to new conditions and ideas. The Swiss citizen tends to be soberly calculating at the polls as well as at his place of business. Newfangled theories do not appeal to him in comparison with the time-tested customs of his nation and his canton. The result is a citizen and a country that at times have progressed slowly in political development, but whose strength of purpose, civic accomplishments, and democratic steadfastness are an example for other countries.

Citizen Soldier. The Swiss are a soldierly people with a strong antimilitarist bent of mind. The federal constitution forbids the maintenance of a standing army, but every male citizen who is physically and mentally fit is drafted for military service, which is divided into annual short periods of intensive training. This militia system is maintained with a minimum of professional army officers, and on the principle that the military is subject to civilian direction.

In line with the country's traditional policy of neutrality, the Army specializes in defense tactics. It excels in sharpshooting and mountain fighting, without neglecting modern weapons, including jet planes. Army instruction is made easier by the high educational level of the rank and file, the premilitary stress on physical training, and the lifelong enthusiasm of the average Swiss for sharpshooting contests. Boys from fifteen years up may take federally subsidized courses outside school in the use of weapons. After completion of their military training, soldiers receive their rifles and uniforms as gifts, subject to periodical inspection. All officers up to the rank of colonel are civilians who continue their regular vocations or professions, except for brief training periods. Only the army instructors and the corps and divisional commanders are professional soldiers. Those exempted from military service include members of the Federal Council and clergymen. Members of the federal legislature are often officers. Noncommissioned officers as well as commissioned ones graduate from training schools to which they return periodically for further instruction. Men not in the military service—for instance, residents abroad—pay a graduated exemption tax based upon capital and income, which is divided equally between the Confederation and the cantons.

Military administration is not entirely centralized. The cantons form the infantry and cavalry units, the *Landsturm* of older men for home defense, and the medical, supply, and intelligence services. They commission the officers for these units up to the rank of major. The Confederation forms all the units and staffs not set up by the cantons, especially military communications and transportation. The Federal Council commissions all officers not appointed by the cantons, except the general in command of the Army in times of national emergency, who is elected by the Federal Assembly.

Policy of Neutrality. Upon the close of the "heroic period" of their history, the Swiss turned to a policy of neutrality, which they pursued throughout the Thirty Years War, the wars of Louis XIV, the Wars of Succession, and the Seven Years War. But they were forced by Napoleon I to furnish troops for his campaigns, and their territory served as a battleground. By the Declaration of Vienna of 1815, the neutrality of Switzerland was guaranteed by the leading European powers, and the guaranty has been in force continuously since that time.[14] The powers stated at Vienna "that the neutrality and inviolability of Switzerland and her independence of all foreign influence are in the true interests of the policy of Europe." They confirmed this position at Versailles in 1919 and by the Declaration of London of 1920. The Swiss constitution, in article 102, imposes a policy of neutrality upon the Federal Council.

Swiss foreign policy has been officially described as one of "neutrality and solidarity." The former forbids any political or military alliance. It would make Switzerland's membership in the United Nations possible only on condition that she could keep "permanently neutral" at the same time. While Switzerland cannot join the North Atlantic Treaty Organization, the question of her membership in the European Council is still being debated by the Swiss public. Her extensive political and private international relief work includes her traditional role as the "protective power" of prisoners of war. She does not share in Marshall Plan aid, which she does not need, but belongs to the European Organization for Economic Cooperation.

The Swiss have not depended on the guaranty of their neutrality by foreign countries, but mobilized their manpower for the full period of the two World Wars on an extensive and expensive scale, enforcing respect for their territorial integrity even when surrounded by Nazi Germany, Fascist Italy, and Vichy France. In pursuance of its established policy, the government interned large numbers of French and Polish soldiers who crossed the borders in 1940 and forced or shot down American bombing planes who strayed over Swiss territory. The government has continued to proclaim its firm intention to stick to its traditional neutrality in the current struggle between East and West; but anxious citizens ask how their country could defend its independence against a military avalanche any more than against the masses of the French Revolution. They remember that the Soviet Union has never recognized the neutrality of Switzerland, and they would not count on it if it did.

---

[14] See Zurcher, *op. cit.* above, note 2, pp. 1023 ff.; Sauser-Hall, *op. cit.* above, note 2, chap. 10.

Meanwhile, the voters continue to favor steep military appropriations for national defense, and the government is replenishing the emergency two-year reserve of food and raw materials that it had stored in Alpine caves before World War II. Internationally, the Swiss government cooperates with the European Recovery Plan in its "economic aspects," without stating just how they will be separated from political ends.

Developments and Outlook. In the year of the hundredth anniversary of the constitution of 1848, some Swiss students[15] have called for a return from emergency law to "normal law." They pointed out correctly that decrees were still in force that were based upon the special emergency powers conferred by the Federal Assembly upon the Federal Council in 1939, even in 1933, and in part actually in 1914. To them, this appeared to suggest the need for a constitutional revision—possibly in several stages—that would provide for sufficient federal powers to safeguard the country's existence amid today's dangers, but would do it in a "constitutionally orderly and controlled manner." Public discussion of emergency law as the "opiate of the constitutional state" has since continued—an indication of the healthy state of Swiss democracy.

A need has made itself felt for greater popular interest in basic constitutional questions, in opposition to growing opportunism that rejects concern with "mere questions of form." These constitutional problems are tied up with what some of the country's responsible observers point to with some alarm as a lowered degree of popular interest in civic and political standards, combined with a lack of factual knowledge and a dearth of ethical convictions.[16] It also has been pointed out by them that, on the average, only half of the voters participated in the last eight federal referendums since early 1950, the maximum participation being 53.7 per cent and the lowest 42 per cent on an agricultural proposition. Actually, however, the average vote has never been higher than 62 per cent in recent years. While low voting records in referendums are therefore not a new phenomenon, they suggest to some Swiss observers the need for intensified civic education.

Looking historically at the unfolding of Swiss federalism, one sees a steady constitutional development since 1848 toward an increase in cantonal powers over the individual and, at the same time, a growth, especially since the First World War, of federal jurisdiction at the expense of the cantons, particularly along economic lines. This two-pronged constitutional tendency, it is true, can be observed also in other federal countries, as an expression of the modern service state. In Switzerland, it has been a gradual process without any acute constitutional or political crisis, with results that have been of concern to those who object to *"dirigisme,"* but that have proved acceptable if not desirable to the large majority of the citizens.

---

[15] See report on Professor Werner Kagi's lecture urging a return to the constitution, *Neue Zürcher Zeitung,* February 18, 1948, sec. 6.

[16] See "Die politische Gleichgültigkeit," *Neue Zürcher Zeitung,* May 25, 1947.

PART VI

THE SOCIALIST STATE: THE SOVIET UNION
AND ITS ORBIT

CHAPTER 20

RUSSIA AND MARXISM

1. The Russian Peasant

Land of Peasants. Two principal factors have influenced the development of the Union of Soviet Socialist Republics (USSR). These have been the Russian heritage and the political philosophy of Karl Marx. Both factors are of primary importance to an outsider seeking to understand Soviet political institutions.

The USSR stands where the Russian Empire once stood. As such it has inherited social, economic, and political traditions from old Russia. Perhaps the most outstanding feature of the Russian heritage is the character of the peasantry. Russia had been for centuries, and the USSR remains today, a land of peasants. The industrial revolution came late to Russia. By the end of the nineteenth century, there were only about two million industrial workmen in the whole Empire.[1] Even these were of rural mentality, for the majority retained their ties with the village. They came to the towns at times of slack work in the fields and returned to the farms for summer planting and harvesting, and to live out their old age.

Agricultural work might have developed educated, resourceful, individualistic people, as it has in some parts of the Western world, but it did not do so in Russia. The reverse was true. The peasant heritage of the Russian Empire proved to be a handicap to progress. It spelled illiteracy, bondage, suspicion, and irresponsibility. The Russian peasant thus differs from the American farmer in many ways. Perhaps the most outstanding differences spring from the fact that the great majority of the Russian peasants have only relatively recently become free. A Russian census of 1783 indicated that 94.5 per cent of the male population of the Empire was rural, and of this number only 7 per cent were free men. The others were serfs upon private estates or crown lands.[2] At that very time the United States was building a new nation of free men.

Effects of Serfdom. The Russian peasants were to remain in serfdom almost as long as the Negroes of the United States remained slaves. Not until 1861 were the serfs freed, and even after the emancipation economic ties held

---

[1] The number of factory workers is given by M. I. Tugan-Baranovsky, *Russkaya fabrika v proshlom i nastoyashchem* (3rd ed., St. Petersburg, 1907), p. 342, as the following: 1,318,048 in 1887; 1,582,904 in 1893; 2,098,262 in 1897.

[2] See Alexander Kornilov, *Modern Russian History*, trans. Kaun (New York, 1943), I, p. 26.

400 THE SOVIET UNION AND ITS ORBIT

the former serfs to the land. Serfdom had begun in Russia without the aspects of slavery; but as the years went by serfs became tied to the land and were sold by landlords for personal service the way Negroes were in the slave markets of the United States.[3]   Only a few serfs escaped to the roving bands who fringed the populated areas in the Don and Kuban river basins, to become known as Cossacks.   To descendants of these Cossacks, the Tsars looked for the courageous self-reliance required for the hard police and military tasks of the Empire.   The Soviet government has likewise turned to a new generation of the same Cossacks for its cavalry and for tasks requiring individual initiative.   Such initiative has traditionally been the exception in the Russian character, and historians lay the blame largely at serfdom's door.

Serfdom left a heavy imprint upon the Russian peasant in reducing his opportunities for education.   Peasant schools were established in very small numbers, and these were limited to the primary grades.   A law in 1837 forbade the sending of a serf to a high school or university, and this prohibition was repeated in 1843, except for serfs whom the master was prepared to set free.   The ineffectiveness of the educational system was marked even after the emancipation.   A census in 1897 reported a village population in European Russia of 80 million, of whom 11,431,000 males and 3,923,000 females were recorded as literate.   The proportion of literates among the peasantry is shown by these figures to have been almost 20 per cent on the eve of our century.

Legacy of Suspicion.   Illiteracy and lack of education induced suspicion in the mind of the average peasant.   Documents that he could not read were looked upon with caution.   Laws meant nothing until they were applied, and even then the peasant could not be sure the authorities were following a law that could not be examined or understood by him.   The village priest was the scribe for the community, but he was not infrequently a slim reed upon which to lean, in matters of both culture and politics.   Protection against the government official and the commercial agent lay frequently in the measure of caution that the peasant was able to develop.   He learned to devise excuses for failure of performance and to avoid a face-to-face exposure of such failures.   He learned to postpone unpleasant tasks indefinitely and to plead ignorance when called to account.

Features such as these made themselves felt in the conduct of affairs in old Russia.   The manufacturers who used serfs as workers found them lacking in the discipline of thought and action required for industrial production.   Serfs did not work as well as free men, for they had nothing for which to work.   The danger of serfdom was brought clearly to the fore by the Crimean War.   A serf army proved to be brave, but no match for the free men in the armies of the West.   Even Tsar Nicholas I, who died in 1855 during

---

[3] Cf. Geroid Tanquary Robinson, *Rural Russia under the Old Regime* (London, 1932), p. 44; George Vernadsky, *A History of Russia* (New Haven, 1929), p. 110.

the conduct of the war, appreciated the danger. He told his son, who succeeded him as Alexander II, "I am handing you command of the country in
a poor state." [4]   The basic defect of the old regime was now clearly seen in the
institituon of serfdom.   Serfs had to be freed for the good of Russia, if not
for humanitarian reasons.

Aftermath of the Emancipation. Emancipation brought personal liberty
to the millions of serfs, but it did not eliminate all the causes of peasant suspicion, illiteracy, irresponsibility, and evasion, which had become characteristic of serfdom.   In looking toward freedom, the peasantry wished to escape
all payments for the allotment of land that they were to receive after emancipation.   The landlords, on the other hand, requested payment not only for
the land surrendered for peasant use, but also for the labor that would be lost
when the serfs were freed.   The Emancipation Act of 1861 struck a compromise.   The state was to pay compensation at once to the gentry when
land was surrendered to the peasants, but the peasants who remained on the
land were required to "redeem" it.   This requirement meant that payments
would have to be made to the state extending over forty-nine years.   Even
when the land was redeemed, it was to become the property not of the individual peasants, but of the village community.

The peasants were living in such village communities at the time of the
emancipation, rather than on the individual farms typical of American agricultural areas.   These village communities remained collectively responsible
for taxes and the redemption payments.   The old passport system was continued, under which the peasants remained dependent on their village community, which they could not leave without permission.   The Emancipation
Act, then, held the former serfs in what amounted to communal economic
bondage until the land should be redeemed.

Not until 1906 were the village communities made the subject of a land
reform designed to create a large class of independent farmer-owners.[5]
Under this reform, initiated by Minister P. A. Stolypin, about half a million
such farms appeared.[6]   Even with such a reform, the communal life of the
peasantry was slow to change.   Individualism in the sense in which the
American understands it had hardly emerged before the Soviet system of
organization of agriculture became paramount, with the collective farm as
the principal form of organization.

Quest for Spiritual Ease. The church also served as an important influence upon the peasantry and contributed to its characteristics.   The Orthodox church was never the organizer of social life, as the Catholic parish priest
and the Protestant minister have been in the United States, but it provided
an outlet for the spirit of people who were sorely tried by the burdens of this

[4] See Vernadsky, *op. cit.* above, note 3, p. 151.
[5] For an account of the reforms, see Sir Bernard Pares, *A History of Russia* (3rd ed., New York, 1941), pp. 353 ff.
[6] See Ernest J. Simmons, ed., *U.S.S.R.: A Concise Handbook* (Ithaca, 1947), p. 217.

world. It had been for centuries a church of mystic rites and conservative tendencies. Its control by the tsarist government and its official duties of keeping birth, marriage, and death records gave it an unusual position in the community. Its traditions had become instilled in the peasantry so firmly as to cause resistance to much that was new and even to prevent the adventurous from seeking out a solution to the problems of the community. The church was a restraining influence that tended to accentuate the characteristics derived from serfdom.

With so many weights upon it, the peasantry had much in its daily life from which to escape. Country living in old Russia was dotted with occasions when hard liquor was the accepted means of obtaining forgetfulness. Expenditures in one province for *vodka* were almost equivalent in the 107 families investigated in 1909 to the sum spent for education (aside from taxes), for books, for oil and incense, for gifts to the priests and to the poor, and for weddings and funerals. A government report in 1903 found that not one event in the social life of the community—such as the cutting of the hay, or the local saint's day—could be celebrated without the drinking of *vodka,* and *vodka* was indispensable on every important occasion in the life of the family, such as births, marriages, funerals, the departure of recruits drafted into the Army, and the like. The report might have added that heavy drinking was the rule even after the weekly steam bath, with the lame excuse that it helped restore the liquid to the body.

The historian V. O. Kluchevsky, revered both before and since the Russian Revolution, has written the following of the native type: "By some observers he is accused of lack of straightforwardness and sincerity. That is a mistake. True, he often takes two views of a question, but this seeming doublemindedness arises from the fact that, though his mental process leads him to make straight for his goal (ill-considered though the goal often be), he does so looking to either side of him as he goes, even as his ancestors scanned the surrounding fastnesses they were forced to traverse. 'Beware lest thou strike thy forehead against a wall; none but the crows fly straight,' says a Great Russian proverb. Circumstances and the forces of nature have combined to teach the native of Great Russia to try all roads when making for a given point, and to think and act as he goes along."[7] Kluchevsky's words do much to aid the American to understand the human material with which the USSR has been built.

Variety of Native Stock. The human material with which the Soviet Union has been built is not entirely of Russian or even of Slav origin, however. The Empire was remarkable in the number of national groups that lived within its borders, and the USSR has inherited them. The census of 1939 recorded a total of 170,467,186 persons.[8] Only 58 per cent of these were

[7] See V. O. Kluchevsky, *A History of Russia,* trans. Hogarth (London, 1911), I, 220.

[8] For population statistics and information on natural resources, see George B. Cressey, *The Basis of Soviet Strength* (New York, 1945). Postwar estimates come to 200 millions.

of Great Russian stock. Ukrainians accounted for an additional 17 per cent, and Byelorussians for 3 per cent. These three peoples constituted the Slavic element, totaling a little more than three quarters of the population. The remaining quarter was divided among 166 ethnic groups, only 47 of which numbered more than 20,000 each. Many of these were of Asiatic origin, with different cultures.

Other minority groups were added by the extension of Soviet frontiers during and after World War II, which also increased the number of Slavs by inclusion of the districts absorbed from prewar Poland. The population has probably reached or exceeded 200 million, but it is still three-quarters Slav.

Most of the peoples of the USSR live upon a great plain. This feature is thought to have affected their mentality and even the form of their government. Historians have argued that the rulers of the Empire tried to gather into one the Russian lands and keep them united.[9] In this manner the centralization of the imperial government's political structure is explained. Whether this be a correct explanation or not, the phenomenon of centralization has continued. The USSR is a federation, whereas the Empire was, as defined by its basic law, "unified and indivisible." But there has continued to the present day a strong tradition of looking to the center for guidance and even direction.

National Wealth. Size and wealth of natural resources have always influenced the thinking of those who have guided the land that is now the USSR. Its area of approximately 8,400,000 square miles is twice the area of Europe. From Leningrad to Vladivostok, one travels 5,800 miles across a land mass that has an average breadth of 1,500 miles. In this territory have been found ample resources for agricultural and industrial development with but few shortages. Some of the shortages may be serious, however, in times of crisis. Geographers believe that the Soviet Union is probably short of high-grade copper ores and bauxite and may even have to import oil at a future date. There seems no likelihood of growing sufficient rubber from dandelion or other plants to meet the requirements for natural rubber, and certainly there will be no cocoa or coffee, because of the northerly latitude of the country, most of which is north of the parallel on which lies Winnipeg, Canada.

The resources of manpower and raw materials have given the thinking people of the USSR great confidence in the future of their country, if only the resources can be employed to full advantage. Many of the Soviet planners ascribe the backwardness of their country to the failure of Russian leaders of the past so to utilize these resources as to make them productive for the people as a whole. Dreams of such utilization characterized much of the thinking of the revolutionaries as they arose in the Empire at the end of the

---

[9] See Anatole Leroy-Beaulieu, *The Empire of the Tsars and the Russians,* trans. Zenaide A. Ragozin (New York, 1894), II, 63.

nineteenth century. Dreams of the same sort are characteristic of the leadership of today.

2. Absolutism and Democracy

Tradition of Autocracy. The Russian heritage is many-sided. In the political field, the cornerstone has been the tradition of authoritarianism, exemplified in the Tsar as absolute ruler. Sharp contrast is provided to the words of Thomas Jefferson and of the French Declaration of the Rights of Man by article 4 of the Fundamental Laws of the Russian Empire. This article read as follows: "To the Emperor of all the Russias belongs the supreme autocratic power. To obey his commands not merely from fear but according to the dictates of one's conscience is ordained by God himself."

Had such phraseology been the product of the ministers of a George III, it might not startle American students; but it was not a product of the eighteenth century. It was drafted in the twentieth century, as part of a constitution granted reluctantly to a rebellious people, who had shown by their demands after the defeats suffered by the Empire in the Russo-Japanese War that liberalization of imperial policy was necessary. This constitution of 1906 represented a progressive step in the political life of Russia, and the smallness of the step as compared with Western precedents emphasizes the difference in the political traditions of the Russian and American peoples.

Autocracy was not a superficial development in Russia. It was deeply rooted. Some historians date its origin to the official assumption by Ivan the Terrible of the title of Tsar, or Caesar, in 1547, followed by the establishment of supreme police control after the death of his wife in 1565—by poison, as Ivan thought.

Early Reforms. The civil wars of the period following Ivan the Terrible's death, culminating in the capture of the throne by the Poles in 1605, produced no basic change in the principle of autocracy. When the Poles were finally ousted in 1611 by a noble named Pozharsky and a commoner named Minin, a national assembly was convened to consider who should be Tsar. The choice fell on Michael Feodorovich Romanov, the son of the Patriarch of the Orthodox church. He was enthroned in 1613 to establish the Romanov dynasty, which ruled for the succeeding three hundred years. These centuries were dotted with landmarks of internal reform, but nothing was done to detract from the authority of the Crown. Peter the Great introduced Western culture and techniques of production. He was notable also because he initiated reforms in legal procedure, lifting trials out of the medieval star-chamber proceedings in which they had previously been conducted. In spite of these reforms, Peter enhanced the power of the Tsar in his reign and assumed the title of Emperor in 1721.

When Catherine II ascended the throne in 1762, she was prepared to institute some of the ideas of the French philosophers Montesquieu and Voltaire, but her advisers dissuaded her. For a time it seemed that there might be some emulation of the West, but the matter was put aside under the pressure of a peasant revolution. Thereafter, Catherine preserved and enhanced the authority of the Crown.

A more propitious occasion for the introduction of some measure of constitutional rule appeared to have arrived when Alexander I ascended the throne in 1801, much influenced by events in the West. He commissioned an official, Michael Speransky, to draw up a plan to remodel the whole structure and administration of the Empire. This plan called for the creation of a representative body (*duma*) to be composed of deputies elected indirectly by the population. The citizens of each township were to elect a local duma, from which delegates were to be elected to a county duma. Delegates were then to be selected from among these to a provincial duma, and from each of the provincial dumas throughout the Empire delegates were to be chosen to convene as the imperial duma. Speransky's plan also envisaged the creation of an imperial council, which would have as its function the coordination of the various administrative organs of government. The imperial council was brought into existence in 1810, but the other parts of the plan were put aside in the crisis of the resumed war against Napoleon. After nearly a hundred years they served as a model for the reforms inaugurated under Nicholas II. Curiously enough, the system of indirect representation was carried into the government of the Soviets. The constitution of 1918 established a system of elections to a hierarchy of soviets on a base quite similar to that originally conceived by Speransky.

Era of Indecision. The manifesto of January 1, 1810, inaugurating the partial reforms, restated the principle of autocracy by declaring: "The Russian Empire is governed on the firm foundation of the laws . . . emanating from the Autocratic Power." But the Napoleonic wars had wider effects on political thought. Officers who had seen the West brought home reform ideas and the will to action. Some staged an unsuccessful *coup* and became known as the Decembrists, from the fact that their attempt was made in December 1825 on the accession of Nicholas I. Nicholas opened his reign with the suppression of the Decembrists, thus indicating the temper of his rule, which was to last for thirty years.

Alexander II, known as the Liberator, is remembered not only for his abolition of serfdom, but also for extensive reforms of a social and economic character; in particular, the judicial reforms of 1864. Russia was brought at last to a level of judicial administration generally corresponding to that on the continent to the west. But Alexander did nothing to limit the powers of the Crown. Widespread disappointment was the result, stimulating underground activities that led finally to the Tsar's assassination on March 1, 1881. Pathetically enough, he appears to have been on the verge of instituting political reforms. The assassination ended such projects. Reaction set in immediately, for Alexander III proclaimed his unreserved devotion to the unalterable principles of autocracy.

Nicholas II, who was to be the last Tsar, upon ascending the throne in 1894, brushed aside the hopes for reform as senseless dreams. He failed to notice the forces that were to require a change in 1905. As a result of the autocracy of the Tsars, the peoples of the Russian Empire had no experience with a national parliament until the First Duma was convened in May 1906. In spite of this lack of experience with forms of representation that had been commonplace in the West for more than a century, the Russians were not entirely unfamiliar with agencies of self-government and processes that bore the imprint of democracy.

Local Citizen Participation. Russian procedures of self-government existed during the nineteenth century only at the local level. Two institutions have been pointed to as schools in democracy: the local peasant assemblies and the *zemstva.* The more ancient of these was the peasant assembly. Its origin far antedated the nineteenth century; it has been traced back to the early migration of Slavs from the Carpathians to the Dnieper in the period of the dawn of Russian history. The peasants from very early times elected their village elders for the purpose of dividing the communally owned land into plots for individual use. These councils of elders assumed additional tasks, such as keeping peace among the members of the community. As the centuries progressed, the councils of elders dealt with many matters of local concern. They came to be of such importance that they were recognized by the government at the time of the emancipation of the serfs in 1861 as the agency best suited to the assumption of responsibility for payment of the installments due the state for the redemption of the land. The institution of the council of elders taught the peasant something of the possibilities of self-government on the local level.

The zemstva were created in 1864 as the result of a recommendation of a government commission.[10] This commission had been set up to study the

---

[10] See Alexander Kornilov, *Modern Russian History,* cited above, note 2, II, 96. See also Paul Vinogradoff, *Self-Government in Russia* (London, 1915). As amended in 1890, the statute on the zemstva provided that the deputies to the district zemstva were to be elected every three years as follows: Three electoral meetings were called (1) of hereditary and personal nobles of the district, presided over by the district marshal of nobility; (2) of persons other than nobles who had a right to participate, presided over by the mayor of the county seat; and (3) of representatives of the peasant villages. The number of deputies that each electoral meeting could send to the district zemstvo was established by the statute, using as a measure an estimate of the amount of land that each meeting might be expected to represent. Requirements for participation in the meetings were relatively simple for nobles—namely, that they have the status of a noble; and also for peasants—namely, that they be selected by a meeting of their village family-heads to represent the village. Requirements for participation in the other meeting were complex, namely that a participant own in his own right an amount of land not less than the quantity specified in a table attached to the statute, or that he represent a charitable or educational institution, a trade or industrial association, a partnership or corporation that had owned the specified quantity of land for not less than one year or owned other immovable property valued for tax purposes at not less than 15,000 rubles. Life tenancy was the equivalent of ownership. A woman who owned the requisite minimum of property could vote through a male member of her family, and a minor under twenty-five years of age could vote through an adult, if the minor owned the requisite minimum. Persons who owned not less than one tenth

situation caused by the Act of Emancipation, which had upset the foundations of local government existing under serfdom. The recommendation called for the creation of councils in each district of the most populated provinces, from which representatives would be chosen to sit on a provincial council (zemstvo) to coordinate the work in all districts. Jurisdiction of the councils was limited to care of roads, hospitals, and matters concerned with food. Later the sphere of activity was broadened to include education, medical aid, veterinary aid, and public welfare in general. Authority was limited to nonpolitical fields, but the zemstva proved to be useful as a training ground for public administration and as a source of democratic thinking. As such, they were feared by the autocracy and progressively restricted as their power became apparent.

Repression of Autonomy. The terms of delegates to the zemstva were three years, and meetings were held once a year, under the chairmanship of the county marshal of nobility. An executive committee was chosen at the first meeting of delegates following each new election, and it was this committee that carried the burden of administrative work throughout the year. Similar representative forms were introduced into town government in 1870, but control was again retained by the well-to-do citizens. Representation was allotted to three categories, but the numbers in each category varied widely because the amount of taxes paid was made the basis for the division into categories.

In spite of the care taken to provide a system of elections and control that would assure conservative tendencies, the zemstva soon got out of hand. As early as 1866, the government restricted publicity of their debates and put the organization in each province under the control of the governor. After the assassination of Alexander II in 1881, the zemstva suffered in the wave of reaction. In 1890, the executive committee of each district zemstvo was made into an agency of the Ministry of the Interior, and its actions became subject to complete review and control by the governor of the province. The presidents of the committees were to be appointed by the government, and the electoral system was revised to put the zemstva more firmly under the control of the nobility.

At the turn of the century, the zemstva began to expand their activities into the political sphere. Chairmen of provincial zemstva met in Moscow in 1902 in a semi-official national congress. The meeting called attention

---

of the requisite minimum of property could meet and select as many representatives to participate in the electoral meeting as would have been merited under the statutory rate of representation by the total size of their holdings, had they been pooled. All persons had to be Russian subjects to vote—but some of these were excluded even if they owned the requisite property; namely, Jews, local officials of the prosecutor's office, police officers, persons under sentence or investigation for serious crime, insolvents, the insane, and persons under police supervision even if not imprisoned. Priests could not vote, but the bishop of the diocese could send an *ex officio* representative to the district zemstvo if he desired. Each district zemstvo selected its representatives to the provincial zemstvo. The number to represent each district was set by the statute.

to inequalities of civil rights, hindrances to education, defects of financial policy, and need for a free press. In 1903, the chairmen met again and passed a
resolution calling upon the government to submit all drafts of laws relating
to local questions to the zemstva for discussion prior to enactment. The
congress of chairmen of 1904 called for freedom of the individual and his
conscience, of speech and association, for equal civil rights of all regardless
of class or religion, for elective local government, freedom of education, and
a wider franchise for the zemstva. The Tsar thought the zemstva had
gone too far and told them not again to discuss political questions. The next
year his hand was forced by a revolution, and the people pushed beyond the
local peasant assemblies and the zemstva in their quest of a share in government.

3. Surge of Revolution

Currents of Rebellion. Sporadic uprisings appeared among the peasants
at an early date. The best-known movements were the two that swelled into
such size as to require military campaigns for their suppression. Leadership
in both instances came from the Cossacks. The first of these rebel chiefs
was Stenka Razin, who organized and led a discontented horde up the Volga
in 1667 to raid and pillage until captured and executed in 1671. The second
was Emilian Pugachev, who led a similar band in very much the same territory around the Volga in 1773 and continued until he was caught and sentenced to death in 1775. It was this latter rising that caused Catherine to
depart from her program of liberal reform with which she had come to the
throne.

Although the names of Razin and Pugachev live on in ballads and history,
the efforts of these men to oust the Tsar were isolated and confused by personal issues. It was not until the latter half of the nineteenth century that
a true revolutionary movement appeared. It grew up among the educated
professional classes known in Russia as the *intelligentsia,* many of whose
members became influenced by liberal thought as they traveled abroad or
read the literature of the West. They appreciated that they would remain
ineffective unless they organized a mass movement for their support. Russia
of the 1860's was in no sense a land of workmen. Fuel for revolution, if it
were to be found anywhere, had to be found among the peasantry. The
intelligentsia formed what was later called the *narodnik* movement to enlist
the peasantry under its leadership in a drive for reform. This movement
looked to the village community and the small producing cooperative as the
forms of economic life from which socialism would eventually develop to
save the country.

The narodnik movement went through the debilitating process of factional splits. One wing in 1876 turned to a program of mass uprisings to
overthrow the existing government. The main body held on to a program
of peaceful propaganda of socialist ideas among the peasants. Members

went into the country as teachers, physicians, blacksmiths, and carpenters, but the peasants seemed not to listen. The government arrested the leaders and sentenced them to hard labor. The movement now went underground, but again there was a split, culminating in 1879 with the creation of two groups. One, the "people's will," pushed a program of terror against tsarism and created an organization to spread propaganda among soldiers and workmen. This was the organization that assassinated Alexander II in 1881 and tried to kill Alexander III in 1887. The participants in these terroristic acts were executed. The death of one of them was of historical consequence because of its impact upon a younger brother, later known to the world as Lenin. The other wing, the "black redistribution," tried to adhere to a program avoiding terror and limited to underground propaganda; but the government raided its print shops, and its leaders were compelled to flee abroad. One of these, Plekhanov, was later to have great influence from his place of exile by writing revolutionary material to be smuggled into Russia.

Influx of Marxist Ideas. Soviet schoolchildren are now taught that the narodnik movement failed because it did not appreciate that the workmen rather than the peasants constituted the class that could create socialism.[11] The narodniks are also criticized because they diverted the attention of the workmen and the peasantry from the fight against the ruling class as a whole to the futile assassination of individual representatives. Both lessons have become slogans of revolutionaries who follow the Russian experience in other countries of the world. As the industrialization of Russia spread, factory owners introduced routines copied from the early examples in the West. Working days ranged from twelve to fourteen hours. Wages were low. Safety conditions were lacking. Discipline was maintained by high fines that might accumulate to such proportions that they could never be paid. Maintenance of such conditions caused unrest. Strikes appeared sporadically in the 1870's. The first workmen's organization appeared in Odessa in 1875, to be followed by another in 1878 in St. Petersburg, calling for the overthrow of autocracy, for political freedom, and for socialism. Its leaders were seized by the police in 1881. These efforts were noisy but unsuccessful, and workmen began to wonder why. They turned to the experience of Western movements that seemed to be more successful.

It was into this fertile field that Marxist ideas entered in the 1880's. Plekhanov had formed a group on reaching the outside world after his flight from the tsarist police. It set as its task the propagation of Marxism in Russia. It translated the work of Marx and Engels and brought out tracts on thin paper, to be smuggled across the frontier. Its principal message was that socialism could not be achieved through the peasantry, but that a workmen's movement was required.

Emergence of Lenin. A violent strike occurred in 1885 at a textile mill in

---

[11] See A. V. Shestakov, ed., *A Short History of the U.S.S.R.* (English trans., Moscow, 1938), p. 133.

Orekhovo-Zuyevo. The government called out a regiment of infantry and Cossacks. Many strikers were killed or wounded in the rioting. This was the first bloodletting, and it gave strength to revolutionaries. Social Democratic circles appeared in St. Petersburg, Kazan, Kiev, Kharkhov, and Samara. Small groups, many of them from the intelligentsia, were formed to learn and develop rules for successful operation. In 1889 the Social Democrats in the West united to form a Second International. Its program called for improved conditions for workingmen, but it urged that this program be pressed through parliaments of the various nations. Russia had no parliaments, and so her Social Democrats had no outlet for their endeavors, even if they had accepted the plan proposed.

The course of history is sometimes influenced by strong-willed individuals. Among the Russian revolutionaries several such men were developing at this time. The one to become most famous was Lenin. Although not himself a workman, but a member of the middle-class intelligentsia, he had early become interested in the revolutionary movement and Marxism. The execution of his eldest brother for his part in the attempt to assassinate Alexander III in 1887 influenced Lenin deeply. The ostracism of his family after the execution accentuated his hatred of the society that he held responsible. He set about to study Marxism and the best techniques of organization. This activity earned him expulsion from Kazan University in 1887 when he assumed leadership of a student demonstration. Thereafter, he studied alone, but with such success that he passed the state bar examination in St. Petersburg in 1891. In 1893 he moved to the capital.

Lenin became one of the leaders in the wing of Social Democracy in Russia that opposed the program of parliamentary tactics proposed by the Second International. In 1893 he was part of a Marxist group that called for revolution and insisted that the Second International's program would betray the workmen's cause. He began the fight with the Social Democrats of the West that was to come to full flower in 1919 with the organization of the competing Third International.

Problems of Revolutionary Organization. The tsarist government recognized Lenin's danger and arrested him in 1895, exiling him to Siberia in 1897. He continued to study and write. Meanwhile, his colleagues continued their efforts to organize. Organizations called Leagues of Struggle for the Emancipation of the Working Class were created in key cities with a principal organization in St. Petersburg, which commenced a newspaper that was soon quashed. A meeting of representatives of the various Leagues of Struggle was called in the city of Minsk in 1898. The meeting issued a manifesto urging a fight against capitalism until the complete victory of socialism. It also proclaimed the organization of a national party—the Russian Social Democratic Labor party. The effort was abortive, as the members of the meeting were arrested soon after, but it proved to be a spark. The organization that had been announced came into existence in 1903 and honored the Minsk meeting by calling it the "First Congress of the RSDLP."

In the years following the "First Congress," a great industrial crisis spread throughout Europe. Russia suffered as well with bankruptcy of corporations and unemployment. Strikes were the response, leading up to a clash with the Cossacks in Rostov in 1902. A general strike followed in South Russia in 1903, but it was crushed by the use of troops. Peasants and students rose in sympathy during the same period. The tsarist police tried to direct the movement they could not stop by a practice of introducing agents into the revolutionary circles.

Lenin had returned in 1900 at the beginning of the crisis. He concerned himself immediately with organization, but found considerable differences of opinion about it. Liberal members of the intelligentsia were being attracted at the time to a party called Socialist Revolutionary (SR), which had been formed from the remains of the narodnik groups and concentrated its work largely on the peasants. Some of Lenin's friends, such as Plekhanov, thought that these liberals could be helpful in furthering the revolution and urged that they be encouraged to join the new Social Democratic party. Lenin, taking a position to which he adhered up to this death, answered that liberals were generally halfhearted, cowardly, and ready to compromise with tsarism. Lenin argued with another branch of the Social Democratic movement—"economism." This branch thought it unnecessary for the new party to become a single, highly centralized organization of trained revolutionaries. The "economists" preferred an organization of mass character that would progress with the workmen as they developed a political and social consciousness. In 1902 Lenin wrote a pamphlet entitled *What Is to Be Done,* calling for a vigorous, closely knit party of professional revolutionaries to lead the proletariat, as its vanguard.

Lenin's Doctrine. In the midst of these disagreements on plans and programs, a meeting of the RSDLP was called at Brussels on July 30, 1903. Because of police surveillance the congress moved shortly to London, where it established itself as the Second Congress of the party. Opposition was expressed to Lenin's idea about the necessity for revolution and a dictatorship of the proletariat. Leo Bronstein, known in the party and later to the world as Leon Trotsky, argued that such dictatorship could be accomplished only when the working class had become the majority of the population and had joined the party almost in its entirety. Lenin's view prevailed. But he lost out on the rules to be adopted for membership. He was sure that the party should be a militant, disciplined, centralized organization, which should maintain a clear line of demarcation between members and mere sympathizers. His victorious opponents, including Trotsky, asked for and obtained a vote that anyone could be a member if he recognized the program and promised to render aid. In conflicts developing later in the congress, some of the moderates, who had helped to carry the vote over Lenin's group on the question of membership, walked out. In consequence, in voting for members of the Central Committee of the party and the editorial board of the party newspaper, Lenin's group found itself in the majority. Hence the name "Bolsheviks," while the opposition, at this point in the minority, earned the name "Mensheviks."

Conditions within Russia continued to deteriorate. In February 1904 the Japanese began their undeclared war against Russia. The war went badly for the Tsar's forces. With the mounting defeats disillusion spread, accompanied by new strikes and disorders. In January 1905 a strike developed in St. Petersburg. A priest, Father Gapon, one of the agents used by the government to guide the workers into nonrevolutionary channels, urged the men to present a petition to the Tsar. He led a crowd with the petition—couched in almost medievally submissive terms—to the Winter Palace, but the reception was an order to the troops to fire. "Bloody Sunday" strengthened the hands of the revolutionaries immeasurably, because it seemed to indicate to the average workman that there was no redress, even from the Tsar.

Lenin made use of the incident to call a Third Congress of the party in London. The Mensheviks refused to participate, leaving the Bolsheviks with the opportunity of rescinding the decisions on membership taken in 1903. The rule was adopted that the party should be limited to a disciplined small group of schooled revolutionaries. Sympathizers who would not work as professionals were to be barred. The Bolsheviks also adopted a plan for armed uprising in connection with the political strikes and decided that leadership of the planned revolution should be in the hands of a provisional revolutionary group. The party was thus enabled to take an active part in guiding the barricade fighting that arose with the public demands of 1905 for a national duma and a broad franchise.

4. Soviets—New Instrument of Government

Lesson of the Revolution of 1905. The barricade fighting later known as the Revolution of 1905 proved to be a useful lesson for those who sought the downfall of tsarism. Lenin drew the conclusion from its failure that "the offensive against the enemy must be most energetic; attack and not defense must be the slogan of the masses." [12] But attack required more than leadership of a political party pledged to revolution. It required an organization for the masses, a kind of agency that could bring together those who wanted change, no matter what their party. The events of 1905 gave birth to such a kind of agency in the *soviet,* the Russian word for council.

Marxists in Russia had studied with care the creation of the Paris Com-

---

[12] V. I. Lenin, "The Lessons of the Moscow Uprising," *Selected Works* (English trans., Moscow and New York, 1935), III, 353.

mune of 1871 and the commune itself as a model. Evidence of Lenin's thoughts on the subject is to be found in his statement of 1917 that "the Soviets of workers' and peasants' deputies reproduced that type of state which had been worked out by the Paris Commune." The Paris Commune had been elected on the basis of general suffrage, but as a result of the boycott by some groups of the bourgeoisie and the absence of many well-to-do voters from the city, the membership was primarily representative of the workmen and the lower middle class. Leadership had been among the workmen, in spite of their minority position, owing to the fact that Paris was in the hands of the national guard, composed mainly of proletarians.

When the fighting in St. Petersburg required direction in October 1905, unofficial elections were called among the workmen in all mills and factories by the Socialist parties. The representatives who gathered for the first meeting of the soviet were only forty at the start, but as more groups were represented, the membership reached five hundred. Absence of the middle-class groups, in contrast with the Paris Commune, was explained by the fact that the soviet was not intended as a general government of a whole area, but was solely to provide leadership for the workmen in their struggle. The majority of the St. Petersburg Soviet was in the hands of the Mensheviks; Trotsky was deputy chairman. It is to this fact that the Bolsheviks now lay the blame for the failure of 1905. The Bolsheviks, however, did not quarrel with the form of the soviets, for they had only praise for the soviets that appeared in other cities, notably Moscow, which they controlled. In some of the cities of Siberia, the soviets became the only government for a time, setting up an administrative apparatus for the railways, lands, gold fields, and post and telegraph offices. The revolution was crushed, but the new type of workers' government had proved its suitability to the satisfaction of revolutionary leaders.

Failure of Political Representation. The revolutionary movement subsided as the Tsar's grudgingly conceded program of popular assistance in government was tried. A State Duma was created. The franchise was limited. A second chamber, the State Council, was erected from the agency established by Alexander I a hundred years earlier and placed over the Duma with the same legislative rights. Half its members were appointed by the Tsar and the other half elected from institutions such as the stock exchanges, universities, and zemstva.

In theory no law could be made without the consent of the Duma, but restrictions appeared. The Duma was declared to have no power to amend the fundamental laws; loans and currency were put under the exclusive jurisdiction of the Ministry of Finance; the Army and Navy were retained as prerogatives of the Crown; and parts of the budget were not open to public criticism. The Council of Ministers was permitted to report legislation directly to the Tsar for signature during the recess of the Duma. His sanction was required for any bill before it became law, and he had the right to dissolve the legislative bodies, provided only that they be convened every year.

In spite of the restrictions upon the power of the Duma, the government found it to be a thorn in its side. The First Duma was dissolved in July 1906, and the Second in June 1907. The electoral law was changed to favor property owners; elections were made indirect, except in five of the largest cities of the Empire. Under the changed electoral law, issued without the required sanction of the legislative chambers, the Third and Fourth Dumas were elected in 1907 and 1912, respectively. They proved to be relatively submissive, although there was criticism in considerable measure, for the Dumas presented a welcome platform for the few delegates from the Socialist and Liberal parties who were able to win election.

End of Tsardom. The military disintegration in 1917 provided a new opportunity for the revolutionaries. With the rise of disorder, rioting, and strikes in February in a country weary of the war and on the brink of defeat, the soviets emerged again. Lenin was still in exile in Switzerland, and Stalin in exile in Siberia. Trotsky was also abroad. The bureau of the Central Committee of the Bolshevik party in Petrograd, headed by Molotov, issued a manifesto calling for the continuation of the armed struggle against tsardom and the formation of a provisional revolutionary government. Mobs began to riot on the same day, and the next morning they were joined by the Volkynian regiment of the imperial guard. Prisons were forced. The Duma appointed a provisional committee, representative of nearly all parties, but the Social Democrats were unwilling to join. The freed political prisoners converged on the Duma building and called into the lobby the Socialist members of the Duma. They then formed a Provisional Executive Committee of the Soviet of Workers' Deputies and sent a call to the factories and barracks for election of deputies from the workmen and soldiers for an evening meeting. At the evening meeting, March 12, the soviet was proclaimed and proceeded to elect officers. One of these was Alexander Kerensky, as vice chairman.

In the same evening, Grand Duke Cyril and officers of the Preobrazhensky regiment asked the Provisional Committee of the Duma to assume power. The president of the Duma had already telegraphed the Tsar urging the appointment of a prime minister who had the confidence of the country, but there had been no answer; so the Provisional Committee set about naming the ministers. Two sources of power had appeared, and an effort was made to bridge the gap between the two. Kerensky, who was both a member of the Duma and vice chairman of the newly created soviet was offered the post of Minister of Justice. He assented, in the face of a blanket prohibition by the soviet against accepting office from the Duma, but he obtained what he interpreted as the sanction of the soviet the next day. The chairman of the soviet, Chkheidze, a Socialist, refused the post of Minister of Labor.

The Tsar abdicated on March 15 in favor of his brother, Grand Duke Michael, and at the same time nodded assent to the naming of Prince Lvov as head of the Provisional Government.

Power of the Soviet. The new soviet was formed on the model that had evolved during 1905. The rate of representation was one deputy for every 1,000 workers in the large factories, with at least one deputy from each factory. On the basis of this system, the large factories, in which 87 per cent of the Petrograd proletariat was employed, received 124 seats, and the small factories, employing only 13 per cent of the workmen, obtained 122 seats. It is to this fact that the Bolsheviks lay their minority position. Their influence was claimed as greatest in the large factories. As time went on, the soldier deputies swelled the numbers, with one deputy for each company, until the total reached about 2,500.

The new soviet was in its way a government from its inception, because it possessed power. When the chairman of the Provisional Committee of the Duma had been summoned to Pskov to see the Tsar March 14, the railwaymen's union had refused to supply a train without a permit from the soviet. When this permit was denied, the chairman talked with the Tsar by telegraph, but only after he had obtained an escort from the soviet to the telegraph office.

The soviet began publication of an official newspaper known as the *Izvestiya* of the Petrograd Soviet. In its first number it carried an appeal stating that the soviet considered its principal aim to be the organization of the forces of the people for the complete consolidation of political freedom and popular government in Russia. The paper reported that the soviet had appointed district commissars to establish popular government in the districts of Petrograd. The paper also invited the population of the capital to rally round the soviet, to organize local committees in the districts, and to take over the administration of all local affairs. It called for the complete abolition of the old government and for the convocation of a constituent assembly elected on the basis of a universal, equal, and direct suffrage by secret ballot.

Dual Government. As a result of its assumption of some of the functions of government, the new soviet created a situation in Russia in which dual government existed. The soviet was not widely active at first, although it attempted to limit the Provisional Government's control of the Army. It created a liaison commission to keep the soviet informed of the intentions and actions of the Provisional Government and to bring influence to bear on this government to satisfy the demands of the revolutionary people. It demanded the arrest of the Tsar, who had abdicated but remained free. It informed the Provisional Government that it considered the new oath for the Army and all public servants unsuitable.

On March 27 the soviet published an appeal addressed to all nations of the world, announcing that the Tsar had been dethroned; that Russia was now a democratic country; and that it was time for the peoples themselves to settle the question of peace. Nevertheless, the soviet agreed with the government that the Army should continue the war, though it persuaded the government to issue a peace appeal in the same terms as its own. This relationship of limited cooperation continued until Lenin's return from abroad April 16, 1917.

Growth of the Soviets. In view of its size, the Petrograd Soviet could not function effectively. It therefore created a Central Executive Committee. Even this was too large for general discussion, so that matters of primary importance were decided by an even smaller group—the Presidium of the Central Executive Committee. In this way there came into being a structure of government that has continued to the present day.

The Petrograd Soviet was composed of delegates from two main political parties—the Socialist Revolutionary and the Social Democratic, the latter having two branches, Bolsheviks and Mensheviks. By virtue of the structure of the soviet, a small group of leaders could run it. Owing to the fact that the Socialist Revolutionary party and the Menshevik wing of the Social Democratic party constituted the majority, leadership remained in the hands of the moderates until Lenin's return. At that time he caused the Bolsheviks to break formally with the Mensheviks and to form a separate party. In this independent form, the Bolsheviks were able, by their discipline and their skillful leadership, to gain control of the soviet. Lenin then called for a new slogan, "All power to the soviets," which inaugurated the split with the Provisional Government.

Every town in Russia formed soviets on the Petrograd pattern. They appeared also in the Army and in many villages. The time was ripe for national organization. The Petrograd Soviet called an All-Russian Congress of Soviets to convene June 16, 1917. The tally of the delegates revealed the division of power: Social Revolutionaries, 385; Mensheviks, 248; and Bolsheviks, 105. The Bolsheviks demanded of the new congress that it seize power, but they were unable to sway the national body as they had swayed the Petrograd Soviet. The demand was not accepted, and the Bolsheviks had to bide their time until the next congress. The meeting was not without general importance, however, for it had given birth to an assembly suitable for national government. This new agency needed only strength to seize power.

Seizure of Power. Competition with the soviets was weakening. The Tsar's brother had refused to ascend the throne unless a constituent assembly requested him to do so. The Provisional Government and the soviet had both declared themselves in favor of a constituent assembly, but it took time to organize elections. The Provisional Government called upon the zemstva to prepare the voting lists. This move retarded elections at least until the autumn of 1917, as the zemstva had to be reorganized. The Provisional Government's last act of power was to stage a July offensive against Austria. The offensive failed completely, and Prince Lvov resigned as Prime

Minister, to be replaced by Kerensky. The latter tried to strengthen his position by bringing loyal troops into the capital, but the effort proved disastrous. His commander-in-chief, General Kornilov, turned upon him and marched on the capital to seize power. Historians are not agreed as to whether this was an act of personal ambition, disgust with Kerensky's policies, or sheer misunderstanding.[13] Kerensky had nowhere to turn for support against Kornilov except to the soviet. The soviet came to his aid. The Petrograd garrison under its control stood firm, and the railwaymen misrouted Kornilov's troop trains. The Provisional Government had been saved, but it no longer had any power except that derived from the soviet.

A Second Congress of Soviets was called by the Petrograd Soviet to meet November 2, 1917, later postponed to November 7. Representing workmen, soldiers, and peasants, it met in a capital in turmoil. The Provisional Government, sensing disaster, had made a last desperate effort to prevent a *coup* by ordering the bridges raised between the islands of Petrograd. The effort was thwarted by troops loyal to the soviet. The military revolutionary committee of the Petrograd Soviet announced that the Provisional Government had been overthrown and that power was in the committee. But the Winter Palace with the ministers of the government held out until late evening. Kerensky fled to the armies still fighting Germany at the front. It was during the opening session of the Second Congress that word came of the fall of the Winter Palace. A manifesto was drafted, and the congress adjourned until the next morning when it went about the task of forming a new government.

Power had passed to the soviets, which were a new kind of representative body. They had grown up in a period of strife to represent one part of the population against the classes that held power. They were not representative of all the people, nor intended to be so. The national body was indirectly elected, for delegates came forward from the local soviets and not from the people itself. It may be small wonder that when the new governmental structure was finally adopted, it was a structure of the same character as the agency that had guided the revolution. The soviet system became for the first time the government of a nation.

5. Marxism—Its Opportunity

Control of Production. "We shall now proceed to construct the socialist order." These were Lenin's words as he appeared on the rostrum of the Second Congress of Soviets at the moment of victory. The dream of Marxists had come true. For the first time, men espousing the doctrines of Marx were securely in possession of political power. Viewpoints differed on details, but there was unity on four planks of a platform: (1) smash the old

---

[13] See Vernadsky, *op. cit.* above, note 3, p. 244, for the belief that it was a misunderstanding, and Pares, *op. cit.* above, note 5, p. 475, for the belief that it was disgust with Kerensky's failure to dissolve the soviet.

ruling machine, the state; (2) create a new state, a state of the proletariat; (3) establish new production relations designed to lead to socialism; and (4) educate citizens to discard bourgeois ideology and accept the ideology of socialism as a step toward communism.

The key to the enduring success of the program lay in point three, according to the thinking of the leaders of the Revolution. New production relations could be established only by depriving the bourgeoisie of the ownership of the means of production—land, industry, mines, and forests—and of the means of communication and trade—railroads, telegraph, stores, and banks. Such a program was believed to be the method of removing from the bourgeoisie the only source of power with which it might be able to regain control of the state.

Looking toward a Blueprint. Lenin had begun to prepare a guidebook for the revolution while awaiting his opportunity to lead it. During July 1917, while he was hiding in a hut in Finland, he drafted the first part of the guide, which he entitled *State and Revolution.* He never finished the analysis of the events of 1905 and of the revolution of March 1917 culminating in the abdication of the Tsar. The approach of his party's opportunity to gain power brought him back to active leadership before the text was finished. As a result, the Revolution was fought with a handbook not yet completed. There was no precise blueprint for the long-range future. Marxism provided ideological guidance, but it was indefinite in detail.

The leadership of the Revolution was not in agreement on detail. In the soviets, composed of three major parties, only the Bolsheviks were thoroughly determined to proceed quickly, no matter what the cost, short of losing power. The Second Congress of Soviets by its first decree set up an executive branch of government called the Council of People's Commissars "to govern the country until the meeting of the Constituent Assembly as a Provisional Workers' and Peasants' Government." Lenin was made chairman. Policy was still to be guided in the main by another body created by the congress on the same day—the Central Executive Committee. This was to be the steering committee of the congress, to meet more frequently than the congress itself. By these decrees, the old state apparatus was replaced by a new one, springing from the soviet system of working-class representation. The initial step had been taken to implement the Marxist program.

Economic matters were next on the agenda.[14] Land was the principal subject of concern. The Revolution had been fought under the slogan "peace, land, bread." The decree on land issued by the Congress of Soviets on November 8 attacked ownership. But the decree was a compromise between the desire of the Bolsheviks to eliminate all private ownership of land and the attitude of the left of the Socialist Revolutionary party representing the old *narodnik* view of dividing the land among the peasants. In consequence,

---

[14] For details on the program relating to property, see John N. Hazard, "Soviet Property Law," *Cornell Law Quarterly,* 30 (1945), 466 ff.

the decree annulled without compensation the right of ownership only of large landed property, placing it at the disposal of regional agricultural committees and district soviets until the constituent assembly should act. Land of the peasants and such Cossacks as had been simple soldiers was not made subject to confiscation. Not until February 1918, when the Bolsheviks gained the ascendancy, did it prove possible to enact a decree entirely satisfactory to them. Under the second decree on land, all property right in the land, subsoil, forests, and livestock was abolished, and the land transferred without compensation to the use of the toiling population.

Economic Transformation. Other economic matters were left by the Congress of Soviets for its Central Executive Committee and the Council of People's Commissars to deal with. Banking was declared a state monopoly and all private banks merged with the State Bank in December 1917. The interests of small depositors were guaranteed in their entirety. Trading in the stock of private corporations and the payment of dividends by these corporations was forbidden soon after. In January 1918 the principle was extended. Bonds issued by former governments of Russia were annulled, as were government guarantees of private obligations. Exceptions were created for holders of government bonds below a certain limit and for holders of short-term obligations and bank notes.

City land and buildings became the subject of decrees in August 1918. Ownership of large houses in cities above middle size was abolished. The small owner was left untouched. A similar distinction between large and small owners had occurred in the decree on merchant ships of January 1918. Merchant fleet corporations were nationalized, together with their fleets, but small owners of fishing boats and small cooperatives that used their fleets solely to provide a living for the members of the cooperative were exempted.

Nationalization of private industry progressed more slowly. It took time for workmen to learn the complex details of industrial management. Immediately after the Revolution, a decree created workers' committees to exercise control over those managers who had retained their positions. Certain very large industries were nationalized by name, but no general law was enacted until June 1918, when all large enterprises were nationalized without compensation to the owners. Smaller enterprises were not touched for two years. In November 1920 all industries having more than five workmen with mechanical tools or ten workmen without mechanical tools were nationalized. The principle of nationalized enterprise was relaxed in 1922 for some years to aid reconstruction after the civil war, but it was fully restored in even more restricted form with the introduction of the Five Year Plans in the late 1920's. It has remained a cornerstone of Soviet economic policy ever since.

Steps toward Retention of Power. The Bolsheviks established their power firmly on the basis of state ownership of the means of production, but it had to be solidified in the political sphere as well. The old regime's minor officials were numerous and skillful. The newcomers to power had no such numbers of skilled administrators and specialists. It took time to train new officials; meanwhile, the old ones had to be utilized. Supervisors whose loyalty to the new scheme of things was unquestioned were placed in strategic positions. Little by little, the positions under them were filled by new people, or in some cases by former minor officials who accepted the new program. In this way the outlook of the old regime was eliminated from the governmental machinery.

By the summer of 1918 an electoral law had been enacted that completed the measures designed to assure retention of power. The franchise was extended to "all persons who earn their livelihood by engaging in production, socially useful labor, and all persons who are engaged in household work, which enables the aforementioned persons to perform their production work." It included also soldiers and persons of working-class origin kept from work because of disability. It specifically excluded persons hiring labor for profit or living on income not derived from their own labor, private traders and middlemen, monks and priests, policemen of the former regime and members of the royal family, the insane, and criminals deprived of rights by law or court sentence.

The electoral law put not only the Russian people but the world at large on notice that representative government in Russia was to be of quite a new type. Marxist political thought had gained a laboratory in which it could work out its future.[15]

---

[15] For a discussion of the character of Marxian political thought and the extent to which it has influenced Soviet policy, see Barrington Moore, Jr., *Soviet Politics—The Dilemma of Power* (Cambridge, 1950) and R. N. Carew Hunt, *The Theory and Practice of Communism* (New York, 1951). For American influences, see Max Laserson, *The American Impact on Russia, Diplomatic and Ideological, 1784-1917* (New York, 1950). On the revolutionary development, see Bertram D. Wolfe, *Three Who Made a Revolution* (New York, 1948), and E. H. Carr, *History of Soviet Russia*, I: *The Bolshevik Revolution, 1917-1923* (New York, 1951).

CHAPTER 21

THE ONE-PARTY SYSTEM

1. Party Monopoly

Three political parties shared victory in the seizure of power that by the Russian calendar is known as the October Revolution, but only one has survived. The Socialist Revolutionaries and the Mensheviks have given way to the Bolsheviks. The passing of two of the three parties is not mourned in Soviet political writings. The reason is partly one of political theory. Stalin stated it to Mr. Roy Howard in an interview in 1936. He said:

We have no contending parties any more than we have a capitalist class contending against a working class which is exploited by capitalists. Our society consists exclusively of free toilers of town and country—workers, peasants, intellectuals. Each of these strata may have its special interests and express them by means of the numerous public organizations that exist. But since there are no classes, since the dividing lines between classes have been obliterated, since only a slight but not a fundamental difference between various strata in socialist society has remained, there can be no soil for the creation of contending parties. Where there are not several classes there cannot be several parties, for a party is part of a class.[1]

Stalin's thought is so foreign to American thinking and experience that it has been hard for us to accept the idea. In the United States, the political arena has generally been shared by two large parties, in which voters of all classes may be found, regardless of how "class" is defined. In Europe, however, the class basis of party life has long been more conspicuous. For instance, although Prime Minister Attlee of the British Labor party wears an "old school tie" and springs from the propertied classes, the determining fact is that the core of his party is usually seen in the workman, whereas the core of the Conservative party is usually seen in the larger-scale property owner. If one accepts the Marxist thesis, expressed by Stalin to Mr. Howard, that political parties reflect a class structure, then the conclusion follows that if a society were to eliminate all but one class, there would be need for only one political party to represent it.

Party and Opinion. Americans have been troubled by the Marxist ex-

---

[1] For a slightly different English translation, see B. J. Stern and S. Smith, *Understanding the Russians* (New York, 1947), p. 11.

planation that is outlined in Stalin's words. An American labor delegation that interviewed Stalin in 1927 asked, "In what manner can the opinions of the working class and of the peasantry, as distinct from the Communist party, find legal expression?" [2] Stalin met the question by saying that there was, of course, conflict of opinion among the workers and the toiling masses of the peasantry, and that this was to be expected because all people do not think alike. But then he went on to say that the nature of the conflict of opinion differed from what it had been before the Revolution. Before the Revolution, conflict arose over questions about the desirability of overthrowing tsarism and breaking up the capitalist system. After the Revolution, conflict of opinion revolved no longer about the overthrow of the government, but around questions about the improvement of government agencies and of their work.

Even if there had still been conflict over the desirability of socialism or over the Soviet system of government, Stalin's explanation makes clear the extent to which variation in opinion will be countenanced and may find expression within a one-party system. Conflicts of opinion have occurred in Soviet history, but they have not taken the form of efforts to create a separate political party to compete with the Communist party. They have occurred within the single political party, especially during the formative period of the 1920's. Some of these conflicts arose over what the monopoly position of the Communist party actually meant.

Status of the Party. Nothing in the law established the Communist party as the only legal political party until the enactment of the constitution of 1936. Its monopoly status was preserved on the basis of the theoretical position that one class requires only one party to represent its interests, and also on the basis of political custom. The Socialist Revolutionaries and the Mensheviks withdrew from the government within a few months after the Revolution under strong Bolshevik pressure. No other groups have since tried to organize themselves as political parties.

The constitution of 1936 introduced the right of citizens to unite in public organizations. Only one political party is mentioned, the Communist party; it is declared available to the "most active and politically conscious citizens in the ranks of the working class and other sections of the working people." The omission of an explicit statement of a right to form other political parties has been taken to establish the legal monopoly of the Communist party.

Scope of Party Membership. Only a small percentage of the population of the USSR has joined or been permitted to join the Communist party. Membership at the time of the October Revolution is said to have been 200,-000. It has grown slowly since then. By 1930 there were only 711,000 members and 1,261,000 candidates. By 1940 the total number of members and candidates had risen, but only to 3,400,000. By the end of the war, at the

---

[2] See Joseph Stalin, *Leninism* (English trans., Moscow, 1934), I, 373.

time of the first postwar elections in 1946, the total number of members and candidates was announced as being 6,000,000.[3]   Later growth has been small.

Legal monopoly has not meant that only members of the Communist party may hold political office or positions in public administration.   The contrary has been true.   Many persons who are not party members but rank only as sympathizers hold positions of importance.   In the highest governmental body, the Supreme Soviet of the USSR, the percentage of deputies who were members of the Communist party was 83.4 per cent after the elections of 1950. The percentage has been rising slowly in this body in each election since 1937. Owing to the small size of the Communist party, there are simply not enough party members to fill all positions in the government, even if that were desired.   Thus, in the urban soviets, as a result of the elections of 1937, the percentage of party members among the deputies was 42.   In the village soviets, the percentage of party members was less than 20.   It is now higher.

Some idea of the small percentage of party members in public administration may be gained from an analysis of the housing administration in the city of Moscow.   In 1942 only 12.9 per cent were members of the Communist party.   In 1943 the figure had risen, but only to 14.7 per cent.[4]   A different situation has existed in the Army.   In 1936, just prior to the great increases in size required by the war, the over-all percentage of party members and members of the Communist Youth League in the Army was 40.   The officers corps included a much higher percentage of party members, varying in the infantry from 96 per cent of the corps commanders to 63 per cent of the platoon commanders.   In contrast with most superior court judges, only 47 per cent of lower court judges were party members in 1949.

Resolution of the Class Struggle.   Those who participate in government without being members of the party are called "nonparty Bolsheviks" to indicate their adherence to the principles for which the Communist party stands, even though they lack party membership.   These men and women are by no means considered socially inferior, although they cannot expect to rise to the very top of the political and administrative structure of government.   Positions as ministers of the government and presiding officials of the soviets seem to be reserved by custom, although not by law, for members of the Communist party.

Mr. Roy Howard asked Stalin how the one-party system in the USSR differed from the one-party system in Nazi Germany or Fascist Italy.   Stalin replied:

Under National 'Socialism' there is also only one party.   But nothing will come of this fascist one-party system.   The point is that in Germany, capitalism and

---

[3] For further details, see John N. Hazard, "The Soviet Government Organizes for Reconstruction," *Journal of Politics*, 8 (1946), 261 ff.

[4] See D. L. Broner, *Ocherki Ekonomiki Zhilishchnogo Khozyaistva Moskvy* (Moscow, 1946), p. 53.

classes have remained, the class struggle has remained and will force itself to the surface in spite of everything, even in the struggle between parties which present antagonistic classes, just as it did in Spain, for example. In Italy there is only one party, the Fascist Party. But nothing will come of it for the same reasons.[5]

Stalin's thought seemed to be that the Soviet one-party system is different because it is built on the essential base for a one-party system—namely, a society in which there is only a single economic class. Soviet leaders believe that one-party systems maintained under conditions of capitalism must fail because they rest on economies where conflicting economic classes still exist.

2. The Party's Program and Methods

Verbal Symbols. The key to the program of the Communist party is to be found in its name. When the party was organized in Russia at the turn of the twentieth century, it took the name of the Russian Social Democratic Labor party. This move was in keeping with the acceptance by Marx and Engels of the term "social democrat" to indicate political parties that favored their views. The split of opinion in the party in 1903 produced two wings, "Bolshevik" and "Menshevik." The wings grew to be separate parties in fact, although official separation did not occur until after the abdication of the Tsar and the return of Lenin to Russia in 1917. Even then the label RSDLP remained, with indication of the Bolshevik or Menshevik wing in parenthesis following the title.

At the time of the formal separation of the Bolshevik wing and its assumption of the position of an independent political party in April 1917, Lenin proposed that the name be changed, dropping the term "social democrat."[6] He argued that it was scientifically incorrect because the party looked beyond socialism to communism; and that it was also incorrect because it included the term "democrat," which indicated a type of state. Communism was to witness the "withering away" of the state; therefore no term that referred to a type of state appeared appropriate. Use of the old term seemed to Lenin to endanger the further progress of the Revolution because it would prevent the revolutionary people from using their initiative to build something new.

Lenin's plan for a change of name was not accepted until the Seventh Congress of the party in March 1918. At that time, all agreed that the change was appropriate, provided that the name "Bolshevik" be retained in a parenthesis after the title "Communist party." This retention would indicate to all that there was continuity of policy and would identify the party by means of a word that had acquired broad meaning in the Revolution.

Preamble of Intentions. In addition to adopting a name for the party that would indicate its objective of communism, the Seventh Congress created a commission to revise the program to bring it into accord with the aims of the party that had achieved power. Preparation of the program required

---

[5] See *op. cit.* above, note 1.
[6] See V. I. Lenin, *Selected Works* (English trans., Moscow, 1935), VI, 72.

one year. The draft was presented to the Eighth Congress of the party in March 1919. It was an extensive revision of the program that had been in effect since 1905. Sharp debate arose among party members over the draft. Lenin said that it was more than a program for Russia.[7] "Our program will provide powerful material for propaganda and agitation; it is a document which will lead the workers to say: 'Here are our comrades, our brothers, here our common cause is being accomplished.'" The program of 1919 has remained in effect to the present day, although the progress of events in the USSR has made some of its paragraphs obsolete.[8] This fact has been recognized by the party. A commission was created at the Eighteenth Party Congress in 1939 to redraft the program. The war intervened, and the new draft has not yet been brought forward.

The propagandistic nature of the party program inspired a general introduction, stating broad aims of the party, such as attainment of the highest type of democracy; expropriation of presses, premises, and paper from the bourgeoisie so that the proletariat might exercise its freedom of expression; liberation of women from the burdens of antiquated methods of housekeeping; abolition of the negative features of parliamentary government, especially the separation of legislative and executive powers; continuation of unity between workmen and soldiers, but establishment of certain privileges for the industrial proletariat as the more concentrated, united, and educated section of the toiling masses hardened in battle, though these privileges over the peasantry were to be temporary. During this privileged period, the industrial workmen were to use their position to unite the backward and scattered masses of village proletarians as well as the middle-class peasantry. Finally, the party was to fight bureaucracy in the state machinery by having all members of each soviet serve in rotation in the various departments.

Basic Principles. Subsequent paragraphs of the party program dealt with specific questions. The fullest equality of all nationalities was proclaimed, and a federative form of government proposed. Efforts toward separation of nations from other oppressing nations were to be supported, but only if the class requesting separation was the more progressive. The Red Army was to be filled exclusively with proletarians, to indicate its undisguised class character. Military training and education of the Army was to be conducted on the basis of class solidarity and socialist education. Court organization and procedure were to be simplified, and judges elected by the working masses. The schools were to be transformed into instruments for a communist regeneration of society, and education was to be made free for all children of both sexes up to the age of seventeen.

Religion was treated in a paragraph declaring the aim of the party to be the final destruction of ties between the exploiting classes and the organizations of religious propaganda. At the same time, the party was to help the toiling

---

[7] *Ibid.*, VIII, 46.

[8] For the text, see William E. Rappard and Others, *Source Book on European Governments* (New York, 1937), v-7 ff., and James H. Meisel and Edward S. Kozera, *Materials for the Study of the Soviet System* (Ann Arbor, 1950), 100 ff.

masses to liberate their minds from religious superstition. Party members were admonished to avoid offending the religious susceptibilities of believers, since such offense would only lead to the strengthening of religious fanaticism.

Economic principles were covered in a section that opened with a paragraph calling for expropriation of the bourgeoisie and transfer of all means of production into the property of the Soviet Republic. Socialized industry was to rest on the trade unions, which were urged to free themselves from their narrow guild outlook and to transform themselves into large productive combinations. The party demanded of all toilers assumption of responsibility. The trade unions were to play the principal part in establishing a new socialist discipline. Agriculture was to be organized on a socialist basis with emphasis on communes, but also with all possible encouragement to agricultural cooperatives. Distribution was to be on a national scale, with elimination of private trade. Banking was to be monopolized by the state and transformed into a mechanism for general economic accounting. The ultimate aim was abolition of the bank in the financial sense and its utilization as a central bookkeeping department of the communist society. The party was to work toward the abolition of money and a shift from personal taxation to direct use of part of the income derived from the various state monopolies as state revenue. There was to be the maximum increase and improvement in housing, social security, and public health.

Rules of the Party. The party program of 1919 foretold much of what was to happen in subsequent years, even in the face of unanticipated chaos caused by a civil war and the Second World War. The most marked departures from the program have occurred in the field of money, banking, and finance. It has not been found possible to proceed swiftly to the abolition of money and personal taxation. Banks still have many banking functions as well as being accounting agencies. It may well be that party leaders today would not set such goals in a new program.

The program is accompanied by the rules of the party. As a pamphlet stated in 1945, "For the Bolshevist Party the Rules and the Program are as one—the inviolable basis of Party life and structure, the guide to action. . . . The Rules are the Constitution of the Party." The program sets forth the short-term and long-term objectives. The rules provide the outline of the organization that is designed to achieve the objectives. Unlike the program, the rules have been amended quite often. Although the program could, in effect, be amended by individual decisions taking the form of party directives, the whole tradition of constitutions is that a significant change in the body politic for which they are written requires a formal change in the constitution itself. On the other hand, changes in the rules since the Revolution have occurred in 1919, 1922, 1925, 1934, and 1939.[9]

---

[9] For an English translation of the Rules of 1939, see Meisel and Kozera, *op. cit.* above, note 8, 310 ff.

Throughout the years of the postrevolutionary existence of the Communist party, the essential core of the rules has remained the same in spite of changes in the text. The main changes have come not in the structure of the party, but in the requirements governing admission to membership and the conduct of members within the party.

Destruction of National Partitions. Marxist "internationalism" is reflected in party structure. The conduct of Social Democratic parties in the First World War, when each voted to support its own government, was the spark that ignited a fire in Lenin's mind. This thought was later to develop into the Third or Communist International, but it came to the fore in the structure of the party in Russia as well. Since 1903 Lenin had opposed nationalist blocs within the Russian party. He denied to the Jews and the Polish workmen the request that the party be constructed on the principle of federation of national groups, each one to be largely autonomous in its internal discipline and operations while conforming to a general plan set by the federal agency. Stalin wrote a pamphlet at this time in which he said: "We want to unite the proletariat in one party. . . . We want to destroy national partitions."

Lenin's view prevailed. The party has grown into a strongly centralized organism, whose basis is not nationality but unity of class. This principle has sometimes been misunderstood, particularly because the government was organized along national lines and was federal in form. The Party Congress of 1919 made the position clear. It was pointed out that while the Ukraine, Latvia, Lithuania, and Byelorussia existed as individual republics, the rule must be different within the party. The congress called for a single centralized Communist party with a single central committee, to which the party organizations in the Ukraine, Latvia, Lithuania, and Byelorussia should be completely subordinate, in exactly the same manner as provincial party organizations within the Russian republic itself.

In furtherance of this principle the party rules have established all-Union agencies, which direct the party as a whole. These consist of the Party Congress, the Party Conference, and the Central Committee. The congress is to be convened in regular sessions not less often than every three years. Actually, longer periods have intervened. The Eighteenth Congress was held in 1939, and none has been convened since. Delegates to the congress are sent forward by the party organizations in each of the provinces of the Russian Soviet Federated Socialist Republic and in each of the other republics. In this way the status of party organizations within the smaller republics is clearly indicated as being the same as that of party organizations in the provinces of the RSFSR. Special congresses may also be called on the demand of not less than one third of the total membership represented at the preceding Party Congress.

Main Organs of the Party. Powers of the Party Congress are those of an agency of supreme authority: election of a Central Committee and a Central Auditing Committee; revision and amendment of the program and rules of the party; determination of tactical lines and the principal questions of current policy; and approval of reports of central organizations. Congresses last for about ten days and occur seldom. The fact that the party has functioned without a congress since 1939 without any apparent difficulty indicates that the congress is not a nerve center.

The Party Conference is defined in the rules as meeting in intervals between congresses, and not less often than once a year, on call of the Central Committee. There was a meeting in 1941, but no meetings have been convened during recent years. The conference is a group composed of the chairmen of provincial and republic party committees and their principal assistants, providing a link between the central authorities and the men in the field without necessitating the attendance of full delegations in Moscow. Its principal duty is to keep the membership of the Central Committee full, by replacing men who have dropped out or whom it wishes to remove. It selects replacements from a panel of alternates named by the preceding Party Congress, but it may not so replace more than one fifth of the members of the Central Committee. In this way extensive change in leadership at any one time is prevented. The conference may also make decisions on party policy, but its power is definitely restricted, for such decisions require ratification by the Central Committee before they are binding on party organizations. The party operated successfully throughout and after World War II without the annual party conference, which attests the limited significance of the latter, like that of the congress.

The third all-Union party agency is the Central Committee. Here one finds the source of policy determination and the center of party organization. By the rules, the Central Committee is required to meet not less than once every four months. During intervals between congresses, it guides the entire work of the party. It also appoints editorial staffs for the central party press and confirms such staffs appointed by local party agencies to publish the local party press. The Central Committee's principal importance lies probably in the fact that it is the link between the party and the government. Under the rules, "The Central Committee directs the work of the central soviet and public organizations through the Party groups in them."

Specialized Party Agencies. The work of the Central Committee is segregated in accordance with the various functions of the committee. These functions are the concern of four bureaus and five administrations. The bureaus concern themselves with the determination of general policy—the Political Bureau; the planning of organization to provide for execution of general policy—the Organizational Bureau; the execution of the plan of organization—the Secretariat; and the checking upon fulfillment—the Commission of Party Control.[10] The five administrations deal with personnel,

---

[10] No official listing of members of the principal agencies of the Communist Party has been made public for some time. The composition is believed to be as follows: Political Bureau—Stalin, Molotov, Kaganovich, Mikoyan, Khrushchev, Andreyev, Voroshilov, Beria, and Malenkov.

propaganda and agitation, organization and instruction, agriculture, and schools.

Because the determination of policy catches the attention of the world, the Political Bureau is often called by outsiders the most important agency in the party and the key to power. Those familiar with the importance of administration may take issue with this contention, for execution of policy often proves the key to success or failure. The relationship between different factors is apparently appreciated by the highest party leaders, for Stalin sits on both the Political and Organizational Bureaus and is the principal party secretary as well.

The fourth all-Union party agency is the Central Auditing Commission. Although its functions have not attracted general attention, it would appear from the rules to perform two: those of an auditor, auditing accounts throughout the party, and also that of reviewing the proper and expeditious handling of all party affairs.

Regional and Local Agencies. Central agencies always catch the eye. This often results in the ignoring of the work of the local agencies. Within the Communist party, the agencies below the all-Union level perform vital functions. They provide the bricks and mortar with which the party structure is built and held together. Within each province of the RSFSR and each of the other fifteen non-Russian republics, the top party position is held by the provincial conference or, in the non-Russian republics, the republic congress. No republic congress exists in the RSFSR. Each provincial conference or republic congress elects a central committee, with which it maintains the same relationship to be found between the All-Union Party Congress and its Central Committee. The duty of the provincial or republic agencies is the organization and guidance of all party institutions within their territories.

Below each provincial or republic level, there are two steps. The higher one is the district (or city) conference. The lower is the primary party organization, often known in early party writings as the party cell. These do the footwork of the party. The district (or city) conference, which meets every year, selects a plenum, to meet every one and a half months, and also a committee with an executive bureau which is in constant session. Each district (or city) executive bureau provides the rallying point for the secretaries of all primary party organizations within its district. It is from this desk that policy directives are distributed each morning. It is here that decisions are made that allow no time for reference to higher authority. It is

---

with Shvernik, Bulganin, Kosygin, and Suslov as candidates; Organizational Bureau—Stalin, Malenkov, Andreyev, Kaganovich, Khrushchev, Shvernik, Bulganin, Suslov, Mikhailov, Shatalin, Kuznetsov, Cherbakov, Ponomarenko, Patolichev, Andrianov, and perhaps Aleksandrov, with Merkulov, Chernousov, Poskrebyshev, Pospelov, Yudin, and Vasilevski possibly as members or as candidates; Secretaries of the Party—Stalin, Khrushchev, Malenkov, Suslov, and Ponomarenko. See Boris Meissner, "Stalinistische Autokratie und Bolschewistische Staatspartei," *Europa-Archiv,* 6, no. 4/5 (March 1, 1951), 3757-9; George K. Schueller, *The Politburo* (Stanford, 1951).

this desk that directs the local party press and makes certain that party policy is adequately presented in local nonparty organizations, such as the trade unions, the cooperatives, and the collective farms. It is this desk that keeps the register of all party members in the district.

Primary party organizations are relatively small. They are created not in geographical districts, such as those from which deputies to the soviets are elected, but in places of work, such as mills, factories, state farms, collective farms, machine tractor stations, universities or schools, Army and Navy units, and administrative departments of government. If there are less than three party members in such a place of work, the one or two members combine with members of the Communist Youth League to form an organization. If there are more than a hundred party members in the place of work, the primary party organization may be divided into sections so as to provide simplified administration and the close association desired of party members. If there should be more than five hundred party members at a place of work, two or more individual primary party organizations may be formed in the same place of work, but only with the consent of the All-Union Central Committee of the party.

Volunteer Effort. Work in party agencies is usually performed as a personal contribution and in spare time outside the hours of regular employment, whether as factory workman, teacher, soldier, or collective farmer. Only a few full-time paid executives are permitted, and such permission is granted only if the organization has over a hundred members. Funds to pay executives and meet other party expenses are provided by dues. In addition to a small initiation fee, each member pays 20 kopecks of his monthly wages up to 100 rubles, and 3 per cent of wages above 100 rubles monthly.

Selection of deputies to each level in the structure is by the indirect method. The primary party organizations send delegates to the district (or city) conferences. These conferences then send delegates to the next higher body, and the process is continued until the top is reached. Since 1939 the selection of delegates has been by secret ballot. Before that time it was by show of hands.

3. Party Democracy and Discipline

Stimulation of Discussion. The Communist party takes great pride in the dual principle of democracy and discipline that it has developed under the name of "democratic centralism." The evolution of the principle has been stormy. Some party members felt that the all-Union party agencies should not interfere in the work of local organizations, but should leave the local organizations much autonomy, subject to reports of general progress. Lenin took a strong stand against this position in 1903, arguing that matters of general interest might be dragged into a local situation. He felt it necessary to permit the Central Committee to intervene in local affairs, perhaps even against local interests, if it proved necessary in furtherance of general party objectives.

The rule of centralized authority has become clearly established within the party. But party leaders state that centralism, in the sense of a single fully empowered guiding center in the party, must not destroy the autonomy of subordinate organizations. Leaders recognize the desirability and even need of preserving personal initiative and independent thinking on the local level, if the party membership is to remain imaginative and not lose its power through requirements to the effect that every idea come from the center. To remind itself of the proper balance between central determination and local initiative, the party has devised its principle of "democratic centralism." A definition appears in the rules. The principle includes electoral choice for all leading agencies of the party; periodical accountability of the party agencies to their respective congresses or conferences; strict party discipline; subordination of the minority to the majority; and the absolutely binding character of the decisions of the higher bodies upon the lower bodies.

Party democracy is defined by the rules as involving the free and businesslike discussion of questions in individual organizations or in the party as a whole. Thus, under the rules, the member may say what he thinks wise, but subject to restrictions as to the manner in which he says it. The rules provide that extensive discussion, especially on an all-Union scale, of party policy must be so organized that it cannot lead to attempts by an insignificant minority to impose its will upon the vast majority of the party, or to attempts to form factional groupings. The Communist party plainly excludes the right to form minority blocs. Practice has shown that the individual must rely solely upon his own persuasiveness in the meeting itself in which his idea is presented. He is not permitted to make deals before the meeting through which the support of others is gained for his point of view.

Factionalism and Discipline. A split of opinion on the right to form factions was the cause of one of the historic arguments in which Trotsky and Bukharin participated. Trotsky wrote later in his *Revolution Betrayed:* "The present doctrine that Bolshevism does not tolerate factions is a myth of the epoch of decline. In reality the history of Bolshevism is a history of the struggle of factions. And, indeed, how could a genuinely revolutionary organization, setting itself the task of overthrowing the world and uniting under its banner the most audacious iconoclasts, fighters and insurgents live and develop without intellectual conflicts, without groupings and temporary factional formations?"[11] Present-day Soviet leaders do not quarrel with the idea of constructive debate, but they do oppose the formation of factional groups. There can hence be no doubt about the meaning of party democracy.

Discipline within the Communist party has impressed all students of the

---

[11] Leon Trotsky, *The Revolution Betrayed* (New York, 1937), p. 94.

Soviet system. The requirement of discipline springs from the historic conflict of opinion in 1903 over membership requirements. Lenin's principle, excluding mere sympathizers from party membership, has remained the rule. Only those who are willing to accept the program, work in a party organization, submit to party decisions, and pay dues may be considered for membership. The preamble to the rules, as amended in 1939, defines party work in precise terms: "The Party demands from its members active and self-sacrificing work to carry out the program and rules of the Party, to fulfill all decisions of the Party and its bodies, to insure unity within the Party and the consolidation of fraternal international relations among the toilers of the nationalities of the U.S.S.R., as well as among the proletarians of the whole world."

Enforcement of Discipline. Discipline is indicated in provisions for its enforcement, although this is not the sole index. There may be, and probably is, a mental discipline of great force, resulting from a thorough belief in the objectives and techniques of the party. This belief is a very real factor in the Communist party, for no one is encouraged to join or remain in the party against his will. It is hard, of course, to determine how many party members accept discipline out of understanding and how many because they fear social and political ostracism or worse in the event of expulsion.

Penalties relate to entire party organizations or to individual members. A primary party organization may be censured or even dissolved if it fails to carry out a decision of a superior organization, or commits any other offense regarded as criminal by the party. An individual may be subjected to censure in the form of an admonition or a reprimand, or by public announcement. He may be temporarily removed from party work or recalled from his position in a government agency. He may be expelled from membership, with the resulting stigma. If his actions include a violation of the criminal code of the Soviet state, the party reports this fact to the responsible administrative and judicial organs for appropriate trial. Even without such violation, he faces the concentration camp if he is viewed as "dangerous."

Members of the Central Committee of the party, or alternates, are especially protected against lightly considered disciplinary action. Penalties cannot be exacted unless approved in a meeting of the plenum of the Central Committee by a two-thirds majority. Expulsion from party membership is always a grave matter—somewhat like excommunication to a churchman, like cutting out the central core of interest around which life revolves. Practical considerations enter, too, for an expelled party member will find closed in the future any positions of responsibility and importance. Life becomes drab and even difficult to sustain in more than a subsistence manner.

Control over Party Membership. To provide for constant checks on loyalty as well as execution of decisions, the rules call for continuous cleansing of party ranks. The party arranges for periodic review of the record of each member. Matters may be brought out from the distant past, and excellent work is required to redeem one who has deviated sharply from the party program at some early date. The thought of this periodic cleansing is sufficient to keep the average member alert to his responsibilities.

Membership is not gained easily. Rules have always required that applicants be supported by recommendations of party members, who are held responsible for the good quality of their recommendations. Before the amendment of 1939, the rules clarified the extent of responsibility by saying: "Those giving unsound recommendations are liable to Party penalties, including expulsion from the Party." Since the amendment in 1939, no such clear threat of penalties appears, but the tradition of responsibility is such as to make it unlikely that a recommendation will be given lightly.

The number of required recommendations has varied from time to time. Before 1939 applicants were placed in categories, graded in accordance with anticipated loyalty to party principles. The preferred category was industrial workmen with a record of more than five years in production. The second preference went to a group composing industrial workmen of less than five years in production, agricultural workers on state farms, army men coming from industrial work or collective farms, and engineers and technicians working not in the front office but in the shops. The third category covered a group including collective farmers, members of artisans' cooperatives, and elementary school teachers. The fourth category covered all other employees, except former members of political parties other than the Bolshevik. These latter fell in a fifth category, for which requirements were more rigid. For each category, the number of necessary recommendations was progressively greater, or greater backing was needed from members with long experience in the party. The fifth category, comprising former members of other parties, required five recommendations, two of which to be from persons who had been Bolsheviks before the Revolution; the applicant was also required to have the endorsement of the Central Committee of the party. The amendment of 1939 made all categories equal, except the fifth. The change was explained as being in keeping with the development of the peasantry and other groups to the point where they could be accepted as being equally as loyal and determined as industrial workmen. For all but the fifth category, requirements were relaxed to endorsement by three party members of at least three years' standing.

Admission Standards. A candidacy of one year is required after admission, during which the candidate studies the party's history, its policy, and its techniques of operation and takes part in assigned tasks. Those who pass the strict tests are admitted to full membership by decision of a general meeting of the primary party organization, following ratification by the district (or city) committee.

Wartime procedures relating to admission were less strict than those existing before World War II. In the darkest days, when the Germans had pushed to the Volga, many young heroes were admitted because of their valorous record. As a result of the flood of admissions of this sort, and the death of many party members in the perilous tasks they were assigned to perform, membership characteristics changed. In 1946 it was reported that two-thirds of the members and candidates on the rolls had been admitted during the preceding five years. The wave of admissions had resulted in a lowering of the average age of members and of the level of education. Before the war only 8.9 per cent of the candidates and members had been under the age of twenty-five. After the war 18.3 per cent were under the age of twenty-five, and 63.6 per cent were under the age of thirty-five. This fact meant that two thirds of the members had been born since the Revolution or not long before. Of the 6,000,000 members and candidates in 1946, only 400,000 had a university education; 2,750,000 had an incomplete or complete high school education; and the balance of 2,900,000 had not reached high school. It is a matter of concern to party leaders that the new recruits to membership be educated in party principles promptly or be expelled, so that the party may regain the disciplined and skilled type of member characteristic of its ranks before the war. Attendance at party refresher schools has been required.

Party influence is exerted by party members in all nonparty agencies, whether they be those of government, or trade unions, cooperatives, collective farms, schools, and the like. Under the party rules, members who find themselves in such agencies are required to organize a caucus. Problems are considered as they are expected to arise or after they have arisen unexpectedly. Agreement is reached on the desired policy, sometimes with the help of a call upon high or intermediate party agencies. Thereafter, each member is bound by party discipline to support the view adopted in caucus and to work for its achievement. In this manner, as the disciplined minority of the people, the Communist party is in a position to exert influence far in excess of the numerical strength of its membership.

Intellectual Guidance. Party members at the various levels are aided in following the thinking of party leadership by the reports of the Administration of Propaganda and Agitation of the Central Committee of the party. This administration studies basic directives of the Political Bureau of the party, and prepares commentaries in detail upon aspects of social, cultural, and political life in which party members are expected to influence the attitudes of the communities within which they live and work. In such a way the central agencies of the party are able to inform members of party policy on all points of their daily activity. The members in turn are prepared to take a principal part in the formation of public opinion.

There have been occasions when the Administration of Propaganda and Agitation has failed to perform its function of policy guidance in the manner desired by the highest party leaders. An example is found in the events of the summer of 1947. At that time the chief of the Administration of Propaganda and Agitation was criticized and ultimately ousted for his failure to translate the party's basic principles into the details of his history of Western

European philosophic thought. The history was being used as a guide by editors, authors, critics, and teachers, so that it had more influence than one might expect of a philosophical treatise in many other countries. The criticism of the book came from one of the members of the Political Bureau, who explained in a speech the extent to which the book's approach could not be accepted. He indicated through this criticism the outlines of the approach that the Political Bureau wished for the readers of the Soviet press.[12]

The outlines of the criticism of this book on philosophy spread to other fields and resulted in criticism of novels and music. Authors and composers were directed to be critical of cultural eccentricities in all forms of art as symptomatic of decadent bourgeois society outside the USSR, and to cultivate forms that would inspire the people for whom the Revolution had been fought.

4. Support from Youth

Winning the Rising Generation. Party policy is supported not only by members of the Communist party. There has long been a system of youth organizations, which not only support party principles but provide the means of training large numbers of young men and women for political work. As the training has progressed, party membership has been recruited increasingly from these groups. They are three in number: Komsomols, Pioneers, and Little Octobrists.

Youths from the ages of fifteen to twenty-six may join the All-Union Leninist Communist League of Youth, known generally as the Komsomols. During the revolutionary months of 1917, many of the young men and women who took part in the Red Guard belonged to youth organizations formed spontaneously. In October 1918 the groups were brought together in a first Congress of Bolshevik Youth Organizations, with 22,000 members. With the end of the civil war, the impetus of military action was lost, and no peacetime objective sufficiently strong to attract youth had been developed. Communist party leadership then devised the plan of rallying youth around a program of sport, education, health, publishing, and—most important of all—special industrial projects.

The peacetime program proved effective in attracting adherents and in completing important industrial projects. By 1926 the number of members had grown to 1,612,000. By 1935 the total was 5,500,000. On the eve of the German attack on the USSR in 1941, it was 10,500,000, and by the opening of 1951 about 12,000,000. Projects such as the construction of a new industrial city in the Far East were given to the Komsomols to perform. The city was named Komsomolsk in their honor. The Moscow Subway was also made their special project, and many Komsomol members were employed in its construction, either full-time or on holidays and weekends.

---

[12] For the criticism, see A. A. Zhdanov, "Vystuplenie na diskussii po knige G. F. Aleksandrova 'Istoriya Zapadnoevropeiskoi Filosofii,'" *Bolshevik*, no. 16 (June 24, 1947).

Program of the Komsomols. As a result of the growth during the war, a large percentage of relatively inexperienced youths was admitted to the Komsomols. In the liberated Ukraine 70 per cent of the Komsomols at the end of the war were of less than two years' standing, which, to the general secretary of the Komsomol in 1946, appeared as a challenge to leadership. The Komsomols have always been stronger in cities among the children of industrial workmen than in the country, where few peasant youths joined in the early years.

The program of the Komsomols has been amended frequently to keep it abreast of the times. A comprehensive revision occurred in 1936 to conform to the changed conditions created in 1936 by the new constitution of the USSR. The revision made it the principal objective of the organization to assist the Communist party in the education of youth and children in the spirit of communism. More changes occurred in 1949. The Komsomols are called the "auxiliary and reserve" of the party. The program defines several sub-aims, such as organizing the study of Marxist ideas, explaining the harm of religious prejudices and superstitions, and exposing chauvinism and nationalism—terms mainly applied to the West or to "reaction."

Komsomols also perform work of a nonpolitical nature. Members are to spread culture among youth, especially by extending literacy; to strengthen discipline in the schools by fighting against bad behavior and also by organizing extracurricular activities; to encourage physical training; and to participate in socialist reconstruction, which includes strengthening the family. Finally, the Komsomols have the task of defending the Soviet fatherland, a task to which the whole membership devoted itself in World War II.

Structure of the Komsomols. Putting it generally, the Komsomols have the duty of making clean living good politics. In performing this task, the organization was particularly successful before the war. The young man or woman who hoped to rise on the political ladder knew that a reputation for drunkenness, loose living, uncleanliness, or slighting of school work would close the door to them. This fact has had a marked effect upon the morale of the country. Although the enormous disruptions of the war did much to throw Soviet society back several years, the plenum of the Komsomols in 1944 revitalized the work in the schools. *Pravda* editorialized: "Some Komsomol organizations still live in their yesterdays and work with inertia. This practice has fallen behind the growth of the demands of life . . . the Komsomol organization must aid the teacher and strengthen his authority." The teacher's hand was strengthened at the same time. No student may now be admitted to the Komsomols unless the opinion of his teacher or class director has been obtained.

The pattern of organization of the Komsomols is similar to that of the party. Cells are formed in factories, offices, schools, the Army and Navy, and collective farms. Each cell reports to a district (or city) committee of the Komsomols. The committees report, in turn, to provincial committees in the

RSFSR and to republic committees in the fifteen smaller republics. These are directed by the rules to send delegates every two years to an all-Union conference at Moscow, which elects a central committee to carry on the burden of work. Owing to the fact that the structure parallels that of the party, members of the Komsomols work in the same places as do party members and in close relationship with them. The work of the Komsomols is carried out under the direct leadership of the party. Guidance is required by the rule that the central committee of the Komsomols be directly responsible to the Central Committee of the party, and by the provision of the rules that "the work of local organizations of the Komsomols is directed and controlled by the corresponding regional, republic, city, and district party organization."

Membership in the Komsomols. Membership is easier to achieve than membership in the Communist party, but it is not granted quickly. Every application must be supported by recommendations of two members of one year's standing or of one party member. Those who recommend an undesirable candidate are "held responsible for it." No period of candidacy is compulsory. Boys and girls from the age of 14 may themselves apply for membership. Dues must be paid, and the member must be available at all times to perform any work assigned to him. After reaching the age of twenty-six, members may remain in the organization with an advisory voice, but if they are selected as delegates to the top agencies, they have full rights with the younger members.

Democracy and discipline are treated in the same way as in the party. There is freedom of discussion within the organization, but "only up to the time the decision on the subject is adopted by the organization." Discipline is bolstered by penalties, including expulsion. Members who wish to join the party are bound to find that their record in the Komsomols is of utmost importance in influencing the decision of party authorities. Those youths who want to join the party between the ages of eighteen and twenty must come forward from the membership of the Komsomols.

Tasks of the Pioneers. The Pioneers were organized in 1923 from youths of both sexes between the ages of ten and sixteen. Admission is easy, being open equally to any child, although the child must show possibilities of development during a two-month period of candidacy. Even when the party drew a distinction for its membership between industrial workmen and other categories of applicants, the Pioneers made none on the basis of social origin. Membership figures jumped from about 1,000,000 in 1925 to about 13,000,000 in 1949. Komsomol influence is felt by the Pioneers, for the latter are organized into brigades which are attached to Komsomol cells. One of the members of the Komsomol cell is the brigade leader for the Pioneers.

The role of the Pioneers was defined in 1932 as "the task of developing a socialist attitude toward study, labor and communal activities in the Pioneer ranks and among children." In substance, the Pioneers have the same general political and cultural task as the Komsomols, but it is performed by means of techniques designed to appeal to the younger element, which the Pioneers represent.

Tasks of the Little Octobrists. The Little Octobrists are organized from children between the ages of eight and eleven. Their relationship to the Pioneers and even to the Komsomols is close, for they are organized in "links" and "groups." Links contain five children, to whom a Pioneer is assigned as leader. Five links form a group, to which a Komsomol is assigned. Tasks of the Little Octobrists take no precise form, but the leaders try to instill in the children, by group games and the assignment of small duties, a sense of association and responsibility.

Each of the three main youth organizations overlaps the age at which members may enter the next. This system provides a means of adjusting promotion to the varying rates of maturity of young people. It avoids any gaps in the political and cultural life of the member as he progresses. Each organization has accepted in the past fewer members than the one below, indicating that not all move to the next-higher organization. Some youths have not wanted to assume the greater responsibilities and greater sacrifices required in the higher organization. Others have not been able to meet the more stringent selection for membership.

Much has been said of discipline, but greater emphasis is on good leadership. The best leader is believed to be the one who interests and convinces his charges, rather than the one who frightens them or trains automatons. Not all young people believe what they hear from their leaders, but most of them seem to do so. This fact the Communist party considers a key to its strength, which would never have existed if its support were to be based solely on compulsion.

5. Mass Support

Supporting Organizations. The vast majority of Soviet citizens do not belong to the Communist party or its youth organizations. Out of a total population of some 200 million people, probably no more than some 40 million belong to these organized political groups, and only 6 million of these are adults. Support for party policies must be found in other agencies besides the party and its youth organizations. Stalin has said that the dictatorship of the proletariat cannot be accomplished without the aid of the labor unions, the cooperatives, and the soviets. "The proletariat . . . needs these organizations because without them it would suffer inevitable defeat in its fight for the overthrow of the bourgeoisie, for the consolidation of its power and for the building of socialism . . . ." [13]

The soviets constitute the government itself. The trade unions and cooperatives are neither organizations of the party nor part of the government, but they support each. The importance of the trade unions is emphasized

---

[13] *Op. cit.* above, note 2, I, 275.

by the constitution, which lists them first as one of the organizations in which citizens have the right to unite. Their task has been defined as being a "school of communism," as forming a link between the advanced and backward elements of the working class, as uniting the masses with their vanguard. The influence of the trade unions may be measured further by the fact that on the eve of the last war, in 1938, the membership numbered over 22,000,000, out of a total number of workmen and employees of 27,800,000.[14] By 1949 there were 32,000,000 members out of a higher total.

Early Role of the Labor Unions. Agreement has been hard to reach among Soviet leaders as to what the character and role of the labor unions should be. After the Revolution, the factory committees that had supervised the election of delegates to the first soviets were combined with the labor unions. The policy of the Bolsheviks was to bring labor unions completely into the institutional structure of the new Soviet state. During the civil war, the unions became recruiting centers and aided the government in this way. With the advent of a reconstruction program calling for a limited return to controlled private enterprise, known as the New Economic Policy or NEP, there were private employers and state employers. Lenin felt that under conditions of limited capitalism the labor unions should represent the workmen in opposition to private employers. Trotsky wanted to organize the labor unions like an army and incorporate them formally in the state machinery as government agencies designed to ensure industrial discipline and common action. The decision was made in December 1921 to keep the labor unions independent, with the basic task of improving the material conditions of their members, not only by resisting exploitation by private employers, but also by rectifying faults that resulted from bureaucracy in the state machinery. Lenin knew that administrators of state-owned industry could be expected to require some check upon their administration.

Introduction of the first Five Year Plan, which became effective in 1928, brought the role of the labor union to the forefront of discussion. Private employment was then practically extinguished. Workmen could think no longer in terms of resisting a private employer. Their task was cooperation with the state administrator in a common endeavor. State planners set wages in accordance with the ability of the national economy to pay them. Higher wages could not result from pressure groups, but only from increased production and reduced production costs, outside the factor of wages.

Promoting Socialist Competition. Tomsky, who had been president of the All-Union Central Council of Trade Unions, argued in 1928 that the unions should remain free to press for further improvements in the material conditions of their members. He thought it incongruous for a union to direct its members toward increased production. Production seemed to him

---

[14] See F. Koshelev, *Pravo na Trud—Velikoe Zavoevanie Trudyashchikhsya SSSR* (Moscow, 1946), 27. For an evaluation, see Isaac Deutscher, *Soviet Trade Unions* (New York, 1950).

to be the task of management. He felt that unions should not be put in the position of representing both labor and management. Tomsky was opposed by the Communist party, and he was retired from union leadership. The All-Union Central Committee of Trade Unions required union members to concern themselves with the problem of increasing production. The Sixteenth Party Congress in 1930 decided that it was the duty of the unions to take the lead in promoting socialist competition to improve production.

Pressure for production is not the sole duty of unions. Lenin saw the need for checks upon overzealous or corrupt state managers. Unions came to aid in providing this check, not in the form of strikes, but by attention to detail in the administration of policy as set by the highest agencies of party and government. Individual problems raised by workmen are discussed with management by the shop committee of the union in each plant. If a dispute arises, representatives of the union sit with an equal number of representatives of management on a conciliation commission to hear the case. The union local does not try to change the law, which defines in detail every matter of basic concern between management and labor—such as hours, wages, safety provisions, social security, and health protection. If changes in law are required, they are debated and decided upon in the highest agencies of party and government, not imposed as a result of strikes.

In 1933 the unions were given the additional function of administering the social insurance program. In this way they became something of an administrative branch of the government itself. But the unions have not ceased to be significant instrumentalities through which the opinion of the labor public is brought to the attention of policy-makers in the party. Unions also serve as a main channel through which party policies may be explained and millions convinced of their desirability.

Structure of Labor Unions. Soviet labor unions are organized in places of employment, rather than by crafts cutting across industry lines. Members have a common bond, not in being carpenters or bricklayers, but in that they are all employed by, let us say, the steel industry, or in the administration of justice, whether they be jurists or charwomen in the courthouse. With time, the unions have spread over the whole USSR. The organization of each union resembles in structure the Communist party, with an all-Union congress of the trade union at the top and conferences in each province of the RSFSR and in each of the other republics. Every conference has an executive committee. Below these are the conferences in each district or city with their executive committees, and further below the units in each factory, composed of a factory (or local) committee, and usually several shop committees and a number of *profgrupps,* each led by an organizer.

To coordinate the work of all unions on a national scale is the main function of the All-Union Congress of Trade Unions, composed of delegates sent forward by each union in approximate proportion to its size. The congress, which has numbered some 2,000 delegates, meets every other year and elects an All-Union Central Committee of Trade Unions. It is this body that conducts the work of liaison between the agencies of government and party on the one hand and labor unions on the other. Important labor legislation—such as that of 1938, which lengthened the work day and restored the six-day week—has been introduced to the public by explanation from the chairman of the All-Union Central Committee of Trade Unions. The close relationship between the unions and the government and party has also been indicated. A trade union representative sits on the Economic Council of the Council of Ministers and on the Organizational Bureau of the Central Committee of the party.

Coordination is provided not only at the top, but at each level in the structure of the individual unions from the district up. This coordination is achieved through a district or city Trade Union Council to which each union sends delegates. The same procedure is followed in the formation of the provincial council in the RSFSR or a republic council in the other republics.

Membership and Finance. Membership is open to workers and students. Admission is granted in a meeting of the membership committee, at which two thirds of the members must be present. The applicant must also be approved by the shop committee, or the factory committee if the factory is too small for shop organization. Expulsion from membership is permitted only in extreme cases, when a member has proved himself lacking in discipline in important matters. Prior to 1937 the class approach also applied to the unions. Those up to then deprived of the franchise were denied membership in the union. The All-Union Central Committee of Trade Unions countermanded the earlier rule in July 1937. It declared that in view of the changes made in the constitution of 1936, opening the franchise to all, "the restriction on the admission to membership in the Trade Unions of persons working as workmen or clerks in enterprises or offices because of their social origin or their past activity is abolished, except for persons deprived of electoral rights by a court."

Dues for union members are fixed at 1 per cent of wages, including overtime, to be paid monthly. Receipt is given by a stamp pasted in the trade-union book of each member. By a change in rules in October 1940, election of delegates to higher union bodies was to be by secret ballot and by vote on each individual candidate, rather than by a list of candidates presented to fill the places available on the whole delegation. Voting for individual offices, such as president and vice president of factory and shop committees, president and secretary of district (or city) conferences, and provincial or republic conferences, remained subject to the old rule calling for a show of hands.

Recognition of Cooperatives. Cooperatives had been an important form of organization in old Russia from shortly after the emancipation of the serfs, just as they have been and still are in much of Europe in general. Because of their link with the private enterprise system, they were viewed with doubts immediately after the Revolution by some party members. Lenin put an end to such doubts in 1923. He wrote: "Our cooperatives are looked down upon with contempt, but those who do so fail to understand the exceptional significance of our cooperatives, first, from the aspect of principle (the means of production are owned by the state), and second, from the aspect of the transition to the new order by means that will be simplest, easiest, and most intelligible for the peasantry." [15]

The constitution of 1936 recognized the importance of the cooperatives, for it listed cooperatively owned property as one of the two forms of socialist property—the other being the property owned by the state itself. Soviet legislation has protected cooperatively owned property on the same basis as state property, which has meant higher penalties for those who steal or destroy cooperatively owned property than for those who violate private ownership.

Cooperatives have existed primarily among the peasantry. But they have played an important part in city life in the form of workers' consumer cooperatives until 1935, and in the construction and management of apartment houses until 1937. They have been and remain the principal form in which agriculture is conducted. In 1933, cooperatives, called collective farms, tilled 73.9 per cent of all tilled land. By 1937, 18,500,000 peasant families belonged to such collective farms, which represented 93 per cent of all peasant families in the USSR.

Since that time the percentage has increased. Production cooperatives in which village people united to make articles for local consumption, such as furniture, rugs, hand tools, harnesses, clothes, and the like, have also been important. In 1933 they accounted for 7.17 per cent of the total value of large-scale industry in the USSR for that year. Although their importance declined in the years leading up to the last war, they regained their position when state industry was diverted largely to the production of munitions. In 1946 the government re-emphasized their importance by placing the burden of local industry largely upon their shoulders.

Cooperative Organization and Management. The structure of cooperative societies is almost alike in each field of activity, although different laws apply. Consumer cooperatives may be taken as typical. Since 1923 membership has been voluntary. On the local level, workmen or peasants engaged in the same general activity, together with members of their families over the age of fourteen, are permitted to join, unless they were from the classes deprived of electoral rights. As in the labor unions, this restriction lost validity after the constitution of 1936 had been enacted. Members meet to decide questions of policy and elect the management of the cooperative for a one-year term. All members over sixteen may vote.

Capital of the cooperative is composed of the property transferred to it at

---

[15] *Op. cit.* above, note 6, IX, 402.

the time of its formation, which is sometimes the property of a former cooperative or of a village soviet. Capital also comes from initiation fees and the "shares" that the members contribute and that remain to their credit. Profits and other income in excess of what amounts to wages of members who work for the cooperative are also credited to capital to reduce prices. There is no distribution of profits. The amount that members contribute as their share of the capital of the cooperative is set by the general meeting in accordance with capacity to pay, within a fixed range. Any member may resign and be paid his share from the treasury. Each cooperative must adopt a charter conforming to the model established by law. The cooperative has the rights of a legal person, so that it may make contracts and sue and be sued in court.

Consumer cooperatives may join the unions of consumer cooperatives at the district level. The latter in turn send delegates to unions on the provincial level in the RSFSR and on the republic level in the smaller republics. These bodies send delegates to another at the top, called *tsentrosoyuz* of the USSR, which maintains liaison with agencies of the Communist party and the government, as the All-Union Congress of Trade Unions and its central committee provide liaison for the labor unions. Authority is maintained for the higher agencies by means of a provision that each level may give orders that are binding on its members and may enforce these orders by removing from office, elective or other, any official of the lower level.

Structure of Collective Farms. The agricultural cooperative associations, known as collective farms, admit any peasant sixteen years of age or older, in accordance with the provisions of the Model Charter for the Collective Farm, adopted in 1930 and amended in 1935.[16] The members meet periodically and every two years select an administration of from five to nine persons, depending on the size of the association. The administration selects a president. Under normal conditions, selection of a president is the concern of the members alone, for it is the declared policy of the government to favor the development of initiative and self-reliance among members. But if a cooperative association fails to function well, the government considers that the interests of the country are endangered by the loss to production and the unrest in the association. It places skilled executives of the Ministry of Agriculture in the post of president until healthy conditions are restored.

New members are admitted on nomination of the administration by the general meeting of members. The general meeting on a two-thirds vote may also expel recalcitrants. In such an event, the expelled person may appeal to the executive committee of the district soviet for reinstatement. Both

---

[16] Full details of collective farm law may be found in Vsesoyuznyi Institut Yuridicheskikh Nauk NKYU Soyuza SSR, *Kolkhoznoe Pravo* (Moscow, 1940). See also Gregory Bienstock and Others, *Management in Russian Industry and Agriculture* (New York, 1944). For a discussion of the details relating to the use of land, see John N. Hazard, "Soviet Property Law," *Cornell Law Quarterly*, 30 (1945), 466 ff.

the complainant and the president of the cooperative association must be present at the hearing.

Remuneration is provided members by distributing a share of the production of the cooperative association. The share varies in size according to the estimate by the general meeting of the importance to the association of the type of work performed and the number of days the member has worked. In consequence, there are wide variations in the share that the various members receive each year.

Benefits of Collective Farms. Produce of an agricultural cooperative association is sold to government agencies in accordance with annual contracts negotiated on the basis of a rate of delivery established by law. The contract amount of produce is paid for by the state agencies at a price that is lower than that of the open market. The difference between the contract price and that of the open market might be thought of as a tax levied on the association for the use of the state-owned land. Any produce raised in excess of the quantity obligated in the contract is available for sale in the open market. On market days in the nearest town or city, the cooperative association operates stalls and sells for its benefit.

Members of agricultural cooperative associations are permitted by the model charter to cultivate a garden plot that is assigned from the state-owned land for the use of each household. The household is also permitted to raise barnyard animals in limited quantities. The produce from such a garden and the animals are under the law the personal property of the individual household, as is the house in which the household lives. Such produce and animals may be disposed of to augment family income.

Integration of Collective Farms. The agricultural cooperative associations were once joined together in a hierarchy leading up to a *kolkhoztsentr* at the top in the republic. Since 1932, however, this system has been abolished, and each agricultural cooperative association now stands alone. Direct relations are maintained by it with the land department of the village soviet of its area. The village department is responsible to the land department of the district soviet. The latter accounts to the land department of the provincial soviet, which reports to the Ministry of Agriculture of the republic. As a result, state agencies control the activities of the agricultural associations. They may set aside any act of the associations that is contrary to government policy.

To meet the strain of reconstruction after World War II, a Council for Collective Farm Affairs was created September 19, 1946, as an agency of the Council of Ministers of the USSR. The new council is composed of the Minister of Agriculture of the USSR and leading figures from party and government. It has the task of devising policy for the agricultural cooperative associations. To aid its liaison with lower echelons, the council maintains its own representatives in republics and provinces. These representatives are free of any dependence upon local authorities. The council may enforce its policies by issuing orders binding upon all government agencies and the agricultural cooperative associations. The cooperative movement in agriculture thus has been integrated with the government. Similar integration has been occurring since World War II with respect to other types of cooperatives.

Combination of small agricultural cooperative associations into large units was begun in 1950. The announced purpose was to extend large-scale mechanized agriculture and at the same time take a step toward the ultimate urbanization of the countryside. To some Soviet students, bringing together the collective farmers in large communities and housing the peasant families in city-type apartments accords with Marx's admonition to draw the cities and the countryside close together. In so doing the peasants might be expected to lose much of their individualism and to accept with less opposition than has been evident in the past the collectivist social order planned by the Soviet leadership.

The practical result of the attempt at urbanization of the peasantry was to separate many farm families from their homesteads and from the small garden plots behind these homes. Some outside observers have seen in this change a move toward a pattern more like that of the state farm in which the peasants work as employees of a state enterprise, a "land factory," rather than as joint property-owners in a cooperative association. In 1951, however, Soviet periodicals reported serious peasant opposition. Soviet spokesmen declared that the farms would still be amalgamated for agricultural purposes, but peasants would not be moved from their cottages among the fields.

Such adjustments in policy in the face of actual friction shows that the government is by no means in absolute control of the allegiance of the people. Postwar interviews of Soviet citizens who have fled the USSR cast doubt on the complete effectiveness of the Communist party in obtaining mass support. Some former Soviet citizens have felt that dissension has reached such proportions that a large-scale military test would result in the break-up of the Soviet system. All such testimony presents problems of evaluation, of course, since the witnesses could be hoping to gain acceptance in lands that want no immigrants with any trace of communist leanings. Moreover, the particular individuals may not be representative of the mass they have left behind. Dissension must certainly exist, as evidenced by the numbers of persons held in concentration camps. Yet by closing channels of communication so that domestic propaganda has almost no competitors, and by organizing the mass agencies discussed above, the percentage of dissenters may be kept sufficiently low to be within the reach of police control. There is little to suggest that revolution has a chance of rising from among the masses.[17]

---

[17] See Merle Fainsod, "Controls and Tensions in the Soviet System," *American Political Science Review*, 44 (1950), 266 ff.; David Dallin, *The New Soviet Empire* (New Haven, 1951).

CHAPTER 22

GOVERNMENTAL STRUCTURE AND POLITICAL CONTROL

1. Constitutional History

Introduction of the Soviet Principle. Mass participation in the administration of the state was an objective enunciated by Lenin. Policy guidance was to be provided by the small Communist party, but execution of policy was the task of the people, organized as a government. The party was the pilot. The ship of state was to be manned by the millions of nonparty members. Although the principles of government were in mind, the permanent form that they were to find had not yet been decided upon. The revolutionary soviets, united in a congress, had seized power on November 7, 1917, but the government that the congress created was declared to be provisional. The Socialist parties that had guided the Revolution were committed to proceed with the elections for a constituent assembly to determine the character of Russia's permanent government. It was this assembly for which the masses had looked since the abdication of the Tsar.

Elections were held for the constituent assembly in November 1917 on the basis of the lists of candidates drawn up by the numerous splinter parties and the three principal parties of the Revolution. The voting produced a body in which the moderates were in the majority. Of the 703 deputies, only 168 were Bolsheviks. A draft decree had been prepared by the Bolsheviks for submission to the constituent assembly, making permanent the soviet form of government adopted provisionally November 7, 1917. The non-Bolshevik majority of the constituent assembly refused, however, to recognize the Council of People's Commissars as the legal government. Debate on this point ensued on the first day of the session, January 18, 1918. The Bolshevik delegates withdrew, and at 1:30 in the morning of January 20 the Central Executive Committee, installed by the preceding Congress of Soviets, decreed the dissolution of the constituent assembly.[1] A Third Congress of Soviets was called. On January 28 it issued the decree originally prepared by the Bolsheviks for the constituent assembly. The soviet system of government became the permanent form of government for Russia. The Congress of Soviets became the supreme power. The Central Executive Committee, elected by it to serve between sessions, continued as its deputy, and the Council of People's Commissars continued as the administrative body.

---

[1] See George Vernadsky, *A History of Russia* (New Haven, 1929), p. 257; Harry Dorosh, *Russia's Struggle for Democracy* (Bridgeport, 1939), pp. 85 ff.

The decree of the Third Congress of Soviets carried over into the state a form that had been a weapon of revolution, not a device intended to represent all the people after the revolution had been won. This fact was made clear in a Declaration of the Rights of the Toiling and Exploited Peoples, issued by the congress. It stated that "exploiters can have no place in any of the agencies of authority. Power must belong wholly and exclusively to the toiling masses and to their plenipotentiary representatives—to the Soviets of Workers', Soldiers' and Peasants' Deputies." [2]

Toward a Soviet Constitution. Russia was still fighting for its life with Germany at the time of this congress. The first peace negotiations had failed, and the Germans had renewed the advance. The spring of 1918 was disastrous. It was not a propitious time to draft a new constitution, even though the Central Executive Committee had been directed to do so by the Third Congress of Soviets. Not until April 1918 was a drafting commission appointed, and not until July was the commission prepared to present a draft to the Fifth Congress of Soviets, which was then sitting.

The new republic's first constitution presented no surprises. The drafting commission had heard many proposals, several of them considerable departures from the system of government adopted during the seizure of power. The chairman of the commission, Sverdlov, had expressed the opinion that the commission was free to consider all these and adopt whatever form of government seemed best. He said that the commission should act without regard to existing declarations or measures, except that it should take as a guide revolutionary experience and a socialist sense of justice, and should consider that it was formulating a document of an agitational and propagandistic nature to be considered in a world setting. Stalin, as a member of the drafting commission, reminded it that it had been instructed by the Third Congress of Soviets to do its work on the basis of the declarations of that congress. The commission finally adopted his suggestions and made its task the elaboration of the basic declarations.

Bases of Soviet Federalism. Rights of national minorities had long been the concern of Bolsheviks. Stalin had come to be the principal student and spokesman for the minority policy of the party even before the Revolution.[3] With the formation of the Council of People's Commissars in November 1917, he was named Commissar of Nationalities. His influence was considerable on the federal form of government that was developed from the start for the Russian Soviet Federated Socialist Republic. National minorities within the boundaries of the Republic were granted the right to use their own language in public administration, the schools, the courts, and the press. In his

---

[2] For sources in translation, see William E. Rappard and Others, *Source Book on European Governments* (New York, 1937) and James H. Meisel and Edward S. Kozera, *Materials for the Study of the Soviet System* (Ann Arbor, 1950).

[3] See Joseph Stalin, *Marxism and the National Question,* published originally in 1913; English translation included in Joseph Stalin, *Marxism and the National and Colonial Question* (Moscow and New York, 1935).

writing before the Revolution, Stalin had emphasized this right as essential to the solution of the minority question. The principle has remained a guiding one to the present day.

The Russian Empire had included more territory than that which became the RSFSR. The formerly Russian areas of Finland, Poland, the Baltic provinces, the Ukraine, Byelorussia, and Central Asia were outside the boundaries of the RSFSR. Considerable parts of these areas, except for Central Asia, were occupied by the Germans. Finland, Poland, and the Baltic provinces obtained independence with the end of hostilities and parted with the revolutionary path taken by the Russians. Bolshevik hopes that at least the Baltic states would retain the soviet system of government that had appeared for a while in parts of them were dashed. The outcome was different, however, in the other areas. The Ukraine and Byelorussia adopted the soviet form of government and enacted constitutions in 1919. The areas south of the Caucasus Mountains were delayed in formulating their plans by civil war and foreign occupation. In 1921 Azerbaidjan adopted its constitution as a soviet socialist republic. In 1922 Armenia and Georgia followed suit with similar constitutions.

The Central Asiatic areas presented a variation. They had been largely nomadic and feudal. Industries had never developed as in other parts of the Russian Empire. This meant that there were almost no industrial workmen. Communist leaders concluded that there was no possibility of establishing a socialist economy under such conditions. Although the Moslem Khans and Emirs could be ousted, the people were not prepared for more. Bokhara and Khorezm (formerly known as Khiva) became soviet republics and were recognized as independent in 1920. In 1922 they adopted new constitutions, constructing their governments on the soviet model but omitting any declaration of socialist principles.

Pressure for Union. One who had not studied the policies and techniques of the Communist party might find it remarkable that the republics that arose around the RSFSR should adopt essentially the same form of government. Although each chose its own constitution, worded in its own way and in its own language, the substance was without variation. Each republic was, however, under the leadership of men trained in Marxism, who were members of the Communist party. It would follow that the approach would be as identical with that developed in the RSFSR under conditions of revolution as the conditions of different national economic development permitted.

The experience of the independent republics was like that of the American colonies. They could not live separately. The need for union was felt both in the economic and in the military field. The common problems of administration required union, too. Stalin explained later[4] that union on a volun-

---

[4] Joseph Stalin, *Leninism* (English translation, Moscow, 1934), I, 382.

tary basis in one federal state had been possible precisely because the Bolsheviks had granted the right of self-determination of nations, eliminated suspicion among the various nationalities by conceding independence, and then let the economic, military, and administrative situation convince the masses of the need for union.

Moves toward union appeared early. In January 1919 the temporary government of the Ukraine raised the question of an economic exchange with the RSFSR. In May 1919 the Ukraine issued a decree directing that military operations be carried on against the common enemy in cooperation with all existing soviet republics. In January 1920 the Ukraine extended to its own territory the laws of the RSFSR relating to transport, mails, telegraph, military organization, production, labor, and social insurance. In the same year, Byelorussia voted to send delegates to the meetings of the Congress of Soviets of the RSFSR and to unite its commissariats with those of the largest republic. In April 1920, Azerbaidjan made the same request. These steps involved administrative mergers.

Foundations of the Soviet Union. A series of treaties was concluded by the RSFSR with the other republics in 1920 and 1921, merging all their commissariats of military and naval affairs, foreign trade, finance, labor, railways, posts and telegraph; other agencies formed a Supreme Council of National Economy, which conducted large-scale industry. Diplomatic representation was merged in 1922 in preparation for the Genoa Conference, which was to be the first meeting with the countries of Central and Western Europe since the Revolution. Only formal union remained to be accomplished.

The Communist parties of the various republics appointed committees to work out the form of union. A general plan was prepared and accepted by the Central Executive Committee of the party in October 1922. Each republic called its congress of soviets together to hear the plan explained and to select delegates to a meeting of all republics to consider and adopt the plan. Events south of the Caucasus moved rapidly to put matters in readiness for union. The three republics of Armenia, Azerbaidjan, and Georgia formed a federation called the Transcaucasian Soviet Federated Socialist Republic, and adopted a constitution on December 13, 1922. Each of the three participating republics retained its identity, with a constitution and a government of its own, but they had created over them a federal government. It was explained long after that this had been done to accustom the three peoples, long hostile to one another, to work together in matters of local concern.

As a result of the merger of the republics south of the Caucasus, delegates of the Transcaucasian Soviet Federated Socialist Republic, rather than delegates of the three individual republics, met in Moscow December 29, 1922, with delegates from the RSFSR, the Ukrainian republic, and the Byelorussian republic. The four republics adopted a "treaty of union" and a provisional draft of a declaration indicating the outlines of government. The next day the delegates met again as the First Congress of Soviets of the Union of Soviet Socialist Republics to review the declaration and treaty and to elect a Central Executive Committee of 371 members and 138 candidates. The congress declared Moscow to be the capital of the USSR. The union had become a reality. The new Central Executive Committee prepared a draft of the federal constitution and put it into effect on July 6, 1923. Final approval was given by the Second Congress of Soviets of the USSR on January 31, 1924.[5]

Union and Constitutional Revision. The union was open to others to join, and others accepted the invitation. Bokhara and Khorezm combined with other neighboring areas to enter in 1924, as the Uzbek and Turkmen republics. The Tadzhik republic entered in 1929, having developed in an area that had formerly been a part of the Uzbek republic. These seven republics remained the only union republics until 1936. There were lesser peoples, however, who had a measure of autonomy commensurate with their size and stage of development. Most of these were within the RSFSR. They spoke languages that were not of the Slav family, and several of the peoples were not racially Caucasian. Their governments were designated as autonomous soviet socialist republics, autonomous regions, and national districts. All were permitted to use their own languages in public administration, the courts, and the schools. The higher two of the three types had representatives in one of the subdivisions of the Central Executive Committee of the Union Congress of Soviets, but they were on a plane inferior to that of the union republics. Their powers were limited more extensively, and they had no constitutional right to secede.

The development of socialized industry and collectivized agriculture altered Soviet society. Changes in social and economic structure were thought to require a change in the constitution. When the party leaders met at the regular February meeting of the full Central Committee in 1935, the decision was made to amend the constitution. The Central Committee transmitted the proposal to the Congress of Soviets, as the supreme agency of government. The congress, which was sitting in Moscow at the same time, directed its Central Executive Committee to draft a new text, with provision for further democratization of the electoral system. Drafting proceeded in a commission under Stalin's chairmanship, and in May 1936 the Central Executive Committee received the result. The draft was accepted for publication and printed in the press June 12, 1936.[6] A special congress to discuss it was called on November 25, 1936. Action was speedy

---

[5] For an English translation of the text, see Rappard and Others, *op. cit.* above, note 2, v-88 ff. and Meisel and Kozera, *op. cit.* above, note 2, 152 ff.

[6] See *Izvestiya*, no. 136, June 12, 1936. An English translation was published in the *Moscow News* (weekly edition) of June 17, 1936, and in brochure form by the Cooperative Publishing Society of Foreign Workers in the U.S.S.R. (Moscow, 1936).

at the session, and the second constitution of the USSR emerged December 5, 1936.[7]

Adjustments in the Structure of the Union. Two of the minority peoples by 1936 had progressed sufficiently in their development to enter the Union as union republics; they emerged as the Kazakh and Kirghiz Soviet Socialist Republics. The Transcaucasian Soviet Federated Socialist Republic was dissolved, and its three constituent parts of Armenia, Azerbaidjan, and Georgia entered the Union on an equal basis with the older members. This brought the total union republics to eleven.

The principle of preserving a distinctive governmental form was continued for such minorities as were of lesser size, or of less advanced cultural development, or were living within a union republic. Autonomous soviet socialist republics, autonomous regions, and national districts were thus preserved. By 1946 these totaled nineteen, nine, and ten, respectively, most of them being within the borders of the RSFSR. Three autonomous republics were disestablished after the war on grounds of treasonable activity.

With the approach of World War II, the USSR expanded its territory by a series of diplomatic and military moves. Five more territories were brought into the union as union republics to raise the total to sixteen. These were the Karelo-Finnish, Estonian, Latvian, Lithuanian, and Moldavian Soviet Socialist Republics, all of which were absorbed in 1940.

2. Rejection of the Separation of Powers

Principle of Concentration. Soviet writers express an aversion to the separation of powers, especially in the form of checks and balances between the legislative, executive, and judicial branches of government as found in the constitution of the United States. The Soviet argument is that this principle was developed in accordance with the theory of Montesquieu as a means of limiting the absolute power of the King of France. Soviet political scientists contend that in a state where only one class survives, there can be no class conflict, and hence there is no need to limit one branch of government by another. All branches are thought to work in the same interest.[8]

Soviet dislike of the separation of powers does not mean that all business of government is carried on by one agency. Even though the Congress of Soviets in the RSFSR, and after 1922 the Congress of Soviets on the federal level, were the repositories of all power at their respective levels—legislative, executive, and judicial—both delegated functions of the executive and the judiciary to agencies named for the purpose. These agencies acted on behalf of the congress and were responsible to it. They could not, therefore,

---

[7] For an English translation of the text as adopted December 5, 1936, see Rappard and Others, *op. cit.* above, note 2, v-107 ff. For an English translation of the text as amended to 1950, see Meisel and Kozera, *op. cit.* above, note 2, 242 ff.

[8] See Andrei Y. Vyshinsky, *Sovetskoe gosudarstvennoe pravo* (Moscow, 1938), 296. The English translation published has the title *The Law of the Soviet State* (New York, 1949).

attempt to check the power of the congress at any point. The principle of organization around a single source of power continued under the constitution of 1936. At that time a Supreme Soviet replaced the Congress of Soviets on the federal and republic levels, but the change in name and structure left unaltered the principle of concentration of power in a single body.

Lack of Sharp Division of Functions. Clear demarcation of functions between the various agencies of government has not been characteristic of the Soviet system. When the Second Congress of Soviets of the Russian Republic in 1917 created a Central Executive Committee to represent it between sessions and a Council of People's Commissars to administer policy, the relationships between the two agencies were not precisely defined. The possibility of establishing a distinction was further hampered by two facts. Many of the same people sat in both bodies. The crisis of the time required quick and decisive action by the Council of People's Commissars without reference to the Central Executive Committee—an agency both large and unwieldy, not created for twenty-four-hour daily duty. It had no technical experts, moreover. Because of the overlapping of functions between the two organs, some of the members of the constitutional commission proposed in the summer of 1918 that the Central Executive Committee and the Council of People's Commissars be combined. But the proposal was not accepted.

The discussion over the powers of the Council of People's Commissars in 1918 pointed to some practical problems that arose again when an agency of similar name and function began operating in the federal government in December 1922. Matters came to such a pass that Stalin said before adoption of the constitution of 1936: "It is time we put an end to a situation in which not one but a number of bodies legislate. Such a situation runs counter to the principle that laws should be stable." [9] Since 1936 the rule has been established that the Supreme Soviet and its Presidium legislate, and the Council of People's Commissars—the Council of Ministers since 1946—is limited to action as the executive.

No single head of state has ever been provided for by Soviet constitutional law, either elected by the people or appointed by the Congress of Soviets—or after 1936 by the Supreme Soviet. Some of the functions of a titular head of state, such as the receiving of ambassadors, are performed by the chairman of the Presidium of the Supreme Soviet, or earlier by his predecessor in the Presidium of the Central Executive Committee, but these are only formal functions. There is no President of the USSR.

Structure of the Judiciary. Two court systems have emerged, federal and republic. The latter is the backbone of the judicial structure. In the union republics, the system is three-stepped, with people's courts at the local level, provincial courts at the intermediate level, and a supreme court at the top. The smaller union republics omit the provincial step, as do all the autono-

---

[9] Joseph Stalin, "Leninism," *Selected Writings* (New York, 1942), p. 402.

mous republics. The basic principle is established that there is a right of appeal to one higher court only. The court of original jurisdiction may be any of the three, depending on the gravity of the crime or the nature of a civil suit. A statute specifically defines the jurisdiction.[10] Even though there is an appeal as of right to only the next-higher court, the record of a case may be called for by still higher courts. This step is taken as a result of the periodic review by the presiding justice of the work of lower courts, or as a result of notice from the prosecutor that justice has not been done.

Federal Courts. Federal courts are headed by the Supreme Court of the USSR. They are concerned with special types of problems cutting across boundaries of the republic—namely, transport and national defense. The military courts have four grades: division, corps, army or flotilla, and military district, front or fleet. All grades have original jurisdiction, depending on the military rank of the accused to be tried. Jurisdiction is not limited to military personnel, but extends even in peacetime to all civilians who commit acts of treason, espionage, terror, arson, explosion, or like crimes. These courts have no civil jurisdiction. In wartime all civilians are subject to the jurisdiction of military courts in areas declared theaters of war. The level at which they are tried depends on the seriousness of the offense.

The transport courts in the federal system are of two types: railroad and water, with three steps defined in area by individual railroad systems or river basins. Jurisdiction extends to criminal acts directed toward the disorganization of labor discipline and other crimes upsetting the normal work of transportation, whether the accused be an employee of the transport system or an ordinary citizen. The same rules of appeal apply in the federal courts as in republic courts, except in wartime. When a military court sentences a criminal, there is no appeal in wartime; but no sentence of death may be carried out until seventy-two hours have elapsed after informing by telegraph the presiding justice of the military college of the Supreme Court of the USSR and the chief prosecutor of the Army or Navy. Both railroads and water transport were militarized in the past war, so that their courts became military courts. This development meant that all three judges on the bench at a trial were professional judges, instead of a single professional judge and two lay judges as in all civilian and military courts of original jurisdiction in peacetime. In all courts the rules of the Code of Criminal Procedure are binding upon the conduct of the trial.

Federal Supreme Court. The Supreme Court of the USSR may not declare legislation unconstitutional. The Supreme Soviet is its own judge of what legislation amounts to an amendment of the constitution and re-

[10] See Judiciary Act of 1938, *Vedomosti Verkhovnogo Soveta SSSR,* no. 11, September 5, 1938. In general, see Harold Berman, *Justice in Russia* (Cambridge, 1950). For an analysis of the judicial system and the office of the Prosecutor General, see John N. Hazard, "Soviet Agencies of Law," *Notre Dame Lawyer,* 21 (1945), 69 ff.; Hazard and Harold L. Weisberg, *Cases and Readings on Soviet Law* (New York, 1950).

quires a two-thirds vote rather than a simple majority. Before 1936 the constitution provided that the Supreme Court might recommend to the Central Executive Committee that a law or an order of a commissariat of the federal government, or of the Council of People's Commissars, or of any other central agency of the Union be voided as unconstitutional. No explicit statement of this power was placed in the constitution of 1936. The court may still, however, be asked for advice on questions of constitutionality. There is no published report of such a request.

The Supreme Court of the USSR is divided into colleges specializing in military, rail transport, water transport, criminal, and civil cases. The colleges hear appeals from the supreme courts of the republics when the latter have sat as courts of original jurisdiction, and from the highest military and transport courts. They also review cases below these levels, when called to their attention by the prosecutor or by their own presiding justice. Finally, the colleges have original jurisdiction over crimes of national importance, such as the treason trials of Bukharin, Radek, Pyatakov, and Yagoda before World War II, and over other cases selected by the presiding justice of the Supreme Court because of the national importance of the question involved. When sitting as appellate colleges, the bench is composed of three professional judges. When sitting as colleges of original jurisdiction (except in the case of the military college), the bench is composed in the usual way—that is, of one professional judge and two lay judges. A panel of twenty-five lay judges is appointed by the Supreme Soviet for the purpose of providing lay judges for such cases.

A board of review called a plenum, composed of the sixty-nine professional judges of all the colleges, in addition to the presiding justice and the vice presidents, convenes not less often than once every two months. The plenum hears protests brought by the Prosecutor General of the USSR or by the presiding justice, and often reverses its own colleges. It also issues guiding orders for court practice on the basis of matters that are reviewed.

Federal Prosecutor General. A separate agency of law created by the constitution is the Prosecutor General of the USSR. He is named by the Supreme Soviet of the USSR for the longest term constitutionally defined— namely, seven years. The Prosecutor General names in turn the prosecutors of each of the republics and approves the nominations made by these of prosecutors of the provinces, districts, and cities. The prosecutors are distinguished from the courts in the republics in that they do not owe their positions to the soviets at the various levels and are not responsible to any local agencies whatsoever. From top to bottom the prosecutors provide an independent centralized agency of the federal government. They are not even responsible to the Ministry of Justice or to the Supreme Court. The Prosecutor General reports directly to the Supreme Soviet. This position of independence is designed to lift the prosecution above local fear or favor.

The Prosecutor General of the USSR is directed by the constitution to

ensure strict observance of the law. He is concerned considerably with trans-
gressions of bureaucrats. He may protest to the Supreme Court cases in
which a defendant has received a sentence in a lower court which seems too
severe and consequently harmful to the prestige of the state in so far as prestige rests upon a reputation for justice. The Supreme Court's decisions indicate that this duty of intervention is apparently taken seriously, for a good
many cases that have been reversed—often on behalf of the defendant—have
come to the attention of the Supreme Court as the result of the protest of the
Prosecutor General.

3. Policy Determination in the Union

Federal Powers. Powers were distributed between the federal government
and the republics in the first federal constitution in a manner that was not
unfamiliar to students of government in the United States. In both the
USSR and the United States, only the federal government may coin money,
regulate citizenship in the Union, settle disputes among republics, maintain a postal service, and establish standards of weights and measures. The
first constitution of the USSR also corresponded to that of the United States
in placing in the federal government sole power to declare war, conclude
treaties, and conduct diplomatic relations.

The similarity between the powers of the federal government in the two
countries is not present in the economic powers granted to each. The USSR,
which bases its national economy upon state ownership of the means of
production, transport, distribution, and banking, places corresponding power
in the federal government. The first constitution empowered the federal
government to develop a general plan for the entire national economy; to
establish general principles for the development and use of the soil, mineral
deposits, forests, and waters; to direct transport and telegraphic services;
and to conduct foreign trade.

There were some notable omissions from the first federal constitution.
No bill of civil or civic rights was included. These matters were left to the
republics to control. Not until the second federal constitution were human
rights and the franchise defined in the federal document.

Role of the Supreme Soviet. Power is wielded in the federal government
by a Supreme Soviet. Until 1936, the Congress of Soviets and its Central
Executive Committee operated as the principal federal agencies under the
first constitution. The Supreme Soviet was patterned closely on the early
Central Executive Committee. It is bicameral, as the Central Executive Committee had been. One chamber, entitled Soviet of the Union, represents the population on a strictly proportional basis of one deputy for
every 300,000 inhabitants. The other chamber, entitled Soviet of Nationalities, represents the republics in a manner somewhat similar to representation in the United States Senate. Each of the 16 union republics is represented by 25 deputies, regardless of its size or the number of its citizens.

Each autonomous republic is represented by 11 deputies, each autonomous region by 5 deputies, and each national district by 1 deputy. In the elections of 1950 to the Supreme Soviet, there were elected 678 deputies to the Soviet of the Union and 638 to the Soviet of Nationalities. Terms of deputies are four years, although owing to the war no elections were held until 1946 after the elections of 1937.

Meetings of the Supreme Soviet are called twice a year and last usually for a week or less. During the war longer intervals occurred between sessions. As in any large legislative body, work is done in committees. Each chamber selects the members of three committees at the beginning of each session to be concerned with legislation, budget, and foreign affairs. Either chamber may initiate legislation, and agreement of both is required before a proposal becomes law. Both chambers meet simultaneously and often gather in joint session to hear a report. If disagreement occurs, the measure is referred to a committee of both chambers. If disagreement continues even in committee, the matter is referred back to both chambers. If disagreement persists, the Supreme Soviet is dissolved and a new election held.

Power of the Presidium. To decide policy questions and issue provisional legislation during the period between sessions of the Supreme Soviet, both chambers in joint session elect a Presidium, composed of a president, secretary, 16 vice presidents representing each of the union republics, and 15 other members. The Presidium is in a strategic position, for it interprets laws and even issues decrees; appoints and removes ministers; appoints and removes the higher commands of the armed forces; proclaims a state of war in the event of armed attack on the USSR during an interval between sessions of the Supreme Soviet; orders general or partial mobilization; ratifies international treaties; appoints and recalls Soviet diplomats; and proclaims martial law in particular localities or throughout the USSR. Experience has demonstrated that the Presidium is the principal agency of government in determining policy, for its actions concern every field of interest and take effect immediately, subject only to subsequent ratification by the Supreme Soviet, which may not meet for months.

Evidence of the power of the Presidium of the Supreme Soviet was particularly marked immediately after the Second World War. It became necessary to hold elections to the Supreme Soviet, which were three years overdue. The Presidium not only set the date; it proceeded to enact changes in the electoral law that amounted to amendments to the constitution. It raised the age of deputies to the Supreme Soviet from eighteen to twenty-three. It added new electoral districts to both chambers of the Supreme Soviet by decreeing that Soviet Army units abroad should be represented in each chamber by a deputy for every 100,000 voters. The decrees changing the franchise and the system of representation were presented to the Supreme Soviet when, elected under the new rules, it was subsequently convened. The decrees were then adopted formally as constitutional amendments.

Procedure of the Supreme Soviet. Analysis of the stenographic reports of sessions of the Supreme Soviet indicates what is done. If the record of the first postwar session (March 1946) is taken for examination, it will be found that the first matter of business was organization—election of a chairman for each chamber, approval of rules, adoption of an agenda, election of a credentials committee, examination of credentials of deputies. Then followed a session of each chamber to hear a report on the activities of the Presidium from its secretary. The report was identical in each chamber, and the decrees of the Presidium issued since the preceding session were affirmed.

Both chambers then met in joint session to hear a report of the chairman of the State Planning Commission on a proposed fourth Five Year Plan. At the conclusion of the report, it was announced that discussion would proceed in each chamber meeting separately, but the joint meeting continued to hear the resignation of the Council of People's Commissars, of which Stalin had been chairman. A woman deputy from a district in the Ukrainian Republic rose to make a speech in support of a proposal moved by her that a unanimous vote of confidence be given the retiring council. She proposed that Stalin be asked to form a new government and to present a list to the Supreme Soviet for approval. Her proposal was adopted unanimously by a voice vote.

A deputy from a district in the RSFSR then rose to propose that the name of the Council of People's Commissars be changed to Council of Ministers, since the old name, adopted at the time of the Revolution to mark the complete destruction of the former state apparatus, was no longer desirable. Restoration of the name of minister would establish a clear distinction between heads of government departments and lower officials who were also called commissars. This proposal was also adopted unanimously by voice vote.

Action on the Five Year Plan. Discussion in each chamber of the proposed fourth Five Year Plan produced several reports from deputies on the outstanding problems of their districts, coupled with praise of the work done by people in the district. Some of the speeches were critical of the plan. For example, a deputy from the Georgian Republic said that the plan did not take sufficiently into consideration the extent to which cities had deteriorated during the war, nor the lack of health resorts and of good quarters for scientific personnel. He commented that the plan's 35,000 square meters of new dwelling space for the Georgian Republic would not be enough even to keep pace with demolition and deterioration. He proposed that the figure be raised to 70,000 square meters.

The chairman of the State Planning Commission closed debate in each chamber with the same remarks. He stressed that the requested additions to the plan could be made only if manpower, raw materials, tools, and construction were made available. Since planning required study and time, he proposed that the Council of Ministers consider the proposals. He reminded his listeners that under the general plan there would be a series of annual plans. If any goals were exceeded by performance, an opportunity would be presented for doing some of the additional things requested.

The plan as originally submitted was voted on by sections and passed unanimously by voice vote. A proposal was made and accepted in the Soviet of Nationalities to appoint a commission of eighteen to put the plan into the form of law. In the Soviet of the Union, a commission of nineteen was appointed for the same purpose. Each chamber then organized a budget committee, a foreign affairs committee, and a committee on legislation.

Action on Other Kinds of Business. Both chambers concluded the session with a final joint session. They adopted an amendment to the constitution reducing the number of members of the Presidium of the Supreme Soviet to thirty-three, so as to make it easier to assemble. They heard and adopted the proposal of a group of deputies from Moscow, Leningrad, and Kiev, and the Azerbaidjan, Uzbek, and Latvian Republics to elect a list of nominees as members of the Presidium. The chairman then read Stalin's list of ministers to constitute the new government under Stalin's chairmanship. The list had been brought in by request of the preceding sitting. The Supreme Soviet decided to vote on the list as a whole, and approval was given by voice vote. A deputy then proposed a list of professional judges for the Supreme Court. It was accepted, as was a panel of lay judges for the same court. A candidate for the position of Prosecutor General of the USSR was proposed and accepted. All proposals had received prior party approval.

A commission was appointed to incorporate in the constitution in their proper places the amendments that had been made in the text since 1936. The chairman then announced that as all matters on the agenda had been acted upon, the meeting was adjourned. It had lasted seven days, with two days of recess.

Foreign affairs are rarely discussed. In 1950 a "Partisans of Peace" report was used to obtain a resolution advocating peace and security. In 1951 a law making warmongering a crime was passed. No issues are raised over government proposals of this sort.

Countersignature of the Communist Party. Decrees involving basic policy sometimes bear the imprint of the Communist party as well as that of the issuing authority. This policy began in 1931, apparently as a way of reminding party members to give special attention. Although the practice was very irregular in the early 1930's, it reached a high point in 1935, with 16 per cent of all decrees appearing in the Collection of Laws and Orders of the USSR bearing the signature of the secretary of the Central Committee of the Communist party as well as that of the chairman of the Council of People's Commissars. In recent years Stalin has held both positions.

Most of the decrees bearing both signatures related to agriculture. Trade, education, and industry also received such attention. Although the Communist party does not legislate, its direct influence on legislation is manifested in this manner as well. The practice illuminates again the close relationship between the party and the government.

4. Policy Determination in the Republics

Right to Secede. Republics preserved for themselves several powers when they united in 1922. The first federal constitution provided that the union republics were limited in sovereignty only to the extent that they might not exercise powers granted the federal government. They retained the right to secede. The second federal constitution had continued these general principles. Stalin emphasized the right to secession in his commentary on a proposal to remove the right from the draft of the constitution of 1936. He argued that "to delete from the constitution the article providing for the right of free secession from the USSR would be to violate the voluntary character of this union." He went further to comment: "It is said that there is not a single republic in the USSR that would want to secede from the USSR, and that therefore Article 17 is of no practical importance. It is, of course, true that there is not a single republic that would want to secede from the USSR. But this does not in the least mean that we should not fix in the constitution the right of Union Republics freely to secede from the USSR." [11]

Stalin's thought was expanded in his comments on a proposal that autonomous republics be transformed into union republics on reaching the proper level of economic and cultural development. He argued against the proposal by pointing out that a people cannot become organized as a union republic if it is surrounded on all sides by territory of the Union. The reason Stalin gave for this rule was that a "Union Republic must be in a position logically and actually to raise the question of secession from the USSR. And this question can be raised only by a republic which, say, borders on some foreign state, and, consequently, is not surrounded on all sides by USSR territory." [12]

The legal right to secession does not preclude the Communist party from opposing exercise of the right. Some clue as to what party policy might be is found in Stalin's advice in 1913. He was speaking to his colleagues in the Social Democratic parties of Europe. He said: "The right of self-determination means that a nation can arrange its life according to its own will. . . . It has the right to complete secession. . . . This, of course, does not mean that the Social Democrats will support every demand of a nation. A nation has the right even to return to the old order of things; but this does not mean that Social Democrats will subscribe to such a decision if taken by any institution of the said nation." [13] The party attitude was again clearly ex-

---

[11] Joseph Stalin, "Report on the Draft Constitution of the USSR," *op. cit.* above, note 9, p. 399.

[12] *Ibid.*, p. 400.

[13] *Op. cit.* above, note 3, p. 19.

pressed by Stalin in 1917 in a report to his party.[14]   He explained: "A people has a right to secede, but it may or may not exercise that right, according to circumstances.   Thus we are at liberty to agitate for or against secession, according to the interests of the proletariat, of the proletarian revolution. Hence the question must be determined in each particular case independently, in accordance with existing circumstances, and for this reason the recognition of the right to secession must not be confused with the expediency of secession in any given circumstances."

Federal Integration.   While remaining within the Union, the republics of the USSR are subject to close integration with the federal government. Budgets of republics have to be incorporated in the federal budget for approval by the Supreme Soviet of the USSR.   Taxes of any lower authorities have to be approved as a part of the budget.   Principles of criminal and civil legislation were made the province of the federal government under the first federal constitution.   The codes, however, were enacted and amended by the republics themselves.   This situation was changed by the constitution of 1936, which transferred the criminal and civil codes and the codes of criminal and civil procedure to the jurisdiction of the federal government.   The intervention of the war prevented enactment of all-Union codes, and work was not resumed by drafting commissions until after the war.   The new Baltic republics simply adopted the codes of the RSFSR when they became part of the Union, pending promulgation of an all-Union code.   Codes of family law and labor law remain the province of each republic, subject to the requirement that they adhere to general principles established by the federal government.

The bill of rights and the electoral law remained within the legislative power of the republics until 1936.   At that time they were written into the new federal constitution.   The form of government of each republic was also outlined in the constitution in accordance with a pattern similar to that of the federal government.   The only difference was the unicameral structure of the Supreme Soviet in each republic.   The other familiar institutions were prescribed—a Presidium of the Supreme Soviet and a Council of People's Commissars.

To provide conformity each republic amended its constitution after adoption of the first federal constitution[15] and again after adoption of the second. Details about representation in the unicameral supreme soviets appear in the republic constitutions.   Deputies are selected on the basis of population in ratios determined by the size of the republic.   Thus, in the RSFSR there is one deputy in the Supreme Soviet for each 150,000 of the population. The Ukrainian Republic provides for a ratio of one to 100,000; the Byelorussian, of one to 20,000; the Georgian, of one to 15,000; and the Azerbaidjan,

---

[14] *Ibid.*, p. 64.
[15] For an English translation of the constitution of the RSFSR of 1925, see Rappard and Others, *op. cit.* above, note 2, pp. v-67 ff.

of one to 10,000. Sessions of the supreme soviets are called for twice a year, and the presidiums act between sessions.

Functions of Supreme Soviets of the Republics. Examination of the stenographic records of the Supreme Soviet of the RSFSR at its meetings of 1941, 1944, and 1945 will suggest the matters with which the republics are concerned. The session of 1941, in addition to organizational matters, discussed and approved a budget for the republic for 1941, and also approved the decrees of its Presidium issued since the last meeting of the Supreme Soviet. The session of 1944 performed the same functions, besides creating new commissariats in accordance with the authority granted by amendments to the federal constitution in 1944. The session of 1945 again concerned itself with the budget of the republic and the interim decrees of its Presidium. It is clear that the major business is discussion and approval of the budget.

The budget question was raised by the presiding officer in 1945 by calling upon the Council of People's Commissars for presentation. The first speaker was the Commissar of Finance, who reviewed the results of the preceding two years and gave a summary of the main items of revenue and expenditure, in comparison with the original budget estimates. Receipts were 102.7 per cent of the estimates, and expenditures 98.7 per cent. The minister also referred specifically to the financial agencies of local bodies that had made the best records. Mechanically, the budget for 1945 was presented in much the same manner as in other countries.

The chairman of the budget commission of the Supreme Soviet followed the Commissar of Finance. He praised the performance of the past two years and stated that the budget commission had reviewed the report of the Council of People's Commissars without finding major corrections to make. The budget commission had reached the conclusion that the republic's budget was in conformity with the federal government's budget. The speaker noted the main points of difference between the current proposals and the budget for the preceding year, remarking especially on the increase of receipts from local sources.

Effecting Changes in the Budget. Proposals of the budget commission for changes in the budget were presented next. They were divided into such categories as industry, communal economy, forestry, trade, entertainment places, education, and public health. It was proposed that industry reduce costs and increase its proceeds payable to the republic by 27,500,000 rubles. Communal economy was to contribute to the state 24 million rubles more by utilizing premises to better advantage. Expenditures on dormitories for factories and hotels were to be increased by specified amounts. As to places of entertainment, the commission believed that it was reasonable to expect higher returns from the admission tax in view of past experience and the increase in the number of theaters. On public health, the commission proposed an increase of 6,900,000 rubles to improve equipment in schools of the Commissariat of Health.

A general comment was made to the effect that the budget commission had found in every field of national economy some untapped reserves of income. The chairman analyzed in detail the work of the various commissariats to prove his point. He called for action, criticizing the financial agencies for relaxing their fiscal supervision over the economic agencies of the state. Then followed discussion from the floor. Many deputies rose to discuss the work in their districts since the last meeting of the Supreme Soviet. Some criticized the supervisory work of the commissariats. A delegate from the Moscow province assailed the Commissariat of Finance over a procedure that made it very difficult to carry out the local budget. A delegate from the Chuvash autonomous republic took to task the Commissariat of Fuels for delays in developing the peat industry. Some of the commissars rose to report what had been done to improve specific conditions criticized at the previous session of the Supreme Soviet.

The budget was finally approved with all the changes recommended by the budget commission. Some outsiders believe the budget report is staged to give the appearance of parliamentary influence on legislation. Others think it a genuine nonprofessional check on the work of professionals in government departments. Debate does not arise over the direction to be followed on questions of major policy. The direction has already been decided. The questions open for discussion are those relating to the improvement of public administration so that set objectives may be achieved more rapidly and efficiently.

Step Toward Increased Autonomy. Until 1944, the trend of Soviet constitutional policy was toward strengthening the authority of the federal government. The second constitution, providing for all-Union codes of law in four main fields, for an all-Union bill of rights and electoral law, and for transfer of many administrative responsibilities to the federal level, had been an important step in this progression. It came, therefore, as a surprise to outsiders when the Supreme Soviet of the USSR amended the constitution in 1944 to permit the union republics to establish commissariats for defense and foreign affairs. Ever since the first constitution, and by treaty before that, military and foreign affairs had been handled by federal commissariats.

The amendments of 1944 provided that each union republic has its own military formations, and that each has the right to enter into direct relations with foreign states, to conclude agreements with them, and to exchange diplomatic and consular representatives. The federal government retained its commissariats of defense and foreign affairs. It was charged with the defense of the USSR, the direction of all the Union's armed forces, and the establishment of the principles to govern the organization of all military formations of the union republics. It was also charged with "the representation of the Union in international relations, conclusion and ratification of treaties with other states, and the establishment of the general procedure in the mutual relations between the Union Republics." Clearly, the authority of the

federal government was still paramount in these fields, but sufficient authority was transferred to permit two of the republics, the Ukrainian and the
Byelorussian, to seek and obtain membership in the United Nations. Joint
voting of the two republics with the USSR on issues coming before agencies
of the United Nations has been common.

Since 1944 there have been no further changes in favor of greater authority
for the republics. On the contrary, certain administrative developments have
strengthened the federal government's authority. The committee on higher
education, which had guided policy from the federal level, became a federal
ministry in April 1946. Traditionally, education had been a matter for the
republics, subject only to general policy guidance from above.

5. Provincial and Local Government

Initial Controversy. Debate over the character and authority of local
soviets was hot between the Socialist Revolutionaries and the Bolsheviks in
the early months of the Revolution. The former were sufficiently strong to
require the addition of an article to the draft presented by Stalin to the Third
Congress of Soviets in January 1918. This article stated that "all local matters are decided solely by local soviets." The authority of the central soviets
was limited to the regulation of relationships among the local soviets, to the
settlement of disputes among them, and to the handling of questions that
could be solved only for the country as a whole.

The constitutional commission met early in April to carry out the mandate
of the Third Congress of Soviets for a draft of a first constitution of the
RSFSR. At that time the Socialist Revolutionaries, through their influence
in the Commissariat of Justice, caused that department to propose a draft
providing that local soviets should not be both administrative agencies and
policy-making bodies, but only leaders of local administration. This draft
stated that legislative and executive powers should be separated, arguing that
the unity of both in the soviet system was its basic inadequacy.

The Socialist Revolutionaries lost out in the drafting commission in both
their efforts, as well as in an effort to keep representation in the national soviets on an equal basis for peasantry and workmen. They saw in centralized authority, in the combination of policy and administration in the local
soviet, and in weighted representation in favor of urban workers the end
to their power as representatives of the peasantry. They took the fight to
the floor of the Fifth Congress of Soviets, but without success. On July 6,
1918, they broke openly with the Bolsheviks and withdrew from participation in the government. The path was clear for the Communist party to
introduce its own conception of local soviets, though with an eye to the inertia and conservatism of the peasantry, which required slowness in change.

Basis of Representation. Local soviets were comprised of persons elected
directly by the inhabitants for the short term of three months. This term
was designed to bring everyone in rotation the opportunity to serve in gov-

ernment. The local soviets in country districts selected a few of their number to attend district soviets; these, in turn, selected some of their number to attend provincial soviets, on the basis of one deputy for every 25,000 inhabitants in the country districts and one deputy for every 5,000 voters in the cities. Some of the city soviets were represented directly in the provincial soviets, without the intervening step of the district.

The basis for representation in the provincial soviets, then, was different —inhabitants in the country were balanced by much smaller numbers of voters, excluding those deprived of electoral rights as bourgeois elements, in the cities. This was the measure to which the Socialist Revolutionaries had objected most. The provincial soviets selected a few delegates to attend the Congress of Soviets of the RSFSR. Elections thus were indirect, and weighted to the disadvantage of the peasants. These principles were carried over into the federal government. They remained the rule until the constitution of 1936 changed it to make elections direct for all soviets at any level and to readjust the ratio of representation for city and country so that it would be similar for each.

Decrease of Policy-making Authority. The policy-making authority of local soviets was reduced by degrees from the principle established by the Third Congress of Soviets in January 1918. Both the constitution of 1918 and the subsequent constitution of 1925 of the RSFSR gave the local soviets the authority "to settle questions of local importance within their respective territories." The first constitution of the USSR made no reference to the authority of local soviets, leaving it to the republics to determine. The second constitution changed this, by providing that "the Soviets of Working People's Deputies direct the work of the organs of administration subordinate to them, ensure the maintenance of public order, the observance of the laws and the protection of the rights of citizens, direct local economic and cultural organization and development, and draw up local budgets."

The formula of 1936 was not to mean that local soviets are but rubber stamps. Experience over the years has shown that they exercise considerable initiative. Although their proposals often require approval from above, the superior levels are amenable to argument. Local soviets concern themselves with matters of public health, education, trade, urban improvement, and new construction. They make up a large body of citizens, elected since 1936 for two-year terms, who supervise the administrative departments that in the fields reserved for the city soviets do the actual work. The chairman of the executive committee of the Taganrog city soviet has recently given a helpful picture of urban soviet activity.[16]

Conducting Local Soviet Business. Taganrog's city soviet has 370 deputies. Of this number, 177 are workmen, 132 employees of state institutions, 36 engineers and technical workers, 14 students, and 11 housewives. Al-

[16] See Konstantin Agapov and A. Aksarov, "Functions of Local Soviets," *U.S.S.R. Information Bulletin* (Embassy of the U.S.S.R. in the U.S.A.) 7, no. 7 (April 30, 1947), 16.

together, 85 are women. The soviet meets monthly, with all deputies participating, and decides questions of policy relating to the administration of the city. As a means of executing its decisions, it elects by open vote at the first session every two years a secretary and a chairman. The chairman appoints members of the executive committee, submitting their names to the soviet for approval. These become the chiefs of the various departments and commissions. The chairman heads the executive committee. Members of the executive committee generally belong to the soviet. Departments in Taganrog exist for municipal economy, trade, local industry, finance, health, social security, public education, and general administration, besides a planning commission.

As liaison between its full membership and the departments, the soviet creates specialized permanent commissions. There were nine of them in Taganrog, corresponding to the eight departments and the planning commission. It is the permanent commissions of the soviet, composed of deputies who devote their spare time to them, that act as a link with the public and as a source of special information and advice to the soviet when its full membership meets to discuss questions of administrative policy. Deputies choose their commissions, generally on the basis of the work in which they are professionally engaged. Teachers, students, and writers usually choose the commission on education. Accountants choose the finance commission. Experts from among the city electorate are called in for advice. Ten to twenty per cent of the members of the soviet belong to the commissions.

An example of the initiative taken by local soviets is evidenced by an experience in the city of Komsomolsk. The streets had deteriorated so badly under the neglect occasioned by the diversion of all materials to the war effort that by 1944 many were pitted with holes. The city soviet drew up a plan for repair and presented it to the provincial soviet in Khabarovsk for consideration. The plan was fully documented with engineering details and estimates of cost, and experts from the city soviet journeyed to Khabarovsk to explain details. Approval was gained, and next the matter was referred to the Supreme Soviet of the RSFSR, because of the magnitude of the expenditure. The experts of the city went to Moscow with the folders of supporting materials, and were successful in obtaining the needed funds.[17]

Metropolitan Soviet Government. In the largest cities there are district soviets in the various urban districts or boroughs, as contrasted with the ordinary administrative district. A report from the chairman of one of the district soviets in Moscow outlines the work.[18] The Kirov district soviet in the city of Moscow has 186 deputies, who meet in plenary session every two months. It has eight standing commissions on housing, municipal serv-

---

[17] The incident was recounted to the author by the chairman of the Komsomolsk city soviet during a visit to the city in 1944.

[18] See Nikolai Pichugin, "Work of District Soviets," *U.S.S.R. Information Bulletin* (Embassy of the U.S.S.R. in the U.S.A.) 7, no. 8 (May 14, 1947), 18.

ices, trade, schools, public health, eating places, industry, and the budget. As a rule the commissions meet twice a month, each headed by a deputy with considerable experience in the subject. As examples of their activities, the industrial commission put forward a new scheme for utilizing the byproducts of the textile mills and clothing factories. The commission on municipal services drew up a plan for the conversion of the district to the use of gas fuel. The school commission organized individual aid to children who had fallen behind in their studies owing to the war and evacuation. The Kirov district soviet has the usual executive committee and the customary administrative departments. The number of departments is not set by law, but left to the needs of the district, with changes from time to time.

The district executive committee of eleven members meets weekly. It may have on its agenda such items as questions of guardianship, applications for allowances to mothers of large families or unmarried mothers, requests for apartments, arrangements for the sale of soft drinks, and a review of the fulfillment of the plan for installing gas in apartments.

Lenin's hope of bringing everyone into local government has not been attained to the full, but there are many who participate in the three levels of local soviets—provincial, district or city, and village. As a result of the elections of 1939 to lower soviets, 1,400,000 deputies were elected to fill places on the various levels from the province down. There were 63,183 village soviets, 3,572 district soviets, 1,301 city soviets, and 103 provincial soviets. An additional 21 soviets appeared in the specially organized districts of the Far North, called *okrugs*.

6. The Electoral System

Elimination of Discriminating Exclusion. Elimination of discrimination on the basis of social origin or occupation was the principal innovation of the second federal constitution adopted in 1936. The provisions of the electoral law previously incorporated in the constitutions of the union republics were supplanted. The republics amended their constitutions to conform. All citizens of the USSR who have reached the age of eighteen, irrespective of race or nationality, religion, educational and residential qualifications, social origin, property status or past activities, have the right to vote. The only exceptions are insane persons and those who upon conviction by a court have been judicially deprived of political rights as part of the penalty.

Elimination of discrimination was not achieved unanimously. The principle of discrimination had been firmly implanted in the minds of citizens at the time of the Revolution. The soviets had remained representative only of the workmen and poor or middle-class peasants. The extent of the influence of this idea may be gauged by a proposal made for inclusions in the draft of a new constitution, to which Stalin referred critically in 1936. The proposal aimed to disfranchise ministers of religion, former White Guards, all the former rich, and persons not engaged in socially useful occupations. A variant was that if these classes of persons were not disfranchised, they should at least be restricted to the right to elect, but not be elected.

Stalin opposed continued discrimination. He told the Congress of Soviets discussing the draft: "The Soviet government disfranchised the non-working and exploiting elements not for all time, but temporarily, up to a certain period. There was a time when these elements waged open war against the people and actively resisted the Soviet laws. The Soviet law depriving them of the franchise was the Soviet government's only reply to this resistance. Quite some time has elapsed since then. During this period we have succeeded in abolishing the exploiting classes, and the Soviet government has become an invincible force. Has not the time arrived for us to revise this law? I think the time has arrived." [19]

Loss of the Vote by Foreigners. The number of persons who could not qualify under the electoral rules before 1936 had been decreasing with the advance of both collectivization of agriculture and industrialization. The totals were given as 4.9 per cent of all adults in 1929, 3.9 per cent in 1931, and 2.5 per cent in 1934. These figures make it clear that the percentage of those barred from the franchise was a small minority by 1936. Most of them had been able to gain admission to the franchise during the years since the Revolution, by giving up the employment of labor for profit, by abandoning private trade, or by discarding a profession that disqualified its practitioners.[20] The political system was not exclusive, except for members of the former royal family and employees or agents of the former police force, of the special corps of gendarmes, and of the tsarist secret service.

Only one group was placed in a less advantageous political position by the constitution of 1936 than it had enjoyed previously. This group was composed of foreign workmen employed by Soviet state industry or agriculture who had not acquired Soviet citizenship. In the first electoral law of the RSFSR and in the electoral law continuing up to 1936, no distinction was made on grounds of foreign citizenship in the right to vote or even to be elected, provided that the foreigner met the requirements of working-class origin that applied to all. This practice was the result of the Soviet government's desire to appeal to workmen of the world and to emphasize solidarity of class as opposed to national political divisions. With the disappointments of the 1920's in the slow rate with which revolution spread to other countries, and with the further discovery in the 1930's that foreign governments had apparently used the opportunity for espionage, policy changed. No report was ever issued on the subject, but foreigners simply lost the vote in 1936, regardless of social origin or occupation.

Establishment of Direct Election. Direct elections were the second innovation of the constitution of 1936. No longer were the people to vote only for deputies to village or other local soviets, who in turn selected deputies

---

[19] *Op. cit.* above, note 9, p. 403.
[20] See John N. Hazard, *Materials on Soviet Law* (mimeographed, New York, 1947), pp. 94 ff.

to the next higher soviet, and so on. The public was to vote directly for deputies at every level, including the top. This change presented some mechanical problems in elections for deputies to the Soviet of Nationalities in the Supreme Soviet. The constitutional commission had attempted to avoid such problems by providing that deputies to the Soviet of Nationalities be chosen not by the people themselves, but by the Supreme Soviet of each union republic, autonomous republic, autonomous region, and national district, in a manner reminiscent of the election of members of the Senate by the state legislatures prior to the seventeenth amendment to the constitution of the United States. Stalin recommended that the proposed change to direct elections be accepted even for the Soviet of Nationalities.

Mechanical inconvenience resulted, for every voter in the USSR is now presented with at least two ballots in voting for the Supreme Soviet—one for his representative as a citizen of the Union in the Soviet of the Union and the other for his representative as a citizen of his union republic in the Soviet of Nationalities. Citizens of autonomous republics, autonomous regions, and national districts have three ballots to mark, including one each for the two higher levels, because these three types of lower governmental organization exist within a union republic and are not sovereign in the sense of the latter. A citizen, for instance, of the Bashkir Autonomous Soviet Socialist Republic, which is within the boundaries of the RSFSR, will vote on different-colored ballots for a deputy to the Soviet of the Union and for two deputies to the Soviet of Nationalities. Of the two, one is to become a member of the delegation of eleven deputies representing the Bashkir Republic, and one is to become a member of the delegation of twenty-five deputies representing the RSFSR in the Soviet of Nationalities.

Other Innovations. Secret elections were the third innovation of the constitution of 1936. This rule was to have repercussions. The rules of both the Communist party and the trade unions were later amended to require secret election of deputies to the next-higher bodies of these organizations. Secret elections did not mean secret voting within the various elective bodies, once they were elected. The show of hands or voice vote continued in the soviets in deciding matters of policy and in selecting presiding officials or members of committees.

A fourth innovation was that deputies were to represent geographical areas in the local soviets. This was an innovation in the light of the instructions issued under the previous electoral law embodied in the constitutions of the union republics, which had said only: "The methods of holding elections as well as the participation in the elections by the trade unions and other labor organizations shall be determined by the All-Russian Central Executive Committee of Soviets or its Presidium." Under the instructions applicable to the old system, elections were ordered to be held in "production units (enterprises, offices) or trade unions." For those who would not be reached in this way, especially "artisans, housewives, cab drivers, and others," the instructions provided that voting should be conducted at any production unit or trade-union meeting to which they wished to go, or at any meeting in a country district. The principle was clarified in the official handbook for election commissions, which were directed so to organize election precincts as to unite that number of electors that is necessary for the election of one deputy. The handbook added, however, that a trade union should not ordinarily constitute an electoral precinct for one deputy, unless its members were scattered among many small industries or with individual employers, such as domestic servants. The deputies were not to be direct representatives of the trade unions on the soviets.

In the country districts, if a village was too small to have one deputy, its members were to be combined with a neighboring village or villages to constitute enough inhabitants to elect one deputy. Norms were set at varying rates for the local soviets. In the instructions that were still in effect in 1936, cities of up to 3,000 inhabitants were to have one deputy in the city soviet for from 15 to 20 voters. This ratio was altered progressively in proportion to the greater size of cities, until a top ratio of one deputy for from 400 to 500 voters was established for cities with from 400,000 to 550,000 inhabitants. In Moscow and Leningrad the ratio was one deputy for 1,500 voters. In villages the standard rate was set at one deputy for 100 inhabitants, but it was provided that a village soviet should not exceed 100 members and should not be much smaller than the optimum number. If it became necessary to change the ratio of representation to keep to the optimum number of 100 deputies, the central executive committee of the province was to notify the central executive committee of the republic.

Aftermath of Functional Concept of Representation. This discarded system of elections has influence even today on the new system adopted in 1936. For that reason it deserves examination. The fact that under its provision deputies were elected to local soviets by voters who were working together in the same factory or office, or by a trade union representing scattered members of the same profession, caused the deputies to feel that they were representatives of trades, professions, or a common employment interest. The city soviets were made up of what amounted to representatives of each principal industry in the city and of the larger trade unions. In the villages the deputies, of course, represented largely the interests of the peasantry. The city soviets developed the character of bodies containing a cross section of local activities.

Deputies in higher soviets were meant to represent geographical areas, rather than professional groups, and they did to a greater extent, because of the indirect system of elections. But it seems logical to suppose that their members were still primarily conscious of their own professional activities, with which they were most familiar. Thus, the higher soviets, too, were cross sections of the major professions or occupational strata of the population. For example, the Eighth Congress of Soviets, which adopted the new constitution in 1936, represented three main groups, as follows: 42 per cent of its membership were workmen, of whom 19 per cent were directly employed in industrial production; 40 per cent were peasants, all of whom were collective farmers; and 18 per cent were intelligentsia. This composition compared with a composition of society that was reported in 1937 as being 34.7 per cent workmen or clerks; 60.1 per cent peasants, of whom all but one twelfth were collective farmers or artisans; and 4.2 per cent others, including Army, pensioners, and so on. These figures do not separate workers and intelligentsia, but they do indicate the extent to which representation was weighted in favor of the city.

Unchanged Method of Nomination. The constitution of 1936, besides declaring that elections for local as well as all other soviets should be by geographical areas, also provided a nominating procedure. It looked familiar to students of the former electoral system. The right to nominate was granted to trade unions, cooperatives, youth organizations, and cultural societies, as well as to the Communist party. In practice, workers in factories and offices, students in universities, collective farmers on their collective farms, and soldiers in their units make nominations. The groups correspond almost exactly to those that had previously been the voting units.

In the first round of nominations after the adoption of the constitution of 1936, the initiative was usually taken by the trade-union organization in the nominating group. A general meeting was called in the factory hall or yard. The leader of the union's factory committee made a speech explaining the purpose of the meeting. Nominations were called for. A voice called for attention, and someone came forward to place a name in nomination. Sometimes it was one of the nation's leaders. Sometimes it was one of the outstanding workmen of the plant. Further nominations were called for. There being none, the name was forwarded to the electoral commission of the precinct.

Residence in the precinct was not a requirement for nomination, so that names from near and far were transmitted to the electoral commission for the precinct. The electoral regulations provided that the names of candidates be printed on the ballot with occupation, party affiliation, and name of nominating organization. A candidate could run in only one district, so that he or she had to choose one if nominated in several and be withdrawn from all other lists. An election with competing candidates seemed to be expected.

Absence of Election Contests. Stalin had explained to Roy Howard in March 1936 that a one-party system did not mean that there would not be several candidates for a deputy's seat. He had said: "It is evident that election lists will be put out not only by the Communist Party, but by all kinds of public and nonparty organizations. And we have hundreds of these. . . .

You think there will be no election contests. But there will be, and I foresee very lively election campaigns." [21]

The form of ballot set forth in the regulations contained a heading, "Cross out all but one name." The official election poster, indicating in a series of drawings the steps to be taken in voting, showed a man entering a private room and being directed to cross out all but one name. But the multicandidate elections did not occur. After the nominations had all been filed with the electoral commissions charged with the preparation of ballots, all but one name for each deputy's seat were withdrawn. The ballot was printed with only one name.

No outsider knows what happened, but a surmise is possible. The time was December 1937. Hitler's aims had become plain to the Soviet leadership by that time. Disaffection had appeared in the Red Army itself. Even the chief of the federal security police had been arrested, tried, and executed. The nation seemed to be in serious danger. Apparently, the leadership decided that it was no time to introduce election contests to a people that had not seen such contests since the voting for the constituent assembly in 1917, and who had had only a decade of experience before that with the process.

Choice of Single Candidates. One wonders how the choice of the single candidate is made. Some clue is provided by a conversation with a provincial leader in 1944. He said that the party organization in each province reviews the nominations and selects the final candidates in an effort to send to the Supreme Soviet a delegation that is representative of the interests and activities of the province. In this way workmen, collective farmers, aged and young people, women, and the intelligentsia are apportioned so as to provide a reasonable balance.

Such an arrangement is reminiscent of the results achieved by the election of deputies from occupational groupings before 1936. It may be that twenty years of experience with the former system, together with the difficulties of introducing a multicandidate election, induced party leaders to devise a procedure that would have results comparable to those achieved previously.

The one-candidate practice which has developed in the USSR deprives Soviet elections of meaning for those who live in countries enjoying a two- or multi-party system. Choice of candidates, even between persons of similar political faith but with different personal qualities, is denied. The primary, which guarantees choice between individuals also in communities where a single party has a tradition of political power within a two- or multi-party system, is missing. For these reasons Soviet electoral procedures have been found wanting in democratic elements by most American students of the Soviet system.

---

[21] See "An Interview with Stalin," in B. J. Stern and S. Smith, *Understanding the Russians* (New York, 1947), p. 11. For greater clarity and fidelity to the Russian original, the last two sentences of the quotation are taken from the English translation published in Moscow in 1936.

CHAPTER 23

SOCIALIST ADMINISTRATION AND THE PUBLIC INTEREST

1. Inherent Administrative Problems

A Collegial Executive. The public interest, in his own frame of reference, had been the declared motivation of the Marxist since the *Communist Manifesto.* The Russian Revolution presented the first opportunity to try out theory in the hard school of practice. The earliest decrees of the Congress of Soviets and its agencies laid the base that Marxists had said was necessary to permit the public interest to be served by the achievement of abundance. Land, industry, banking, and large-scale trade were socialized, as fast as the leadership believed it possible to introduce the new legislation. The second step was administration. Unproductive property would have been valueless. The state began to organize the largest administrative structure the world has ever known.

Administration of the affairs of state was made the business of the Council of People's Commissars by the first decree of the Congress of Soviets after the fall of the Winter Palace in 1917. It has remained the business of the same agency ever since. Only a change in name has occurred, and that change to the designation of Council of Ministers is very recent, having been decreed in 1946.

The Council of People's Commissars, as originally instituted for the Russian Republic, looked much like the Cabinet in parliamentary democracies. There were the chairman, Lenin, and commissariats of Foreign Affairs (Trotsky), Nationalities (Stalin), Interior (Rykov), Education (Lunarcharsky), Agriculture (Rilyutin), Labor (Shlyapnikov), Army and Navy (a committee of Avseenko, Krylenko, and Dybenko), Commerce and Industry (Nogin), Finance (Skvortsov), Justice (Oppokov), Supplies (Teodorovich), Posts and Telegraph (Avilov), and Railway (not filled). Economic matters were not yet sufficiently pressing to require many administrative departments of government for segments of state industry.

Changing Character of the Council of People's Commissars. The character of the Council of People's Commissars changed markedly after 1917 as industry developed. The structure of the council changed also with the formation of the Union, calling for the creation of commissariats in the new federal government and necessitating the meshing of activity on the all-Union and republic levels. Some of the problems of relationship were met by, creating committees and commissions within the Council of People's Commissars to provide federal guidance, leaving administration the responsibility of agencies in the republics.

The first federal constitution placed in the Council of People's Commissars of the USSR authority to enact decrees with binding force throughout the Union, in accordance with powers given it from time to time by the Central Executive Committee.[1] Obviously, the council was to stay within the limits of federal power created by the constitution. The council was further authorized by the constitution to review decrees and orders issued by the central executive committees of the republics. In its own actions, it was responsible to the Central Executive Committee of the USSR and to its Presidium. Both agencies could revoke or suspend orders of the Council of People's Commissars. The council was required to notify the Presidium of the Central Executive Committee within three days of the issuance of a decree so that there might be an opportunity for review.

Republics were given recourse against decrees and orders of the Council of People's Commissars of the USSR. Through their central executive committees and presidiums, they might protest decrees and orders of the council to the Central Executive Committee of the USSR. The execution of a decree protested in this manner was not suspended, however, awaiting a decision of the Central Executive Committee.

Categories of Commissariats. Two classes of commissariats were created by the first federal constitution, "all-Union" and "federated," both on the federal level, but the latter in a close functional relationship with comparable agencies on the level of the union republics. In addition, there remained in the republics certain commissariats that had no administrative link with the federal government at all.[2] The two classes of commissariats created by the constitution and the one relating to each republic alone constituted the three types of commissariats that have been characteristic of the Soviet system ever since. The only change in the intervening years has been a change of name from "federated" to "union republic." This change occurred in the second federal constitution in 1936.[3]

The distribution of specific activities among the three categories of commissariats has been based on the nature of the function to be performed. Some functions have been moved from one category to another as administrative experience seemed to require. The effort has been to find an administrative mechanism that would suit the type of activity concerned. When the activity transcended the boundary lines of republics, the "all-Union" form would be preferred. When it was desired to introduce a measure of regional

---

[1] For an English translation of the text, see William E. Rappard and Others, *Source Book on European Governments* (New York, 1937), pp. v-88 ff.

[2] See Rappard and Others, *op. cit.* above, note 1, pp. v-67 ff.

[3] See Rappard and Others, *op. cit.* above, note 1, v-107 ff. For the text as amended to 1950, see James H. Meisel and Edward S. Kozera, *Materials for the Study of the Soviet System* (Ann Arbor, 1950), 242 ff.

responsibility, linked with central planning and administrative review, the "federated" or "union-republic" type would be preferred. When the matter was of purely regional or local concern, requiring national attention only to see that the results were integrated with any national program that was planned, the "republic" type was made use of.

Distinction between the categories of "all-Union," "federated" or "union-republic," and "republic" jurisdiction can be made clearer by an examination of the commissariats created by the first federal constitution. The all-Union commissariats were those relating to foreign affairs, Army and Navy, foreign trade, railways, posts and telegraph. The federated type were those relating to labor, finance, inspection (auditing), supplies (collection of agricultural produce from the farms), and the Supreme Council of National Economy (planning and administration of industry). The republic type dealt with agriculture, justice, education, health, and social insurance.

Industrial Commissariats. Development of the Five Year Plans emphasized the increasing importance of state-owned industry. The Supreme Council of National Economy required expansion to manage the rising administrative load. With the formation of the Union, the council had been placed in the same category as a federated commissariat. There was thus a Supreme Council of National Economy in the federal government and one of similar name in each republic. Administrative divisions within the councils attended to supervision of the various branches of industry. In 1932 a sharp change in practice occurred. The Supreme Council of National Economy in the federal government was transformed into a Commissariat of Heavy Industry of the all-Union type. It was shorn of its responsibility for consumer goods and wood products. To direct the consumer goods industries there was created a Commissariat of Light Industry of the federated type. To provide the corresponding commissariats required in each republic under the federated type, the supreme councils of national economy in each republic were transformed into commissariats of light industry. Wood products were placed under a newly created Commissariat of Forest Industry of the all-Union type.

Breakdown of the Supreme Council of National Economy into commissariats relating to activities that had formerly been combined in a single agency began a process that proved popular. Time and again since 1932, industrial commissariats have been divided and later subdivided as industry has grown. As a result of this process, the Council of People's Commissars of the USSR grew from the twelve commissariats listed in the first federal constitution to a total of fifty-nine ministries in April 1947. Soon thereafter a trend to combine developed. By June 1950 there were thirty ministries of the all-Union type and twenty-one of the union-republic type. The number of ministries of a republic type varies with each republic, in accordance with the kinds of activity carried on in each. Since the constitutional amendment of 1947, no list of these appears in the federal constitution, but prior to the amendment four were listed—local industry, municipal economy, social security, and motor transport.

Agencies Attached to the Council of Ministers. Ministries are not the sole agencies represented in the Council of Ministers. By amendment to the first federal constitution, commissions and committees became attached to the Council of People's Commissars.[4] The number of committees has grown sharply in the years since the first appeared, but the number of commissions has been reduced, as when the Soviet Control Commission became a ministry and the State Planning Commission became a committee in 1948. The State Planning Committee has inherited the planning functions originally created in 1921 but not actively exercised until the first Five Year Plan was drafted within it.

Of the committees, several now have voting seats on the Council of Ministers. These are the State Planning Committee, the State Committee for the Material-Technical Supply of the National Economy, the State Committee for Introducing Advanced Techniques into the National Economy, the State Committee for Construction Affairs, and the Committee for Art Affairs. Committees have the administrative form of all-Union ministries; but the Committee for Art Affairs is organized like a union-republic ministry, with committees of the same name attached to the Council of Ministers of two union republics. The names of some of the committees indicate their activities—weights and measures, geological affairs, broadcasting, and Stalin Prizes. Several agencies have the same status without the name of committee, such as the Academy of Sciences of the USSR, the new agency TASS, and State Arbitration.

In addition to committees and the few remaining commissions, there are still further agencies attached to the Council of Ministers. These are called chief administrations, and concern themselves with such matters as the northern sea route, civil aviation, hydromatics, conservation and restoration of forests, and geodetics and cartography. There is also a category designated

---

[4] A complete list of the chief administrations, administrations, committees, commissions, and councils attached to the Council of Ministers in 1946 is given in I. I. Evtikhiev and V. A. Vlasov, *Administrativnoe pravo* (Moscow, 1946), pp. 28-29. It is as follows: (a) *Chief Administrations:* Northern Sea Route, Civil Aviation Fleet, Hydro-Meteorological Services, Geodetics and Cartography, Forest Patrol and Replanting, Supply of the National Economy with Petroleum Products, Supply of the National Economy with Lumber and Wood, Oxygen Industry, Supply of Coal, Artificial Liquid Fuel and Gas, and Affairs of the Producing and Consuming Cooperatives. (b) *Administrations:* Moscow-Volga Canal. (c) *Committees:* Physical Culture and Sport, Standards, Weights and Measures, Radio and Broadcasting, Restoration of the Economy in Regions Liberated from the German Occupation, Architectural Affairs, Stalin Prizes in Literature and the Arts, and Stalin Prizes in Science, Military Science and Invention. (d) *Commissions:* State Commission on the Civil Service, and Exemption from and Deferment of Compulsory Military Service. (e) *Councils:* Council for Affairs of the Russian Orthodox Church, Council for Affairs of Religious Sects, Council for Affairs of the Collective Farms, and Technical Council for Mechanization of Labor Capacity and Heavy Work. (f) *Others:* State Arbitration, Telegraph Agency of the Soviet Union (TASS), and Academy of Sciences of the USSR.

simply as administrations.

Ministerial Organization. The principal problem facing Soviet administrators has been the organization of an administrative structure which would
permit them to keep close to the activity of each division under their control.
The early practice was to create many vertical divisions within a few ministries. Since each of the industries administered dealt with different types of
activity, there developed as many divisions with their subordinate subdivisions and sections. It has been reported that no man heading a ministry of
this type had sufficient comprehensive knowledge to follow the activities for
which he was responsible. In 1934 the rule was established that the range of
responsibility must be reduced. This was to be achieved, in part, by placing
operating functions outside the ministries in agencies of a corporate character
and, in part, by narrowing the field of jurisdiction of each ministry. Thus
ministries were to be divided, either on the basis of different types of activity
or, if no such division was possible, on the basis of an arbitrary geographical
line, as between the coal industry in the eastern and western regions. Two
ministers then carried the administrative responsibilities that one had previously carried, with as much contact between them as could be maintained.
Each reported directly to the Council of Ministers.

The administrative task of Soviet ministries has been a familiar one—
namely, to provide centralized direction while preserving sufficient authority
in the lower levels to stimulate the exercise of imagination and initiative.
The magnitude of the task has been increased under the Soviet system of
socialism because the economy of the country is administered very nearly in
its entirety by the state. The economic stimuli and restraints that accompany the private enterprise system are not present in the same form. Planning replaces the stimulus for growth or retraction that in private enterprise
economies is furnished by hope of profit or fear of loss. Yet planning would
quite possibly have no chance of success under the weight of top-heavy bureaucratic administration, if some means were not found to spread responsibility among many persons on different administrative levels, and to develop
structures and procedures to make control as simple as possible.

Failure to achieve an efficient system of administration is appreciated in
the Soviet Union as a source of great danger to a state that is trying to prove
to its people and the world that its system of economics and government is
the best, to be emulated by others. It is considerations such as this that
prompt a Soviet textbook on administrative law to tell its readers: "The
questions are not solely technical. They always have political importance
of primary interest." [5]

2. *Quest for Administrative Efficiency*

Experiment with Functional Organization. All states maintain agencies
of government designed to improve the efficiency of government. The

[5] *Sovetskoe administrativnoe pravo* (Moscow, 1940), p. 61.

United States has its Bureau of the Budget in the Executive Office of the President. Its activities go beyond the preparation of budget estimates for submission to the Congress. They include, as an integral part of the budgeting function, the devising of administrative structures and techniques designed to reduce the cost of administration and improve the results. The USSR places this responsibility in its Ministry of Finance, as Britain puts it in the Treasury. The Ministry of Finance of the USSR is responsible for preparing the organization chart for each ministry and for determining the size and character of its staff. This work is necessarily performed in collaboration with the administrative experts in the ministry concerned, for they live with the problems every day. When the agency is of a republic character only, the supervision is performed by the Ministry of Finance in the republic.

Whether commissariats should be organized on a functional or area basis has been one of the major questions faced by Soviet planners. The USSR has tried various approaches. Prior to 1934, emphasis was placed upon the functional division. A commissariat would be divided into units that would carry on the administration of a single type of activity in the various fields in which the commissariat worked. These might be construction of plants, transportation, repairs, drilling, pumping, refining, and so forth.

The ineffectiveness of the functional organization was brought out at the Seventeenth Congress of the Communist party in 1934. It was argued that functional organization had failed because distribution of directing functions between several divisions required endless agreements between chiefs of each to decide questions of over-all administration; because there arose from the distribution of functions an absence of unified direction and responsibility in operation, with an opportunity to evade responsibility by blaming another division; and because the lack of definition of rights and duties of the chiefs of functional divisions made it necessary for a local official to confer with a whole group of people when he sought an answer to the simplest question relating to an activity within his jurisdiction.

Structural Reform. A complete reorganization of the administrative mechanism of the Soviet state was ordered by the Communist party in 1934. The functional system of organization was to be abolished. It was to be replaced with the principle of the "production branch." Under this arrangement, the production branches were to be made responsible for everything in the sphere of work to which they were assigned. All the other parts of the organization that were specialized in character were to serve them—such staff or auxiliary services as administrative planning, statistical accounting, legal review, personnel management, the secretariat, and so forth. These services were denied the right to reach directly down to the production enterprises at the bottom level. They could conduct their operations only through the production division, which controlled the agencies at the bottom—manufacturing gasoline or locomotives, or training engineers, as the case might be.

Federal Field Representation. Efficiency ranks high among the objectives of the ministries. Each ministry of the all-Union type maintains in each union republic a regional agency. This agency is not part of the administrative system of the republic. It is responsible solely to the federal ministry. The agent's position in the union republic in which he works has varied. In the first federal constitution it was provided that the agent, though not responsible to the government of the republic, was to have a seat in its Council of People's Commissars. In this capacity he might be granted a consultative voice or even a vote equivalent to that of the members. His voting status was to be determined by the Central Executive Committee of the union republic concerned or by its Presidium.

The position of the agents of all-Union commissariats was improved by the second constitution of 1936, for in it they were listed as members of the councils of people's commissars of the union republics. They were also given the same voice in voting as the commissars. Thus, since 1939, the All-Union Commissariat of Foreign Trade has had its regional agent in the Council of People's Commissars in each union republic; so has the All-Union Commissariat of Communications. In the case of the All-Union Commissariat of Government Stocks, agents are located also in the provinces and even in the districts to supervise the delivery from collective farms of the produce due under the law.

The revision of the constitution in 1947 eliminated the provision that agents of the all-Union ministries should sit on the Council of Ministers of each union republic. It is not explained whether this elimination means that they no longer may sit, or whether it is only the removal of an explicit statement about the point, in keeping with the elimination from the constitution of the listing of the membership of the Council of Ministers in each republic, leaving the composition for each republic to decide as it desires.

Two-way Relationships. Authorities on lower levels are not without influence in the affairs of enterprises of all-Union ministries that are located in their territories. A coal mine in Karaganda, for instance, which is operated by the Ministry of Coal Industry of the Eastern Regions, is physically located in the Kazakh Soviet Socialist Republic. The republic, within the limits of its governmental interest, has the right of control and review over the activities of the mine administration, as has the local soviet within whose area it lies. This provision is particularly necessary because at many points the activities of the mine management bear upon the operation of municipal services or upon labor relations within the republic, and proper coordination is essential to efficient operation.

The scope of subjects on which the work of all-Union ministries is intertwined with the interests of the republics may be sensed when one looks at the listing of these ministries set forth in the revision of 1950 of the constitution of 1936. They are the ministries for aviation industry, automobile and tractor industry, foreign trade, Navy, munitions, geology, town development, food and material reserves, machine and instrument construction, agricultural stocks, maritime fleet, petroleum industry, metallurgical industry, industry of the means of communication, railways, river fleet, postal service together with telegraph and telephone, agricultural machine construction, machine tool construction, construction of machines for the building and highway-construction industries, construction of machine building works, shipbuilding, construction of engines for transportation, labor reserves, construction of heavy machines, construction of heavy industry enterprises, coal industry, chemical industry, electric industry, and electric stations.

Relations of Union-Republic Ministries. Ministries of the union-republic type in the federal government have their counterparts in each republic. On each level, the minister sits as a voting member of the Council of Ministers. The minister in the republic has a dual responsibility, unlike agents of all-Union ministries who may sit beside him, for he is responsible to the Supreme Soviet of the republic, which appoints him, as well as to the ministry in the federal government that has the same name as his.

The federal ministry prepares the over-all plans for the operations in the sphere of activity concerned. It even operates directly some of the largest plants of the industry. The chief operating responsibility is shouldered, however, by the ministry in each republic. In this way less centralization results than in the case of the all-Union type of ministry. Production is intended to be more responsive to local availabilities, requirements, and tastes.

A listing of the ministries of the union-republic type, as they appear in the revision of 1950 of the constitution of 1936, will indicate their functions: internal affairs, armed forces, higher education, state security, state control, public health, foreign affairs, moving picture industry, light industry, forest industry, timber and paper industry, meat and dairy industry, food industry, building materials, fishing industry, agriculture, state farms, trade, finance, justice, and cotton growing.

Organization of Planning. Planning of the national economy on an all-Union basis has required special agencies of coordination. At the federal level is the State Planning Committee attached to the Council of Ministers. The chairman has a vote in the council. In each union republic and autonomous republic, there is also a State Planning Committee. The chairmen of these committees are voting members of the Council of Ministers in which they sit. The provinces, districts, and cities, too, have planning committees attached to their executive committees, with the status of departments. In 1941 the three kinds of lower planning committees were given full power to plan for local industry, using local raw materials, in accordance with tasks set by their republic.

Liaison between the lower planning agencies and the federal State Planning Committee is provided by a group of traveling agents of the committee. They have no responsibility to the governments at the republic or lower levels, but operate as inspectors and guides to make certain that uniform statistical techniques are being followed in reporting the data with which the federal government must work, and also that local planners understand the regulations, old and new.

The varying levels of planning agencies are created to meet the ever-present problem of combining effectively centralized direction and utilization of local personnel with its knowledge of local conditions. The State Planning Committee of the USSR prepares figures for the national plan on the basis of questionnaires returned from local planning agencies to report performance and estimate developments. Reports are also obtained from various ministries, which since 1928 have included planning units in their structure. These units are responsible to the minister, but they must operate in accordance with methodology established by the State Planning Committee of the USSR. In performing their functions, such ministerial planning units have the right of direct communication with the federal State Planning Committee for close and speedy collaboration.

Attainment of the National Plan. The national plan develops as a synthesis of the reports and proposals flowing from the various types of lower planning agencies. When it is completed by the federal State Planning Committee, it is taken before the Council of Ministers for comment, correction, and ultimate approval. Thereafter, the Council of Ministers presents the proposed plan to the Supreme Soviet of the USSR for discussion and approval.

Upon approval by the Supreme Soviet, the national plan is divided into its component parts. Those parts that are the responsibility of the republics are forwarded to each. It is then the responsibility of the State Planning Committee of each republic to work out the detail necessary to achieve the objective. The Council of Ministers of the republic next reviews and accepts the completed plan and presents it to its Supreme Soviet for examination and adoption. After that has occurred, it is the task of the planning committees of provinces and districts to see that the detail necessary for performance by agencies under the supervision of the provincial or district soviet is elaborated and communicated to these agencies.

Execution of plans for the industries under the jurisdiction of all-Union ministries is planned directly by the ministries. No problems of detail are sent to the republics for attention. Execution of plans for industries under the jurisdiction of union-republic ministries is outlined in its primary features by the federal ministry, and the detail is filled in by the ministry in the republic. Execution of plans for the ministries of the republic type is the task of the Council of Ministers of the republic alone.

3. Provincial and Local Soviets as Administrative Agencies

Federal Principles. Not all administrative functions are carried out by ministries of the federal government through agents responsible to the ministries alone. A considerable amount of related activity is carried on by provincial and local government. This work is in the hands of the soviets of working people's deputies, which combine functions of both policy-making and administration.

The authority and responsibility of the soviets in the provinces, autonomous provinces, districts, cities, and rural localities is defined in broad outline by the federal constitution. It states that the executive and administrative organs of these soviets are the executive committees elected by them, consisting of a chairman, vice chairman, secretary, and members. The constitution gave the executive committees dual responsibility. It declares: "The executive organs of the Soviets of Working People's Deputies are directly accountable both to the Soviets of Working People's Deputies which elected them and to the executive organ of the superior Soviet of Working People's Deputies." Thus, the executive committee of a village soviet is responsible to the executive committee of the district soviet, as well as to the village soviet. The executive committee in the district is in turn responsible to the executive committee in the province, as well as to the district soviet.

Constitutional Provisions of the Republics. Greater detail about the responsibilities and structure of lower soviets is provided by the constitution of each union republic. For instance, the constitution of the RSFSR gives to an executive committee on the higher level the power to annul or suspend decisions and orders of the executive committees of lower soviets. In its form of 1945, the constitution provided that provincial soviets would establish particular departments of their executive committees, including those for land, finance, trade, public health, general matters, education, local industry, communal economy, social insurance, highways, artistic affairs, building materials, fuel-making industry for local use, and motor transport, as well as a planning commission. In addition, there might be departments for light industry, textile industry, food industry, timber industry, state farms— all provided the union-republic commissariat of the same name approved. The same constitution stated that the all-Union commissariats and the union-republic Commissariats of Internal Affairs and State Security were permitted to organize their own agencies in the province, responsible to them alone, but with seats on the executive committee of the provincial soviet.

Responsibility of departments under the executive committees of the provincial soviets is dual again. The next-higher level is the Council of Ministers of the union republic. The chiefs of departments are therefore subordinate in their activities and responsible to the union-republic commissariat concerned with their affairs as well as to the provincial soviet.

Status of City Soviets. Middle-sized and large cities are treated in a special way because of their size. Middle-sized cities report directly to the provincial soviet, rather than through the intermediary level of a district soviet. Their department chiefs in consequence are responsible to the departments of the same name under the provincial executive committee, and to the city soviet as well.

Moscow, Leningrad, Kiev, Minsk, Vitebsk, Gomel, Mogilev, Baku, Tbilisi, Poti, Erevan, Alma Ata, Kaunas, Vilna, Riga, and several other large cities report directly to the supreme soviets of their republics, rather than through a province. Hence, their department heads are responsible to the corresponding ministry of the republic. They are simultaneously responsible to the city soviet that elected them. In this way the ministries of the republic maintain direct supervision of departments in the large cities.

Hierarchical Unity of Administration. As a result of this interlocking administrative hierarchy, the union-republic ministries and the republic ministries show a series of functional relationships running from the top to the bottom of the structure within each province. Except in very unusual cases, the work to be done is not done by agents of the central authority of the republic, but by the local executives who know local resources and limitations.

Constitutional restrictions upon federal power limit the agency of the federal government in some countries to advice and suggestion. A notable example in the United States is the Department of Agriculture. In dealing with farmers it generally must rely on powers of persuasion, sometimes augmented by the use of funds to pay farmers for crops they do not plant. Soviet administrators who study the American system are often surprised by the results and wonder how the right kinds of crops are produced each year.

The USSR has no such division between central and local powers. As a Soviet textbook on administrative law remarks: ". . . the difference between central and local organs of administration in the Soviet system of administration is devoid of any importance in principle—the Soviet system of administration is a unit."[6] This fact is explained by Soviet writers as resulting from the unity of class to be found in all agencies of Soviet authority. Both local and central bodies are agencies of the dictatorship of the working class.

4. Management of Economic Enterprises

Trial and Error. Management of industry, transport, and trade is not conducted directly by ministries or by departments of executive committees of local soviets. Government corporations perform the actual operating job. This arrangement to meet the complex problems of operating a vast empire of state-owned industry grew out of experiences and mistakes after the first large private enterprises had been nationalized in 1918.[7]

---

[6] *Op. cit.* above, note 5, p. 52.
[7] For a review of the background, see John N. Hazard, "Soviet Government Corporations," *Michigan Law Review*, 41 (1943), 850 ff.; Gregory Bienstock and Others, *Management in Russian Industry and Agriculture* (New York, 1944).

Management of these enterprises was attempted by divisions of the Supreme Council of National Economy. The divisions, or *glavki* as they were called, operated by methods designed to preserve the maximum centralization, excluding any opportunity for independence of any sort for the individual enterprise. The times were trying; local management was still usually composed of the former plant directors, in whose loyalty to the new system of government the revolutionary leaders had little confidence. The development also conformed to the thinking of the day, reflected in the view of the Communist party that money relationships were to be done away with as quickly as possible.[8] From the higher responsible authority, which was another glavk, the glavki received all raw materials required. These were distributed by the glavki among the enterprises subject to the control of each. All products of the enterprises were delivered for further processing to the state in the person of other glavki, or to state distributing agencies for use by the population.

As smaller-sized industries were nationalized, the Supreme Council of National Economy in December 1920 began to transfer such industries to the provincial authorities. These created in each province a provincial Council of National Economy. The glavki of the Supreme Council of National Economy retained regulation and control of the smaller-sized industries to conform to the national plan, but direct administration was provided locally. The largest enterprises remained under direct operating control of the glavki. This arrangement was designed to carry out a directive of the Ninth Congress of the Communist party, held in March 1920.

Effect of the New Economic Policy. The needs of the Army during the civil war of late 1918 to 1920, including the defense of the country against the Poles in that year, upset plans for orderly administration. A special agency was created to supply the Army. It worked in closest relationship with the Supreme Council of National Economy and the Commissariat of Agricultural Provisions. Priority was given to military needs. The civilian public received only what was left.

The period of reconstruction, introduced by adoption of the New Economic Policy (NEP) to become effective in early 1922, brought an extensive change in administration as in everything else. Any hope of eliminating a money economy was set aside. Small-scale private enterprise was reintroduced to aid in restoring the devastated economy as quickly as possible. The decree creating the NEP put state industry on an accounting basis. State enterprises were to buy supplies for money locally and to sell products locally through their own agencies.

Lenin declared that state enterprises were now given the task of proving their worth in competition with the enterprises of the private sector. In line with the new approach, a decree of April 1923 authorized the creation

[8] See Rappard and Others, *op. cit.* above, note 1, pp. v-29 ff.

of state trusts to conduct the industrial operations of the state. Each trust was given independence in conducting its operations within terms to be set in a charter. Each was to operate on the basis of commercial accounting, with the objective of making profits. The trust was given the status of a juridical entity, which permitted it to assume obligations, to sue and be sued, to acquire property, and to take part in trade. Its capital was assigned by the state agency to which it reported. It could sell its products where it liked at prices agreed upon with the buyer, being merely required to give preference to state agencies and cooperative organizations. The only other restriction was that it could not exercise its independence in civil trade in opposition to the interests of the proletarian state. General supervision over trust activities was provided by the Supreme Council of National Economy or any other appropriate commissariat.

The trust system, though developed for industry, soon spread to other fields. It was adopted for some agricultural activities, for conducting municipal services such as streetcars and water supply, for the administration of health resorts, for the management of municipally owned apartment houses, and for the operation of river transport and trading enterprises. By the time the first Five Year Plan was in preparation in 1927, the operation of the economic affairs of the state was in the hands of the trusts.

Development of Managerial Responsibility. The introduction of the first Five Year Plan brought a significant change in the objective of the trusts. By decree of June 1927, profit-making was replaced by the objective of fulfillment of the plan. Now profits were important only as a means of checking on the efficiency of administration, thus aiding in control over performance of the plan. The second change of importance in 1927 was the organization of the factories and mills, administered by the trusts, as government corporations in their own right. This step was designed to free the lower links in the hierarchy of industrial administration from higher control over details, which the trusts had been exercising in many instances. The responsibility of the plant director was increased when his factory became a government corporation, which made it a juridical entity responsible for its activities.

Development of managerial responsibility had been a problem from the beginning. Early revolutionary measures had created committees of workmen in the plant to watch a director whom the workmen did not trust, but whose skill they needed. As general managers left or were removed, the committees assumed managerial functions. There developed what came to be known as the "collegium system" of management. This system proved early to be ineffective. There was no effective responsibility when all were responsible, and no audacious plan of management when each issue had to be debated and voted upon.

Lenin saw the danger early. He said in December 1918: ". . . the transition from administration by a collegium to personal responsibility is the

task of today." The Ninth Congress of the Communist party in 1920 repeated the statement, calling for the administration of industry on the basis
of the responsibility of particular individuals for specific branches of activity.
But the change to personal responsibility was difficult to make. The collegium system had become firmly entrenched, and in some minds it was a
symbol of the democracy of the Revolution. Workmen wanted no personal
authority in a director to boss them as owners or managers had done before
the Revolution.

Call for Managers. The Fourteenth Party Congress in 1925 issued rules
for the reorganization of industry to prepare the way for socialist advance.
The first rule called for the adoption everywhere of the principle of personal
responsibility in all spheres of production. It was recognized that there
must be a top level, a last center to which questions of supreme importance
might be referred; but it was also recognized that this need did not exclude
the possibility of lower centers where questions of operating policy were
to be decided.

It was one thing to establish the principle of personal responsibility and
another to find men capable of such positions. Stalin explained: "It is frequently asked why we have not attained individual management. We have
not got it and will not have it until we have mastered technique. We will
not have real individual management until there are among us Bolsheviks
who are thoroughly familiar with the technical questions, economics and
finance."[9] The collegium system of management died slowly. Not until
1934 was it ordered liquidated in all spheres of Soviet economic work, except
for elected Soviet organs. It was not gone permanently, however, for with
the treason trials of 1936-8 and the party cleansing that accompanied them, a
collegium was established in each commissariat. Yet this collegium did not
manage. It was only advisory to the commissar, who was fully responsible
for any decisions taken in accordance with or contrary to its advice. These
advisory collegiums continue to this day.

Advice of Factory Organs. Management is also advised by the primary
party organization of the Communist party and the factory committee of the
labor union in the plant. Before 1937 this advice was provided through the
medium of a rather formal but unofficial organization called the "triangle,"
composed of representatives of management, party, and union. By a decision of the Communist party of 1929,[10] management was declared directly
responsible for fulfillment of the plan and all industrial tasks, and all its
orders were obligatory upon everyone in the plant, regardless of party or
union position. On the other hand, management was directed to take into
consideration the opinion of party and union organizations in decisions

---

[9] See Joseph Stalin, "Speech Delivered at the First All-Union Conference of Managers of
Soviet Industry, February 4, 1931," *Leninism* (Moscow, 1933), II, 364.

[10] Reported in *Pravda,* September 7, 1929, and reprinted in L. Gintzburg, A. Kosteltsev, and
V. Khitev, *Sovetskoe khozyaistvennoe zakonodatelstvo* (Moscow, 1934), part I, 83.

about personnel. In the event the local party or union representative disagreed, he could appeal to higher authority, where the matter could be taken up with the commissariat concerned, or even with the Council of People's Commissars or perhaps the Central Committee of the party. The decision of management was to be put in effect in the meanwhile, however, and remain in effect until a decision reversing it was received through administrative channels.

The triangle was present and active everywhere until the surge of strict disciplinary measures, which developed with the advent of war conditions. Stalin criticized the triangle in 1937 as interfering with discipline and the personal responsibility of management. No party order was issued dissolving the triangle, but it faded out of the picture after Stalin's criticism. Thereafter, the party representative in the plant or the factory committee could report independently to their own higher levels if they did not approve the decision of management. Still, they could not put on the manager the moral pressure of the meeting of the triangle committee, in which he was outnumbered.

Effecting Managerial Responsibility. Responsibility accompanies power. A chapter of the criminal code about economic crimes[11] includes various provisions relating to heads of state or local agencies and enterprises. A penalty of up to two years imprisonment may be imposed by a court if there has been lack of economic organization owing to carelessness or insufficient attention to assigned tasks. The penalty may be from five to eight years imprisonment if a director, a chief engineer, or a chief of a department permits production below compulsory quality standards.

Pay varies in accordance with responsibility. To induce competent persons to assume responsibilities from which they might otherwise recoil in view of the difficulties involved, a system of sharply graduated wage scales was introduced in the middle 1920's and greatly expanded under the Five Year Plans. Directors and department chiefs receive not only high salaries but also certain emoluments designed to improve their efficiency, such as automobiles and chauffeurs, comfortable apartments, a preferred position in the distribution of rationed articles, and national recognition in the form of medals and prizes.

Government Corporations. Organization of industry, trade, transport, state farms, and other agencies operated by the state as government corporations has introduced many features familiar to lawyers in the United States. Each government corporation operates under a charter, granted by the ministry within which the corporation is organized and registered with the Ministry of Finance of the federal government or the republic, depending on

---

[11] For an English translation, see *The Penal Code of the Russian Socialist Federal Soviet Republic, Text of 1926* (London, 1934). Subsequent amendments appear in the Russian-language editions published by the Ministry of Justice of the USSR at intervals under the title *Ugolovnyi kodeks R.S.F.S.R.*

the corporation's administrative affiliation. Organizations of purely local importance are also run as government corporations, the charter being registered with the executive committee of the local soviet.

Powers of the corporation are defined in its charter. The state property that it is to administer is inventoried, and the inventory made part of the charter. The property becomes the capital for which the corporation is responsible. The corporation has an official seal and an official name. To protect other government corporations or individuals who may deal with it, publication of notice of registration is required in the newspaper of the region. If the corporation is of all-Union importance, the notice appears in the official publication of the Ministry of Finance.

Liquidation of the corporation may occur only if it seems desirable for planning reasons. These reasons may result from a change in the needs of the economy, or the desirability of a merger with some other corporation or of creating two or more corporations out of the one, or finally because the corporation had proved that it cannot make money, and it seems inexpedient to subsidize it from the state treasury. If liquidation occurs, notice must be published immediately. A liquidating commission receives claims against the corporation. Assets not sufficient to meet all claims are distributed in accordance with a priority established by law. This priority places wages, alimony payments deducted at source, and claims of labor unions first; then follow taxes, claims of other state enterprises and cooperatives, and finally all remaining claims.

Accounting Procedure. Property control has presented the most difficult problems to government administrators. During the NEP, state trusts were required to introduce cost-accounting methods. The principle has been continued ever since for government corporations. Uniform accounting is prescribed by the Ministry of Finance, and manuals of instruction are issued for bookkeepers. Reports are required monthly and annually. They must be filed, in the form of a balance sheet and a profit-and-loss statement, with the Ministry of Finance and the branch of the state bank at which the corporation keeps its account.

Such a system of accounting requires that all goods be assigned values at which the raw materials are charged in and the finished products charged out. The setting of these values is the function of the planning agencies of the state, which consider the cost of production of the raw materials and the cost of production of the finished products, including labor costs, amortization, and any other expenses incurred in the production process. The cost may also be influenced by taxation, such as the turnover tax, which is fixed by the state to obtain revenue and also to influence consumption of the articles taxed. A margin is then left by the planners so that a well-administered government corporation will show a profit at the end of the year.

Submission of profit-and-loss statements permits officials of the Ministry of Finance to tell quickly what is the state of operations. If loss appears, either the management is not as effective as it should be or an error was made in computing the prices of the product. A review will indicate which was the situation, and corrective measures may be taken. If a good profit is shown, either the management has performed better than was expected or there has been an accounting error. A review again will clarify the reason, and the management may be promoted or paid a bonus as the case may warrant. If no unexpected profit or loss is evidenced, no review is required, except at rare intervals and by way of sampling.

Accounting as Control. Soviet lawyers point out that the accounting system differs from that of capitalism in that it is operated not to make profits for investors, but as a measure of automatic control over efficiency of management. It involves, however, many concepts familiar to traders in a capitalist economy. For example, Soviet government corporations place trade-marks and trade names upon their products. This practice is designed to present the consumer with the opportunity to select his preferred brand at the store, and thus indicate to the producer whether his product is satisfactory. In case there are enough commodities of a given type to exceed the demand of the consumers, the undesired commodities will be left on the store shelves, and prices may have to be reduced to move them. This reduction will be reflected later in the profit-and-loss statement of the producer, and attract the attention of the inspectors in the Ministry of Finance. Consumers may thus influence efficiency of production as reflected in quality of a product.

Economic accounting as a means of checking on efficiency requires a method of allocating a loss to the responsible agency if it does not fall there in the first instance. All relations between government corporations are defined in contracts executed by their directors. These contracts implement the national plan and provide the detail that no master mind could comprehend and dictate, such as exact specifications, dates and places of delivery, cost and quantity. If a delivery does not occur in accordance with the contract, the corporation that suffers loss as a result sues the one that has violated the contract. The damages will permit the corporation that has not been at fault to show the results expected, whereas the corporation that was at fault will present a profit-and-loss statement that will attract the attention of inspectors.

Arbitration Tribunals. In the early years, disputes of this kind went before the regular courts, but in 1931 a change was introduced. It was thought that courts were unnecessarily rigid in their procedures and not sufficiently skilled in large-scale business operations. A special system of tribunals, presided over by professional arbitrators, was established. Within each commissariat, a tribunal, responsible to the commissar, heard disputes between corporations under the jurisdiction of the commissar. For disputes between corporations under the administrative supervision of different commissariats, other tribunals, called state arbitration, were attached to the Council of People's Commissars.

Directors of both corporations that are parties to the dispute, or their representatives, sit with the professional arbitrator. An effort is made to obtain performance of contractual obligations, if that is possible. The plan, and hence the good of the nation, require that commodities be fabricated and delivered. Money damages will correct a balance sheet, but they will not replace performance. Only if the tribunal decides that performance cannot be completed or would be too late are damages awarded. Provisions of contract law enunciated in the civil code are applied by the tribunals, and negligence on the part of a corporation is determined under the same principles as would be applied in any court of law elsewhere.

If failure to perform a contract involves elements of wilfulness, gross negligence, or poor judgment on the part of plant directors, the arbitration tribunal discovering this fact notifies the prosecutor to take up the case through the criminal courts. Plant managers are held to high standards, for the criminal code provides that careless attention to duties resulting in harm to state property is a crime punishable by imprisonment up to two years. Production of goods of a quality below contractual or governmental standards carries with it a penalty of imprisonment for a period of from five to eight years. In each case the court sentence may not be the end of the matter.

The industrial life of the Soviet Union shows that achievement of the Communist party's expressed goal of abolition of money seems to be far in the future. Administrative procedures indicate how conventional money-cost accounting is used in Soviet economic relationships. The same reliance on money is evident in Soviet public finance. State industry is taxed on production to provide over sixty per cent of the public budget, the balance coming from governmental loans, personal income taxation, and lesser sources.

Factors of strength and weakness may be seen in the Soviet administrative system. Centralization makes possible quick changes of direction following policy decisions, but the cumbrous machinery brought into being by centralization gives rise to red tape and loss of personal initiative in supervisors at lower levels. Soviet authorities seem convinced that the advantages of centralization outweigh the disadvantages, and that the disadvantages can be lessened by competent management. On the other hand, Tito of Yugoslavia, who has seen the problems at first hand in his own economy, has come to the conclusion that centralization is the cancer of socialism.

CHAPTER 24

INDIVIDUAL INTERESTS AND
COLLECTIVE NEEDS

1. Civil Rights and Duties

Collective Organization and Personal Freedom. Soviet socialism requires extensive machinery to conduct the business of the state. Millions are employed directly or indirectly by government. Discipline has been found necessary, and rules controlling these millions are many. The individual may seem lost in the movement of the masses.

But Soviet leaders point out that they are not unmindful of the individual. On the contrary, they say that their rules and regulations of today are designed to increase production to the point of abundance, and to educate the masses to adopt a disciplined social consciousness that will ultimately require no enforcement of rules. They anticipate that when abundance is achieved, when there are enough homes, clothes, food, and means of recreation, and when society has developed its own self-discipline, the individual will come into his own. They believe that only under the socialist system of economy can such a result be achieved. Marx gave them the keynote: "Only in the collective can the individual find the means and the opportunity to develop his inclinations in all directions; in consequence, personal freedom is possible only in the collective." [1]

Acknowledgment of Rights. A bill of rights was proposed by Lenin for the first constitution of the RSFSR in 1918.[2] It was designed to appeal to the workmen of Russia and of the world, to indicate the changes that the Revolution had brought—the rights of the individual in the new state. The first bill of rights opened by assuring liberty of conscience. It declared the church separated from the state, and the school from the church. It recognized freedom of religious and antireligious propaganda. The Orthodox church had been a state church for centuries, supported by taxation to supplement contributions and income derived from church lands. Its leaders had worked closely with the state; they had often been intolerant. The church performed functions for the state in keeping public records. As a result, it meant something important to many workmen to have the church removed from its preferred official position—as it had been in the West over a century earlier.

---

[1] Karl Marx, "German Ideology," *Sochineniya* (Moscow, 1933), IV, 65.

[2] For an account of the introduction of the articles before the drafting committee, see G. S. Gurvich, *Istoriya sovetskoi konstitutsii* (Moscow, 1923), p. 79.

Bolsheviks had always been critical of religion, for—like most other Marxists—they thought religious belief to be contrary to the evidence of science. They also felt that the preaching of meekness had discouraged the masses from rising in opposition to oppression. For these reasons they wanted to spread antireligious teaching—not only to dispel religious influences in the minds of the workmen and peasants, but also to cause the hierarchy of the church to disintegrate for lack of popular support. The article in the bill of rights relating to religion had, therefore, important political implications.

Civil Liberties and Class. A group of articles in the bill of rights professed to safeguard freedom of expression, including freedom of the press, of assembly, and of association. Tsarist Russia had annulled these freedoms by means of vigorous censorship and police action. Trade unions had grown with difficulty, and strikes had been repressed with bloodshed. Turning the table on the old regime was popular, and the new articles offered the promise that this would be done.

But the first constitution of the RSFSR did not see human rights in the same light as Thomas Jefferson had seen them. It did not assume the time appropriate to establish complete freedom of expression for everyone, regardless of his class background. The continuing struggle of the Revolution was still very real. Marxists had taught that a revolutionary victor must be on the alert for counterrevolution. Counterrevolution had occurred after the French Revolution and after several others. The means of expression in Russia were not to be laid open to all. The articles on civil rights in the constitution made this clear by beginning, "for the purpose of assuring the workers real freedom of expression of opinion," and "for the purpose of assuring the workers real freedom of assembly." It was the workers who were to have the freedom and not the ousted classes. Another article declared it the task of the state to provide the workers and poor peasants with complete, general, and free education. Again, emphasis was laid on the political aims of the Revolution. The article guaranteed nothing like education for all, regardless of class, or general freedom of education.

Civic Obligations. The bill of rights was prefaced by a general article that made clear the manner in which the rights were to be exercised and warned everyone against their abuse. It read: "The basic task placed during the present transitional moment on the Constitution of the RSFSR is the establishment of the dictatorship of the city and village proletariat and the poorest peasantry in the form of a powerful All-Russian Soviet authority with the objective of complete suppression of the bourgeoisie, the elimination of the exploitation of man by man and the installation of socialism under which there will be neither division into classes nor a state authority." The same principle was stated in another article, which reserved for the RSFSR the right to deprive individuals or groups of rights which they exercised contrary to the interests of the socialist revolution.

The bill of rights ended with a statement of duties. Soviet political the-

orists have always said that the rights promised in the constitution cannot
be assured unless the citizens assume the duties necessary to preserve the
Soviet system.[3] An article recognized work as a duty of the citizen. Work
was required in accordance with the slogan "He who does not work shall
not eat." Another article declared it the duty of all citizens to defend the
socialist fatherland. It established compulsory military service.

Economic Rights. No bill of rights was incorporated in the first federal
constitution, but the constitutions of the republics, amended after adoption
of the federal constitution, carried bills of rights almost identical with those
adopted in 1918. The constitution of the RSFSR of 1925, for instance, did
little but change the wording of the article on religion to exclude the right of
religious propaganda while preserving the right of atheists to engage in
propaganda.[4]

Economic rights appeared for the first time in the bill of rights of 1936,[5]
part of the new federal constitution. A chapter entitled "fundamental rights
and duties of citizens" opened with the right to work, and continued with
the right to rest and leisure, and to maintenance in old age, as well as in case
of sickness or loss of capacity to work. It has been the Soviet thesis that only
a socialist economy can provide such rights, since government in a private
enterprise system cannot compel employers to retain workmen indefinitely
on the payroll. Soviet theorists argue that a government must itself be
the employer to be able to guarantee that work will be found.

Restriction of Personal Freedom. Inviolability of the person and of the
home and secrecy of correspondence were also included in the bill of rights
for the first time in 1936. The code of criminal procedure of each republic
had earlier established the rules defining the extent to which the individual
is protected. According to these codes, a person may be held under guard
before trial only when the crime is particularly serious. Arrest is always by
written order, except when the person has been seen committing a crime
or when a suspect attempts to flee; but a written order must be prepared
thereafter as authority for continuing to hold him. If arrest occurs illegally,
the arrested person may appeal directly to the Prosecutor General of the
USSR, who maintains a special section to examine such complaints in accordance with his constitutional duty to see that the laws are observed.

If prosecution is decided upon, there must be a specific indictment citing
the evidence, including the names of witnesses to be called.[6] The accused is
guaranteed the right of counsel of his choice. At the trial itself, the accused
must be present at all times unless he is hiding. He may cross-examine wit-

[3] See Andrei Y. Vyshinsky, *Sovetskoe gosudarstvennoe pravo* (Moscow, 1938), p. 573.
[4] For an English translation of the text, see William E. Rappard and Others, *Source Book on European Governments* (New York, 1937), pp. v-67 ff.
[5] See *ibid.*, v-107 ff.; also James H. Meisel and Edward S. Kozera, *Materials for the Study of the Soviet System* (Ann Arbor, 1950), 261 ff.
[6] For a discussion of the details, see John N. Hazard, "Soviet Criminal Procedure," *Tulane Law Review*, 15 (1941), 220 ff.

nesses and introduce evidence. Not only is the sentence reversible if procedural rules are violated, but those officials who violate them may be prosecuted under the criminal code. The reports of court decisions indicate that numerous cases of reversal for violation of procedure occur, and also some prosecutions of judges for wilful violation of procedural rights or criminal neglect in performing their duties.

In analyzing Soviet treatment of civil rights, one finds that the officials pay constant attention to their major duty of protecting the state. In consequence, a warrant may be issued for an arrest or search, or the prosecutor may consent to the censoring of personal mail with varying alacrity, depending upon the danger assumed to exist for the state. Since the state has faced crises during most of the period of its existence, Soviet justice has earned for itself a reputation for severity and inattention to procedural safeguards. Nevertheless, Soviet jurists urge a different attitude if the state is to attract supporters at home and abroad, or even to retain respect among its citizens. Evidence during the middle 1930's and again since the war indicates that attention to procedural law increases when expectation of danger is lessened.

Right to Question. The constitution grants opportunities to citizens to disclose irregularities in government. The Supreme Soviet is authorized to appoint commissions of inquiry and investigation on any matter. It is made the duty of all institutions and public servants to comply with the demands of these commissions and to submit to them the necessary materials and documents. The federal constitution also authorizes members of the Supreme Soviet of the USSR to address questions to the Council of Ministers or any individual minister. The records of the Supreme Soviet, however, indicate no occasion when either procedure has been used. During the first months after adoption of the constitution of 1936 public questions to commissars were printed in the press, together with answers. For instance, questions on foreign affairs were raised. The Commissar of Foreign Affairs was asked in 1937 the basis on which Japan continued to fish in Soviet waters in the Pacific. He was also asked what measures were being taken to bring back the crew of a Soviet freighter believed to have been in Spanish waters during the period of strained Soviet-Spanish relations. He gave factual details, citing the Treaty of Portsmouth and supplementary agreements in response to the first question, and in response to the second the measures taken through Italy in view of the absence of diplomatic relations with Franco.

The Commissar of Foreign Trade was asked why imports during 1936 from Germany were greater than exports to that country. He replied by stating the terms of the credit agreement of 1935, and his expectation that Soviet purchases would be reduced as the credit was exhausted. Technical matters appeared in questions to the Commissars of Light and Heavy Industry. They were asked what was being done to assure women good-quality silk stockings and why oxygen was not used in nonferrous metallurgy and in the chemical industry. Answers provided details. Some questions were directed to the leading agency of the cooperatives, which is not part of the government, although it maintains close liaison with it. Citizens wanted to know why the model charter of producer cooperatives had not been changed to permit persons not of working-class origin to join, in view of the provisions of equality established in the constitution of 1936. The co-operatives were also asked why they did not construct new apartment houses.

Questions of this formal nature ceased with the war. But there are many letters to the editor. The press provides a means through which aberrations of local officials have been brought to the attention of headquarters.

2. Career Officialdom and Responsibility

Applicability of General Laws. Regulation of recruitment of civil serv-ants and protection of their positions has passed through different stages. In the early days, when all economic activity was conducted by the state and when there was no precise thinking on the control of administrative costs, the government service grew rapidly. The New Economic Policy changed the situation. Its emphasis upon costs of operation, accompanied by the inauguration of a system of indirect administration of economic enter-prises through the device of the government corporation, resulted in efforts to reduce personnel in governmental positions.

A system of classification of positions and control over the size of personnel was established by an agency known as Workman-Peasant Inspection, later to become a commissariat. The task was simplified by the fact that the state had enacted detailed laws on the employment of labor in 1922. Gov-ernment employees in administrative agencies and commissariats were placed in the same general category as workers in production. In conse-quence, many of the same laws applied to them as to the industrial employees of government corporations. Tenure, compensation, working hours, and social insurance were, and still are, regulated by the code of labor laws, which is subject to frequent amendment.

Special Legislation. Particular conditions existing in the civil service ne-cessitated the enactment of a few special laws. Shortly after the code of labor laws became effective, there were enacted "temporary rules of service in state offices and enterprises." Even though called "temporary," the law remained in force up to World War II, and is actually still in effect. It provided that no one could be employed in state offices or enterprises if his employment was forbidden by a court sentence, and that two persons of close family relation-ship should not be employed in the same agency if one would be under the other. Exceptions to this rule designed to combat nepotism were granted by a law of 1923 for the post office and the telegraph agency, and for teachers, artists, musicians, doctors, agronomists, and other professions—in so far as a special exception proved desirable. Such exceptions were later extended to meteorologists and laboratory workers. Needed skills thus had preference.

Establishment of categories of wages was the subject of the second special law relating to the civil service. In the absence of a general wage law for industrial workmen, the law of 1925 on the categories of wages for civil servants was the first of a long series that was to culminate in 1938 with a law establishing fixed categories of salaries and wages for all activities, and requiring every commissariat and central agency of the USSR to observe them.

Nomenclature and job descriptions were required by the law of 1925 for all government employees. The system had to be uniform throughout the entire government service, so that the same work in any agency would be called by the same name and be entitled to the same pay. The job descriptions were to be written up by the Commissariat of Worker-Peasant Inspection; the salary scale to accompany the descriptions was to be prepared by the Commissariat of Labor in agreement with the Commissariat of Finance and other interested government agencies. Payments above the fixed norms were permitted in exceptional cases on agreement among the Commissariats of Trade, Finance, and Inspection.

Change of Control Agencies. The principle of classified positions and fixed wages in relation to them has remained the rule of the Soviet civil service, although the agencies that control it have changed. In 1935 a Central Commission on the Civil Service was created in the Commissariat of Finance to administer the law. In a sense, the commission was above even the Commissariat of Finance, in that its members were named and approved by the Council of People's Commissars directly. This independence was demonstrated in June 1941, when the Central Commission on the Civil Service was made an independent commission of the Council of People's Commissars.

Personnel at headquarters of each of the ministries and other central agencies of the USSR, including headquarters of the cooperatives and the social agencies, must be approved by the Central Commission on the Civil Service. The over-all limits on the number of employees permitted on the field levels of the various ministries are also set by the commission. Distribution of personnel within the field agencies remains the task of the minister or of the chief of each central agency. Control over compliance with the rules and limits on personnel remains with the Ministry of Finance. Its inspectors, in reviewing budget statements and accounting data, also check into the state of personnel management.

Classification systems for types of workers that are very large in number and importance often go before the Council of Ministers and the Central Committee of the party for approval before publication. Thus, in 1942, a decree on a new classification schedule for medical workers was signed by both government and party bodies. The same procedure was followed in 1943 for teachers.

Classification Process. Considerations to be used in placing civil servants within classifications have been set forth in law. They include the work to be performed, the qualifications of the employee, and the responsibility to be assumed. The work is defined largely by objective factors, such as the number of beds in a hospital to be supervised, the number of visits a doctor receives at a clinic, or the number of pieces of mail to be handled. Other factors are years of service, special education, and degrees received. Wages for the same type of position increase in accordance with years of service. If the clinical worker has a degree of candidate of medical science, his basic wage is increased; if he has a degree of doctor of medical science, his basic wage is increased twice as much.

Other factors considered include the danger of the work and the location. A doctor in a psychiatric ward will receive substantially more than doctors in ordinary wards. A doctor in the areas of the Far North also will receive an increase. If a person is an eminent specialist, no fixed rules apply to salary. A special classification may be set up for him alone on the approval of the ministry concerned, but not to exceed 150 per cent of the highest classification in the profession. The Council of Ministers may in special cases approve still higher salaries.

Examination and Recruitment. No single examination is given throughout the country from which panels of qualified aspirants are compiled to provide the source to which chiefs of government offices are required to turn in recruiting new personnel. Each ministry is permitted to conduct its own examining and recruiting. No restriction exists on the examining process, except that the selection must not be based upon racial, religious, or sex prejudice. If biased choice occurs, prosecution is indicated, because prejudice in the selection of personnel violates the constitutional guaranty of equality.

Most specialists come to their positions through the specialized schools conducted by the ministries—foreign affairs, foreign trade, justice, public health, and various types of engineering. These schools are conducted in addition to the general system of education, in much the same manner as the Department of State of the United States trains career officers in its Institute after they have been admitted to the foreign service. Each ministry either trains its recruits itself or requests the Ministry of Education to train a certain number of specialists. Candidates for available positions apply to the schools for admission. Those with gold and silver medals from the middle school are admitted without examination. Those with lesser grades are admitted by competitive examinations. At the end of the training period, a graduate enters the ministry at the level established for beginning specialists and takes the assignment offered. Probationary service in the ministry is required for three years. If an aspirant withdraws before that time or refuses to accept his assigned post, he is prosecuted.[7]

Intermediate skilled workers are recruited in large measure by the personnel office of the ministry or other agency. In 1940 this process was regular-

---

[7] For a discussion of the civil service, see chap. 4 of I. I. Evtikhiev and V. A. Vlasov, *Administrativnoe pravo* (Moscow, 1946).

ized for industry and transport to some extent by a law requiring urban and village centers to send forward youths for training in technical schools for industry and transport. Assignment of the graduates of these schools is the duty of the Ministry of Labor Reserves. Those assigned must work four consecutive years at the place they are referred to for employment.

Control over Personnel. Wartime laws increased the control of state agencies over employees. Permission had to be obtained before leaving a position, which could be denied except in cases of ill health or withdrawal to enter a technical training school. Workers in military industries were frozen in their jobs. Professional people and skilled workmen were required to proceed to any place to which they were assigned. Funds for bonuses and travel expenses of families were established. At the end of the war, some of these restrictions were abandoned. But the pressure for reconstruction kept several of them in force.

Dismissal may be accomplished in accordance with the rules of the code of labor laws.[8] These rules permit dismissal in the following cases: complete or partial abolition of an office or reduction in its work load; stoppage of work for a period of more than one month because of production problems; incompetency; recurrent failure to perform duties assigned without a satisfactory reason; commission of a criminal offense in connection with the work; failure to be present at work for one day without excuse; and displacement by a reinstated person formerly performing the functions of the incumbent. During the war, tardiness of twenty minutes was made equivalent to absence of one day; thus, it became a reason for dismissal, and also for prosecution.

3. Employment Security

Prohibition of Strikes. Almost all citizens, except those in the cooperative societies in agriculture or industry, work for the state, either directly or indirectly in government corporations. Good morale requires that they be given protection on the job. There must be means of airing grievances and enforcing one's rights under the law. The Soviet system provides an extensive mechanism for this purpose.

The individual and his labor union may not conduct unauthorized strikes against management, and authorization would be highly exceptional. Under legislation freezing certain classes of workmen in their jobs and inaugurating the labor draft, many individuals cannot even leave their place of employment without subjecting themselves to criminal prosecution. The forms of labor pressure on management familiar in capitalist countries are therefore not available to large masses of workmen. In Soviet political theory such means of pressure need not be available because both management and workman have the same class interests. If management goes beyond the law, it has be-

---

[8] For annotations bringing the code up to 1947, see N. G. Aleksandrov, E. I. Astrakhan, S. S. Karinskii, and G. K. Moskalenko, *Zakonodatelstvo o trude, Komentarii,* pod. red. I. T. Golyakova (Moscow, 1947).

trayed its trust, and orderly measures are available to the workman to enforce his legal rights.

Main Areas of Conflict. Sources of conflict between state management in industry or office and workmen are reported as being generally these: management has committed an act believed by the workmen to be illegal; the workman appears to management to be too backward to perform his assigned task; counterrevolutionary elements have tried to sabotage operations; and the individual workman has taken matters into his own hands because his labor union has overlooked his complaints concerning bad working conditions or violations of the law.

A court case chosen at random presents an example of a type of dispute.[9] A carpenter refused to report to work on a holiday even though ordered to do so. He thought the director's order illegal. He was dismissed and prosecuted, since the industry was a war industry. The court found him guilty, declaring that the director's order was binding until revoked. The carpenter was advised that he should have worked and protested through one of the established channels for redress.

Procedure for Labor Protest. Three ways of protesting against management exist for the workman: resort to the conciliation commission, redress from the court, and administrative appeal. Each method is open only for certain kinds of disputes. The conciliation commission handles most cases. It is composed of an equal number of representatives of management and the local committee of the labor union. Decisions are reached only on agreement of both parties. Jurisdiction relates to the conditions of work—wages, piecework rates, necessity of overtime work, granting of regular and supplemental vacations, transfer to other work, spoiled production, incapacity, compensation for use of a tool belonging to the workman, failure to achieve the required norms of production, issuance of special clothes, money, or food, payment for idle time at a machine, payment for time spent in preparing for piecework or for closing, payment for incomplete piecework, deduction from wages for harm caused the enterprise, payment of compensation for vacations withheld, payment during an apprenticeship, payment of premiums and overtime, and fulfillment of contract terms relating to living quarters.

Disputes must be presented to a conciliation commission within a fixed brief period of time. If agreement cannot be reached and the question is one of law, the workman may take the matter to the local people's court, which hears and decides it, subject to appeal to the next-higher court. Even an agreed decision of a conciliation commission may be contested, but only by appeal to the All-Union Central Committee of Trade Unions, which reviews the decision to determine whether there has been a violation of law or false evidence. It may not rehear the case to determine whether the facts were determined correctly by the conciliation commission. The people's court may

---

[9] See Case of Musienko, decision of December 10, 1944, *Sudebnaya praktika verkhovnogo suda S.S.S.R., 1944* (Moscow, 1944), III (IX).

review decisions of the conciliation commission if it believes them wrong, but the workman has no right to compel such review.

Violations of labor law also go before the people's court without prior submission to the conciliation commission. Disputes have been many over the distinction between cases that may be brought directly to a people's court and those that must first go before a conciliation commission. Court rulings have defined the dividing line. It has sometimes been thin, as when the Supreme Court of the USSR decided that suits over premiums may be brought before a court without prior submission to a conciliation commission only if the premium is a periodic payment measurable by objective standards, not if it is a nonrecurring one. Some disputes may not be brought before either a conciliation commission or a court. These concern matters over which management is given sole discretion and no objective standards of measurement exist. An example appeared in the report of a case of the Supreme Court of the USSR on a worker's appeal claiming that management had unjustly refused him permission to leave his job into which he had been frozen by wartime law. The Supreme Court held that this matter was solely within management's jurisdiction. The workman's remedy, if he believed that the refusal was unfounded, was to appeal to management's superiors—if need be, to the minister himself.

Record of a Case. The relative position of commissions and courts and the attention paid to problems of individual workmen may be illustrated by a case reported in 1938.[10] Manager Belyaev had worked for fourteen years in the consumer cooperative system. He was dismissed from his position as store manager in Medyn on the ground that for a long time he had refused to accept promotion to a more responsible position, and also because his father had formerly been a middleman and not a workman. The case was brought by Belyaev before a conciliation commission, which agreed with the dismissal.

The local people's court then examined the case because the labor inspector felt that the decision was wrong. The court refused to restore Belyaev to his position on the ground that he was an "outsider," the son of a man deprived of his rights. The court thought that he should have been dismissed as part of the campaign being conducted to reduce losses in the cooperative stores, since he was a doubtful character because of his background.

The provincial court affirmed the decision of the people's court. The president of the Supreme Court of the RSFSR then took an interest in it and asked the College for Civil Affairs of the Supreme Court to review the decision. The result was a reversal. The college said that the reasons for dismissal violated the code of labor laws and were simply not understandable. It stated also that persons who have worked honestly in the cooperative system may not be dismissed if they have not contributed to the losses of the system. Belyaev was illegally dismissed, and the Supreme Court ordered that he be reinstated with payment of wages for the period he was out of work.

[10] See *Sovetskaya yustitsiya*, 1938, no. 9, p. 22.

Safeguards against Arbitrary Managerial Decisions. An indication of the types of cases litigated was made by a commission of labor-union lawyers in Leningrad in 1938. They examined 273 cases in the people's courts. Their findings showed that 145 cases dealt with payment of wages; 99 with reinstatement after a dismissal that the workman believed to be illegal; 25 with damages resulting from injury caused by action of management that the workman believed negligent or willfully illegal; and 4 with removal of a disciplinary censure.

Protection from arbitrary action of state agents as employers is viewed as a matter requiring special consideration in a socialist state. State ownership of the means of production, transportation, and trade requires protection of the individual from injustice on the part of state managers if the bulk of the workmen is to be satisfied. Government is a participant in industrial relations, and assumes direct responsibilities.

Administrative Redress for the Citizen. Protection of the individual from arbitrary action of state administration, quite aside from employer-employee relationships, is also a concern of Soviet law. Administration by municipalities or state agencies of most of the urban housing has brought forth a large volume of law designed to regulate distribution in such a fashion that there may be a maximum of satisfaction and a minimum of injustice.[11] A case will illustrate the role of the courts. An action for eviction had been brought by the All-Russian Society for the Blind against an occupant of one of the buildings managed by the society. The grounds were stated to be the interest of the group. The lower court held for the society. The Supreme Court of the RSFSR, upon review of the decision, declared that the reason was not adequate to support an action of eviction. It said that if it were imperative that the individual be ousted, the society could not avoid its duty to find other suitable quarters to which he might be moved.

The law on the preservation of the housing fund of 1937 contains a restatement of the general principles protecting the individual against the state administrator. It provides that an occupant may be evicted without provision of other premises only if a court finds (*a*) that the occupant, or a member of his family, systematically destroys or damages the premises or places of general use; (*b*) that the occupant, or a member of his family, by their deportment makes it impossible for other occupants to live in the same apartment or room; or (*c*) that the occupant does not pay rent for three months.

Balance of Interests. Individual preference is not allowed to stand in the way of prompt action in cases where the supporting facts are not in dispute. Administrative procedures, rather than court procedures, are prescribed in certain types of cases. These relate to hotel occupancy by the day, or dormitories or barracks maintained for transients or students, after a period of study has ended; houses threatened with collapse; school buildings; hospitals;

[11] For the details of housing law and the cases cited, see John N. Hazard, *Soviet Housing Law* (New Haven, 1939).

clinics; sanatoria; dispensaries and medical stations; and apartment houses operated by government corporations specifically for their employees, in which apartments are provided only on the basis of a contract of employment. In all these cases the management is alone responsible, entitled to eviction when it becomes necessary or the occasion for the occupancy terminates, as when health is regained by a patient in a hospital, or a contract of employment that gives tenancy terminates legally.

Innumerable court cases have arisen over specific situations. Many of them arose during World War II in connection with the transfer of population from one area to another to escape the enemy. The cases and the regulations issued to control these situations indicate an effort to balance the requirements of the community with the interests of the individual. It is clear that a matter such as one's living quarters is of major concern to every citizen of the Soviet Union. State administrators, in the interest of the state itself, are directed to act impartially and with strict fairness in meeting the needs of all.

4. Restraint of Recalcitrants

Crimes against the State. Protection of the individual from arbitrary action by state officials, whether they be employers or administrators, is one task of the law. Another task of the law is to protect the state from nonconformists who are dangerous to its continued existence. Soviet criminal codes define the objective of penal legislation as being the protection of the socialist state and the established order against socially dangerous acts. Specific articles define certain acts as criminal and provide limits within which a court shall sentence the guilty. Crimes against the state are believed most dangerous and are placed first. The list opens with counterrevolutionary crimes, defined as acts aimed to overthrow, undermine, or weaken the authority of the soviets or of the administration. These acts include any armed uprising, invasion, or seizure of power, communication with a foreign government with counterrevolutionary intent, rendering assistance to that part of the international bourgeoisie seeking to overthrow the Communist system, inducing a foreign government to declare war, and espionage.

Acts committed without counterrevolutionary intent but shaking the foundations of the state administration or the economic strength of the USSR or its republics are placed second in importance. Various specific situations are listed, including the incitement of mass disorders accompanied by pogroms; banditry; breach of labor discipline by transport workers; evasion of military service; evasion of taxes in time of war; propaganda intended to arouse racial or religious hatred or discord; counterfeiting; and professional smuggling. In contrast to the first group of crimes, for which the death penalty was prescribed by the codes, the maximum penalty for the second group was set as generally ten years' deprivation of freedom. A third category of crimes includes nonpayment of taxes in peacetime, concealment of property from assessment, public insult to a representative of authority, willful slaughter of cattle, criminally careless treatment of a tractor or horse, and infringement of the laws on nationalization of the land. Penalties for some of these acts are only fines, or sentences usually limited to two or three years' imprisonment.

Danger to the state threatens not only from acts such as those listed, but also from acts which upset order and the confidence in ability to maintain order. As in all systems of government, Soviet criminal codes provide penalties for murder, rape, bodily injury, bribery, larceny, embezzlement, and harm to property. Penalties are increased sharply if the property is that of the state or of a cooperative.[12]

Operation of the Criminal Law. Penalties are designed to provide for rehabilitation of the criminal, if at all possible. For that reason, it is only in rare cases and in relatively recent years that imprisonment was inflicted. For most offenses the penalty has been confinement in a correctional labor camp. Even murder, for which many states impose a penalty of death, has carried a maximum term of ten years in correctional labor camps. The death penalty was reserved for cases where rehabilitation seemed impossible or the danger to the state too great to permit taking the chance inherent in any program of rehabilitation. In 1947 the death penalty was abolished for all crimes committed during peacetime, but in 1950 it was restored for serious crimes endangering the security of the state.

Prosecution based on analogy to an article of the criminal code has been permitted when an action not defined as a crime or defined as of minor importance appears to a court to be more dangerous to the state than the code foresaw. This provision was inserted when the Revolution was still young. As the Soviet system became more thoroughly established, the Supreme Court ordered that analogy be applied sparingly. Courts were advised to confine analogy to the scope of the prescribed penalty only and no longer to apply it to an act not defined as a punishable crime.

The last war caused re-emphasis upon the analogy provision. An example of its application is provided by an order instructing courts to treat the illegal distillation of liquors as an offense of greater seriousness than had been thought to be warranted when the code had been drafted. The code's penalties for this offense were a maximum of one year in a labor camp or a fine. The instruction stated that in wartime liquor could disrupt production for the front, and its illegal manufacture could thus be harmful to the state.[13] The reverse of the rule also applies, to relieve a person from the application of a penalty if an act defined as a crime in the code is not believed to be socially dangerous at the time it is committed or at the time when the penalty is to be exacted. Many cases reach the Supreme Court that lead to the conclusion

---

[12] For an English translation of the text, see the *American Review on the Soviet Union*, 8 (October 1947), 89-90.

[13] For a discussion of such wartime laws, see John N. Hazard, "The Trend of Law in the U.S.S.R.," *Wisconsin Law Review*, 1947, 223 ff.

that a person sentenced by a lower court should be released, because the act no longer seems dangerous.

Extrajudicial Sanctions. Prosecution of those accused under the criminal code proceeds in court in accordance with the safeguards of procedural law. There is, however, another sort of protection of the state, outside the courts and apart from the established codes of law. It is the protection provided by the Ministry of the Interior—the principal relic of the turbulent days of the Revolution, which were characterized by Lenin when he said: "I have discussed soberly and categorically which is better, to put in prison several tens or hundreds of instigators, guilty or not guilty, or to lose thousands of Red Army men and workers? The first is better. And let me be accused of any mortal sin whatever and of violating freedom. I admit myself guilty but the interests of the workers still win out." [14]

Origin of the special jurisdiction of the Ministry of the Interior can be traced back to a decree of June 1919. It gave the Extraordinary Committee known as the *cheka,* created in 1918, discretionary powers to impose penalties, including death in areas of martial law. The cheka could exercise its power against persons charged with political or semipolitical offenses, such as treason, espionage, participation in counterrevolutionary activities, willful destruction of railroad property, and so forth.

The cheka was authorized to conduct a trial in its own tribunals and to convict persons found guilty. It was not required to follow judicial procedure; its tribunals had no relationship to the regular court system, which was concerned with crimes not related to politics. But the judicial powers of the cheka were short-lived. An act of April 1920, after the counterrevolution had declined, dispensed with the right of the cheka to try suspected persons and execute them. This power passed to revolutionary tribunals, which followed a measure of legal procedure and conducted public trials, even though they were quite informal. The accused was denied the right of counsel, however, and one of the members of the bench had to be a member of the provincial department of the cheka.

From Cheka to OGPU. The special conditions of the NEP resulted in the creation in 1922 of a State Political Bureau known as the GPU. This agency replaced the cheka, which passed out of existence. The GPU was permitted to inflict punishment at its discretion in a nonjudicial manner, even by shooting "all persons apprehended while participating in a banditry raid or armed robbery." Otherwise its powers were generally less extensive than had been those of the cheka. The agreement in December 1922 to form a union contained a provision that there should be a supervisory agency in the federal government to coordinate the work of the GPU in each republic. This supervisory agency, called the OGPU, was given a seat on the Council of People's Commissars of the USSR. The organization was placed under the

---

[14] V. I. Lenin, in *op. cit.* above, note 1, XXIV, 241.

supervision of the Prosecutor General, who at that time was attached to the Supreme Court.

The OGPU had large powers in connection with the program of liquidating the *kulaks* as a class by decree of 1931. It was in charge of the process under which many of the well-to-do peasants resisting collectivization of agriculture were sent into exile in Siberia, Central Asia, or the Far North. It also was to operate the industrial, construction, or mining projects to which the exiles were sent. About May 1934 this process began to come to its conclusion; a decree authorized the OGPU to recommend restoration of civil rights to kulaks who had proved their worth by excelling in production.

The OGPU was transferred to the newly created Commissariat of Internal Affairs, the NKVD, by a decree of July 1934, and its court college was abolished. All cases that the NKVD investigated thereafter were not to be tried by it but ordered transferred to the regular courts when the preliminary investigation had been completed. Special colleges were created in the provincial courts, the supreme courts of the republics, and the Supreme Court of the USSR to hear cases formerly going before the OGPU tribunals. The special colleges were bound by the same rules of criminal procedure as were all courts, but they differed from the regular courts of original jurisdiction in that the bench of three judges was composed of three professionals, rather than of the one professional and two lay judges provided in the regular colleges.

Development of the NKVD. The NKVD, by virtue of the decree of 1934, received special jurisdiction as follows: "Under the People's Commissariat of Internal Affairs there are organized special boards to which shall be given, under a special statute relating to it, the right to apply through administrative procedures measures of exile, banishment and confinement in a corrective labor camp for periods up to five years and expulsion from the USSR." In 1935 the first federal constitution was amended to eliminate all reference to the OGPU, so that its name was completely obliterated from the laws.

With the federal constitution of 1936 the special colleges in the provincial courts, the supreme courts of the republics, and the Supreme Court of the USSR were abolished. Jurisdiction over the cases they had formerly heard passed to the federal military courts or the military college of the Supreme Court of the Soviet Union. Up to the war, steady progress occurred away from the special procedures and powers that the cheka had originally possessed. Political cases that amounted to overt acts punishable under the criminal code were tried in the regular courts. The NKVD remained as an extraordinary means of eliminating the persons who committed no defined crime, but who because of their attitude toward the efforts of the regime were believed to be undermining its position and threatening its security.

The danger brought by the war restored the NKVD to increasing power. When the Germans attacked, and regions of the country were declared to be military theaters, jurisdiction over crime of all types passed to the military courts of the federal system. The responsibility was apparently more than these courts could undertake to perform, for by a joint order of the Commissariat of Justice and the Prosecutor of the USSR, dated June 24, 1941, jurisdiction was handed over to military tribunals of the NKVD. If the case related to labor discipline and there were no military tribunals of the NKVD conveniently near, the Army's military court had jurisdiction. With the return of life to peacetime conditions after the war, the military tribunals of the NKVD were abolished in most areas. The special boards created under the decree of 1934 continue, however, for the country as a whole. They are made up of representatives of the Minister of Internal Affairs, the head of the chief administration of the militia, and the Minister of Internal Affairs of the individual union republic. The Prosecutor General of the USSR or his representative must also be present at board meetings. Millions of people are said to have been put through this procedure, which has been assailed before agencies of the United Nations.

5. Control of Administration by Complaint

Voice of the Press. Few questions appear to worry Soviet leaders as much as the possibility that the large administrative organization of the state will become callous and inattentive to the needs of citizens. The press is relied upon as the thorn in the side of the bureaucrat to remind him of his obligations to the public. Large papers maintain staff or nonprofessional correspondents throughout the country. Each of them—workmen and collective farmers, housewives and newspaper reporters—help in the task of exposing maladministration, inattention to the public, red tape, delays, and incompetence, by writing for their papers. Officials often do not know the reporters are in the community. They are sufficiently effective in their search for flaws in administration to be feared.

The function of the nonprofessional and professional journalists has been supported by the agencies of law. The Commissariat of Justice issued a circular in 1932 requiring the courts to listen to the voice of the press. Judges must meet with press representatives from time to time to discuss what has been done to investigate complaints. A quarterly report must be made to the presidium of the Supreme Court of a republic on action taken upon each complaint. The work of the local police must be looked into not less than twice a month by the prosecutor's office, either by its own agents or through the newspaper reporters' association.

Decisions of the Supreme Court of the RSFSR indicate the extent to which the press has been effective in exposing maladministration and abuse of power. The court has held that if a newspaper correspondent is murdered because of his exposure of an official, the act is to be punished as a terrorist act. If persons whose actions are criticized in reports sent to the press succeed in destroying the reports intentionally before publication, their action is to be treated as socially dangerous and punished under the criminal code. Disclosure of the names of persons sending complaints to a newspaper for publication is equal to revelation of confidential facts, and punished as a criminal of-fense. Such actions would scarcely have occurred if letters of complaint to the newspapers were of no importance. Moreover, prosecution of officials often occurs for excess of authority as well as failure to use authority to guard against harm.

Deputy Reports and Complaint Bureaus. Further avenues of control over bureaucratic officials lie with the deputy of the district in the Supreme Soviet of the republic or of the USSR. Deputies are required by the constitution to make reports to their constituents. Newspapers in the region carry the re-ports. Deputies are paid a stipend for expenses of their office correspondence through which citizens may express their grievances or obtain action by pros-ecution.

Still another means of control is to be found in the complaint bureaus that every soviet is required to maintain. Citizens may call to complain about of-ficials. The importance of these complaint bureaus has been emphasized by a report of a meeting of the Presidium of the Supreme Soviet of the USSR on October 19, 1946, in which the chairman of the provincial soviet of Krasnodar was reprimanded for failure to maintain a complaint bureau and for negli-gence in attending to the requests of individuals. He was ordered to install a complaint bureau immediately.

Quest for Popular Support. Measures of this nature suggest the concern with which Soviet leaders approach the task of making the socialist system popular with the people. They obviously appreciate that no state, no matter how well equipped with means of compulsion, can proceed to attain its goals without wasting its strength if it lacks the confidence and support of most of its people. In times of crisis the people will accept restrictions and excuse official indifference, but over a period of years there must be improve-ment if support is to continue. The Russian people has endured an experi-ence of privation and restriction for centuries, and it has been taught sacrifice for the promise of Marxism. Nevertheless, there is a limit beyond which a people cannot be hurried or asked to continue sacrifices. Soviet leaders find it necessary to become specialists in sensing the point at which the limit may be reached. They cannot go faster than the masses will permit. The gauges of pressure available in complaint procedure are instruments on the bridge of the ship of state, with the aid of which the leaders navigate.

Nature of the Soviet Leadership. There may be still another pressure gauge in the character of the political leadership itself. It is an intangible factor, but the possibility of its existence cannot be ignored. It may exist by virtue of the fact that the first generation of political leaders were born the sons and daughters of the common people. They chose to become profes-sional revolutionaries when such a choice meant political oblivion, social ostracism, or even exile. It was not a choice that men primarily interested in careers would make. Some did become "careerists," but most identified their lives with a cause, continuing to act in what they believe to be the interests of that cause. Devotion to that cause may well act as a restraint upon their personal aspirations and keep them mindful of the feelings of the people in whose name they profess to act. They came from the workmen and peasantry whom they now lead, and the reactions of the people cannot be hard for them to imagine.

Since the Revolution a new generation of junior leaders had risen to the intermediate positions. Fame, social position, comforts, and even relative wealth have been the rewards of those who have accepted the discipline of the party. These have gone to some heads, but it must be clear to careerists of the more recent vintage that although the party as an institution may be expected to have a long life, individuals within the party do not necessarily share it. There is no hereditary position of leadership, whether by blood, property, or service. The reserves of the future are to be found in the people itself. Meanwhile, the policy of those who guide the country will probably be restrained by an inherent conception of what the people will tolerate.[15]

The character of the present Soviet leadership is much debated in the United States. Some believe, on the basis of interviews in European displaced persons camps, that Soviet leaders are today mostly narrow in perspective and mindful only of continuing themselves in power and of satisfying their personal ambition. Certainly, the evidence includes much that suggests a degeneration in the leadership groups. There is indication of a loss of faith in the success of world revolution as preached by early Marxists. If this be so, men may live solely for what they can exact from society in the way of comfortable living, personal glory, and material rewards.

If such testimony represents the general situation, the Soviet system may well be doomed. One must note, however, that scientific check upon impressions of this character is no longer possible when frontiers are closed, and travel and study on the scene restricted for all but those who share Soviet hopes and expectations. Serious travelers before World War II doubted that reports of degeneration and cynicism then current were trustworthy. It remains an open question whether the intervening decade, accompanied as it was by the destructions and degradations of war, has nurtured a new generation unlike their fathers. Will this new generation when it reaches power manifest conclusively that Soviet leadership has lost its vitality, as the leadership of other revolutions lost faith and purpose in the succession of generations?

---

[15] For a discussion of social factors and leadership trends, see Julian Towster, *Political Power in the U.S.S.R.* (New York, 1948).

CHAPTER 25

SOVIET CONSOLIDATION—BLUEPRINT FOR THE FUTURE?

1. Socialism in One Country

Creating Conditions of Socialism. Political leadership in all states pursues objectives toward which it guides the citizens, but there are few bodies of leaders that have as definite a goal as have the leaders of the USSR. Marxism is the intellectual heritage of the Russian Revolution. It calls for state directed socialism, and ultimately stateless communism. It defines in general terms what form of organization society is to take. It sets forth the prerequisites to any effort to achieve its objectives. It calls for collective ownership of the means of production, for a smashing of the old state apparatus, and for the creation of a new one of a different type drawing its support from workmen and small peasants. But Marxism goes no further. It has remained for revolutionary leaders to draw their own blueprint of measures to reach the final objective. They have been handed no blueprint by the thinkers of the past. They have had to face new situations and new problems that Marx and his associates could not have foreseen.

The first and major task of the new state arising in Russia in 1917 was to create the conditions of socialism. This immediate objective was considered of primary importance. The leaders of the Revolution appreciated that they could not expect to hold the support of the people unless the new state were to introduce a new economy more productive than the old. The proof would be better homes, clothes, food, and services than the masses had seen before the Revolution. Soviet leaders knew that their program would require time, but they believed in the inevitability of success. Their whole study of history and economics led them to this conclusion, which gave them assurance during the stormy period of civil war and foreign intervention when everyone could see that economic conditions were worse than they had previously been.

Steps were taken at home to prepare for socialism. The leaders also counted for success partly on events abroad. They expected the industrial power of Germany to be seized by the proletariat. This move would have linked agrarian, semi-industrialized Russia and its wealth of raw materials with highly industrialized Germany. The combination would have aided reconstruction and the speedy development of a socialist economy in Eastern and Central Europe. Proof was expected to be conclusive, not only to the peoples of these regions, but to the peoples of the world, that socialism could do more for the masses than capitalism.

Failure of Revolution Abroad. The dream of spreading revolution failed to materialize. The executive committee of the Workers' and Soldiers' Soviet of Greater Berlin seized power November 11, 1918, but it was short-lived. The soviet republics that declared themselves in some other areas of Germany, notably in Munich from April 7 to May 1, 1919, were suppressed by government troops. The soviets that emerged in Austria in 1918 had no voice in national affairs; they served only to preserve discipline in the Army and to combat profiteering in foodstuffs and housing. The soviet republic in Hungary lasted from March 21 to July 31, 1919, but failed under pressure from within and without. Even in the RSFSR it proved necessary to reintroduce a limited measure of private enterprise with the New Economic Policy in the wake of the civil war.

Support from abroad was not forthcoming. Conditions at home had degenerated. Lenin was a practical man. He had demonstrated that preservation of the advance of the Russian Revolution came first when he insisted on peace with Germany at any price in March 1918.[1] He told his followers that the revolutionary parties must complete their education. Having learned how to attack, they must now understand how best to retreat.

Basic Controversy. Lenin's colleagues did not all agree with him. Some, including Bukharin, Pyatakov, Radek, and Preobrazhensky, felt that the new Soviet Russia would have to push through in support of a revolutionary German proletariat or it would itself go down in defeat. These men saw no hope of building a socialist economy in the East alone. Their school of thought was nicknamed "left communism."

One of the most ardent advocates of the strategy of support of revolutionary movements in Western Europe was Leon Trotsky. He believed that the construction of socialism and the consolidation of the dictatorship of the proletariat were impossible in Russia without the direct support of the proletariat of Europe. In his later *History of the Revolution,*[2] he devoted much space to a justification of his position. He wrote: "The problem of a socialist society cannot be abstracted from the problem of productive forces which, at the present stage of human development, are world-wide in their very essence. The separate state, having become too narrow for capitalism, is so much the less capable of becoming the arena of a finished socialist society. The backwardness of a revolutionary country, moreover, increases for it the danger of being thrown back to capitalism."

The record seems to indicate that Lenin looked forward to complete success only after revolution had come to Western Europe. Yet he was faced with the very practical problem of deciding to give up or go on as best he could.

---

[1] See Louis Fischer, *The Soviets in World Affairs* (New York, 1930), I, 72.

[2] Leon Trotsky, *The History of the Russian Revolution* (New York, 1936), III, app. 2, 397 ff.

He followed the line of thought he had set forth in 1918: "It is in our interest to do all that is possible to take advantage of the slightest opportunity to postpone the decisive battle until the moment (or till after) the revolutionary ranks of the single, great, international army have been united." [3]   This principle had been accepted by the Communist party, but there was much opposition. Even Lenin did not call for the abandonment of efforts to bring about world revolution. He sponsored the creation of a Third International to organize and direct the proletariat of other lands. For some years it continued to press militantly for world revolution. Not until 1924, with revolution more remote than ever, and in the face of the pressing need for the USSR to restore her economy under conditions of peace, did the Third International begin its swing to other tactics—the tactics of the "united front."

Liquidation of the Opposition. A decision that the country was able to build socialism even though surrounded by capitalist nations, and under conditions of the NEP, issued from the Fourteenth Party Congress in December 1925. Kamenev and Zinoviev, who were very active in the Third International, opposed this view but were voted down. The effort to complete the construction of socialism in one country was hailed as successful by Stalin at the Seventeenth Party Congress in 1934.[4] He announced that experience had shown that it was entirely possible for socialism to achieve victory in one country. Yet the opposition was not silenced. The men who had declared the effort doomed to failure continued to oppose it. In the end they were tried for attempting to call in outside aid in a plot to unseat those who were committed to the prevailing policy, and they confessed "errors."

The trials of the proponents of world revolution at any cost spread over three years prior to the war. Zinoviev and Kamenev were tried in 1936. Bukharin and Radek were tried in the last trial in 1938. In all of the trials, Trotsky's name was linked with treason, but he was abroad and could not be tried in person. Now all argument had ceased over the need for the USSR to center its attentions on its own development and to create political institutions with that goal in mind. National self-protection loomed as the next main task with the rising menace of Hitler. It led to the Nazi-Soviet pact of 1939.

Lesson of World War II. Emphasis upon construction at home did not mean that the international proletarian cause was lost sight of. World revolution was still a goal, but its attainment became associated in the minds of Soviet leaders with the retention of power in the USSR as a prerequisite. Reliance on the workers of Germany, even with the large Communist vote, was thought to be ineffective to stop Hitler.

A final effort was made to enlist the aid of the German workmen when the attack on the Soviet Union began. The Soviet press of October 16, 1941,[5] printed a "plea to the German people and the German Army," signed by the

---

[3] V. I. Lenin, "Left Wing Childishness and Petty Bourgeois Mentality," *Selected Works* (English trans., Moscow, 1936), VII, 357.

[4] See Joseph Stalin, *Problems of Leninism* (English trans., Moscow, 1940), p. 516.

[5] See *Izvestiya*, no. 245 (7621), October 16, 1941, p. 3.

Central Committee of the Communist party in Germany, whose members were taking refuge in the USSR. Excerpts indicate the strength of feeling: "German workers, are you not ashamed that you have not impeded Hitler in carrying his war against the only socialist state in the world, that you are forging in the factories weapons to be used against the country where the owners are the workers and peasants? Do you not understand that at the same time you are forging the chains of an even worse slavery?" The plea ended with the words: "Soldiers, end the war. Refuse to fight. Workers, hamper the war machine of Hitler with all your strength."

No response came forth. There must have been many Soviet citizens who thought that the policy of their leaders had been vindicated. The USSR had been built into a country that did not have to rely on the revolutionary workers of all the world for its continued existence. No help was rendered by proletarian movements abroad. What help there was came from the great private enterprise countries of the United States and the British Commonwealth.

2. World Revolution Reborn

New Communist World Leadership. The chaos following World War II gave Soviet leaders cause to plan again for world revolution. The situation had changed greatly from the one which had dictated a program of building socialism in one country. The years of retreat were over, during which the emphasis had been placed upon internal Soviet strength. But an organized high command of international revolution was not available to implement a new policy. The Communist International (Comintern) no longer existed. It had been disbanded by vote of its executive committee in 1943, following eight years of relative inactivity.[6]

Elimination of the coordinating agency of world revolution did not mean, however, that there was complete lack of coordination. Many of the men who had staffed the old Comintern remained. With the end of the war, it became possible for most of them to return to their homelands. They took up the leadership of the Communist parties in their countries, and often assumed high positions in the postwar governments. Their parties had won considerable popular support by strong opposition to German occupation. They often had popular appeal in contrast to their unpopularity before the war.

The names of the leaders indicate the new relationship that emerged between political activity in Europe and the old Comintern. Dimitrov, head of the Comintern when it was disbanded, returned to Bulgaria to lead the Fatherland Front. Wilhelm Pieck, who had represented the German Communist party in Moscow for years, went back to Germany. Palmiro Togliatti, active in the Comintern as Ercoli, assumed leadership in Italy. Thorez returned to France. Rakosi appeared again in Hungary. Gottwald, who had

---

[6] Congresses of the Comintern were held in 1919, 1920, 1921, 1922, 1924, 1928, and 1935. No congresses were held from 1935 to the date of dissolution in 1943.

sought refuge in Moscow during the war, took the party reins in Czechoslovakia.

Troublesome Factors. The men who returned to their homelands after
the war had been trained in the same school. They believed in the same
interpretation of Marx. They had studied the successful application of his
political theory in the USSR and had learned techniques. There was little
likelihood of disagreement among them about basic directions for their countrymen to follow. The directions had been drawn in outline by the Comintern in its various programs, the last of which had been published in 1928.[7]
Yet there were some new factors that were to cause them trouble. These
emerged from the necessity of appealing for votes in parliamentary elections
in which the principal competitors of the Communist parties were parties
which also relied upon workmen for support—namely, the Social Democratic parties.

Communist leaders in all lands felt that the Social Democratic parties were
misguided. The Social Democrats argued that socialism might be achieved
through the ballot. They thought it was entirely possible to persuade enough
voters to elect Social Democratic deputies to parliaments in order to secure a
majority for nationalization of the means of production and thus introduce
socialism. Communists were certain that time would prove the impossibility
of voting socialism into existence, because of the strength of opposition still
inherent in the groups that favored the private enterprise system of capitalism.
But time was flying, and with each day recovery moved forward, solidifying
the position of the Social Democratic parties and strengthening even the parties of the center and right who wanted no socialism whatever.

Communist training had been to mold history, while utilizing the trends
in the development of the productive system. In order to mold history, it
was necessary to gain adherents quickly. These could be torn from other
parties only if some of the appeals were those that excited the nationalism of
the voters. It mattered not that Communists did not themselves believe in
such appeals. They had been trained in the Leninist tradition enunciated at
Zimmerwald in 1915 that class loyalty must be above national loyalty. Nevertheless, new votes were to be obtained only by catering to national aspirations. Thus, situation after situation arose in which Communist parties were
driven to support slogans that had no lasting interest for them. Most Italian
workmen would not have understood a party that was willing to let Trieste be
delivered to Yugoslavia. French workmen would not have flocked to a
party that did not support traditional French interest in the Saar and in Germany. Many German workmen would have thought a political party treasonable that agreed to let France have an inch of German soil. Communist
parties found themselves taking positions on these national aims that were in
direct opposition to one another. This situation brought down upon them

---

[7] For an English translation, see *Blueprint for World Conquest* (Human Events, Washington
and Chicago, 1946).

the ridicule of those outsiders who had a chance of studying all the programs.

Birth of the Cominform. In the face of such situations, and in view of the new position of Communist parties in Eastern Europe as the party of the government, a new organization came into being. Delegates from a considerable part of Europe assembled in Poland in 1947 to hear reports on the international situation and proposals of policy direction.[8] There emerged from the meeting the Communist Information Bureau, with headquarters first at Belgrade in Yugoslavia.[9] The new agency, known colloquially as the Cominform, is not as closely knit as was the Comintern. Its rules indicate that the member parties have greater autonomy, but it too is designed for coordination. The rift with Tito indicates that the Soviet Union is a dominating influence in the Cominform. The Cominform has become the new high command of the program of world revolution.

No published statement has appeared since the war to indicate how the program for world revolution is to be pressed. Soviet arms have aided Communist parties in Eastern Europe, yet the program of the former Comintern stressed forces other than marching armies. It called for guidance by the Communist party in developing economic forces and educating workmen to their condition and opportunities, so that they might fight their own revolutions. The Comintern spoke of the recurrence of depressions and mass unemployment in the capitalist world, and predicted that capitalist states would come to war in seeking markets that might permit industry and agriculture to continue at high productive levels and avoid crises. The question has arisen whether the Soviet leadership has changed the basis of its tactics for world revolution since the Comintern program was adopted in the 1920's. Soviet sources have stated no doctrine of world revolution through armed intervention, but events in the Far East have erupted into war, and the USSR has been heavily implicated, although its troops have not appeared on the field of battle. It now seems clear that if native communists can stir up serious local unrest, and if native guerrilla or other military forces can be developed in sufficient strength to have a chance in a civil war, the Soviet Union will be ready to supply military advice and even arms if the area's strategic and political importance warrants it.

3. Soviet Foreign Policy and the Russian Heritage

Window to the West. Concern for the preservation of the country has been a factor in the formulation of policy both by the Tsars and by the Soviet

---

[8] For communiqué, declaration, and resolution of representatives of the Communist parties of Yugoslavia, Bulgaria, Rumania, Hungary, Poland, USSR, France, Czechoslovakia, and Italy, see *Bolshevik*, no. 19 (October 15, 1947). For an English translation of the principal speech, see A. Zhdanov, *The International Situation* (Foreign Languages Publishing House, Moscow, 1947).

[9] The official publication of the Cominform is entitled *For a Lasting Peace and for a People's Democracy*. It is published in English, as well as in the other main languages. After the Cominform rift with Tito of Yugoslavia in 1948, the headquarters of the Cominform were moved to Rumania.

leaders. This concern has been accompanied by a determination to maintain avenues of communication with the world. Historians place great emphasis upon the fact that Russia is a land island—so large that it has been isolated from the influence of other parts of the world, yet unable, like an island in the sea, to maintain easy communication with the outside.

Peter the Great opened his "window on the Baltic" in 1703 by founding the city of St. Petersburg. Wars were fought by him with the Swedes to maintain Russia's approaches to the west and with the Turks to maintain a foothold on the Sea of Azov. His policy was continued by Catherine II in her wars with Turkey during the latter half of the eighteenth century in which she demonstrated her determination to keep open a route through the Black Sea. These drives have remained established policy of the Russians ever since.

Threat of Invasion. Access to the outside world had its counterpart in invasion of Russia. Imperial Russia was the prey of conquerors, the most recent of which were Napoleon and Wilhelm II. Armies swept across her plains from Europe. Russians marched to oppose them, sometimes moving beyond her borders, as when Alexander I made peace in Paris in 1814. The second great invasion of modern times was not met successfully, for the armies of Nicholas II went down to defeat, and the Russian republic was forced into the humiliating peace of Brest Litovsk in 1918.

Invasion did not end with the First World War, for most of the great powers intervened in Russia between 1918 and 1924. Armies entered Russia from the north through Archangel and Murmansk, from the south through Persia and across the Black Sea, from the Far East through Vladivostok and Manchuria, and from the west across the plains of Poland. Russian generals and admirals joined these troops of other countries, for the attack was not upon Russia as such, but upon a political ideology that had become intrenched in Russia.[10]

Resistance was offered to the intervention by many who today are among the leaders of the USSR. Stalin and Voroshilov commanded in the defense of Tsaritzyn, now Stalingrad. The Red Army was born and matured in these conflicts. It seems quite likely that such exasperating experiences have left indelible memories in the minds of Soviet leaders, and are now shared by millions of younger citizens who have fought through the Second World War. Fear of invasion has become a cornerstone of Soviet thinking.

Fear of Insecurity. Some impression of the extent to which Soviet leaders weigh the importance of maintaining routes of access to the outside world and of closing routes of invasion can be gained from Stalin's speech at the time of the Japanese surrender in 1945. Referring to the defeat of imperial Russia by the Japanese in 1905, he said: "As is well known, at that time . . . Japan took advantage of Tsarist Russia's defeat to wrest Southern Sakhalin

---

[10] For accounts of intervention, see William S. Graves, *America's Siberian Adventure, 1918-1920* (New York, 1941); Sir Bernard Pares, *A History of Russia* (3rd ed., New York, 1941).

from Russia, to strengthen her hold over the Kurile Islands, thus locking all outlets to the ocean in the east and consequently also the outlets for our country to the ports of Soviet Kamchatka and the Soviet Sea of Okhotsk."

In considering the prospects for the USSR in the light of its gain of southern Sakhalin and the Kurile Islands, Stalin observed: "They will serve . . . as a means of direct communication of the Soviet Union with the ocean and as a base for the defense of our country against Japanese aggression."

Bulwarks in the East, South, and West. Soviet foreign policy seems to have been directed in the first instance toward guarding the USSR from attack. The Kurile Islands have been acquired. In addition, Korea, the northward path of invasion from Japan, has been blocked at a point sufficiently far south to prevent landings in Vladivostok from the Korean peninsula.[11] Treaties with China have restored the former tsarist naval base of Port Arthur, which protects the USSR from a landing to thrust through Manchuria.[12] The Chinese government has been brought into a treaty pledging combined action with the Soviet Union against any Japanese attack in the future.[13]

The former Chinese province of Outer Mongolia has been recognized by China as independent. As a People's Republic, it has concluded a treaty with the USSR under which mutual defense against aggression is guranteed.[14] Soviet efforts in the Middle East have not been so successful, for Iran has failed to ratify an agreement granting the USSR an oil concession, which the latter probably looked upon as a means of preventing any repetition of the events of 1919, when the British moved into the Transcaucasian regions. The Soviet Union has not ceased trying to safeguard this portal. The same may be said of Soviet policy toward Turkey. The enemy of the Tsars has remained the enemy of the USSR. Repeated Soviet notes have demanded a position in control of the Straits and even the right to a fortress to guarantee that position.

The Black Sea countries of Bulgaria and Rumania have come within the Soviet security system under treaties of mutual assistance.[15] Their loyalty to the USSR has been made more secure by the coming to power of the Com-

---

[11] Soviet troops accepted the surrender of Japanese troops north of the 38th parallel. See *Department of State Bulletin,* 13 (1945), 812. The Korean intervention of Chinese communists in 1950-51 appears to have been an attempt to push the bulwark southward, perhaps with the hope that Korea might serve as a center for Far Eastern communist activity.

[12] For the texts, see *ibid.,* 14 (1946), 282; as for Communist China, see treaty of February 14, 1950.

[13] Treaty of August 14, 1945; see *ibid.,* 14 (1946), 201; as for Communist China, see treaty of February 14, 1950.

[14] Treaty of Friendship and Mutual Assistance, dated February 27, 1946. For the text in English translation, see *ibid.,* 14 (1946), 968. The treaty constituted an extension for ten years of the Protocol of Agreement between the USSR and the Mongolian People's Republic, dated March 12, 1936, which expired in 1946. For the text in English translation, see Harriet L. Moore, *Soviet Far Eastern Policy, 1931-1945* (Princeton, 1945), p. 185.

[15] For an account of the postwar treaties between the USSR and Bulgaria and Rumania, see *Department of State Bulletin,* 15 (1946), 392.

munist party within each country.   Depth has been added to this position
by similar events in Albania, Yugoslavia, Hungary, and Czechoslovakia.[16]
Poland's policies have also been coordinated with those of the Soviet Union.
The principal plank of her foreign policy has been the maintenance of
friendly relations with the USSR.   The Baltic republics have become union
republics of the USSR itself.   Only Finland has lagged behind, but by a peace
treaty, close economic ties, and a mutual assistance pact, she is bound to stay
outside any coalition against the USSR.

Policy toward Germany.   The division of Germany after the war presented several possibilities to Soviet leaders.   Most of East Prussia, once a
bastion of the Junker class, was occupied and made an integral part of the
USSR.   The remainder of East Prussia was turned over to Poland.   With
Soviet support, Poland has also obtained a large segment of eastern Germany
in which lay much of German industrial strength and natural resources.
Most of the German population has been expelled.

Policy in the zone of Germany occupied by the Soviet Union seems to have
been the product of two inevitably conflicting motives: winning friends to
the Soviet way of life and obtaining economic resources needed for reconstruction at home.   The winning of friends has been attempted by support of
the trade unions, and by programs that have gained sympathy of workmen
and peasants elsewhere in Eastern Europe—expropriation of estates and industrial plants.   At the same time the USSR has indicated its serious need
for German resources by combining the factories claimed as reparations into
a familiar pattern of industrial corporations, and by pressing for maximum
production regardless of the cost in good will among the Germans who work
in them.

Soviet policy in occupied Germany as a whole has varied with conditions,
but there is probably a hard core.   The aim has seemed to be to prevent Germany's ever rising again to attack the USSR, either as an independent power
or as a member of a coalition of other powers.   When it has looked to Soviet
eyes as if western Germany would remain hostile and subject to the influence
of other powers, the USSR has closed the zonal frontiers and fought to prevent the other powers from unifying Germany in opposition to the USSR.
At the same time, the Soviet Union has tried to keep open the door for a
united Germany at some future time, if union seems possible on a basis advantageous to the USSR.   Thus, Soviet policy has remained fluid.

Participation in International Bodies.   Soviet participation in international
organizations has evidenced some of the same aims.[17]   The USSR has shown

---

[16] Examples of the treaties of mutual assistance which the USSR has signed with the states
of Eastern Europe are those with Yugoslavia and Poland.   For an English translation of the
Yugoslav treaty, see *American Review on the Soviet Union,* 7 (May, 1946), 80.

[17] For an account of the record during the formative months, see John N. Hazard, "The
Soviet Union and the United Nations," *Yale Law Journal,* 55 (1946), 1016 ff.   For the Soviet
attitude on one of the issues of long-term concern, see John N. Hazard, "The Soviet Union
and a World Bill of Rights," *Columbia Law Review,* 47 (1947), 1095 ff.

a determination not to permit any of the international agencies to take action that might be interpreted as an entering wedge into the Soviet belt of national security. Since Marxists have always felt that political power rests upon economic power, Soviet opposition has extended to the area of economic plans as well as to that of political plans. The USSR has been active in the affairs of the United Nations, but has consistently opposed any move that might subject her to action of a hostile majority. In consequence, Soviet use of the veto in the United Nations has become increasingly frequent.

Soviet fear of Western antagonism is deeply rooted. Clemenceau tried to build a strangulating *cordon sanitaire* around the Russian republic after the First World War. Within a generation Hitler rushed into a crusade against Bolshevism. Soviet leaders expect the cry of the crusader to be raised again, especially as the example of Marxist socialism is followed by other European countries, and in Asia as well.

For outsiders Soviet motives are hard to analyze. Current events can be interpreted as indicating either a Soviet desire to maintain a security belt or to provide theaters to stage eventually a large-scale expansion by military means. Few students of Marxism expect the Soviet Union to resort to warfare as long as its leaders remain convinced of the effectiveness of the Marxist formula for spreading revolution. But no one knows how strongly historic Russian urges toward expansion may have taken hold in the minds of Soviet leaders and how far temptation to rush events by war may sway decisions. Whatever the motives, the USSR has determined to maintain a powerful state at home. It is this determination that has presented some basic difficulties in political theory, and also has reflected upon Soviet domestic policy.

4. State Power and Classless Society

Establishment of Socialism. The federal constitution of 1936 declared at the outset that the Union was a socialist state. This was not the first time socialism had been proclaimed. The first federal constitution had spoken in its preamble of the "camp of socialism." The constitution of the RSFSR in its form of 1925 had said the same thing. Yet everyone knew that the constitutions of the early 1920's were stating only objectives, not achievement, for the NEP was at its height. There were many elements of private enterprise and capitalism in the country.

The constitution of 1936 had been drafted in accordance with a resolution of the Seventh Congress of Soviets of the USSR in 1935, calling for a reflection of the existing class relationships created by the emergence of a new socialist industry, the elimination of the kulaks, the victory of the system of collective farming, and the acceptance of socialist property as the basis of Soviet society. In the minds of Soviet leaders, socialism had been achieved. The first constitution of the RSFSR of 1918 had said that the basic task was the "establishment of socialism, under which there would be no division into classes, no state." Soviet leaders heralded the achievement of the goals by 1936—classless society and socialism. Yet there remained compulsion, the police, the courts, criminal law, legal sanctions in civil law, and the Army. These were elements which Engels had characterized as the "state." They were the apparatus of coercion, which he had predicted would "wither away" when the classless society was achieved.

End of the State? The situation clearly required consideration. There was an apparent conflict between policy as stated by Engels and the contemporary fact. The problem required consideration not only by the Soviet leadership, but also by those students who have sought to estimate the future course of the USSR. Varying opinions appeared among Soviet political theorists. Some thought that with the achievement of a classless society and socialism, it was time to find manifestations of the withering away of the state, which Engels had foretold in his *Anti-Dühring*.[18] He had declared the goal, but he had left open the question of the means and time of the disappearance of the state. He had written in general terms: "The government of persons is replaced by the administration of things and the direction of the process of production. The state is not 'abolished.' It withers away."

Lenin had also spoken in general terms on this subject. Some of his statements[19] seemed to imply a gradual process of disappearance. Thus, "The expression 'the state withers away' is very well chosen, for it indicates both the gradual and spontaneous nature of the process." Also, "There can be no question of the exact moment of the future withering away—the more so since it must obviously be a rather lengthy process."[20] There was another statement of Lenin's[21] that indicated that the process would not be so gradual. On the "axiom" of the revolutionary dictatorship of the proletariat during the transition period between capitalism and communism, he said: "Up to now the axiom has never been disputed by socialists, and yet it implies the recognition of the state right up to the time when victorious socialism will have grown into complete communism."

Two alternative views were developed as to how the process of withering away would occur. One of them was Stalin's. The other was associated with Bukharin, who believed that the withering away would occur progressively during the transitional period, with the army disappearing first of all. The influence of the latter approach was strong on the jurists who concerned themselves with the development and administration of law. They felt that law as an instrument of compulsion would begin to disappear soon after the

---

[18] See Friedrich Engels, *Herr Eugen Dühring's Revolution in Science* (English trans., Moscow, 1934), pp. 314-15.

[19] V. I. Lenin, *The State and Revolution* (special ed., New York, 1932), chap. 5, sec. 2, pp. 74 ff.

[20] *Ibid.*, chap. 5, sec. 1.

[21] See quotation in footnote, Karl Marx, *Critique of the Gotha Programme* (English trans., Moscow, 1937), p. 28.

revolution. They expected administrative rules for a socialist economy to emerge as a matter of greatest importance, in accordance with Engel's statement that government would give way to the administration of things.

Stalin's View. The jurists put their theory into practice by drafting a statement of general principles to be used by judges in dealing with criminals who broke the rules of society. This statement was expected to replace the criminal codes in effect in each republic, with their detailed definition of specific crimes and allocation of specific penalties. The new draft was not enacted to replace the codes, but it had great influence and caused provisions of the codes to be ignored. The jurists likewise stopped paying much attention to the civil code, as a relic of bourgeois society that was of but passing interest; thus they undermined respect for the code and strict observance of its articles.

A remark was made by Stalin in his report to the Sixteenth Party Congress in 1930 that was destined to have great importance in the resolution of the problem of the withering away of the state. Stalin there was pointing out that at this stage the party favored extensive development of national cultures so that ultimately there might be a unification of cultures. He illustrated his thought with the following comment on the withering away of the state: "We are in favor of the state dying out and at the same time we stand for the strengthening of the dictatorship of the proletariat, which represents the most powerful and mighty authority of all forms of state which have existed up to the present day. The highest possible development of the power of the state, with the object of preparing the conditions for the dying out of the state—that is the Marxist formula. Is it 'contradictory'? Yes, it is 'contradictory.' But this contradiction is a living thing and completely reflects Marxist dialectics." [22]

Bukharin's school of thought continued to be popular, especially among the jurists. Stalin's statement, though the complete negation of Bukharin's view, went unnoticed for a time. Instead of assuming that the state would soon die out gradually, Stalin expected it to become even stronger before it ceased to exist. He felt this interpretation to be in harmony with Marxist dialectics.

Settlement of the Issue. Stalin's thesis seems to have been overlooked by the jurists until 1937. Then they were sharply criticized for having failed to note two elements—(1) that the USSR as a socialist state was daily threatened by the capitalist states, headed by Hitler's Germany; and (2) that there were still differences between agricultural work and industrial work even though classes had been eliminated. There was a third element that argued against the Bukharin school of thought; private ownership of consumption goods was still to play a main role in raising the level of production as required by Soviet programs. The best citizens had come to be those

---

[22] Joseph Stalin, "Report to the XVI Party Congress (1930)," *Leninism* (English trans., Moscow, 1934), II, 342.

who contributed most to production. One of the inducements to maximum production was the differentiated wage scale of "socialist competition." Those who produced the most for society were paid most. If this income was to be of value, it had to be protected, and also the property acquired with it. The civil code had the function of regulating the use of property, and the criminal code of protecting it.

The constitution of 1936 emphasized this consideration by guaranteeing personal ownership of income from work, savings, dwellings, subsidiary household economies, household furniture, and articles of personal use and convenience. It guaranteed also the right of inheritance. It was clear that law was to play an important part in society. Those who had thought otherwise were removed from their posts. Stalin's thought of 1930 became the policy of the land.

Questions arose as to what the function of the state in a socialist society should be. Stalin reported on this subject to the Eighteenth Party Congress in May 1939. He pointed out that death in 1924 had prevented Lenin from enlarging upon his *State and Revolution* to develop the theory of the state on the basis of Soviet experience. Stalin went on to say that "what Lenin did not manage to do should be done by his disciples." He then reviewed the experience of the past to reach the following conclusion: "The state acquired the function of protecting socialist property from thieves and pilferers. The function of defending the country from foreign attack fully remained; consequently, the Red Army and Navy also fully remained, and the punitive organs and the intelligence service, which are indispensable for the detection and punishment of the spies, assassins, and wreckers sent into our country by foreign espionage services. The function of economic organization and cultural education by the state organs also remained, and was developed to the full. Now the main task of our state inside the country is the work of peaceful economic organization and cultural education. As for our army, punitive organs, and intelligence service, this edge is no longer turned to the inside of the country but to the outside, against external enemies." [23]

State and Communism. One further question was raised. If socialism could be and had been developed in one country, and if the state as an apparatus of compulsion were to exist under socialism, what was to be the future of the state once communism had been achieved, and could communism be achieved by one country?

Stalin responded to this question by saying that the answer depended upon the conditions to be found in the world. In his words: "We are going ahead towards communism. Will our state remain in the period of communism also? Yes, it will, unless the capitalist encirclement is liquidated and unless the danger of foreign military attack has disappeared. Naturally, of course,

---

[23] Joseph Stalin, "Report to the XVIII Party Congress," *Leninism* (English trans., New York, 1942), p. 474.

the forms of our state will again change in conformity with the change in the situation at home and abroad. No, it will not remain and will atrophy if the capitalist encirclement is liquidated and a socialist encirclement takes its place." [24]

The factor which determines whether the state remains under communism seems to be the future of the dominant capitalist economies. It is unlikely that Soviet leaders at the time of Stalin's report in 1939 believed the "capitalist encirclement" to end in the immediately foreseeable future.

[24] *Ibid.*

CHAPTER 26

VARIATIONS ON THE SOVIET THEME: DANUBIAN GOVERNMENTS

1. Trends and Problems

Shadow of the Soviet Union. The end of military operations in World War II did not bring either temporary truce or permanent peace to the small nations in Danubian Europe. Largely as a disturbing heritage of the war, the six countries of the Danube valley are torn today by serious political dissensions and deep-seated economic problems. Internally they have persisted in the unhappy state of a "frozen" civil war. In foreign affairs their principal worry is how much they will be affected by the clash between the Soviet Union and the Western world. This feeling of internal instability and external insecurity has induced them to resort to a strange assortment of political devices. In the domestic field one finds that constant intimidation, frequent violence, and occasional assassinations are widely recognized means of governmental action, whereas internationally "good neighbor" policies appear merely as infrequent and individual exceptions.

A main complicating factor has been the continued presence of Soviet occupation troops and officials. At least four of the recent national elections in the Danube valley have been held in countries partly or wholly occupied by the Soviet Union—namely, Austria, Hungary, Rumania, and Bulgaria. Soviet troops also occupied Yugoslavia and Czechoslovakia for several months, but had left before the voting took place and a more or less stable postwar government was formed. Although no Danubian country actually witnessed a setback of the Communist party, it is certain that the Communists would have a considerably stronger popular following in Austria and Hungary had those two been evacuated by the Russians. Until the outside pressure grew unbearably strong and resistance became impossible, Hungary in particular seemed anxious to rely on a rather conservative government. The comparatively "free and unfettered" elections of November 1945 expressed a serious dissatisfaction with the occupation practices of the Red Army and Soviet officials.

On the whole, postwar political development in Central-Eastern Europe has taken three forms. The two extremes are marked by evolutionary and revolutionary types of government; more recently a transitional form has emerged. Revolutionary methods were most thoroughly adopted by Yugoslavia and Bulgaria, and evolutionary development has characterized the

522

first two years of postwar Czech politics. Hungary and Rumania are in a transition stage, with their political life and government increasingly exposed to the overwhelming pressure of the occupying power. In these two countries the far-reaching changes so characteristic of other governments of the area are being carried out slowly, by surgical operations of growing seriousness, until eventually both countries will fit in with the general pattern of present-day Eastern Europe.

Similarities of Development. Revolutionary methods have taken the form of unusual political processes applied to individual governments through generous use of tangible and intangible coercion and incentives, particularly through the substantial backing of the Soviet Union. The results are well known and obvious. The "monolithic" one-party state appears, controlled by a Communist majority or, in exceptional cases, even a minority. Political power is exercised by the party hierarchy, and seemingly all-inclusive popular fronts are formed to take charge of every aspect of national life. The revolutionary methods originally used to assume power are next conveniently obscured or hastily legalized. Government by party monopoly then enters its full postwar bloom. The few countries of an evolutionary type of political development stand in strong contrast. Here one notes the emergence of fairly liberal provisional groups, which are succeeded by governments chosen through meaningful elections, freely participated in by most democratic elements. Unhappily for Central-Eastern Europe, this form of political progress is almost extinct at present, although of great interest to the student of politics.

The fabric of the three basic patterns is complicated by the diversity of political terminology. In Hungary the Smallholders party wielded the balance of parliamentary power for a period of two years, and in Czechoslovakia the National Socialists long remained vocal in governmental matters. In Yugoslavia Tito's followers belong to the People's Front; in Bulgaria the Fatherland Front is in absolute control; in Albania the Democratic Front party rules; and in Rumania the Plowmen's Front, led by a former capitalist, wealthy Petru Groza, scored a resounding victory in abolishing the monarchy and establishing a people's republic. The various governmental patterns and political "fronts" display a considerable measure of similarity. An interesting difference lies in the ideological intensity, the political coloring of individual countries. As one moves toward the east and south of the European continent, this color gets steadily clearer, more and more pronounced, until it finally assumes an obvious "crimson hue."

Impact of Power Politics. Because of the many similar features, none of them entirely superficial, observers of the Danubian area are prone to oversimplify the political picture. One attractive cliché refers to Soviet communism in six guises, to the endless and dull repetition of a single uniformity throughout Eastern Europe. Actually, Danubian Europe is an area characterized by complex political forces and deep historical contrasts. The contrasts are further aggravated by the widely divergent policies and objectives that guide the Big Two—the United States and the Soviet Union.

American foreign policy toward Danubian Europe progressed through two distinct phases of development. There cannot be much doubt about the fundamental benevolence of American policy as it unfolded during the first three years after World War II. The most significant illustration was the wholesale release by the United States of some 600 river boats, vital to the Danube trade of their owners in Czechoslovakia, Hungary, and Yugo-slavia. American occupation authorities also returned the gold reserves of Austria and Hungary, thus contributing to an essential stabilization of the currency in the two countries. Furthermore, at the Paris peace con-ference of 1946 the United States insisted that a general clause be inserted in the peace treaties for Eastern Europe, containing definite guarantees that all nations would have equal trading rights on the Danube. Follow-ing the Czechoslovakian *coup d'état* of February 1948, the second phase of American diplomacy expressed itself in a systematic disapproval and vig-orous denunciation of the new Eastern European "people's democracies." This policy was forcefully documented by a refusal to sign trade agreements with Soviet satellites, by protests against the persecution of church digni-taries, and by energetic negotiations in the case of American citizens illegally imprisoned by Eastern European governments. In general, the United States clearly emphasized its determination to counteract the spread of Sta-linist Communism by all available diplomatic means short of war.

Soviet policies, on the other hand, have consistently been guided by three major objectives. The first is to prevent use of the Danubian states as po-tential bases for aggression against Soviet territory. This negative point leads to the further policy of destroying the former ruling classes as dan-gerous forces that might be harmful to Soviet security. Such class destruc-tion was in many cases promoted by long-delayed social reforms, like land redistribution and the encouragement of organized labor. In addition, the Soviet government demands that its people be compensated for the military and economic ravages of World War II at the expense of the countries of Central-Eastern Europe. It is clear by now that the resources of this region are largely used to aid in the postwar recovery of the Soviet Union.

Characteristics of the Danubian Area. In view of its new function as a Soviet security zone toward the west, the Danubian area, comprising over 300,000 square miles, assumes great strategic importance. It is geographi-cally centered around the Danube river, which flows over 1,800 miles from the Black Forest in southwestern Germany to the Black Sea. The upper reaches of the Danube are in Bavaria, the rich agricultural region of south-ern Germany; 250 miles from its source the river enters Austria, the eastern-most outpost of Anglo-American influence. From then on it cuts across areas in the Soviet orbit—Czechoslovakia, Hungary, Yugoslavia, Bulgaria, Rumania, and a strip of the Soviet Ukraine.

The river, in normal times one of the busiest trade routes of continental Europe, is a vital economic factor in the lives of about 75 million people. Political boundaries break up the unity of the Danube valley proper; the six states were formerly parts of the Turkish and Hapsburg Empires. Austria is the smallest, both in area and population. Czechoslovakia's 50,000 square miles hold about 13 million people. Hungary spreads over an area of 35,900 square miles and has a population of almost 9 million. Yugoslavia's area is 96,000 square miles, and her population 15,700,000. Located at the lower end of the Danube, Bulgaria has an area of 42,800 square miles and a population equal to Hungary's. Rumania, with an area of 91,900 square miles, is the most populous; her people were estimated in 1951 at 16 million.

2. Czechoslovakia

A Hopeful Beginning. Politically, a predictable and planned development characterized Czechoslovakia's early postwar reconstruction. In a Danubian Europe full of bitter ideological strife, Czechoslovakia served as the prototype of evolutionary political progress. There were no occupation troops in this country except for a short period, and the notorious manifestations of big-power pressure had to enter from the outside. A moderate form of internal political independence helped Czechoslovakia to achieve temporarily a large degree of stability, which was further enhanced by the fortunate coincidence that, practically alone of all formerly enemy-occupied countries, there was no profound cleavage here between the resistance movement at home and the legally constituted government in exile abroad.

The enthusiasm with which the returning government was received in Prague best displayed the fundamental unity of Czech politics. The non-partisan and unanimous endorsement of Eduard Benes as President of the postwar republic further accentuated the absence of serious political disagreements and the Czechs' natural tendency toward coalition and compromise. The first wave of postwar enthusiasm thus produced conditions of political stability that made for rapid reconstruction under auspices of a constitutional democracy soon to come to an end.

Stature of the President. The Czechoslovakian Republic was a parliamentary state based on constitutional development. The postwar republic reverted to its condition of 1920, when the first Czech constituent assembly successfully completed the arduous task of constitution-making. The document of 1920 was modified in only a few details. The highest governmental and executive power was again shared by two organs, the President of the Republic and a Cabinet appointed by the President and responsible to Parliament. Legislative power was vested in the two houses of Parliament. The broad authority of the Chamber of Deputies and the Senate bore out clearly the legislative supremacy and the monopoly of lawmaking by Parliament as the foundation stones of the reign of justice contemplated by the constitution.

Yet the President's powers were so impressive that Czechoslovakia actually displayed an admixture of presidential government.[1] The head of the state came to enjoy authority within five different but equally significant spheres of government. In international relations the President represented his country in all negotiations with other states. He concluded and ratified international treaties, with the exception of certain military or territorial arrangements that could be carried out only with the consent of Parliament. The President declared the existence of a state of war, but had to submit peace terms to Parliament for its approval. In matters of civil administration, he possessed broad powers. He appointed and dismissed the Prime Minister and members of the Cabinet, university professors, and higher civil servants; and he had jurisdiction over the entire civil service. In the military sphere, the President was Commander-in-Chief of all the armed forces of the Republic. In the legislative realm, he was empowered to dissolve Parliament. He had the further right to call extraordinary sessions if he deemed it necessary. He also had a limited suspensory veto of legislation. In the judicial sphere, the President was empowered to appoint all higher judges, acting on the proposal of the Cabinet. He could grant pardons in penal and disciplinary cases.

The President was elected for seven years by a joint session of both houses of Parliament. The fundamental stability of Czechoslovakia is revealed by the fact that throughout her existence as a republic the country had only two presidents, Thomas G. Masaryk (1920-35) and Eduard Benes (1935-48). The outstanding personality and character of these two men lent the presidency a special—almost supraconstitutional—significance, which was of inestimable value in setting the course of domestic politics in the turbulent years of the past decades.

Cabinet Responsibility. The Cabinet was closely connected with the presidency in every phase of the government. According to the constitution, the Cabinet exercised all executive powers except those expressly reserved for the President. Its authority explained the insistence of Czechoslovakia's

---

[1] Cf. M. W. Graham, "Constitutional and Political Structure," in R. J. Kerner, ed., *Czechoslovakia: Twenty Years of Independence* (Berkeley, 1940), chap. 7, 119 ff. In the general field of recent Danubian political developments, material is scattered and not always adequate. Several excellent British publications seem to be the main exceptions. Hugh Seton-Watson's *Eastern Europe Between the Wars, 1918-1941* (Cambridge, 1946) and his *East European Revolution* (London, 1950) are first-rate surveys. Among recent reference works published by the Royal Institute of International Affairs, *Central and South-East Europe, 1945-1948*, edited by R. R. Betts, and a document collection entitled *The Soviet-Yugoslav Dispute* (London, 1948) are valuable. On specialized aspects of Eastern European politics, cf. M. Dewar's *Soviet Trade With Eastern Europe, 1945-1949* (London, 1951), F. Dvornik's *The Making of Central and Eastern Europe* (London, 1949), and Fitzroy Maclean's *Eastern Approaches* (London, 1949). In the American bibliography of Titoism, Hamilton Fish Armstrong's *Tito and Goliath* (New York, 1951) and Josef Korbel's *Tito's Communism* (Denver, 1951) are recent and noteworthy. For general discussions of the postwar politics of Central-Eastern Europe, cf. *Soviet Satellites* (University of Notre Dame Press, 1949) and Andrew Gyorgy, *Governments of Danubian Europe* (New York, 1949).

present-day Communist party on appropriating for itself as large a number of ministerial seats as was possible within the framework of the early coalition.

The Cabinet had two distinctive powers: the right to initiate legislation and the authority to issue decrees. The legislative initiative of Cabinet ministers did not completely bypass the President; for, as a matter of practice, all government bills were brought before the President for his consideration. This procedure helped to limit the use of the presidential veto to extreme and unusual cases.

The government's decree power was distinctly limited. Under the constitution of 1920, decrees could only be issued for the execution of a specific statute, and then only within the framework of that statute. Even so, as one author rightly observed, "the absolute predominance of the Cabinet over the President in this important sphere of governmental powers naturally greatly strengthened the position of the Cabinet." [2]

Bicameralism. The Czech constitution was based on a division of political functions. The legislative branch occupied a coequal position with regard to the executive. The bicameral legislature was called the National Assembly, with legislative primacy accorded the lower house. In all budgetary and financial matters, for example, the Chamber of Deputies had exclusive right to final legislation. The Senate was intended in the main to furnish fuller deliberation.

One of the real differences between the two bodies derived from the age qualifications for membership, the minimum set for the Chamber being thirty years, whereas the senators were to be at least forty-five. To the difference in age was added that of size, the Chamber having a membership of 300 against the Senate's 150. Owing to these differences, the weight of parliamentary power lay in the Chamber, which was the scene of compromise and conflict throughout the early postwar years.

Postwar Political Parties. The political parties of Czechoslovakia tested their vitality in May 1946, in the country's first election after liberation. Most of the bewildering party divisions of the prewar era had disappeared. The number of competing political parties was sharply reduced, as a result of agreements among the party leaders and the strong denunciation of the former system by President Benes. In his widely read *Democracy Today and Tomorrow,* Benes criticized the evils resulting from an excessive number of parties and urged their reduction as "a manifestation of real patriotic statesmanship." Consequently, a compromise was devised, and a rather oversimplified division of left and right parties established, with a center group to hold the precarious balance of political power. The four most important national parties thus recognized were the Social Democrats, the National Socialists, the People's party, and the Communists.

---

[2] Edward Táborsky, *Czechoslovak Democracy at Work* (London, 1945), p. 26.

The most significant move was the authorization granted to eight separate parties to participate in the elections. Because of the political bitterness and open animosity between the Czech areas proper and Slovakia, these official permissions were carefully distributed between four Czech and four Slovak parties that were cleared of the taint of collaboration with German occupation authorities. In general, a far-reaching disfranchisement of collaborators took place; for example, the entire Agrarian party, from which so many prominent statesmen and prime ministers had come, was banned along with the more notorious Hlinka party, the National Democrats, the fascist Stribrny, and various local German and Magyar minority parties. The thorough process of political cleansing was justified by the particular significance of the first postwar elections. The interim government of the country, which had just returned from several years of exile in London, felt that every step leading toward the renewal of a formal legal order would have to be carefully safeguarded.

The chief hope of Benes' liberal-minded government was based on Communist abstinence in 1945. The Communists did not take the country in their hands, although they probably could have. The survival of Czechoslovakian democracy appeared again more dependent on the international situation than on domestic issues. Following the withdrawal of the Red Army, completed by December 1945, a feeling of hope and confidence pervaded Czech public opinion. The wave of optimism was further enhanced by a formal interparty agreement stipulating that Benes resume his prewar constitutional position as President of the Republic.

Communist Victory and Strategy. As a result of the elections of May 1946, in which the Communist party gained about 36 per cent of the total vote, a tightly disciplined Communist nucleus succeeded in replacing the Cabinet of the colorless Socialist fellow-traveler, Zdenek Fierlinger. The Communist prewar leader Klement Gottwald assumed the Prime Minister's position, and under his aggressive direction the party gained stronger representation in the government than even its high percentage of votes originally warranted. In addition to the prime ministership, the Communists by 1947 had acquired all the portfolios dealing with the economic bases and the general control of reconstruction, with the exception of foreign trade. Communist ministers were in charge of public information, finance, agriculture, international trade, social welfare, the interior, and national defense. Although the head of the Foreign Office had been usually a nonparty appointment, the candidacy of Jan Masaryk was strongly supported by the Communists, who also managed to apply direct pressure on him by insisting on a Communist under-secretary under him. In keeping with the coalition character of the four-party government, the remaining three groups were still given a fairly liberal representation in the Cabinet. The National Socialists held the ministries dealing with education, justice, and foreign trade, whereas the extreme left wing of the Social Democrats, the party that had lost most conspicuously since prewar days, retained the portfolios of industry and food. The latter were entrusted to the Social Democrats merely for the purposes of immediate political expediency, and thus involved a short-lived compromise arrangement.

A period of temporary truce reached its end by the latter part of 1947, bringing with it a remarkable stiffening of the Communist party's attitude and a gradual abandonment of the restrained and cautious tactics, which had been so unusual in Danubian politics. In spite—or because—of tougher partisan methods and increased pressure from the Soviet Union, the Communists appeared to grow weaker in Czechoslovakia than they had been in the summer of 1946. The new phase of political strategy caused violent reactions even within the Communist party, whose democratic elements suddenly realized that they were the "displaced persons" of an undemocratic movement. Prime Minister Gottwald was forced to acknowledge the difficulties his party had encountered. He stated that reaction was at work within the entire National Front, attacking particularly three governmental key organs —police, agriculture, and public information. According to Gottwald, the results of national reconstruction were wholly unsatisfactory because of the political atmosphere prevailing within the coalition itself.

Simultaneously, Communist circles expressed the hope that the party would be able to strengthen its status in certain pivotal provinces and areas of obvious ideological resistance. As a primary step they advocated the necessity of winning an absolute majority at the next elections, in the interests of the Czech people and state. In the Prime Minister's words: "The crux of the Communist struggle for a majority lies in the country, where the farmers must be won over." From the party's viewpoint, Slovakia was the weakest point of the Republic. The Communists' most obvious target was the Slovak Democratic party, which in May 1946 succeeded in obtaining 62 per cent of the vote against the Communists. With a majority of Catholic and conservative peasants, the area dominated by the party had to be strongly regimented if the position of the Communists were to be ensured. Throughout 1947 the Communist party made public accusations of high treason and of subversive activities with regard to those Slovaks abroad who had favored the Hitler-created independent Slovakia and opposed the reestablishment of the united nation. The Communists thus "hoped to isolate the Slovak Democratic party from the other non-Communist Czech parties, which had never had great sympathy for the rather loose Slovak conception of state unity."[3] A pattern of arrests, purges, plots, and trials unfolded in Slovakia, clearly setting the stage in this crucial area for a Communist-inspired "revolution from above."

Communist Seizure of Power. The foundations of Czechoslovak democ-

---

[3] Ivo Duchacek, "The February Coup in Czechoslovakia," *World Politics,* 3 (1950), 518 ff. On theoretical disagreements between Czechs and Slovaks, cf. Vladimir Clementis, *Panslavism, Past and Present* (London, 1943).

racy were abruptly destroyed in February 1948. The Communist party took over complete control in a violent but speedy *coup d'état*. The delicate equilibrium of the governmental coalition was decisively upset when all but Communist ministers were forced to resign. A new Cabinet was formed, still under the leadership of Klement Gottwald, but including only prominent Communists and sympathizers. Purges conducted by the Minister of the Interior, Vaclav Nosek, effectively weakened the two principal political parties opposing all-out Communist rule—the National Socialists and the People's party. These two historic parties and the formerly powerful Slovak Democrats were practically eliminated from the scene of domestic politics.

President Benes hesitated for several crucial days before sanctioning these changes, which transformed his country into a full-fledged Communist state. Under increasing pressure he finally approved of the new Cabinet; the President, Prime Minister Gottwald stated, "did not arrive at his decision easily, but had to accept the will of the people." The Social Democrats had to enter into all-out cooperation with the Communists. Promising blind obedience, most of their leaders voted for a merger with the Communist party. Led by treacherous Fierlinger, the Social Democrats sanctioned the suicide of their own party on April 18, 1948.

Two important factors seem to have precipitated the Czech crisis. The main challenge was the Marshall Plan for European reconstruction, which gave the Communist parties under direct Soviet protection an incentive to accelerate the drive toward complete consolidation. The other motivating force was an impending general election. The Czech Communists were faced with the possibility of losing prestige and parliamentary strength. They had to move rapidly to destroy the constitutional frame of Czech postwar democracy. In staging the *coup* of February 1948, they served their own ends but erased Czechoslovakia's familiar political physiognomy. When a Communist-designed constitution replaced that of 1920, President Benes refused to sign the new document. He resigned in May 1948 and died shortly thereafter. By unanimous vote of Parliament, Klement Gottwald was chosen Benes' successor as third President of Czechoslovakia. Gottwald, in turn, was followed by Antonin Zapotocky, powerful leader of the national trade-union organization, who assumed the Prime Minister's position in June 1948.

Early Economic Recovery and Economic Plans. Czechoslovakia's Two Year Plan was one of the most important Danubian variations of recent Soviet Five Year Plans. Officially introduced January 1, 1947, it is a blueprint for economic planning designed to bring about the country's industrial recovery. Fulfillment of the plan calls for raising the level of industrial production to 110 per cent of the standard of 1937. The project is built around three main goals. The most significant of these is increased economic productivity through nationalization of industries, whereas another aim is the thorough modernization of equipment and improvement of labor conditions. Finally, tight control and revision of the country's entire foreign trade structure is embodied in the plan, with import regulation of essential raw materials and export subsidies of manufactured goods. This control is inevitable if Czechoslovakia is to maintain her position in the world markets. The country's ability to increase production, or even to maintain it at present levels, depends on being able to buy the raw materials and semifinished products that normally comprise more than 60 per cent of total imports. Such imports, in turn, depend on ability to export above the prewar level in a country that suffered six years of continued enemy occupation and lost about 30 per cent of its highly skilled industrial workers. To counteract these initial difficulties, an elaborate administrative machinery was established. Three members of the Cabinet were granted sweeping authority to mobilize management, capital, and labor in an all-out effort toward recovery. The Ministers of Commerce, Finance, and Foreign Trade were thus given joint responsibility for carrying out the plan and for coordinating its various phases. Following the Soviet pattern, a State Planning Office was set up to take charge of the actual planning business, and a State Office of Statistics was organized to collate information on results and progress of the plan.

The success or failure of this process was tied in with the extent of industrial nationalization. The Two Year Plan envisaged the eventual nationalization of 70 per cent or more of Czechoslovakia's economy, with industrial councils—made up of representatives of government, labor, and management —controlling the distribution of raw materials and manpower in each branch of industry. Nationalization was drastically extended by the Five Year Plan announced in October 1948. Soviet influence asserted itself in every major provision of the new plan, which stresses the development of the steel, chemical, and electrical industries. Large new plants are to be erected throughout Czechoslovakia, such as the steel works at Moravska Ostrava, a powerful chemical combine for coal distillation, synthetic oil plants, and four important new electric power stations. In general the accent is on accelerated development of heavy industries, at the expense of the well-developed and highly specialized consumers industries. Along with neighboring Poland, Czechoslovakia now seems to serve the purpose of a satellite workshop aiding Soviet heavy industry.

Foreign Orientation. Considering the interwar record of Western powers and the dangerous aggressiveness of neighboring Germany, Czechoslovakia had chosen the Soviet Union as her most reliable ally. In the Kosice Program of 1945, and again in later conferences, the four coalition parties agreed on one fundamental principle of diplomacy—the vital necessity of close cooperation with the USSR. For the Czechs, the Soviet Union is not a power whose vast dominion lies largely outside Europe, but a partner-nation that has committed itself to the defense of a new European system east of the Rhine. This conviction and the desire to participate in a Russian-inspired, preferably Slavic, bloc proved early to be the greatest obstacle to satisfactory relations with the West. The country's liberation by the Soviet Army, rather than by General Patton's forces, caused Czechoslovakia to adapt her policy to the Soviet Union. When the war ended, the United States was committed, mainly through its active participation in UNRRA, to assist in the rehabilitation of the newly liberated, war-devastated countries. The initial phase of American policy aimed at securing faithful observance of the Yalta agreement, guaranteeing democratic governments and free elections in Eastern Central Europe. Although this strategy was not so complete a failure in Czechoslovakia as in neighboring Poland, Hungary, and Rumania, American diplomats at Prague proved powerless to combat the insistent political maneuvering of the Communist party. For Czechoslovakia the Marshall Plan developed into a test case. A country that was not allowed to participate in the plan, despite much sincere popular sentiment for a Western *economic* orientation, could no longer be regarded as free or independent. On this point, the Communist *coup* was affirmative.

3. Hungary

Constitutional Development. Hungary, prototype of a transitional form of governmental development, today is in a more precarious position than any of her Danubian neighbors. Hungarians have not fought for liberation as did the Yugoslavs, nor does their country enjoy the political prestige of Czechoslovakia, accumulated through twenty years of democratic experience. Hungary has no oil, no significant trade routes, few such strategic lines of communication as run through Rumania and Bulgaria, and no well-defined political boundaries that also afford strategic defense, as has Turkey. Hungary also mismanaged her political affairs in World War II, including even the final withdrawal from actual military operations.

On February 1, 1946, an official proclamation by the first democratically elected National Assembly unanimously terminated the 945-year-old Hungarian monarchy and declared Hungary a republic. With the simultaneous emergence of a fairly representative government, the cycle of Hungarian constitutional development seemed to have entered a new phase. In the brief span of thirty-four years the country had passively witnessed six basically different phases of political evolution—from monarchy to republic (1918-19), from a liberal order to communism (1919), then to varying forms of personal dictatorship (1920-44), a sudden return to at least a temporarily republican type of government (1944-47), and finally a Communist dictatorship thinly concealed by the artificial political slogan of a "people's democracy" (since 1947).

The interregnum between the two rather tentative experiments in republicanism gave Hungary nothing but political immorality, and a thoroughly bankrupt economy. Exercise of royal power actually ceased on November 13, 1918, when Charles I abdicated. In the ensuing vacuum, a republican regime was formed under the leadership of Count Michael Károlyi, a well-known Hungarian liberal. His government within a few months yielded to a ruthless Communist dictatorship under Moscow-trained Béla Kun, which "followed a pure Russian world-revolutionary model, with chaotic experiments in socialization, dreams of the *sovkhozes,* and occasional hysterical outbursts of terrorism. It was short-lived, but it made a deep impression on Hungary's conservative soul." [4] Afterwards, Nicholas Horthy, a former admiral of the Austro-Hungarian Navy, succeeded in establishing a reactionary and semiparliamentary system of government. Although Horthy's regime excelled in the misuse of constitutional forms, a certain political normalization was accomplished under the ten-year tenure of Prime Minister Count Stephen Bethlen. But Bethlen's successors, particularly General Julius Gömbös, brought about a regression to political and social feudalism. Reaping the full harvest of Hungary's revisionist aspirations, these regimes helped to pave the way toward a thoroughgoing German orientation of the country. The regency of Horthy collapsed in the autumn of 1944, following his sudden request for an armistice with the Red Army.

Budapest was still under siege when a new provisional government in Debrecen set about reconstructing the country's political life. In December 1944, elections for a provisional National Assembly were held in the territories freed from the Germans. The new Assembly swiftly confirmed a provisional government, which succeeded in keeping itself in political power for about a year. The first election after the complete liberation offered a choice from among six political parties ranging from Conservative to the ubiquitous Communists. The most significant constitutional step was the inauguration of the Republic by the new National Assembly in its first parliamentary sessions. The law on "Hungary's form of government" declares that the power of the state rests with the Hungarian people, who exercise their legislative power through the democratically elected National Assembly. The document also states that "the Republic guarantees to its citizens the natural and inalienable rights of men." The enumeration, in the words of one writer,[5] sounds like the Bill of Rights and the Four Freedoms rolled into one.

Outline of Government. The Hungarian constitution of 1949 radically alters the previous fundamental document. The constitution proposes to construct a new political and economic system by destroying the liberal-democratic features of the postwar order. Theoretically, a unicameral Parliament exercises popular sovereignty; in practice, however, the Presidium is the most important organ in the country's public life. Consisting of a

---

[4] Oscar Jászi, "The Choices in Hungary," *Foreign Affairs,* 24 (1946), 456. Permission has been granted by the editor of the *Review of Politics* (Notre Dame, Ind.) to use for this section parts of Andrew Gyorgy's article on "Postwar Hungary" (July 1947).

[5] George A. Lanyi, "Hungary Aims at Liberty for All in Republic," *Christian Science Monitor,* Feb. 5, 1946, pp. 1 and 6.

President, several vice presidents, and about twenty members elected by Parliament, the powers of the Presidium are those generally attributed to a chief of state. The President of the Presidium fulfills the ceremonial functions of the President of a republic. In addition, the Presidium serves as a steering committee for Parliament, passes on the constitutionality of all laws, directly controls the appointment and activities of the Cabinet, and closely supervises the work of high judicial officials. The Presidium thus assumes the place of the previous National Assembly and overshadows both the Cabinet and the President. With the combination of legislative, executive, and judicial functions, it represents the Stalinist concept of "state authority" in its most complete form.[6]

These constitutional features are supported by restrictive legislation. A governmental decree of June 1946 provided that the right of supervising political associations shall be exercised by the Minister of the Interior. Simultaneously, a law on the "defense of Hungarian democracy" defined as criminal any incitement against the republican form of government, against a race or religion, or against the equality of all citizens. This law served as the basis for the trials of war criminals in Hungary; its provisions were applied in setting up the juridical procedure for the people's courts.

Postwar Parties. The composition of the first postwar coalition government corresponded roughly to the results of the election of November 1945. Of the 5 million votes cast, the Smallholders party polled well over 2½ million. The combined votes cast for the Communist and Social Democratic parties barely exceeded 1½ million. Obviously, the election had inflicted a significant defeat upon the two leftist parties, particularly on the Communists, while temporarily assuring the Smallholders party of a decisive majority. The coalition government was built around nine members of the Smallholders party and four members each of the Social Democratic and Communist parties.

The constitutional impact of the election was considerably deflated by the prior agreement of the three main political parties to continue their coalition *regardless of election results.* This political maneuver displayed a strange "ballot-proof" attitude and an autocratic appraisal of the role of national elections in parliamentary government. According to its official interpretation, the agreement "was absolutely necessary to maintain national unity. There were such serious problems to be solved that none of the parties could attempt to undertake the task alone. For this reason . . . the major parties of the Hungarian Independence Front have agreed to maintain the coalition

---

[6] See C. E. Black, "Constitutional Trends in Eastern Europe, 1945-1948," in *Soviet Satellites* (Notre Dame, 1949), 32 ff. For a survey of other satellite constitutions, cf. arts. 34-37 of the Bulgarian constitution (1947), arts. 41-46 of the Rumanian constitution (1948), and arts. 73-76 of the Yugoslav constitution (1946).

government after the elections. Their unity was also characterized by the fact that discussions about the formation of the coalition government began on the day of the elections."[7] This prematurely formed government was under the titular leadership of Zoltán Tildy of the Smallholders party, but in reality the reins of power were tightly controlled by a new political leader. Through a flexible arrangement that permitted him to become Deputy Prime Minister without portfolio, Mátyás Rákosi of the Communist party wielded the decisive influence in the Cabinet after the politically meaningless election of November 1945.

The weakness of native liberal peasant movements has been most consequential. Obviously, neither in Hungary nor in the surrounding Danubian countries is the majority of the peasantry adequately represented by the parties of either left or right. Between the two World Wars, only one liberal peasant group, the Independent Small Farmers party, had moments of political influence under the effective leadership of Gaszton Gál; but generally the small landholders, who should have formed the political backbone of the country, were gradually reduced to the role of an impoverished and underemployed proletariat. The Smallholders party was run by townsmen, and never represented the economically submerged or depressed elements of the peasantry.

Communist Engineering. The idea of a coalition of the left has had several aggressive champions. The core of the Hungarian Communist party is a group of about eighty trained leaders who have come to wield almost all actual political power and direct the daily conduct of the nation's affairs. Most of them have managed to retain their original Soviet citizenship. All the influential members of the party have spent several years in Moscow, partly because the Horthy government never tolerated their presence in Hungary, partly to complete the process of political indoctrination and education for eventual leadership. Rákosi spent most of the interwar period either in the Soviet Union or in Hungary's jails, which were unusually receptive to any Communist. His first large political role was participation in Béla Kun's revolution of 1918-19. In 1920 Rákosi quietly emigrated to Russia, returning to Hungary in 1925 as leader of the illegal Communist party. He was arrested soon after his return and condemned to eight years in prison. When he had completed his first prison term, charges were brought against him of "uninterrupted revolutionary activities." This time (January 1937) he was sentenced to life imprisonment. Under increasing Soviet pressure, the government finally released him, and in 1940 exchanged him for several Hungarian agents held in Soviet prisons. Rákosi again returned to Hungary in January 1945, as official leader and secretary general of the Hungarian Communist party. Since November 1945 he has been a member of the government as one of the three Vice Prime Ministers.

[7] István Száva, *New Hungarian Domestic Policy* (Budapest, 1946; pub. in English), pp. 34-35.

For the past six years, Rákosi has been the guiding power and top policy-maker of the Communist party. At first his attitude was one of conciliation and of professed belief in coalition. In June 1946, for example, Rákosi emphatically declared that his party did not aim at dictatorship, but at "effective collaboration in a concentration of national forces." This statement implied the tactical decision of continuing participation in the three-party coalition, which had largely achieved the primary ends of reconstruction—land reform, currency stabilization, and gradual nationalization.

By the spring of 1947, Communist party tactics revealed a drastic change. A second phase of *Gleichschaltung* was launched, coincident with the slow withdrawal of the Red Army occupation troops, the signing of the satellite peace treaties, and the increase in political interest and economic pressure from the West. The ultimate purpose of this phase was all too clear, particularly as the shaky coalition government collapsed almost immediately under its own weight. Now the Communists took over.

Economic Reconstruction. The Hungarian Three Year Plan, officially announced in June 1947, was to restore industry to the level of production of 1938. This comprehensive plan was prepared by experts of the Social Democratic and Communist parties with the cooperation of two former Hungarian professors of economics, Jenö Varga of Moscow and Nicholas Káldor of London. Administrative details of the plan closely paralleled Czech, Polish, and Yugoslav projects, which proposed to reach the economic levels of the last peacetime year by intensive national effort of two to five years of agricultural and industrial reconstruction. Two features were prominent in the Hungarian plan: the nationalization of mines and industry, and the establishment of new labor unions as a means of broadening the worker's participation in the country's economic life.

Coal mines were first on the nationalization list. The economic argument was based on the fact that "the supply of energy is a monopoly, and this monopoly cannot be left in private hands." Nationalization of coal mines was logically followed by that of all other sources of energy and of power plants, many of which were owned by foreign corporations. In this respect the same aggressively antiforeign methods were used that proved so successful in Rumania and Czechoslovakia.[8] Next was the nationalization of heavy industries, applied only to the largest enterprises, such as the Ganz-Danubius, Bauxite, and Rima-Murányi machine, steel, and metallurgical plants. By 1948, however, a far more drastic step was taken when all industries employing more than a hundred persons were expropriated by the state. In December 1949, all firms employing more than five persons were nationalized, leaving only the handicraft industries in private hands. The process of nationalization was considerably accelerated by the recent Hungarian Five Year Plan, officially proclaimed to cover the period of 1950-1955. Compre-

---

[8] For the first official announcement of the government's action, under the heading "Forced Nationalization of Hungary's Heavy Industry," cf. *Magyar Nemzet*, Nov. 24, 1946.

hensive government decrees were drafted for banks and for firms engaged in the distribution of agricultural products. Simultaneously, the entire field of domestic and foreign trade was brought under the control of a Supreme Economic Council, headed by the economic "trouble-shooter" of Hungary's Communist regime, Zoltán Vas.

Hungarian reparations have included nearly all the country's production of capital goods. Through "joint economic collaboration" agreements, Soviet control has penetrated the economic structure. Particularly far-reaching are the agreements about oil and bauxite production, Danube shipping, and civil aviation. Capital and management are as tightly controlled as if these economic sectors had been actually nationalized by the government. Soviet occupation authorities have also acquired majority holdings in banks, insurance companies, mining corporations, and most of the remaining privately owned factories. Elaborate executive decrees were issued to give adequate legal basis to these joint agreements and to earmark the use of most industrial production for reparations.

Looking Ahead. Hungary today is in the twilight zone of Europe's southeast. Her domestic politics mirror the fundamental tensions among the world powers. The early postwar era has seen a moral and economic transformation of the country spurred on by liberal reform moves. Fair national elections resulting in an acceptable coalition government based on the Smallholders party, neither ultraconservative nor revolutionary; a thorough land reform; a reasonably free press; a stabilized currency; and a moderately successful process of industrial nationalization—these were promising landmarks at the beginning of the road toward reconstruction.

Yet the forces responsible for such results were gradually destroyed by the rising influence of the Communist party, which brought internal disruption and social crisis. Liberation was affected by an oppressive military occupation. When the coalition government gave way, Communist domination reduced all other parties to silent partners. The newly won freedom of the press gradually disappeared as one party emerged as the final arbiter. Nationalization led to elimination of former managements and to a tight system of production discipline. Soviet propaganda also contributed its share to the tenseness of the political atmosphere, though the Russians with time effectively destroyed a great deal of the original good will widely felt for them after liberation.

Hungary's political position is determined by her peripheral location in Central-Eastern Europe. In this area the Soviet Union has claimed strategic security. Guided by a broad interpretation of this concept, the Soviet Union has compelled neighbor countries to accept its choice of governmental leaders and methods of administration. National planning, industrial recovery, and financial stabilization are strongly encouraged, in order to meet the enormous reparations and bolster up the one-way movement of goods to the USSR. The entire field of domestic affairs is gradually subordinated to the dictates of foreign interests. Once again Hungary is a satellite nation.

4. Yugoslavia

Postwar Constitutional Development. Yugoslavia today is the strongest single military power in the Danubian area, with relatively the most stable form of government. Behind the façade of a People's Front, the government of Marshal Tito is entrenched, rigidly controlling every aspect of the country's political and economic life. In spite of its revolutionary features, however, the postwar Yugoslav state presents a distinct phase in the political evolution of the South Slavs.

A new constitution, first outlined in 1943, was adopted by the constituent assembly in January 1946. The constitution replaced the earlier unitary state with a new federal structure. The Federal People's Republic of Yugoslavia is divided into six full-fledged republics—Serbia, Croatia, Slovenia, Macedonia, Montenegro, and Bosnia, each with its own government and a certain amount of authority. Legislative authority is vested in a People's Assembly composed of two houses, the Federal Council and the Council of Nationalities, both of equal jurisdiction. The Federal Council is elected by all citizens on the basis of population; for every 50,000 inhabitants one deputy is elected. The Council of Nationalities is chosen on a territorial basis, each republic being allotted thirty members, the smaller autonomous provinces twenty, and the smallest geographic units, the autonomous regions, fifteen. Regular sessions of the People's Assembly are convened twice a year, in April and October. Its none-too-well defined sphere of powers is generally that of adoption of bills introduced by the government.

The Presidium of Parliament is a completely new institution in the country's constitutional life. The People's Assembly chooses the Presidium, which is the formal executive organ and performs some of the most important state functions. Its activities are like those exercised by the Presidium of the Supreme Soviet of the USSR, convening and dissolving the People's Assembly, ordering elections, proclaiming and interpreting all federal laws, ratifying international treaties, appointing and recalling members of the foreign service, declaring general mobilization and a state of war.[9] The Presidium consists of a president, six vice presidents, a secretary, and thirty members. At present the top leaders of Yugoslavia's Communist party, the ministers of the central government, and the premiers of the six individual republics all belong to the Presidium. Its comprehensive functions emphatically illustrate the fact that the constitution provides for no separation between executive and legislative powers. In a way, as one author puts it, "this in itself does not represent a departure from the past, since Yugoslavia was previously governed on the basis of . . . the fusion of the legislative and ex-

---

[9] Article 74 of the Constitution of the Federal People's Republic of Yugoslavia of 1946 enumerates under seventeen headings the functions of the new Presidium.

ecutive powers."[10]   As long as government officials and Cabinet ministers form the membership of the Presidium, they will be responsible *for* themselves as administrators, and *to* themselves as executives.   In line with this concept of responsibility, personal liberties, though guaranteed in theory, are under practical limitations clearly outlined by the constitution.   Profascist writing is prohibited; papers may not incite national hatred nor recommend the overthrow of the government by force; no one may write against friendly states or issue any publications financed from abroad.

Collectivist Planning.   The constitution devotes a separate chapter to social and economic organization.   All economic activities of the state point toward intensive socialization and long-range national planning.   The concept of property is redefined; private property is radically limited and subject to expropriation at any time.   The means of production now belong either to the state or to the cooperatives, whose number and national significance have increased steadily since 1945.   The progress of socialization was speeded up considerably by transferring into national property such resources as minerals, waters, and all means of communication and transportation.   A "general economic plan" is outlined in broad features; the state is to direct the economic development of the country in accordance with this plan.   In so doing, the government is to rely primarily on the assistance of syndicalist organizations and similar cooperative groups of the working people.   The national program is entrusted to a Commissioner of Economic Planning, who is a member of the Cabinet.   The commissioner and the Ministers of Industry and Finance are responsible for the state-controlled reconstruction of Yugoslavia's economy.   In November 1946 Marshal Tito personally announced a new Five Year Plan "to help transform Yugoslavia from an agricultural into an industrial country."

Collectivist planning is usually incompatible with the existence of commercial organizations or landed interests.   The constitution prefers to go around the corner by forbidding expressly only "cartels, syndicates, trusts, and similar organizations created for the purpose of dictating prices, monopolizing the market, and damaging the interests of the national economy." Maximum size of private landholdings is rigidly established by law, subject to the sweeping pronouncement, "The land belongs to those who cultivate it."   The state has taken over for redistribution all lands that were owned by banks, joint stock companies, churches and monasteries, and German citizens and collaborators.   Beyond these initial measures, the status of the land has not been fully determined.

People's Committees.   People's committees elected by the citizens of towns and villages play an important role in local government and administration.   Their task is to ensure the maintenance of public order, the execution of the laws, and the protection of the rights of citizens.   Through these administrative organs, both state and party authorities can exert a direct influ-

[10] Alex N. Dragnich, "Yugoslavia's New Constitution," *Current History*, 10 (1946), 421 ff.

ence on individual communities. Members of the people's committees are also local agents of the Communist party.

The mass appeal of the constitution is clearly expressed in its declaration that "it is the duty of the people's committees in the execution of their general and local duties to rely on the initiative and wide participation of the masses of the people and workers' organizations." The constitution also provides for people's courts headed by a Supreme Court as the highest organ of justice, with judges and jurors elected by the People's Assembly. Much power resides, however, in the public prosecutors, who supervise all agencies of the state in the application of the law and are active on every level of national and local administration. Their role is paralleled by that of the military prosecutors, appointed by the Commander-in-Chief and active within the broad framework of the state's military organization. On the whole, then, the Yugoslav constitution of 1946 is a fairly true copy of the Soviet constitution.

Tito's People's Front. Describing the new constitution, Marshal Tito observed in 1946 that "the relationship between people and authority has changed in new Yugoslavia so that there is no longer a conflict between them, but a political and organizational unity."[11] This professed unity presents a marked contrast to the wartime partisan movements in which amorphous groups were temporarily welded together by the revolutionary tactics of the Communists. Although initially dependent on the political and moral support of Western democracies, Tito's followers soon devoted their full energies to a thorough reorganization of the country. Today complete Communist direction is maintained through a powerful and effective party system —the People's Front.

This organization, officially described as a coalition of several political parties, consists mostly of a thin texture of names and leaders, all of them directly controlled by the Communist party. A cleverly simulated national front, it includes the remnants of several historically familiar prewar parties, now claiming to represent various democratic or socialist groups. The regime apparently intends to bring new classes of people into the political life, using the People's Front as a convenient cloak. Before the war, a large part of the nation—nearly all the workers, most of the peasants, and the entire leftist intelligentsia—were essentially excluded from politics. They belonged to no party, because no political group was interested in their ideas and aspirations. It is questionable, however, whether the present organization of the party system allows them a larger area of expressing their beliefs. In addition to a Communist nucleus, the People's Front today includes small representations of the Republican party, the Agrarians, and the Croatian Republican Peasant party, which used to be a potent factor in national poli-

---

[11] Tito restated this idea in a later and even more significant speech given at the Second Congress of the People's Front of Yugoslavia, September 27, 1947. See special reprint by Yugoslav Embassy, Washington, D. C.

tics under the leadership of Dr. Machek. Some of the present-day parties, like the meticulously selected pro-Tito factions of the Croatian Republicans, seem to be artificially fostered by the government in order to give the impression of a multiparty system. Opposition is impossible in a government of this type. It is not surprising that the principal leaders of Tito's opposition are either dead or in exile.

In spite of the frequently repeated official label, according to which the People's Front is "a coalition of all progressive and uncompromised parties," the real center of political power lies outside this group. The Front is a mere variation of the strategy to weaken political parties of the moderate left and the center by the simple device of including them in the government.[12] The parties then share all the burdens and responsibilities without the advantages of power. The same pattern of "divide and rule" has emerged in Rumania, Yugoslavia, and Bulgaria. It is now in process of full application in Czechoslovakia and Hungary.

Three Principal Agencies. Yugoslavia's present regime is not a personal dictatorship, but a government by oligarchy whose authority radiates from three important agencies. These are the federal Cabinet, the Army, and the secret police—the latter an expression of the ever-present power of the Communist party. The party exerts a great deal of its aggressiveness through the Cabinet. The key positions are safely held by Communists, who fill at least nine of the major portfolios in a Cabinet of twenty-eight ministers. The nucleus of power is formed around three Communists: the Prime Minister, the Minister of War, and the Minister of the Interior. Being in charge of the entire police system, the latter is a particularly formidable figure in the political hierarchy. This position is held by Colonel General Rankovich, head of the dreaded secret police, recently camouflaged by the name of State Security Administration, or UDB. The other leading spokesmen of the Cabinet are Edvard Kardelj, Foreign Minister of the regime and its representative in the councils of peacemaking, and General Milovan Djilas, in charge of all party affairs and active as Tito's personal deputy.

Party and government are safely linked. The most powerful figures of the Cabinet are also members of the Communist Committee of Seven, which is closely patterned after the *Politburo.* Both Cabinet and Committee of Seven are directly responsible to Marshal Tito in his dual capacity as head of state and leader of the Communist party. The most paradoxical feature of this governmental system is that the top members of the party have not attempted to legalize their *de facto* control. Only Tito's official position is well defined; he serves as leader of the movement, and officially his principal titles are those of secretary general of the Communist party, Prime Minister, Minister of National Defense, and Marshal of Yugoslavia.

Foreign Policies. Yugoslavia's postwar foreign policies are determined, to a large extent, by her geographic location in Southern Europe. Astride a gi-

---

[12] Cf. the reprint of the speech by Marshal Tito, cited above, note 11, pp. 17-18.

gantic highway linking Europe with Asia Minor and the East, the country is partly Mediterranean, partly Central European, and partly Balkan. It lies open in every direction and is subjected today, as in the past, to pressure from all sides. As it is easily accessible from the sea, maritime countries will look toward it to protect their interests in the Mediterranean and the Middle East. Land powers, on the other hand, will become increasingly interested in the rich mineral and other resources of Yugoslavia. Until the recent break with the Cominform, the rulers of Yugoslavia accepted the leadership of the Soviet Union, based on the active cooperation of all major Slavic countries. In June 1948 the Cominform unexpectedly denounced the leadership of the Yugoslav Communist party. Tito and his top lieutenants were accused of retreating from Marxism-Leninism by undertaking wrong policies both at home and abroad. The Yugoslav regime categorically rejected the Cominform charges. Tito's administration did not back down or weaken its hold on the people even after the Cominform moved its headquarters to Bucharest to operate without Yugoslav participation. The schism between Tito and the Cominform marks the first publicized fissure in Russia's Eastern European bloc.

In its Yugoslav version, Tito's defection presents a challenging dilemma. On the one hand, his regime is intent on perpetuating its independent position in international politics, preserving itself against both the impact of Soviet imperialism and Western political influence. On the other hand, it wants to retain a revolutionary government fired by extravagant ideological aims and economic ambitions.[13] The pursuit of these conflicting aims leads to significant compromises which complicate and deepen the political mystery of Titoism. Alone politically, the Yugoslav regime had to give up its isolated position toward the West and engage in friendly overtures to the United States and Great Britain. Under Eastern pressure Tito was forced to make drastic allowances to the policy of rigorous independence so proudly stressed by his lieutenants.[14] Across his frontiers the Soviet satellites wage their war of nerves with unabated enthusiasm; at home economic troubles accumulate and the standard of living—already very low—can only be maintained with the greatest difficulty. This complex set of pressures tends to drive Tito closer to the United States, to the camp of his "class enemy" which he professes to abhor.

5. Common Problems

Titoism and Soviet Control in Eastern Europe. Official admission of the Soviet-Yugoslav break in June 1948 marked the appearance of a singularly

---

[13] See George Adamkiewicz, "Tito, Titoism and the West," *International Journal* (Winter 1949-1950), 38 ff., and Edward Crankshaw, "Tito and the Cominform," *International Affairs* (April 1950), 208 ff.

[14] A characteristic recent statement came from Edvard Kardelj, Yugoslavia's Foreign Minister, who asserted in Maribor (Slovenia) on February 26, 1950, that "Yugoslavia refuses to surrender its independence and to submit itself to foreign domination and exploitation." *Borba*, March 1, 1950, 2.

grave threat to Moscow's Eastern leadership. Tito's refusal to obey Soviet orders clearly implied that for the first time Communist leaders had succeeded in challenging a well-established international hierarchy without losing their own lives or the control of their party members. Even when judged by its precarious lifespan of a few years, Titoism carries with it the hope that satellite Communist parties will increasingly embark on the road of determined political deviation.

Recent developments in Eastern Europe seem to justify both Western expectations and Eastern anxiety in mirroring the recurrent waves of actual or potential Titoism throughout the satellite world. Large-scale purges in Bulgaria and Czechoslovakia, carefully synchronized with the tightening of a Soviet-organized military network in these two countries; reports of unrest and party purges in Poland and Rumania; continual flareups between church and state in Hungary—these serve as timely indications that in the Eastern European satellite states the everpresent elements of political dissatisfaction have been kindled into resistance by Yugoslavia's deviation.

Fired by its opportunism and practical flexibility, Titoism asserts a genuine vigor in assailing the existing conceptual order of Stalinism. In Eastern Europe it causes the Soviet-instilled waves of patriotism to recede considerably. Satellite propaganda faces the arduous task of dispensing the Soviet version of nationalism—loyalty to the USSR—and of creating popular support for it. Judged on the basis of recent tensions and symptoms of conflict, Titoism helps to establish channels for latent sources of resentment toward Stalinism and its control of the Danubian and Balkan areas.

Federative Plans. The deep ideological rift between East and West has intensified the urgency of federation in Europe. The organization of Europe depends at present on the relationships between big powers and small nations, and on the expression of regional political interests. Most recent projects usually extend only to Western Europe. A Western bloc would then face a regional group of similar dimensions, on the pattern of an Eastern Europe composed of the Soviet Union, Finland, Poland, the Soviet zone of Germany, and the Danubian states.

The significance of a Danubian or Balkan federation is obvious in the light of the division in the organizational structure of Europe. Such a federation could effectively serve as a shock-absorber for either side. Were it able to remain free of encroachments, it would in the long run unite rather than further split the peoples of Europe. Before the Communist *coup* in Czechoslovakia, the late President Benes expressed this thought in a speech in which he stated that "we cannot gauge accurately the present strength of Slavic solidarity. . . . Culturally we are Europeans. We shall never ally ourselves exclusively with the West but will always attempt to do so with both East and West." [15]

As the subsequent events in Czechoslovakia showed, the most serious hand-

---

[15] "Eine Rede Beneschs," *Neue Zürcher Zeitung*, May 4, 1947.

icap facing federations is the actual or threatened domination by neighboring large powers. In the recent past, Nazi conquest frustrated all attempts at an effective and fairly independent federation in the Danubian area. At present, the region is being transformed into a closed economic and political system, working in rhythm with Soviet methods and developments. A Soviet-sponsored Danubian or Balkan federation would not serve as a bridge between East and West.

Anti-Western Trends. With the rapid emergence of the Soviet Union as the dominant power in Danubian Europe, the intensity of anti-Western feelings has increased perceptibly. Anti-Western propaganda, as one writer observed, is "an ideological holy war of words. Britain in particular is denounced as a cruel, oppressive, war-mongering, and reactionary power. Absolutely no credit is given to social reform in Britain. . . ." [16] The campaign is principally directed against the United States and Great Britain, its weapons ranging from a blackout of information to sharp diplomatic notes criticizing and denouncing American and British policies.

Military Integration. Anti-Western sentiments are also implicit in Soviet sponsorship of a gradual internal militarization of the entire area. This process is encouraged in several directions simultaneously. General military service has been made compulsory in each of the Danubian republics; new standing armies have appeared, led by Soviet-trained generals. The latter are not only instrumental in consolidating their power and purging the army under their command, but are assuming an ever increasing share of influence in civilian matters. Military leaders are consulted on most important policy decisions of the government, and are members of the tightly organized "inner circle." This is particularly true in Rumania and Bulgaria.

The military development of Eastern European countries is coordinated through formal and comprehensive military alliances, of which the Soviet-Bulgarian, Soviet-Rumanian, and Czech-Polish treaties are the prototypes. A close military network has been formed, with headquarters in Bucharest, where numerous meetings of Soviet and satellite army staffs were held during the years 1948-1951. Soviet leadership is the salient factor in the process of Eastern European military integration.

---

[16] Hugh Seton-Watson, "Jugoslavia Today," *International Journal,* 2 (1947), 161. See also the writings cited above, note 1.

PART VII

PART VII

RECONSTRUCTION GOVERNMENT:
CHINA AND JAPAN

CHAPTER 27

IDEOLOGICAL DYNAMICS OF THE POSTWAR FAR EAST

1. Japan's New Way

Occurrence of the Unbelievable. Imagine that Alexander the Great had created a lasting Grecian world—so stable that the empire still sprawled from Copenhagen to the Sahara, from Baghdad to Madeira, as recently as 1912. Imagine that Plato, Virgil, Shakespeare, Cervantes, Molière, Goethe, and Ibsen had all written essentially the same Greek language, and that all culture had taken on a common form. Only an obdurate Britain, let us imagine, stood independent—defying the Grecians in a language written with Greek letters, quoting Greek authorities, old and new, in defense of Britannic rights. Such a Britain would be toward Grecian Europe in much the position of Japan toward China; and Scandinavia, long contested between Grecian and Britannic power, might lie helpless like a Korea between the two of them.

In the Grecian world the common law and the common religion might long ago have permitted the withering away of most of government. But the Grecian culture, nine tenths adopted by independent Britain, would help her to be tough and organized in order to survive the perils of power and independence. In both worlds—the sophisticated, weary, sagacious old continent and the resolutely independent islands—the common culture would bind each to the other in an unbreakable web of ancient hatred and equally ancient admiration. But the Grecians would accept the admiration of the Britannic people without feeling need to return it. Now add the unimaginable—that Aztecs with atomic power defeated the Britannic empire—and the Far East stands historically parallel to Europe.

Japan is still there, with 147,000 square miles as against the 120,000 of the British Isles, with 84 million Japanese as against 51 million English, Scots, and Irish. The Japanese still look west toward the enormously long coastline of China, with the hook of Korea reaching down almost to touch their strategic Straits of Shimonoseki. Like the British, the Japanese have a vast ocean at their backs, with a single power dominating its islands and the far shores—the United States. And a representative of that power sat in Tokyo, giving Japan commands—Japan, whom no nation had successfully invaded until 1945! Two thousand and more years of contact with China had never led to

Japanese conquest of China, nor Chinese conquest of Japan; but less than a hundred years after the first tentative American official visit, an American official held effective dominion over all Japan.

Historic Influence. Japan is the most nearly unique nation of the world in more than one respect.[1] She is the only country to possess a ruling family whose lineage runs back into the prehistoric. Moreover, the mind of Japan is one that has been formed in centuries of isolation. Japanese therefore have a keen sense of their superiority over other peoples—a superiority proceeding from appreciation of their own national character. Through most of the years of their national history, they kept to themselves. As late as 1775, when a tiny England with some 6 million inhabitants was lording it over the Atlantic, an immense Japan with about 30 million extended her authority not a single league outside the coastal waters. Again, it is likely that the largest city in the world in 1800 was one that Napoleon never thought of conquering: Tokyo, then called Yedo, and thoroughly free from imperial dreams.

The reasons for Japan's modernization—the swift transition to Western economics and technology—are to be found in the centralized police state with its direction and authority; in the high intelligence and patriotism of the Japanese, who had the good sense to see the danger that threatened them if they remained "backward," and the national morale to do something about it; in the farsighted leadership of a knightly class, which generally accepted transformation of its status from feudal to money power; in a ruler who was able to add to the functions of pope those of emperor, and thus to focus upon himself symbolic loyalty to an extraordinary degree; and, above all, in the genius of the Japanese for imitation.[2]

The defeat of Japan in 1945 was her reward for playing the Western game of power politics. One aspect of the combined archaic-modern Japanese ideology and social system—ultranationalist militarism—was now discredited. Japan's best was not enough. Her final defeat arose pre-eminently from her haste to achieve a modern equivalent of her ancient security. The militarists who led Japan to war had been able to play on two of the most pronounced

---

[1] For a scholarly short history of Japan, see Edwin O. Reischauer, *Japan: Past and Present* (New York, 1946). A classic of British scholarship is Sir George Sansom's *Japan: A Short Cultural History* (New York, 1943). See also D. C. Holtom, *Modern Japan and Shinto Nationalism* (rev. ed., Chicago, 1947); Ruth Benedict, *The Chrysanthemum and the Sword: Patterns of Japanese Culture* (Boston, 1946).

The author of Part VII of the present book wishes to report the research and re-thinking of his own work made possible by a demobilization grant from the Social Science Research Council in 1946. He must also acknowledge the contributions made by Professor Ardath Burks, of Rutgers University, and Dr. Djang Chu, of the School of Advanced International Studies, Washington, D. C. Dr. Djang is a Chinese classical scholar and an American-trained Chinese political scientist with wide administrative experience; Professor Burks is a Japanese-language expert. Their help amounted to collaboration, in so far as the original research for this part was concerned; for the final product Professor Linebarger assumes sole responsibility.

[2] For an outstanding description of a complicated process, see E. Herbert Norman, *Japan's Emergence as a Modern State: Political and Economic Problems of the Meiji Period* (New York, 1940).

characteristics of the Japanese people: their sense of insecurity and their corresponding stress upon loyalty.[3]

Character of Japanese Aggression. Japanese aggression (1931-45) was not the invention of cold-blooded bankers and Cabinet ministers plotting the preservation of ill-gotten gains. It was a turbulent, loosely organized movement both inside and outside Japan. The militarists were centered in the Army and in reservists' and veterans' organizations, supplemented by secret societies and opportunist politicians. In the bad sense of the word *popular* (that is, in the sense of "vulgar and mob-like"), Japanese aggression was a deeply popular movement. It could claim the support of the plain peasantry in much the way that Hitler's national socialism could claim to be *völkisch*.[4]

The parliamentary Japanese had tried to have their cake and eat it too; they had installed limited democracy but had used the schools to inculcate fanatical nationalism. In the 1920's and 1930's coarse-minded soldiers and shoddy politicians took the government away from the moderates. The *gumbatsu* (militarist clique) and the peasantry could unite in opposing the heartbreaking inequities of parliamentarism and capitalism, and in turning to the illusory decisiveness of war.

The war was the testing ground, and the militarists lost—utterly and irretrievably. The new Japanese constitution has now prohibited armies, navies, and all other military facilities within Japan; but the constitutional provision is not so effective as common sense. Japan may fight Russia on the American side, or America on the Russian side; but she is not apt again to fight on her own. Therefore, the Japanese are back where they started in the 1920's, though much worse off—with a Parliament that is neither very noble nor very important, a capitalist system with only a fragile prosperity, and a democracy that gives legitimacy to a depressing *status quo*.

Japanese Parliamentarism. Japanese parliamentarism was not only discredited by the militarists who seized power for the China adventure and the Pacific war; it is still being discredited today. The interrelationship of parliamentarism and capitalism, under the peculiar conditions of Japanese state-tutelage of both, was plain from the beginning. The two structures were of one piece. But the Americans tended to identify Japanese capitalism with wickedness because business had gone to war, together with the whole of the country. The great family concerns were held up as monsters of iniquity. A program of reform was undertaken that attempted to break down Japanese business to units that had long been found unprofitable in the United States.

With the militarists politically extinct as militarists (though not necessarily as citizens or patriots), and with the old business-Parliament groups sitting

---

[3] Cf. Hugh Borton, *Japan since 1931* (New York, 1940); Charles B. Fahs, *Government in Japan* (New York, 1940).

[4] The Army-reservist-veteran tie-up is explained in Kenneth Colegrove, *Militarism in Japan* (Boston, 1936). The character of Japan as an enemy is discussed in Joseph C. Grew's books, *Report from Tokyo* and *Ten Years in Japan* (New York, 1942 and 1944). The Soviet view is presented in O. Tanin and E. Johan, *Militarism and Fascism in Japan* (New York, 1934).

out the duration of foreign displeasure, dynamic new leadership in Japan has had to come from party and professional groups. Unfortunately, these groups do not have a tradition or a mission commensurate with their tragic responsibilities. Unwilling or unable to launch a great social crusade, they are also incapable of demonstrating their loyalty to ancient tradition.

New Purposes. Ideologically, then, Japan can be expressed in contrasts. The Japanese respect power; since the Americans were powerful enough to whip them, they must have the ingredients of power. An American general, who splendidly epitomized the military life, admonished them to renounce war. An American government encouraged them to seek the material and moral benefits of democracy without giving intelligible indication of what position Japan will be expected to fill in the world twenty years from now.

The one socially functioning group of institutions that first showed postwar vitality was the labor movement. But, anywhere in the world, labor unions are more effective in upgrade economic situations than in downhill ones. Labor movements can become partners in a capitalist system and bring labor to a mature role in such a system; but they cannot do so if capitalism itself is half-wrecked or near bankruptcy. Labor movements can also overthrow capitalism and create socialist or communist governments, but it is not practical for them to do so in the face of military prohibition while foreign warplanes are on every airfield. Labor is availing itself of the opportunity to mature in Japan, but even labor has no political goal that seems tied to economic reality.

Japan is therefore a temporary ideological void—a land of questions without answers, duties without purposes, politics without policy. The foreground of the Japanese stage is filled with a passable performance of "democracy"—by order. But the background is dark. The Japanese have retained their Emperor and their bureaucracy; they have obtained a better educational policy than they ever had before. Yet their ideological positions are unlike those of China, where two powerful regimes fought out the basic issue with gunfire. All Japanese ideologies, with the exception of the Communist, are discreet. They stay within the limits of what the foreign authorities permit; they are sensitive to what General MacArthur so recently approved or disapproved. Under renewed peace and independence, this must change.

2. Current Japanese Ideologies

Repudiated Militarism. Facts, not choices, have totally repudiated militarist ideology. In its own way it was persuasive—far more reminiscent of the Hearstian nationalism of the United States (1905-25) than of the later and subtler manipulations of a Goebbels.

The militarists propounded the notions of *kokutai,* a special and very high kind of national entity that existed only in Japan; of *kodo,* the "way of the Emperor," a divine path of polity; of *hakko ichiu,* "eight corners, one roof," or the brotherhood of men under Japanese sponsorship; of *Dai Toa Kyoei*

Ken, "Greater East Asia Co-Prosperity Sphere," or the liberation of East Asia from white colonialism and capitalism into Japanese hegemony; of the "Showa restoration," or a second step forward, this time from false Westernization to the true essence of Japan.[5] These militarist ideas enjoyed genuine appeal as long as world events, as twisted and interpreted by a controlled press, made them seem real.

Middle-to-Left Politics. Political views run all the way from the middle to the left. The middle is made up of those prewar parliamentary elements that have survived militarist purges, wartime hazards, and the conqueror's purges. Connected with the bureaucracy and with what is left of business, the middle aims at getting along with the occupation and making the best of democracy. The left proper depends upon the new labor unions and upon the prewar Socialist parties, together with Christians, intellectuals, land-reform advocates, and other pleaders of special and worthy causes. The extreme left consists of the Communist party and its fellow-travelers.

Prewar parties were replaced in the summer of 1940 by the *Taisei Yokusan Kai* (Imperial Rule Assistance Association, or IRAA), into which everything of a public or patriotic character was gathered, all the way from political parties to youth camps, from labor unions to "cultural" organizations.[6] With the end of war, the politicians rushed out from this confinement and regrouped themselves in "parties," carefully named so as to please the Americans and ensure the political survival of their "founders."

These parties were not successors to the old major parties. Rather, the Liberal (*Jiyuto*) and People's Democratic (*Kokumin Minshuto*) parties of today represent an almost random assembly of prewar politicians from either the *Minseito* or the *Seiyukai,* the former "two big parties." Thus, the Democratic party includes the Machida faction of the Minseito and the Nakajima faction of the Seiyukai, along with elements of the prewar leftist Social Mass party.[7] The Liberals and Democrats are now, in general, "progressive" in the ordinary American sense of the term. As reorganized in 1947, the People's Democrats—who have no links with the Stalinist "popular democracy" —reconcile some of the old Minseito connections with the role of mild opposition. A few non-reorganized Democrats vote with the People's Cooperatives.

This parliamentary survival is significant. The party politicians did not,

---

[5] The general background of the militarist ideology is given in H. F. MacNair, *The Real Conflict between China and Japan: An Analysis of Opposing Ideologies* (Chicago, 1938) and J. Paul Reed, *Kokutai: A Study of Certain Sacred and Secular Aspects of Japanese Nationalism* (Chicago, 1937). On militarist revival, see Nobutaka Ike, " 'National Socialism' in Japan," *Pacific Affairs,* 23, No. 3 (Sept., 1950), 311-314. "Militarism," like other western terms of political science has meanings in Japan that flow from the national environment.

[6] See *Army Service Forces Manual M354-2A, Civil Affairs Handbook, Japan, sec. 2A, Government and Administration* (Washington, released 1948) on wartime government.

[7] See Robert K. Reischauer, *Japan: Government—Politics* (New York, 1939); Harold S. Quigley, *Japanese Government and Politics* (New York, 1932); Harold Zink and Taylor Cole, eds., *Government in Wartime Europe and Japan* (Boston, 1942), chap. 9 by Kenneth Colegrove.

before World War II, hold a decisive position in Japanese politics. Policy was not made in the Diet, but in the general staffs, the joint military agencies, the Privy Council, and the service ministries. Hence, the parliamentarians of the prewar middle, today on the extreme right of a purged Japan, now possess those powers that they had held in title but never in fact before. They have the opportunity to make reformed capitalist democracy work—if they can figure out how to do so and have the character to lead wisely.

Socialists and Communists. The prewar radicals have become the mild postwar left—constitutional and moderate. Japan's Socialist party (*Nihon Shakaito*) became the largest party in the Diet and took the premiership in June 1947, with a coalition Cabinet that included leftist members of the Democratic party. Going back to the founding of a Socialist party in 1901, which lasted one day, and to a welter of splinter parties in the 1920's, all of which were swept into the militarist fronts or into oblivion during the war, the Socialists in the new setting opened their ranks to everyone weary of prewar parliamentarism and of wartime militarism. The result was that their party is in Japan almost the kind of amalgam that the New Deal represented in the United States. Whereas the Socialists borrowed the left wing of the Democratic party in order to form a coalition Cabinet in 1947, their own left wing joined the Communist party in opposition. The coalition under Socialist leadership was succeeded in 1948 by one under Democratic leadership with about the same membership. Japanese socialism has roots in the past in so far as the old imperial system—in contrast with capitalism—already represented the halfway point to socialism. Add patriotism to the subordination of property rights to ethical requirements, and there is in Japan a frame of mind that has been military-socialist and may be democratic-socialist or imperial-socialist in the future.[8]

The Japanese Communists—alone of all formal political groups—never joined the militarists, always remained in opposition, worked for the Allied powers before 1945, and opposed continuation of the Emperor. Called *Nihon Kyosan To,* the party was first organized in 1922. The founder was a certain Tokuda (given name, Kyuichi), whom the government kept locked up from 1928 until 1945. He came out brimming with ideas. The American occupation welcomed the Japanese Communists returning from exile and prison. With deteriorating relations between the United States and the Soviet Union, the Communists came out poorly. Their leader-from-exile, Nozaka Sanzo, was caught between the Scylla of the occupation and the Charybdis of the Politburo. In 1950 he was under attack from both the Cominform and occupation-inspired police raids. The top command went into hiding, leaving a Temporary Central Guidance Committee (*Rinji Chuo Shidobu*) to carry on.

---

[8] On the ideological spectrum there must be grouped with the Socialists the still less dogmatic and even more Japanese *Kydo Minshu To* (People's Cooperative Party), a left-of-center group that arose from the widespread Japanese cooperative movement.

3. Chinese Communism

Native Roots. In China, communism has won the mastery of a population at least twice and more nearly three times that of the USSR, and for control of a territory extending—even after the loss of Outer Mongolia to Soviet patronage—over more than 3½ million square miles as against the Soviet Union's 8. The power of communism in modern China is amplified many times by two special features of Chinese political life: (1) the traditional Chinese dependence on ideological control rather than organized governmental direction; and (2) the equally traditional Chinese deviation into fanaticism in times of governmental corruption and popular discontent.

Marxism marches in China as a religion—as *the* scientific religion which reconciles morality with public health, land reform with human purpose, anti-imperialism with the history of the future. The Chinese peasant who turns to communism is not getting more food, a higher standard of living, or the better material life. He is getting a cause. The Communists give him purpose, action, psychological release, modernization, the salvation of mankind—all in one package. But communism is nowhere self-generating in China. It never breaks out among the untouched common people. It spreads as predictably as does a bacterial infection—by the actual transplantation of commando gangs, killers, shockers, arousers, who get things going. The Chinese Soviet Republic occupied a large and populous area of Southeast China for years (1927-35); the Nationalists reclaimed it.[9] After Nationalist reconquest, the area had been loosely garrisoned, and yet, from among the millions of people with firsthand memories of Chinese Communist rule, no new Communist rebellion arose until the approach of Red Regulars.

Communist Organization. Organizationally, Chinese Communists follow the familiar pattern. They have the Soviet principle of "democratic centralism"—under which the topmost leaders may ratify their own decisions by demanding and winning plebiscitary assent through a pyramid of indirectly elected, carefully managed party organs.

More frankly, perhaps, than communists anywhere else in the world, the Chinese Communists knew that the party and its military had the control of authentic power, and that governments—even communist ones—were mere means of applying control. As a result, the Chinese Communists kept in their party a first-rate managerial structure, though even unimportant people could criticize important Communist leaders within the limits of official policy, and beside it, a loose political structure of area relationships, modest enough to appeal to Chinese and world opinion.

Personal Leadership. The Chinese Communist top leadership is a sesquiduumvirate—the rule of two and a half men. And an ominous fourth leader has joined them.

---

[9] The outstanding general discussion is Harold Isaacs, *The Tragedy of the Chinese Revolution* (London, 1938), which is Trotskyite in outlook. A 1951 edition (Stanford) is more balanced.

Mao Tse-tung corresponds to Stalin the Ideologist, Historian, and Objective Scientist. Chu Teh, the Chinese Red general, is the equivalent of Stalin the Strategist, Generalissimo, and Friend of the People. Chou En-lai, one of the most brilliant and personable men of modern times, is not quite in the duumvirate and not quite out of it, possessing as he does the role of Stalin the Diplomat and Negotiator.

Mao is a serious and competent Communist thinker, within the rigid limits of Stalinist orthodoxy. Chu Teh, field commander, admired by the late Brigadier General Evans Carlson of the United States Marine Corps, gives the studied impression of not caring much about Communist ideology, but he never gets in trouble with it. A hard-working, clearheaded, and audacious strategist, he runs whatever kind of war he is told to carry out and does it well. Before he became a Communist, he was a rich, opium-sotted warlord with a harem full of concubines; it was sheer will power that made him decide to do something worthwhile with his own life. In Chu there is exemplified the tremendous drawing power of communism-as-purpose, rather than of communism-as-economics. In sharp contrast, Chou En-lai is a slight, voluble, pleasantly friendly man. He feels sure enough of his position to make quips about Stalinist orthodoxy, or to concede points on common-sense grounds. It was he who virtually hypnotized a whole succession of American officials in China, with the exception of Generals Hurley and Wedemeyer.

A different man, as tedious and repetitious as the Russian Communist dignitaries whom he sedulously imitates, is Liu Shao-chi. Unfortunately for Chinese civilization, Liu has risen to sharp prominence since the proclamation of the People's Republic. He has become second only to Mao as the cryptogogue of party mysteries, the enunciator of the subtleties of the Marxist-Leninist line in China.

There is an important difference between the two men. While Mao is subtle and gifted in his own strange way, Liu is the party bully on a grand scale. During 1950-1951 Liu worked hard to become the most slavish Moscow stooge in the satellite world. His diatribes against Chinese cultural traditions and American "imperialism" masked an immense appetite for cruelty and a monumental capacity for coarse fanaticism.

Is Mao's outlook basically the same? The hope for "Titoism" sprang up among American friends of Red China long before Tito himself dreamed of it. Mao thus far has combined deep loyalty to Marxism-Leninism with a resolute admiration for himself and his immediate followers; his self-esteem does not permit him the most degrading imitations of Russia. He never quite calls Stalin a god; he would rather reserve that status for himself. Liu Shao-chi has performed the political miracle of remaining acceptable to Mao while serving as China's chief adulator of Russia. Ominously, his rising power presages a growing dependence of his country on Moscow.

Chinese-Russian Contacts. Chinese communism remained long separated from Russian communism by Nationalist forces. Only a thin corridor through Jehol provided connections with the USSR. Hence, the heavy hand of Moscow simply did not manage to reach Chinese Communist areas too frequently. Furthermore, the Chinese Communists have the tremendous advantage of speaking, reading, and writing Chinese—a language that is as difficult for the Russians as it is for Americans. The Kremlin is apt to get late, partial, and garbled information on what Chinese communism is doing at any given moment in a particular local situation. Until the Chinese intervention in Korea, Moscow appears to have been content to let Chinese Communists work out their own destiny in their peculiar but effective Chinese way.

This statement does not mean that the Chinese Communists have ever challenged Moscow on a basic point of policy. Chinese communism has had its schisms and purges, and the party as a whole has gloried in being part of a world movement. With all that, the Chinese Communists are the only Communist party of the world today to admix a non-Marxist ideology with their official party thought. Like the Kuomintang, they were for long committed to the support of the *San Min Chu I,* the "three principles of the people" set forth by Sun Yat-sen. This lip-service arose from the fact that Dr. Sun himself founded the first Kuomintang-Communist coalition, the further fact that the junior of his two widows was always a supporter of Chinese communism under the "coalition" slogan, and the final consideration that the Communists are free to interpret Dr. Sun *correctly. Correctly* means that they may take the nearest handy quotation from Sun Yat-sen to paraphrase Stalin.

4. Ideological Position of the Kuomintang

Characteristics of the Kuomintang. The Kuomintang is a bundle of contradictions. It included virtually all the non-Communist leadership of China. In power, it stood for the *status quo,* but talked the language of revolution. Never well enough organized to become fascist, it is a sufficiently closed entity to provide an operating political machine.

The name *kuomintang* is now so old that it is found in American dictionaries. The three Chinese words *kuo* and *min* and *tang* mean, loosely, nation, people, and party. The term *Nationalist* has been used so long by English-speaking Kuomintang leaders themselves, as a matter of semantic shorthand, that the untranslatability of the European concept "nationalism" has been forgotten by Chinese and Westerners alike. Sun Yat-sen himself, in calling for nationalism, used the phrase *min-tsu,* roughly equivalent to "race nation." But it is apparent from the general context of his thinking that he was talking about something much more nearly equivalent to the term "civilization" as it has been used by Mr. Arnold Toynbee—a way of life, a political-ethical-religious-semantic system usually possessing a definite ethnic and territorial base.

Sun Yat-sen. Sun Yat-sen is most commonly recognized in the Western world for the most dismal disappointment of his political life—his brief and unhappy tenure as first provisional President of the Chinese Republic, from January 1 to March 10, 1912. Actually, Sun never held great political power until just before he died. The effect of his revolutionary, modernizing work was ideological and cultural. If his proposed synthesis of Chinese and Western political and moral values goes into effect, Sun will have given his name and personality to a great new way of life among mankind. Born in 1866 near the old Sino-Portuguese city of Macao, Sun went as a boy to the Hawaiian islands, where he faced Western material progress with precocious soul-searching. He became a Christian and a democrat. Returning to China, where he was married by command of his family to a girl of his own yeoman-farmer class, he studied medicine in British Hongkong and is probably the first Chinese in all history to have obtained the Western degree of M.D. It is no accident that he was a doctor. Medical knowledge gave him the spiritual authority to prescribe for other people's ills; Western medical progress made him believe that keen thought and hard work could solve any human problem; his British-Hawaiian-American background gave him the political self-assurance to attack the Manchu Empire in China.

Sun tackled the job of revolution in his late boyhood. He was a magnetic man. Often he converted people to his cause in a single short interview. He proceeded idealistically against incredibly adverse odds; but he proceeded shrewdly and hopefully, and won. From 1885 to 1911 he worked first with friends and then with the antidynastic secret societies, weaving together the overseas Chinese communities and the progressives at home.[10] He wanted the people to have less liberty and more government, less traditionalism and more progress, less psychological security and more strategic security. The revolution caught flame in the fall of 1911. The Manchus, who had ruled China for centuries, were overthrown with almost casual ease. The Republic was proclaimed. But after a few weeks' tenure of the presidency, Sun yielded the government on a "coalition" basis to the only remaining holders of real power: the commanders of the modernized soldiery. Once in power, the militarists remained under the leadership of their "strong man" (Yüan Shih-k'ai) until 1916. Then the strong militarist died, and China lapsed into shameful and useless civil war. Sun Yat-sen's revolution of 1911 had swept away the traditional authority, creating not progress but anarchy.

Undismayed, Sun started again. He changed his league of conspirators into a parliamentary party and then back into a revolutionary league; *Kuomintang* is merely the latest of its many names. He sought help from the French, from the Japanese, from Chicago and New York bankers, from Woodrow Wilson, and finally from the Bolsheviks, who had come to power

---

[10] The first date is his own. In a manuscript in the author's possession (unpublished), Sun wrote: "My mind was made up to overthrow the Ching [Manchu] dynasty and to establish the Republican form of Government in 1885 when China was defeated in the war with France. Henceforth I utilized the schoolroom as the headquarters of my propaganda, and used the medical profession as a medium of association with the different classes: thus ten years rolled by as a day."

in Russia. The Russians were the only ones who responded; Sun they regarded as a transitional Asiatic leader from the anti-imperialist revolution to the Communist-led revolution. Sun, who was very Chinese, said that he was a Communist and added that Marxism was a mistaken philosophy. The Leninist agents did not argue the point. They came down to Canton, where Sun ruled over about one fiftieth of the Chinese Republic, and began to give the Kuomintang the organizational touch. As long as he lived, Sun was loyal to the Communist-Kuomintang coalition. During his much-traveled, revolutionary life, he had married an Americanized Chinese girl, his first wife not having much appetite for tumult and conspiracy. The veteran leader and his young wife symbolized awakening Asia. Brilliant Russians joined students, army officers, old conspirators, college professors, and every other kind of Chinese in launching another Chinese revolution—the revolution of 1922-27, which put both Communists and Kuomintang in power.

Chiang—Party Leader. Revolutions start with principles and end with orders-of-battle; to succeed, they must take military form. The new military leader was a young man named Chiang Kai-shek, who soon became one of a triumvirate of Kuomintang leaders. When Sun Yat-sen died in the midst of his final revolution on March 12, 1925, power passed into Chiang's hands. His civilian coadjutors, Hu Han-min (whom he ran out of office in 1931) and Wang Ch'ing-wei (whom jealousy drove to treason as Japan's quisling in World War II), could not hold power without him.

Chiang had been educated at the imperial military school for modernized troops; he had been sent to Japan and had served, honorarily, as a Japanese second lieutenant; he had played a minor role in the revolution of 1912; he had been a spy, a businessman, a recruiting officer, a politician, all in turn. Sun had sent him to Moscow to learn all the tricks of the Communist trade —infiltration, double talk, conspiracy, sedition, provocation of riots, exploitation of labor unrest, and so on. Chiang came back and created, with the help of able Russian officers, an army that had a purpose. Preceded by swarms of agitators and propagandists, the army united Southern and Central China by 1927. The Communists began to debate whether "history" had any further need of Chiang. Thanks to his Moscow training, Chiang understood them and led the Kuomintang in a sharp swing to the right in 1927. Doing so, he became the political as well as the military head of Nationalist China.

Kuomintang Principles. The ideology that Sun Yat-sen left permitted divergencies. Its only textual form is that of stenographic notes from sixteen lectures given by Sun just before he died.[11] Its Chinese name is Three (*San*) Popular or Democratic (*Min*) Ideas or Principles (*Chu I*). *Min-tsu* ("race nationalism") teaches that Chinese civilization must become a patri-

---

[11] Paschal M. d'Elia, S. J., *The Triple Demism of Sun Yat-sen* (Wuchang, 1931) is the translation with the greatest amount of explanatory and critical apparatus. A good literal version is that of Frank Price, *San Min Chu I*, various editions.

otic, *governed,* democratic state if it is to survive; that it should reconcile Chinese morality and sagacity with Western science (Sun leaving the problem of *how* to his successors, who have quarreled about it ever since); that China should be strong, revolutionary, pro-Soviet, pro-Japanese, peaceful, and progressive. *Min-ch'üan* ("democracy" or "popular power") postulates that men are naturally unequal, being divided into seers, implementers, and obeyers; that the people could know what they wanted and should have the power (*ch'üan*) to choose, but that the people could not be counted on to know how to get what they wanted, since they lacked the technical capacity (*nêng*) to use political means for chosen ends; that a better democracy than any now known could be created by a *five*-power division (executive, legislative, judicial, administrative, censoral) which reconciled the ancient Chinese systems with American, Swiss, and British practice; and that since the people were manifestly unable to start real democracy without training, the Kuomintang should fight for power (first stage of revolution) by military means, should train the people in constitutional government (second stage), and should then abdicate in favor of elected officials (third stage). *Min-shêng* (essentially untranslatable, but sometimes rendered as "the people's livelihood") was a humane, intelligent empirical collectivism, philosophically combining the merits of socialism and free enterprise.

Various modifications have appeared on the level of political argument or controversy. The unhappy genius and later quisling, Wang Ch'ing-wei, who ended his life under the bungling knives of Japanese surgeons, issued his own doctrinal variety to show that the *San Min Chu I* had pan-Asiatic elements more important than any other. Generalissimo Chiang Kai-shek, in his remarkable confession of views entitled *China's Destiny,*[12] skews Sun's doctrine around to fit the austere, conservative, patriotic tradition to which Chiang has dedicated his life. On the other hand, the tireless Communists have proved not only that Sun's heritage is Marxism in a crude and local form, but that each later variation of Stalinist policy was what Sun Yat-sen *really* meant.

Party Changes. The Kuomintang in form is still much like the Communist party of the Soviet Union (Bolshevik), from which its organization was copied in the days of the first coalition. The Bolshevik imprint did not matter. What matters, Chinese think, is the man, not the rule; the purpose, not the law; the fact, not the formula. Hence, formulas are almost always immaculately tidy in Chinese public affairs: they are rarely subjected to the test of practical application.

The Kuomintang started as a league of conspiring Chinese rebels. It became a loose-knit *camarilla* of progressives grouped around Sun Yat-sen. During the revolution of 1922-27, it turned into a dynamic and disciplined revolutionary party. From 1928-48 it lapsed into an aspect of Chinese offi-

---

[12] Available in an "official edition" with an introduction by Lin Yut'ang and in a Marxist "liberal" edition (both New York, 1947).

cialdom. It was about as dangerous to belong to the Kuomintang as it is to go to church on Sunday in Topeka, Kansas. What was said in the Kuomintang meetings was inspiring, but the participants had all heard it before. "The political crisis is terrible, leadership is needed, officials must be honest, the people must be energetic, the nation must survive, and Sun must be venerated." Everybody listened; everybody made the appropriate group responses; then everybody except the Generalissimo went home and had lunch. Chiang, like a dissatisfied Savonarola, stalked about in a frenzy of unappeasable zeal.

Loss of Party Zeal. Disappearance of party zeal accounts for the Kuomintang's most serious political mistake of recent years—the failure to compete with the Communists for leadership of the guerrillas behind the Japanese lines. But the Kuomintang, although able to support a starved, under-equipped, low-morale, but still tremendous army, simply did not have its own fanatics who would seek death and glory behind the Japanese lines, beyond occasional adventurers. Even these were discouraged by the fierce cruelty with which the Communists met them. Decrying "civil war" at the top of their voices, the Communists attacked every Kuomintang unit that tried to join them in the "fraternal struggle" for freedom. When the war ended, the Kuomintang "ordered" the Communists to evacuate areas that the Communists had taken from government troops or from the Japanese. But the party had only words.

In 1944 the Kuomintang had a fiftieth anniversary celebration; the post office issued special stamps. In 1945 the Kuomintang held its Sixth National Congress in Chungking (May 5 to May 21) and listened to speeches, adopted irreproachable resolutions that no one expected to have literal effect, and then elected new committees. No significant change of tempo was observable.

Present Kuomintang Power. In the past few years, the question of the extent of the Kuomintang's ideological appeal to the people of China was one of the most important matters in Far Eastern affairs.

A good case can be made for the argument that the Kuomintang is washed up; but it is a case with loopholes. The Nationalists possess only the territorial bases of Formosa and a few islands—physical, along the coast; and political, in the form of guerrilla islands on the mainland. But the Nationalists have moral opportunities; these might develop.

In the Korean combat zone in 1951, one could find both ex-Nationalist and Communist prisoners of war who regarded the Kuomintang as the pre-eminent alternative to Communist power. Furthermore, the Kuomintang is the only rival to the Communists to possess an official and articulated ideological creed, and it still has the capacity Sun Yat-sen had for organizing overseas Chinese communities. The Chinese prisoners took Chiang much more seriously than did their American interrogators. He was a real second choice.

Minor Parties. The minor parties are small groups that control not a single county, not a single regiment, not a single battalion of police. They have English-speaking leaders, pious ambitions, violent invective for the Generalissimo, and much American approval. Their patron saint is the junior Mme. Sun Yat-sen, a lady who has by now been continuously non-Communist and pro-Communist longer than any other living person. She long remained a nominal member of the Kuomintang while giving her support to anyone who would oppose her brother-in-law, Chiang. The chief military leaders of the minor parties include Li Chi-shen, a "toothless tiger" now eking out a sinecure in Communist China, and Fêng Yü-hsiang, the "Christian general," who was burned to death on a Russian ship in 1948. Their aggregate party forces are minute indeed as against the millions who adhere to the Kuomintang or communism. Minor parties became temporarily important on the advent of quasi-constitutional government, however, because each of the two great parties desired to give itself a democratic flavor by exhibiting sympathetic satellites. There were a great many of these minor parties. All of them lacked guns, wealth, or practical political effect. Of these, the most serious lack was that of weapons. Military control of an area has involved control of its economics and politics as well.

According to the organic law of 1931, the Kuomintang was the sole legal political party in the Chinese state. During the long anti-Japanese party truce, the Kuomintang remained the sole party before the law, but in the atmosphere of wartime tolerance a number of minor parties appeared.[13]

Important among them were the Third party (*Ti-san Tang*), composed of Nationalists and Communists who, disloyal to their respective parties, sought to maintain the long-lost coalition of 1922-27. Moral and idealistic, but hopelessly obscure and ineffectual, the party had one trump card—the benevolent patronage of the junior Mme. Sun Yat-sen. The Chinese National Socialist party (*Kuo-chia Shê-hui Tang*) was literally a mildly nationalist socialist party, not at all resembling its Nazi namesake; it later took the more appropriate name of Social Democratic party (*Shê-hui Min-chu Tang*). The Young China party (*Ch'ing-nien Tang*) was democratic and progressive in intent; it owed much to French inspiration. A further grouping was provided by sponsors of rural rehabilitation and of vocational education, each of whom set up pressure organizations to effect their ends; they were recognized by the government as minor parties. In March 1941 these splinter parties formed a united front, mildly pro-Communist in character, under the name of Federation of Chinese Democratic Parties, revived in September 1944 as the Democratic League (*Min-chu T'ung Mêng*). The League included the Third party, National Salvationists, the two other reform groups, the Youth party, and the Social Democrats.

When the Nationalist-Communist split was made final in the early autumn

---

[13] For a description of minor parties as of 1940, see Paul M. A. Linebarger, *The China of Chiang K'ai-shek* (Boston, 1941), pp. 175 ff.

of 1947, the minor parties had to make a real choice. Most of them remained within the framework of the national government, but a substantial portion of the Democratic League went over to the Communists. The Nationalists had been appeasing their tame minor parties with profuse offers of jobs— including a guaranteed minimum membership in the National Assembly, a share in the Cabinet, pro rata assignments to the public payroll, and so on. The Kuomintang appeasement of minor parties went to such a length that Kuomintang party members, running as private individuals and against party orders, beat some of the inept and unknown minor-party democrats whom the Kuomintang leaders wished to have elected as a loyal opposition. In the National Assembly there resulted the weird scene of democratically elected Kuomintang members being denied their seats because the Kuomintang leadership had already promised those same seats to persons who had been considered "anti-Kuomintang democrats" by the American government. In the end the elections were annulled, and the Generalissimo, with a hopeful eye on United States foreign policy, announced that China would never accept foreign political interference. Chinese sanity and humor were never better demonstrated than in the press despatch which announced that the dissident Kuomintang delegates, outraged and humiliated, had vowed to go on a hunger strike—on a "light diet."

When the Communists finally consolidated their power after 1948, the political decline of the minor parties was rapid. Under the loose hegemony of a respectability-seeking Kuomintang, there was a future ahead of them. They had bargaining value when they faced the Generalissimo, because they possessed the ability to make his regime acceptably "democratic" in appearance to the non-Communist nations.

The Communists held little with such nonsense. Though minor parties exist within the area of the People's Republic, the security requirements of the war in Korea tightened up Communist police control of all independents, no matter how nominal or timid their independence might be. The minor parties exist as the obedient echo of an increasingly rigid Communist line. They are mercilessly purged if they live up to the hopes of a popular front which animated their most honest leaders to join the new regime.[14]

---

[14] On the development of Chinese politics under Mao's regime, see the pertinent sections of Ch'ien Tuan-shêng, *The Government and Politics of China* (Cambridge, Mass., 1950), a long, bitter, biased book by a heart-broken liberal. Accounts of recent leaders and events can be found in works by Robert S. Elegant, Robert Payne, Freda Utley, George Moorad, Graham Peck, Harrison Forman, Anna Louise Strong, and Jack Belden; most of these have a case to prove. A detached document is *Communism in China,* prepared by George S. Pettee for the Bolton subcommittee of the House Foreign Affairs Committee (Washington, 1949).

CHAPTER 28

SOURCES OF POWER IN THE
POSTWAR FAR EAST

1. The Eggshell of a Democratic Japan

The Nonrevolutionary Liberation. Japanese democracy was born under the auspices of the twice infamous Prince Higashikuni—hated in China because he commanded the troops who went mad in the horrors of the Nanking massacre, unforgettable in Japan because he was the imperial clansman designated to accept Japan's profoundest shaming. Made Premier for the explicit task of conveying the imperial command to surrender, Higashikuni came to power on August 17, 1945. The words of the Emperor's message commanding and explaining surrender were still echoing in every street. Japan had lost "according to the dictate of time and fate." The penalty was to be paid by "enduring the unendurable and suffering the insufferable." The key to Japanese survival had been discipline. Yet the outside world was unprepared to see that discipline make a 180° change of direction and move phalanx-like into freedom. The Japanese showed in 1945 ability to stay conquered, to remain united, to "endure the unendurable" without flashes of revolt which might have led to the consummate ruin of their sovereignty.

Democracy was commanded by the Emperor, who had the right, over and above all law, to command his own people as he saw best. If he chose to deny his own divinity later, so much better the proof that his imperial person was peculiar, above all need of fable or justification. Democracy was also the command of the Allied powers. The victor is the victor; the Japanese expected homage and obedience from the peoples they whipped; when they themselves were whipped, they expected to render these in turn. Finally, since the victors were themselves "democratic" (China and Russia being dubious cases), there was in democracy something that conduced to power—to actual tangible triumph. Democracy "worked"—it had worked on Saipan, Iwo Jima, Okinawa—in a way that the Japanese were willing to acknowledge, to study, and to imitate. If totalitarianism had led to defeat, something must have been wrong with it. Hence, the Japanese turnabout combined tradition, discipline, and a shocking admixture of sentiment and realism.

Never was a revolution less revolutionary. Totalitarianism demobilized rapidly and in good order; with transparent hopefulness, the militarist and ultranationalist politicians grouped themselves into parliamentary "parties" to fit the new role of things. Imperial Army generals sang the blessings of peace. The change came from the top, the Cabinet; and the top above that, the Emperor; and the top above him, Allied military power. The Japanese government held back long enough to make sure that the United States would in fact accept a conditional surrender, leaving the Japanese government intact. Moreover, the Americans also saved face for themselves by calling the process "unconditional surrender."

Allied Controls. The structure of Allied controls was shown from the very beginning. Troops were to have duties of security and garrison. Military government was to be supervisory in name and advisory in effect. The Americans were to send experts to show the Japanese how to avoid chaos, civil war, further ruin; they were to lead the Japanese every step of the way. Pre-eminently significant was the structure on each side. Theoretically, the Japanese government obeyed Allied orders; actually, the Japanese have been suggesting or initiating much of the practical policy ever since the first weeks of surrender. Theoretically, viewed from the outside, the Allied control is Allied; actually, it is American. Thus, an "Allied military government" of Japan has remained a Japanese government of Japan with American protection and assistance. The key to Japan was the man bearing the title of Supreme Commander for the Allied Powers. He represented the historical accident of a Western military institution emerging at just the right historical moment to meet a Japanese political institution: the theater commander and the more-than-mortal monarch. The theater commander of World War II represented an Anglo-Saxon experiment in absolute monarchy. No order applied without being applied by him and through him, subject to his interpretation. This process happened to fit the need of Japan superbly well.

The Supreme Commander for the Allied Powers, until April 11, 1951, happened to be MacArthur, but it was office as well as personality that fitted him for the job of being super-Emperor for Japan. The formal controls —Far Eastern Commission (FEC); Allied Council for Japan; State-Army-Navy-Air Coordinating Committee (SANACC), later superseded by the National Security Council—were, in the most correct sense of the word, *formal*. They dealt in generalities, not specific cases; in intentions, not practices; in the policy that can be put into legal words, not in policy that can be seen retrospectively in the wake of action. The theater commander retained the substance of the responsibility—one-man military and general policy.

From the personality, juridically considered, of the Supreme Commander for the Allied Powers (SCAP), there grew an office which bore his name, with 9, later 13, staff sections: Economic and Scientific, Civil Information and Education, Natural Resources, Government, Legal, Civil Intelligence, Public Health and Welfare, Civil Communications, Statistical and Reports, Office of Civilian Property Custodian, Civil Transportation, Adjutant General (Military), and Office of Procurement Agent. In addition to these special sections, there were at the level of the Chief of Staff a Diplomatic Section and a Public Information Section.

These agencies were not ministries in a military government. They watched; they supervised, to a very limited extent; they helped; they collaborated; but they did not govern. The governors were the Japanese; the supervisor was MacArthur; the United States was the chief power responsible; the four greater Allies were represented in the Allied Council for Japan, which met in Tokyo; all of the Allies assembled as the Far Eastern Commission in the former Japanese Embassy in Washington, D. C. The presiding officer of the Allied Council for Japan was usually the political advisor to SCAP, a veteran American diplomat; the chairman of the Far Eastern Commission was an American, a soldier or diplomat; the secretary of the commission was also an American.

"Allied controls" therefore meant a special new Japanese-American relationship, in which Japan became a quasi-dominion, largely self-governing, in an implicit United States Combine of Nations. The "Allied" capacity to overrule MacArthur on any tangible measure was not substantially greater than the "Allied" capacity to overrule Soviet authority in Rumania, Bulgaria, or Hungary, before the peace treaties were signed. Authority was plainly in American hands. And the principle, rigorously applied but rarely expressed outside military staffs, on which Americans held the authority, was total delegation of military authority to a single man. A named Japanese monarchy from the past had met the nameless Theater monarchy of the present.

Connecting Link. To the supreme command of MacArthur, Japanese authority extruded an institution through which the substance of power could flow. It was called the Central Liaison Office (CLO), and it was established by the Japanese before the formal American arrival.

As SCAP became increasingly dependent upon liaison with the Japanese ministries appropriate to the problems at hand, CLO was abolished on February 1, 1948. The Foreign Ministry (*Giamusho*), long one of the most vigorous diplomatic units of our world, put matters in their right perspective by setting up its own Liaison Bureau for this function.

Liaison kept the overlord happy; that was the Japanese design. It furnished information, arranged meetings, accepted commands, and in general performed the functions of both chancery and grand secretariat. The Japanese rendered MacArthur's name as *Makasa.* Himself virile, autocratic, flamboyant, decisive, he made a tremendous impression on them; few other men could have fitted into the job of being an emperor's emperor quite so neatly or effectively in the course of great crises. Japanese history has never before had anyone like him; Japanese admiration for *Makasa* remains great.

The One Perfect State. The Japanese government returned, therefore, to that state of uterine bliss which some Freudians posit as the original datum of all human security. It was shielded on all sides by overwhelming power. No invaders could touch Japan. No revolution could occur in the face of Allied guns. No policy could fail. Under these circumstances the Japanese, who are not without a wry official humor of their own, undertook to make Japan a state somewhat better than perfect. They not only disarmed but renounced all war forever, along with all military establishments and training. What better device could have been found to remind the Americans that when American military force moved out, the Japanese had nothing whatever to keep other forces from moving in? For the time being, Japan spent more on the occupation armies (chiefly American, but with some British detachments) than she had ever spent on her own forces in time of peace. But this cost would some day go off the Japanese budget, possibly leaving the Japanese defended by the United States without the cost of a single sen.[1]

The pleasures of irresponsibility can be exaggerated. But, out of castastrophe, the Japanese have come very near to doing the best they could; that, in itself, is a remarkable accomplishment.

2. Violence in Postwar Japan

Violence in Japanese Ethics. China and Japan stand in sharp contrast to each other in terms of their ideological response to violence. To the Chinese, violence has long been brutalizing and ineffectual; even Chinese warfare has emphasized wit rather than attack. The Chinese writer Sun Tzŭ, in his Art of War written about 500 B.C., said categorically: ". . . to fight and conquer in all your battles is not supreme excellence; supreme excellence consists in breaking the enemy's resistance without fighting." [2] Moreover, the Chinese have extolled peace in their political life to such an unprecedented degree that modern Chinese soldiery takes on high morale only when infused with German, American, Russian, or Japanese doctrines. But in Japan the soldier was not at the bottom of the scale; he was at the top. Weapons seemed not vulgar but glorious. Chinese classics extol men like Ch'u-k'o Liang, who frightened away his opponents by pretending to have hidden troops when he had no troops at all. Japanese classics extol the forty-seven ronin, who led lives of poverty and dissoluteness until they could catch their dead master's

---

[1] The chief official source for material on present-day Japan is Supreme Commander for the Allied Powers, Summation of Non-Military Activities in Japan, General Headquarters, Supreme Commander for the Allied Powers (Tokyo, monthly, numbered serially with a new number for each monthly issue). The official "diary" of political aspects of the occupation, particularly as seen in the rôle of the SCAP Government Section, is Political Reorientation of Japan, September 1945 to September 1948, Report of Government Section, Supreme Commander for the Allied Powers (Washington, 1949), 2 vols. The Department of State Bulletin includes most major policy materials on Japan as approved by FEC. The Loochoo or Ryukyu Islands are reported in Commander-in-Chief, Far East, Summation of United States Army Military Government Activities in the Ryukyu Islands, General Headquarters, Commander-in-Chief, Far East (location presumably Tokyo, issued bimonthly, each issue bearing a new serial number). The Commander-in-Chief, Far East, was at first General MacArthur, later General Ridgeway, this time in a purely American and not an Allied role. An excellent general summary is contained in the Department of State Publication No. 267, Far Eastern Series 17, Occupation of Japan: Policy and Progress (Washington, 1947).

[2] Quoted from the Lionel Giles translation as reprinted in Major T. R. Phillips, ed., Roots of Strategy: A Collection of Military Classics (Harrisburg, 1940), p. 26.

enemy off guard and murder him—being rewarded with forty-seven honorable deaths, and great memories.

The strain of violence in Japanese institutions and thinking has shown its good side in *bushido*, the "way of the warrior," which ranks with the most refined and literally noble chivalric codes. Its bad side has been shown in the class application of violence, by the upper classes against the lower, and in the undisciplined, frantic cruelty that Japanese may commit when placed in positions of political or military unfamiliarity. Nor did the Japanese confine their application of violence to external situations. Assassination, because of its feudal connotations, was one of the chief means whereby the militarist cliques of the 1920's and 1930's drove Japan's liberalist leadership from power. Beatings and tortures were administered on a scale which would have horrified a world that had not yet heard of Auschwitz or Komi. The courts were so thoroughly intimidated that assassins were often acquitted amid public acclaim.

Political Assassination. Violence reached its peak in the attempted murder of the whole Japanese Cabinet by the military extremists in February 1936.[3] The conspirators were junior officers who seized command of regiments in the Tokyo metropolitan area. Under the influence of ultranationalist propaganda, they undertook a *coup* that in some respects resembled that of the Russian Decembrists of 1825. Patriotism and an urge "forward" on the part of young idealists played a part. But in the Tokyo case, the tenor of the times made the fascistic road seem the forward one. Some of the most eminent, conservative, and wealthy men in Japan were killed on this occasion. It marked the final submission of the antimilitarists. Henceforth, the two major sections of the ruling class—the *gumbatsu* (military clique) and the *zaibatsu* (business interests), along with the bureaucrats—hid their disagreements. The leftists never organized a corresponding degree of counterviolence. They realized that the militarist-traditionalists held the whip hand, and that bloodshed from the left would merely signal disproportionate reprisals from the right, both official and unofficial.

It was the identification with official militarism, and in turn with the government and the Emperor, which made the official nationalists so vigorous in Japan. Without the Army and Navy to spur the ultranationalists, they would not have gone far. The old leaders whispered their regrets to the American Ambassador, in a number of instances, when they were in mortal terror despite their eminence in title, wealth, and official position.

Changing Outlook. The imperial rescript of surrender removed the purpose from militarism. If the Emperor could no longer be worshipped as Commander-in-Chief; if the Army and Navy were no longer special and *above* the ignoble civilian government; if the Japanese code of strength pointed up to a pinnacle on which there stood General MacArthur—under

---

[3] See the vivid account given in Joseph C. Grew, *Ten Years in Japan* (New York, 1944), pp. 169 ff.

these conditions the whole ideological impetus to socially sanctioned violence was lost.   With an abrupt reversal of character the Japanese hooted their own defeated homecoming troops in the railway stations.[4]

More recently, a group of informed Japanese agreed that there was no tangible evidence of current activities of the old secret societies.[5]   Not a single patriotic murder has been reported.

3. Authority and Wealth in Postwar Japan

A Sober Capitalism.   The power in Japan that made for war was, economically, the fusion of governmental-political-financial strength into a reasonably well-disciplined solidarity.   Capitalism in Japan never had its ruthless individualists, its opulent lechers, its squandering eccentrics.   Japanese capitalism was dry, civic, functional; it made tremendous profits and plowed these back into investment.   Western commentators who decried the high rates of return on Japanese investment could never charge the Japanese owning classes with malodorous conspicuous waste.   The greatest capitalists chose an actual scale of living not too far removed from that of the American middle classes.

The sobriety and patriotism of Japanese capitalism arose from its unique sense of national responsibility.   It was the economic and intellectual limitations of this capitalist class that committed Japan to overseas trade and over-industrialization.   When the American-British-Chinese-Dutch doors were slammed in its face, it was this class that yielded to the extremists and militarists.   The great capitalists would not have gone to war on their own; they might have opposed the militarists if they had been sure of their share of world trade.   But when their own armed services, anticapitalist in word but less so in deed, showed Japan a way out, the capitalists went along.

Economics under Occupation.   The occupation helped Japan by correlating her national status with American strategic protection, by providing the Japanese with American defenders against any forays from the mainland, by advising the Japanese on dismantlement of their war machine, and by furnishing experienced personnel to show them the appropriate American techniques in a variety of skills.   But occupation was more costly than Japanese military budgets at their costliest in time of peace.   Moreover, the economic burden was two-sided.   There was also the fact that the Americans turned upon Japan the crippling threat of reparations—along with the reparations already seized, in the form of Japanese-owned property abroad,

---

[4] For a general examination of the Japanese character, and the type of personality that makes such changes possible, see Geoffrey Gorer, "Themes in Japanese Culture," *Transactions of the New York Academy of Sciences,* ser. II, 5 (March 1943), 106 ff.

[5] See S. Abe and Others, "Nihon no Chika Seifu" ("The Underground Government of Japan"), in *Nihon Hyoron (Japanese Review),* Tokyo (March 1948), 50 ff.   For another type of "invisible" government, see Harry Emerson Wildes, "Underground Politics in Post-War Japan," in a symposium entitled "Post-war Politics in Japan," edited by Harold S. Quigley, *American Political Science Review,* 42 (1948), 1149 ff.

in every nation of the world except for Switzerland, Sweden, Spain, and one or two other smaller countries.

The American reply to Japan's first surrender offer stated categorically: "The armed forces of the Allied Powers will remain in Japan until the purposes set forth in the Potsdam Declaration are achieved." The Potsdam Declaration had promised Japan permission to maintain industries that would "sustain her economy." After the peace treaty Japan will have much more sovereign liberty; she may have less to eat unless the American and Japanese governments are minded to be both friendly and careful with each other.

Fundamental Problems. The basic problems that must be worked out before Japan is ready for the future include that of the economic cost and actual provision of Japanese defense. An undefended frontier is not practicable along strategic Soviet borders. Japan is disarmed. How can she be defended? Who will pay for it? Indeed, how will a ruined and over-populated country re-establish its position in world trade? Will the American market welcome "cheap" Japanese goods? Will the Indian, Chinese, and Southeast Asia markets of Japan be available again? The likelihood is small, but how then will Japan live?

Again, how can a nation's economy expand to meet the "democratically" demanded standard of income that the Americans call "widened," with a loss of dominions and colonies, a loss of all overseas investments, and a rising population? Are there any alternatives to increased foreign trade? Will any area of the world be prepared to accept sizeable Japanese immigration? If the Japanese are to obtain raw materials, how shall they get that "access to, as distinguished from control of," these that the Potsdam ultimatum held forth to them? Moreover, if the general economic system, although perhaps above subsistence requirements, remains unsatisfactory to the human beings who have to live inside it, how are the Japanese going to reconcile their democracy with omnipresent depression and fear of chaos?

4. Class and War in China

Contrasting Approaches. In Japan, the managerial class faces the problem of an imposed *transformation* on an unparalleled scale. In China and Formosa, two rivals fight over the prospective *creation* of a viable economic system. The Communists have almost won. In neither part of China is the old scholastic-familist pattern of management effective; nor have Kuomintang or Communists succeeded in creating an economic system that works on an extensive scale. The Nationalists have moved part-way toward creation of a modern government as the political framework for a modern economy, but they got that far at the price of reform. The Communists have rushed forward into reform, and were wise enough to leave national modernization to the maturing of their regime.

Nationalist China produced many of the modern "good things" that the

West has developed—serums, radio and telephone equipment, electrical goods, and canned foods, for example. But it did not produce them on a grand enough scale to meet the demands of the masses. Most of China produces virtually nothing that could not have been manufactured in the Mexico of 1850. But what it produces it distributes justly.

Cycle of Peasant Revolts. Thomas Taylor Meadows pointed out one hundred years ago that the Chinese had made constitutional the process of rebellion; they had worked out traditions which governed even such explosives as class violence; they had developed ethics that enveloped revolution. The Chinese Communists are in the peculiar position of being heirs and explôiters of this tradition, and at the same time the native voice of the Marxian world religion. The Nationalists were slowly driven by their partial conquest of power into much of the old *defensive* position, rather than the *rebellious*. Completely interpenetrating, the Chinese revolutionary process has (in Communist hands) mixed the traditions of old China, the drive of anti-imperialism, and the Stalinist dogma.[6]

In political terms, the Chinese Communist rebellion has run fairly far through the full cycle, since spontaneous revolutionary movements are out of the question with military power polarized. But there are countervailing factors of extreme importance that modify the old pattern of class struggle. In the past the rebels had no aim other than that of becoming "good" rulers, and the only standard for "good" was one or the other interpretation of the Confucian tradition. Political redress had no other criteria of honor, wealth, or fame, which fell outside Confucian standards. The result was that the fanaticism by which rebellions were promoted almost invariably vanished upon the advent of victory. Today rebellion is a "science" of permanent effort intent upon guiding its own victory.[7]

Positive Growth. The particular phase of disunity that the Chinese are now undergoing is distressing; but in the balance sheet of China's political development, the present general situation represents a distinct improvement over previous decades. On the positive side one may enter the following: China has had governments, first under Chiang and now under Mao, more nearly national and more nearly *government* than anything seen on Chinese soil for many centuries. The Chinese possess the most professional all-Chinese armies to exist since the sixteenth century. They have been freed of all unequal treaties, save for the Portuguese holding at Macao, the British Kowloon leases, and the reconstituted tsarist Russian privileges in Manchuria—exceptions which, though irritating, cannot impede eventual Chinese unification. The Chinese had in the Nationalists an experienced

---

[6] Cf. Paul M. A. Linebarger, *Government in Republican China* (New York, 1938), pp. 63, 84-86.

[7] Much of this chapter is taken from Paul M. A. Linebarger, "The Complex Problem of China," *Yale Review*, 36 (Spring 1947), 499 ff. The editors of the *Yale Review* have given permission for re-use of this material.

and, in some ways, modern-minded leadership and have now what is probably the finest Communist party in the world today. The new regime shows itself most plainly as a national Communist successor-government to the Nationalists in its handling of the war in Korea—a military campaign which, waged on foreign soil, emotionally redressed a century of defeat.

On the other side of the balance sheet are China's tragic defects. Some defects are new. The Communist rule, whatever its military or economic benefits, is costing the Chinese people a terrible price in cultural discontinuity and the down-grading of education—when Chinese education is actually a key to the future. Military adventures in Korea and Indochina eat up the savings which began to accrue with the end of internal war. Economically, Communist benefits were expensive to China after 1949; after 1951, they came to verge on the prohibitive.

Nationalist Class Function. In their social and economic function, the Nationalists long made the pretense, as did the Communists, of transcending class interests and of representing all classes in the struggle against Japan. With that they had little difficulty in the first five years of the war, since inflation discounted farm debts and the inward migration created a boom throughout most of unconquered China. From 1942 onward, however, their failure to block the continued Japanese advance, the resulting military uncertainty, and the complete land and sea blockade, quite aside from excessive issue of paper money, caused the Nationalist economic position to deteriorate.

That economic position rested more on the mercantile classes and on "modernized" capitalism than it did on the old-fashioned landlords. A good case is often badly overstated in showing Chinese politics to be the product of an agrarian economy, as though all Chinese affairs were reducible to landlord-usurer-taxgatherer terms. It is true that China is the greatest farming country on earth; but it is equally true that China throughout the ages, being the biggest country, has always been one of the largest of urban nations. No one would try to analyze Roman history in terms of the *latifundia* alone, when the cities were so plainly evident as fulcra of power. But some Western writers frequently discuss even present-day China as though its hundreds of great rich cities did not exist. The mercantile spirit in China is important; when the country acts, it acts through cities, both economically and strategically. The significant thing about the Nationalist war against Japan was that it was city-based.

The Nationalists, thinking of cities, favored first their officials; secondly, their army; and thirdly, the mercantile and financial groups in society. As the war progressed in China—the only Allied country to suffer severe Axis victories as late as 1944—the morale of the Nationalist areas dropped. In common with all downgrade slides of morale, this situation brought out the worst traits of those adversely affected: selfishness, insane shortsighted-ness, an almost hysterical indolence in the face of danger. Nationalist China was thoroughly defeated in the hour of victory. It was demoralized, half-bankrupt, disoriented when triumph came from the outside. Nothing was easier for the world—and for the Chinese Nationalists themselves—than to forget China's initial contribution to the common victory.

Communist Class Basis. On the Communist side, the class basis was entirely different. It comprised one of the most intelligent and effective applications of Marxist theory ever made. The Communists adopted an economically moderate policy of total land reform, based on the assumption that if the cities did not have to be fed, the land could flourish. As the coastland cities were occupied by the Japanese, the Communists saw readily that the drain of goods to cities could be cut off on grounds of patriotism. The resulting surplus gave the Communists local prosperity, whereas such segmentation brought bankruptcy to the Nationalist economy wherever it operated at or behind the Japanese front lines, because the mercantile and urban system was predicated on China-wide relationships. The Communists created a huge chain of primitive economic areas, set up autarchy in each of them, and used the surplus to meet local needs. Communist areas did not offer to feed the starving Nationalist armies. Instead, they fed light Communist forces, together with a well-organized militia.

The Communists had to survive between Nationalist China and Japanese-occupied China. On the one side, they were pressed by Japanese and their political puppets; on the other, by the Nationalist blockade. Under pressure of the need to survive, they developed. Their politics never called for replacement of the national government; they could afford to call for unity, since they had to bear none of its burdens. For a while they shared power with non-Communist elements on the basis of a united front, and worked out a formal division of one-third Communist, one-third pro-Communist "Kuomintang," and one-third pro-Communist "nonparty" membership for their most important organs of government.

In their areas the Communist leaders developed a sound economy from which to expand. Their small-scale primitive autarchies worked well, but would not have worked at all if the Communists had not managed them with a combination of sharpness and tact. Moreover, the Communists had large cadres of incorruptible leaders. They preserved the foundations of the Marxist doctrines, while accommodating the doctrines to the currently accepted common-denominator slogans of "democracy," "freedom," and so on. They eliminated opposition, whether Nationalist or Japanese, by lumping both under the heading of "profascist treason." The Nationalists held cities, roads, rivers, railroads, canals. The Communists swallowed territory. The Japanese occupation was a thin spiderweb spread out over Eastern and Northern China, and in its early phases cut off many Nationalist islands. The Communists went in and organized these areas. How they did it is a matter of dispute. But the disputes have died, leaving a trail of bitterness all over the anti-Communist world.[8]

The tragic facts remain. Nationalists and Communists did not struggle honorably in competition, demonstrating their ability to govern well. The Nationalists, in 1948 and 1949 as their mainland power died, governed so badly as to provide no serious alternative to the Communists. The Communists won because they opposed bad government—while doing everything possible to make sure that the Nationalist government *stayed* bad.

Tendency and Outlook. The rôle of class cannot be demonstrated in the fall of the Nationalists and the rise of the Communists. For a while, in 1950, the Far East was presented with the astonishing sight of two anti-pathetic Chinas, both of which throve as a result of reciprocal challenge and the momentary but immense benefits of peace. Nationalist Formosa went ahead with real land reforms, genuine military regrouping, and workable local elections. The Communist mainland had cities more operative, more stable, than the most sanguine non-Communist would have thought possible.

Then came the Korean war. The "populist" character of the Communists faded under pressure. Harsh government—traditionally hated in Chinese history—reappeared after a mild opening. Totalitarianism moved forward.[9] The Nationalists, in their turn, saw their destiny blow away in the hurricane of world struggle.

Not only is power changing in China; the sources of power themselves are changing. One of those changes is the ever-increasing effect of Washington and Moscow politics on the internal affairs of China.

---

[8] The anti-Chiang case was stated by the Department of State in *United States Relations with China* (Washington, 1949). The case against the State Department's case, in turn, is best presented by Freda Utley, *The China Story* (Chicago, 1951). The case against Freda Utley had been put by Owen Lattimore in *Ordeal by Slander* (Boston, 1950). The case against Owen Lattimore is well stated by Nathaniel Weyl, *The Battle against Disloyalty* (New York, 1951). The case *for* a buoyant or hopeful program is conspicuously absent.

[9] See the epitome by H. Arthur Steiner, "Perspectives on the Chinese Revolution," *Social Science*, 25 (Oct. 1950), 215-222. For the present author's views, see "Communist China: Some Observations," *South Atlantic Quarterly*, 50 (Apr. 1951) 159-166, and "The China of Mao Tse-tung," *School of Advanced International Studies Alumni Review*, 1 (Winter 1950), 4-8.

CHAPTER 29

GOVERNMENT IN JAPAN

1. The Emperor as an Ex-God

Life by Prescription. Hirohito (he possesses no surname), Emperor of the Showa period, has not had a happy life. He was born to be a god and a constitutional Emperor. He entered upon mortal existence in 1901. His reigning grandfather, the Meiji Emperor, was driving Japan forward with ruthless intelligence and excellent advice toward modern ways.

From the moment of his birth until today, it is reported, Hirohito has had but twenty minutes of genuine privacy, when he was not under the official and worshipful scrutiny of other Japanese. As crown prince, visiting Paris, he gave his escort the slip on the Paris *metro*. For the remainder of his life, he has had less privacy than the Washington Monument in Washington, D. C.

His father, an amiable person, was subject to unconcealable mental deficiencies that made a regency necessary. But prince, regent, or Emperor, Hirohito has never had his own way. No one even knows what his own way would have been; it is too late now. Hirohito, like almost all other Japanese, has simply done what he was told.

Living up to the Meiji Constitution. But if all Japanese do what they are told, who tells them what to do? Part of the answer, especially for the Emperor, could be found in the Meiji constitution, in which one reads: "The Empire of Japan shall be reigned over and governed by a line of Emperors unbroken for ages eternal." [1] The chief author of this constitution of 1889 was the great jurist-statesman-prince, Ito Hirobumi, who in his classic commentaries, by way of exposition, declared:

Since the time when the first Imperial Ancestor opened it, the country has not been free from occasional checks in its prosperity nor from frequent disturbances in its tranquillity; but the splendor of the Sacred Throne transmitted through an unbroken line of one and the same dynasty has always remained as immutable as

---

[1] Prince Hirobumi Ito (Count Myoji Ito, translator), *Commentaries on the Constitution of the Empire of Japan* (3rd ed., Tokyo, 1931), p. 2. This serious and competent work represents a high spot in the preparation of clear, though formal, Asiatic state documents. The most recent statement on the Japanese constitution is Harold S. Quigley, "Japan's Constitutions: 1890 and 1947," *American Political Science Review,* 41 (1947), 865 ff. The great bibliographies of von Wenckstern, Nachod, and Praesent, compiled in English and German by German scholars, provide a reasonably complete guide to all Western-language materials down to 1935.

that of the heavens and the earth.   At the outset, this Article states the great principle of the Constitution of the country, and declares that the Empire of Japan
shall, to the end of time, identify itself with the Imperial dynasty unbroken in lineage, and that the principle has never changed in the past, and will never change
in the future, even to eternity.   It is intended thus to make clear forever the relations that shall exist between the Emperor and His subjects.

By 'reigned over and governed,' it is meant that the Emperor on His Throne
combines in Himself the sovereignty of the State and the government of the country and His subjects.   An ancient record mentions a decree of the first Emperor in
which he says—'The Country of Goodly Grain is a State, over which Our descendants shall become Sovereigns: You, Our descendants, come and govern it.' . . .
[Several quotations from historical fables omitted.]   The word *shiroshimesu*
means reigning over and governing.   It will thus be seen that the Imperial Ancestors regarded it as their Heaven-bestowed purpose of a monarchical society to
reign over the country and not the people, and not to minister to the private wants
of individuals or of families.   Such is the fundamental basis of the present Constitution.[2]

This document is one scarcely typical of modern jurisprudence, yet it represents the deliberate, careful writing of a thoroughly sane man with an
excellent grasp of world affairs.   Even the English form of the capitalized
His, carefully used by the authorized Japanese translator, is an accurate reproduction of the letter and spirit of the Japanese original.   The constitution was a religio-juristic statement, not a politico-juristic one.   Throughout Hirohito's lifetime, it has served the twofold purpose of preserving him
as a divinity and defining the juridical and administrative relationships of
the complicated modern state that operated in "His" name.   Japanese authors never tired of proclaiming the "peculiarity"—meaning the set-apart-
ness, the implicit sacredness, the unique ever-rightness—of the Japanese ruler
and state.   One jurist who, after deep thought, decided that for the purpose
of erudite juridical theory, in the Germanic line of Hegel, the Japanese Emperor could be considered an organ of the Japanese state, eventually lost his
seat in Parliament and almost got killed.   Most Japanese writers adopted the
ecstatic tone of the learned Japanese professor who explained, for the Eng-
lish-reading public, that the Emperor's more-than-sovereign state

. . . is in perfect accord with the ideas of our national structure, which has
remained ever unchanged since the foundation of Japan.   It is in perfect accord
with the Sun Goddess' Edict issued on the occasion of the descent of the Heavenly
Grandson on this land.   It is in perfect accord with all the historical facts on
record. . . . [The Emperor], in the sphere of the provisions of the Constitution,
is the holder of the power to rule over and govern the country, and compared with
the sovereigns of other countries, He has the unique position of being the absolute
center of the nation and of the state.[3]

---

[2] Ito, *op. cit.* above, note 1, pp. 2-4.
[3] Fujii Shinichii, *The Essentials of Japanese Constitutional Law* (Tokyo, 1940), pp. 115, 122.

Emperor-God and National Need. In terms of mass propaganda and its recipients, this Japanese attachment of the Emperor represented a reserve of security against the powerful but corrosive Western semantic references that modern social and political skills had forced upon the Japanese. Applying borrowed political terms, they feared for their own dignity and self-respect. They held back a reserve of alleged "uniqueness" that could, at any given point, be set against shortcomings in their adopted Western pattern of behavior. No matter how Western a Japanese became, no matter how ludicrous or inadequate he might appear in his economic, political, military, or other public behavior, he always had the indefinable mysteries of the Japanese Throne into which to retreat.

The Emperor-as-god was a reflection of the deep inward uncertainties put into the personalities of Japanese in national childhood. Great insecurity begets need for dependence; dependence requires reverence; reverence requires, in turn, irreproachability. If the ruler is to be beyond reproach, the vulgar process of actual government must be removed from his hands. If a political system is to be kept immaculately perfect, it therewith becomes doomed to be a show, not a reality. "The government" in Japan was therefore left intact by giving it nothing to do; the process of government was transferred to vulgar and dirty places behind the scenes, where disagreement and human conflict could go on. When this *de facto* process began to take on dignities, the Japanese purified it, too, and moved practical politics elsewhere.

Dualism of Government. Japan therefore has normally had at least two governments, sometimes as many as four, one behind the other. The topmost was the visible empire; the one at the bottom was that of the vulgar characters who actually had to make politics work. In the period of the virtually autonomous shoguns, for instance, government was usually something like this: The imperial government was visible, sacred, and inactive. The shogunal government was partly visible, respected but not sacred, and thoroughly active. Local government, possessing the most telling effect, had no spiritual reference attached to it. Under the Meiji constitution, the official constitutional procedure got so thoroughly involved with sacredness that the Cabinet risked lese majesty when it tried to *govern*. It was admonished to look nice out front, while the Privy Council and the military determined the hard-and-fast policies behind the scenes. Under the conditions of a new "democratic" dispensation, it is not impossible that the MacArthur machinery will some day be moved up front, operating with tremendous *éclat* in full view of the world, while real politics—like a mother cat hiding her kittens again—goes somewhere else in Japanese national life.

Denial of Godship. The godship of Hirohito has now been officially denied by the principal character. In a carefully phrased imperial rescript issued on New Year's Day 1946, the Japanese court pleased both MacArthur and the Japanese by reaffirming the Emperor's solicitude for his people, and then adding:

We [the Showa Emperor, Hirohito] stand by the people and we wish always to share with them in their moment of joys and sorrows. The ties between us and our people have always stood upon mutual trust and affection. They do not depend upon mere legends and myths. They are not predicated upon the false conception that the Emperor is divine and that the Japanese people are superior to other races and fated to rule the world.

With their blend of psychologically needed sense of peculiarity and empiricism in thinking, the Japanese could well accept this statement as true in one sense while disbelieving it in another. It was true that the Emperor was not "divine" in the way people had thought; otherwise, how could the Americans have won? It was obvious to any fool that the Japanese were not "superior" to the B-29 pilots or to General MacArthur himself; otherwise the Japanese would be parading down Pennsylvania Avenue, rather than U.S. troops down the Ginza. But that did not mean that Japan was no longer a very special kind of state, with a special kind of ruler. It merely meant that Japan had to excel in some other direction. What direction was a question ultimately to be decided when the armed American kibitzers had gone away.

The Emperor was an ex-god, but he nevertheless represented an institution not found elsewhere in the world. He was still entitled to reverence and obedience. Hirohito was doomed to stay where he was born—up above the real politics. He was still the *tenno*—the *tien huang* in the Chinese ideographs, the "heavenly lord." The "heavenly lord" was not sacred; he was merely heavenly.

2. The MacArthur Constitution

Obedient Overlord. The sacred desuetude of the Japanese Emperor does not mean that Hirohito has been powerless. The Emperor, in the tradition of Japan, has vast latent power, whose first limitation is the nature of the Emperor's own personality. Three rulers have governed Japan since the restoration of the throne and the beginning of modernization. The Meiji period brought forth a genius; the Taisho, a sick madman; and the Showa, the present period, gave Japan an obedient official with a taste for natural science. The life of the new constitution, in course of time, will be shaped by Akihito, who will ascend the throne with his head full of childhood memories of fire-rain, MacArthur, and Mrs. Elizabeth Vining, the tutoress nominated by SCAP for him. But it is a fair presumption that Akihito, like Hirohito, is apt to obey. The constitution is set within the framework of the Emperor's religio-social power—a power that could be abolished legally every day for a decade without undergoing serious diminution *unless* there were concurrent ideological change within Japan.

Thus, the paradox of the Japanese written constitution lies in the fact that it is a footnote to a moral constitution possessing much higher authority. The moral constitution conveys almost illimitable powers to the Emperor.

A strong Emperor, therefore, could do almost anything, if he went about it step-by-step and shrewdly. But there is neither a strong Emperor on the throne now nor any serious prospect of one in the near future. Hence, the imperial power is perpetually in reserve.

Use of the Emperor's Power. This reserved power is sought by groups that try to transcend the letter of the existing constitution. In the days of Meiji, Taisho, and early Showa, the structure of government looked like the accompanying chart. The visible government was the "constitutional" one

VISIBLE AND INVISIBLE GOVERNMENT OF PREWAR JAPAN

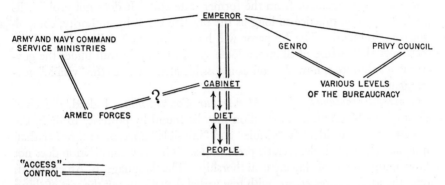

—the line from Emperor to Cabinet to Diet to electorate. But the invisible government was dual toward the end of "parliamentary" Japan, military and civilian. The Army and Navy, whose highest agencies were the Board of Field Marshals and Fleet Admirals (*gensui-fu*) and the Supreme War Council (*gunji sangi-in*), used these agencies as cover for real power. Actual power was exercised by the top men in the staffs in Tokyo—such as the respective chiefs of staff, the military education chiefs, the Army and Navy ministers who were the channel of the military to the Cabinet. Since the Army and Navy ministries represented outside forces, they stood above the Cabinet, taking part only on a veto basis. In the end they dominated.

On the civilian side of the government, the Privy Council and other non-parliamentary institutions (such as the Imperial Household Ministry and the Lord Privy Seal) reached their peak in a peculiar institution which never met as an agency, could not accept new members, and transcended all the "constitutional" offices. This institution was the *genro,* the elder statesmen whose prestige arose from their having been advisers to the Meiji Emperor. The *genro* stood very near the throne; their invisible power was so great that it came to be visible. When they died, one by one, the institution lapsed.

Shinto Disestablishment. The old invisible government is now gone; the pattern of the new is not yet in evidence. Meanwhile, the new constitution, fruit of defeat, had modified not merely the text but the context of the old in a very basic respect. Since December 15, 1945, Shintoism has been officially disestablished as the Japanese governmental religion. This move might be compared to that which left a Vatican state standing on the official understanding that it was purely secular and involved no particular religion.

By direction of SCAP, state Shinto was abolished altogether. The national shrines became the property of religious associations, unless divorced from ceremonial religion and turned into mere artistic treasures. The teaching of Shinto as the national cult in the schools has ceased. But the heart of the change was disestablishment, not abolition. Japan has been compelled to become officially secular. But the persuasiveness of national respect is carried to exaggerated lengths in Japan. Disestablishment removes official protection and encouragement from the former state cult. It does not prohibit its public or private practice so long as the practice is not by authority, compulsion, or command. The Emperor will have to be unofficially holy; and the ecclesiastical structure of Shinto, a loose system formerly well under the government's thumb, is now shut off as a possible alternative to the "visible" government.

General Framework of the MacArthur Constitution. Indeed, the chief merit of the MacArthur constitution may be found by posterity to lie in the earnest attempt to identify "visible" and "invisible" government, rather than in its naïvely explicit democratic pretensions. The new constitution does not show many signs of Japanese authorship. The language is American in tone; the ideals expressed are, with few verbal deviations, not the sort of thing one would expect of Japan, however defeated and regenerated. It seems quite possible that the constitution has been the work of well-meaning Americans on the SCAP staff, who upon completion let the Japanese modify "their" constitution in various details.[4] For instance, the abrogation of all "peerage" means that the *kuge,* the oldest, most loyal, and most harmless nobility in the world, will be deprived of all titles at the end of this generation. Similarly, an awkward bicameral legislature is retained, on the model of most American state governments, even though the House of Peers loses its class basis and becomes a House of Councillors without acquiring a valid sectional foundation.

In constitutional law, Japan has been transformed, as it were, into an imperial Arkansas or Utah. It seems likely that the Japanese, without the wholesome but quaintly unhistorical American advice they were given, might have veered in the direction of some kind of Asiatic neodemocracy on the model of Dr. Sun or of India.

Formal Source. "We, the Japanese people, . . ." wrote some anonymous

---

[4] The knowledgeable journalist Noel Busch, however, states categorically in his *Fallen Sun: A Report on Japan* (New York, 1948), pp. 52-53, that the constitution was written by Prince Konoye before he committed suicide, and was later revised by SCAP. For an official reply to the rumors that the constitution was originally written in English, see James W. Hester, "What Is the Origin of the New Constitution?" *Worudo (The World),* 2, no. 6 (June 1947), 16-17, statement in English and Japanese, from *Political Affairs Bulletin,* no. 2 (March 1, 1947), prepared in SCAP.

American on a typewriter, "do proclaim that sovereign power resides with the people and do firmly establish this Constitution." The author or authors overlooked the absurdity of the inference that a constitution deriving from "the people" in Japan would have the characteristics of this one. The document goes on with a good deal of rhetoric, none of it playing upon those particular strings of tragedy, nobility, romance, and chivalry which have stirred Japanese emotions for more than a thousand years. It is rather as though a new American constitution opened with the statement: "Swearing to keep our emotions benevolent, and to observe the rightful relations between elders and juniors, we, the families of America, ordain a better community life in the name of morality, decency, and the common resolution."

The Emperor's position is restated as that of "the symbol of the State," not the source of authority as under the Meiji constitution. He is declared appropriately to be "deriving his position from the will of the people with whom resides sovereign power."

Imperial House Law. Real and substantial reform lies in another clause: "The Imperial Throne shall be dynastic and succeeded to in accordance with the Imperial House Law passed by the Diet." The old Imperial House Law was proclaimed by the Meiji Emperor; its modification was left to "the Emperor, with the advice of the Imperial Family Council, and of the Privy Council." The Diet was left out. In purely juristic terms, the new provision puts the ultimate *Kompetenz-Kompetenz*—the saying of who's going to say what's the last word in law, and when the last word is really the last—in the hands of the elected Parliament.

Before the new constitution came into effect, the Imperial Family Council, together with the old Privy Council, had the final word in this matter. The present Imperial Family Council, established under the postwar Imperial House Law passed by the Diet like any other law,[5] has a greatly changed composition. It comprises two members of the imperial family, the president and vice president of each house of the Diet, the Prime Minister, the chief of the Imperial Household Agency (*Kunaicho*), the chief justice and one other justice. In the hypothetical case of an Emperor desiring to disavow the constitution, this body could dethrone him and put some other imperial heir on the throne. If the Emperor had subverted the council, the latter, established by law, could be abolished by a single legislative act of the Diet and replaced by a new one composed of whatever members the Diet wished. Theoretically, therefore, it should not take more than a day for Japan to become a republic in fact by removal of the Emperor. No other modern monarch, not even the British or the Swedish king, has been placed so completely at the legislative mercy of his subjects.

In practice, this provision means that skulking reactionaries around the imperial palace can easily be smoked out by any Diet that has the moral stamina

---

[5] The new Imperial House Law was one of the first laws passed by the Diet (January 16, 1947) which gave practical effect to the modified status of the Emperor.

to make the effort. No longer can authority—without check on the process —disappear upward into agencies that are so close to the Emperor as to lie beyond parliamentary interpellation, but so far from the Emperor as to leave him clear of responsibility for their acts.

Renunciation of War. The new constitution also declares:

Aspiring sincerely to an international peace based on justice and order, the Japanese people forever renounce war as a sovereign right of the nation and the threat or use of force as means of settling international disputes.

In order to accomplish the aim of the preceding paragraph, land, sea, and air forces, as well as other war potential, will never be maintained. The right of belligerency of the state will not be recognized.[6]

However strange-sounding, this provision appears to be one of the few in the constitution that is—perhaps unintentionally—in keeping with Japanese tradition. It is characteristic of the Japanese to seek uniqueness, to go on fighting their ancient battle for identity. A Japan that strove to unite the world under a Shinto-Confucian mythology by means of undersea infantry and *kamikaze* planes is quite aptly succeeded by a Japan that goes to the uttermost of the other extreme. Uniquely world-conquering Japan got whipped; uniquely nonmilitary Japan can now sit back and await the world's praise.

Position of Parliament. Bolstered by as fine a listing of rights as one can find in the constitution of the USSR, the Japanese have also acquired a handsome Parliament or Diet. The new constitution conveys primary authority directly to this body, and then prescribes in explicit detail the relationship between Parliament and Cabinet. In particular, the Prime Minister "shall be designated from among the members of the Diet by a resolution of the Diet."

The new constitution must properly be seen as reinforcing and reaffirming pre-existing Japanese parliamentary tendencies rather than installing new institutions. The "democratization" of the Japanese would be comparable to the *ad hoc* parliamentarization of South Korea, if it were not for the fifty-odd years of acquaintance with the *intents* of parliamentary practice that the Japanese have had under the constitution given them by their Meiji Emperor.

Judicial Provisions. Japanese courts, in general, have shown in the past a commendable spirit of professional zeal and integrity. Extensive specialization of legal skill had already developed before the impact of the West, and the Japanese were usually accustomed to accord law a higher place in society than did the Chinese. In the Meiji period the European forms of jurisprudence and adjudication were relied upon in setting up Six Codes (*Roppo*), but the content and spirit of law were largely Japanese. Generally, however, law and its application through the courts and the legal profession in Japan had much in common with the West.

---

[6] This, with all other quotations from the text of the constitution, is taken from State Department, *The Constitution of Japan*, Publication No. 2836, Far Eastern Series 22 (Washington, 1947).

The new constitution confers upon the Supreme Court two new elements of strength: full independence from the executive and judicial review of "constitutionality." This unfamiliar concept the Japanese had to translate by the cumbersome phrase *Kempo ni tekigo suru ka shinai ka*. It is likely that Japanese judges, considering their professional traditions, will be extremely reserved in exercising judicial review.[7] After the provision had stood for two years the Supreme Court timorously overruled a lower jurisdiction on constitutional grounds—in this case, the inadmissibility of a dubiously voluntary confession.

Decentralization. Local self-government, which in the organized sense has amounted almost to anarchy in the case of China, has had feeble traditions in Japan. With modernization, the old principalities of the *daimyo* (feudal lords, kinglets) were centralized into a prefectural system, but the people had little more self-government than before.

Centralization is often a prerequisite of enforced progress toward a stated goal; Meiji Japan started off with a high degree of centralization. The MacArthur constitution now provides for direct local management of local concerns. Here again, there is a demonstration of the external approach to Japanese politics. Neighborhood associations (*tonarigumi,* corresponding to the Chinese *pao-chia* system) have been wiped out because they had been misused by the militarists; brand-new principles of "local autonomy" were enunciated. The Ministry of Home Affairs was abolished December 3, 1947.

Amendment. The new constitution is very easy to amend. A two-thirds vote of the Diet, followed by popular approval either in a special referendum or in the next general election, leads to proclamation of the change by the Emperor "in the name of the people."

Under the Meiji constitution, the amendment had to be sent to the Diet by imperial order. Then, with at least two-thirds of the whole membership of each house present, a two-thirds majority was required to pass the amendment; and no amendment whatever could be passed during a regency. Prince Ito said: "The Constitution has been personally determined by his Majesty [*sic*] the Emperor in conformity with the instructions transmitted to Him by His Ancestors, and He desires to bequeath it to posterity as an immutable code of laws, whose provisions His present subjects and their descendants shall obey forever. Therefore, the essential character of the Constitution should undergo no alteration." [8]

3. The Parliamentary Cabinet System

Continuity. In China, government has not yet existed in the modern sense; in Japan, it continued. Despite defeat and reform, the most striking

---

[7] Japanese terms are taken from Yanagizawa Yoshio, *Nihonkoku Kempo Chikujo Kogi* (*An Explanation of the Japanese Constitution*) (Tokyo, 1947). For a delightfully anecdotal and well-illustrated description of Japanese law, see John Henry Wigmore, *A Panorama of the World's Legal Systems* (Washington, 1928; reissued, 1936), pp. 459 ff.

[8] Ito, *op. cit.* above, note 1, p. 140.

feature of Japanese life and government is the element of continuity. Though the unprecedented did happen, public affairs went on. One could set down the old government and by a process of stripping away arrive at the new, as the next chart shows.

COMPARISON OF GOVERNMENT IN JAPAN,
BEFORE AND AFTER OCCUPATION

SCAP

EMPEROR————*Central Liaison Office*————⌐
[later, Foreign Office
(Genro)   *Liaison Bureau*]

(Various Joint Staffs   (Privy Council, Lord Privy
Army Ministry,   Seal, Imperial Household
Navy Ministry)   CABINET   Minister)
Ministries

(Home Affairs Ministry, Overseas Affairs Ministry)

DIET

(House of Peers)   *House of Councillors*   House of Representatives

URBAN PREFECTURES   *Elected Governors*   RURAL PREFECTURES
Home, Police, and Educa-   Home, Police, and Education Departments   tion Departments

PREFECTURAL ASSEMBLY   PREFECTURAL ASSEMBLY

COUNTY GOVERNMENTS   CITY GOVERNMENTS
Townships or Towns, Villages   Wards, Precincts

Note: Agencies in parentheses are abolished; agencies in italics are new.

Structure and Powers of the Diet. The Diet, once "talking society" (*Gikai*), is now raised to "national meeting" (*Kokkai*). The upper house is no longer the House of Peers (*kizokuin*), open only to nobility, persons enjoying the officially expressed esteem of the government, or selected candidates voted on by the rich. It is now the House of Councillors (*sangiin*), voted upon by the whole people. The House of Representatives has not changed its name (*shugiin*). The change in the Diet is more one of environment than of composition or organization. The new constitution provides a considerable number of innovations, but these apply to an institution that was a going concern before the improvements were made. For example, the House of Representatives, elected for a four-year term, can overrule, by a two-thirds vote, rejection or amendment by the House of Councillors, whose members are elected, half at a time, for a six-year term. Again, dissolution of "the Diet" as a result of a Cabinet crisis means only that the House of Representatives must face re-election; the House of Councillors is closed for the interim. If the two houses of the Diet fail to agree on a Prime Minister, the decision of the shorter-lived chamber shall apply after ten days.

More substantial are the requirements that place definite power and responsibility in the hands of the Prime Minister. He must be a member of the Diet, and must appoint a Cabinet whose majority are members of the Diet. He may remove Cabinet members at will—subject to the inevitable parliamentary hazard of a vote of nonconfidence. The members of both houses are elected by the whole electorate. Discrimination against voters on grounds of "race, creed, social status, family origin, education, property, or income" is prohibited.

Each house of the Diet elects its own officers and sets up its own committees. The Diet is explicitly stated to be the "highest organ of state power," but the Cabinet, in specific terms, is given the normal range of executive power. The Prime Minister and those of his colleagues who are members of the Diet must respond to interpellation in either house, no matter whether they are members of that house or not. Organizationally, there soon arose far too many special and standing committees; in 1948 a new Diet act cut the number of committees down to fifteen, one for each main administrative field.[9] The unofficial Interparty Negotiating Committee has continued to maintain its overriding time-saving control of the parliamentary calendar.

Legislative-Executive Relations. The intimacy of the legislative-executive relationship is heightened by the extensive use of parliamentary vice ministers—one for each ministry from each house. In the prewar system, each ministry had one administrative vice minister from the career service and a parliamentary vice minister to make sure that the Diet was informed of matters that the ministry might undertake. The parliamentary contact with the executive is the Prime Minister, since the remainder of the old executive (Emperor, Privy Council, armed services) for all practical purposes is wiped out. The only thing that the Showa Emperor does is to ceremonialize convocation, dissolution of the popular chamber, appointment of prime ministers as designated by the Diet, proclamation of elections, and so forth. Hirohito has been very discreet in his use of the convocation speech. Instead of making a policy speech written for him by the incoming Cabinet, as is the British custom, he has spoken briefly and in a noncommittal manner. His address in January 1948 read in full:

It is my great pleasure to meet with you here at the opening ceremony of the Second Session of the National Diet. It is the most important duty for fulfillment

[9] Kyodo news service broadcast for domestic Japanese audience, Tokyo, April 11, 1948. For list of the original twenty-one standing committees of the Diet, before reduction, see Oike Makoto, *Shin Kokkai Keisetsu* (*An Explanation of the New Diet*) (Tokyo, 1947), chap. 9. Oike was chief clerk of the Diet.

STRUCTURE OF GOVERNMENT IN PRESENT-DAY JAPAN

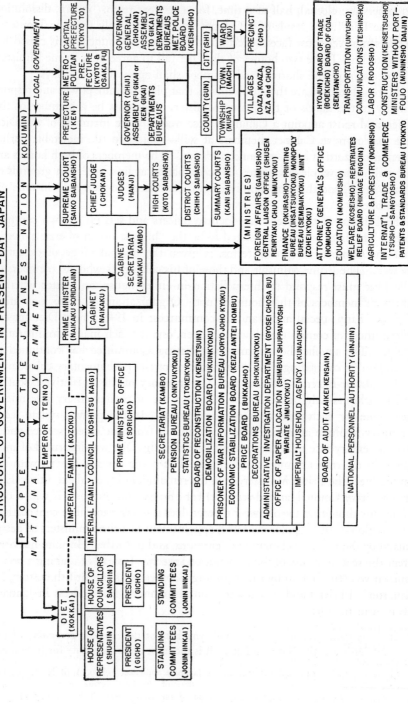

by us, the people of Japan, to tide over the serious economic crisis now confronting us, to promote the national morale befitting a cultural nation, to build up a democratic and peace-loving nation, and thus to win the confidence of the world.

I earnestly desire that the National Diet will fully achieve its mission as the highest organ of State power, and that the people, with due recognition of the current situation of the country, will make their best efforts for the rehabilitation of our Fatherland.[10]

The Meiji constitution contained a provision to the effect that when the Diet failed to vote a new budget, the government automatically carried on with the budget of the preceding year. The new constitution provides explicitly that every expenditure or state obligation be upon authorization of the Diet only. This provision means that although in the prewar practice a resolute but unpopular government could get along without the Diet for a while, the postwar system gives the Diet complete power in fiscal as in all other matters.

Parties and Diet Procedure. Some tendency toward "invisible government" may be observed in the way the Japanese make their new postwar Diet run smoothly. Under the liberalized election procedures and the hastily reconstituted party system, they have not had single-party majorities in either house. From the summer of 1945, just before VJ Day, to the summer of 1951, there were six prime ministers: Admiral Baron Suzuki Kantaro (Suzuki being the old nonmilitarist conservative who paved the way to peace); Prince Higashikuni Naruhiko; Baron Shidehara Kijuro; Mr. Yoshida Shigeru; Mr. Katayama Tetsu (Katayama was Japan's first Christian Premier); and Mr. Ashida Hitoshi. An additional shuffle once in a while, not involving a change of prime ministers, sometimes led the press to count in an additional Cabinet. Thus Yoshida came back with his second Cabinet in October 1948, and his third Cabinet after the elections of January 1949. In each case the Diet, relatively placid, waited for arrangements to be consummated until it could have a complete solution to legalize. It was the party organizations that consummated the arrangements.

Japanese political parties were divided in these first years into four roughly equal blocs—Liberals, Democrats, Socialists, and all others. Thus, the Liberals and Democrats (the prewar center, now the right) held approximately half the seats, the Socialists a quarter, and the other parties (Communists, cooperatives, still more minor parties, and independent deputies) the remaining quarter. In the House of Councillors the independent element was higher. But instead of waging their fights on the floor, the parties dealt directly and informally with one another.

Organizationally, the parties projected themselves into the houses of Parliament, not out from them. Most parties have developed rather elaborate party bureaucracies. The Social Democratic party, for instance, had built the or-

---

[10] Tokyo radio, Kyodo release in both English and Japanese, January 21, 1948, 12:30 A.M., E.S.T.

ganization shown in the next chart. With such organization, the parties can meet through their respective secretaries general and name a Prime Minister with the reasonable certainty that the Diet will give legal ratification to their action.

INTERNAL ORGANIZATION OF THE JAPANESE SOCIAL DEMOCRATIC PARTY, 1948

PARTY MEMBERSHIP

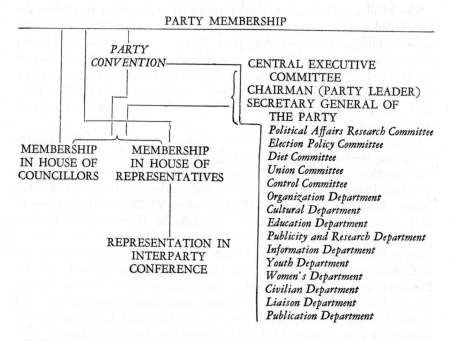

Political Flux and Party Bureaucracies. Although it is entirely possible that the party bureaucracies, outside the reach of constitution and law, may some day become the quick-reacting actual government of Japan, thus relegating the "democratic" system to noble somnolence, this development has by no means taken place so far. In the first place, Japanese parties are still extremely factional. Torn by the legitimacy of democratic dissension within a traditional solidarity, the Japanese politician never knows how seriously he dare take his own politics. Secessions and reunions are frequent; it is not uncommon for a Diet member to change parties right in the middle of a session, without feeling obliged to resign. Also, the ideological politics have operated within a comfortable impotence sustained by SCAP finality in real power. The conquerors were perpetual bucktakers.

Again, the new constitution is just beginning to make itself felt in actual working politics. In 1948, for instance, the House of Councillors rudely suggested that it would nominate a Prime Minister anyhow if the lower house would not make up its collective mind. The House of Representatives

slapped the Ashida nomination right back in the Councillors' face and refused to fuss further with a joint committee of the two houses that was to
have made the nomination unanimous. It is thus possible that Japanese democratic politics, feeling their way along new routes, will discover the unprecedented fact that visible politics is just as useful as invisible.

Prospects of Parliamentary Leadership. To the leadership that has been
displayed thus far, mild praise can be given. Suzuki, who led the fight
for peace, was purged from public life by an American order, whereas Higashikuni, who took over when peace came, was not purged, although he had
commanded infamously at Nanking. Konoye, who got along famously with
MacArthur for a while, was a *kuge* prince who had ridden the tide in with
the militarists and then proposed to ride it out with democracy. When a
purge order belatedly overtook him, he had the dignity to commit suicide.
Yoshida was an old centrist politician; Katayama, the Christian Prime Minister, was leftist and moderate. Ashida, a somewhat tougher and wilier career
politician, took over from him. The six premiers have had thankless tasks,
with both Japanese and Americans watching them. Sublime leadership can
scarcely be displayed in fulfilling the terms of an ignominious surrender.

In the face of a deep uncertainty as to the direction of future political fashion in Japan, one may guess that modish politics will not turn to the houses
of the Diet for its living models whom young, bright, ambitious, public-
spirited Japanese would wish to follow. It is more likely that some kind of a
new *genro* will emerge, possibly from among the ranks of the present party
bureaucracies, with the aspiring leader trying to wrap himself in mystery,
goodness, sagacity, and a certain detachment from the working political
scene. Perhaps such men could give to parliamentarism the stability, direction, and purpose which machinery as such will always lack, and which
"democracy" cannot obtain by chill constitutional fiat.

4. National and Local Administration in Japan

Record of Responsibility. The Meiji constitution did not provide for a
specific responsibility of the Cabinet to anyone, despite the statement of
Prince Ito that the ministers were responsible to the sovereign, the Emperor
himself.[11] Being answerable to an authority who in turn was not answerable to anyone except the gods and his ancestors, the prewar Japanese cabinets
had to work at the meeting point of many different forces: the Emperor, the
Imperial Household Ministry, the Privy Council, the various military and
naval commands, the Ministry of War, the Ministry of the Navy, and the
Diet. In actual practice, the foreign parliamentary example was such as to
encourage the Japanese in two directions: (1) acknowledgment of responsibility of the Cabinet and the Prime Minister to the Diet; and (2) recognition
of the primacy of the Prime Minister, literally the Minister President of the

[11] Ito, *op. cit.* above, note 1, p. 92.

State, a title adopted in imitation of the imperial German chancellorship, which also aimed at dual responsibility—to ruler and to Parliament.[12]

Whenever parliamentarism and anti-oligarchy ran high, the Japanese cabinets tended to hold themselves responsible to the Diet. When the *genro* (in the early days) or the militarists (in the latter days of the Meiji constitution) wished to drive an unpopular or untested policy ahead, it was always possible to hide governmental responsibility behind the "responsibility" of the Emperor, who could never be questioned. Or it was possible to frustrate incoming civilian cabinets by withholding from them those generals and admirals on active service who were needed for the service ministries to complete the roster. It may therefore be said that prewar Japanese cabinets were *always* responsible to the persons who could speak in the name of the Emperor, *usually* responsible to the service ministries, and *sometimes* responsible to the Diet.

Under the new constitution, this situation is entirely changed. The Cabinet is explicitly subordinated to the Diet. The old agencies, which used to interfere with the direct Diet-Cabinet relationship, have now been abolished altogether. New interferers have not yet appeared.

Structure of the Cabinet (Naikaku). The Japanese Cabinet is a multiple executive responsible directly to the Diet, which is a body combining legislative authority with the role of "highest organ of state power." In two respects, the present Japanese Cabinet is peculiar. First, it has developed, as administrative offshoots of itself, a large complex of nonministerial facilities— agencies that in other times would have been attached to the imperial household, the Privy Council, or the service ministries. Apart from the eleven recognized and distinct ministries, the Cabinet has the following agencies nominally attached to the Prime Minister: (1) Cabinet Secretariat (*Naikaku Kambo*), headed by a Secretary General (*Kambocho*); (2) Prime Minister's Office (*Soricho*) and *its* Secretariat (*Kambo*); (3) Pension Bureau (*Onkyukyoku*); (4) Statistics Bureau (*Tokeikyoku*); (5) Board of Reconstruction (*Kensetsuin*); (6) Demobilization Board (*Fukuinkyoku*); (7) Prisoners of War Information Bureau (*Furyo Johokyoku*); (8) Economic Stabilization Board (*Keizai Antei Hombu*); (9) Price Board (*Bukkacho*); (10) Decorations Bureau (*Shokunkyoku*); (11) Administrative Investigation Department (*Gyosa Chosei Bu*); (12) Office for Allocation of Paper to Newspapers and Publications (*Shimbun Shuppanyoshi wariate Jimukyoku*); (13) Imperial Household Agency (*Kunaicho*); and (14) Board of Audit (*Kaikei Kensaiin*). The Central Liaison Office having been abolished, its functions are carried on by the Foreign Office. A National Personnel Authority (*Jinjiin*) has also been added.

The peculiarity is that the Cabinet is very definitely centered around the Prime Minister. In practice, he and his colleagues may come into office to-

---

[12] See Woodrow Wilson's account of this institution in his *The State* (Boston, 1902), pp. 268-69. See also Charles B. Fahs, *Government in Japan* (New York, 1940), pp. 71 ff.

gether, but the new constitution gives him the explicit power of appointing them, subject to the proviso that a majority of them be members of the Diet. Constitutionally, he "exercises control and supervision" over the whole of the executive, and his countersignature is needed for all laws and Cabinet orders. The ministries are: (1) Foreign Affairs Ministry (*Gaimusho*); (2) Ministry of Finance (*Okurasho*); (3) Attorney General's Office (*Homucho*), replacing the Ministry of Justice (*Shihosho*); (4) Ministry of Education (*Mombusho*); (5) Ministry of Welfare (*Koseisho*); (6) Ministry of Agriculture and Forestry (*Norinsho*); (7) Ministry of International Trade and Commerce (*Tsusho-Sangyosho*); (8) Ministry of Transportation (*Unyusho*); (9) Ministry of Communications (*Teishinsho*); (10) Ministry of Labor (*Rodosho*); and (11) Ministry of Construction (*Kensetsucho*). Each ministry (*sho*) is headed by a minister, with two parliamentary vice ministers, an administrative vice minister, and a minister's secretariat (*Daijin Kambo*).[13]

The current flow of authority is thus very plain in Japan. The Diet is responsible to the electorate. The Prime Minister is made closely responsible to the Diet; and both the ministries (through parliamentary vice ministers) and the Diet itself (through standing committees, one for each of the major Cabinet fields) have created organs to ensure parliamentary supervision and executive liaison. Finally, the Cabinet as a whole is not permitted to diffuse its answerability throughout the imperial government, but remains the constitutional instrument of the Prime Minister himself. It would be difficult to go further in making administration responsive to the popular will.

Administrative Changes. In addition to the elimination of the great independent policy-making agencies, such as the Imperial Household Ministry and the Privy Council, three of the most important prewar ministries have been abolished. The first two of these are the Army and Navy ministries, which formerly were not only autonomous, but—resting upon their separate military pyramids—had an effective veto power over the Cabinet. They became ministries and then mere bureaus in the Demobilization Board, and finally disappeared altogether in October 1947. Even though Japan's return to a formal state of peace presumably conveys the rights and moral obligations of national self-defence, little in the nature of armed services has yet been established. The constitution may be in the way.

The third of the missing ministries is the Home Ministry (or Ministry of the Interior, *Naimusho*). Like its surviving Chinese counterpart, the Home Ministry used to be the national agency for controlling or supervising all regional or local government. The Japanese have customarily followed the

---

[13] The sequence of this and the preceding list is taken from SCAP, *Organization Report*, mimeographed, as of October 1, 1947, p. 160, and corrected by press and radio broadcast material down to summer, 1951. The Japanese terminology is taken from Takabe Yoshinobu, ed., *Jiji Eigo Nenkan* (*Jiji English-language Yearbook*) (Tokyo, 1943), and corrected by current press materials. Recent changes have been checked against materials released by the Information Division of the National Personnel Authority (*Jinjiin*).

Franco-British model, rather than the American-German, of having the national administration superimposed directly over the prefecture or county, with no state or *Land* in between. Toward the very end of the war, the Japanese did experiment with regional government offices, which grouped a number of prefectures together into "provincial" governments. But these were established for the obvious military purpose of having fissiparous authorities that could spring to autonomous life in the event of an American landing. As soon as the threat of a fighting invasion disappeared, the regions were abolished as summarily as they had been created. Until its abolition December 31, 1947, the Home Ministry returned to the position it occupied under the old constitution. At present Japan has been converted from a highly unitary police-type of state into a nation marked by extraordinary legal freedom of its smallest local governments.

New Agencies. The addition of new agencies directly under the Prime Minister seems to be a practice deriving in part from Japan's wartime experience with emergency controls, and copied in part from the wartime developments in the United States. The Cabinet Secretariat is, in loose terms, the equivalent of the Executive Office of the President—an administrative staff group to render central advisory and recording services. Some of the new boards in the same category are as important as any ministry. The Economic Stabilization Board has been a storm center of practical politics, since it has had to attempt the impossible—the creation of prosperity in a country stripped of trade, colonies, markets, and credit, and simultaneously drained by the cost of a high-standard-of-living occupation force. The Price Board has been kept in operation by SCAP. The Board of Reconstruction undertakes a task that in Japan is beyond the capacity of any single administrative agency. The Imperial Household Ministry, formerly so important that it stood beside and above the other ministries, has been turned into the Imperial Household Agency and put under the Prime Minister. For the latter, the odd assortment of agencies under him, some very influential, is a burdensome additional responsibility.

Most important of the postwar agencies was the Central Liaison Office (CLO—*Shusen Renryaku Chuo Jimukyoku*), created before the American arrival. On August 26, 1945, Domei, the official press source, said that Okazaki Katsu had been made chief of the CLO. Okazaki, till then head of the Foreign Office research section, had been a wartime spokesman. A career bureaucrat, he received the mission to make the conquerors feel at home. The CLO became the umbilical cord connecting the Empire of Japan with the Supreme Commander for the Allied Powers from whom all basic policy flowed. The CLO was a twin agency to the old Foreign Ministry (*Gaimusho*), into which it was absorbed in 1948. This absorption delicately indicated that Japan's relations with the occupation were "external affairs."

Work of the Central Liaison Office. For administrative purposes, the CLO was connected with both the Prime Minister's Office and the *Gaimusho*.

Many of the most competent or promising young officials in Japan's present career diplomatic service were put on detail for a half year or year to the CLO, where they learned diplomacy the hard way—by taking orders from SCAP, answering SCAP's questions, evading SCAP's more difficult or troublesome demands. In its own organization, the CLO was set up under a president with the rank of minister, with two vice ministers, a secretariat with secretarial and translation sections, and seven divisions: general, political, economic, transportation and communications, accommodation, repatriation, reparations. In addition, it had local liaison offices at critical locations and local liaison committees at various others. The CLO did its job with much skill and sensitivity, easing the strain of converting surrender into cooperation.

To handle the new agencies as well as the old ministries, the Japanese Cabinet includes various ministers with special assignments. In the early summer of 1950, for instance, it had eighteen members, if the Prime Minister is counted as being in the Cabinet as well as over it. Eleven represented the regular ministries. The remaining seven included four ministers without portfolio in charge of economic matters, the chief Cabinet secretary (*Naikaku Shoki Kancho*) serving as a minister without portfolio (*Kokumu Daijin* or *Muninsho Sho*), the director general of the Economic Stabilization Board, and the new head of postal administration (*Yugeisho*). This eighteen-man team had to meet the workload imposed on it from four directions: from the SCAP authorities up above; from the Emperor, who can be presumed to have bothered it very little; from the Diet, which can be counted on to create a good deal of work; and from the administrative pyramids below it.

Administrative Morale and Traditions. Of the various governing elites that existed in prewar Japan, the bureaucracy (*kambatsu,* literally "clique of officials") has come through with the least damage. The capitalists were long persecuted, not as capitalists, but as economic war criminals under the rubric of *zaibatsu.* The imperial court clique has been returned to innocuous desuetude. The nobility is permitted to keep its titles for this generation only; and, along with the dissolution of the House of Peers, the new constitution explicitly provides that no governmental function shall attach to a title of nobility. The military clique (*gumbatsu*) has been disgraced by failure. But the officials go right on, provided they remained reasonably noncontroversial and obscure during the war.

Ethics and formalism are probably the two chief characteristics of Japanese bureaucracy. Both these traits have their roots in the language itself, as well as in the Sino-Japanese tradition of government. It is not possible to achieve official position without knowing the language more than passably well—and the language, being ideographic, involves a tremendous effort of memory, a discipline of personality, an apperception of ethics for its mastery. To be an official, one must start as a scholar and proceed onward. That is sum and substance of the Confucian tradition, most strikingly exemplified in the magnificent bureaucracy of the T'ang, which represented one of the high points of governmental sophistication and accomplishment.[14]

Chinese and Japanese part company, however, when it comes to the character of the scholar-official himself. To the Chinese he is the civilian gentleman. The Japanese official has a marked trace of the national character: fierce courage, utter loyalty, and a deep though vague spirituality. Both Chinese and Japanese differ from Westerners in that they do not expect officialdom to be plain in the common man's terms; do not consider that government should explain itself to the governed in the same language in which these explain things to one another; and do believe that talent, training, and virtue entitle the officials to public office from which no rude electorate should presume to eject them.

Effect of Institutional Inertia. In action the consequence is that much of government goes "by the book." The Sino-Japanese bureaucrat knows perfectly well that it is no use explaining his action in everyday terms; the language of government, most of the time, cannot be translated into those terms without losing much of its richness. The important thing for him is that he abide by the institutional formula, much as American lawyers and judges find formulas when they act impersonally in civil or criminal cases. But the Chinese-Japanese bureaucratic formula differs from the Western legal formula in that it does not seek to be impersonal; in line with the Confucian tradition, it attempts to be correctly personal. Even in Japan, which has had much more actual government over the ages than has China, ideological control is always the companion to legal authority.

Japanese bureaucracy is still functioning. It cannot be replaced save through social revolution. The officials have not shown themselves less eager than the whole of the population to accept the novelties of the SCAP period, but they have much more to unlearn than the common man. In many instances they follow old "militarist, feudal" practices, not because of willfulness or reactionary conspiracy, but simply because they have spent most of their adult lives doing things in a set way. Western critics have been quick in attributing to institutional inertia the character of personal scheming.

Composition of the Civil Service. The Japanese officialdom even today bears the imprint of the T'ang exemplar. Basic grades exist independent of the particular employment, at any given time, of the individual official. In this respect Japanese bureaucracy, along with the Chinese, has been centuries ahead of the American or British, which began to accord rank (apart from the particular assignment) only in the twentieth century. In the West, this structural grouping developed in the military far earlier than in the civilian services of government; a major, for example, remained a major, no matter what he was doing. The Japanese bureaucratic grades are defined first in

---

[14] The T'ang bureaucracy is admirably described in Baron Robert des Rotours, *Traité des Examens* (Paris, 1932). It was the T'ang that the Japanese most revered and copied.

terms of the appointing authority, and secondly in terms of levels within each major grouping. There are four major levels of Japanese officials, of which the fourth, the topmost, is usually considered an extension of the third, next below.

Grade for grade, examinations have been considerably more difficult than for positions in government employment in the United States. Tenure has been safeguarded, and the cultural tradition itself supplements the salaries paid to civil servants. The bureaucrat is a person of dignity; he is apt to be pompous in the lower grades. Unlike China, where the civil service went entirely to pieces with the dissolution of the Empire in 1911-12 and is only now being painfully reconstructed, Japan has a bureaucracy which possesses great *esprit de corps*. It could give great strength to effective leadership.

On the negative side, the capacity of the bureaucracy for survival is shown in the frustration or failure of the various attempts made to reform the civil service during the occupation period. The Socialist cabinet (1947-1948) of Premier Katayama made the most vigorous attempt, following up on the work of an American group of consultants who had been asked to come to Japan for the express purpose of reforming the bureaucracy; this group was the United States Personnel Advisory Mission which went to Japan in 1946 and reported its recommendations in 1947.

The result was the National Public Service Law, promulgated in October 1947 and put into effect July 1, 1948. But the law was less than satisfactory. General MacArthur himself encouraged its revision in a letter to the Premier on July 22, 1948. Yet distance of mind between Americans and Japanese— with bureaucrats, military or civilians, on both sides—made it possible to postpone action. Deep reform of the Japanese bureaucracy did not take place in the early years of the occupation, when American intellectuals found in Japan a country needing a New Deal, with the opposition cowed, disgraced, eclipsed or even hanged. Policies were pushed through which could not possibly have been enacted for the United States itself by its Congress in its right mind. The shrewd and experienced Japanese officials counted on a turning of the tide in social or political experiment. The tide did turn.

Under independence, it is possible that the new National Personnel Authority (*Jinjiin*) will be able to carry on a program of sustained and practical improvements and reforms. It is difficult to predict any impressive change as long as the future of Japan is so uncertain within an uncertain balance of world power. One can only be sure that wholly Japanese reforms will differ in both substance and form from joint SCAP-Japanese reforms.

Administration of Economic Controls. After World War II, almost every nation faced the twofold problem of economic unbalance requiring more and more control, and economic strain leading to demands that "nonproductive" government personnel be reduced. Under the aegis of SCAP, the Japanese continued a considerable number of regulatory devices, such as the Economic Stabilization Board and the Price Board. These in turn stemmed from the elaborate controls that developed after the first Manchurian crisis of 1931,[15] and reached their consummation of intricacy and penetration during the war years themselves. Under occupation the Japanese were unable to let a free capitalism assure them prosperity by competition in the international markets; they had no diplomatic relations, little foreign trade, meager credit, and few friends. Therefore, they were in the position of administering poverty, needing and getting real but hidden American economic aid.

The Japanese have continued to hope that foreign capital would become available to them, if admitted on relatively favorable terms.[16] Japanese interest in this direction included both foreign private investment and the possibility that the government might be authorized by SCAP to float a postwar loan through British or American banks. Meanwhile, the burden of the occupation was being met through increase of the currency. The printing press provided a constant self-collecting tax for the needs of the emergency; and the budget showed no prospect of ever being balanced.

Early in 1948, the Ashida Cabinet set up a Temporary Administrative Reform Council for the purpose of integrating the various sudden reforms made: (1) during the actual surrender; (2) under the orders of SCAP; (3) on account of democratization; (4) because of decentralization caused by the establishment of local autonomy; and (5) in response to economic need.

Under the Yoshida Cabinets, particularly in 1950 and 1951, the processes of decartelization were finally arrested, and the reverse—ending the disabilities of the purged wartime leaders, including economic managers—was carried to its conclusion. These measures, together with the Korean war, stimulated business.

Local Government Structure. The greatest change in the pattern of Japanese government has been the divorce of the prefectures from the central authority. This change reverses a trend that dates back to the consolidation of the Tokugawa overlordship in the early 1600's. The Meiji modernization from 1868 onward merely substituted a new European brand of centralism for an old indigenous one; the only opponents were the feudal knights (*samurai*), who were suppressed by warfare during the Satsuma rebellion of 1877. Even the most progress-minded reformers never urged federalism for Japan. To such reformers before the war, democracy meant control of the central government by the people, not emancipation of the local governments from the central.

Yet it is precisely this which has been agreed upon as the keystone in the Allied plan for democratizing Japan. Central-local relationships in prewar Japan looked straight-lined, as the accompanying chart demonstrates. Un-

---

[15] A careful study of these developments is provided by Fahs, *op. cit.* above, note 12.

[16] For example, the official news agency listed a six-point plan, attributing it to "economic circles in Japan." The plan gave recognition to the fact that nationalistic discrimination against foreign capital would lead nowhere, and to the need for giving foreign investors a preferred and assured status. Tokyo radio, Kyodo release in Japanese to Japan, February 4, 1948, 3:40 A.M., E.S.T.

der each prefecture there were cities or counties, the latter subdivided into towns or townships, with villages underneath. Every square yard of Japan is thus governed by a city, town, or township. The term *prefecture* is itself the loose equivalent of two Japanese terms, *fu* (for the urban prefecture) and *ken* (for a prefecture other than urban). A *ken* might be heavily settled and possess cities, but it did not become a *fu* unless it ranked as one of the out-standing cities of Japan.

Save for Tokyo, which as a capital (*to*) had special status, all the prefec-tures of Japan worked under the Home Ministry. Each *fu* or *ken* had a gov-ernor who was appointed by the central government, theoretically on a career basis, but actually on a basis of political choice. An almost impotent prefec-tural assembly assisted in the making of the budget and had to authorize local

CENTRAL-LOCAL RELATIONSHIPS IN PREWAR JAPAN

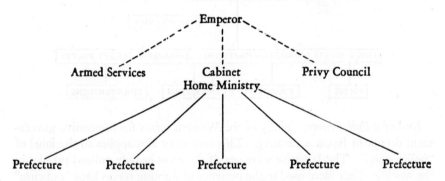

debts. But the day-to-day business of regional-local government was super-intended by the governor under the authority of the Home Ministry in Tokyo. Only the city of Tokyo enjoyed a relatively high degree of munici-pal freedom. This of itself was a reflection of the T'ang tradition, which pro-vided that the capital city of the Empire, in its special capacity as the metropo-lis, should be given special administrative status.

New Local Government. As a result of the occupation, the prefectures have emerged as self-government bodies. The local governments under them have remained relatively unchanged so far as their formal relationships to one another are concerned. A normal *ken* is still organized on the old pattern, which includes three departments under a governor, and the sub-ordinate local governments filling out the map, as the next chart indicates.

In going from complete centralism to complete local autonomy, the Japa-nese are finding themselves losers as well as gainers. A high degree of cen-tralization is not necessarily incompatible with democracy, particularly where the country is small, homogeneous, and crowded. With decentralization, the Japanese enjoy the immediate benefits of less interference of a police-state kind, but they also lose the benefits of a nation-wide, experienced civil service for the administration of local affairs. For example, all local government procedures of importance were formerly automatically standardized; they all came under the Home Ministry. All local career bureaucrats were nationally employed civil servants. The result was that unevenness, nonstandardization, and inequalities of service tended to be ironed out quickly. Now the Japanese are having to experiment with the half-voluntary types of standardization, where officials possessing no authority over one another meet for the purpose of finding improved methods of doing the government's business.

ORGANIZATION OF THE PREFECTURE IN POSTWAR JAPAN

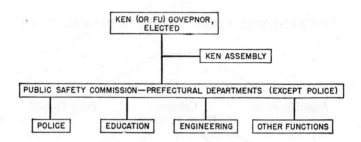

End of a Police State. Many of the Western terms for oppressive government do not fit Japan accurately. This statement also applies to the label of "police state." The Japanese were one of the most heavily policed peoples in the world. They were used to the presence of fighting forces kept "in being" for domestic needs. Government spying on private citizens dates back to the beginnings of Japan. The use of central registration was universal. The ordinary Japanese citizen was registered with the police at birth, supervised while he grew up, watched for signs of sedition in early manhood, snooped and reported on throughout his life, and locked up by the police whenever it suited their convenience—even though this convenience applied for the most part only where there was "suspicion." Yet the Japanese combined a scientific approach to ideological blockade with internal supervision to the degree that special officers at Yedo (later called Tokyo) followed the progress of the American Revolution at a time when ordinary Japanese were punished for any attempt to study overseas countries. The officialdom maintained, through intensely supervised trade with the Chinese and the Dutch, a peephole on the outside world.[17] The quaint Japanese, whom Gilbert and Sullivan ridiculed in *The Mikado,* knew a great deal more about Gilbert and

[17] Cf. Harley Farnsworth MacNair, *The Real Conflict Between China and Japan* (Chicago, 1938), which describes the premodern formation of ideological traits that made modern Japan nationalist and militarist; and C. R. Boxer, *Jan Compagnie in Japan* (The Hague, 1936), which tells of the closely guarded relationships of Japanese and Dutch at the peephole port of Nagasaki.

Sullivan's world than those two ever dreamed they did. The Japanese authorities made it a point to *know* things. There was nothing in Japan that was legally or morally exempt from official investigation or official interference.

Given these conditions, the present decentralization of police is a change bound to have revolutionary cultural consequences if it lasts. The age-old centrality of Japanese police was broken with the police reforms of 1948. No longer was there a Home Ministry designed to watch, check, and punish Japanese who strayed an inch from the ordinary course. No longer were policemen in Japan free to exercise their authority over the individual with ultimate accountability only in some high-up secret office in Tokyo. No longer were levels of police superimposed one upon the other, each more clandestine, more powerful, and more regular than the lower. The Japanese took the plunge, and sought to reduce policing from its ancient role of maintaining right thinking and right being to its modern role of keeping the visible public peace.

Most Japanese were not accustomed to the idea that police should be reduced to the level of a community service, instead of being maintained at the height of a national monitoring system. A sharply reduced state police under restricted national authority is now connected with the courts through the Attorney General's office, no longer the powerful Ministry of Justice.

After Occupation, What?   The peace treaty is bound to change the morale as well as the legal status of Japan. Barring miracles, the treaty cannot do much to change strategic or economic fact.

Japan will necessarily add to the difficult problems of a special American-Japanese relationship the additional problems of her return to the raw materials and markets of Asia and her re-entry into the community of civilized nations. She has already been negotiating hard-headedly with the Bonn government of Germany. Given a chance, she will make her way.

But that way is encompassed by the framework of American air and naval power, and by the presence of American land forces in Korea. The new Japanese military organization, courteously called the National Japanese Police Reserves (NJPR), cannot possibly replace United States power as the defender of Japan.

Japanese politics, and even the governmental structure, will for the immediate future remain that of an Asian nation threatened from the mainland by a European-Asian power bloc and protected by American power. It is not likely that Japan could support a defense system capable of stopping the Soviet Union in the East without acquiring a new Asian empire to support that defense system. From defense needs spring economic cooperation and some kind of political partnership. Japanese politics will never again concern Japan alone; it is an American problem as well. Americans will, if they are wise, listen sympathetically and with interest to Japanese expressions of hope, need, or purpose.

CHAPTER 30

GOVERNMENT IN CHINA

1. The Position of Chiang Kai-shek

Two Heads of State: Chiang and Hirohito. No two national leaders could differ more from each other than do Hirohito, the Showa Emperor, and General Chiang Kai-shek, President of the Republic of China, which is now on Formosa. Chiang himself was sixty-five years old in 1951, relaxed and youthful in manner, though chronologically older than his or any other Chinese republic. His Republic was in its year XL, and virtually eclipsed by a new Communist "People's Republic" under Mao Tse-tung.

By contrast, Hirohito was fifty in 1951; his family still held their pre-historic throne. For his part, Chiang came from poor gentry, with a very common surname. Hirohito was the son of a god-king. Chiang was a boy when his father died; Hirohito's father went mad. Chiang married twice, has two sons and some half-Russian grandchildren. Hirohito married once and has an heir, the crown prince Akihito, who is pure Japanese. Chiang sought power; Hirohito inherited it.

In World War II, the two men nominally fought each other. Chiang, who won, sees his country ruined, bankrupt, disunited, and invaded. Hirohito, who lost, exchanges courtesies with his conquerors and has one of the world's greatest military forces protecting him and his country against rebellion or invasion. Chiang speaks Japanese, but there is no record of Hirohito's speaking vernacular Chinese. Both men have received a kind of worship. Each has been the target of assassins. Few seem to like Hirohito; fewer hate him much. But throughout the world, many take sides for or against Chiang. Neither man has much private property. Both like to write the old Chinese ideographs. They do not write each other.

Hirohito is not called Mikado, except by some antiquarians or ritualists. Chiang is not officially a generalissimo and never was one; he has been "Commander-in-Chief of the Army, Navy, and Air Forces of the Republic of China." Chiang has usually been known as "the Chairman," sometimes as "the Party Chief," and now as "the President." [1] Hirohito reigns over a vast

---

[1] In Chinese, *Wei-yüan-chang* (from his chairmanship of the Military Affairs Commission), *Tsung-ts'ai* (in the Kuomintang as party), and *Tsung-t'ung,* respectively. In each case the surname would precede the title. Chiang Chieh-shih (pronounced in Cantonese as Chiang Kai-shek or Chiang K'ai-shek) was the name under which he first became famous. It is rarely heard in China. Chiang Chung-cheng is the formal name under which he holds office. Chinese use many different given names, following the surname, but they use them only one at a time, which makes things confusing for historians, creditors, and policemen. A recent Chinese government order tries to pin all Chinese down to the one-man one-name rule.

empire, which he ruled perhaps only for those few minutes in which he gave his divine and irrefutable command to surrender; it may well have been the one definite political act of his life. Chiang presided over a much larger empire and tried to run everything in it, all the way from prescribing fashions, dictating curricula, admonishing half the people he met and encouraging the other half, not to mention waging almost forty years of intermittent war against other Chinese. Hirohito's country, thought of as being small, has almost twice the population of France. Chiang's country, now held mostly by Mao Tse-tung, is the largest political unit in the world, with about 450 to 500 million people. Chiang's own China is shrinking. Hirohito's Japan has shrunk.

Legacy of Sun Yat-sen. From such a comparison, it would be easy to conclude that Chiang rose by his own strength, with no tradition or authority behind him. That would not be true. Chiang's government is under the moral authority of a dead man who has been declared—formally and officially—to be the superior of Chiang in perpetuity. That sainted ruler is Sun Yat-sen.[2] He framed a doctrine that operates after the manner of the Confucian tradition, though its net effect—despite Sun's protestations—is at variance with the primacy of ideological control that existed under the Confucian system. Sun left a double legacy. First, he left a tradition of turmoil and disorder, justifying not merely rebellion but social and ideological revolution, on the ground that the old China would not have survived imperialist oppression without renewed dynamics from within. Second, he left, together with the example of charismatic personal leadership, a positive code in the *San Min Chu I,* which comprises both an ideology for thinking about government and programs for doing the governing.

Sun Yat-sen's place in world history is not yet certain. If his ideas and principles, as embodied in the institutions of a non-Communist China, re-emerge in the course of the present world struggle, he may show up as having been one of the most important men of our age. The prime responsibility for making those ideas survive is Chiang's. Chiang inherited both parts of Sun's legacy—the revolution that exists in fact, which Sun himself helped to bring about, and the program for consummating the revolution. Inheriting a revolution is an easy way to get power, but a hard way to maintain it. Since he took over the revolution, it has been Chiang's task to be organizer of the revolution. The beginning of a revolution is often an occasion for an excess of joy, a removal of old oppressions; but to finish the revolution is rarely a happy experience. Today Chiang is still in the position of a hypothetical Trotsky facing a hundred million organized followers of Stalin, or of an imaginary Napoleon with most of France still in the hands of Danton or Robespierre. Chiang is one legitimate heir of the revolution. He has suc-

---

[2] Sun is still *Tsung-li* (Leader) of the Kuomintang, even though dead; Chiang is junior to him with the title *Tsung-ts'ai* (Chief).

ceeded in seizing and keeping the mantle of Sun Yat-sen, and even lets himself be called leader (*lin hsiu*) on occasion. But China is vast and his enemies hold it; his "China" is Taiwan (Formosa) and a few dozen guerilla-held counties on the mainland. Chiang is China's unifier, but the China he unified is Mao's.

Warring Heirs to the Revolution. The opposition to Chiang challenges his reasonable demand for unity with the equally reasonable statement that unity could be accomplished soon if conditions under Chiang became good—democratic, prosperous, happy, free. Both statements are reasonable, and neither makes sense. It is impossible to impose unity by force alone in an area which is spiraling downward in social and economic conditions. It is equally impossible to seek attainment of the ideal as a prerequisite to unified authority when the state provides the only means by which improvement can be planned, organized, decreed, and enforced.

Hence, there exists in Chinese politics also the stereotype of Chiang, political leader of a power-seeking government, still mouthing the slogans of a long-past revolt while the Communists simultaneously profess revolution. Chiang asks all Chinese to struggle "with oneness of heart for the complete realization of the aims of our revolution." [3] The Communist leader, Mao Tse-tung, agrees in saying: "New political force, new economic force, new cultural force are all Chinese revolutionary force, and are in opposition to old politics, old economics, old culture." [4] The difference between Chiang and the opposition lies in the politico-military truism that the creation of governmental power restricts the further freedom of the creator to act as a revolutionary. He is committed by his own victories. He must preserve what he has won, and the more he wins, the more he is tied down. Each victory brings with it obligations toward those followers who have been most effective and loyal. Chiang failed at last through too much success.

Life of Chiang. In 1906, when Chiang was eighteen, he was sent to the first Chinese officers' training school established by the imperial authorities at Paotingfu. On the basis of his record there he won a military scholarship to study in Japan. Part of his studies included a tour of duty in the Imperial Japanese Army. After four years in Japan—his longest residence abroad—he got back to China in time to play a part in the fighting and politics of the revolution of 1911-12. During the following ten years (1913-23) he did many things. He was in business. He was an undercover agent for Sun's movement. He is reported to have joined the Green Gang of Shanghai. Finally, he went to Russia, on Sun's personal nomination, spending almost a year there and getting the exceedingly intensive training in subversion, assassination, propaganda, guerrilla warfare, and other useful arts, which the Soviet authorities were offering to promising young Asiatics.

---

[3] Chinese Ministry of Information, *The Collected Wartime Messages of Generalissimo Chiang Kai-shek, 1937-1945* (New York, 1946), II, 770.

[4] Mao Tse-tung, *Hsin Min-chu Chu-i Lun* (*Discourse on the New Democracy*) (Yenan, 1944), p. 53.

Returning to China, he set up the first politically indoctrinating officers' school, the Huangpu Academy (written Whampoa from the Cantonese). He made such a good impression by his exercise of politically conscious military command that he became commander of Sun's limited troops. From there he stepped up into the Kuomintang triumvirate which, with the death of the old leader, succeeded to Sun's position in 1925. Since then Chiang has got rid of his two colleagues, driving one to heartbreak and the other to treason. He has turned Christian. He broke with the Communists in 1926-27, made up with them during 1936-45, and broke with them again in 1946. His few and infrequent retirements from politics have been events; each time he "retired" the chief question was, "How will he come back?" He has occupied almost all top positions in the national government and has had a strong voice in its direction. •

But Chiang himself is not even dictator. He has always had to bargain for power with the different military, economic, and social groups among which power was diffused. As a state-building leader, he has seen more and more power accrue to officialdom as such. He has not often been despotic, and probably could not be efficiently despotic on a large scale even if he wanted to try. His present vestigial post is his most explicit one legally— President under the constitution, with authority not from the Kuomintang but from "the people." Without copying each other, Stalin and Chiang made the identical transformation of their personal roles in World War II. Each began as boss of a dominant party; each ended as official head of his state. But Stalin's power has grown and Chiang's has waned.

Character and Associates. Chiang's power has rested on his activity, not on his attitudes. He is not a political philosopher and utopist, like Sun Yat-sen, who could stir men by his depth and insight. Nor is Chiang a saint like Gandhi, who embodied an idea until the whole world recognized his personality and the principle of *satragraha* as an accomplished artistic unity. Chiang has power because he got it and kept it. To get and keep power, he has had to show qualities of political and military leadership, and even of ethical stature, but these have always rested on his not taking the chance of waiting. Chiang had been on the offensive—till he lost.[5] Yet few other governments have had as stable an elite as Nationalist China, from 1928 to 1948. Almost everyone important twenty years before was still important, unless dead; and almost everyone of any importance had moved slowly upward in the official circles. There were right and left wings, some of whose members

---

[5] A penetrating but bitterly hostile view of Chiang is presented in Theodore H. White and Annalee Jacoby, *Thunder out of China* (New York, 1946), pp. 118 ff. An official biography, which omits all disturbing essentials, is Hollington K. Tong, *Chiang Kai-shek: Soldier and Statesman* (Shanghai, 1937), 2 vols. A competent newspaperman's presentation is Robert Berkov, *Strong Man of China: The Story of Chiang Kai-shek* (Boston, 1938). Perhaps the most thoughtful book about Chiang is Gustav Amann, *Chiang Kaishek und die Regierung der Kuomintang in China* (Heidelberg and Berlin, 1936). Amann, a German writer and technician, was a good friend of the Generalissimo's. A bibliography on Chiang would now make up a fair-sized book. There is a recent life by the talented Chinese poetic writer, S. I. Hsiung.

exchanged sides. Wang Ch'ing-wei, the darling of the liberals in the 1930's, became the quisling of the Japanese. The son of Sun Yat-sen, Dr. Sun K'ê (Sun Fo) had always held a post of dignity and importance; he was not dispensable, until the end.

Chiang's family relationship to Sun has counted for a great deal. Sun married one of the Soong sisters; H. H. K'ung married the oldest; Chiang, the youngest. These three, with their brothers, have been exceedingly important in the national government, although friends and critics disagree as to whether they have been a hindrance or a help to good government. The family connection is not united; Mme. Sun is a Vice President in the Peking regime, while her brother-in-law is the enemy President beyond the shores. The Soong family has been as stable in power as the aged group from Dr. Sun's circle, which comprises the heart of the government. By getting a "half-outside" Premier and an "outside" Vice President in 1948, the Nationalists underwent what seemed a radical transfer of power. To be sure, stability has its penalties. The Generalissimo, whatever office he has occupied, has been playing a game of musical chairs with his lifelong associates. Every now and then they all change places, but when the time comes to grab seats, they are all back in—the same people, though now twenty or thirty years older than they were at the beginning. Their responses to danger are affected by their age. A New Life Movement preaches ethics and confidence. But the Nationalist leaders are unnecessarily afraid of labor unions, a free press, and foreign opinion.

No new blood has come into the government for many years, with the exception of a few professors and other experts entering below the Cabinet level during the war. Chiang's position is stable, and the government that gives it form cannot be told apart from Chiang's own power. There are definite indications, however, that the process of modern government has come to stay in China, even though any particular regime in any particular form must face return or demise. All parties, including the Communists, agree on application of many of the essential methods of government. The military systems have matured. Communications have developed under a growing technological capacity. Even law, though used peculiarly by Communists or Nationalists, has gone far to replace traditionalism.

2. The Search for Constitutional Form

Family and Village. For more than thirty years the Chinese have been drafting "modern" constitutions. One noble document has succeeded another without any of them being applied. Throughout this time, the Chinese common people have had rights—sometimes protected, sometimes not—but the rights were not those listed in the various constitutions. They were traditional rights arising from concepts of Chinese social behavior and usually enforced through intergroup pressure, not through the government. Fifty years ago, most Chinese still lived their lives below the ordinary reach of government. The imperial bureaucracy ended at the *hsien*. With less than 2,000 *hsien* units for all China, and with a population somewhere above 400,000,000, a rough arithmetical average would show more than 200,000 in each *hsien*—a unit variously translated as "district, prefecture, county." The *hsien* normally had one regular career official, who was assisted by fiscal agents, military detachments of very low quality, and equally low-grade clerks. The *hsien-chang,* in the normal course of events, did not even try to govern. He was the ambassador of the central government to the people. The people took care of themselves.

They did so through institutions that depended neither on law nor on constitutions. The institutions existed by the imprescriptible rights of common sense, as exemplified in the Confucian tradition. For the essential minimum of social security, decent burial, police protection, and related rights, every Chinese was the member of a family. The family got him out of trouble, sheltered him when he was unemployed, fed him when he was hungry, locked him up in a back room if he went mad, talked him into committing suicide if he were caught in a felony, and in general lived his life with him.

For purposes of community life, most Chinese were also members of villages. The villages had governments that ran to all types—just as a single block, in an American street today, can provide living samples of almost every form of government known by nations in the past: families are open-hearted, secure, and constitutional in some cases; in others they are oppressive tyrannies; in still others, near anarchy. Some village governments were township meetings, others, councils of elders; some were ruled by esteemed, moral old men; others by oppressive and venal bosses.

Government by Association. Finally, the Chinese had *hui. Hui* can most simply be described as *combinations.* The six main categories included: (1) fraternal societies; (2) insurance groups; (3) economic guilds of producers, dealers, transporters, and the like; (4) religious societies; (5) political societies, usually secret and normally subversive; and (6) volunteer militia and vigilante organizations.[6] Wherever family and village did not apply sufficiently widely or specifically, a *hui* was sure to be formed. Credit, insurance, common worship, numbers games, hired-out murders—almost anything could be arranged through one of the many private societies that existed below the attention of the government. The old government dealt with the people on terms of aloofness and collective responsibility. The people responded by working out their lives without much reference to government. Sun Yat-sen, not realizing how swiftly his own teaching had overtaken him, suggested in his doctrinal lectures that the Chinese move toward nationalism

---

[6] Cf. J. S. Burgess, *The Guilds of Peking* (New York, 1928); Paul M. A. Linebarger, *Government in Republican China* (New York, 1938), p. 138.

by starting with unions of families. It then seemed to be a practicable way.

With government nonexistent or at the most extremely dilute, it was impossible for the Chinese to follow the Japanese example of redoing the laws to make a constitutional government. The revolution that ended the empire was a revolution against inadequate authority, against a social system rather than a political one. The real revolution did not get under way until well after the Republic had come into nominal existence. It was the civil wars, the technological advance, foreign trade, modern education, communism, Christianity, and a thousand other forces all thrown together that shook down the Chinese world. Between 1900, when the old system still worked for most of China, and 1940, when it had broken down in its essentials for most of China, the great revolution took place.

The limits of government as a *social* institution had to become known before government as a *political* institution could be grasped and arranged. China's need of government today is attested by the almost complete breakdown of the old institutions in all fields—fraternal, religious, military, political, and economic. Families no longer command; sons cannot be counted on to obey. Kinsmen do not meet their clan obligations unless they feel like it. The people are far less confident of their freedom from government and far more dependent on government—whereas in the old days they turned to passive resistance whenever it suited them. The Chinese of today expect things of government that no Chinese ever expected from the state before: cholera inoculation, education, postal service, sound banking, police protection, political rights of speech and assembly.

Early Constitutions. The first Chinese written constitution was issued August 27, 1908. It represented a bewildered attempt by the Manchu court, controlled by the dying, despotic, once competent Dowager Empress Yehonola, to contend with forces that no palace attendant really understood. The outcome was an imitation of the Meiji constitution.[7]

The first republican constitutions varied in form, with the presidential-parliamentary motif predominating. The first, temporary document conveyed power to a National Council that was not elected but was composed of persons who had to be selected by the *de facto* revolutionary governments of the provinces.[8] Thus, military governors, or provincial assemblies, or revolutionary juntas set up the first government. The Chinese Revolution,

---

[7] An outstanding book on Manchu government is P. C. Hsieh, *The Government of China (1644-1911)* (Baltimore, 1925). The last phase of Chinese imperial government is described in tremendous detail in H. S. Brunnert and V. V. Hagelstrom, *Present-Day Political Organization of China* (Shanghai, 1912). The imperial government collapsed in the republican revolution while this vast administrative guide, originally written in Russian, was on press.

[8] Cf. H. M. Vinacke, *Modern Constitutional Development of China* (Princeton, 1920), p. 124. See also the detailed historical study by Pan Wei-tung, *The Chinese Constitution: A Study of Forty Years of Constitution-Making in China* (Washington, 1945); and the juristic discussion by W. Y. Tsao, *The Constitutional Structure of Modern China* (Melbourne, 1947).

like the American revolutionary process of 1775-76, began with the convocation of representatives from existing units of government, and not with a
mob uprising or a plebiscite. The temporary constitution was succeeded by
a variety of constitutions that veered toward high presidential authority and
even paved the way for General Yüan Shih-k'ai's attempted change from
President to Emperor in 1915-16.

Governmental Succession. In American diplomatic history, governmental
succession in China ran from the Empire (till 1911) to the Peking—presidential and warlord—republic (till 1928) and the Nationalist government
under Chiang from 1928 on. In the history of the Kuomintang, the succession ran from the Empire to the revolutionary government set up in Nanking
in 1912, thence to the parliamentary republic under Yüan Shih-k'ai, thence
to the rump governments established at Canton by Sun Yat-sen, to the leftist
coalition "Kuomintang" government at Wu-han, and finally to the Nanking
government of 1927 (co-existing with the Wu-han regime for a period of
months), which remained at Nanking until recently, except for its wartime
exiles, first back to Wu-han (1938) and then to Chungking (1938-45).

Thus, "Nanking government" has meant the national government under
Chiang's leadership, save for the years 1938-45. From 1938 to 1940, the term
referred to a local pro-Japanese puppet government (Reformed Government
of China), and from 1940 to 1945, to the ostensibly national puppet government of the secessionist Kuomintang leader Wang Ch'ing-wei (Reorganized
National Government of China).[9] Every single one of these governments
had some kind of constitution or organic law, and almost all such documents
were highly progressive in tone.

The first constitutional government on Sun Yat-sen's formula, headed by
Sun himself, was a simple military junta at Canton, with a group of the anti-
dictatorial, pro-Sun members of the Peking Parliament giving the regime
the color of parliamentarism. Unrecognized by any outside nation, it served
simply as the governing facility for Sun and his military associates of the moment. It is this junta, however, which the national government sees as its
own legitimate forerunner.

Nationalist Government, Soviet in Form. The loose constitutional pattern
of the junta at Canton was actually more closely adapted to political reality
than were the pretentious parliamentary façades of the North. There the
Republic gradually faded out amid the struggle of the warlords, until only a
foreign office, a few tax offices, and a statistical bureau were left, none of
them possessing actual jurisdiction even over the capital city of Peking. But
before Sun died, his military governments were discontinued in favor of a

---

[9] Paul M. A. Linebarger, *The China of Chiang K'ai-shek* (Boston, 1941), pp. 183 ff., gives
the dubious genealogies of these puppet governments as the author traced them through interviews with the traitor officials.

significant experiment—the creation of a soviet government by a non-communist party.[10]

In token of its ideological orientation, this government called itself the National*ist* Government. In organization it followed the Russian pattern. Actual power was held in the hands of principal committees, though the beginnings of Sun's five-power system were put down on paper. The structure was effective as an instrument of revolution, but the principles of Sun Yat-sen, calling for the first revolutionary phase of conquest to be succeeded by one of tutelage, required the adoption of a provisional version of the five-power system.

Period of Tutelage (1928-47). By virtue of a constitutional program entitled *Outline of Political Tutelage*, formulated and promulgated on October 3, 1928, the Kuomintang vested in itself all the rights of the electorate, pending the ultimate creation of elected popular government, and gave itself as a party a monopoly of political power. Thus, in establishing a one-party regime, it followed the Communist party of the Soviet Union and the Fascist party of Italy. In the Year XX of the Chinese Republic (1931), the National Government was provided with an organic act by the Kuomintang, together with a group of basic ordinances (December 30, 1931), which also defined the party's relationship to the government. The Organic Act (*Yüeh-fa*) is sometimes referred to (in English) as the provisional constitution.

For China, this was a long-lived constitution. Under it, supreme power was vested in the party organization of the Kuomintang. A party congress elected a Central Executive Committee and a Control Committee, which in turn managed a *Chêng-chih Wei-yüan-hui* (usually translated as Central Political Council). This agency, though a party creation, was as much the constitutional master of China as if it had been a corporate autocratic monarch. In time of war it yielded to a slightly different version of itself called the Supreme National Defense Council (*Kuo-fang Tsui-kao Wei-yüan-hui*), but the power relationships remained the same. The principal characteristic of government in this entire period was the growth of actual administration, giving content to constitutional form, and the modesty of the formal constitution in contrast with the overambitious attempts of the early Republic.

Outline of Government. The chief governmental facility—under the Central Political Council of the Kuomintang—was a Council of State (*Kuomin Chêng-fu Wei-yüan-hui*), rising over both the five component *yüan* and the ministries, which were one echelon further down, mainly under the Executive *Yüan*. This triple-echelon organization of government was a distinct

---

[10] The only Western work to study this important point is Arthur N. Holcombe, *The Chinese Revolution* (Cambridge, Mass., 1930). P. Miff's *Heroic China* (New York, 1937), apparently a digest of the same author's *Kitaiskaya Revoliutsiya* (Moscow, 1932), fails to make any mention of it. Wang Shih-chieh, in his *Pi-chiao Hsien-fa* (*Comparative Constitutions*) (Shanghai, 1937), pp. 653 ff., describes this phase clearly in his analysis of the *Chêng-chih Wei-yüan-hui* (usually translated as Central Political Council), but does not use the Soviet analogy in any express form.

Chinese innovation. The chairman of the Council of State was *ex-officio* the head of the government. Sun's five-power structure was recognized in a basic division of functions into executive, legislative, judicial, examination, and control branches, each a *yüan*.

The written constitution did not change much during the period of tutelage, but the government acted like a very light boat in which a very heavy man changes position. Wherever the Generalissimo went, power went too. When he was President of the Government (as chairman of the Council of State), that office held great power. When he was president of the Executive *Yüan*, the chairman of the Council of State tended to become a purely titular office. On occasion, Chiang held neither of these offices, working merely as head of the Kuomintang and as joint chairman of its Supreme National Defense Council and the Military Affairs Commission, which was the highest military organ of the government. But the offices not occupied by Chiang continued to fill constitutional roles. Successive presidents of the Executive *Yüan* did in fact behave like premiers in parliamentary republics. Without the experience provided by this period of tutelage, there would be no Chinese at all who were familiar with a national administration. The pattern set slowly, but it did set.

Within the one-party state, a limited experiment was carried on in representative government. The government, at Kuomintang command, created a People's Political Council (*Kuo-min Ts'an-chêng Hui*),[11] to which a fairly representative group of delegates was appointed. Kuomintang members, Communists, representatives of minor parties, and eminent nonparty citizens learned the arts of interpellation, of budgetary analysis, of administrative and political investigation, of legislative committee action. The official lawmaking body, the Legislative *Yüan*, served as a collegial chamber of legal experts for the drafting and planning of law.

End of Tutelage. A draft constitution, quite similar to the one finally adopted in 1946, was issued for study on May 5, 1936, 5/5/XXV in the Chinese calendar—the Double Five draft. For ten long years the government was diverted by war, by the uncertainty of the Communist issue, and by the irresoluteness of Kuomintang leaders when faced with actual democracy. It kept postponing the calling of a National Assembly (*Kuo-min Ta-hui*)

---

[11] Often referred to as PPC, its English initials. This body is not to be confused with the PCC, the People's Consultative Conference (*Chêng-chih Hsieh-shang Hui-i*). The PCC was an *ad hoc* constitutional organ, largely set up at the instance of the United States representative, General George C. Marshall. It was composed of eight Kuomintang representatives, seven Communists, eleven representatives from minor parties, and nine nonparty men. It was able to agree on liberalizing the proposed constitution (Double Five draft, as amended in 1946) to include unqualified guarantees of popular rights, the rights of provinces to draw up their own provincial constitutions, the creation of a popularly representative Legislative *Yüan* for the constitutional government, and the declaration of Cabinet responsibility to the Legislative *Yüan* acting in the role of a parliament. But the PCC was unable to stop the civil war, to bring Nationalists and Communists together in agreeing on a constituent assembly for the enactment of the Constitution, and to create a climate of good faith.

to consider the draft and then to adopt this or a similar constitution, thus changing *the* party into *a* party. The final decision to go ahead with the holding of the assembly provided the reason for the break between Kuomintang and Communists in 1946. The Communists, foreseeing an assembly in which they could not possibly have a majority, raised objections that were legally entirely proper—the irregularity of *Kuo-min Ta-hui* elections, for example—but that were not germane to a global struggle for power. On November 15, 1946, the assembly did meet.

Its composition was peculiar. Nine hundred and fifty delegates had been elected ten years before, in rather sloppy elections. Four hundred further members were scheduled to be added by new indirect elections. Seven hundred more were arbitrarily assigned to the chief political parties—200 for the Kuomintang, 190 for the Communists, 120 for the minority-party coalition of the Democratic League, 100 for the China Youth party, and 90 nonpartisan citizens of eminence. The Communists and the pro-Communist majority of the Democratic League refused to participate on these terms.

Review of the New Constitution. A Chinese administrator and political scientist, writing in a critical and detached vein, has provided a general critique of the constituent assembly and the new constitution that merits extensive quotation.

Meeting of the Assembly. The assembly met November 15, 1946. The draft constitution was acted upon November 22 by the old Legislative *Yüan* and transmitted to the assembly, which had already opened discussion of the outstanding questions. On November 28 President Chiang, officially representing the national government before the assembly, presented the draft. This was enacted on December 25, Christmas Day, 1946. On New Year's Day of 1947, the new constitution was proclaimed in force.

In the main, the assembly retained the liberalized amendments to the government draft which were recommended by the People's Consultative Conference. Discussion was at times both intense and prolonged. There was no serious objection to the one really unique feature of the constitution, its official basis in the ideology of Dr. Sun Yat-sen, which provides for the five powers of government, the four rights of the electorate, and the three principles of the people. Under the new constitution, the four rights of the electorate should go into effect immediately, but election is the only one which seems practical now, and it would be surprising if even the elections worked 100 per cent in a country which never had the ballot before. Putting the constitution into effect—even limited effect—was a major political adventure, and the assembly performed this task.

Brief Résumé of the Constitution.[12] Dr. Sun taught that in order to have effective control over the government, the electorate should possess four political rights: election and recall, initiative and referendum. In local self-government, these four rights are to be exercised directly by the voters; and in the central government, indirectly through a national assembly.

---

[12] Much of this discussion is based upon the various comments made at the time (and published in the Chinese press) by the former World Court judge, Dr. Wang Ch'ung-hui.

As to the five-power system of government, there should be, besides the executive, legislative, and judicial powers, two additional ones—namely, the power of examination and the power of control. Roughly, the first refers to a system of open competitive examination for the holding of public offices, and the second to a system of impeachment of, and supervision over, public functionaries. These correspond to the ancient Chinese institutions of the mandarinate and the censorate. The point to be emphasized is that these two powers should be raised to an equal status with the other three. In other words, there should be five branches of government—five *yüan*, independent of, though coordinate with, one another.

The salient features of the constitution may be briefly summarized as follows:

(1) *Equality of all persons and racial groups.* All racial groups are declared to be equal. All persons irrespective of sex, religion, race, class or party affiliation are equal before the law. There is to be universal suffrage and secret ballot. Men and women attaining the age of twenty have the right to vote. It is worth noting in this connection that in order to assure women's representation in the National Assembly and the Legislative *Yüan,* a minimum number to be prescribed by law are to be women.

(2) *Guaranty of personal liberties and rights.* Practically all personal liberties and rights that can be found in a modern bill of rights, including a *habeas corpus* provision, are guaranteed. In addition, the responsibility of the state for illegal acts of public officers is recognized.

(3) *The National Assembly.* The National Assembly is to be the supreme organ of the people. Its members are elected mainly on the basis of territorial and professional representation. They serve for a term of six years, subject to recall. The National Assembly elects the President and the Vice President of the Republic and it may recall them. It has the power to amend the constitution. Eventually, it may, in accordance with its own rules of procedure, exercise the right of initiative regarding national legislation.

(4) *The President.* The President is elected for six years, and can be re-elected only for a second term. He appoints the president of the Executive *Yüan* (the equivalent of a Premier) with the consent of the Legislative *Yüan.* Upon the Premier's recommendation, he appoints ministers with or without portfolio. Generally speaking, the President has the powers and functions that usually belong to the chief executive of a republic.

(5) *Five Branches of Government.* (*a*) The Executive *Yüan* is composed of a president (Premier), a deputy president, heads of different ministries and commissions, and a certain number of ministers without portfolio. (*b*) The Legislative *Yüan* is unicameral. Its members are elected mainly on the basis of territorial and professional representation for a three-year term, and are both eligible for re-election and subject to recall. (*c*) The Judicial *Yüan* is the highest court of justice. Its president and judges are appointed by the President with the consent of the Control *Yüan.* (*d*) The Examination *Yüan* has charge of the examination for civil service and other related matters. Its members are appointed by the President with the consent of the Control *Yüan.* (*e*) As to the Control *Yüan,* its main functions are impeachment of, and supervision over, public functionaries, auditing, and approval of appointment of certain high officials. Its members are elected by provincial assemblies for a term of six years.

(6) *Relationship between the Executive and Legislative Yüan.* The Executive *Yüan* is responsible to the Legislative *Yüan* in the following manner. In case of a difference of opinion about questions concerning basic policy, legislation, the budget, or treaties, the Executive *Yüan* may, with the approval of the President of the Republic, veto resolutions of the Legislative *Yüan.* If the Legislative *Yüan* overrides the veto by a two-thirds vote, the Premier has either to abide by the resolution or to resign. Abiding by the two-thirds vote of overriding the veto is one of the characteristics of the presidential system. The modification introduced in the present constitution is that there is a Premier to face the legislature. The Premier may, instead of yielding to the will of the legislature, choose to resign, in which case he assumes his responsibility as under the parliamentary system. In other words, this is a mixed presidential and parliamentary type of government.

(7) *Division of Powers between Central Government and Provincial Governments.* The powers of both the central and provincial governments are enumerated. As to unenumerated matters, they belong to either government according to their nature—that is, whether they are national in character or not. In case of dispute, the Legislative *Yüan* determines where the power shall reside.

(8) *Local Self-government.* The province and the district (*hsien*), respectively, are the large and small units of local self-government. In each there is to be a popular assembly. The provincial governor as well as the district magistrate is to be elected by the people. A province may adopt its own self-government law. Under the district government the people may exercise the rights of election and recall, initiative and referendum. There are other provisions to be put into practice in accordance with the General Principles of Provincial and District Self-Government, to be determined by law.

(9) *Fundamental National Policies.* Fundamental national policies are divided into national defense, foreign relations, national economy, social security, education and culture, and border regions. Maintenance of national security and world peace is to be the objective of national defense; observance of treaty obligations and of the charter of the United Nations is expressly provided for. Other fundamental policies include: equitable distribution of land and control of capital; protection and limitation of private property; taxation of unearned increment; government control of public utilities and other enterprises of a monopolistic nature; allocation of minimum percentages of the national and local budget for educational, cultural, and scientific purposes; opportunity of employment for persons capable of work; special protection of working women and children; establishment of social insurance; and so forth.

(10) *Interpretation of the Constitution.* The power to interpret the constitution resides in the Judicial *Yüan.* Any law whether national or local may be declared unconstitutional by the Judicial *Yüan.*

Critique of the Constitution. To the Communists, the constitution is an illegal document produced by an assembly in which the people of the Communist-held areas are not represented. After the convocation of the assembly, General Chou En-lai made a statement defending the Communist party's nonrecognition policy towards the assembly and denouncing the assembly as an illegal one-party organ. . . .

But in all fairness, in a country like present-day China, where democratic tradition is lacking, the achievement of a constitution which is fundamentally democratic is at least a sizable advance. This is to the credit of Generalissimo Chiang, who insisted that the assembly should adopt a constitution based on the principles generally accepted by all party leaders at the People's Consultative Conference. If the government can make the constitution function in the spirit of its authors, it should set China on the path to democracy and honest government. . . .[13]

3. The Nationalist Governmental Structure, to 1948

Present Political Meaning. The Nationalist governmental structure of 1947-1948 represented the highest level to which noncommunist government has been carried by Chinese. Its battered remnant on Formosa—improved and simplified but localized—remained recognized by the United States as the *de jure* government of China and retained China's seat in the United Nations.

This structure is worth some attention even now because—first of all—it is *the one alternative to Chinese Communism which did in fact exist as a government national in scope.* It failed, but it did exist. Others were talked about, dreamed of, hoped for, but they did not come into being.

The last mainland Nationalist government gives Formosa its claim to represent China to the Chinese people and to the world. The mainland government fell rapidly; conceivably it may rise equally rapidly. Whether this government comes to power with the same name and leaders or not, it is the one alternative to communism which most Chinese have ever known. In addition, it is worth remembering as a strategic fact. Its defects help explain the triumph of communism in China, and the weakness of its merits—wonderful on paper but difficult to fulfill in life—explain that triumph even further.

Most Chinese are governed by Mao, whose troops, by "volunteering" in Korea, may have uncorked bottled lightning. Chiang fell because he underestimated the Communists; Mao could fall if he really underestimated the United States. The Mao government was reasonably stable and prosperous in 1950; after the Korean hostilities deepened it became much more tyrannical and poorer. The Nationalist mainland government is—as a government—a phantom, but its Communist successor is by no means a thousand-year Reich more permanent than Hitler's—or Stalin's.

The Italian anti-Fascists of 1930 were aged has-beens whom no one, it was said then, would ever notice again. Italian elections, Italian parliamentarism —they were archaeology. Fascism had come, and come to stay. But Mussolini hung dead in a public place, and the forlorn has-beens came back to very real power and leadership. The Formosa Nationalists have more territory, more troops, more help than were ever possessed by the anti-Hitlerites or anti-Fascists. Nationalist China may be eclipsed; it may be dead. The present cannot answer—only the future. This was the government a Na-

---

[13] Revised text of a lecture given by Dr. Djang Chu in May 1947 at the School of Advanced International Studies, Washington, D. C. Dr. Djang had been present in Nanking at the time of the assembly and was familiar with the proceedings as an observer at first hand.

tionalist China would have had, did begin to have, as a variety of democracy, just before the downfall of Chiang's mainland power.

Transition Government. There was an unusual year between the adoption of the new constitution and the establishment of government on a non-monopoly basis. The constituent assembly of 1946 disbanded when it had sanctioned the constitution. Now it was up to the Kuomintang to develop formulas for relinquishing control. This task was carried out in the midst of civil war, with the result that the change was less substantial than it presumably would have been in peacetime. The next chart shows the intermediate form of government created for the specific purpose of moving from a one-party state to a multiparty democracy. The Council of State became the ruling body. It was changed from its previous status of recipient of policy from the Kuomintang to being a multiparty collegium superintending all of the national government.

On April 18, 1947, the government—by command of the Kuomintang's still controlling dominant committees—proclaimed a new organic law taking itself out of Kuomintang hands. A year and a day later (April 19, 1948), the first elected National Assembly in turn elected Chiang as the first Chinese chief of state to hold office by election. Within that year political progress was made, though in a discouraging military and economic context. Following the government's self-proclaimed autonomy from the Kuomintang in April 1947, the Council of State met with a new membership. It now had 40 members. The five *Yüan* presidents sat *ex-officio.* Of the remaining 35 seats, the allocation was on a party basis, as follows: Kuomintang, 12; Young China party, 4; Social Democratic party, 4; independent leaders, 4; reserved for the Communists and pro-Communist Democratic League, but unoccupied, 11.[14] The Council of State on April 23, 1947,[15] promptly appointed a new Cabinet that included non-Kuomintang representation. The same general multiparty composition appeared in other organs of the government.

The Kuomintang proceeded in the spirit of the novel situation by abolishing the governmental role of its special organ for policy control, the Central Political Council. It transferred to the government the quasi-governmental party ministries—such as the Kuomintang Ministry of Information, which had functioned throughout World War II as China's *national* propaganda facility. The special monopoly-party features were stripped away. The San Min Chu I Youth Corps went out of existence. The policy-making officers of the corps were rewarded with correspondingly high posts in the Kuomintang party proper, which added a Youth Department (*Ch'ing-nien Pu*). What was left was a party organization that still bore the imprint of the elaborate structure developed by the Russian Communists and exported in

[14] The government in this phase is described by Chen Chih-mai, "The Postwar Government in China," in Taylor Cole and John Hallowell, eds., *Postwar Governments of the Far East* (Gainesville, Fla., 1947), pp. 503 ff.

[15] Dates through May 1947 are taken from the *Ta Kung Pao,* Shanghai (leading independent newspaper). Later dates are usually from *The New York Times.*

the 1920's. But the Kuomintang, at the opening of constitutional government, was not much more elaborate than the Japanese Social Democratic
party.

End of Transition. In June 1947 even the civil war was given more definite legal status. The Supreme Court issued an order for the arrest of Mao
Tse-tung as the rebel leader of an illegal party. The Democratic League
was not rendered illegal until October 28, after the government charged that

TRANSITIONAL ORGANIZATION OF THE CHINESE GOVERNMENT, 1947–48

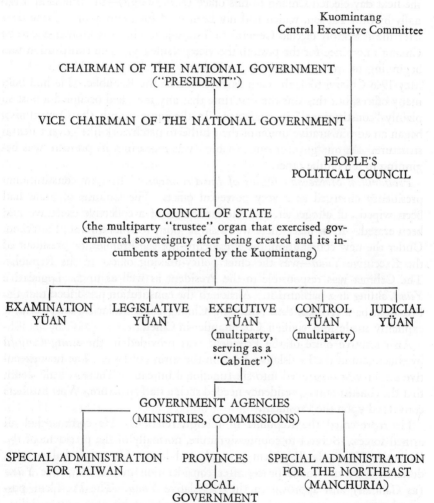

Kuomintang
Central Executive Committee

CHAIRMAN OF THE NATIONAL GOVERNMENT
("PRESIDENT")

VICE CHAIRMAN OF THE NATIONAL GOVERNMENT

PEOPLE'S
POLITICAL COUNCIL

COUNCIL OF STATE
(the multiparty "trustee" organ that exercised governmental sovereignty after being created and its incumbents appointed by the Kuomintang)

| EXAMINATION YÜAN | LEGISLATIVE YÜAN | EXECUTIVE YÜAN (multiparty, serving as a "Cabinet") | CONTROL YÜAN (multiparty) | JUDICIAL YÜAN |

GOVERNMENT AGENCIES
(MINISTRIES, COMMISSIONS)

SPECIAL ADMINISTRATION   PROVINCES   SPECIAL ADMINISTRATION
FOR TAIWAN   FOR THE NORTHEAST
                                                    LOCAL   (MANCHURIA)
                                               GOVERNMENT

Note: In a strict sense, the Kuomintang continued to exercise all powers of sovereignty as
under the theory of tutelage. By a self-denying ordinance, it appointed the multiparty bodies
and thereafter did not give the government direct commands. Its members, however, had
comfortable pluralities in all main organs of government.

members of the league had been participating in espionage and other para-military activities for the Communists.

The first regular election for the National Assembly came on November 21-23, 1947, with 165 million voters registered, according to the official announcement. Elections for the Legislative *Yüan,* also first in the history of this body, were held in January. On March 29, 1948, the National Assembly opened with 1,369 of its 3,045 seats filled. Attendance improved considerably as the sessions continued.

On April 18 the Assembly voted emergency powers to the President and the next day elected Chiang to this office (*tsung-t'ung*)—the title held originally by Sun Yat-sen, which had not been used for many years. Nine days later the Assembly elected General Li Tsung-jên, who was known not to be Chiang's nominee for the post, to the vice presidency. The constitution was beginning to work, but nobody could know whether it would succeed. In May 1948 Chiang took the oath as President of the Republic. He had held many offices, but this was the first time that any man had occupied a post so plainly "constitutional" in character. In the same month the Communists began an administrative union of their hitherto patchwork-like governmental structure. As one government in China was maturing, its pressure was beginning to tell on the other.

Presidential Status and Office of the President. The new constitutional presidency emerged as a very powerful office. The Council of State had been wiped out altogether, and the last traces of a collective executive had been erased. In its place there was a single post, with its own staff attached. Under the new constitution, the President—not the Premier, or president of the Executive *Yüan*—was the chief policy-making officer of the Republic. The Cabinet was responsible to the President as well as to the Legislative *Yüan,* sitting as a parliament. Although the constitution prescribed that the President be a civilian, thus removing Chiang from titular military rank, it explicitly made him civilian Commander-in-Chief.

An executive office of the President was provided in the *tsung-t'ung-fu* by enactment of the Legislative *Yüan* in the spring of 1948. The new executive center was organized into six functional bureaus. There is little doubt that the constitutional presidency needed such a staff structure. Vast business converged upon the President.

He represented the Republic in foreign relations. He commanded all armed forces. Subject to countersignature, normally of the president of the Executive *Yüan,* the President promulgated laws. He concluded treaties, declared war, and made peace, after consideration in the Executive *Yüan* (as Cabinet) and approval in the Legislative *Yüan.* The President possessed emergency powers which he could exercise on his own responsibility, subject to automatic review by the Legislative *Yüan* within one month after declaration of the state of emergency. He resolved differences between *Yüan* presidents. As to conditions of tenure, the constitution stipulated that to qualify for the presidency, a citizen must be forty years of age. Both the President and the Vice President could seek re-election for a second six-year term; nothing was said about a third.

Role of the Constitutional Cabinet. In the last months of Nationalist mainland power, the functions of the Cabinet were conducted by the Executive *Yüan* (including narrowly the executive officers at the top, and broadly the entire pyramid of administration). The Cabinet was formed, however, around the president of the Executive *Yüan* (Premier); it was not the Cabinet of the President himself.

Responsibility of the Executive *Yüan* to the Legislative *Yüan* was not contemplated in the early plans for the five-power system. It was assumed that the National Assembly (*Kuo-min Ta-hui*) would sit as a policy-decreeing and not merely as an electoral and constituent body. The constitution reversed this idea, compelling the members of the Executive *Yüan* (ministers and other department heads) to submit to interpellation. Responsibility was more fully provided by a negative device. The Legislative *Yüan* had power to ask the Executive *Yüan* to alter its policy. With the approval of the President, the Executive *Yüan* could request the Legislative *Yüan* to reconsider its resolution. In that event a two-thirds vote was needed to sustain the resolution calling for "altered policies." If the motion were carried, the head of the Executive *Yüan* had the alternative of abiding by the requested change or of resigning from office. If this were parliamentary responsibility, it was of a tenuous kind—not one that could be enforced with a compelling vote of nonconfidence. The permitted intervention of the President lent color to the suspicion of the leftists that the Chinese constitution of 1946, in its essentials about responsibility, is not very far ahead of the Meiji constitution of 1889.

Functions of the Legislative Yüan. The Legislative *Yüan* of the period of tutelage was an experiment—a nonelective, nonrepresentative, noncameral legislative body. Legislation was prepared by panels of experts, not by committees of politicians. It was submitted to the government through a chief legislative bureaucrat, not a balloting chamber. The new Legislative *Yüan* was a limited unicameral national Parliament. Members served three years. The constitution authorized laws that were to provide a certain number of seats reserved for women. Representation was both on a territorial and on a national-occupational basis.

The president of the Legislative *Yüan* was elected from among the members. He thus changed from director general of legislative drafting to the mere speaker of a chamber.

The new Legislative *Yüan* started out, from the Chinese point of view, "making trouble." Its members, formerly docile and studious jurists, had become a pack of politicians overnight, putting questions to the government, demanding investigations of this and that, and in general creating an uninterrupted uproar. In this there could be seen an encouraging hint of the eventual operational success of elective democracy in China. The Legislative *Yüan,* however, held no more power than was normal for a national parliament. It was not, like the Japanese Diet, the supreme organ of the state. Indeed, under the *yüan* system, its legislative powers were surrounded not by threefold but by fivefold checks and balances.

Examination and Control. Under the Double Five draft of a constitution, but not under the document enacted, the Examination *Yüan* would have had the authority to hold examinations also for *elective* candidates for public office. Left to this *Yüan* were the conduct of all civil service examinations and the prescription of qualifications for public functionaries and for members of the learned professions. During the entire period of tutelage, the *Yüan* occupied itself with extremely dignified inactivity. It continued to work like that while Nationalist China was falling.

The members of the Control (or Censoral) *Yüan* were elected by provincial and municipal assemblies. According to Sun's theory, there should be in government a body of men with the power to "raise any issue publicly"— along with the authority to audit and to impeach. The Control *Yüan* was this body. In the period of tutelage, it worked by use of teams that went through both the central and the field offices of the government. Under the Control *Yüan* there was also the Ministry of Audit, which checked the spending of public funds; the Ministry of the Budget, under the Executive *Yüan,* controlled the allocation of funds. Unfortunately, both budgeting and audit forever ran behind administrative emergencies of various kinds, and were disastrously ineffective.

The new constitution provided that the Control *Yüan* was to exercise "the powers of consent, impeachment, ratification, and auditing." By consent was meant the approval by this *Yüan* of various appointments listed in the constitution; for example, the Examination *Yüan* was composed of a president, vice president, and members appointed by the President of the Republic with the consent of the Control *Yüan.* The Control *Yüan,* acting as a chamber in the exercise of its impeaching authority, could impeach the President for trial before the National Assembly. The members of the Control *Yüan,* elected for six-year terms, elected their own president and vice president.

Ministries and Commissions. The Nationalist ministries and commissions are shown on the accompanying chart. The last change from wartime practice was the dissolution of the monstrously overgrown Military Affairs Commission, which for a while operated as a sort of duplicate national government. It was replaced by the new consolidated Ministry of National Defense.[16]   The list of principal agencies in 1948 (June 1) comprised National Defense, Finance, Industry and Commerce, Land Administration,

---

[16] *The Chinese Year Book* and *The China Handbook,* both of which are annual English-language reference publications issued by the Chinese authorities, will be found to contain descriptions of the official organization and duties of the various ministries.

Health, Foreign Affairs, Communications, Food, Water Conservancy, Interior, Education, Justice, Social Affairs, and Budget.

In a few cases these designations are not self-explanatory. Land Administration was concerned with cadastral surveys, land reform, the planning of taxes in kind, and similar measures. Water Conservancy represented the historic Chinese preoccupation, grown from great urgency, with irrigation and river problems. Interior had control of the entire local and municipal

ORGANIZATION OF THE CHINESE GOVERNMENT, JUNE 1, 1948

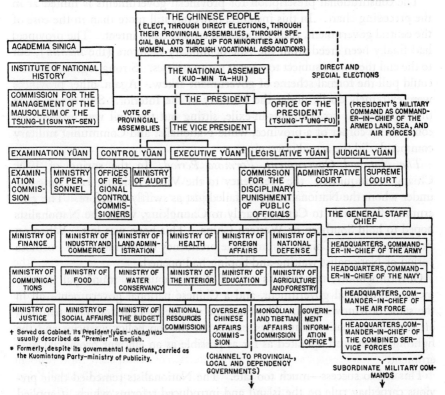

Note: Practically, the Kuomintang still exercised a predominant influence through the majority its members held in policy-making bodies of the government. This influence was in part vitiated by the independence shown by individual party members once they got into elective office. Juridically, the party-government relationship had been erased altogether.

system of the country—subject to whatever checks distance, local elections, or practical politics might impose. In this role, the Ministry of the Interior was still what it used to be for Japan—the supervisory agency of a government that had plenary powers at the center. Social Affairs dealt with associations of all kinds, including labor unions, welfare agencies, organized social work, and the like; its official control of labor unions had been one of the sore points exploited by the Communists for many years.

Along with these ministries under the Executive *Yüan,* there were various commissions, such as the Resources Commission.

Provincial Government. Great hopes were entertained by many for a long time that the government might revise the entire provincial pattern of the country, making the provinces smaller in size and more numerous. But no results came of these hopes. Small provinces were proclaimed in the Northeast. The traditional large provinces—each about the size of a European country—have remained elsewhere in the country.

The constitutional prescription for provincial governments is hinted at in the preceding chart. In this instance, however, still more than in the case of the central government, reality remained remote from intent. The provinces had finally been freed from the rule of military dictators (the *tuchün*), but to the end they were subject to a great many stresses. Strong regional leaders could pull the formal scheme of government askew. Again, other provinces were extremely docile under the Ministry of the Interior. Still others were timid provincial governments-in-exile, sitting out the civil war in some inconspicuous corner of a province, while Nationalist and Communist military commands did the actual governing.

The National Government, Formosa Period. In the spring of 1949, Chiang "relinquished" the presidency to the Vice President, Li Tsung-jên, under whom the Nationalist forces failed just as swiftly as before. The government fled partly to Canton, partly to Chungking, while the Nationalists hoped to hold Southern or Western China. This hope was lost. When on February 28, 1950, Chiang resumed the presidency on Formosa, the Formosa period of Nationalist waiting-and-hoping had opened.

Governmentally, the island's city of Taipei houses a municipal government, a provincial government, and a Chinese national government—all in the same downtown area. The Formosa regime in 1950 and 1951 trimmed off superfluous national agencies, except for the top policy agencies and the fighting forces, and operated as far as possible as an efficient provincial government.

This led to success—much too late. The Nationalists remedied their previous carpetbag rule on the island and introduced reforms which, if applied five years earlier on the mainland, might have stalled Communism. But the reforms were possible precisely because Formosa was an island small enough not to overstrain the Nationalists, and prepared by fifty years of strict but honest Japanese colonial administration.

Within the Kuomintang, moves toward reform gained momentum. A Reform Committee was set up to reorganize and to simplify the party, so as to resume the Nationalist revolution.

The most critical agencies of all are, of course, the secret ones. These are the Kuomintang underground in Communist cities, the Kuomintang guerrillas in the countryside, the mainland Kuomintang leaders who must—if anyone can—keep the Nationalist cause alive in China proper. The Formosa propaganda line exaggerates all these so thoroughly that it is easy to dismiss them as chimerical. The truth would concede more. Formosa is a cross between a loyalist satrapy and a government-in-exile, with the latter role likely to increase only if the Nationalists show superhuman qualities or if the Communists commit great blunders.

4. The Communist Party as a Competing Government

Fostering Cohesion. The Chinese Communist party, in one very significant respect, is an institution that has learned a lesson thoroughly. From 1927 to 1937 the approach of the party was overtly and fiercely political. The red flag flew every place it could be run up. The language was changed in the schools. Coins were minted and banknotes printed, even under the most extraordinary circumstances, not because the Communists needed the money for spending, but because they wanted extensive circulation of proof of their own existence. The Chinese Soviet Republic defied not only the national government, but the entire world as well. Recognized by no one, not even by the USSR, it was a "state" maintained at terrific cost of life and energy by the fighting fanatics of the Chinese Communist vanguard. They had to fight hard. The National Government had the advantages of international recognition, foreign commerce, foreign credit, foreign munitions, and even Italian, German, and American military aid of one kind or another. The Chinese Communists did not allow their government to die, but in an epic migration dragged it six thousand miles across China. Only afterwards did they realize that in putting political form ahead of economic content they had paid too high a price for power.

From 1937 onward the Chinese Communists carefully avoided political and juridical commitment on aims and forms. Even when they fought the national government, they did not proclaim a government of their own. Even in issuing currency, they did so under the color of "local" and "emergency" authorities, keeping each local authority separate from the other.

Unifying factors were: (1) the Chinese Communist party, and (2) the Chinese Communist military command. The latter used whatever cover name the Nationalists gave it—such as Eighth Route Army, Eighteenth Army Group, and so on. The Chinese Communist party never called itself anything else. For covert and clandestine operations, it used the names of pro-Communist groups or merely had its members introduce themselves as "liberals." After the civil war went to full scale in 1947, the Communist armies began to call themselves "democratic" or "liberation" forces of one kind or another. They avoided looking too Communist, or seeming to be anything more than spontaneous, disconnected, separate, local uprisings of patriots.

Class Economics as Reality. This noticeable change of governmental procedure can be understood readily in terms of Marxist semantics operating in the pragmatic intellectual environment of China. The Chinese Communists did not have to contend with formal government as much as did the Communists of the West. Agreeing with the Russian or German or American Communists that what really mattered was full economic control, they were able to disregard government on a much larger scale than did Western Communists. A whole procession of American and British visitors to the Chinese Communist areas came to see and praise the local governments that the Chinese Communists had created.[17] The praise was deserved —but not for the institutions. It was the men behind the institutions, with their indifference toward mere forms of government, who had earned the praise.

Like other communists, the Chinese Communists regard governments as mere screens for the true and occult power behind all government—the unalterable dictatorship exercised over men's moods and thoughts by the pervasive influences of "class realities." Just as the Nazis were taken in by their own pseudoscientific view of the world, the Communists are taken in by their theories of personality and history.

The Communists have created a new heaven and a new earth out of their curious magic. They transfer all blame in the world to selected devils; they achieve a moral certainty not known by history; in their darkest hours they are comforted by the belief that they *know* what is going to happen. Such "knowledge" is based on the selective, capricious, unqualified acceptance of certain phenomena as determinative. Religion, politics, literature, art—all these, they say, stem from class relationships.

The People's Republic. Communist governmental structures operate, therefore, in a context unlike that of any other present-day government. They are the artistic creations of men who doubt government while extolling control. While continuing to praise their own handiwork, the major Communist leaders operate through less formal controls.

The Chinese Communist regime is a new kind of government for China. It appears to have at least four times as many officials in South and Central China as the Chiang regime had at its most heavily staffed times. It tries to reach deep into society. Though the new government went through the motions of making itself a successor-state to republican China, the actual control of society is still for most purposes vested in the military command or in the party itself.

In a sense this represents a new and efficient kind of Asian communism, ranging beyond the state model of the USSR. The power which is held by military party authorities is exercised frankly by them. The old Chinese margin between "political" and "social" was never distinct; under the Peking regime—the capital having been restored to its Ch'ing dynasty location and

---

[17] Edgar Snow, *Red Star Over China* (New York, 1939), is the most noteworthy of these. George E. Taylor is one qualified political scientist to have studied the Communist governmental forms, but even his *The Struggle for North China* (New York, 1940) presents the historical rather than the institutional aspects of the Hopei-Shansi-Chahar border region.

name—the Chinese Communists are making a fanatical but intelligent attempt to find their own answers to the problems of communism. The Chinese Communist movement is too big, culturally, physically, militarily, to be a "satellite" of Russia in the abject Czech, Bulgarian, or Polish sense. Red China is at the least a very slight junior to Russia.

From the outside the similarity between Red China and the Soviet Union is great; from inside out, it is not so great. It would be foolish to describe the People's Government in its own self-advertised terms as a "people's democracy." But it would be equally foolish to assume that it will break with the USSR merely because it is different.

The institutions of Red China themselves are still rudimentary: instead of the five-power system, a one-power system of government; the adulation of a leader, in this case Mao Tse-tung, who carries the title *Chu-hsi* (Chairman, or "President"), but not such titles as *Tsung-t'ung* and *Wei-yüan-chang,* usually borne by Chiang; a temporary agency, so "temporary" that provision is made for triennial meetings; a Central People's Government Council, to which ministries, the military, regions, and courts are all directly appended; a State Administrative Council, serving as Cabinet with its chairman acting as Premier.[18]

More significant are the great regions, modern versions of the enormous vice-royalties of the last Empire, and even more strikingly re-creations of Chiang Kai-shek's "war areas," which take a major military and political role above the level of the province but below the nation. China has, in effect, been made into a chain of Manchurias, multiprovincial groupings, each of which is larger than most nations, each of which is overwhelmingly Chinese, each of which exercises autonomy while preserving central command.

Facing the Issue. The Communist leaders have shown themselves fanatical, intelligent, honest, cruel—and contemptuous of what American usage means by "civilization." They are achieving great political changes, and are doing so at immense cultural and economic cost. It is too early to tell whether they are building a new world or a new hell for the Chinese.

The fall of Nationalist China was the greatest triumph of Marxism since 1917. Chinese Communism will hardly outlast world Communism if world Communism attacks the Free World and is destroyed in the encounter. There is a chance that China's political future will be settled by Chinese in China and in Formosa. If that chance grows, the challenge to be communist and human, revolutionary and Chinese, repressive and hopeful—all the opposites at once—will face Peking as a similar challenge once faced Nanking. The Kuomintang triumphed and was undone by the shallowness of its success. No one can know now about the new Peking. The drama is not over. This is the scene in which dark deeds are done.

---

[18] There are various descriptions of this structure of government, notably those by H. Arthur Steiner in several American journals, and under his editorship in the September 1951 issue of the *Annals of the American Academy of Political and Social Science.*

PART VIII

LATIN AMERICA: MEXICO AND BRAZIL

CHAPTER 31

MEXICO: FROM REVOLUTION
TOWARD CONSTITUTIONALISM

1. Unity and Diversity in Latin American Politics

Appropriate Caution. In any study of government in Latin America it is essential to heed the warning that the late Dr. Leo S. Rowe, for many years Director General of the Pan American Union, placed at the beginning of his classical treatise on Argentina:

One of the most serious obstacles to the scientific study of the political institutions of South American countries has been the tendency to group them in one class and to regard their history as succession of revolutions and dictatorships. Any serious study of the political institutions of these countries must at the outset recognize: (1) That it is impossible to study South America *en bloc.* Fundamental differences in mode of settlement, in colonial organization, and in social development subsequent to independence have determined in each the form of government and the content and operation of political institutions. (2) That the successive revolutions and dictatorships which have occurred in many of the countries of South America must be studied as integral parts of their constitutional development, possessing a far-reaching institutional significance and in many cases marking the successive stages in the advance of the political system toward a more democratic basis through the recognition of popular rights as against class privilege.[1]

What Dr. Rowe here says specifically of South American countries is applicable also to all Latin America, including Mexico. Indeed, to one trying to understand the Latin American political scene in its startling contrasts, it must soon be apparent that from the outset a multiplicity of factors caused characteristic differences among the several republics, and that these differences were almost immediately reflected in institutional development.

Geographic Influences and Economic Bases. Physical environment has provided controlling conditions for the formation of states and their political structure. The range of the *cordillera*—called the Andes in South America—binds all Latin America together, but it also divides the area into two unequal parts. The mountains have long impeded east and west movements, and even today there is but one land route traversing the southern

[1] L. S. Rowe, *The Federal System of the Argentine Republic* (Washington, 1921), p. 3, quoted by permission of the publishers (Carnegie Institution).

continent. On the other hand, the isthmus of Panama has always served as gateway to the whole west coast. Moreover, climatic conditions in large parts of the mountain range, which has an average height of some 10,000 feet and extends in width to 400 miles, are much alike. The temperate uplands attracted, even in precolonial times, much larger numbers of people than the tropical coast and plains. Hence, the settlement of the South American hinterland has always been sparse, and its exploration by white men was long delayed.[2]

Closely related to geographical formation is the distribution of natural resources. Since the *cordillera* contains the greatest mineral deposits of the continent, the interest of early conquerors and later settlers was directed mainly toward that region. Up to recent times, the industrial evolution of Latin America was largely dependent on the location of these deposits and their proximity to ocean ports.[3] Only as the exploitative interest of the colonial regimes and subsequent stagnation in the young republics made way for the initiative of traders from Europe and North America was a new direction given to the industrial growth of the Latin American countries. This turn was intensified when, about the middle of the last century, political consolidation had progressed far enough to encourage more vigorous economic enterprise than had prevailed under the traditional, often sluggish, system of plantation agriculture.[4]

At the same time, Latin American governments began to recognize eco-

[2] Generalizations of this sort require many qualifications. Here the most obvious ones would concern the southernmost part of the continent, which includes Chile, Argentina, Uruguay, and a corner of Brazil. For the geography of Latin America, see William L. Schurz, *Latin America* (New York, 1941), pp. 15-35; Preston E. James, *Latin America* (New York, 1942); R. H. Whitbeck, F. E. Williams, and W. F. Christians, *Economic Geography of South America* (3rd ed., New York, 1940).

[3] The mining of gold, silver, mercury, copper, and diamonds was already the pivot of colonial economic activity, and demand has been rising. The exploitation of ferro-alloys and non-ferrous metals, such as tin, manganese, and chromium, began late in the nineteenth century; that of guano, nitrogen, and iodine somewhat earlier.

[4] On the conditions of agriculture, see Schurz, *op. cit.* above, note 2, pp. 155-78, and Frank Tannenbaum, *Whither Latin America?* (New York, 1934). Despite extensive mining and incipient industrialization, agriculture is still the basic economic activity in all Latin America. Brazil, for instance, is agricultural to the extent that more than 70 per cent of its population is engaged in farming and stock-raising. It is the world's largest producer of coffee, although the export share of coffee has been declining: in 1929 it comprised 71 per cent of all Brazilian exports, but in 1939 only 40 per cent. Further, Brazil is the second largest world producer of cacao, ranks third as regards corn, and fourth as to tobacco; its cotton production takes fifth place in the world economy. Brazil is also the fifth largest stock-raising country in the world, and the third in hog-producing and in the production of goatskins. Mexico's agriculture, too, is highly diversified, since variations in soil and climate have permitted many types of production, ranging from henequen fiber in the tropical plains to wheat on the highland plateaus. Cotton is mostly consumed in the country, but henequen, sugar, coffee, vegetables, and fruit are exported in considerable quantities. Latin American governments have lately taken an interest in the promotion of agriculture mainly under two aspects: increase of productive efficiency and reform of land tenure systems that for centuries have encumbered farming in Latin America. With respect to overcoming the social effects of *latifundismo*, Mexico stands out as the leader of the other republics.

nomic possibilities and responsibilities, which caused them to pay more attention to the augmentation of national wealth. In this development the building of railroads by foreign investors, together with the increased demand of new industries in Europe and the United States for raw materials, played a major part. Conversely, the population growth in those industrial countries widened markets for Latin American agriculture. Unfortunately, the resources of the individual Latin American republics are not so richly diversified as to give them equal chances of economic and social development. Most of the republics live by the export of a small number of staple products, which may be agricultural or mineral. This situation has made them extremely sensitive to economic fluctuations abroad and has gravely affected political institutions that depend on a degree of social and economic stability. Moreover, the paucity of coal resources, besides that of capital, has constituted a check on industrial development. Yet industrialization and the raising of living standards in all the republics are widely stressed as the next goal of Latin American advancement.[5]

Settlement and Colonial Organization. Early colonization followed on the whole the road suggested by geophysical structure—up the valleys onto the highlands and along the coasts of the Caribbean and the Atlantic. The Spaniards laid the groundwork for a permanent colonial government as soon as they had conquered Mexico. But the interest of the Portuguese in their American domain developed slowly, centering at first in a small number of coastal settlements. The white man exploited the services of the Indians inhabiting the adjacent high plateaus as much as feasible or, wherever they did not meet the demands of the new plantation culture, introduced Negro slaves from Africa, creating in due course a new racial mixture. In the interior Indians were allowed to vegetate without suffering much outside interference. Thus, the Brazilian hinterland, constituting more than one third of the land mass of the continent, has remained one of the most thinly populated territories in the world. The more populous coastal sections, however, came to represent a great variety of ethnic groups, including a heavy percentage of Negroes and mulattoes. Mexico, whose historical course was merely interrupted by the Spanish conquest, still is a predominantly Indian country, with some 30 per cent pure and about 60 per cent mixed Indian blood. Recently, most Latin American governments have made attempts to promote the welfare of the Indian population. The Mexican Revolution spearheaded this movement by embodying in its program the policy of Indian rehabilitation, thus bringing the bulk of the population into the political picture. Generally speaking, the problem of

---

[5] For brief surveys of the resources and economy of Latin America, see Schurz, *op. cit.* above, note 2, pp. 147-251; Seymour E. Harris, ed., *Economic Problems of Latin America* (New York, 1944); George Soule, David Efron, and Norman J. Ness, *Latin America in the Future World* (New York, 1945); J. Fred Rippy, *Latin America and the Industrial Age* (New York, 1944); and, especially for the foreign trade of Latin America, Paul R. Olson and C. Addison Hickman, *Pan American Economics* (New York, 1943).

integrating the diversified strains of population with the existing political systems has added to the ferment of Latin American politics, especially as the demographic composition became more complex with new waves of immigration.

Since the first European settlers of Latin America were Spanish and Portuguese, the political institutions of their home countries were carried into Mexico and into Central and South America[6]. As for Spanish America, this meant in effect extremely strong centralization under the Crown, with the church as a powerful auxiliary. "The general aim of the Spanish colonial policy was primarily to keep the colonies in a continual state of dependency upon the mother country, and to exploit them for the benefit of Spain."[7]   Not only was social and economic growth retarded under such a system, but the development of self-government was impossible except on the local level, and even there only to a very limited degree. In Portuguese Brazil, however, central organization was lagging. To be sure, a governor general or a viceroy was placed over the whole colony, but because of the vast expansion of territory and the lack of communications he wielded little actual power, and decentralization at a rather early stage was the logical consequence. Local initiative in government therefore had wider opportunities in Brazil than in the Spanish colonies. The *senado da camara,* or municipal council, was an important local arm of the government, to which many viceregal functions— even the regulation of money and prices—were delegated. Also, from the beginning the church had less influence in Brazil than in Spanish America.

Characteristics of Political Evolution. Out of this general pattern the Latin American republics evolved. Where Spanish rule had obtained, the process was not a natural transition, but a revolt whose effects might well be called illogical in some respects. Having the examples of the American and French Revolutions before them, the Spanish Latin Americans eagerly took up the new ideas under the delusion that they could be translated at once into reality. But there was no actual experience in democracy, and the movement remained in the stage of constitutional blueprinting. The consequences are reflected in the continuous alternation between dictatorship (*caudillismo*) and revolution so characteristic of Spanish America, and in the frequent apathy of the masses toward the strife and violence between political factions. In time, however, compromises were worked out through which a semblance of popular government was attained under republican institutions. Mexico and Brazil [8] represent such trends in two major respects:

---

[6] For historical background, see Dana G. Munro, *The Latin American Republics: A History* (New York, 1942), with a useful bibliography; A. Curtis Wilgus, *The Development of Hispanic America* (New York, 1941); C. H. Haring, *South American Progress* (Cambridge, Mass., 1934). On the racial problem, see Frank Tannenbaum, *Slave and Citizen* (New York, 1946).

[7] Wilgus, *op. cit.* above, note 6, 191, quoted by permission of the publisher (Rinehart).

[8] Mexico and Brazil are the most populous states in the Latin American orbit. Out of a total now estimated at close to 160 million, the population of Mexico is approximately 25 million and that of Brazil more than 50 million, or about 16 and 32 per cent of the whole, respectively.

First, they are conspicuous examples of some important stages in Latin American political development. Second, both countries have increasingly become laboratories of social and economic experimentation that has also affected their political outlook.

Both republics also illustrate the problem of federalism. Centrifugal tendencies under a federal system may lead to the reassertion of central authority for the control of states and other sections. This development may facilitate the rise of dictatorship, as happened in the case of Brazil, where the seizure of power by Vargas was successful mainly as a move against sectionalism and state rivalries of long standing. Hardly any incentive for federalism existed in the political structure of the old viceroyalty of New Spain. Federalism in the successor states could therefore originate only in special circumstances. This it did in Argentina, where political and economic jealousy between Buenos Aires and other parts of the country filled the first five decades of republican existence with conflict and unrest. In the same way, the long and varied history of federalism in Mexico owed its inception to a compromise designed to reconcile the interests of the new national state with the ambition of local *caudillos* to retain regional authority for themselves.

A historically related transformation concerned the position of the individual in the state and in society. Through constitutional reforms, including the extension of the suffrage, an approach was made toward overcoming the traditional contradiction between class privilege and popular rights. The year 1917, when Mexico adopted its present constitution, has been called "probably the most significant date in the whole panorama of Latin American constitutionalism." The principles and provisions of that constitution "have been borrowed in varying degrees by almost every Latin American constitution subsequently drafted," and therefore "may be regarded as symbolically Latin American rather than narrowly Mexican." [9] In fact, the Mexican constitution of 1917 was but the reflex of profound social and economic changes, or of the belief in the necessity of such changes. Under different circumstances, Brazil also went through several stages of social reform—characterized by such measures as the emancipation of the slaves—and of economic advancement. Both countries, then, are outstanding examples of the manner in which Latin America adjusted itself to changed world conditions and concepts and, by political action, promoted national welfare in the framework of indigenous culture.

Order and Revolt. In the federal republics of Latin America, the presidency has become the focus of centralization. Often this movement reached a point where the question had to be raised of how much reality there was in the federal system, especially because presidential government has generally prevailed. Such predominance of the executive easily lends

---

[9] Russell H. Fitzgibbon, "Constitutional Development in Latin America," *American Political Science Review,* 39 (1945), 518 ff., quoted by permission of the editor.

itself to the growth of totalitarianism. Even where, as in both Mexico and Brazil, the powers of the legislative branch are amply defined and on the whole respected, totalitarian traits, in the name of order, may enter the political system through back doors, such as one-party control of the electorate, manipulation of public opinion, and suppression of civil rights.[10]

A counterpart to strong-man government is the periodic character of revolutionary disturbances in Latin America. "Revolutions" frequently function as the means whereby political factions decide on personal leadership and ascendancy to power; or they may be manifestations of conflicts about issues vested with deep emotional feelings. In this sense, indeed, a "divine right of revolution" has been asserted as an attribute of Latin American politics. It is in that same context that the fervid interest taken in politics by Latin American university students must be considered. Outbreaks of political passion in the student bodies time and again have signaled impending storms.

Mexico and Brazil in the International Scene. In World War II, Mexico's position was clear. President Manuel Avila Camacho's government cooperated closely with the United States and with the United Nations. Likewise, Brazil, notwithstanding the ideological affinity of its then regime for some of the dictatorships of Europe, immediately established effective collaboration with the United States and never faltered in giving all possible support to the Allied nations. By their wartime actions and by fostering hemisphere agreements, such as the Act of Chapultepec in 1945, both countries have decisively contributed to the "Pan-Americanization" of the Monroe Doctrine. Together with the other Latin American republics, they have been looking forward to a commitment of the United States to participate on a large scale in their programs of economic development. But at the recent inter-American conferences—those of Rio de Janeiro in 1947 and of Bogotá in 1948—the United States took the position that the reconstruction of Europe must have priority. Although this decision was highly unsatisfactory to all Latin American governments, Brazil and Mexico did not resort to obstruction as attempted by Argentina. They have backed up the European Recovery Program, conscious of the fact that in carrying through this program the United States and Europe would need large quantities of products of which Latin American countries have exportable surpluses.

In the affairs of the United Nations, Mexico and Brazil have increasingly supported the course of the United States, though with some important exceptions. Brazilian and Mexican statesmen have gained for their countries great international respect. Both countries are effectively represented

[10] See the discussion of this problem in Karl Loewenstein, *Brazil under Vargas* (New York, 1942), 369 ff.; also 121 ff.

in some of the specialized agencies set up under United Nations auspices.

Mexico was honored by seeing its former Foreign Minister, J. Torres Bodet, elected Director General of UNESCO; and the two countries were chosen members of the United Nations Security Committee that was to draw practical lessons from the war in Korea.

Outlook for Democracy. There is today a definite trend in Latin American constitutional development to bring the facts of political life and constitutional theory into a more realistic relationship. As social forces heretofore passive or neglected drive forward into the political arena, Latin American experience has indicated the need for such readjustment. If portents tell, it may well be that the age of old-fashioned political liberalism with its zeal for legalistic construction is coming to a close.

Nevertheless, the discrepancy between constitutional formulae and governmental practice will remain a characteristic of Latin American politics for some time to come. The particular cultural setting in which it has flourished does not vary with changes in governmental machinery. But there is now an awareness of a new situation, which calls for "realism" in matching the political heritage with the needs and, indeed, ideals of living men. A seasoned observer has summed up this transformation as follows:

In spite of local setbacks . . . democracy has made very substantial, though unequal, gains in Latin America. . . . This progress has been the result of a variety of factors. The decline of illiteracy, due to extension of the public-school system, has widened the electoral base of democracy, since the ability to read and write is a common qualification for voting. . . . The rise of a middle class of citizens, consisting largely of members of the professions, small businessmen, and independent farmers, has formed a strong nucleus of democratic opinion in the more advanced republics. Similarly, wherever industrialization has proceeded on a considerable scale, factory workers and allied labor groups have become conscious of their political interests and assertive of their rights.[11]

This statement holds true despite recent neofascist or ultraconservative developments in some countries, Argentina being a striking example. That trend indicates another lag in adjustment between social exigencies and the political order, to be overcome by time and circumstances, with democracy the likely winner.

2. The Making of Modern Mexico

Political and Social Antecedents. Spanish colonial rule involved oppressive authority in Latin America for colonists and aborigines alike. This was so especially where office purchase and the corruption pervading colonial government enabled subordinate officials to exact unjust levies. Moreover, since all land in the colonies belonged to the Crown, the Indian was deprived

[11] Schurz, *op. cit.* above, note 2, p. 138, quoted by permission of the publisher (E. P. Dutton). Cf. "Pathology of Democracy in Latin America; A Symposium," *American Political Science Review*, 44 (1950), 100 ff.

of his patrimony and made a virtual slave, though outright slavery became less frequent as the colonies developed. Most important was the practice of placing each native village under a Spanish settler, known as the *encomienda* system.[12] Legally abolished in the eighteenth century, it was in fact continued under the plantation economy of the *haciendas*,[13] whose size still increased in the first decades after independence.

The white intruders and the Indians soon intermingled. Today the majority of Mexico's population is held to consist of the mixed race (*mestizos*). During the Spanish regime, the mestizos were subjected to all manner of discrimination, legal and social. They could not hold public office, were excluded from higher education and the professions, and lived as craftsmen and laborers. By contrast, the pure-blooded descendants of the early Spanish settlers—called *criollos* or Creoles—were in possession of the mines and valuable lands. They formed the upper class and naturally aspired to political power. But power was mostly in the hands of the "peninsular" Spaniards —those born abroad. They could depend for support on the viceregal administration. Furthermore, the mercantilistic and monopolistic trade policy of the mother country held back economic development, much to the detriment of the Creoles. The latter therefore harbored a deep resentment against the peninsular Spaniards and their colonial administration.[14]

Independence under a Federal Constitution. It was the overthrow of the Madrid government by Napoleon I and the subsequent revolution in Spain that brought things to a head also in New Spain. Mexico's hero of independence, the priest Miguel Hidalgo, raised the standard of revolt on September 16, 1810. He and his successor, Morelos, failed, and both had to pay the supreme penalty. But the movement they had started could not be arrested for long. When in 1820 another revolution in Spain brought a fresh wave of liberal ideas to the fore there, the conservative Creoles of Mexico, supported by a large part of the clergy, decided that separation from the European dynasty would be the lesser evil. A Creole officer, Agustín de Iturbide, succeeded in reaching a compromise with the forces still pursuing the more radical ideas of Hidalgo. This understanding was implemented in the Plan of Iguala, which provided for the establishment of a limited but independent monarchy, maintenance of the position of the Catholic church with all privileges of the clergy, and equality of Spaniards and Mexicans before the law. Iturbide managed to have himself elected

---

[12] Munro, *op. cit.* above, note 6, p. 34, describes the origin of the *encomienda* as follows: "Each village was to be placed under the protection of a Spanish colonist, who was to see that the Indians were instructed in the Christian faith, and was to be recompensed by the tribute that the Indians were required to pay . . . ." Quoted by permission of the publisher (Appleton-Century).

[13] The term *hacienda* means farm or estate and signifies large private property.

[14] For the historical development of Mexico since independence, with many references to the constitutional questions, consult Munro, *op. cit.* above, note 6; Ernest Gruening, *Mexico and Its Heritage* (New York, 1934); Henry B. Parks, *A History of Mexico* (Boston, 1938); and, for the period since 1910, Frank Tannenbaum, *Peace by Revolution* (New York, 1933).

Emperor by the constituent assembly, but after a few months on the throne he was forced to abdicate early in 1823.

On July 19, 1824, a constitution was adopted that established a federal republic, composed of nineteen states and four territories. The document contained a bill of rights and followed the pattern of the United States, with certain deviations. A President and a Vice President were to be chosen for four years by the state legislatures, a bicameral Congress and a Supreme Court were to be set up, and the states were to frame their own constitutions. Roman Catholicism was declared the state religion; the exercise of any other religion was prohibited. The constitution also provided for a Council of Government to act when the Congress was not in session. This last arrangement was to be of more than transitory importance in the constitutional development of Mexico.

From here on, five periods in the political history of Mexico may be distinguished. The federal republic established in 1824 lasted till 1834. It was followed by a centralized scheme, which in 1846 gave way to a restoration of federalism. A new constitution was framed in 1857 and remained in force until 1917. In that year the constitution was adopted under which the federal republic of Mexico—*Los Estados Unidos Mexicanos*—is living now.

Reaction and the Rise of Juárez. Soon after the constitution of 1824 had been put into effect, the conservative forces turned against it. Their opportunity came when under a liberal administration a series of anticlerical laws were passed that brought certain church property under government control and deprived the church of its exclusive position in the educational field. A revolt followed. The new Congress, dominated by the conservative element, passed the so-called Seven Laws of 1836, which actually replaced the constitution of 1824, abolishing the federal form of government and extending the presidential term to eight years. As a check on dictatorial aspirations, provision was made for a "supreme conservative power" (*poder conservador*), consisting of a citizens' commission to supervise the government.

There were continual internal conflicts in the ensuing years, with external involvements to boot. The revolt in Texas (1835-36) and the so-called Pastry War with France (1838-39) led to various experiments in dictatorship, in which the repeated ascendancy of the famed military leader Santa Anna was the outstanding factor. When war broke out with the United States in 1846, Santa Anna was forced to accept restoration of the federal constitution. As the war took a bad turn for Mexico, Santa Anna had to abandon the presidency. He came back in 1853, proclaiming himself dictator and setting aside the constitution, but fell definitely from power in 1855.

The opponents of the dictator had been successful with a popular appeal embodied in the Plan of Ayutla. This step initiated the long struggle between powerful classes hitherto dominant in Mexican political life and those elements that now demanded a voice in government. The main issue was at

first the power of the church, whose influence was on the side of the privileged classes. Hence, the liberals saw in the church and the professional
army officers, both supporters of Santa Anna's regime, their principal enemies.
The new president, General Juan Álvarez, the first Indian in that office,
agreed with the Plan of Ayutla. He was backed by the intellectual leader
of the liberal movement, another full-blooded Indian, Benito Juárez, who,
as Minister of Justice and Ecclesiastical Affairs, fathered the so-called Juárez
Law limiting the jurisdiction of military and ecclesiastical courts. But
opposition was strong, and after only two months in office, Álvarez was
compelled to resign in favor of Ignacio Comonfort, his Secretary of War.
Although a *moderado*, Comonfort promulgated the Lerdo Law, enacted
by Congress in 1856, which broadened the attack on the church by requiring it to sell all land not actually used for religious purposes; at that time,
little less than one half of all valuable land in the republic was church property. Several other laws restricting the power of the church were adopted,
and the Jesuit order was suppressed.

Policies of Juárez. The Juárez and Lerdo Laws were incorporated in a
new constitution, proclaimed February 5, 1857. The constitution was revolutionary in character. It ensured freedom of speech, of the press, and of
worship. Suffrage was extended to all male Mexicans twenty-one years of
age (or eighteen, if married) who had an honest means of livelihood.
The vote was indirect in presidential and senatorial elections.[15] Most important, perhaps, the federal form of government was reaffirmed, the country
being reorganized into twenty-three states and one territory. The federal
principle was weakened, though, by certain clauses. Thus, the Congress
was granted power to remove state governors by impeachment, and disputed
elections in the states were to be decided by the federal Supreme Court.
This shift of powers opened the door to much central manipulation in state
affairs. Above all, it highlighted the concept inherent in Mexican federalism
that the nation is supreme and the states are dependent on it for whatever
powers they may exercise. It is probably correct to say that under this
constitution the later dictator, Porfirio Diaz, could establish himself almost
within the law. But the essential thing was at the moment that federalism
was thought to offer an effective check to control by the conservatives or a
caudillo who might have conservative support.

As it was directed against them, the conservatives and the church strenu-
ously opposed this change. A civil war ensued, known under the name of
War of the Reform, which lasted for three years. When Comonfort had
tried in vain to reach a compromise with the opposition leaders and resigned,
Juárez claimed the presidency. He obtained the recognition and support of
the United States. In July 1859 he issued a series of stern decrees disestab-
lishing the church, confiscating its property not yet sold under the Lerdo

---

[15] The federal Congress was unicameral at first, but a Senate was created in 1874.

Law, suppressing all religious orders and monasteries, and instituting the civil registration of marriages, births, and deaths.[16] After the conservatives had been defeated, an election was held in January 1861, and Juárez became constitutional President.

In the following year, while Juárez was trying to restore peace at home, the French intervention began, which lasted until 1867. During this period the conservatives, identifying their cause with that of the foreigners, forfeited the remainder of the credit which they still had with parts of the Mexican public. Juárez easily gained re-election in 1867. His enemies attempted to mobilize the popular fear of dictatorship. Nevertheless, by congressional choice, Juárez succeeded himself again in 1871. He died a year thereafter, whereupon the office fell to the president of the Supreme Court, in accordance with the constitution. The leader of the opposition, Porfirio Diaz, revolted when the new President, too, secured another term in 1875. Diaz finally assumed power in 1877 under the Plan of La Noria, which explicitly forbade re-election. After an interval of one term, however, in which he yielded the presidency to one of his friends, Diaz regained it in 1884 and stayed in the presidential office until 1911.

Rule of Diaz. From the constitutional angle, the long rule of Porfirio Diaz was wholly anomalous. True, he was careful not to contravene openly the constitution of 1857 and had elections held regularly. To remove the sting of unconstitutionality from his own tenure, he caused the constitutional prohibition against re-election to be eliminated, and the presidential term was lengthened to six years. Election results, incidentally, had always been disputed and "corrected" in Mexico if they did not fulfill the expectations of the political bosses. Now they were dictated from the national capital. The church benefited from concessions in the enforcement of the Juárez laws and from the return of some of the property already seized. Under the absolute rule of Diaz, federalism was in eclipse. The states and their governors were without effective power; governors, indeed, were appointed and removed at the president's pleasure.

In the field of administration, Diaz brought about various wholesome reforms. He reorganized the civil and consular services and remodeled the budget system by abolishing certain taxes and other practices that had survived from the Spanish regime. But the secret of his success has to be sought in the economic sphere. Economic conditions were chaotic when the dictator took over. Seizing his opportunity, he initiated a sweeping program of rehabilitation, did away with internal customs barriers, and placed the currency on a gold basis. The credit of Mexico improved so much that in the early years of this century the government could raise funds

---

[16] This group of decrees became known as the Laws of Reform. Since the foreign invasion and Maximilian's empire intervened, these "laws" were not immediately enforced in their entirety, but several of the anti-ecclesiastical measures were incorporated in the constitution in 1874 and others served as the basis for similar provisions in the constitution of 1917.

to acquire a controlling interest in many of the country's railroads. Investments of foreign capital multiplied, new industries developed, communications expanded, Mexico's silver industry regained its former position in the world market, and the nation's foreign commerce flourished generally.

From the inside, however, the matter looked different. There was, to be sure, a comparatively large group who derived benefits from the Diaz system. Property in land or commercial enterprise was firmly protected under "law and order" maintained with political strong-arm methods. Not only political opposition but labor agitation and strikes were summarily dealt with by the Army and police. Foreign capitalists felt secure as they had never felt before in Mexico or, for that matter, almost anywhere in Latin America. But the natives were paid the same wages as decades ago; as the price level was rising, their living standard decreased while peonage, or debt slavery, increased. The great landowners were allowed to destroy the village communities by acquiring their lands.[17] It is estimated that the concentration of landownership reached the point where 2 per cent of the population owned 70 per cent of the land, and in some states up to 98 per cent of the rural families were entirely landless.[18] Much of the land and many mining properties had been transferred to foreigners, which caused resentment even among upper-class Mexicans.

3. The Revolution of 1910 and the Constitution of 1917

Madero and Civil War. The Diaz regime collapsed with unexpected suddenness after an energetic opposition had emerged in the election of 1910. Francisco Madero, scion of a wealthy family with liberal ideals, gained the presidency. While in prison, he had drafted the Plan of San Luis, which called for redistribution of land among the peasants and other reforms. But once in office, Madero seemed to have forgotten what he had himself demanded, and relied on the Army for support against prospective counterrevolts by the partisans of Diaz and other rivals. This reliance proved to be the wrong policy, however, mainly because of the personal character of the Army's commander, General Victoriano Huerta, who betrayed the President and had him murdered on February 23, 1913. Huerta made himself President. He received support from Mexican conservatives and foreigners who looked forward to the restoration of government along the lines of the Diaz regime.

Several years of turmoil followed. Since Huerta encountered firm resistance not only from the Mexican constitutionalists under Venustiano Carranza, but also from President Woodrow Wilson, his situation was soon

---

[17] This process had been inadvertently facilitated by Juárez, who in one of his reform laws undertook to abolish communal ownership so as to foster small-scale private ownership and operation; but this intent turned out to be illusory.

[18] From a paper by Ramón Beteta, *Aspectos economicos del plan sexenal* (Mexico City, 1935). The author became Minister of Finance of Mexico.

untenable. He resigned in July 1914 and left the field to Carranza. But Carranza's leadership was disputed by groups of revolutionaries among whom Francisco ("Pancho") Villa and Emiliano Zapata, a radical peasant leader, were outstanding. After much bloodshed and diplomatic maneuvering,[19] Carranza, who had been recognized as the *de facto* President of Mexico by the United States, succeeded in consolidating his position. A constituent assembly met at Querétaro December 1, 1916. In two months it wrote a new constitution, which was promulgated on February 5, 1917.

Revolution by Constitution. The impulse of the Revolution soon transcended such causes as the defense of constitutionalism and the rights of the individual.[20] To the constitutional law of the past, representing the classic liberal tradition, there was now added the principle of socialistic evolution. From the pragmatic viewpoint, any administration that hoped to command the lasting support of the people would have to make a visible contribution to the realization of the revolutionary program. This requirement has remained the basic law of Mexican politics. It accounts for the insistence, official and nonofficial, on the continuing character of the Revolution. Social philosophy and political dynamics were thus directly related in a collective version of democracy. An ideology born of the deficiencies of an obdurate social order has become the guiding principle in the process of approximation to new social demands. Yet a frame of republican traditions is given and the essential meaning of limited government maintained.

As part of limited government, federalism was permanently associated with the leftist movement, whereas centralism had become an attribute of rightist or conservative politics. This fact was again manifest when the assembly at Querétaro decided to retain the federal principle. But the theory underlying the federal constitution of Mexico as well as the constitutions of its states—now twenty-eight in number, besides three territories and the Federal District—is that the authority of the states is restricted to internal state concerns without effect on other states. There are, therefore, no powers inherent in the states that could not be nullified—because they might affect other states—or superseded by congressional action, as coming within the purview of the general (federal) interest. Consequently, Congress, by virtue of powers granted it under the federal constitution, in many instances has legislated for the states in an all-inclusive manner.

Wherever the revolutionary current breaks forth in the Mexican constitu-

---

[19] It was during these disturbances that a United States force under General Pershing was sent into northern Mexico. Villa's troops had perpetrated savage acts against Americans, killing citizens and burning part of the frontier town of Columbus, N. M.

[20] The liberties of the individual are elaborately stated in the constitution of 1917, especially in chap. I, "Of the Individual Guaranties"; II, "Of the Mexicans"; and IV, "Of the Mexican Citizens." Of the 136 articles of the constitution, a little less than one half were taken from the constitution of 1857; others were modified; and the remainder embody new principles. An English translation of the constitution will be found in Russell H. Fitzgibbon, ed., *The Constitutions of the Americas* (Chicago, 1948).

tion—above all in the fields of agrarian reform, labor legislation, and general economic control, and in matters concerning the church and its influence on education—the same directness of congressional responsibility will be found. In most other respects, the powers of the states and the restrictions placed upon them are more orthodox. Thus, the states, under their own constitutions, formulate their budgets, may exercise police power, create public offices, and regulate municipalities. But they may not make treaties with foreign governments, coin money, or interfere with interstate transit and commerce.

Changes in Constitutional Structure. As regards the formal structure of government, a few significant changes were laid down in the new constitution.[21] They were due to a desire to circumscribe more closely the powers of the President and to make him more responsive to the popular will. The principle of indirect voting was abandoned in favor of direct election of the chief executive and the legislature, in the Union as well as in the states. The office of Vice President was dropped; in the event of the resignation or disability of the President, the Congress elects a provisional President. This provision gives the legislature added power to break up existing political combinations in an emergency. A Cabinet is specifically provided for in the constitution, its membership consisting of the heads of the eleven executive departments. Members of the Cabinet must appear before Congress to report on matters under their jurisdiction; they may attend legislative sessions but may not vote.[22] In several respects the functions of the President and his Cabinet officers whom he appoints are about the same as in the United States, although the appointing and removing power of the Mexican President is somewhat broader. Furthermore, he has an item veto over legislation.

According to the constitution, the President as well as any member of the Congress may introduce bills into either house. The most striking feature in regard to legislative initiative, however, is that the state legislatures also have the right to introduce bills in Congress. With respect to legislative control of the executive, a persistent problem of Mexican politics had been how executive power might be limited during a congressional recess. All too often this condition had been used to prevent the legislature from reassembling. A solution was attempted by inserting into the constitution a provision for a Permanent Commission to which certain interim functions were entrusted, not unlike the Council of Government under the constitution of 1824. The commission, to be composed of fifteen deputies and four-

---

[21] The Mexican Congress consists of the Senate and the Chamber of Deputies. The Chamber is renewed every three years; its members are elected on the basis of population and number 147 at present. The Senate is composed of 2 members from each state and 2 from the federal district, making a total of 58 senators.

[22] William S. Stokes, "Parliamentary Government in Latin America," *American Political Science Review,* 39 (1945), 524, has pointed out that here the constitutional separation of powers has been modified toward cabinet government.

teen senators, was to go on with the business left by the regular session, call special sessions, confirm judicial recess appointments, appoint a functionary to take the President's place during his absence, and control the use of the national guard outside the boundaries of their respective states or territories. This check on arbitrary actions by the chief executive has, it appears, adequately served its purpose.

Constitutional Amendments. The judicial system of Mexico shows a surprising similarity to that of the United States, considering the fact that the legal basis is different; for, as in all Hispanic American countries, not common law but Roman law in the form handed down and modified by the Spaniards and the Napoleonic code is applied by the Mexican courts. The jurisdiction of the Supreme Court and the other federal courts of Mexico is approximately the same as that of the corresponding courts in the United States. The original text of the constitution of 1917 provided for election by Congress of the judges of the Supreme Court. But in 1928 an amendment was passed that empowered the President to appoint the judges, subject to Senate confirmation. Members of the circuit and district courts are nominated by the Supreme Court.

Other constitutional amendments, adopted in 1928 and in 1933, concerned the extension to six years of the President's term of office, with reaffirmation of his ineligibility for re-election, and analogous extension of the terms of senators and deputies to six and three years, respectively, with no immediate re-election. The four-year term for the President had furnished too frequent stimulation for disturbances of the political scene. Neither had it permitted the incumbent administration enough time to show advancement of the revolutionary program—the overriding task to which all Mexican officials are pledged. On the other hand, it was found desirable to coordinate the life-span of the legislature and the mandates of its members with the presidential term. Congress now is renewed in its entirety at the time the President is elected. This rearrangement of terms has made for greater political stability and more consistent collaboration among the main branches of government.

Social Questions in the Constitution. Aside from governmental structure, the most pressing problems which the new constitution was expected to settle were those that had given impetus to the whole revolutionary development. There was foremost the land question. If the social status of the *peones* was to be advanced, a thorough agrarian reform had to be sanctioned by the constitution. Limits to property claims had to be set where such claims would conflict with the public interest or, more precisely, with the new collective philosophy acknowledging the right of all citizens to a share in the land and other national wealth. Likewise, the scope and specific means of the land reform would have to be defined as closely as agreement on the ultimate purpose might permit.

Obviously, the people whose welfare was the object of such a program could make wise use of their extended rights only if they were also given knowledge enabling them to understand their new condition. The Mexican revolutionaries therefore amplified their opposition to the church as one of the great landowners by opposition to its influence in education. As things stood, this opposition called for special regulations about the possession of land by the church and governmental control of educational institutions and programs.

Another element was the influence that foreign investors and managers had gained in Mexican affairs through their association with the past regime. Here was the point where the social-revolutionary drive merged with a new nationalistic attitude. The question how far foreigners might be permitted to go in exploiting for their own benefit the soil and other resources of the republic became of decisive importance. There was also the problem of labor. It concerned the relationship of the worker to his native employer almost as much as to the foreigner. Both had a private interest in profit, whereas from the national point of view the issue was the raising of a people long neglected.

Agrarian Reform. A sense of urgency runs through the constitution of 1917, as the leaders realized that fate had knocked at the Mexican people's door. This sense should partly account for the fact that some of the provisions about the land question, the church, education, and labor went far beyond what seemed to be called for, and that they represented postulates rather than devices for immediate use. Nevertheless, they formed the basis for later stages of the Revolution.

The land question was dealt with in a long article of the constitution. This article provides that the lands and waters within the territorial limits of Mexico belong originally to the nation, which has authority to transfer them to private hands. Expropriation is legal where it serves a public interest, but compensation must be granted. The nation has the right to impose upon private property standards of public convenience and to regulate the utilization of national resources. The equitable distribution, control, and conservation of the national wealth is declared a constitutional purpose of legislation. Therefore, the government is authorized to prescribe procedures for the division of uncultivated lands as well as for the development of lands in production. Where common lands previously had been taken away from villages, the proceedings were declared null and void; and the nation assumed the obligation to donate land, by dividing large estates, to villages having no verifiable claim.[23] No religious organization may hold, acquire, or administer real property. Nor may any commercial or industrial

---

[23] This provision was to ensure the continuity of a land act passed in 1915, under which the *ejidos* were established, i. e., agricultural communities to which parcels of land were granted in collective ownership. This is the form in which, to a large extent, the agrarian reform has been implemented. Ejidal procedure was placed on a permanent basis by the Agrarian Regulatory Law of April 10, 1922. A National Agrarian Commission, in cooperation with state commissions, decides on the claim of villages to ejidal lands. The initiative for the establishment of ejidos has to be taken by the village communities themselves.

enterprise own agricultural lands. The state governments are authorized to determine the maximum size of private landholdings. National ownership of all subsoil deposits and minerals was expressly affirmed. Foreigners who want to acquire land or obtain concessions for the development of natural resources must agree not to invoke the protection of their home governments in matters relating to such privileges extended by Mexico. The restrictions imposed on foreigners are supplemented by the President's authority to expel without judicial process any foreigner whose presence in the country he may deem inconvenient, and also by prohibition of all monopolies.

Church, Education, and Labor. The separation of church and state had already been enacted in the constitution of 1857, and Juárez had gone even further, but enforcement had been lagging. Now, again, all religious institutions were divested of privileged status, and the clergy relegated to the role of an ordinary profession to which special regulations should apply. The number of priests was to be determined by the state legislatures in accordance with local requirements. Members of the clergy—who must be Mexican-born—may not vote and are not eligible for public office; they may not carry on any political activity whatsoever. The government's permission must be obtained for the dedication of new churches, and religious organizations may not be landowners. Moreover, all education was declared to be secular. An amendment of 1934 explicitly states: "The education imparted in the country will be socialistic, and all religious doctrine will be excluded . . . ." Both primary and higher education are provided by government, federal and state. Primary education is compulsory and free. Licensed private educational institutions must conform to programs of study approved by public authorities.

As for labor, constitutional provision is made for maximum hours, for restrictions on the employment of women and children, for minimum wages, and for profit-sharing. Local councils were empowered to fix wage rates and the rate of profit-sharing; disputes were to be resolved by a conciliation and arbitration board established in each state and by a national board in the last instance.[24] Other clauses declared the equality of sex and nationality as to pay and called for wholesome working and living conditions, including housing, to be supplied by the employer. Freedom of organization, for both workers and employers, and the right to strike are guaranteed. Peonage and all forms of debt servitude—including any compulsion to patronize company stores—are outlawed.

Appraisal. In such sweeping provisions the Mexican constitution went

---

[24] These boards are composed of equal numbers of employer and worker representatives, with one government member. They have jurisdiction over all controversies between capital and labor. The original constitution did not provide for a federal conciliation and arbitration board, which was created by constitutional amendment in 1933. Other constitutional amendments, adopted in 1929, vested the sole responsibility for labor legislation in the Congress and postulated a national social security law that would include life, unemployment, health, and accident insurance.

far ahead of any other organic legislation of that time. If one should ask what the impelling motive was, the answer does not come easily. Marxist ideology, to be sure, has gained considerable currency in parts of the Mexican labor movement; as this movement grew, it developed intellectual and personal affiliations with foreign and international organizations. But at the time the constitution was written, such connections had hardly been established. Since the late years of the Diaz regime, industrialism had been growing. With it entered syndicalist and socialistic ideas, mostly from Spain. This knowledge, however, had been limited to a small circle of intellectuals and labor leaders, whose influence in the constitutional convention was practically nil. Yet there were others who wished to utilize the labor question as a lever against foreign interests in Mexico. A document embodying the most progressive principles of labor legislation in Europe, the United States, and even Australia had been worked out with Carranza's consent. This program was seized upon by a few forceful personalities at the convention for their own ends, which were political rather than social.

On the whole, the thinking of the men at Querétaro was unburdened by intellectual scruples. As they were groping for something new, it happened that they used a terminology foreign to Mexican conditions. Even then, however, it was true that, as President Cárdenas said almost twenty years afterward when he tried to define the direction in which Mexico was traveling, the Mexican Revolution "departs from state communism, because our people are not the kind to adopt a system that deprives them of the full enjoyment of their efforts, nor do they want to substitute for the individual boss the boss state." Repudiating state socialism and communism, Mexico has been directing its efforts toward the establishment of an order called socialistic in which workers' and peasants' cooperatives may be destined to play a major role. Respecting the Mexican people's strong sense of personal freedom and its traditional distrust of concentrated power, the constitution of 1917 has so far adequately served as the instrument of government under which the national evolution could proceed.

4. Political Dynamics

Early Struggles. When the constitution of 1917 was promulgated, acute possibilities of renewed domestic and foreign involvement soon became apparent. Carranza's moderation and President Wilson's sympathetic attitude did not mitigate the threat to foreign interests implied in the constitution. A diplomatic controversy with the United States began when in 1918 a tax decree required that the oil companies recognize Mexico's public ownership rights in the subsoil resources. But when General Alvaro Obregón had succeeded Carranza, a *modus vivendi* was reached in 1923, whereby claims of American citizens to land coming under the beginning agrarian reform were to be placed under arbitration. Oil properties, for the time being, were protected by a decision of the Mexican Supreme Court that made the constitutional restrictions inapplicable in cases where the surface landowner had shown by some "positive act" that he wished to exploit the oil underground. This compromise effected, the United States extended recognition to Obregón's government, who now was enabled to draw on the support of the United States against a counterrevolutionary revolt of conservatives under the leadership of Adolfo de la Huerta, aided by parts of the Army and the clergy. The revolt was suppressed, and the victor, General Plutarco Elias Calles, followed Obregón in the presidency.

Under Obregón some attempts had been made to put into effect the various reforms demanded by the constitution, especially the land reform. Calles pursued this course with vigor. He was supported by the Labor party, at that time the CROM (*Confederación Regional Obrera Mexicana*). When in 1926 the Catholic bishops issued a statement rejecting the religious articles of the constitution, Calles decreed that all Catholic schools and convents be closed and all priests register with the authorities. The church refused compliance. Catholic laymen rose in rebellion, confident of moral support from the United States. But the rebels were overpowered. Official relations with the United States improved when United States Ambassador Dwight Morrow successfully mediated in land and church affairs. The Mexican Supreme Court again came to the aid of the oil companies by declaring a recent petroleum law unconstitutional and forcing new legislation, in 1928, which gave the oil companies concessions unlimited in time.

From Calles to Cárdenas. Calles retained effective power until 1934. In the presidential election of that year, the party of the revolutionary movement—the *Partido Revolucionario Mexicano* (PRM)—presented as its official candidate the *mestizo* General Lázaro Cárdenas. He won the election against a left socialist and a rightist "independent democratic" candidate.

Under President Cárdenas the revolutionary movement gained new momentum. At a party convention in December 1933, PRM had authorized a Six Year Plan by which a "cooperative economic system tending toward socialism" was to be promoted. Cárdenas at once took measures for putting the plan into effect. This effort brought him into conflict with Calles, who went to the United States, where he made speeches critical of the alleged communist trend in Mexico. When Calles returned late in 1935, the clash between his followers and the government had reached menacing proportions. But Cárdenas gave short shrift to the opposition, and Calles was finally deported to the United States.

Throughout this and other crises, it was evident that Cárdenas was intent on carrying out loyally the revolutionary program, especially the Six Year Plan, but that he was also determined to keep order in the country. In October 1935 he stated that Mexico welcomed the investment of foreign capital to promote industrial expansion, and would treat investors fairly. On the other hand, it was under his administration that the railways were expropriated and, in 1938, turned over to the railroad labor unions for operation.

Likewise, in the same year the North American and British oil companies were expropriated after the Mexican Supreme Court this time had upheld the government's action in ordering a substantial wage increase throughout the industry. The expropriation measure itself, with a mandate for compensation, was unanimously declared valid by the same court on December 2, 1939. These properties, too, were handed over to the unions for operation.[25]

Progress of Reform. Beginning early in Cárdenas' administration, the distribution of land was speeded up. The agrarian reform was never lost sight of as the core of the program for economic democracy, although administrative and political difficulties had greatly hampered its execution over the years. By the end of 1933, some 19 million acres had been allotted to villages with about 750,000 families. When Cárdenas left office in 1940, the number of heads of families benefited by land grants to villages had increased to 2 million, and the amount of land distributed had risen to about 70 million acres.[26] On the labor front, the provisions of a far-reaching federal labor law enacted in 1931 were being enforced with increasing effectiveness. Collective bargaining strengthened the position of the industrial worker generally. Specific minimum wages became established in many states. Moreover, the requirement that 80 per cent of the employees of all industrial and commercial concerns be Mexican citizens was more and more widely observed.

The ranks of the labor movement, however, were split in the years of the Cárdenas administration. The political tradition of the movement had been rather conservative, comparatively speaking. Now, in 1936, a new *Confederación de Trabajadorcs Mexicanos* (CTM) was founded by an ambitious young leader, Vicente Lombardo Toledano, who envisaged a further transformation of the Mexican social system into one of industry-managing workers' cooperatives, much along the lines tried shortly afterward in the case of the railroads and the petroleum industry. In fact, cooperative management was making headway in many municipal services and several industries. Moreover, the idea of establishing cooperative farms for the production of

---

[25] For a brief survey of the oil controversy with the United States and Great Britain, see Wilgus, *op. cit.* above, note 6, pp. 419 ff. Mexico refused to have the matter arbitrated, as suggested by Secretary of State Hull, since it was considered a domestic one by the Mexican government. An agreement was finally reached whereby Mexico acknowledged a debt to the North American oil companies of about $24,000,000. This debt was paid, less an amount allowed for counterclaims by Mexico, and the last check of $4,500,000 delivered to the United States Department of State on September 30, 1947. Other claims of United States citizens against Mexico—mostly from the expropriation of lands and mines—were adjusted by payment of a lump sum of $40,000,000.

[26] The figure given above includes large tracts of pasture and woodlands for communal use. Since 1941, titles to crop land have been passing to individual peasants, but communal operation has continued. In 1937 the government asserted that 45 per cent of the Mexican people were living on communal lands which were eventually to be brought under the reform program.

commercial crops was introduced. Unquestionably, labor had become a powerful factor to be reckoned with in any design for the political future of the country.

Party Organization and Methods. The position of labor was enhanced by the influence that the CTM wielded in the councils of the leading political party, the *Partido Revolucionario Mexicano* (PRM).[27] It would be wrong to say that Mexico is a one-party state in the usual sense. For minority parties have been coming and going, constantly contesting the power of the PRM. Among these were leftist groups, such as the New Revolutionary party, which made its appearance in 1938 with a program of wholesale collectivization of agriculture, and various rightist movements, of which the *Unión Nacional Sinarquista* received international attention.[28] But the PRM alone obtained semi-official status, by an executive decree issued in 1937 under which every government employee must contribute a fixed percentage of his salary to the party. Thus, the party became firmly entrenched, claiming to be the authentic guardian of the revolutionary tradition. Today it is in undisputed control of both houses of the Congress and most state legislatures.

Historically, the party was founded as a vehicle of political organization for the urban workers who considered it their special role to consolidate and further the achievements of the Revolution. From urban centers the organization has spread, carried forward by a deliberate attempt to unify social action and to see to it that local governments would fall in line with the new national policies. Branches of the party organization reach out to the most remote sections of the country, establishing close collaboration with state and municipal authorities. In Mexico City, seat of the party's general headquarters, an elaborate machinery, paralleling in some respects that of the government itself, functions under the supervision of the Central Executive Committee; to this the state central committees each delegate one representative. The Central Executive Committee controls the state and local organizations of the party, with farm committees in the rural communities at the bottom of the pyramid.

In general, nomination by the party is tantamount to election; and most

---

[27] At the party convention in 1946, where Miguel Alemán was nominated as the official candidate, the name was changed to *Partido Revolucionario Institucional,* or PRI (usually pronounced simply *pree,* as that sequence of letters in Spanish would indicate).

[28] Sinarquism was founded in 1937, as a pro-Catholic, antidemocratic movement, and later turned into a political party, against the will of its principal sponsor, Salvador Abascal. Under its political leader, Manuel Torres Bueno, the organization built up a membership of two to three million farmers, small businessmen, and other lower-middle-class people. The similarity of its structure and aims with the fascist parties of Europe suggested the rise of a Mexican fascist movement. In 1944, the organization played up an alleged Communist plot, engaged in insurrectionist activities, and exposed itself to treason charges. It had little popular support in the elections of 1946, and in 1949 the government canceled its registration as a political party. There have been several totalitarian groups of the fascist variety in Mexico; one of them was a branch of the Spanish Falangist movement.

officials who are responsible for policy-making and coordination of the various governmental services are approved by the party. Its leadership has been astute and adaptable; although the party exercises far-reaching control over the policies of the government, in the main it has respected constitutional forms and democratic procedure. To secure and broaden its popular backing, the party has instituted "internal primaries" for the selection of its candidates and has worked continuously toward activation of the suffrage in backward regions of the country. It allowed women to vote for the first time in the party primaries of 1937. Through congressional action in 1946 it extended woman suffrage to municipal elections. In 1948 compulsory voting—in accordance with requisite qualifications—was instituted.

Retrenchment and War. New party developments came to the fore in the presidential election at the end of Cárdenas' term. The chief contenders were General Manuel Ávila Camacho, the official candidate, and General Juan Andreu Almazán, who claimed the support of eighteen "independent" parties, although he, too, was a member of PRM. It was evident, however, that Almazán had the support of many conservatives and other rightists. After the election, both candidates claimed victory; the *Almazanistas* revolted in several places. The issue was clinched when the United States indicated that it considered Camacho constitutionally elected, and delegated Vice President-elect Henry A. Wallace to take part in the inauguration of the new President on December 1, 1940. Camacho immediately took occasion to proclaim his friendship for the United States and his willingness to cooperate in hemisphere defense. He also expressed his desire to deal fairly with both capital and labor, and promised protection for the rights of foreign investors. Soon thereafter the government announced a four-point program to curb excesses of labor unions and to revise certain expropriation practices. It also emphasized the need for foreign help, especially of technicians, in developing the country's production potential.

The new President brought about a sharp change in the management of the nationalized railroads by returning it to the government. The railroads were placed under a seven-member board on which labor had but three elected representatives. The expropriation of landed and other property, which had been under the exclusive jurisdiction of the executive, was made subject to the control of the courts. Steps were also taken to transfer land titles on a large scale to individual peasants and to increase the allotments so that they would furnish subsistence.[29] Mexico appeared on its way to more settled conditions, which had begun to arouse anew the interest of financial circles in the United States. But World War II naturally upset all plans of normal development. Prices soared as imported goods became more and more scarce and other countries, especially the United States, were willing to

---

[29] The insufficient size of land allotments to individual families under ejidal procedure had been one of the weakest points in the agrarian reform and called forth much criticism. Cf. Frank Tannenbaum, *The Mexican Agrarian Revolution* (New York, 1929).

pay almost any price for the country's products. A revival of labor unrest followed. The President was personally successful in pacifying labor, but the administration was firm in dealing with union leaders who seemed to endanger success of the defense program. But the war was not all strain. War needs caused several new industries to develop, especially in the chemical field. A Federal Commission for Industrial Promotion was established for the purpose of supervising capital investments and preventing foreign interests from building up monopolies. At about the same time, in 1944, a national insurance system was adopted and set up first in the Federal District; its extension to other parts of the country was projected.

New Trends under Alemán. When in 1945 the end of Camacho's term approached, again a rightist candidate, former Foreign Minister Ezequiel Padilla, faced a man backed by the PRM. Its official candidate was Miguel Alemán, former Minister of the Interior, who like Padilla stood for cooperation with the United States, but was known as "a little more to the left" than Camacho. With the prestige he had acquired as a diplomatic figure in the Chapultepec and San Francisco conferences, Padilla hoped to gain considerable support, but he was tagged with the label of subservience to the United States by his opponents. Even then his following showed that PRM control was neither absolute nor total. The official party took heed and announced at the height of the campaign that it would cease deducting contributions from government pay envelopes. Under the new name of *Partido Revolucionario Institucional* (PRI), the party underwent a thorough internal reorganization. The "most peaceful election in Mexico's history" gave Alemán a three-to-one victory over Padilla.

In his inaugural, Alemán pledged himself to enlarge the nation's irrigation program and give greater credit facilities to agriculture and industry. About 10 per cent of the budget was soon earmarked for irrigation projects, besides large credits extended by the United States Export-Import Bank in 1950. The President further advocated the creation of a National Colonization Commission to effect a large-scale resettlement program. He spoke out against foreign oil interests, declaring that his administration would not readmit them in any exploitative or managerial capacity, but would welcome capital investments on a sound business basis to increase the output of the nationalized petroleum industry. Industrialization and a better distribution of wealth he pronounced to be his supreme objectives.

Both Camacho and Alemán have preserved the progressive tendencies of the Revolution. The spirit of rebellion and radicalism is checked by experience. But Mexico is young. The masses of its people are just awakening to a fuller grasp of their possibilities, in a new synthesis of past and present that is still waiting to be consummated on the level of full achievement.

Constitutional Process and the Church. Confronted with the impact of the Revolution, the church eventually decided on a policy of waiting and seeing. It has remained noncommittal in the most recent stages of Mexican political development and thereby indirectly supported the regime of President Alemán.

Since the turbulent happenings of early revolutionary days, various attempts at reconciliation had been made. An agreement having been reached on the registration of priests and on religious instruction in church buildings, the churches were again opened in 1929. New difficulties arose in 1932 when the government enforced a law whereby the clergy in the Federal District was limited to one for every 50,000 inhabitants. There was open resistance when in 1934 the law ordering secular and "socialistic" education went into effect. Since President Camacho's regime, however, the church has enjoyed comparative freedom within the limits set by the constitution and on the understanding that the clergy would abstain from any political activity. Actually there is freedom of worship for all religions.

Education as Collective Enterprise. One of its cherished prerogatives, it is true, the church had to abandon without prospect of ever recovering it. This was its role in education. In order to enlist the informed cooperation of the people for whose sake the political reforms were enacted, public education had to be brought right down to the lowliest laborers in the rural communities. This process, moreover, would have to reach not only children but adults as well in a country one third of whose population was illiterate. Elementary teaching, therefore, had to be connected with the teaching of arts and crafts and agricultural methods. Such goals meant struggling against extraordinary odds—which included the lack of trained teachers and communications with the isolated villages, and the variety of native Indian languages that the government wished to preserve rather than destroy.

Where there were, in 1929, 14,700 primary schools for about one million pupils, there were, in 1949, 24,625 primary schools with three million students. Compared with conditions in 1910, when the six hundred schools provided for only 70,000 pupils, the figures show that within a short span of time great strides were made. The latest, most comprehensive attack on illiteracy was initiated by the Camacho administration and has been conducted continuously for a number of years. With sixty-six "literacy missions" operating throughout the country in 1947, the campaign claimed the active help of all who could read and write to teach these arts to at least one of their compatriots. Thus, one of the great human problems facing the Mexican people has been tackled—by government decree but with the aid and cooperation of the whole community. It is this kind of collectivist achievement in which modern Mexico takes pride.

5. Outlook for the Future

Mexico in World War II. Long before World War II broke out, Mexico, because it was consciously leftist and progressive, served as one of the chief obstacles to fascist hopes for the control of Latin America. Official Mexico's aversion to becoming a partner in a plot destructive of hemisphere solidarity was matched perhaps only by the stubborn independence of Vargas' Brazil toward any attempts to mobilize profascist and pro-German leanings in the interest of Hitler's Reich. In this respect both Cárdenas' and Camacho's leadership was unequivocal, in spite of the political and economic difficulties engendered by the expropriation measures. There were considerable tensions inside Mexico that might have caused the country's course to waver or change if it had not been for the determination of the administration to abide by the inter-American commitments underwritten at the conferences and meetings of Lima (1938), Panama (1939), Havana (1940), and Rio de Janeiro (1942).[30] Tensions resulted mainly from "fifth column" activities of foreign colonies, especially the relatively large and Nazi-dominated German business community in Mexico City, and of indigenous elements who were fascist by persuasion or would accept support from any quarter to undo the work of the Revolution. Among the dissatisfied elements was also the small but aggressive group of Communists on the extreme left wing of the labor movement, who often collaborated with Axis agents until the Nazi armies turned against Soviet Russia. Rightist intrigues, however, received no encouragement from the church, which seconded the government's stand against any kind of totalitarian encroachment; it later urged all good Catholics to cooperate loyally in the prosecution of the war.

Mexico severed relations with the Axis powers immediately upon the attack on Pearl Harbor. A joint Mexican-United States defense commission to prepare mutual aid plans in case of attack was set up in January 1942. On June 5, 1942, Mexico signed the United Nations Declaration, and its declaration of war late that month closed the front of all the countries between the Rio Grande and the Panama Canal giving full support to the United States. The government's cautious but determined policy followed the trend of public opinion, which became more militant as the war progressed. Compulsory military training was introduced in 1942, and in December 1943 President Camacho declared that Mexican forces were ready to give active assistance to the Allied powers.[31] Finally, in April 1945, a Mexican air squadron left for the Pacific and saw some action in the Philippines.

Of greater importance was Mexico's contribution on the economic front of World War II. It supplied large quantities of minerals and other strategic materials, foremost to the United States. Mexico was in a particularly favorable position to make up for the loss of European markets by turning all its surpluses over to the rich northern neighbor whose requirements were well-

[30] For the principal decisions of these gatherings, see the chapters on Pan-Americanism in Wilgus, *op. cit.* above, note 6, and Pan-Americanism and the War in Munro, *op. cit.* above, note 6. The story of later developments is told in *Inter-American Affairs,* an annual survey published since 1941 (ed. Arthur P. Whitaker; New York, 1941 and after).

[31] Under lend-lease agreements of 1942 and 1943, the United States governments undertook to supply equipment for the new Mexican Army and helped in the rehabilitation of the railroads. Mexico assisted the United States all through the war in guarding frontiers and coastal areas, and by exercising vigilance over foreigners.

nigh insatiable. Besides, as shortages of all kinds developed on both sides of the frontier, a number of new industries came into being that gave to Mexican labor good wartime wages and to capital good wartime profits. All in all, Mexico had a considerable share of wartime prosperity, which was also expressed in favorable trade balances and the accumulation of foreign exchange reserves such as Mexico had never seen since prerevolutionary days.[32]

Postwar Economic Crisis. When the war was over, however, the artificial character of the boom became obvious. The cost-of-living index rose more than 360 per cent from January 1943 to April 1946, and currency circulation increased, with the end not in sight. The favorable trade balance vanished into its opposite, and the foreign exchange hoard quickly shrank. True, wartime prosperity had enabled the government to liquidate the major part of Mexico's external indebtedness and to reduce the internal debt. But new credit needs arose as imports increased over exports, food shortages had to be relieved, wage raises were demanded by the workers, and government expenditures mounted.

Unrest was inevitable. A wave of strikes, which had set in when deliveries of defense materials to the United States tapered off, reached menacing proportions in 1946. One of the government's worries was to keep industries going that had produced for the war program and attracted manpower from the villages to the cities. The number of industrial workers was at an all-time high. Under such circumstances, the country became fertile ground for Communist activity. Fortunately, efforts to increase production in the agricultural sector of the economy were paying off while food demands remained high.

Generally, the foremost task for Mexico was the expansion of the national economy. As President Alemán stated in his report to the Congress on September 1, 1947, the solution of Mexico's problems depended on the development of natural resources and the increase of the market for the growing domestic industries. He warned that economic cooperation with the United States—now again under the peacetime good-neighbor policy—must not be one-sided, but that Mexico, having made great sacrifices for victory, had the right to expect help in its postwar predicament. Such help was not lacking, but like most Latin American countries Mexico felt that what the United States offered did not come up to expectations. Meanwhile, the Mexican government practices self-help to the best of its ability. In order to stem an inflation that in 1951, under the stress of new threats to world peace, had raised the price level 300 per cent above that of 1940, the government restricted credit, froze commodity prices, and took other emergency measures.

Record of Nationalization. As to the goals of the Revolution, results of

---

[32] The trade balance had been in Mexico's favor from 1903 to 1913, but the disturbances of the civil war and later the world depression caused great financial difficulties. A ten-year moratorium on the internal debt was declared, the silver standard was adopted, and in 1930 a moratorium on the foreign debt was effected, which lasted until 1934.

social reform in agriculture seem to indicate that the break-up of large estates and the establishment of cooperative farming communities have given a sizable portion of the Mexican people the chance for self-development where before there had been none. The record of industrial socialization, on the other hand, showed that collectivization of management through the unions —as the term "socialization" was at first understood—did not work. Nor was nationalization—that is, management by government—able to avoid conflicts. These brought the workers squarely up against public authority and compelled the government to take strong disciplinarian measures. Moreover, the workers had to accept restrictions and wage regulations that did not leave them with much of that once cherished feeling of ownership. This was especially true when in December 1946 President Alemán dismissed, "in the national interest," fifty leaders of the oil labor unions as the ones responsible for an illegal work stoppage, and was backed up in this and similar actions by public opinion.

It would be wrong to conclude, however, that industrial nationalization was a failure. The railroads had deteriorated under union management, but considerably improved under government direction. That progress can be made under nationalization has been proved in the case of the oil industry, whose production, after a temporary decline, has constantly increased. It has been pointed out by the partisans of nationalization that at the same time the workers were receiving more in wages than they had been paid by the foreign oil companies; and general working conditions were improved under government auspices. What solution Mexico would find for its struggle to build a partly collectivized economy into a democratic system of government and to integrate its widely divergent social components with one another was still an open question.

Mexico's Foreign Policy. In accordance with domestic contingencies, Mexican foreign policy has been directed toward the establishment and maintenance of good relations with the United States and other nations in the concert of powers. Moreover, political relations with the neighbor in the north were amply cemented by President Truman's visit to Mexico in March 1947, and President Alemán's return visit to Washington two months later. Mexico, however, does not propose to yield to the United States in matters in which it has a long-standing interest of its own. It demanded to be heard in the peace conferences with the enemies in World War II. At San Francisco, in 1951, it became one of the signers of the peace treaty with Japan. Even before that, the state of war with Germany had been terminated.

In various Pan-American meetings and conferences of recent years, Mexican statesmen have had a leading part. At Rio de Janeiro in 1942, Mexico's delegation was in the forefront of those pressing toward a united hemisphere policy in the conduct of the war as well as in postwar matters of common interest. At the Inter-American Conference on Problems of War and Peace in Mexico City three years later, Mexico exerted a notable influence in framing the Act of Chapultepec, whereby the hemisphere solidarity forged in war was to be extended into peacetime. Likewise, after the Rio (Petropolis) conference of August 1947, Mexico underwrote the obligations created for all American states in the Inter-American Treaty of Reciprocal Assistance. This treaty gave permanent form to provisions for "reciprocal assistance and American solidarity," as envisaged in the Act of Chapultepec, through a system of collective defense measures against possible aggression.

For the Ninth Pan-American Conference held at Bogotá in April 1948, Mexico had prepared a draft charter for a reorganized inter-American system, which was a major contribution to the Charter of the Organization of American States as finally adopted. On two important points, however, the Mexican representatives at the conference expressed clearly their government's disagreement with certain other Latin American states and the United States. When the issue of communism was raised, Mexico joined Venezuela and Guatemala in declaring that the real threat to democratic institutions on this continent emanated from the right rather than from the left. A compromise formula was at last adopted in which the condemnation of communism was complemented by references to "any other form of totalitarianism." Reconstruction and development provided the other issue on which Mexico disagreed with the United States. With most other Latin American countries, Mexico protested against the priority given to European reconstruction by the United States. But at the emergency meeting of the American Republics in March 1951, Mexico aligned itself with a concerted program for supplying strategic materials in the defense of the West and joined in political and military cooperation for that purpose.

Mexico's Role in the United Nations. Mexico's part in the United Nations was determined by the fact that it was a charter member. It held a seat in the Security Council for one year (1946), the first of the Council's existence, and was elected member of the Trusteeship Council. Mexican representatives have also served on other such bodies, notably the Economic and Social Council and its offspring, the Economic Commission for Latin America.

At the United Nations Conference on Trade and Employment at Havana, the Mexican Finance Minister, Ramón Beteta, as chairman of the committee on economic development again presented forcefully the Latin American viewpoint, objecting to the United States plan for the International Trade Organization because "it would prevent the industrialization of the Latin American nations." These countries signed only after they had secured exceptions about import restrictions and preferential tariff agreements that seemed to them indispensable for safeguarding their own development. In the Atomic Energy Commission, Mexico submitted a plan for control with which it hoped to bring the United States and the Soviet Union together in a compromise; but the plan failed of acceptance. In all basic questions of policy, however, Mexico has stood by the Western nations; its record here, as in the Pan American Union and the Organization of American States, founded at the Bogotá Conference of 1948, has been one of cooperation and constructive criticism. The new Cultural Council set up by the latter organization held its first meeting in Mexico City in September 1951, in conjunction with the 400th anniversary of the founding of the National University of Mexico. And the first model school in a world network of centers for the training of specialists in basic education, significantly, was established by UNESCO at Patzcuaro, on Mexican soil, in the same year.

Summary and Prospects. Modern Mexico has gone through several upheavals that cut its history into a number of more or less fragmentary parts. Political and social turmoil began, as in most Latin American republics, in the wake of independence. Soon, however, Mexico became the champion in Latin America of popular rights and collective defense against the inequities of class privilege. Setbacks were caused by foreign intervention and the vicissitudes of internal struggle between highly articulate social camps. The country's march toward political, social, and economic emancipation of its people culminated in a revolution whose extraordinary intensity was bound to be discharged in a progression of shocks. But the issues of the Revolution were given permanence in a constitution conceived at the height of tension.

The constitution of 1917 was imbued with the ideas of a world to come— it was anticipation, not fulfillment. Upon enlightened statesmanship devolved the task of fusing the revolutionary currents in the constitutional frame. Fortunately, the nation has had a succession of presidents who understood this crucial problem. Moreover, the majority of its people appear to realize that their future depends largely on social self-discipline and patience allowing for consistent development. Thus, what has been called "the natural event of the Revolution" may be conceived as but a phase of the nation's historical advance, without loss of continuing actuality. The Revolution is irreversible. The hopes that it has aroused it strives to fulfill.

One long-range choice Mexicans must surely make is this: Would they insist on their own course, mindful of the strength that had been theirs in brave solitude? Or would they integrate their domestic scheme with a world that had offered them little support but needed harmonious adjustment more than ever to uphold and develop the common welfare? Indications are that Mexico will preserve the essentials of the democratic order while advancing on the road of industrial evolution toward full maturity. With extremes of wealth and poverty, inflation, and other economic and social ills besetting it today, Mexico is marching alongside the nations of the Western World because this course serves best its own national interests.[33]

---

[33] For recent publications, containing also ample references to further literature, see below, p. 677, note 20.

CHAPTER 32

BRAZIL: FROM DICTATORSHIP
TOWARD CONSTITUTIONALISM

1. The Making of Modern Brazil

Legacy of Tradition. As European politics in the wake of the Napoleonic wars determined much of the fate of Mexico, so they played a decisive role in the case of Brazil. But the immediate result was contrary to the Spanish-American experience. Whereas developments in New Spain led directly to independence and republicanism, the occupation of Portugal by French troops in 1807 brought about in Brazil a temporary consolidation of Portuguese rule with the home government. The transfer of power from the mother country to the colony—with the removal of the royal family and many nobles of the court from Lisbon to Rio de Janeiro—became a success mainly because that shift put an end to colonial repression and had a liberating effect on Brazilian life. Although Portugal's colonial rule had on the whole been relatively mild when compared with that of Spain, social and economic conditions in Brazil were even more backward than in some of the Spanish possessions. Techniques and methods employed on the plantations and in the mines were most primitive; slavery was a legally acknowledged fact; and the intellectual level of the population as a whole was extremely low. Contact with foreigners had been negligible during most of the eighteenth century, owing to a policy of rigid exclusion pursued by the home government. The stirring literature of that period was unknown to Brazilians, since only religious books were imported; and the country itself did not have a single printing press. Upon his arrival in Brazil, the Prince Regent—later King João VI—at once lifted restrictions on foreign trade and domestic manufacture,[1] established a printing press and schools for medicine and law, a library, hospitals, a national bank, and other facilities. He also invited distinguished foreigners and generally opened the country to outside influences.

Because of the weakness of central organization, local government had played a significant part in the earlier Brazilian development.[2] A trend countering this diffusion of authority had seemed to set in only a few decades before the end of colonial rule, when the Marquis of Pombal, Prime

[1] In 1810 a trade treaty with England was signed, which laid the foundation for later British predominance in the economic life of Brazil.
[2] See the introductory section to chap. 31.

654

Minister of King José I of Portugal, instituted a new regime under which the viceroy held real power over the provincial governors. This innovation prevented the colony from disintegrating into a number of semi-independent states and filled the Portuguese dynasty with a new interest in Brazil. Conditions there had been deteriorating because early depredations by foreign invaders and frequent inner disturbances, together with events in Portugal itself, had impaired the position of the mother country as a colonial power.[3]

Now, under Pombal's reform, administration was improved and corruption subdued. The Indians of Brazil were given their legal freedom; the Jesuit order was expelled but other immigration encouraged. Moreover, in 1763 the capital was moved to Rio de Janeiro. By that time Rio had replaced the old ports of Recife (Pernambuco) and São Salvador (Bahia) as the principal export outlet of the country; for the gold and diamond findings in Matto Grosso, Goyaz, and Minas Geraes—hinterland of Rio—were gaining in importance over the sugar industry of the North, which suffered by competition from the British, French, and Dutch West Indies. When in 1777 Pombal's regime fell, the colonial government reverted to its former evil and inefficient practices. A movement for independence, republican in character and stimulated by the ideas of the French and North American revolutions, gathered some force in Minas Geraes in 1789, but remained abortive. Thus, the question of Brazil's future was left open when the new century dawned. Soon the assemblage of Portuguese political and military power on the colony's soil made success of an independence movement well-nigh impossible.

Independence through Monarchy. In spite of promising beginnings in both the domestic and foreign fields, King João soon met with difficulties that had much to do with social and economic rivalry between the native Brazilian element and the newcomers from the Iberian peninsula, who were gaining a reputation for meddlesomeness and arrogance. A revolt in Pernambuco, seat of fierce local patriotism, had to be suppressed with military force. Complications of a more serious nature arose when a revolutionary assembly in the homeland, inspired by the Spanish revolution of 1820, demanded the return of the royal family. Finally, the King yielded, leaving his son Pedro as regent in Brazil and exhorting him to place the crown on his head if Brazil—as the King expected—should become an independent nation. Less than one year later, in 1822, Pedro faced the alternative of

---

[3] For general and historical background, see the works by W. L. Schurz, D. G. Munro, A. C. Wilgus, and C. H. Haring, *cit.* in the preceding chapter. A panorama of social conditions in the colonial age is presented by Gilberto Freyre in *The Masters and the Slaves* (4th ed., New York, 1946; published first in Portuguese under the title *Casa-Grande e Senzala,* Rio de Janeiro, 1933). For more recent developments, consult Herman G. James, *Brazil after a Century of Independence* (New York, 1925), and Karl Loewenstein, *Brazil under Vargas* (New York, 1942). The last-named work contains a thorough discussion of constitutional issues; as regards the republican pre-Vargas constitution, see Herman G. James, *The Constitutional System of Brazil* (Washington, 1923). Compendious analyses of the Brazilian scene will be found in Gilberto Freyre, *Brazil: An Interpretation* (New York, 1945); Lawrence F. Hill, ed., *Brazil* (Berkeley, Cal., 1947); T. Lynn Smith and Alexander Marchant, *Brazil* (New York, 1951).

whether he, too, should obey a legislative order to return to Portugal, abandoning Brazil to its former status as a mere colony, or whether he should give in to a popular request not to leave the country but to serve as its symbol of independence. He chose the latter course, and assumed the title of Perpetual Defender and Protector of Brazil. On September 7, 1822, he decided upon a complete severance from the mother country. A call for a constituent assembly had been issued. Pedro announced that he would accept the constitution that the assembly was to draw up, and was proclaimed constitutional Emperor of Brazil. The remaining Portuguese troops were driven from their last stronghold within another year. Thus, independence was achieved through apt use of the monarchy as a vehicle of public pressure.

The monarchical system marked the first period of the independent existence of Brazil. Owing to circumstances that seemed fortunate even to many contemporaries, the monarchy lasted for the greater part of the century. It was followed by a republic, which sustained itself until in the early thirties of our century it was submerged in the maelstrom of the great economic depression, world-wide in scope and consequences. A dictatorship was born that pretended to be transitory but had some of the earmarks of a daring continuing experiment. Still it did not rise above the level of what has been called the "most successful example of authoritarian government in the Western Hemisphere." With its demise in 1945, a new period of constitutional development was initiated; it is that of a democracy seasoned by experience and limited by safeguards against the repetition of excesses that might lead to its overthrow by powerful personalities or groups. *Caudillismo,* in the sense in which it has been a phenomenon of some regularity in Spanish-American republics, has remained the exception in Brazil, though some basic conditions seem to favor it. Among these conditions are, first of all, the feudalistic structure of Brazilian society shared with the other Latin American countries, a structure built upon large-scale plantation economy and an unbroken tradition of slavery for the majority of Negroes who were brought into the country in huge numbers during almost three and a half centuries.[4]

Another factor is the uneven distribution of population, making for spotty concentrations that might have come, one by one, under the sway of a "leader" and be welded into a machine under his command. In Brazil, more than elsewhere, however, the plantation economy meant self-sufficiency of the individual manor with all its dependents, and therefore offered less ground for political activity. Moreover, the larger centers of population were almost all at or near the seacoast, where they were rapidly urbanized and where com-

---

[4] At the end of the colonial regime (1808), the population of Brazil was about 3.5 million, of whom at least two fifths were Negro slaves. The Negro population was about half of the total in 1830, and still in 1865 slaves made up a quarter of the country's inhabitants. In 1888, the population had increased to 15 million; but owing to various legislative reforms and widespread manumission, the number of slaves was reduced to fewer than 700,000. Race mixture has taken place on a large scale, so that now the pure white element is slightly in a minority, most of it resident in the southern states.

mercial intercourse caused people to acquire a comparatively rational, if not cosmopolitan, outlook. Consequently, the formation of parties and factions proceeded on the pattern of existing political divisions rather than through media of national appeal. This tendency, effective up to most recent times, was powerfully supported by the diversified history of the Brazilian states as provinces of the old colony. Nevertheless, Brazil as a whole, with its distinct periods of development, has exhibited a greater variety of governmental forms than most of the Latin American republics.

First Constitution. In keeping with his promise, the new Emperor, as Pedro I, accepted a constitution that had been submitted to the municipal councils for approval. But it was not the one drafted by the constituent assembly. Several northern provinces had boycotted that assembly, which cast doubts upon its competence as a representative body. When it also refused to do the Emperor's bidding, he dissolved it by armed force and had a constitution drafted by a commission consisting of men appointed by him. It was their work that Pedro finally swore to adhere to on March 25, 1824. In truth, however, he disregarded it and continued to exercise absolute power. Nor did he pay much attention to the will of the legislature when it met at last, after several delays. Naturally, this attitude aroused the liberal opposition that had been growing in various parts of the country, and led to open hostility in a new Congress which met in 1830. Belated attempts to placate both politicians and the public failed. In the following year, Pedro was ready to give up; he abdicated in favor of his infant son, who later became Emperor under the name of Pedro II. The latter occupied the Brazilian throne until 1889, when a federal republic was proclaimed. Meanwhile, the constitution of 1824 remained the supreme law of the land, but the role it played in the political life of the country changed significantly.

That constitution made Brazil a hereditary, limited, and representative monarchy on the European model of the period. It established a unitary and centralized system whereby the provinces could be "subdivided as might be demanded for the good of the state." All questions arising between the executive and legislative were to be decided by the Crown as the ultimate arbiter. The legislature consisted of two houses: a Senate, whose members were appointed for life by the Emperor from a list of candidates chosen by indirect elections; and a Chamber of Deputies chosen for four years by electors named by popular vote. Roman Catholicism was the official religion, but others were "permitted."

For nine years following the overthrow of Pedro I, a regency—at first of three men elected by the Congress—groped its way through a maze of factional antagonisms, in order to secure the constitutional basis of the new nation. In terms of political alignment there were, on the one hand, radical federalists and republicans, and, on the other, the conservative element supported by Portuguese landowners who had cast their lot with independence. As during this period the general condition of the people advanced by greater economic activity and improvements in education and internal communications, the liberal forces finally had their way. In 1834 an act of Congress—the so-called *Acto Addicional*—replaced the three-man regency by one single regent, elected by universal indirect suffrage. At the same time, the constitution was amended so that the provinces would have the right to choose their own assemblies, levy taxes, and conduct their local government. Only the provincial governors, or "presidents," were henceforth to be appointed by the central government.

Thus, progressive and federalist tendencies asserted themselves, in the line of the Minas Geraes revolt of 1789 and Pernambuco's ill-fated attempt of 1824 at a "confederation of the equator." As the constitution now stood, it represented a liberal triumph over the absolutism of the preceding period. To be sure, the political system was far from democratic in the modern sense. The suffrage was very limited, and all national elections were indirect and could be controlled by the central government through its appointed officials in the provinces. The rights of the provinces in self-government were restricted even though the provincial legislatures could, by repassage of a law, override the veto of the provincial governors, and even though legislative action in some fields was not subject to executive sanction. Unfortunately, autonomy received a severe blow when a separatist and republican movement in Rio Grande do Sul provoked a long-drawn-out civil war, calling forth conservative reaction against the financial powers granted to the provinces. A weakening of provincial self-government for the whole Empire was the consequence. Meanwhile, the liberals, anxious not to lose what constitutional guarantees had been gained, succeeded in putting an end to the regency. At their insistence, the Congress in 1840 declared the majority of Pedro II, of whom it was hoped that as Emperor he would lend continuity and stability to constitutional development.

Pedro II and Parliamentary Government. Such hopes were not misplaced. The young Emperor turned out to be a constitutional prince of the highest caliber. During his long reign Brazil progressed in every field of human endeavor, attaining the stature of an internationally respected power and one of the most liberal monarchies of that day. Pedro was highly popular, owing to his personal character as well as to the enlightened ways of his regime. Contemporaries spoke of the latter as a "crowned democracy." It was imperial in that the sovereign himself was the real head of the government, making the more important decisions and personally supervising the work of his ministers. But there was no arbitrariness; the rule of law was strictly observed. Although some serious disturbances of the political order occurred in the early years and many party shifts took place during Pedro's reign, peaceful constitutional procedure was safeguarded, in striking contrast to the turbulence in other Latin American countries. Administration became more efficient and more honest than it had ever been before in Brazil. Freedom of speech and press existed to a degree that elicited admiration on the part of many European travelers. Thus, a tradition of political liberalism and public order, combined with administrative efficiency, became part of the country's political heritage.

Even under these happy circumstances, constitutional development did not stagnate. Pedro's political fortunes were helped by a reform that permitted him to adapt his rule to public opinion without losing prestige or power. That was the constitutional amendment adopted in 1847, by which the office of Prime Minister was created and the Cabinet members were made responsible to the Congress, instead of to the Emperor. The idea of parliamentary government had been ventilated during the regency by several writers and politicians, such as Bernardo de Vasconcelhos. Now it was to be put into institutional practice. As it turned out, both the Emperor's eminence as political leader of the nation and the fact that elections were artfully managed to suit his aims rendered the experiment somewhat illusory. But it showed the turn toward democratization of the monarchy. In the same direction lay the Saraiva law of 1880, through which direct voting for deputies was introduced and the suffrage broadened. Two Cabinets had to be ousted before Pedro saw this project adopted by a resisting Congress. The opposition included, besides a republican group among the liberals, the landed aristocracy, whom Pedro had antagonized by his consistent stand against slavery, and the church, which was apprehensive of his philosophical and scientific propensities.[5]

Pedro's prestige was at its height when in 1870, after a war lasting six years and involving heavy sacrifices, victory was finally attained over Francisco López of Paraguay. But this war left in its wake more than moral and financial exhaustion. Businessmen were dissatisfied with the government's conduct of economic affairs. Actually, agricultural production had greatly increased, many new industries had got under way, and the foreign trade of the country had more than doubled by 1860. The war and the depression of the early seventies, however, caused dislocations in the budget and currency system that it took many years to clear up. On the other side, the more aggressive liberals thought the Emperor's reforms inadequate and the pace of political progress too slow. Agitation for a republic increased and gained currency among the younger officers of the Army, especially through the teachings of Benjamin Constant, a professor at the military school at Rio. From 1870 on, republican clubs were widely organized, and periodicals appeared that advocated a republican system, with the federal principle as its complement. But the test came with the further evolution of the slavery issue.

End of the Monarchy. In 1845 the British Parliament had passed the

---

[5] The breach with the church came when the Pope's condemnation of the Masonic order led to conflicts in the course of which the government prosecuted and imprisoned two bishops. Nor did it help that Pedro encouraged the translation of Charles Darwin's *Origin of Species* for study in Brazilian institutions of learning.

Aberdeen Act, which was to end slave traffic on the high seas and would have permitted the seizure of slave ships even in Brazilian territorial waters. In face of this threat to national sovereignty, Pedro insisted on the passage of a law by the Brazilian Congress effectively suppressing the slave trade. The Civil War in the United States gave new impetus to a drive for abolition, but the most that could be achieved was adoption in 1871 of the Rio Branco law, which declared all children henceforth born of a slave mother to be legally free. This act alienated a large body of the Conservative party. Simultaneously, agitation for complete abolition continued, and an attempt to enact a law to that effect was defeated by only seven votes in 1884. A year later, however, the Congress freed all slaves over sixty years of age, and further steps leading toward wholesale emancipation were being considered; several northern provinces released the slaves in their territories by independent action. When a Conservative Cabinet came into power, a last effort was made to save the institution of slavery for the landowners. But large numbers of slaves simply left the plantations, and the Army refused to help in recapturing them.

At about this time the Emperor went on a trip to Europe and left his daughter, Princess Isabel, in charge of the government. She and her husband, member of a former ruling family of France, were even more ardent abolitionists than Pedro and seized their opportunity to bring matters to a head. Isabel appointed a new Prime Minister, who in May 1888 succeeded in having a law passed whereby all the remaining slaves were freed. For the "property" thus taken away from the plantation owners there was no compensation. The majority of Brazilians rejoiced at the action taken, naming the liberation measure the Golden Law, but the landowning class was deeply resentful and lost all interest in upholding the monarchy when the crisis came.

Upon his return from Europe the Emperor saw that further concessions would have to be made to meet the mounting agitation for a republic. Another Prime Minister, Viscount of Ouro Preto, submitted to the Congress a fresh program of reforms. It tended in the direction of federalism by granting autonomy to the provinces, and abolished life tenure in the Senate, with further extensions of the suffrage. But now it was too late. The Army had grown restive and resisted openly when the government ordered the transfer of certain regiments, held to be of doubtful loyalty, to distant parts of the country. The revolt was led by General Deodoro da Fonseca, allied with Benjamin Constant and other republican leaders. Under such leadership, the Army on November 15, 1889, occupied the palace and other buildings in Rio while the Emperor was at his summer residence. When later the same day Pedro returned to the capital, he found a revolutionary government installed—almost without bloodshed—and himself deposed; he left the country immediately. Meanwhile, as one of its first acts, the new provisional government had issued a proclamation announcing reorganization of the country on a federal basis.

Constitution of the Republic. For the next five years, till 1894, the government of the young republic was headed by military men, being in fact a dictatorship. The so-called military question, which had its origin in the Paraguayan war and the political role of army officers under Pedro II, has continued to plague Brazil intermittently and with varying effect. Once civilian rule was established, however, it has held its own against attempted encroachments of the military. Indeed, more recently, when authoritarian government threatened constitutional integrity, it was in part due to resistance from army quarters that the trend was checked. Therefore, it can well be said that military rule as a governmental type "never obtained a hold over the country." [6] Even after the events of 1889, the provisional (military) government undertook at once sweeping reforms aiming at a modernization of the political system and eventual constitutional consolidation. The complete separation of church and state was effected by decree in January 1890 and civil marriage instituted. Likewise, the judicial system was overhauled, and a new and humane criminal code was promulgated. On the first anniversary of Brazil's "bloodless revolution," a constituent assembly met to draft a new constitution. It was modeled on the example of the United States, and put into force February 24, 1891. Although it provided for popular and direct elections of the President, under transitional provisions the constituent assembly itself chose General Deodoro da Fonseca as first President. But he did not prove equal to his task. The Vice President, another general, served out the first presidential term under considerable friction with enemies and disillusioned adherents of the regime. When in 1894 the first popular election of a chief executive took place, the presidential office was laid into civilian hands. There it remained during the liberal republican period— with the only exception of the presidency of Marshal Hermes da Fonseca, a nephew of Deodoro, which was a dismal failure (1910-14). Even under unfavorable conditions, such as the lack of a firm federalist tradition and recurring economic difficulties, the Republic, on the whole, gave the people a sense of constitutional process that has outlasted the digressions of a later time.

The constitution transformed Brazil from a unitary state into a federal republic composed of twenty states, identical with the former provinces, and named the United States of Brazil. The functions of government were divided among its three branches.[7] The legislature consisted of a bicameral Congress—a Chamber of Deputies whose members were elected on a population basis, and a Senate with three members from each state. All elections,

---

[6] Loewenstein, *op. cit.* above, note 3, p. 15.

[7] The constitution to a large part represented the work of Ruy Barbosa, Brazil's foremost constitutional lawyer of that time, who was an admirer of North American political institutions. Besides the twenty states, the federal system comprised the Federal District with the capital, and the Federal Territory of Acre, ceded by Bolivia in 1903. Later Vargas increased the number of territories to seven by subdividing some states. But under the constitution of 1946 the number was reduced by two; Acre was promised statehood as soon as it could meet a stated financial condition.

like those for President and Vice President, were to be direct, the suffrage being extended to all male citizens twenty-one years of age. Certain qualifications, however, especially that of literacy, in practice limited the number of eligible voters to a small percentage of the population. Legislative terms were three years, but the presidential term was fixed at four, with no immediate re-eligibility of the President. As for the executive branch, its new position determined the character of the whole; the idea of parliamentary government was dropped in favor of the presidential system of the northern model. Ministers of state, or Cabinet members, were to be appointed by the President and responsible to him. The judicial system, again, resembled that of the United States. The power of judicial review was recognized and explicitly vested in the Supreme Federal Tribunal. A detailed bill of rights was attached to the constitution, and the separation of church and state was affirmed. Each state was to be "governed by the constitution and laws which it may adopt, the constitutional principles of the Union being respected." The states, in their organization, also were directed to assure "the autonomy of the municipalities in everything respecting their peculiar interests."

As is obvious from the historical circumstances, the federal form of Brazil was a reaction to the previous "highly centralized unitary type of organization." [8] The very origin of federalism, however, was closely associated with the growth of the republican idea. It is due to this direct connection, perhaps, that there was neither an assured "sovereignty" of the states with largely undefined powers, as in the North American Union, nor a strict limitation on the authority of the federal government in dealing with the states. On the contrary, the doctrine of implied powers was explicitly asserted in the constitution. Furthermore, the President was given authority to decree a state of siege, which was in fact often used to suspend civil rights in states that gave political trouble to the federal government. There was finally the interventor system, which later developed into a powerful means of enforcing the policies of an authoritarian regime. The primary purpose of the latter device was to ensure that any state contravening principles of the federal system would be put back to its proper position. In such cases the President was required to appoint a federal interventor, who superseded the state governor till conditions were remedied. On the other hand, the states had autonomy in matters that in other federal unions are delegated or reserved to the central government. Particularly, the states' right to levy tariff duties at their borders was of great consequence, since it led to rivalries amounting sometimes to economic wars within the country.

Politics and Depression. Brazil had only one permanently organized political party, called Republican, which controlled the elections. The first three civilian Presidents came from the state of São Paulo. The fourth and several later Presidents were from Minas Geraes, besides two others from

---

[8] See James, *op. cit.* above, note 3, p. 1. For the development of federalism, see also Harvey Walker, "Federalism in Brazil," *State Government,* 18 (1945), 43 ff.

the "small" states of Rio Grande do Sul and Parahyba. On the whole, the political weight had shifted from the northeast to the center and south of the country, in accordance with relative increase in population and wealth. A working arrangement was established by which leadership in federal affairs alternated between São Paulo and Minas Geraes. In both, local bosses commanded the support of party machines as well as state militias not unlike private armies. Although the interests of the smaller states were often neglected, the nation generally prospered, with coffee and—up to 1912— rubber furnishing the basis for a steady increase of exports. Moreover, under a brilliant Minister of Foreign Affairs, Baron of Rio Branco, a number of boundary disputes with other South American states were peaceably adjusted so that both the external and domestic situation of the Republic augured well for the future when World War I broke out.

The war, with grave economic dislocations due to sharp decreases in exports and imports, and the subsequent depression caused political difficulties from which Brazil never fully recovered. Coffee "valorization"—a scheme of market and price support similar to that practiced in the United States under the Agricultural Adjustment Act—had been initiated in São Paulo earlier. Since Brazilian rubber had been crowded out from the world market by the more profitable production of the Far East, the problem of coffee became still more important in the postwar depression. In 1922 valorization was instituted permanently, although without restriction on production, which had been a feature of the earlier plan. When two very large crops were followed by the collapse of world prices after Black Friday in October 1929, valorization broke down and left the country and the government in financial turmoil. Discontent was directed especially against the São Paulo faction, which happened to be in control of the central government at the time, as responsible for the failure of valorization. President Washington Luis, himself a *Paulista,* aggravated the situation by naming Julio Prestes, another man from the same state, as the official candidate for the election in 1930. Now the leaders of Minas Geraes, who considered the President's choice a violation of their arrangement with São Paulo, threw their support to the opposing candidate, Getulio Vargas, governor of the "small" state of Rio Grande do Sul and chief of the hitherto powerless Liberal party. After the election of May 1, 1930, in which Prestes was the victor, the Liberals refused to recognize the result, claiming fraud, and rebellions occurred in several states. Vargas and his followers occupied the capital and forced President Luis' resignation. On October 30, a revolutionary *junta* made Vargas provisional President of the Republic.

2. *The Vargas Dictatorship*

New Constitution. Vargas' rise to power marked the end of the hegemony of the large states. But he, who often prided himself upon his "political realism," knew perfectly well that he was in danger as long as resistance to his regime could come from uncontrollable legislatures, or from courts of law interfering with his exercise of executive power. Consequently, only a few days after his installation he issued a decree suspending the constitution and dissolving all federal, state, and municipal legislative bodies. The courts were deprived of the function of judicial review. All powers were united in the presidential office, "until a constituent assembly should deliberate on the reorganization of the country." Interventors replaced the state governors. A special court with jurisdiction over "political crimes" was to be established. The trend of things to come was indicated. For more than a year the people waited for the constituent assembly to meet, and at last rebellion flared up in São Paulo. Eventually, the promised assembly convened. The new constitution was promulgated July 16, 1934.

This constitution declared the federal republic reestablished, but in reality the powers of the states were appreciably reduced. Besides the jurisdiction over labor legislation and public lands, a great part of ordinary police power was taken away from them; and the interventor system remained. There were, however, a number of new features, some of which were concessions to the socio-democratic "spirit of the age," whereas others tended simply to preserve the predominance of executive power under the pretense of constitutionalism. Among the former may be counted the introduction of proportional representation; the enfranchisement of women and lowering of the voting age to eighteen years; the revival of ministerial responsibility to the Congress, with Cabinet ministers to appear and report whenever the Congress so demanded; and, finally, the prohibition denying re-eligibility to the President. Also, the power of the judiciary to nullify laws deemed unconstitutional was restored. As the most striking innovation ensuring the hold of the executive over the legislature, the number of popularly elected deputies in the Chamber was to be supplemented by fifty members appointed by the President from occupational panels representing agriculture, industry, commerce, public employees, the liberal professions, and workers' and employers' syndicates. Here a step was clearly taken in the direction of the corporate state of Mussolini, which was to become even more important as a model for later developments in the Vargas period.

The President's power was further enhanced by reducing the legislative functions of the first Chamber. Like the former Senate, this Chamber consisted of the representatives of the states, now only two for each, against the former three. But under the new prescription, the Chamber was to serve mainly as the *poder coordenador,* without well-defined authority. There was attached to the constitution a section on "the economic and social order," containing various items such as provisions for an eight-hour working day, a minimum wage law, and prohibition of child labor. A decidedly nationalistic tendency was manifest in the clauses restricting concessions for the exploitation of natural resources to Brazilians or Brazilian companies, curtailing the admission of foreigners to the learned professions, and setting up a quota system for immigration.

Reaching the Goal. The constitution of 1934 was in many respects a progressive document, especially in its social features. It did strengthen the powers of the federal government to the extent that little remained of a federal system, and the rigidity of presidential rule was intensified, parliamentary qualification notwithstanding. But it was a compromise product, since many of the liberal constitutionalists of the preceding period were still among the members of the constituent assembly. Vargas, it is said, did not like the new constitution; for it did not give him what he most desired or considered necessary—above all, permanency and absoluteness of his regime. As soon as the assembly had ended its work, he declared himself in favor of revision, though he did not immediately take further revolutionary action. He was elected President by the assembly, which perpetuated itself by assuming the role of the first Congress under the new constitution. But after he had crushed an allegedly Communist-inspired revolt in two eastern seaboard states, he secured late in 1935 the adoption of a constitutional amendment that gave him the power to declare "a state of grave internal commotion" whenever authorized by the Congress to do so; during such an emergency the chief executive was empowered to suspend all constitutional guarantees.[9]

The presidential election set for January 3, 1938, approached. In October 1937 Vargas requested the Congress to authorize "a state of grave internal commotion" on the contention that a "Communist revolt" was imminent. The Congress obliged, and under that authorization Vargas postponed the election. Next, on November 10, 1937, he prevented the Congress by military force from holding further sessions. He told the people by radio that he had dissolved the Congress and that the constitution of 1934 had been replaced by another one, coming into effect that same day. Thus, the *Estado Novo* (New State) was born by *coup d'état,* yet without a shot being fired and with everybody taken by surprise except a small group of insiders, among whom was Francisco Campos, Minister of Education, author of the new constitution and known for his adherence to totalitarian doctrines.

Political Reality. In restrospect, it would be easy to dismiss an analysis of the constitution of the *Estado Novo* with the remark that it was a "ghost constitution," that it existed only on paper, and that its essential provisions never attained living reality.[10] What the constitution really amounted to was revealed in its concluding article, where, among other things, a state of national emergency was declared as part of the constitution. The end of the emergency therefore was made dependent on the adoption of a constitu-

---

[9] The view that at least at that time the "communist" danger was used as a pretext but had little reality is supported by several authorities. Writing in 1941, Hubert Herring, in his *Good Neighbors* (New Haven, 1941), p. 139, says: "In reading Brazilian news, bear in mind that all enemies of Vargas are 'communists.'" See also Loewenstein, *op. cit.* above, note 3, pp. 30 ff.

[10] See Loewenstein, *op. cit.* above, note 3, especially 46 ff., for an exhaustive and thoughtful presentation of Vargas' first regime in its several aspects. Since no incisive change took place in the remaining years of the dictatorship, that work—written in 1942—may be considered the classic on this period of Brazil's political history in the English language.

tional amendment. Elections for a new legislature, which would have to collaborate in the amending process, could not take place before the constitution had been accepted by a plebiscite. But when, or whether at all, the President would order such a plebiscite nobody knew. Unlimited in time, the state of emergency was unlimited in scope as well. For, "until the National Parliament meets," said the constitution, "the President of the Republic shall be empowered to issue decrees on all matters of legislation for the Union." These simple words, Loewenstein has pointed out, embodied the essence of the *Estado Novo,* and the other 186 articles were "legal camouflage." President Vargas was the constitution and "the law." Still, more than paper existence must be attributed to the written document where, and to whatever extent, the program of social aims proclaimed through the constitution was given material fulfillment. And this actually was a good deal.

Irrespective of Vargas' intent, there were several circumstances that might have defeated any sustained effort to implement his "grand design." In particular, for the greater part of his rule World War II intervened, which threw its shadow far ahead. Vargas also faced economic problems of grave urgency—problems still hanging over from World War I and aggravated by the world depression. Both factors were intertwined in political unrest that led to renewed internal friction when the year 1938 opened. A Brazilian fascist movement, called Integralist, had been breeding on middle-class discontent since the early thirties and gained considerable following in later years. Operating quite in the open and using the well-known trappings of fascist mysticism—including a green version of the ubiquitous fascist shirt as well as anti-Semitic slogans—it felt encouraged by the authoritarian character of the regime. In the latent conflict between world powers, Vargas, the leaders of the movement hoped and thought, was veering to the Axis side. There is no doubt that the movement was supported by the German government, through its embassy in Rio, and by German and other pro-Axis elements within the country.

Vargas, however, had early cast Brazil's lot with the United States and waited his opportunity to strangle the home-grown fascist hydra. Political parties had been forbidden by decree in December 1937, and political activity by foreigners was strongly curtailed a few months later.[11] As they

---

[11] The decree-law prohibiting political parties made Brazil in fact a nonparty state, in contrast to the one-party system of the major fascist countries. Subsequently, many additional measures for the control of aliens, for the "Brazilianization" of the large groups of foreign stock, especially the German and Italian element in the southern states, and for the "nationalization" of economic life were taken. Nationalization, however, meant merely the ownership of national resources by Brazilian nationals and did not imply collective or government ownership; on the whole, economic liberalism remained the determining outlook of the regime. For details, see Loewenstein, *op. cit.* above, note 3, pp. 133-211. Some of the more stringent measures were obviously conditioned by the war and were therefore of a transitory nature. Several were tacitly rescinded in the constitution of 1946, though others left a lasting impress on Brazilian life—e.g., the one ordaining that primary schooling shall be given only in the national (Portuguese) language, which has been affirmed in the post-Vargas constitution of 1946.

sensed the true nature of Vargas' feelings toward them, the *Integralistas* became his most active enemies. In May 1938 they struck, trying to seize the presidential palace and the dictator himself, but the revolt resulted in woeful failure. The German Ambassador now was declared *persona non grata* and sent home. These events eliminated the last organized opposition. At about the same time the economic situation was relieved through far-reaching measures. By changing control methods and reducing certain taxes, the government permitted the price of coffee to fall, which encouraged exports and restored a larger share of the world market to Brazilian producers than had been theirs since early depression days. But in the following year the European phase of World War II put new strains on the Brazilian economic and social system.

Aims, Methods, and Instrumentalities. A strong tradition of legalism, which is an attribute of all Latin American nations and the Brazilian in particular, required that even Vargas' personal regime be clothed with the symbols and appurtenances of lawfulness. In this regard, the constitution of 1937 provided everything that was necessary, and more than that. Legalistic verbiage reached a point where, at least to foreign observers, it appeared as if only cynicism could account for the ingenuity of constitutional construction. What Vargas presumably had in mind was, above all, a thoroughgoing modernization of his country, which would enable the Brazilian people to make full use of their natural opportunities, to reach higher standards of living and education, and to secure for themselves a better and more influential position in the hemispheric concert and among the nations of the world. Impatient with the vagaries of the democratic process, he often avowed his belief in the need for "streamlining" government in accordance with blueprints evolved by the contemporary dictators of Europe. He sided with the latter when they claimed that democracy was a good thing for the well-to-do and saturated peoples of the earth, but that others had to toil and sweat under strict "social discipline" if they would ever achieve a position where they could afford such "luxury." He did not, however, subscribe to the tenets of totalitarianism as a way of life, although some of his most prominent followers no doubt did. The easygoing character of the Brazilians and their sense of esthetic values would have been a formidable barrier to the "total state," and the dictator-realist was aware of those *imponderabilia*.

To accomplish his aims, Vargas did better than merely proclaim absolute rule by the "President." According to the constitution, the chief executive was to be elected for six years indirectly, through an electoral college, and might succeed himself; he also could nominate his successor. Indirect elections were likewise reintroduced for the Chamber of Deputies, whereas the Federal Council—formerly the Senate—was in part to be appointed by the President. A National Economic Council, composed of employers and employees, was to advise the Congress and the President on economic and social matters. The longest article of the constitution dealt with rights of the individual, giving a long list of them. Twenty articles concerned the "economic order." They were followed by special provisions about public officials, national security and defense, and one on constitutional amendments. As far as constitutional limitations through elective bodies were concerned, however, they were illusory because none of the legislative organs "created" by the constitution were ever set up—with the exception of a committee that functioned during the last years of the regime as a semblance of the proposed National Economic Council. Legislatures in the states and municipalities also had ceased to exist. Constitutional guarantees and rights for the individual were limited "by the exigencies of the safety of the State and the Nation," and altogether suspended under the state of emergency lasting to the end of the *Estado Novo*. In fact, during the emergency the President was empowered to detain or banish from the country, without trial, anyone suspected as "dangerous," to censor all communications, written or oral, and suppress the right of assembly.

Under these conditions Brazil was entirely ruled by executive decree. Legislative and executive functions were fused in the hands of the central government, with corresponding effects on the states. The interventor system was retained and extended. The position of the interventors was legalized by a special decree-law issued in 1939, which showed a striking similarity to the system in Nazi Germany. In each state administrative departments were set up. They performed a supervisory function on behalf of federal executive departments and assisted the interventor—as a "political" official directly responsible to the President—with technical advice and services. The administrative departments in the states also controlled the municipalities. Prefects, appointed by the interventors, had the same position as the latter in the states. These measures spelled the end of state and local self-government. Moreover, a large number of commissions, councils, and executive boards with jurisdiction in various fields—such as several industries, labor, immigration and colonization, and sports—played an important part.

Among the "independent agencies" of this kind, the Department of Public Administration, popularly known as DASP *(Departamento administrativo do Serviço Publico)*, was outstanding because of its central position in the administrative establishment and its accomplishments. It was a central staff agency for the management of the Brazilian civil service, but its functions were broader than those of the United States Civil Service Commission in that it was charged also with other functions, such as continuous study of the structural organization of the government and the maintenance of liaison with the public, receiving complaints and suggestions for the entire administration. Owing to the establishment of DASP, the Vargas regime was generally credited with a serious attempt to introduce modern administrative methods to Brazil.[12] The "legislative" and ordinance-making activity

---

[12] Walker, *loc. cit.* above, note 8, concludes: "It is high time we began to study Brazilian progress [in civil service reform] as an index to future action in our own United States." A

of the central government and its agencies reached huge proportions; Loewenstein found that early in 1942 the number of federal decrees had long passed the four-thousand mark. More important from the long-range viewpoint, the regime effected a comprehensive reform and unification of the legal codes, criminal and civil, including commercial law, and the codes for the administration of natural resources, mining, fishing, and other matters.[13]

Social and Economic Reforms. In accordance with the precepts of modern dictatorship, the *Estado Novo* employed special devices to safeguard its security against enemies of the regime, and to control public opinion on whose support it depended for undisturbed existence as well as for the execution of its reform program. Although the Tribunal of National Security (*Segurança*) antedated the *Estado Novo* by more than a year and originally was to deal with crimes against the external security of the state, it was clearly established to bolster dictatorial rule. To serve this purpose better, its jurisdiction was later enlarged to embrace all sorts of "political crimes," such as "conspiracy" against "the public powers," and its status changed to that of a "permanent institution." Apologists of the regime and cautious legalists have pointed to the comparatively mild practice of the court and absence of the worst abuses such as have characterized analogous tribunals in other authoritarian countries. But there is no doubt that the legislation on which the *Segurança* based its activity sharply departed from the rule of law of which Brazilians had once been proud. Yet the dictator never failed to realize that at least as important as measures of suppression was the management, if not outright manipulation, of public opinion. Therefore, another agency, the Department of Press and Propaganda, was charged with the task of "public enlightenment" and of enforcing censorship of the press by application of a code which, on the face of it, made every journalist or editor an agent of the government. Although uniformity of view was not demanded, there were many ways to compel compliance with official policies.

realistic appraisal would seem to be that by Loewenstein, *op. cit.* above, note 3, p. 105. At any rate, DASP gave convincing proof of Vargas' zeal for improvement of administration. Students looking for more detailed information on the administrative organization and methods of modern Brazil will find such material in F. Morstein Marx and Bryce Wood, "The Brazilian Civil Service," *Inter-American Quarterly*, 2, no. 4 (1940), 42 ff; Loewenstein, pp. 59 ff.; H. Reining, Jr., "The Brazilian Program of Administrative Reform," *American Political Science Review*, 39 (1945), 536 ff.; Harvey Walker, trans., and Arizio de Viana, *Budget-Making in Brazil* (Columbus, O., 1947). Current volumes of the *Handbook of Latin American Studies* (annually since 1936, Harvard University Press) should be scanned for relevant titles in English and Portuguese.

[13] Although the *Estado Novo* is gone, its administrative and legal attainments have endured to the extent that agency activities and legislative enactments were found compatible with the new constitution of 1946. This means, in effect, that the Vargas codes have been kept in force, with certain exceptions, and that many of the executive boards and commissions, especially DASP, are still in existence, though their authority is in general restricted to advisory and planning functions. The administration of justice, in its various branches—including the power of judicial review, inherent in the Brazilian system since the beginning of the Republic—has of course been freed from the encumbrances of "interpretative legislation" and other interference on the part of the executive.

Likewise, in tune with Vargas' oft-proclaimed admiration for Franklin D. Roosevelt's New Deal and his own intention to raise the living standard of the Brazilian people,[14] the regime was extremely active in promoting economic and social advancement. It is difficult to assess the share of the Vargas government in the upsurge of business activity that marked the immediate prewar years in various industries—as building and mining—and in some branches of agriculture. But the government did take effective measures to help industrialization, such as the founding in 1940 of a steel industry with assistance from the United States Export-Import Bank; to improve production methods in agriculture through scientific research, internal colonization, and reclamation; and to advance communications. Even greater efforts were directed toward social reforms. It is in this sphere that the regime seemed most visibly to emulate the principles of "corporativism" as practiced in Mussolini's Italy, but in addition other contemporary examples—including that of the United States—stimulated Brazilian legislation.

A Ministry of Labor was established early. Although the proposed syndical organization of capital and labor remained largely in the blueprint state, strikes and lockouts were forbidden. Decree-laws modernizing labor conditions were issued and a number of social services established, which have given the workers a limited sense of security—at least in urbanized regions reached by the arm of supervisory governmental agencies. A minimum wage law had been enacted in 1936; it was incorporated in the constitution and reinforced by later decree legislation. Paid vacations; protection against dismissal without indemnity, except for cause; maximum hours; higher wages in industries classified as unhealthful; retirement allowances; limitation of child labor; assistance to pregnant working women and families in general—these were some of the benefits secured to Brazilian labor by the Vargas administration. They account to no small extent for Vargas' popularity among the masses over many years. Finally, as the capping piece, a system of labor courts and boards of conciliation, with a Superior Labor Court at the top, was instituted to administer justice in industrial disputes. Thus, labor relations were placed on a par with the most important branches of the law. Indeed, the system of labor courts—with all the social reforms just mentioned—was included in the new constitution which replaced the document of 1937 after Vargas' fall.

3. Toward Limited Democracy

Vargas' Fall. In the dynamism of its economic and social policies lay the secret of the success of Vargas' "administrative state." Whether the regime actually accomplished a social revolution of incisive importance is a moot question. Social equality has been one of the most conspicuous traits of Brazilian life since the days of Pedro II, in spite of glaring economic differ-

---

[14] In a manifesto of June 1934, Vargas declared: "There are in Brazil three fundamental problems on whose solution progress depends: health, education, and population."

ences. But widespread illiteracy—still at least 55 per cent in 1950—greatly qualifies even now the political attitudes of Brazilians, although under Vargas elementary education was by law free and compulsory, and notable efforts were made to enforce minimum standards. Moreover, the country is still predominantly agricultural, notwithstanding its rapid progress in industrialization. It is hence not surprising that active opposition to the long-entrenched dictatorship crystallized in one of the groups that had been traditionally articulate in politics. There was considerable restlessness in the Army and in the populace at large, especially among students, when in the winter of 1944-45 it became increasingly doubtful whether Vargas would fulfill his promise to hold elections as soon as the war was over. In addition, people were harassed by thoughts of new and even greater economic difficulties. The war had brought prosperity to some and a somewhat higher living standard to many, but all realized that adjustment to peacetime economy would be particularly hard for Brazil as a producer of goods that would have no market in an impoverished Europe. Brazil being the only Latin American country that had dispatched combat troops to Europe,[15] the Army was naturally filled with pride, and intent on making its voice heard in decisions on the future.

Vargas was urged from several quarters to return to constitutional government. He finally yielded, naming December 2, 1945, as the day on which a constituent assembly was to be elected, and declaring that he was not a presidential candidate. He also removed restrictions on the freedom of the press and assembly and released political prisoners. With his Cabinet he agreed that General Eurico Gaspar Dutra, the Minister of War who had helped usher in the dictatorship, should become his successor. The opponent was General Eduardo Gomes, who voiced the suspicion that Dutra would merely act as a "front" for his "boss" and continue the latter's policies. Both candidates offered liberal platforms to the public. Still, a number of military leaders doubted the seriousness of Vargas' intentions. On October 29 their troops occupied all strategic buildings in the capital, and an officers' delegation "suggested" to Vargas that he relinquish office immediately. Vargas complied. The Chief Justice took over temporarily, securing full freedom for the elections, which were held on the appointed day. For the first time the suffrage as broadened by the constitution of 1934 was in use, producing an electorate three times as large as in any previous election.[16] Vargas' man, General Dutra, won. He was inaugurated as the new President on

---

[15] Brazil declared war on the Axis in August 1942. Military cooperation with the United States for hemisphere defense had begun as early as 1939; it became extremely close in later years when Brazil granted air and naval bases in its territory and its naval forces patroled the South Atlantic. Early in 1944 an expeditionary force of two divisions was landed in Naples, Italy, where it entered the fight on the side of the United States Fifth Army. As regards United States lend-lease, Brazil ranked fifth of all nations; its share was about $320,000,000.

[16] In 1922, in a population of more than 30 million, only 1,306,000 were registered voters. Out of 47 million, 7,500,000 went to the polls in 1945.

January 31, 1946. The constituent assembly went to work writing a new constitution. It was promulgated September 18, 1946, "in the 125th year of Independence and the 58th of the Republic." The assembly continued itself as the first Congress.

Back to Federalism. Dutra's Social Democratic party had control of both houses of the Congress; it was therefore mainly responsible for undoing what was objectionable in the *Estado Novo.* Political activity having been revived, the majority party was faced by opposition parties on the right and left: a National Democratic Union whose leader was the speaker of the Chamber of Deputies, Octavio Mangaveira; and a Labor party led by Vargas, now a senator from his home state. Vargas soon turned against his former associate, the new chief executive. The new constitution, however, had revived the principal features of the old republic. The interventors in the Vargas version were gone, having made room for state governors and legislatures elected by the people. Gone were presidential authoritarianism, centralized administration with its claim to exclusiveness, and—most important for the citizen—the *Segurança* and other "constitutional" encroachments upon the rights of the individual. "The United States of Brazil," said the first article of the constitution, "under the representative system maintain the Federation and the Republic."

To be sure, there was no going back to the type of extreme decentralization that had been the misfortune of pre-Vargas federalism. The interventor system as such was not abolished. But it was strictly circumscribed as to its conditions—mainly the maintenance of constitutional guaranties and legal process, the preservation of the financial integrity of the states, and the suppression of civil war—and as to the methods of its implementation and control by the legislative power. The once vexing problem of tariff duties levied by the states was settled by a compromise, with the states allowed to tax exports of their production abroad up to a maximum of 5 per cent *ad valorem.* This change was an improvement even over the Vargas constitution, which had permitted 10 per cent, but it is held to be inadequate by those who would rather have that state privilege done away with altogether. The Union has the power over foreign relations, war and peace, defense, amnesty, drought and flood control, postal services and communications, the "national plan of transport," and the right to grant concessions for development in the two latter fields. Further, the Union retained exclusive power of legislation in all matters covered by the civil, penal, and procedural codes, and as regards electoral and labor law. The same rule applied to expropriation, coastwise shipping, foreign and interstate commerce, money and credit, naturalization and the admission of foreigners, and conditions for the exercise of the professions. But the states govern themselves by their own constitutions and laws, since to each state all powers are reserved "which are not implicitly or explicitly forbidden" by the federal constitution. In many matters the Union and the states have concurrent powers; certain taxing rights—besides that on exports abroad—are reserved for the states. The autonomy of municipalities is likewise ensured, the constitution regulating the major aspects of their relations with the states.[17]

Other Features of the Constitution. It is evident that the new constitution builds upon its predecessors, especially those of 1891 and 1934; but even the constitution of 1937 yielded some significant incentives. The new constitution has 218 articles, but its language is on the whole concise and to the point. Its main provisions regarding suffrage were taken over from the document of 1934, and the system of proportional representation has been retained. Registration and voting are compulsory for both sexes. No immediate re-election of the President and Vice President, and of governors and mayors, is permitted. All elective officials in the Union and in the states, including the President, hold office for five years, whereas legislative periods last four. The arrangement for three senators from each state was restored, the senatorial mandate being for eight years, with membership of the Senate renewable every four years "alternately one-third and two-thirds at a time." The President appoints and dismisses his ministers of state. But several features of parliamentary government have been reintroduced and even been made more explicit. A member of the Congress when appointed minister does not lose his mandate, although his status becomes inactive. Ministers of state may be called before either house for report, and may also on their own initiative appear to request legislative measures. Ministers "are responsible for the acts they may sign, even though jointly with the President of the Republic, or for measures which they may take by his order."

The power of judicial review is defined in considerable detail; and besides the labor courts, permanent electoral courts have been set up. "Individual rights and guarantees" are enumerated at length. Although religious freedom and the separation of church and state are maintained and "marriage shall be civil," marriage is declared indissoluble and "is entitled to the special protection of the state," in accordance with traditional views of the people. Military or equivalent civilian service is compulsory for all Brazilians of both sexes.

Rejection of Laissez Faire and Restrictions on Democracy. Of major interest are some provisions that either utilize ideas introduced into constitutional practice by Vargas or are designed to protect the Republic against a repetition of the experience under that regime. One of these provisions concerns the freedom of thought and of the press. Censorship is abolished, except that "propaganda for war or violent processes to overthrow the political and social order, or prejudices of race or of class shall not be tolerated." But no taxes may be levied from the incomes of teachers and journalists or authors' royalties, since the advancement of cultural standards is a matter of concern to the state.

---

[17] An English translation of the constitution will be found in Russell H. Fitzgibbon, ed., *The Constitutions of the Americas* (Chicago, 1948).

Vargas' plan to make functional (occupational) representation part of the Brazilian system of government is preserved to some extent. A National Council of Economy has been created, its members being appointed by the President with the approval of the Senate. Its functions are "to study the economic life of the country and to . . . suggest measures that the council may deem necessary." A separate section on the "economic and social order" shows a blending of nationalistic ideas with those of state socialism. The right of property is guaranteed, and no expropriation may take place without compensation. But "the use of property shall be conditioned upon social welfare," and the law "may promote the fair distribution of property, with equal opportunities for all." Certain industries and activities may be monopolized by the Union in the public interest. The rights to subsoil wealth are declared to be distinct from surface rights. Concessions for the exploitation of mineral resources and water power "shall be granted exclusively to Brazilians, or to concerns organized in the country." Likewise, all media for the distribution of news must be owned and directed by Brazilians. Legislation dealing with labor and social security is to be governed fully by the principles enunciated in laws decreed by Vargas' former administration, except that the right to strike is recognized, as is that to "professional or syndical association" and collective bargaining.

Political association and organization, however, has recently pointed up peculiar problems. Brazil's history of the last two decades had offered warning examples of how political liberty might be abused to undermine and destroy the very system of which it is the guardian. In writing the new constitution, legislators therefore thought it wise to hedge that liberty with protective restrictions. The constitution says: "The organization, registration, or functioning of any political party or association whose program or action may be contrary to the democratic regime based upon plurality of parties and the guarantee of the fundamental rights of men, is prohibited." Under this provision the Tribunal of Elections, on request by the government, in May 1947 declared the Communist party illegal in Brazil. Later the Congress approved a measure removing from office all persons elected on the party's ticket, which deprived eighteen Communist senators and deputies in the Congress and sixty members of various state legislatures of their mandates. Their leader, Senator Luis Carlos Prestes, went into hiding.[18] The

[18] Vargas was publicly accused of having made common cause with Communists in his home state, Rio Grande do Sul, in order to wrest power from the Dutra forces in control of the state government. The Communist vote had been 586,000—or 8 per cent of the total—in the national elections of December 1945. The Communists' position became more precarious as time went on. A plea for permission to preserve their party as a "civil society" was denied by the Supreme Court; and in October 1948 an investigation of alleged Soviet spying in Brazil led to the arrest of more than one hundred persons. Nevertheless Communist support was said to have played a role in the election of Vargas to the presidency in 1950. This, however, did not prevent him from declaring war on communism at once after his election and from subscribing to Western Hemisphere commitments for the strengthening of internal security against its threat.

constitution would also make it possible, in face of "serious domestic commotion, or facts evidencing its imminence," to invoke martial law, now placed under elaborate legal safeguards. Another safety valve would now finally seem to exist in the power of the federal government to "expel from the national territory any foreigner injurious to the public order . . . ." As in so many other matters, here again the parallel to a clause of the Mexican constitution of 1917 is striking.

4. Current Tendencies

Postwar Crisis. As Brazil was putting its new constitution to the test, political unrest was feeding anew on postwar difficulties. Like other Latin American countries, Brazil had carried a heavy burden of economic aid to the Allied powers during World War II. Its minerals and agricultural produce had been of inestimable value; its industries were geared to war needs; and its civilian population had undergone considerable privations, mainly because of lack of imports. But economic dislocations were greater than the people had realized. True, much money had been made by individuals as well as by the national treasury, in the form of both profits and a large balance in gold and foreign exchange. As war purchases shrank, however, and urgently necessary replacements in the domestic economy were made, dollar reserves declined rapidly. They dropped from an estimated $800,000,000 at the war's close to less than $100,000,000 by mid-1947, forcing the government to resume control of all export-import operations. Inflation and unemployment increased, while the purchasing power of wages steadily diminished. In short, the country sank deeper and deeper into an economic crisis of serious proportions, aggravated by lack of food and transportation.

No wonder, then, that the political balance, too, was disturbed. Brazil turned into a fertile ground for Communist agitation; and Vargas, whose social reforms had not been forgotten by the masses, was still a factor in the political scene. In trying to weather the storm, President Dutra had Congress adopt a five-year plan for development, including mechanization of agriculture and promotion of immigration, while a United States-Brazilian commission worked out ways for attracting new foreign investments. But in the election of October 3, 1950, the impatience of the electorate with delays in the execution of the program became manifest. Vargas, by appealing to the discontented, succeeded in bringing about a landslide vote of 3.8 million in favor of his Labor party and himself, against 2.3 for General Eduardo Gomes, his opponent on the right, with the "official" candidate running a poor third.

Foreign Policy. With its prestige and political position in the world of states Brazil could be well satisfied. Its long-standing rivalry with Argentina had been soothed by the traditional restraint of Brazilian diplomacy and by efforts to establish closer cooperation in fields where the economies of both countries are complementary. Relations with other neighbors and the

United States had been cemented by wartime collaboration. As in the case of Mexico, these relations were governed by mutual commitments entered into at the various Pan-American conferences, especially the Charter of the Organization of American States adopted at Bogotá on May 1, 1948. In the United Nations, Brazil played an active and important role from the beginning. It was elected twice (1946 and 1950) to a nonpermanent seat in the Security Council, became a member of the Economic and Social Council, and participated in efforts to find solutions for the problem of Greece and the dispute between Great Britain and Egypt. At the United Nations Conference on Trade and Employment in Havana (1947), Brazil's policy was that of solidarity with the aspirations of Latin America as a whole, as it has later stressed the need for "reciprocal cooperation" with the United States against one-sided Latin American economic commitments.

The dark spot in this panorama of amiable relationships was Brazil's relation to Soviet Russia. Late in 1946, an incident involving a member of the Brazilian Embassy in Moscow caused anti-Russian riots in Rio de Janeiro. The situation was made worse by mutual recriminations and rising Communist activity in Brazil. On October 21, 1947, Brazil broke with the Soviet Union, asking the Soviet diplomats in Rio to leave the country. The action was but another sign pointing toward a solid front of Latin American nations against Soviet attempts to establish an operating basis for Communist expansion in the Western Hemisphere. In the Far Eastern situation, too, Brazil sided wholeheartedly with the United States, granting a credit to South Korea and remaining opposed to UN membership of Red China.

Summary and Prospects. Brazil's road has been different from the one taken by Mexico. It was only late that circumstances had compelled Brazil to face fully the problems of popular rule. Institutional development in the country had then attained, however, a level where the transition to democratic government no longer involved a radical break with the past. The monarchy established on home ground had fulfilled a carry-over function wanting in other Latin American nations. Moreover, gradually widening experience enabled the dominant class to assume the responsibility that rightfully goes with power. Yet economic and social progress was not long in demanding its due. In the aftermath of war and depression, when existing political machinery seemed unsuited to master the difficulties, the stage was set for experimentation with a "new order" in which social and economic considerations were assigned a conspicuous place. This reversal, perhaps, could be accomplished only under the extremity of dictatorship. Whatever the appraisal of Vargas' case, Brazil was again fortunate in that his regime did not impair the essentially democratic spirit of the Brazilian people. Brazil saved itself for a new era of constitutional government.

A constitution has come to life. It represents a trend toward state socialism, with a nationalistic bent, as initiated by Mexico and increasingly followed by other nations of Hispanic America. The question now arising was how strong in such a setting democratic forms and institutions would prove to be and, in particular, what power of resistance to totalitarian assaults from left and right they might develop under the stress of emergency. Much of Brazil's future would depend on whether its federal system can be effective or whether state rivalries under local bossism will continue to be ruinous.

On the economic front, the treatment accorded foreign capital will perhaps be decisive for the country's further evolution. That Brazil would hold its own against political encroachments if such be attempted by foreign interests seems beyond doubt. But the question of the internal role of the military must yet find a definitive answer if the framework of the present constitution is to endure. Success of the vast development program would offer the best chance for the people to rally in decisive support of civil government. When on January 31, 1951, Vargas as the new president had taken the oath of office, promising "to maintain, defend and fulfill the Constitution of the Republic," he formed a coalition government and placated former opponents through suitable appointments, even to Cabinet posts. His predecessor, General Dutra, came in for lavish praise for heading an administration that was honest and culminated in a "model election." Vargas himself voiced his intent of leading Brazil along the path of orderly evolution, following the examples of Britain and Scandinavia, and thus quieted both the conservative element and those progressives who were apprehensive of his opportunism and former dictatorial zeal.

No doubt the political climate had changed since re-establishment of the republican regime, and certainly the people had no desire for another "great experiment." General conditions, however, were tense and, as the President warned, not auspicious for the "miracles" that the public might have expected of him. Vargas asked Congress for emergency powers to meet economic stringencies caused by the tightening world situation, in which Brazil again was to become an important source of raw materials. At the same time he stressed his wish to intensify cooperation with the United States so as to secure for Brazil the full benefits of President Truman's Point Four program and United Nations technical assistance, especially with respect to the country's agricultural and mineral resources, its transportation system, and the people's health.[19] Ultimate success of Vargas' new administration and, perhaps, the fate of the republic would therefore seem to be contingent also on constructive policies on the part of the United States.[20]

---

[19] For an analysis of Vargas' return to power, see C. H. Haring, "Vargas Returns in Brazil," *Foreign Affairs*, 29 (1951), 308 ff.

[20] The following works, recently published, supply further material on governmental structure and current problems, national and international: Asher N. Christensen, ed., *The Evolution of Latin American Government: A Book of Readings* (New York, 1951); Austin F. Macdonald, *Latin American Politics and Government* (New York, 1949); Arthur P. Whitaker, "Development of American Regionalism: The Organization of American States," *International Conciliation*, No. 469 (March, 1951). A revised edition of William L. Schurz' book, cited above, p. 626, note 2, appeared in 1949.

PART IX

SOVEREIGNTY—ROAD BLOCK
OR STEPPING STONE?

CHAPTER 33

THE CHANGING FACE OF THE NATION-STATE

1. The Governing and the Governed

Growth of National Power. A report on the political behavior of man at the midway mark of the twentieth century would not be seriously incomplete if it confined itself to one pivotal fact. This fact, indeed, is equally self-evident to large masses of people of quite different color, talking quite different languages, and living in quite different parts of the globe. It is the fact that the basic form of political organization is the nation-state—equipped with more power than it ever had before over the affairs of the individual; magnetically pulled, as it were, toward one or the other great constellation of world power; and almost wholly lost to the idea of a single family of nations still so common at the beginning of the century.

The promise of world government, twice bursting into bloom in the immediate aftermath of World War I and World War II, twice wilted quickly in its exposure to the stark realities of postwar international politics. Meanwhile, the mounting burdens of public responsibility, under conditions of an industrial economy both highly organized and very sensitive to disturbances, have continued to fall to national government, steadily adding to its primary role. To the same extent the significance of national subdivisions—such as member states, regions, provinces, districts, counties, and municipalities—has shrunk in the individual's scale of highest needs. In the unabated shift of influence, usually effected without formal revision of the existing distribution of legal authority, national government has been the winner, government on lower levels the loser. Industrial society projects its problems across the whole country. In a national economy, such matters as bank credit, collective bargaining, social security, and price development necessarily extend beyond the local sphere.

Weakness of Popular Control. The unarrested ascendancy of national government broadly parallels a tendency toward concentration of economic control over mass production. Both tendencies are sufficiently marked to remain conspicuous despite their commonplace character. The political implications of these interrelated developments, in turn, are sufficiently thought-provoking to bring to the fore a host of uneasy questions about the position of the individual face to face with national government. The individual's dependence on national government—for prosperity, for a living wage or a benefit payment in lieu of it, for industrial peace, for national secu-

681

rity—has constantly increased. Yet to the same degree that national government has grown to ever more gigantic proportions, the individual, as a political factor, has become an ever tinier dwarf.

For one thing, the more vitally important the integrated contributions of effective government become for each citizen in the machine age, and the more such integration calls for action on the national plane, the less opportunity remains for him to take part in this kind of action. He may feel far removed from the processes by which public policy is determined and those in charge of executing it are kept answerable for their conduct. This dichotomy of need for national government and weakness of control over it is widely sensed today. It has caused increasing anxiety over the gulf between government—more concretely, national government—and the individual, an anxiety shared by both those governing and those governed. From it has risen a strong and almost universal incentive toward critical examination of the workings of modern government.

Pressing Questions. Significantly, such questions are by no means alien to political systems that operate on the totalitarian formula, though there most of the questions take on a sharper emphasis. How thick are the wads of bureaucratic inertia that citizens have to penetrate in seeking modifications in the direction of policy or in the methods of administration or in getting attention for their complaints? How badly hamstrung is the manager of a collective enterprise, looking to the needs of local consumers, by orders and regulations coming down to him from the distant seat of higher control? How effective is the political party in establishing connections between the mass of the people and the machinery of government? How close can the political leadership feel itself to be to the public mind?

An accurate answer would say much about the specific measure of civic cohesion in the one-party state. But in somewhat different form each question can also serve as a test of representative government in free societies. The reason is obvious—both totalitarianism and democracy operate under the cloak of the sovereign nation-state.

Unsolved Problems. Each of these queries points to the central issue of man's relationship with a political structure of extraordinary complexity, extending its levels of decision so high as to make them seem entirely outside his reach. Is the individual irrevocably reduced to the disappointing choice between the greater and the lesser evil on election day? Is he discovering to his horror that while being pronounced sovereign in ceremonial speeches he has actually become the helpless victim of the nation-state? Different political systems, of course, will leave him different degrees of freedom publicly to raise these questions and to attempt an answer. Whatever the range of such freedom, it can hardly be denied that the national integration of government on a unified territorial basis, in combination with the widening functions and responsibilities of public agencies in the affairs of the people, poses a problem crucial to the future of the nation-state.

As it has been in past decades, this problem may be expected to cause everywhere more or less extensive experimentation with a variety of political devices that promise to narrow the chasm between the state and the individual. Here it is more important, however, to bear in mind that the nation-state, though as familiar to modern man as his daily bread, has not yet succeeded in solving its own internal problems. This deficiency grows manifest when we raise the question of the inner balance among the principal organs of national government.

Legislative-Executive Relations. The requirements of balance are nowhere more consequential than in the relations between the legislative power and the executive power. Small wonder that the problem of these requirements, touching as it does the essence of constitutional government, has been pressing toward the forefront of public debate in many countries. But the persistence of the problem is evident not only in political systems built upon the principle of a separation of powers. Even where an institutional separation is lacking, as is the case typically under totalitarian regimes, the residual question of securing enough of an effective equilibrium between representative capacity and executive decision has long plagued political leaders.

Dictatorial supremacy of action may be worth the gamble when speed is the overriding need. But freedom of determination on the part of the leadership may all too easily turn into a cause of disaster when in the making of decisions no firm contact is maintained with the body of public thought. If one were to spot the most outstanding weakness of totalitarianism at any particular point, the point to be mentioned first would be the perilous isolation in which the small nucleus of men exercising highest power reaches its final decisions. The danger of such isolation, once again, puts in sharp relief the fundamental function of the party in the one-party state. As the controlling value of a popularly elected legislature lies not in its wisdom but in its representative character, so the single party is hopefully expected to transmit the sense of the people to the political leadership.

The most alert single party, however, could hardly overcome the deep-freeze effects of the approved political faith upon the people's mind. Totalitarianism, with the executive power as its mainstay, may well claim to be strong in the immediate effectiveness of governmental action. It is distinctly weak in the fragmentary nature of its representative qualities—the popular foundation of its legislative power. The political astuteness of totalitarianism is not broader than the vision and judgment of a handful of leaders who can seek reinforcement only in their best guess at the thinking of the people. By comparison, constitutional government shows far greater strength in making the legislative power the organ of the electorate, thus insuring a high degree of support for public policy in the political sense of the people. Constitutional government has its Achilles' heel in the slowness and fumbling that often mark its utilization of the executive power.

Evolution of the Executive Power. In modern constitutional government, the relationship between the legislative and executive branches has been greatly affected by the steady expansion of governmental functions.[1] This development, involving for the most part the permanent provision of organized administrative activities, has proportionately raised the political stature of the executive branch. Ministering to the needs of various groups of citizens, executive agencies have grown into informed spokesmen of these needs, thus competing with legislators in the inauguration of policy. Moreover, in comparison with the lawmaking branch, the functional responsibilities of executive agencies have led to increased expertship in both subject-matter knowledge and in getting things done. A corollary has been too much diffusion in planning. In order to render possible a responsible general direction and coordination of so many governmental activities, old and new, ways had to be found to strengthen the hand of the constitutional chief executive himself.

The most direct way of making the constitutional chief executive more nearly equal to his tasks has been the creation of staff offices around him. The common rationale of these staff offices is to aid the chief executive in the managerial coordination of all the administrative agencies under his control and in integrating their policies into a coherent government-wide program. Such program and planning staffs, drawing on the knowledge and experience of the entire executive branch, have usually made their entry in budgeting and economic analysis. They have added to the competence of the executive power for assuming the initiative in recommending legislative policy, in particular when the legislature lacks comparable facilities. Seen in broad outline, the constitutional status of the legislative branch as the highest policy-approving body has remained intact. But the logic of dynamic tendencies has produced a shift in responsibility for shaping up governmental programs from the legislative to the executive branch.

It is revealing of the uneasy retrospection characteristic of the current phase of the nation-state that this evolution has often been lamented as an executive usurpation of functions of analysis and planning that are declared to be part and parcel of the legislative process. The lament, it is true, has not made it any less plain that the executive branch is best qualified to present to the legislature, for its consideration and action, an integrated government-wide program based upon the pooled knowledge of governmental administrators and experts. Save under conditions of true cabinet government where the matter is largely academic, the question whether planning and program-making should be organized under legislative or executive auspices is one often regarded as controversial. Besides suggesting differences among levels within the planning process, the alternative raises some issues of respective technical efficiency. Its greatest importance, however, lies in the potential challenge that any executive monopoly of policy would pose to the representative role of the legislative branch. In oversimplified terms, the alternative

---

[1] See above, chap. 1, "Man and the State," sec. 1, "The Value of Comparison."

is sometimes reduced to either having the citizen tell the planner or having the planner tell the citizen.

Effects of the Career Bureaucracy. A related aspect of the same large problem of a balanced structure of political power arises from the working of that inevitable attribute of the service state—the career bureaucracy. Modern merit bureaucracies, because of their professional standards of performance, have been the recipients of substantial grants of authority by the legislature. These bureaucracies manage the mass of public business; and they do a job so creditable on the whole that not too much is left for the citizen to do. In the nation-state of today, those governed see themselves as the customers of public administration, with the administrative process almost completely in the hands of professional government employees. Moreover, organizational size and institutional self-sufficiency always demand a toll. Especially in the national order of magnitude, each executive department is a dominion by itself, unwieldy and intricate, geared to mass operations rather than individual justice. Such a department is also usually tied into the interests of a particular part of the population, which it may come to regard as its clientele.

As the steward of its clientele, the department is in a position to bargain advantageously for legislative support, at least from the legislative committee jurisdictionally paralleling the functions of the department. Interest alignments of this kind may be much stronger than the political cohesion within the lawmaking chamber or its majority. They may be stronger, too, than the hierarchical authority of the chief executive over the leadership of the department. With any such partial paralysis of responsible control, the bureaucratic element, like the interest groups to which it attends as guardian-censor, may emerge virtually exempt from real popular accountability. This result, it should be stressed, would not entail the actual elimination of a single comma from the constitutional charter of representative government. Yet there can be no doubt that defeat of effective public control puts in great jeopardy the individual adversely affected by the activities of the department. He may well feel altogether at its mercy.

Potentialities of Administrative Justice. The position of the citizen in the face of the nation-state's massed power presents itself from a somewhat different angle when the judicial branch is brought into the picture. Judicial review of the constitutionality of legislation, as it has evolved into established practice in the United States, has proved its benefit as a bulwark of some of the individual's most precious human interests. But its capacity for wholesale political obstruction has won judicial review little hospitality outside the American tradition. More widely significant is another weapon in the judicial defense of the individual—the rule of law. Indeed, where there is such defense for him, he does not live under tyranny. Under the rule of law it is axiomatic that public officers be held legally answerable for their official actions. Moreover, it has long been considered necessary that the aggrieved citizen be enabled to obtain redress with dispatch and without oppressive cost.

Self-evident as these postulates may be, it has nowhere been simple to evolve an adequate system of administrative justice. For one thing, legal accountability of administrative authority, and thus appropriate protection of individual rights, had to be balanced against the general welfare. Judicial control should not interfere with the administrative attainment of objectives proclaimed by statute as in the common interest. Perhaps no less important, elaborate prescriptions of administrative procedure might redound to the principal advantage of lawyers rather than of ordinary people dependent on the kind of treatment their condition would rate. Finally, though judicial independence is indispensable, law courts ignorant of the practical side of administrative business are apt to be clumsy in handling this branch of justice.

Significance of the Party System. Of course, the citizen's share in public control is determined not only by the organization and the mechanics of government. One must also look to the operation of the party system to judge the scope of effective popular participation in politics. Without parties, to be sure, there could be neither any kind of popular control nor, as the minimum of institutional security for those governing, a safety valve to register public sentiment. Responsible party government is the most direct way of insuring a satisfactory synthesis of the various interests within the nation. A party system close to the people serves as the very foundation of political representation.

At the same time, parties may be hired agents of particular interests. Parties may embody regional and local points of view at the constant expense of the national good. Parties may also be tightly organized cliques or oligarchies, hostile to free participation by broader groups of citizens and anxious to escape internal democratic control. In the extreme, a party may be the protective shield of the governing against the governed. Even under normal circumstances, however, the citizen's part in the formulation of the party program and nomination of party candidates is usually cut to an infinitesimal slice in national party management.

Defeat of Cooperative Instinct? It is plain, then, that the nation-state, because of its sheer size and might, can pose as a community only in the rhetorical sense. The concentration of authority in national organs, together with the corresponding weakening of the familiar subdivisions of government, has reduced man to an extremely small range of active participation in the formation of national policy and the control of political power. Responsibility for policy determination or executive measures is not easily tracked down. Opportunities for the individual to make himself felt in the procedure by which the national course is set are not easily found. Too much is done for him with his presumed blessing. Too little is he himself supposed to do in government.

This well-nigh universal situation brings up some very tough issues. Has the rise of the nation-state sealed the doom of true self-government? Is man, whatever the constitutional niceties, once again at the bottom of the pile of political power—a subject, who has to take it? Will the nation-state more and more become the warden of the individual—at best benevolent but always firm, ever-present yet also elusively distant? Will birth into one or another nationality take man with inexorable force to each Armageddon that waits on the path of the nation-state? Questions like these are not quieted by a single answer. Few answers, however, could entirely ignore the possibility of so reforming the relationships between man and the state that individual participation in public affairs will be made possible on a much broader scale than is the case today. The cooperative instinct of the individual must be reawakened and channeled toward socially constructive outlets of group action. This action will take politically significant forms only when the pulse of the body politic runs through all its members, when civic status carries with it the full connotation of political membership in a co-operative commonwealth.

Short of such cooperative commonwealth, those governed will probably acknowledge the fairly satisfactory level of effectiveness with which the nation-state devotes itself to the policeman's chores of law and order, externally and internally, and to the regulator's or planner's job of maintaining an operative economy. They may have considerable misgivings about the record of national diplomacy in an age capable of self-destruction by atomic fission or equivalent processes. Yet they will rally to the symbols of the nation when their national feeling is aroused by fear, foreign challenge, or the sense of mission. When not so stirred, they may admit that the nation-state is quite a weight on them—a weight made lighter only by such code of higher proprieties as can be invoked by the individual in seeking refuge from government. The rights of man are an ancient dream that has always remained young. Respect for them in the political mores of the great majority of people is today the most valuable possession the individual can hope for.

2. The Influence of Strain

Democracy and Security. Unimpeded self-development of human beings and free play of collective energies have long been valued as the main supports of a creative and resourceful community.[2] Although endowed with a social purpose, freedom does not admit of organized direction of its spontaneous expressions. Government, acting on a popular consensus, may determine the basic standards of general utility. But the autonomous interaction of individuals and groups within the framework of these standards

---

[2] The following discussion borrows heavily from F. Morstein Marx, "Effects of International Tension on Liberty Under Law," *Columbia Law Review,* 48 (1948), 555 ff., with the permission of the editors of this journal.

can be tampered with only at the price of restricted liberty and dangerous stagnation.

Leaving great latitude to personal initiative, the democratic way of life depends for its full flowering on a considerable measure of ease of mind. A general sense of security must prevail to allow for the potential miscarriage of purpose that goes with diversity of effort. There must be enough ease of mind to ignore the evidence of obstructive stubbornness and incidental waste, to condone the relative slowness in reaching broadly supported decisions for the community as a whole, and to put up with the persistence of residual disagreement in the face of such decisions.

When the general sense of security is shaken, the values attached to the diversity of effort appear in a different light. Sudden awareness of insecurity beclouds accepted rationality. Symbols of unity and interdependence come to the fore, stressing ordered responses to available leadership. Under the spell of crisis, the cumulative effect of man's unsteady emotions and uncertain images of reality resembles an avalanche-like reaction. The greater the psychological pressure, the more striking are its unsettling repercussions. As ease of mind is swept away, traditional attitudes lose their hold on human conduct.

Origin of Restrictive Pressures.   Inroads into the general sense of security may stem from a variety of causes. Some of these causes arise within the national context itself. The harsh impact of economic breakdown associated with the business cycle has engendered periodically acute anxieties, and latent ones that linger on. Such anxieties, in large part, are at the root of the steady expansion of governmental responsibility for the effective operation of the economy. A levelheaded observer, reviewing the European and American development in the depth of the great depression of the thirties, then found the ambit of freedom "rapidly narrowing."[3] Domestic factors, however, are not the only causes that may undermine the general sense of security. Widely felt instabilities of the international order, conveying hints of catastrophe, have the same consequence. Such conditions nag nations into a fierce quest of protection.

Disintegration of the ease of mind that gives the democratic way of life its proper social climate brings forth restrictive pressures. These pressures reflect an intolerance born of fear. Conversely, as the general sense of security returns, the trend is toward relaxation. The far-reaching political significance of the distinction between an atmosphere of confidence and a state of public anxiety is all too obvious. As an official body of inquiry in the United States recently explained with regard to the social and psychological conditions that foster or imperil civil rights: "In a world forever tottering on the brink of war, civil rights will be precarious at best. In a nation wracked by depression and widespread economic insecurity, the inclination

---

[3] Lindsay Rogers, *Crisis Government* (New York, 1934), p. 14.

to consider civil rights a luxury will be more easily accepted. We need peace and prosperity for their own sake; we need them to secure our civil rights as well." [4] To put it more generally, intense emotional strain is likely to seek relief in a powerful urge toward clamping limitations on the democratic process.

Considering the international scene from the vantage point of today, this train of reflections appears far from being academic. References to World War III have become commonplace. Its possibility is real enough to present many countries with a cogent argument for extensive precautionary measures. Such measures are bound to lead to a partial reënactment of a wartime frame of thought. Science and technology have combined to reduce the globe to One World. Its fundamental ideological division into Two Worlds is thus made doubly menacing. The ability of statesmanship to cope with this smoldering paradox of our time is a matter of destiny for millions upon millions of people.

Influence of Totalitarianism. In contemplating the implications of this situation, it is necessary to accord due weight to the dynamic character of totalitarianism. A political system dedicated to the categorical imperatives of a secular religion, totalitarianism is essentially expansionist. It is missionary in spirit and messianic in aspirations. Whatever the changing tactics of its supreme primate, "the temporal Ecclesia of Leviathan is by its very nature bent upon securing the universality of its absolutes. Faced with tangible obstacles, it may for a time acquiesce, but it is bound to resume the pursuit of these absolutes whenever the resistance disintegrates." [5] The limitations on the spread of totalitarianism abroad are basically external rather than internal. The durability of these limitations depends on outside factors and forces.

Under totalitarian auspices, the sovereign state has outdone itself by becoming the ablest "architect of ruin." [6] Yet it is equally clear that consistent action in containing global totalitarianism is beset with grave problems. Such problems not only present themselves in the critical realm of diplomatic and military planning. They also loom in the domestic sphere. One of the hardest of these problems has been posed in the reluctant comment of a historian of warfare: "The atomic bomb and the age of total war make mandatory an increase in military efficiency. This logically means a redirection of all phases of national life toward military strength and the extension of the influence of the military into all phases of life. Yet, how can we thus increase military efficiency without weakening our democracy? How can we prepare for total war without becoming a 'garrison state' and destroying

---

[4] President's Committee on Civil Rights, *To Secure These Rights* (Washington, 1947), p. 133.

[5] F. Morstein Marx, "Totalitarian Politics," *Proceedings of the American Philosophical Society*, 82, no. 1 (1940), 36, quoted by permission of the editor.

[6] Rogers, *op. cit.* above, note 3, p. 135.

the very qualities and virtues and principles we originally aimed to save?"[7]

Tightening of Security Standards. We appreciate the comforting truth that any integrated way of life pulls human behavior into its "own design."[8] That is why we look upon the democratic tradition as something that has identity and continuity. By the same token, however, we would be unable to retain the vitality of this tradition if we placed it in cold storage, as it were, for the duration of an emergency of unpredictable length, extending perhaps over a whole generation. Save for a counterpoise born of alertness, such a long-range emergency would tend to form a design of its own and imperceptibly reshape our conduct. Barring the internal disintegration of foreign totalitarianism, one must be prepared for the conclusion that the success of the Western nations in preventing a World War III by appropriate precautionary measures has its corollary in the prospect of an indefinite period of militant vigilance amounting to quasi-belligerency. This conclusion, at least as a central working hypothesis, must be kept in mind in appraising the influence of strain on liberty under law. Taken only in their current aspects, the tremors that run today through democratic life may seem to be of transitory moment. They warrant particular attention when viewed in the broader perspective of time to come.

One of these tremors is evident in the widespread expansion of standards of internal and external security. The broadening of such standards, of course, has much to do with the underhanded manner in which experts in organized subversion seek to attain their destructive ends. Time-honored procedures based on the worth attached to an honest man's word can turn ineffective in dealing with infiltration and deception. Denial of accusations may be deliberate befuddlement. The canons of propriety respected by revolutionary plotters, in the nature of things, are diametrically opposite to the concepts of integrity commonly upheld.

One area in which the expansion of security standards has been most conspicuous is that of government employment, especially with agencies considered particularly sensitive to fifth-column activities. To proceed along these lines, however, is fraught with considerable difficulties. At a recent legislative hearing of a bill designed to accomplish such ends in the United States, one witness inquired: "What would you do with a person who went around making speeches, who during his speech said that it was the revolutionary right of the people of this country, if they didn't like this government, to dismember or overthrow it? I have read, sir, from the first inaugural of the President of the United States, Abraham Lincoln."[9] He concluded that the bill in question would have prevented the employment in government of Thomas Jefferson as well as Abraham Lincoln.

---

[7] Hanson W. Baldwin, "The Myth of Security," *Foreign Affairs*, 26 (1948), 263, quoted by permission of the editor.
[8] Harold D. Lasswell, *Politics: Who Gets What, When, How* (New York, 1936), p. 30.
[9] For reference, see *loc. cit.* above, note 2, p. 564.

Demand for Solidarity. Speculations of this order demonstrate the range of subtle differentiations that opens up as soon as the meaning of freedom is at issue. When strain and anxiety call forth demands for solidarity, the practice of solidarity presents itself as a principal civic virtue. The people's sense of danger becomes a powerful agent of enforcement. Priority is on public safety, and often with a margin of exaggeration. Popular pressure for common protection is too spontaneous and too sweeping to leave much patience for discriminating attention to individual interests in intellectual liberty that the proverbial average citizen rarely stumbles into in his personal affairs. Such pressure, unorganized but persistent, of necessity exerts great influence upon representative assemblies and responsible executive officials. Through democratic processes it may lead to undemocratic results.

It is worth remembering that the theory of democratic government extends between two poles. One pole is marked by the need for securing protection to the essential integrity of individual personality, the other by the need for achieving a foundation for collective action by resort to majority rule. There is a range of basic balance in the area between these poles, but the boundaries within which balance can be effectively accomplished are not easily defined. Only one thing is certain—that neither purely individual determination nor the decision of a mathematical majority is entitled to claim the last say in what is politically right or wrong. In periods of national relaxation, natural manifestations of diffusion and dispersal in the formation of public opinion operate as safeguards of individual right, especially the right to dissent. In periods of national strain, on the other hand, this right is easily challenged. Among the many, spurred by a spreading sense of insecurity, individual dissent evokes hostile reactions as an apparent act of defiance of solidarity.

Limits to Juridical Defense. For these reasons, the juridical defense of civil liberties is a priceless asset for the individual. At the same time, one should not lose sight of current moves in the direction of a broadened concept of the overriding collective interest. Such moves show an inventive spirit, an inclination to reach beyond established practices of dealing with those who on political grounds seem to offend the public order. New devices and new sanctions of a more flexible nature may go far to draw into themselves an unpredictable number of cases merely upon elusive suspicions. There is hence need for judicial wakefulness and imaginative thought to guard the rule of law.

It must be admitted, however, that it is by no means certain whether in actual fact the juridical defense of liberty will be reinforced by judicial refinement. For one thing, the emotional tensions that play through the entire political system do not leave the judiciary untouched. In past emergencies of great sweep, the courts have never been able to retain complete immunity. On the ultimate issue, the judiciary is likely to acknowledge its obligation to defer to electorates and legislatures as the fundamental sources of public policy. Judicial safeguards ordinarily will have avail only in proportion to such checks on crisis psychology as may emerge from the strength of clear-headed leaders of public thought, and the body of responsive opinion they command.

Exposure of the Individual. Statesmen cannot orate in "neutral colors," it has been said.[10] They must present things as either black or white. In preserving individual rights during a time of stress, the heart of the problem often lies between what is white and what is black. People becoming suspect in the community for one reason or another are usually few. When the few are so few, the many may walk across their bodies without really noticing it.

The conscious culprit, whom one may properly paint black, as a necessity of his sinister business will work hard to appear as white as pure innocence. The assertive individual, who becomes obnoxious merely by speaking his mind, will look quite black to his disturbed audience, although in fact he is as white as his most public-spirited neighbors. As the pretense of the culprit turns from white to gray, he finds himself to his delight in the company of others appearing also gray simply because they have occasionally talked out of turn. Among those who occasionally talk out of turn will be some of the best citizens. In the words of Rebecca West: "The relationship between a man and a fatherland is always disturbed by conflict if either man or fatherland is highly developed. A man's demands for liberty must at some point challenge the limitations the state imposes on the individual for the sake of the mass. If he is to carry on the national tradition he must wrestle with those who, speaking in its name, desire to crystallize it at the point reached by the previous generation. In any case national life itself must frequently exasperate him, because it is the medium in which he is expressing himself, and every craftsman or artist is repelled by the resistance of his medium to his will. All men should have a drop or two of treason in their veins, if the nations are not to go soft like so many sleepy pears." [11]

Maintaining Essential Standards. To see the general need is not enough. One must raise the harder question of what can be done specifically to insure democracy at home. On three particular requirements there will be broad agreement. In the first place, admitting the necessity of exceptional kinds of government action, there is reason to insist upon clear standards to govern the application of effective descrimination to identify those who conspire against the public order. Second, in the process of such identification, there is reason to insist upon the authoritative verdict of full facts. And third, in the manner of resolving remaining doubts, there is reason to insist upon a close approximation of the central maxims of criminal law. No one should be presumed guilty by mere accusation.

All this is doubly pertinent when viewed against the prospect of longer-

---

[10] Rogers, *op. cit.* above, note 3, p. 96.

[11] Rebecca West, *The Meaning of Treason* (New York, 1947), p. 306, quoted by permission of the publisher (Viking Press).

range conditions of external emergency. Seldom has it been truer than to-day that free nations cannot afford to be careless either with their security or with the values that draw their citizens powerfully to the democratic way of life. At a time when for each of these nations political unity is of the essence, there is persuasive reason to restrain unjust discrimination within the people. Indeed, unless the spirit of mass anxiety and individual de-pendence is conquered in time, the nation-state may too soon be too far on the way toward enforcing upon the whole population the well-ordered routines of the reformatory.

Rising Walls. Under conditions of international tension, when most of humanity is being drawn into national causes, the peoples in different politi-cal camps lose sight of one another as parts of mankind, as other human be-ings. Trade between antagonists comes to a stop. General travel becomes well-nigh impossible. There is less and less interchange in the arts and sciences. Who among those millions in the wide spaces of the Soviet Union has personal experience to fall back upon in talking about Americans, for instance? How few throughout all of the United States, for that matter, have that kind of experience in talking about Russians! Half a century ago, nearly all of the countries of the world were open to the visitor, and most of them extended hospitality to the stranger as a matter of course. Today the walls between nations are higher than they have ever been since the ascension of the modern nation-state.

This state of things affects the individual in many ways. In the first place, he obtains his picture of the world increasingly in the perspective of the na-tional interest. His government interprets for him the motives of foreign countries, especially those on the other side of the fence. The printed word, unless it is looked upon as irresponsible, tends to follow pretty closely the lines of national advantage, in part because the national advantage is the nation-state's second nature. As a result, one's own nation acquires some-thing of a monopoly of virtue, while the other nations show varying degrees of evil intent. Within each nation, this point of view is like a sea of glue that slowly spreads to encompass all.

Sovereignty—the foremost characteristic of the nation-state—everywhere enlists the individual as a national partisan. This enlistment is absolute and all-inclusive—indeed, total—under totalitarianism. Under democratic gov-ernment, the individual's enlistment as a national partisan is never total, and in degree dependent on conditions of demonstrable need. Yet it is clear that democracy's commitment to the value of human personality carries with it an important implication. It is the implication that *man's* vision of *man* should never be obscured by the nation-state's demand for national partisanship.

CHAPTER 34

THE INDIVIDUAL AND THE
INTERNATIONAL ORDER

1. The Road to Peace

Utopian Internationalism. No great war of modern times has left the international skies so dark as has World War II. The skies in fact appear darker now than they ever were during the earlier decades of the twentieth century. A world-wide front, including a great power governed by a totalitarian regime, inflicted utter defeat upon three other totalitarian regimes. The result was a striking gain of power for the totalitarian regime in the victorious camp.

It has become fashionable to deplore the marked change in world opinion on the prospects for a peaceful international order that has occurred in the few years since the end of hostilities in World War II. Actually, this change was quite to be expected. Throughout the lands of the United Nations, the psychology of military triumph caused an understandable burst of optimistic sentiments about the future. War-weary peoples threw all their hopes into the beckoning chances of strong machinery for restraining would-be aggressors and for maintaining an international system dedicated to mutual cooperation. But this optimism soared far away from hard realities. It was blind not only to the postwar bases of international politics. It also ignored those conditions of dire need that had made possible a political partnership among countries as different as the Western powers on the one side and the Soviet Union and Kuomintang China on the other.

World-wide Duality. Save for the temporary distraction of battling a common enemy, the oft-acknowledged differences of political mentality and general line of policy between these countries remained unaffected by the pragmatic wartime arrangements among them. Nothing short of a most exceptional kind of political leadership—one that in the circumstances would have been conceivable only among the Western countries—could have prevented the natural drift back toward the old deep-seated antagonisms. The deterioration in the character of international relations during recent years is merely the reverse side of an unarrested return to prewar animosities. But its effect is multiplied by what is an obvious consequence of Western wartime companionship-at-arms with Russia—the tremendous growth of Soviet power, especially in Europe and in the East, near and far. To bemoan the ascendancy of Soviet influence is to take issue with those policies of Western statecraft that gave rise to the United Nations and through concerted effort sealed the doom of Hitler, Mussolini, and Hirohito.

Whatever the moral of diplomatic strategy in World War II, above all the failure to evolve agreement on the postwar world with the Soviet Union at the beginning of the wartime partnership, today's reality is plain. It is that of a globe technologically more nearly unified and more closely inter-dependent in its parts than ever, yet sharply divided into two ideological realms. To stress this appalling truth does not mean that the working of the peacetime machinery fashioned by the United Nations has turned into a sorry laugh.[1] It does mean that neither the existence of this machinery nor the best of good will mustered by individual national representatives in trying to operate it can annul the controlling fact that the world of our day is two worlds divided against each other.

Use of International Bodies. International interests relatively free from political implications—those ranging from the protection of migratory birds to the publication of industrial accident statistics—may well survive the great split. They will retain their standing as feasible objects of international study and management by specialized bodies of the United Nations, as for-merly under auspices of the League of Nations.[2] Yet in general the cate-gorical nature of the antagonism between the two divided worlds is apt with time to reduce these areas of international cooperation, because fewer and fewer fields may be left as clearly devoid of political content. In the political area proper, the organization of the United Nations shows little similarity to a common council. It is more like a barbarian imitation of a medieval tour-nament.

The more prominent bodies of the United Nations may best be compared to open forums where instructed spokesmen of individual nations, in the main dependent on their national points of view, make more or less straight-forward attempts to influence public attitudes within and beyond the boundaries of their own countries. Here, then, is the world stage for popu-

---

[1] For an exceedingly skeptical view of the prospects of world government and an outline of alternative kinds of action open to the United States, see Herman Finer, *America's Destiny* (New York, 1947). A levelheaded analysis is provided by Philip C. Jessup, *The International Problem of Governing Mankind* (Claremont, Cal., 1947). Some of the most acute problems that have arisen in the operations of the United Nations are effectively outlined in Herbert V. Evatt, *The United Nations* (Cambridge, Mass., 1948). See also Leland M. Goodrich, "The United Nations: Its Record of Achievement," *Foreign Policy Reports*, 23 (Sept. 15, 1947), 162 ff., and Eugene P. Chase, *The United Nations in Action* (New York, 1950).

[2] For the growth of international machinery dealing with specialized areas of cooperation, theoretically considered nonpolitical, see Fred L. Hadsel, "Technical and Specialized Agencies of the U.N.—Finance, Transport and Communication, and Trade," *Foreign Policy Reports*, 23 (Nov. 15, 1947), 214 ff.; and "Human Welfare Specialized Agencies of U.N.—Labor, Food, Education, Health, and Refugees," *ibid.*, 23 (Feb. 1, 1948), 274 ff. For the evolution of the early European recovery program, see Harold H. Hutcheson, "International Agencies for European Reconstruction," *ibid.*, 23 (July 15, 1947), 110 ff. An informative discussion of the problem of an international guaranty of individual liberties is offered by Mrs. Franklin D. Roosevelt, "The Promise of Human Rights," *Foreign Affairs*, 26 (1948), 470 ff.

lar diplomacy, as contrasted with open diplomacy—the stage for solemn recital, for argument and rebuttal, addressed to the half-deaf ear of the world. Here is the setting in which governments can maneuver for position by utilizing the procedural devices of formal assemblies. Here is the place where governments can conveniently offset charges against them by counter-charges against those raising the charges. In the perspective of today, to assume any capacity of the United Nations for sustained leadership above the level of national interests is therefore entirely unwarranted.

Uneasy Balance. If lasting peace lacks a secure foundation as long as ideological division gives potency to two worlds, national statesmanship is reduced to a grim alternative. On the one hand, the ideological division could possibly be overcome by force—in so far as resort to force would lead to the destruction of one of the ideological systems, and in so far as thought or faith is ever destroyed by force. Reliance on force entails war, and the logic of war is to strike as soon as the calculus of risk appears to indicate promising conditions for success. To leaders who accept this line of reasoning as compelling, the question of the morality of surprise attack with every means at their command to inflict speedy annihilation upon the opponent would not be deterring; nor would the horrors that the great silent masses of humanity, whether foe or friend, would have to endure.

Remarkably enough in a brutal age, no responsible leader on either side of the ideological cleavage has pressed the logic of this kind of action. The remaining course is one of poise and counterpoise. Such a course argues sternly for a state of preparedness, with physical capacity for producing and maintaining the national armor as the ultimate limit. Each side will care-fully feel for the point beyond which provocation or insult cannot safely be carried. Each side will seek to improve its own position in resources, satel-lites, and zones of hegemony, especially in its relations to such nations as are not yet definitely committed to one or the other camp. Each side will hopefully assume that time will cause trouble for the other side, whether this trouble may take the form of economic recession or collapse on the one hand or of political demoralization or upheaval on the other.

Distant Opportunity? Peace—or absence of major wars—on this basis would be the fruit of a precarious balance between two systems of world power. Without both systems learning to retain such essential balance de-spite reciprocal curses, the thought of imminent catastrophe would loom above every day. With all the inherent dangers, however, and with all the barely sufferable strain on mankind everywhere, even the determined pessi-mist would have to concede at least a slim chance for a state of formal peace continued over years to come.

Perhaps, if and as this extraordinary state endures, a deeper and stronger desire for true peace may rouse itself among the peoples. New opportu-nities may arise for building some kind of common control to check the risky unilateral moves typical of ideological duality. Possibly also, gradual modification in political and economic structures and processes may work on either side of the great cleavage to make the differences between both less rather than more marked. Such a development, too, may furnish a basis for each side to deal with the other in less belligerent terms.

If one strains his imagination, he may conceive of a number of factors that could spell change. The day may yet come when the machinery of the United Nations will have decisive importance. The day may yet come for a leadership international in outlook. Such leadership alone is able to initiate widespread conditions of mind that will render global suicide an assured impossibility.

Essential Conditions of Mind. Conditions of mind to support international equity, quite obviously, will not spring from the fervor of national self-assertion. Nor may one expect them to come forth from the oratory that paints in blatant colors the glory of the nation-state. They are still less likely to emerge from official pronouncements by national governments stating, construing, or clarifying their respective foreign policies. The crucial influence, in the last analysis, is not that of the statesmanlike phrase but that of man's quiet resolve. All roads to peace reach the last milestone in a common appreciation of human qualities, of the individual's value even when he seems swallowed in the great multitude of his kind.

Respect for human individuality, if it is an inner urge rather than a mere lick of civilization, cuts straight across the walls of nationality, class, and color. When guided by their calm judgment, ordinary people are supremely qualified to appreciate the humanity of other ordinary people, whatever language they speak, whatever mores they follow, wherever they live. To such ordinary people, in the depth of their ordinary wisdom, the towering structure of authority on which the nation-state leans its weight may appear as devoid of higher reason or moral purpose as are the barriers in the way toward a peaceful world.

2. Treating the Ills of the Nation-State

Top-heavy Structure. Few who in recent years talked of world government have conveyed to their audiences a reasonably clear picture of the relationship between this kind of government and the individual. World government might be a kind of government many times farther removed from our doorsteps and backyards than is the nation-state. World government might also be many times more heavy-handed and less susceptible of popular control.

If it is to be assumed that the road toward world government leads through the sovereign nation-state, and if the pace of advance will be determined primarily by the formation of favorable conditions of mind among many millions of people, it seems to follow that man's civic experience of living under large-scale structures of power is of critical importance. The more his experience, in thought and dubious afterthought, is adversely affected by the institutional ills of the nation-state, the less likely is his acceptance of a still larger structure of authority. The more his experience reflects effective participation in political affairs, and the more he thus rises above the level of an object of governmental management to the plane of positive citizenship, the less difficult will it be for him to bridge the gulf between his own hopes and worries and a global concept of government.

Bridging the Gulf of Politics. The primary task, from this angle, is a dual one. The gigantic scope and inaccessible character of government in the nation-state must be overcome by drawing the citizenry at many different points and for many different functions into the process of administering public business. It is the cells of government that require attention. For full vitality, each cell must absorb a continuous flow of civic energies. In particular, a fresh search needs to be made for appropriate governmental subdivisions, political as well as administrative. Such subdivisions must be fit to take on, with citizen participation, the highest degree of responsibility compatible with a general integration of policy and management in terms of the whole.

So much now for one side of the primary task. There is also the other side, pointed toward the individual rather than the organization of government. For the individual, the task consists of becoming a conscious political being, one who is reaching for every practical opportunity of playing an effective part in government and administration.

Philosophy of Citizenship. A prerequisite for the individual's active role as a political being in this sense is an operative philosophy of citizenship. Such a philosophy could not simply be constructed from sharp-eyed observation of the "great game" of politics. Nor could it be gained by blind adoption of any given official ideology, which would push the individual into the arms of political bigotry, and surrender his free moral option to the manipulative skill of those who act as the custodians of ideological purity.

In order to avoid such intellectual subjugation to the powers that be, the individual must bring together in his civic philosophy canons of ethics that would infuse concrete meaning into the order of political values. These determinative canons of ethics are the only protection the individual has against the logic of unthinking submission to the gods and clerics of a secular religion administered from above. In order to retain the freedom of his conscience in deciding the ultimate right or wrong of civic action, political man must be able to reach beyond the pragmatic rules ordained by the nation-state for its own immediate purposes. A working philosophy of responsible citizenship calls for a morality grounded in the fundamental distinction between what in general is ethically good and what in general is ethically evil. This kind of civic philosophy is not like a common carrier that discharges the passenger at a chosen destination. It is a frame within which individual judgment must be exercised continuously. It calls for political man to examine his moral sense, to seek his own responsibility, and to be leery of compromising his considered conclusions. Unless he accords his philosophy of citizenship the rank of fundamental doctrine, political man is apt to yield to conflicting pulls—a reed bending with every breeze.

Drawing Government toward the Citizen. Although without coherent civic doctrine there can be no consistency in his thought and action, it is no less true that the individual must also have appropriate outlets for constructive citizenship. Being physically always part of a local setting, he is best equipped to function in this setting. He is most likely to be familiar with the local leverage of group action, or to find out about it. It is much more difficult—and usually impossible—for him to try to be equally effective on a higher level, especially the national level. But with the common trend toward larger units of self-government, the difficulties the citizen has to surmount in attempting to play his part even on the local level are still very real.

One possibility of overcoming these difficulties would be to give renewed recognition in the many-chambered edifice of government to the neighborhood, rural or urban. A middle-sized city comprises many neighborhoods. An average county is made up of a multitude of neighborhoods. In order to invite the individual's active interest in the business of government, it is necessary to carry the government's business nearer his home.[3] Such readjustment in the governmental pattern of the nation-state need not lead to an undesirable fragmentation of policy and administration, especially if an effort is made to differentiate in practical terms among a somewhat larger number of levels of responsibility and decision-making while keeping all levels effectively interlocked.

Training in Cooperation. Neighborhood government and neighborhood administration would challenge and strengthen man's capacity for living and working with others. With all the striking growth of large-scale organization, political, economic, and social, fostered directly and indirectly by the large-scale aspects of the nation-state, most human beings are but dimly alive to the ways and means of cooperative effort and group action. It is a remarkable commentary on the current phase of the machine age that systematic training for civic cooperation has found more extensive attention in the greedy hands of totalitarianism than elsewhere. Formal as well as informal education, if intelligently directed toward this goal, would go far to help

[3] For two sides of the matter in regard to a national valley authority, see David E. Lilienthal, *TVA: Democracy on the March* (New York, 1944), and Philip Selznick, *TVA and the Grass Roots* (Berkeley, 1949). The distance between the present instrumentalities of local government and the ordinary citizen is illuminated in several highly instructive pamphlets published by *Planning* (PEP, London): "Active Democracy—A Local Election," No. 261 (Jan. 24, 1947); "Clubs, Societies and Democracy," No. 263 (Mar. 21, 1947); "Public Relations and the Town Hall," No. 265 (May 2, 1947); "Councils and Their Tenants," No. 282 (May 21, 1948); and "Local Elections: How Many Vote?", No. 291 (Nov. 29, 1948).

man where today his failing is most consequential—in making more productive his relations with others, especially in the pursuit of common ends.[4]

These suggestions look toward particulars. They are only a few, each
elementary. Many other suggestions could be set down, but the full cata-
logue is not needed here. The range of practical possibilities for bringing
government closer to the individual and for making the individual a more
effective participant in political affairs begs for methodical inquiry. Our
era is eminently political, explosively political. Yet the most consequential
processes of political action are out of sight and out of reach for the vast bulk
of mankind. The crying need is for a restoration of the essential bonds of
civic life—bonds that again would effectively link the affairs of government
with those of the individual.

3. The Individual's Part

Seeking Opportunities for Self-expression. Citizenship cannot flower
when the individual has reason to think of himself as a mere pebble kicked
about by the restless feet of government. What is his place in the political
realm? In the wondrous expanse of the nation-state, hidden in the mass
of the governed, he may come to doubt that there is any political role for him
except when fate has lifted him to leadership.

Yet no one will deny that modern government, though all too separate
from the body of the people, shows a high compensatory responsiveness to
public opinion. Public opinion, in turn, however tightly organized it may
be in some of its parts, is a changing composite of opinions emanating from
great numbers of people, some with large influence and most with very
little. Even little influence tells when voice is added to voice. No individual is therefore entitled to the dubious comfort of a set conviction that
his voice amounts to nothing. Each man is able to do something to make
his voice heard among those within hearing. Thus, his voice may gain a
mounting echo. The constant plebiscite of public opinion offers the individual his greatest opportunity for effective political self-expression. Too
few make actual use of this opportunity to the full of their personal potentialities.

Temptations of Convenience. Man cannot honestly acknowledge his
responsibilities as a citizen without simultaneously accepting an obligation
to make his civic influence felt. This is his first step toward playing his part
as a political being. The next step is to train himself to see things right—
to sharpen his eyes, to know enough, to orient his mind in the political
sphere. This is in the main a matter of consolidating his point of view,
bolstered by a working philosophy of citizenship.

Thereafter, the individual must be alert in seizing upon each opportunity
that comes his way for expressing his mind, which is not always merely a

---

[4] Ironically, it is the need of management, not that of politics, that in recent years has been
most instrumental in stimulating inquiries into the mysteries of concerted endeavor.

question of words. Some of these opportunities will fleet by him too fast for prolonged reflection. Undue hesitation would allow them to pass unused. Some other opportunities, when acted upon, will cause eyebrows to rise or disapproval to grow audible. The path of timidity on such occasions would be merely a convenient escape. A very few opportunities can be utilized only at grave risk, but may be of unusual importance. If they are, they must be met. These are simple general rules. Few will disagree with them. All too few, however, with the political frustrations of civic conduct under the nation-state, have made such rules a habitual form of civic behavior.

Need for Civic Courage. One aspect of such steady quest of civic opportunities is discriminating support of political leadership. Availability for public duties and responsibilities is another aspect. Far more important, however, is the individual's mature appreciation that all he says and all he does blend into a pattern of civic behavior—whether positive, negative, or indifferent—that cannot fail to affect the attitudes of others.

If he goes by a dual standard in applying one set of rules in talking about citizenship and another in his actions, he is obviously guilty of subverting civic morality. If he views with alarm all kinds of things without ever bestirring himself to do something about them, he offers at best a sad parody of civic obligation. If he speaks boldly and crawls out of sight as soon as action is in order, he makes a repulsive joke of citizenship. Only when his personal example gives strength to the weak among his fellow-citizens, and vigor to the public interest, can he say with some confidence that he renders fair account of himself as political man.

Basis of Value Judgments. In making himself felt on the right side, the individual must be able to decide between right and wrong. Once again, the vast difference between democracy and totalitarianism becomes conspicuous. The good citizen, in the totalitarian style, knows the right side almost spontaneously—by looking to his country's acknowledged leadership. Being much better groomed in the political scriptures and infinitely more experienced in applying them to the exigencies of power, this leadership is the ordained body to indicate with authority what is right and what is wrong. To trust the individual's own insight, his own conscience, would only lead to "confusion."

Democracy, by contrast, puts its confidence in the commonsense and moral response of ordinary people, of each individual. Man's ultimate freedom—the fountain of all liberties—is his freedom to construct or accept consciously the kind of value system which offers him a basis for deciding himself what is right and what is wrong. Thus, to be a democrat means to meet the obligations that are inherent in the ultimate freedom—to win a basis of responsible choice and to shoulder the burden of responsibility, as man and as citizen.

INDEX

Economic factors, *see* Comparative study
Economic planning, *see* Planning
Economic rights, *see* Liberties
Eden, Anthony, 75
Education, Eire, 180; Germany, 340 *ff.*;
Great Britain, 115, 121 *ff.*, 137 *ff.*; Mexico,
641 *ff.*, 648; New Zealand, 167; South
African Union, 176 *ff.*; *see also* Church and
state
Edward VII, King, 39, 60, 84
Edward VIII, King, 151
Efficiency, *see* Administration
Einaudi, Luigi, 271, 281
Einaudi, Mario, *quoted*, 235, 267
Eire, 148 *ff.*, 179 *ff.*; *see also topical entries*
Eisenhower, General, 346
Eisteddfod, *see* Wales
Ejidos, see Agriculture, Mexico
Election costs, *see* Electoral system
Election results, *see* Electoral system
Electoral system, Australia, 171; Brazil, 674 *ff.*;
China, 611 *ff.*; Eire, 180; France, 213 *ff.*;
Germany, 324 *ff.*, 334 *ff.*; Great Britain,
67 *ff.*; Hungary, 532; Italy, 257 *ff.*, 273 *ff.*;
New Zealand, 167 *ff.*; South African Union,
177; Soviet Union, 421 *ff.*, 464 *ff.*; Switzer-
land, 385 *ff.*
Elgin, Lord, 148
Elizabeth II, 58
Emancipation, *see* Labor; Electoral system
Emergency powers, Austria, 357 *ff.*; Brazil,
662 *ff.*; China, 604 *ff.*; Denmark, 290-291;
Germany, 317 *ff.*; Great Britain, 106 *ff.*;
Norway, 290-291; Sweden, 290-291; Switz-
erland, 394 *ff.*
Emotion, *see* Human element in politics
Empire, British, 146 *ff.*, 166 *ff.*
Empire, French, 217 *ff.*
Empire, Portuguese, 625 *ff.*, 654 *ff.*
Empire routes, *see* Foreign policy
Empire, Spanish, 625 *ff.*
Empiricism, *see* Political theory
Employer associations, *see* Interest groups
Employment policy, *see* Planning
Encomienda system, *see* Local government,
Mexico
Engels, 30 *ff.*, 278, 409, 518 *ff.*
Erlander, Tage, 303
Established churches, *see* Church and state
Estado Novo, see Brazil
"Estates," *see* Interest groups; Nazi regime
Estonian Soviet Socialist Republic, *see* Soviet
Union
Ethics and politics, *see* Political theory
Eugenics, *see* Nazi regime
European rehabilitation, *see* Foreign policy
Evangelical Lutheran church, *see* Church and
state

Examinations, *see* Civil service
Executive, *see* Cabinet system; President
Executive-legislative relations, *see* Cabinet sys-
tem
Expenditure control, *see* Cabinet system; Legis-
lature
Exports, *see* Foreign policy
Expropriation, *see* Nationalization

F

Fabians, 31, 65 *ff.*, 85, 133
Family allowances, *see* Social security
Family system, *see* Local government, China
Far Eastern Commission, *see* Military govern-
ment; Japan
Farmers, *see* Agriculture
Fascist party, *see* Parties
Fascist regime, 253 *ff.*
Federal Assembly, *see* Constitutional govern-
ment; Legislature
Federal Council, *see* Constitutional govern-
ment; Legislature
Federal Diet, *see* Legislature
Federalism, Australia, 168 *ff.*; Austria, 359 *ff.*;
Brazil, 629 *ff.*, 657 *ff.*; Canada, 171 *ff.*;
Germany, 307 *ff.*, 333 *ff.*, 347 *ff.*; Great
Britain, 156-157; Mexico, 629 *ff.*, 637 *ff.*;
Soviet Union, 444 *ff.*, 472 *ff.*; Switzerland,
373 *ff.*; Yugoslavia, 538 *ff.*
Field service, *see* Administration
Fierlinger, 528 *ff.*
Figgis, J. N., 111
Figl, 361, 363; *quoted*, 370 *n.* 12
Films, *see* Moving pictures
"Finance bills," *see* Legislature
Financial powers, *see* Legislature
Financial support, *see* Interest groups; Parties
Fiscal policy, *see* Planning
Fisher, H. A. L., *quoted*, 196
Five Year Plan, *see* Planning
Folksting, see Legislature
Fonseca, Deodoro, 660 *ff.*
Fonseca, Hermes, 661
Food, *see* Agriculture; Planning
Forecasting, *see* Human element in politics
Foreign policy, Brazil, 620 *ff.*, 675 *ff.*; Czecho-
slovakia, 530 *ff.*; Denmark, 303 *ff.*; Eire,
183; France, 244 *ff.*; Germany, 346 *ff.*;
Great Britain, 143 *ff.*, 146 *ff.*; Hungary,
536 *ff.*; Italy, 261 *ff.*, 283; Japan, 547 *ff.*,
593 *ff.*; Mexico, 630 *ff.*, 648 *ff.*; Norway,
305 *ff.*; Soviet Union, 463, 513 *ff.*; Sweden,
303 *ff.*; Switzerland, 393 *ff.*; Yugoslavia,
540 *ff.*
Foreign service, *see* Empire; Foreign policy
Four Year Plan, *see* Planning
Fourier, 31